BIOINFORMATICS

The Machine Learning Approach

second edition

Pierre Baldi and Søren Brunak

An unprecedented wealth of data is being generated by genome sequencing projects and other experimental efforts to determine the structure and function of biological molecules. The demands and opportunities for interpreting these data are expanding more than ever. Bioinformatics is the development and application of computer methods for management, analysis, interpretation, and prediction, as well as for the design of experiments. Machine learning approaches (e.g., neural networks, hidden Markov models, and belief networks) are ideally suited for areas in which there is a lot of data but little theory, as in molecular biology. The goal in machine learning is to extract useful information from a body of data by building good probabilistic models— and to automate the process as much as possible.

Pierre Baldi and Søren Brunak present the key machine learning approaches and apply them to the computational problems encountered in the analysis of biological data. This book is aimed both at biologists and biochemists who need to understand new data-driven algorithms and at those with a primary background in physics, mathematics, statistics, or computer science who need to know more about applications in molecular biology. This edition contains expanded coverage of probabilistic graphical models and the applications of neural networks, as well as a new chapter on microarrays and gene expression. The entire text has been extensively revised.

Pierre Baldi is Professor and Director of the Institute for Genomics and Bioinformatics in the Department of Information and Computer Science and in the Depa[...] of Biological Chemistry in the College of M[...] University of California, Irvine. Søren Bruna[...] and Director of the Center for Biological Sequ[...] at the Biocentrum of the Technical University o[...]

Bioinformatics

Adaptive Computation and Machine Learning

Thomas Dietterich, Editor

Christopher Bishop, David Heckerman, Michael Jordan, and Michael Kearns, Associate Editors

Pierre Baldi
Søren Brunak

Bioinformatics

The Machine Learning Approach

second edition

A Bradford Book
The MIT Press
Cambridge, Massachusetts
London, England

This book was set in Lucida by the authors and was printed and bound in the United States of America.

Library of Congress Cataloging-in-Publication Data

Baldi, Pierre.
  Bioinformatics : the machine learning approach / Pierre Baldi,
  Søren Brunak.—2nd ed.
    p.   cm.—(Adaptive computation and machine learning)
  "A Bradford Book"
  Includes bibliographical references (p.).
  ISBN 0-262-02506-X (hc. : alk. paper)
  1. Bioinformatics. 2. Molecular biology—Computer simulation. 3. Molecular
biology—Mathematical models. 4. Neural networks (Computer science). 5.
Machine learning. 6. Markov processes.   I. Brunak, Søren. II. Title. III. Series.
QH506.B35   2001
572.8′01′13—dc21
                                                                    2001030210

10 9 8 7 6 5 4 3 2

Contents

Series Foreword

The field of bioinformatics, with its interaction between computer science and biology, exemplifies the way that the information sciences are transforming traditional scientific and engineering disciplines. The machine learning methods described in *Bioinformatics*, second edition, are essential tools for this rapidly developing field. Since the publication of the first edition, the amount of biological data requiring automated analysis has exploded: genomes of many important species (including humans) have been completely sequenced, new technologies of DNA and protein arrays have become practical research tools, and other new experimental techniques have been developed for studying the structure and function of proteins. With this explosion of data, many important advances in machine learning have been made, including Bayesian reasoning, maximum entropy methods, Gaussian processes, and support vector machines.

Bioinformatics provides an introduction to the most important information processing problems in computational biology and a unified treatment of the machine learning methods for solving these problems. Students and researchers in biology and computer science will find this a valuable and accessible introduction to these powerful new computational techniques as well as an authoritative reference for implementing and applying the methods. It also provides pointers to many online databases and resources that are essential for research in bioinformatics.

Like bioinformatics, the field of machine learning is interdisciplinary. The goal of building computer systems that can adapt to environments and learn from experience has attracted researchers from many fields, including computer science, engineering, mathematics, physics, neuroscience, and cogni-tive science. Out of this research has come a variety of learning techniques that have the potential to transform many scientific and industrial fields. Several research communities have converged on a common set of issues surrounding supervised, unsupervised, and reinforcement learning problems. The MIT Press series on Adaptive Computation and Machine Learning seeks to unify the many diverse strands of machine learning research and to foster high-quality research and innovative applications.

Thomas Dietterich

Preface

We have been very pleased, beyond our expectations, with the reception of the first edition of this book. Bioinformatics, however, continues to evolve very rapidly, hence the need for a new edition. In the past three years, full-genome sequencing has blossomed with the completion of the sequence of the fly and the first draft of the Human Genome Project. In addition, several other high-throughput/combinatorial technologies, such as DNA microarrays and mass spectrometry, have considerably progressed. Altogether, these high-throughput technologies are capable of rapidly producing terabytes of data that are too overwhelming for conventional biological approaches. As a result, the need for computer/statistical/machine learning techniques is today *stronger* rather than weaker.

Bioinformatics in the Post-genome Era

In all areas of biological and medical research, the role of the computer has been dramatically enhanced in the last five to ten year period. While the first wave of computational analysis did focus on sequence analysis, where many highly important unsolved problems still remain, the current and future needs will in particular concern sophisticated *integration* of extremely diverse sets of data. These novel types of data originate from a variety of experimental techniques of which many are capable of data production at the levels of entire cells, organs, organisms, or even populations.

The main driving force behind the changes has been the advent of new, efficient experimental techniques, primarily DNA sequencing, that have led to an exponential growth of linear descriptions of protein, DNA and RNA molecules. Other new data producing techniques work as massively parallel versions of traditional experimental methodologies. Genome-wide gene expression measurements using DNA microarrays is, in essence, a realization of tens of thousands of Northern blots. As a result, computational support in experiment design, processing of results and interpretation of results has become essential.

These developments have greatly widened the scope of bioinformatics.

As genome and other sequencing projects continue to advance unabated, the emphasis progressively switches from the accumulation of data to its interpretation. Our ability in the future to make new biological discoveries will depend strongly on our ability to combine and correlate diverse data sets along multiple dimensions and scales, rather than a continued effort focused in traditional areas. Sequence data will have to be integrated with structure and function data, with gene expression data, with pathways data, with phenotypic and clinical data, and so forth. Basic research within bioinformatics will have to deal with these issues of *system* and *integrative* biology, in the situation where the amount of data is growing exponentially.

The large amounts of data create a critical need for theoretical, algorithmic, and software advances in storing, retrieving, networking, processing, analyzing, navigating, and visualizing biological information. In turn, biological systems have inspired computer science advances with new concepts, including genetic algorithms, artificial neural networks, computer viruses and synthetic immune systems, DNA computing, artificial life, and hybrid VLSI-DNA gene chips. This cross-fertilization has enriched both fields and will continue to do so in the coming decades. In fact, all the boundaries between carbon-based and silicon-based information processing systems, whether conceptual or material, have begun to shrink [29].

Computational tools for classifying sequences, detecting weak similarities, separating protein coding regions from non-coding regions in DNA sequences, predicting molecular structure, post-translational modification and function, and reconstructing the underlying evolutionary history have become an essential component of the research process. This is essential to our understanding of life and evolution, as well as to the discovery of new drugs and therapies. Bioinformatics has emerged as a strategic discipline at the frontier between biology and computer science, impacting medicine, biotechnology, and society in many ways.

Large databases of biological information create both challenging datamining problems and opportunities, each requiring new ideas. In this regard, conventional computer science algorithms have been useful, but are increasingly unable to address many of the most interesting sequence analysis problems. This is due to the inherent complexity of biological systems, brought about by evolutionary tinkering, and to our lack of a comprehensive theory of life's organization at the molecular level. Machine-learning approaches (e.g. neural networks, hidden Markov models, vector support machines, belief networks), on the other hand, are ideally suited for domains characterized by the presence of large amounts of data, "noisy" patterns, and the absence of general theories. The fundamental idea behind these approaches is to *learn the theory automatically from the data*, through a process of inference, model fitting, or learning from examples. Thus they form a viable complementary approach to conventional methods. The aim of this book is to present a broad overview of bioinformatics from a *machine-learning perspective*.

Machine-learning methods are computationally intensive and benefit greatly from progress in computer speed. It is remarkable that both computer speed and sequence volume have been growing at roughly the same rate since the late 1980s, doubling every 16 months or so. More recently, with the completion of the first draft of the Human Genome Project and the advent of high-throughput technologies such as DNA microarrays, biological data has been growing even faster, doubling about every 6 to 8 months, and further increasing the pressure towards bioinformatics. To the novice, machine-learning methods may appear as a bag of unrelated techniques—but they are not. On the theoretical side, a unifying framework for all machine-learning methods also has emerged since the late 1980s. This is the Bayesian probabilistic framework for modeling and inference. In our minds, in fact, there is little difference between machine learning and Bayesian modeling and inference, except for the emphasis on computers and number crunching implicit in the first term. It is the confluence of all three factors—data, computers, and theoretical probabilistic framework—that is fueling the machine-learning expansion, in bioinformatics and elsewhere. And it is fair to say that bioinformatics and machine learning methods have started to have a significant impact in biology and medicine.

Even for those who are not very sensitive to mathematical rigor, modeling biological data probabilistically makes eminent sense. One reason is that biological measurements are often inherently "noisy", as is the case today of DNA microarray or mass spectrometer data. Sequence data, on the other hand, is becoming noise free due to its discrete nature and the cost-effectiveness of repeated sequencing. Thus measurement noise cannot be the sole reason for modeling biological data probabilistically. The real need for modeling biological data probabilistically comes from the complexity and variability of biological systems brought about by eons of evolutionary tinkering in complex environments. As a result, biological systems have inherently a very high dimensionality. Even in microarray experiments where expression levels of thousands of genes are measured simultaneously, only a small subset of the relevant variables is being observed. The majority of the variables remain "hidden" and must be factored out through probabilistic modeling. Going directly to a systematic probabilistic framework may contribute to the acceleration of the discovery process by avoiding some of the pitfalls observed in the history of sequence analysis, where it took several decades for probabilistic models to emerge as the proper framework.

An often-met criticism of machine-learning techniques is that they are "black box" approaches: one cannot always pin down exactly how a complex neural network, or hidden Markov model, reaches a particular answer. We have tried to address such legitimate concerns both within the general probabilistic framework and from a practical standpoint. It is important to realize, however, that many other techniques in contemporary molecular biology are used on a purely empirical basis. The polymerase chain reaction, for example, for all its usefulness and sensitivity, is still somewhat of a black box technique. Many of its adjustable parameters are chosen on a trial-and-error basis. The movement and mobility of sequences through matrices in gels is another area where the pragmatic success and usefulness are attracting more attention than the lack of detailed understanding of the underlying physical phenomena. Also, the molecular basis for the pharmacological effect of most drugs remains largely unknown. Ultimately the proof is in the pudding. We have striven to show that machine-learning methods yield good puddings and are being elegant at the same time.

Audience and Prerequisites

The book is aimed at both students and more advanced researchers, with diverse backgrounds. We have tried to provide a succinct description of the main biological concepts and problems for the readers with a stronger background in mathematics, statistics, and computer science. Likewise, the book is tailored to the biologists and biochemists who will often know more about the biological problems than the text explains, but need some help to understand the new data-driven algorithms, in the context of biological data. It should in principle provide enough insights while remaining sufficiently simple for the reader to be able to implement the algorithms described, or adapt them to a particular problem. The book, however, does not cover the informatics needed for the management of large databases and sequencing projects, or the processing of raw fluorescence data. The technical prerequisites for the book are basic calculus, algebra, and discrete probability theory, at the level of an undergraduate course. Any prior knowledge of DNA, RNA, and proteins is of course helpful, but not required.

Content and General Outline of the Book

We have tried to write a comprehensive but reasonably concise introductory book that is self-contained. The book includes definitions of main concepts and proofs of main theorems, at least in sketched form. Additional technical details can be found in the appendices and the references. A significant portion of the book is built on material taken from articles we have written over the years, as well as from tutorials given at several conferences, including the ISMB (Intelligent Systems for Molecular Biology) conferences, courses given at the Technical University of Denmark and UC Irvine, and workshops organized during the NIPS (Neural Information Processing Systems) conference. In particular, the general Bayesian probabilistic framework that is at the core of the book has been presented in several ISMB tutorials starting in 1994.

The main focus of the book is on methods, not on the history of a rapidly evolving field. While we have tried to quote the relevant literature in detail, we have concentrated our main effort on presenting a number of techniques, and perhaps a general way of thinking that we hope will prove useful. We have tried to illustrate each method with a number of results, often but not always drawn from our own practice.

Chapter 1 provides an introduction to sequence data in the context of molecular biology, and to sequence analysis. It contains in particular an overview of genomes and proteomes, the DNA and protein "universes" created by evolution that are becoming available in the public databases. It presents an overview of genomes and their sizes, and other comparative material that, if not original, is hard to find in other textbooks.

Chapter 2 is the most important theoretical chapter, since it lays the foundations for all machine-learning techniques, and shows explicitly how one must reason in the presence of uncertainty. It describes a general way of thinking about sequence problems: the Bayesian statistical framework for inference and induction. The main conclusion derived from this framework is that the proper language for machine learning, and for addressing all modeling problems, is the language of probability theory. All models *must* be probabilistic. And probability theory is all one needs for a scientific discourse on models and on their relationship to the data. This uniqueness is reflected in the title of the book. The chapter briefly covers classical topics such as priors, likelihood, Bayes theorem, parameter estimation, and model comparison. In the Bayesian framework, one is mostly interested in probability distributions over high-dimensional spaces associated, for example, with data, hidden variables, and model parameters. In order to handle or approximate such probability distributions, it is useful to exploit independence assumptions as much as possible, in order to achieve simpler factorizations. This is at the root of the notion of graphical models, where variable dependencies are associated with graph connectivity. Useful tractable models are associated with relatively sparse graphs. Graphical models and a few other techniques for handling high-dimensional distributions are briefly introduced in Chapter 2 and further elaborated in Appendix C. The inevitable use of probability theory and (sparse) graphical models are really the two central ideas behind all the methods.

Chapter 3 is a warm-up chapter, to illustrate the general Bayesian probabilistic framework. It develops a few classical examples in some detail which are used in the following chapters. It can be skipped by anyone familiar with such examples, or during a first quick reading of the book. All the examples are based on the idea of generating sequences by tossings one or several dices. While such a dice model is extremely simplistic, it is fair to say that a substantial portion of this book, Chapters 7–12, can be viewed as various generalizations of the dice model. Statistical mechanics is also presented as an elegant application of the dice model within the Bayesian framework. In addition, statistical mechanics offers many insights into different areas of machine learning. It is used in particular in Chapter 4 in connection with a number of algorithms, such as Monte Carlo and EM (expectation maximization) algorithms.

Chapter 4 contains a brief treatment of many of the basic algorithms required for Bayesian inference, machine learning, and sequence applications, in order to compute expectations and optimize cost functions. These include various forms of dynamic programming, gradient-descent and EM algorithms, as well as a number of stochastic algorithms, such as Markov chain Monte Carlo (MCMC) algorithms. Well-known examples of MCMC algorithms are described, such as Gibbs sampling, the Metropolis algorithm, and simulated annealing. This chapter can be skipped in a first reading, especially if the reader has a good acquaintance with algorithms and/or is not interested in implementing such algorithms.

Chapters 5–9 and Chapter 12 form the core of the book. Chapter 5 provides an introduction to the theory of neural networks. It contains definitions of the basic concepts, a short derivation of the "backpropagation" learning algorithm, as well as a simple proof of the fact that neural networks are universal approximators. More important, perhaps, it describes how neural networks, which are often introduced without any reference to probability theory, are in fact best viewed within the general probabilistic framework of Chapter 2. This in turn yields useful insights on the design of neural architectures and the choice of cost functions for learning.

Chapter 6 contains a selected list of applications of neural network techniques to sequence analysis problems. We do not attempt to cover the hundreds of applications produced so far, but have selected seminal examples where advances in the methodology have provided significant improvements over other approaches. We especially treat the issue of optimizing training procedures in the sequence context, and how to combine networks to form more complex and powerful algorithms. The applications treated in detail include protein secondary structure, signal peptides, intron splice sites, and gene-finding.

Chapters 7 and 8, on hidden Markov models, mirror Chapters 5 and 6. Chapter 7 contains a fairly detailed introduction to hidden Markov models (HMMs), and the corresponding dynamic programming algorithms (forward, backward, and Viterbi algorithms) as well as learning algorithms (EM, gradient-descent, etc.). Hidden Markov models of biological sequences can be viewed as generalized dice models with insertions and deletions.

Chapter 8 contains a selected list of applications of hidden Markov models to both protein and DNA/RNA problems. It demonstrates, first, how HMMs can be used, among other things, to model protein families, derive large multiple alignments, classify sequences, and search large databases of complete or fragment sequences. In the case of DNA, we show how HMMs can be used in gene-finding (promoters, exons, introns) and gene-parsing tasks.

HMMs can be very effective, but they have their limitations. Chapters 9–11 can be viewed as extensions of HMMs in different directions. Chapter 9 uses the theory of probabilistic graphical models systematically both as a unifying concept and to derive new classes of models, such as hybrid models that combine HMMs with artificial neural networks, or bidirectional Markov models that exploit the spatial rather than temporal nature of biological sequences. The chapter includes applications to gene-finding, analysis of DNA symmetries, and prediction of protein secondary structure.

Chapter 10 presents phylogenetic trees and, consistent with the framework of Chapter 2, the inevitable underlying probabilistic models of evolution. The models discussed in this chapter and throughout the book can be viewed as generalizations of the simple dice models of Chapter 3. In particular, we show how tree reconstruction methods that are often presented in a nonprobabilistic context (i.e., parsimony methods) are in fact a special case of the general framework as soon as the underlying probabilistic model they approximate is made explicit.

Chapter 11 covers formal grammars and the Chomsky hierarchy. Stochastic grammars provide a new class of models for biological sequences, which generalize both HMMs and the simple dice model. Stochastic regular grammars are in fact equivalent to HMMs. Stochastic context-free grammars are more powerful and roughly correspond to dice that can produce pairs of letters rather than single letters. Applications of stochastic grammars, especially to RNA modeling, are briefly reviewed.

Chapter 12 focuses primarily on the analysis of DNA microarray gene expression data, once again by generalizing the die model. We show how the Bayesian probabilistic framework can be applied systematically to array data. In particular, we treat the problems of establishing whether a gene behaves differently in a treatment versus control situation and of gene clustering. Analysis of regulatory regions and inference of gene regulatory networks are discussed briefly.

Chapter 13 contains an overview of current database resources and other information that is publicly available over the Internet, together with a list of useful directions to interesting WWW sites and pointers. Because these resources are changing rapidly, we focus on general sites where information is likely to be updated regularly. However, the chapter contains also a pointer to a page that contains regularly-updated links to all the other sites.

The book contains in appendix form a few technical sections that are important for reference and for a thorough understanding of the material. Appendix A covers statistical notions such as errors bars, sufficient statistics, and the exponential family of distributions. Appendix B focuses on information theory and the fundamental notions of entropy, mutual information, and relative entropy. Appendix C provides a brief overview of graphical models, independence, and Markov properties, in both the undirected case (random Markov fields) and the directed case (Bayesian networks). Appendix D covers technical issues related to hidden Markov models, such as scaling, loop architectures, and bendability. Finally, appendix E briefly reviews two related classes of machine learning models of growing importance, Gaussian processes and support vector machines. A number of exercises are also scattered throughout the book: from simple proofs left to the reader to suggestions for possible extensions.

For ease of exposition, standard assumptions of positivity or differentiability are sometimes used implicitly, but should be clear from the context.

What Is New and What Is Omitted

On several occasions, we present new unpublished material or old material but from a somewhat new perspective. Examples include the discussion around MaxEnt and the derivation of the Boltzmann–Gibbs distribution in Chapter 3, the application of HMMs to fragments, to promoters, to hydropathy profiles, and to bendability profiles in Chapter 8, the analysis of parsimony methods in probabilistic terms, the higher-order evolutionary models in Chapter 10, and the Bayesian analysis of gene differences in microarray data. The presentation we give of the EM algorithm in terms of free energy is not widely known and, to the best of our knowledge, was first described by Neal and Hinton in an unpublished technical report.

In this second edition we have benefited from and incorporated the feedback received from many colleagues, students, and readers. In addition to revisions and updates scattered throughout the book to reflect the fast pace of discovery set up by complete genome sequencing and other high-throughput technologies, we have included a few more substantial changes.

These include:

- New section on the human genome sequence in Chapter 1.

- New sections on protein function and alternative splicing in Chapter 1.

- New neural network applications in Chapter 6.

- A completely revised Chapter 9, which now focuses systematically on graphical models and their applications to bioinformatics. In particular, this chapter contains entirely new section about gene finding, and the use of recurrent neural networks for the prediction of protein secondary structure.

- A new chapter (Chapter 12) on DNA microarray data and gene expression.

- A new appendix (Appendix E) on support vector machines and Gaussian processes.

The book material and treatment reflect our personal biases. Many relevant topics had to be omitted in order to stay within reasonable size limits. At the theoretical level, we would have liked to be able to go more into higher levels of Bayesian inference and Bayesian networks. Most of the book in fact could have been written using Bayesian networks only, providing an even more unified treatment, at some additional abstraction cost. At the biological level, our treatment of phylogenetic trees, for example, could easily be expanded and the same can be said of the section on DNA microarrays and clustering (Chapter 12). In any case, we have tried to provide ample references where complementary information can be found.

Vocabulary and Notation

Terms such as "bioinformatics," "computational biology," "computational molecular biology," and "biomolecular informatics" are used to denote the field of interest of this book. We have chosen to be flexible and use all those terms essentially in an interchangeable way, although one should not forget that the first two terms are extremely broad and could encompass entire areas not directly related to this book, such as the application of computers to model the immune system, or the brain. More recently, the term "computational molecular biology" has also been used in a completely different sense, similar to "DNA computing," to describe attempts to build computing devices out of biomolecules rather than silicon. The adjective "artificial" is also implied whenever we use the term "neural network" throughout the book. We deal with artificial neural networks from an algorithmic-pattern-recognition point of view only.

And finally, a few words on notation. Most of the symbols used are listed at the end of the book. In general, we do not systematically distinguish between scalars, vectors, and matrices. A symbol such as "D" represents the data, regardless of the amount or complexity. Whenever necessary, vectors should be regarded as column vectors. Boldface letters are usually reserved for probabilistic concepts, such as probability ($\mathbf{P}$), expectation ($\mathbf{E}$), and variance ($\mathbf{Var}$). If X is a random variable, we write $\mathbf{P}(x)$ for $\mathbf{P}(X = x)$, or sometimes just $\mathbf{P}(X)$ if no confusion is possible. Actual distributions are denoted by P, Q, R, and so on.

We deal mostly with discrete probabilities, although it should be clear how to extend the ideas to the continuous case whenever necessary. Calligraphic style is reserved for particular functions, such as the energy ($\mathcal{E}$) and the entropy ($\mathcal{H}$). Finally, we must often deal with quantities characterized by many indices. A connection weight in a neural network may depend on the units, i and j, it connects; its layer, l; the time, t, during the iteration of a learning algorithm; and so on. Within a given context, only the most relevant indices are indicated. On rare occasions, and only when confusion is extremely unlikely, the same symbol is used with two different meanings (for instance, D denotes also the set of delete states of an HMM).

Acknowledgments

Over the years, this book has been supported by the Danish National Research Foundation and the National Institutes of Health. SmithKline Beecham Inc. sponsored some of the work on fragments at Net-ID. Part of the book was written while PB was in the Division of Biology, California Institute of Technology. We also acknowledge support from Sun Microsystems and the Institute for Genomics and Bioinformatics at UCI.

We would like to thank all the people who have provided feedback on early versions of the manuscript, especially Jan Gorodkin, Henrik Nielsen, Anders Gorm Pedersen, Chris Workman, Lars Juhl Jensen, Jakob Hull Kristensen, and David Ussery. Yves Chauvin and Van Mittal-Henkle at Net-ID, and all the members of the Center for Biological Sequence Analysis, have been instrumental to this work over the years in many ways.

We would like also to thank Chris Bishop, Richard Durbin, and David Haussler for inviting us to the Isaac Newton Institute in Cambridge, where the first edition of this book was finished, as well as the Institute itself for its great environment and hospitality. Special thanks to Geeske de Witte, Johanne Keiding, Kristoffer Rapacki, Hans Henrik Stærfeldt and Peter Busk Laursen for superb help in turning the manuscript into a book.

For the second edition, we would like to acknowledge new colleagues and students at UCI including Pierre-François Baisnée, Lee Bardwell, Thomas Briese, Steven Hampson, G. Wesley Hatfield, Dennis Kibler, Brandon Gaut, Richard Lathrop, Ian Lipkin, Anthony Long, Larry Marsh, Calvin McLaughlin, James Nowick, Michael Pazzani, Gianluca Pollastri, Suzanne Sandmeyer, and

Padhraic Smyth. Outside of UCI, we would like to acknowledge Russ Altman, Mark Borodovsky, Mario Blaum, Doug Brutlag, Chris Burge, Rita Casadio, Piero Fariselli, Paolo Frasconi, Larry Hunter, Emeran Mayer, Ron Meir, Burkhard Rost, Pierre Rouze, Giovanni Soda, Gary Stormo, and Gill Williamson.

We also thank the series editor Thomas Dietterich and the staff at MIT Press, especially Deborah Cantor-Adams, Ann Rae Jonas, Yasuyo Iguchi, Ori Kometani, Katherine Innis, Robert Prior, and the late Harry Stanton, who was instrumental in starting this project. Finally, we wish to acknowledge the support of all our friends and families.

Bioinformatics

Chapter 1

Introduction

1.1 Biological Data in Digital Symbol Sequences

A fundamental feature of chain molecules, which are responsible for the function and evolution of living organisms, is that they can be cast in the form of digital symbol sequences. The nucleotide and amino acid monomers in DNA, RNA, and proteins are distinct, and although they are often chemically modified in physiological environments, the chain constituents can without infringement be represented by a set of symbols from a short alphabet. Therefore experimentally determined biological sequences can in principle be obtained with complete certainty. At a particular position in a *given* copy of a sequence we will find a distinct monomer, or letter, and not a mixture of several possibilities.

The digital nature of genetic data makes them quite different from many other types of scientific data, where the fundamental laws of physics or the sophistication of experimental techniques set lower limits for the uncertainty. In contrast, provided the economic and other resources are present, nucleotide sequences in genomic DNA, and the associated amino acid sequences in proteins, can be revealed completely. However, in genome projects carrying out large-scale DNA sequencing or in direct protein sequencing, a balance among purpose, relevance, location, ethics, and economy will set the standard for the quality of the data.

The digital nature of biological sequence data has a profound impact on the types of algorithms that have been developed and applied for computational analysis. While the goal often is to study a particular sequence and its molecular structure and function, the analysis typically proceeds through the study of an ensemble of sequences consisting of its different versions in different species, or even, in the case of polymorphisms, different versions in

1

the same species. Competent comparison of sequence patterns across species must take into account that biological sequences are inherently "noisy," the variability resulting in part from random events amplified by evolution. Because DNA or amino acid sequences with a given function or structure will differ (and be uncertain), sequence models *must be probabilistic.*

1.1.1 Database Annotation Quality

It is somehow illogical that although sequence data can be determined experimentally with high precision, they are generally not available to researchers without additional noise stemming from the joint effects of incorrect interpretation of experiments and incorrect handling and storage in public databases. Given that biological sequences are stored electronically, that the public databases are curated by a highly diverse group of people, and, moreover, that the data are annotated and submitted by an even more diverse group of biologists and bioinformaticians, it is perhaps understandable that in many cases the error rate arising from the subsequent handling of information may be much larger than the initial experimental error [100, 101, 327].

An important factor contributing to this situation is the way in which data are stored in the large sequence databases. Features in biological sequences are normally indicated by listing the relevant positions in numeric form, and not by the "content" of the sequence. In the human brain, which is renowned for its ability to handle vast amounts of information accumulated over the lifetime of the individual, information is recalled by content-addressable schemes by which a small part of a memory item can be used to retrieve its complete content. A song, for example, can often be recalled by its first two lines.

Present-day computers are designed to handle numbers—in many countries human "accession" numbers, in the form of Social Security numbers, for one thing, did not exist before them [103]. Computers do not like content-addressable procedures for annotating and retrieving information. In computer search passport attributes of people—their names, professions, and hair color—cannot always be used to single out a perfect match, and if at all most often only when formulated using correct language and perfect spelling.

Biological sequence retrieval algorithms can been seen as attempts to construct associative approaches for finding specific sequences according to an often "fuzzy" representation of their content. This is very different from the retrieval of sequences according to their functionality. When the experimentalist submits functionally relevant information, this information is typically converted from what in the laboratory is kept as marks, coloring, or scribbles on the sequence itself. This "semiotic" representation by content is then converted into a representation where integers indicate individual positions. The numeric representation is subsequently impossible to review by human visual inspection.

In sequence databases, the result is that numerical feature table errors, instead of being acceptable noise on the retrieval key, normally will produce garbage in the form of more or less random mappings between sequence positions and the annotated structural or functional features. Commonly encountered errors are wrong or meaningless annotation of coding and noncoding regions in genomic DNA and, in the case of amino acid sequences, randomly displaced functional sites and posttranslational modifications. It may not be easy to invent the perfect annotation and data storage principle for this purpose. In the present situation it is important that the bioinformatician carefully take into account these potential sources of error when creating machine-learning approaches for prediction and classification.

In many sequence-driven mechanisms, certain nucleotides or amino acids are compulsory. Prior knowledge of this kind is an easy and very useful way of catching typographical errors in the data. It is interesting that machine-learning techniques provide an alternative and also very powerful way of detecting erroneous information and annotation. In a body of data, if something is notoriously hard to learn, it is likely that it represents either a highly atypical case or simply a wrong assignment. In both cases, it is nice to be able to sift out examples that deviate from the general picture. Machine-learning techniques have been used in this way to detect wrong intron splice sites in eukaryotic genes [100, 97, 101, 98, 327], wrong or missing assignments of O-linked glycosylation sites in mammalian proteins [235], or wrongly assigned cleavage sites in polyproteins from picornaviruses [75], to mention a few cases. Importantly, not all of the errors stem from data handling, such as incorrect transfer of information from published papers into database entries: significant number of errors stems from incorrect assignments made by experimentalists [327]. Many of these errors could also be detected by simple consistency checks prior to incorporation in a public database.

A general problem in the annotation of the public databases is the fuzzy statements in the entries regarding *who* originally produced the feature annotation they contain. The evidence may be experimental, or assigned on the basis of sequence similarity or by a prediction algorithm. Often ambiguities are indicated in a hard-to-parse manner in free text, using question marks or comments such as POTENTIAL or PROBABLE. In order not to produce *circular* evaluation of the prediction performance of particular algorithms, it is necessary to prepare the data carefully and to discard data from unclear sources. Without proper treatment, this problem is likely to increase in the future, because more prediction schemes will be available. One of the reasons for the success of machine-learning techniques within this imperfect data domain is that the methods often—in analogy to their biological counterparts—are able to handle noise, provided large corpora of sequences are available. New discoveries within the related area of natural language acquisition have proven that even eight-month-old infants can detect linguistic regularities and *learn* simple statistics for the recognition of word boundaries in continuous speech [458]. Since the language the infant has to learn is as unknown and complex as the DNA sequences seem to us, it is perhaps not surprising that learning techniques can be useful for revealing similar regularities in genomic data.

1.1.2 Database Redundancy

Another recurrent problem haunting the analysis of protein and DNA sequences is the redundancy of the data. Many entries in protein or genomic databases represent members of protein and gene families, or versions of homologous genes found in different organisms. Several groups may have submitted the same sequence, and entries can therefore be more or less closely related, if not identical. In the best case, the annotation of these very similar sequences will indeed be close to identical, but significant differences may reflect genuine organism or tissue specific variation.

In sequencing projects redundancy is typically generated by the different experimental approaches themselves. A particular piece of DNA may for example be sequenced in genomic form as well as in the form of cDNA complementary to the transcribed RNA present in the cell. As the sequence being deposited in the databases is determined by widely different approaches—ranging from noisy single-pass sequence to finished sequence based on five- to tenfold repetition—the same gene may be represented by many database entries displaying some degree of variation.

In a large number of eukaryotes, the cDNA sequences (complete or incomplete) represent the spliced form of the pre-mRNA, and this means again, for genes undergoing *alternative splicing*, that a given piece of genomic DNA in general will be associated with several cDNA sequences being noncontinuous with the chromosomal sequence [501]. Alternative splice forms can be generated in many different ways. Figure 1.1 illustrates some of the different ways coding and noncoding segments may be joined, skipped, and replaced during splicing. Organisms having a splice machinery at their disposal seem to use alternative splicing quite differently. The alternative to alternative splicing is obviously to include different versions of the same gene as individual genes in the genome. This may be the strategy used by the nematode *Caenorhabditis elegans*, which seems to contain a large number of genes that are very similar, again giving rise to redundancy when converted into data sets [315]. In the case of the human genome [234, 516, 142] it is not unlikely that at least 30-80% of the genes are alternatively spliced, in fact it may be the rule rather than

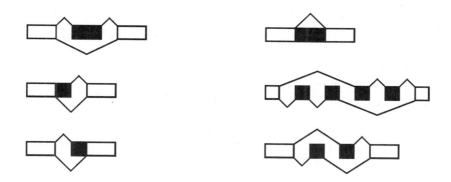

Figure 1.1: The Most Common Modes of Alternative Splicing in Eukaryotes. Left from top: Cassette exon (exon skipping or inclusion), alternative 5' splice site, alternative 3' splice site. Right from top: whole intron retention, pairwise spliced exons and mutually exclusive exons. These different types of alternative pre-mRNA processing can be combined [332].

the exception.

Data redundancy may also play a nontrivial role in relation to massively parallel gene expression experiments, a topic we return to in chapter 12. The sequence of genes either being spotted onto glass plates, or synthesized on DNA chips, is typically based on sequences, or clusters of sequences, deposited in the databases. In this way microarrays or chips may end up containing more sequences than there are genes in the genome of a particular organism, thus giving rise to noise in the quantitative levels of hybridization recorded from the experiments.

In protein databases a given gene may also be represented by amino acid sequences that do not correspond to a direct translation of the genomic wild-type sequence of nucleotides. It is not uncommon that protein sequences are modified slightly in order to obtain sequence versions that for example form better crystals for use in protein structure determination by X-ray crystallography [99]. Deletions and amino acid substitutions may give rise to sequences that generate database redundancy in a nontrivial manner.

The use of a redundant data set implies at least three potential sources of error. First, if a data set of amino acid or nucleic acid sequences contains large families of closely related sequences, statistical analysis will be biased toward these families and will overrepresent features peculiar to them. Second, apparent correlations between different positions in the sequences may be an artifact of biased sampling of the data. Finally, if the data set is being used for predicting a certain feature and the sequences used for making and calibrating the prediction method—the training set—are too closely related to the sequences used for testing, the apparent predictive performance may be overestimated, reflecting the method's ability to reproduce its own particular input rather than its generalization power.

At least some machine-learning approaches will run into trouble when certain sequences are heavily overrepresented in a training set. While algorithmic solutions to this problem have been proposed, it may often be better to clean up the data set first and thereby give the underrepresented sequences equal opportunity. It is important to realize that underrepresentation can pose problems both at the primary structure level (sequence redundancy) and at the classification level. Categories of protein secondary structures, for example, are typically skewed, with random coil being much more frequent than beta-sheet.

For these reasons, it can be necessary to avoid too closely related sequences in a data set. On the other hand, a too rigorous definition of "too closely related" may lead to valuable information being discarded from the data set. Thus, there is a trade-off between data set size and nonredundancy. The appropriate definition of "too closely related" may depend strongly on the problem under consideration. In practice, this is rarely considered. Often the test data are described as being selected "randomly" from the complete data set, implying that great care was taken when preparing the data, even though redundancy reduction was not applied at all. In many cases where redundancy reduction is applied, either a more or less arbitrary similarity threshold is used, or a "representative" data set is made, using a conventional list of protein or gene families and selecting one member from each family.

An alternative strategy is to keep all sequences in a data set and then assign weights to them according to their novelty. A prediction on a closely related sequence will then count very little, while the more distantly related sequences may account for the main part of the evaluation of the predictive performance. A major risk in this approach is that erroneous data almost always will be associated with large weights. Sequences with erroneous annotation will typically stand out, at least if they stem from typographical errors in the feature tables of the databases. The prediction for the wrongly assigned features will then have a major influence on the evaluation, and may even lead to a drastic underestimation of the performance. Not only will false sites be very hard to predict, but the true sites that would appear in a correct annotation will often be counted as false positives.

A very productive way of exploiting database redundancy—both in relation to sequence retrieval by alignment and when designing input representations for machine learning algorithms—is the *sequence profile* [226]. A profile describes position by position the amino acid variation in a family of sequences organized into a multiple alignment. While the profile no longer contains information about the sequential pattern in individual sequences, the degree of sequence variation is extremely powerful in database search, in programs such as PSI-BLAST, where the profile is iteratively updated by the sequences picked up by the current version of the profile [12]. In later chapters, we shall return to hidden Markov models, which also implement the profile concept in a very flexible manner, as well as neural networks receiving profile information as input—all different ways of taking advantage of the redundancy in the information being deposited in the public databases.

1.2 Genomes—Diversity, Size, and Structure

Genomes of living organisms have a profound diversity. The diversity relates not only to genome size but also to the storage principle as either single- or double-stranded DNA or RNA. Moreover, some genomes are linear (e.g. mammals), whereas others are closed and circular (e.g. most bacteria).

Cellular genomes are always made of DNA [389], while phage and viral genomes may consist of either DNA or RNA. In single-stranded genomes, the information is read in the positive sense, the negative sense, or in both directions, in which case one speaks of an ambisense genome. The positive direction is defined as going from the 5' to the 3' end of the molecule. In double-stranded genomes the information is read only in the positive direction (5' to 3' on either strand). Genomes are not always replicated directly; retroviruses, for example, have RNA genomes but use a DNA intermediate in the replication.

The smallest genomes are found in nonself-replicating suborganisms like bacteriophages and viruses, which sponge on the metabolism and replication machinery of free-living prokaryotic and eukaryotic cells, respectively. In 1977, the 5,386 bp in the genome of the bacteriophage ϕX174 was the first to be sequenced [463]. Such very small genomes normally come in one continuous piece of sequence. But other quite small genomes, like the 1.74 Mbp genome of the hyperthermophilic archaeon *Methanococcus jannaschii*, which was completely sequenced in 1996, may have several chromosomal components. In *M. jannaschii* there are three, one of them by far the largest. The much larger 3,310 Mbp human genome is organized into 22 chromosomes plus the two that determine sex. Even among the primates there is variation in the number of chromosomes. Chimpanzees, for example, have 23 chromosomes in addition to the two sex chromosomes. The chimpanzee somatic cell nucleus therefore contains a total number of 48 chromosomes in contrast to the 46 chromosomes in man. Other mammals have completely different chromosome numbers, the cat, for example, has 38, while the dog has as many as 78 chromosomes. As most higher organisms have two near-identical copies of their DNA (the *diploid* genome), one also speaks about the *haploid* DNA content, where only one of the two copies is included.

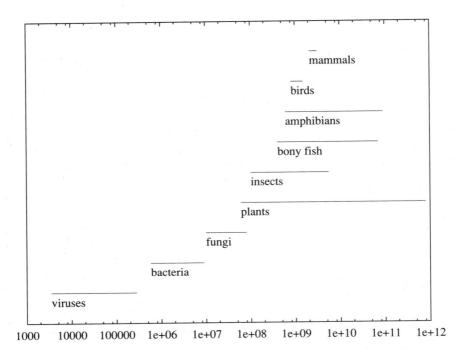

Figure 1.2: Intervals of Genome Sizes for Various Classes of Organisms. Note that the plot is logarithmic in the number of nucleotides on the first axis. Most commonly, the variation within one group is one order of magnitude or more. The narrow interval of genome sizes among mammals is an exception to the general picture. It is tempting to view the second axis as "organism complexity" but it is most certainly not a direct indication of the size of the gene pool. Many organisms in the upper part of the spectrum, e.g., mammals, fish, and plants, have comparable numbers of genes (see table 1.1).

The chromosome in some organisms is not stable. For example, the *Bacillus cereus* chromosome has been found to consist of a large stable component (2.4 Mbp) and a smaller (1.2 Mbp) less stable component that is more easily mobilized into extra-chromosomal elements of varying sizes up to the order of megabases [114]. This has been a major obstacle in determining the genomic sequence, or just a genetic map, of this organism. However, in almost any genome transposable elements can also be responsible for rearrangements, or insertion, of fairly large sequences, although they have been not been reported to cause changes in chromosome number. Some theories claim that a high number of chromosomal components is advantageous and increases the speed of evolution, but currently there is no final answer to this question [438].

It is interesting that the spectrum of genome sizes is to some extent segregated into nonoverlapping intervals. Figure 1.2 shows that viral genomes have sizes in the interval from 3.5 to 280 Kbp, bacteria range from 0.5 to 10 Mbp, fungi from around 10 to 50 Mbp, plants start at around 50 Mbp, and mammals are found in a more narrow band (on the logarithmic scale) around 1 Gb. This staircase reflects the sizes of the gene pools that are necessary for maintaining life in a noncellular form (viruses), a unicellular form (bacteria), multicellular forms without sophisticated intercellular communication (fungi), and highly differentiated multicellular forms with many intercellular signaling systems (mammals and plants). In recent years it has been shown that even bacteria are capable of chemical communication [300]. Molecular messengers may travel between cells and provide populationwide control. One famous example is the expression of the enzyme luciferase, which along with other proteins is involved in light production by marine bacteria. Still, this type of communication requires a very limited gene pool compared with signaling in higher organisms.

The general rule is that within most classes of organisms we see a huge relative variation in genome size. In eukaryotes, a few exceptional classes (e.g., mammals, birds, and reptiles) have genome sizes confined to a narrow interval [116]. As it is possible to estimate the size of the unsequenced gaps, for example by optical mapping, the size of the human genome is now known with a quite high precision. Table 1.2 shows an estimate of the size for each of the 24 chromosomes. In total the reference human genome sequence seems to contain roughly 3,310,004,815 base pairs—an estimate that presumably will change slightly over time.

The cellular DNA content of different species varies by over a millionfold. While the size of bacterial genomes presumably is directly related to the level of genetic and organismic complexity, within the eukaryotes there might be as much as a 50,000-fold excess compared with the basic protein-coding requirements [116]. Organisms that basically need the same molecular apparatus can have a large variation in their genome sizes. Vertebrates share a lot of basic machinery, yet they have very different genome sizes. As early as 1968, it was demonstrated that some fish, in particular the family Tetraodontidae, which contains the pufferfish, have very small genomes [254, 92, 163, 534, 526]. The pufferfish have genomes with a haploid DNA content around 400–500 Mbp, six–eight times smaller than the 3,310 Mbp human genome. The pufferfish *Fugu rubripes* genome is only four times larger than that of the much simpler nematode worm *Caenorhabditis elegans* (100 Mbp) and eight times smaller than the human genome. The vertebrates with the largest amount of DNA per cell are the amphibians. Their genomes cover an enormous range, from 700 Mbp to more than 80,000 Mbp. Nevertheless, they are surely less complex than most humans in their structure and behavior [365].

Group	Species	Genes	Genome size
Phages	Bacteriophage MS2	4	0.003569
	Bacteriophage T4	270	0.168899
Viruses	Cauliflower mosaic virus	8	0.008016
	HIV type 2	9	0.009671
	Vaccinia virus	260	0.191737
Bacteria	*Mycoplasma genitalium*	473	0.58
	Mycoplasma pneumoniae	716	0.82
	Haemophilus influenzae	1,760	1.83
	Bacillus subtilis	3,700	4.2
	Escherichia coli	4,100	4.7
	Myxococcus xanthus	8,000	9.45
Archaea	*Methanococcus jannaschii*	1,735	1.74
Fungi	*Saccharomyces cerevisiae*	5,800	12.1
Protoctista	*Cyanidioschyzon merolae*	5,000	11.7
	Oxytricha similis	12,000	600
Arthropoda	*Drosophila melanogaster*	15,000	180
Nematoda	*Caenorhabditis elegans*	19,000	100
Mollusca	*Loligo pealii*	20-30,000	2,700
Plantae	*Nicotiana tabacum*	20-30,000	4,500
	Arabidopsis thaliana	25,500	125
Chordata	*Giona intestinalis*	N	165
	Fugu rubripes	30-40,000	400
	Danio rerio	N	1,900
	Mus musculus	30-40,000	3,300
	Homo sapiens	30-40,000	3,310

Table 1.1: Approximate Gene Number and Genome Sizes in Organisms in Different Evolutionary Lineages. Genome sizes are given in megabases. N = not available. Data were taken in part from [390] and references therein (and scaled based on more current estimates); others were compiled from a number of different Internet resources, papers, and books.

1.2.1 Gene Content in the Human Genome and other Genomes

A variable part of the complete genome sequence in an organism contains *genes*, a term normally defined as one or several segments that constitute an expressible unit. The word *gene* was coined in 1909 by the Danish geneticist Wilhelm Johannsen (together with the words genetype and phenotype) long before the physical basis of DNA was understood in any detail.

Genes may encode a protein product, or they may encode one of the many RNA molecules that are necessary for the processing of genetic material and for the proper functioning of the cell. mRNA sequences in the cytoplasm are used as recipes for producing many copies of the same protein; genes encoding other RNA molecules must be transcribed in the quantities needed. Se-

Human chromosome	Size
Chr. 1	282,193,664
Chr. 2	253,256,583
Chr. 3	227,524,578
Chr. 4	202,328,347
Chr. 5	203,085,532
Chr. 6	182,415,242
Chr. 7	166,623,906
Chr. 8	152,776,421
Chr. 9	142,271,444
Chr. 10	145,589,288
Chr. 11	150,783,553
Chr. 12	144,282,489
Chr. 13	119,744,898
Chr. 14	106,953,321
Chr. 15	101,380,521
Chr. 16	104,298,331
Chr. 17	89,504,553
Chr. 18	86,677,548
Chr. 19	74,962,845
Chr. 20	66,668,005
Chr. 21	44,907,570
Chr. 22	47,662,662
Chr. X	162,599,930
Chr. Y	51,513,584

Table 1.2: Approximate Sizes for the 24 Chromosomes in the Human Genome Reference Sequence. Note that the 22 chromosome sizes do not rank according to the original numbering of the chromosomes. Data were taken from the Ensembl (www.ensembl.org) and Santa Cruz (genome.ucsc.edu) web-sites. In total the reference human genome sequence seems to contain roughly 3,310,004,815 base pairs—an estimate that presumably will change slightly over time.

quence segments that do not directly give rise to gene products are normally called noncoding regions. Noncoding regions can be parts of genes, either as regulatory elements or as intervening sequences interrupting the DNA that directly encode proteins or RNA. Machine-learning techniques are ideal for the hard task of interpreting unannotated genomic DNA, and for distinguishing between sequences with different functionality.

Table 1.1 shows the current predictions for the approximate number of genes and the genome size in organisms in different evolutionary lineages. In those organisms where the complete genome sequence has now been determined, the indications of these numbers are of course quite precise, while in other organisms only a looser estimate of the gene density is available. In some

Species	Haploid genome size	Bases	Entries
Homo sapiens	3,310,000,000	7,387,490,518	4,544,962
Mus musculus	3,300,000,000	1,527,228,639	2,793,543
Drosophila melanogaster	180,000,000	502,655,942	167,687
Arabidopsis thaliana	125,000,000	249,689,164	183,987
Caenorhabditis elegans	100,000,000	204,396,881	114,744
Oryza sativa	400,000,000	171,870,798	161,411
Tetraodon nigroviridis	350,000,000	165,542,107	189,000
Rattus norvegicus	2,900,000,000	114,331,466	229,838
Bos taurus	3,600,000,000	76,700,774	168,469
Glycine max	1,115,000,000	73,450,470	167,090
Medicago truncatula	400,000,000	60,606,228	120,670
Lycopersicon esculentum	655,000,000	56,462,749	109,913
Trypanosoma brucei	35,000,000	50,723,464	91,360
Hordeum vulgare	5,000,000,000	49,770,458	70,317
Giardia intestinalis	12,000,000	49,431,105	56,451
Strongylocentrotus purpur	900,000,000	47,633,412	77,554
Danio rerio	1,900,000,000	47,584,911	93,141
Xenopus laevis	3,100,000,000	46,517,145	92,041
Zea mays	5,000,000,000	45,978,459	98,818
Entamoeba histolytica	20,000,000	44,552,032	49,969

Table 1.3: The Number of Bases in GenBank rel. 123, April 2001, for the 20 Most Sequenced Organisms. For some organisms there is far more sequence than the size of the genome, due to strain variation and pure redundancy.

organisms, such as bacteria, where the genome size is a strong growth-limiting factor, almost the entire genome is covered with coding (protein and RNA) regions; in other, more slowly growing organisms the coding part may be as little as 1–2%. This means that the gene density in itself normally will influence the precision with which computational approaches can perform gene finding. The noncoding part of a genome will often contain many pseudo-genes and other sequences that will show up as false positive predictions when scanned by an algorithm.

The biggest surprise resulting from the analysis of the two versions of the human genome data [134, 170] was that the gene content may be as low as in the order of 30,000 genes. Only about 30,000-40,000 genes were estimated from the initial analysis of the sequence. It was not totally unexpected as the gene number in the fruit fly (14,000) also was unexpectedly low [132]. But how can man realize its biological potential with less than twice the number of genes found in the primitive worm *C. elegans*? Part of the answer lies in alternative splicing of this limited number of genes as well as other modes of multiplexing the function of genes. This area has to some degree been neglected in basic research and the publication of the human genome illustrated our ignorance all too clearly: only a year before the publication it was expected that around 100-120,000 genes would be present in the sequence [361]. For a complex organism, gene multiplexing makes it possible to produce several different transcripts from many of the genes in its genome, as well as many diferent protein variants from each transcript. As the cellular processing of genetic material is far more complex (in terms of regulation) than previously believed the need for sophisticated bioinformatics approaches with ability to model these processes is also strongly increased.

One of the big open questions is clearly how a quite substantial increase in organism complexity can arise from a quite modest increase in the size of the gene pool. The fact that worms have almost as many genes as humans is somewhat irritating, and in the era of whole cell and whole organism oriented research, we need to understand how the organism complexity scales with the potential of a fixed number of genes in a genome.

The French biologist Jean-Michel Claverie has made [132] an interesting "personal" estimate of the biological complexity K and its relation to the number of genes in a genome, N. The function f that converts N into K could in principle be linear ($K \sim N$), polynomial ($K \sim N^a$), exponential ($K \sim a^N$), $K \sim N!$ (factorial), and so on. Claverie suggests that the complexity should be related to the organism's ability to create diversity in its gene expression, that is to the number of theoretical transcriptome states the organism can achieve. In the simplest model, where genes are assumed to be either active or inactive (ON or OFF), a genome with N genes can potentially encode 2^N states. When we then compare humans to worms, we appear to be

$$2^{30,000} / 2^{20,000} \cong 10^{3,000} \tag{1.1}$$

more complex than nematodes thus confirming (and perhaps reestablishing) our subjective view of superiority of the human species. In this simple model the exponents should clearly be decreased because genes are not independently expressed (due to redundance and/or coregulation), and the fact that many of the states will be lethal. On the other hand gene expression is not ON/OFF, but regulated in a much more graded manner. A quite trivial mathematical model can thus illustrate how a small increase in gene number can lead to a large increase in complexity and suggests a way to resolve the apparent N value paradox which has been created by the whole genome sequencing projects. This model based on patterns of gene expression may seem very trivial, still it represents an attempt to quantify "systemic" aspects of organisms, even if all their parts still may be understood using more conventional, reductionistic approaches [132].

Another fundamental and largely unsolved problem is to understand why the part of the genome that code for protein, in many higher organisms, is quite limited. In the human sequence the coding percentage is small no matter whether one uses the more pessimistic gene number N of 26,000 or the more optimistic figure of 40,000 [170]. For these two estimates in the order of 1.1% (1.4%) of the human sequence seems to be coding, with introns covering 25% (36%) and the remaining intergenic part covering 75% (64%), respectively. While it is often stated that the genes only cover a few percent, this is obviously not true due to the large average intron size in humans. With the estimate of 40,000 genes more than one third of the entire human genome is covered by genes.

The mass of the nuclear DNA in an unreplicated haploid genome in a given organism is known as its C-value, because it usually is a constant in any one narrowly defined type of organism. The C-values of eukaryotic genomes vary at least 80,000-fold across species, yet bear little or no relation to organismic complexity or to the number of protein-coding genes [412, 545]. This phenomenon is known as the C-value paradox [518].

It has been suggested that noncoding DNA just accumulates in the nuclear genome until the costs of replicating it become too great, rather than having a structural role in the nucleus [412]. It became clear many years ago that the extra DNA does not in general contain an increased number of genes. If the large genomes contained just a proportionally increased number of copies of each gene, the kinetics of DNA renaturation experiments would be very fast. In renaturation experiments a sample of heat-denatured strands is cooled, and the strands reassociate provided they are sufficiently complementary. It has been shown that the kinetics is reasonably slow, which indicates that the extra DNA in voluminous genomes most likely does not encode genes [116]. In plants, where some of the most exorbitant genomes have been identified, clear evidence for a correlation between genome size and climate has been established [116]; the very large variation still needs to be accounted for in terms of molecular and evolutionary mechanisms. In any case, the size of the complete message in a genome is not a good indicator of the "quality" of the genome and its efficiency.

This situation may not be as unnatural as it seems. In fact, it is somewhat analogous to the case of communication between humans, where the message length fails to be a good measure of the quality of the information exchanged. Short communications can be very efficient, for example, in the scientific literature, as well as in correspondence between collaborators. In many E-mail exchanges the "garbage" has often been reduced significantly, leaving the essentials in a quite compact form. The shortest known correspondence between humans was extremely efficient: Just after publishing *Les Misérables* in 1862, Victor Hugo went on holiday, but was anxious to know how the sales were going. He wrote a letter to his publisher containing the single symbol "?". The publisher wrote back, using the single symbol "!", and Hugo could continue his

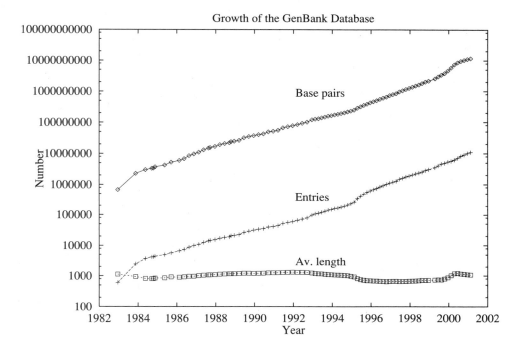

Figure 1.3: The Exponential Growth in the Size of the GenBank Database in the Period 1983-2001. Based on the development in 2000/2001, the doubling time is around 10 months. The complete size of GenBank rel. 123 is 12,418,544,023 nucleotides in 11,545,572 entries (average length 1076). Currently the database grows by more than 11,000,000 bases per day.

holiday without concern for this issue. The book became a best-seller, and is still a success as a movie and a musical.

The exponential growth in the size of the GenBank database [62, 503] is shown in figure 1.3. The 20 most sequenced organisms are listed in table 1.3. Since the data have been growing exponentially at the same pace for many years, the graph will be easy to extrapolate until new, faster, and even more economical sequencing techniques appear. If completely new sequencing approaches are invented the growth rate will presumably increase even further. Otherwise, it is likely that the rate will stagnate when several of the mammalian genomes have been completed. If sequencing at that time is still costly, funding agencies may start to allocate resources to other scientific areas, resulting in a lower production rate.

In addition to the publicly available data deposited in GenBank, proprietary data in companies and elsewhere are also growing at a very fast rate. This means that the current total amount of sequence data known to man is unknown. Today the raw sequencing of a complete prokaryotic genome may—in the largest companies—take less than a day, when arrays of hundreds of sequencing machines are operating in parallel on different regions of the same chromosome. Part of this kind of data will eventually be deposited in the public databases, while the rest will remain in the private domain. For all organisms speed matters a lot, not the least due to the patenting that usually is associated with the generation of sequence data.

1.3 Proteins and Proteomes

1.3.1 From Genome to Proteome

At the protein level, large-scale analysis of complete genomes has its counterpart in what has become known as *proteome* analysis [299, 413]. Proteomes contain the total protein expression of a set of chromosomes. In a multicellular organism this set of proteins will differ from cell type to cell type, and will also change with time because gene regulation controls advances in development from the embryonic stage and further on. Proteome research deals with the proteins produced by genes from a given genome.

Unlike the word "genome" which was coined just after the First World War by the German botanist Hans Winkler [561, 65], the word "proteome" entered the scientific literature recently, in 1994 in papers by Marc Wilkins and Keith Williams [559].

Proteome analysis not only deals with determining the sequence, location, and function of protein-encoding genes, but also is strongly concerned with the precise biochemical state of each protein in its posttranslational form. These active and functional forms of proteins have in several cases been successfully predicted using machine-learning techniques.

Proteins often undergo a large number of modifications that alter their activities. For example, certain amino acids can be linked covalently (or noncovalently) to carbohydrates, and such amino acids represent so-called *glycosylation* sites. Other amino acids are subjected to *phosphorylation*, where phosphate groups are added to the polypeptide chain. In both cases these changes, which are performed by a class of specific enzymes, may be essential for the functional role of the protein. Many other types of posttranslational modifications exist, such as addition of fatty acids and the cleavage of signal peptides in the N-terminus of secretory proteins translocated across a membrane. Together with all the other types, these modifications are very interesting in a data-driven prediction context, because a relatively large body of experimentally verified sites and sequences is deposited in the public databases.

1.3.2 Protein Length Distributions

The evolution of living organisms selects polypeptide chains with the ability to acquire stable conformations in the aqueous or lipid environments where they perform their function. It is well known that interaction between residues situated far from each other in the linear sequence of amino acids plays a crucial role in the folding of proteins. These long-range effects also represent the major obstacle to computational approaches to protein folding. Still, most research on the topic concentrates on the local aspects of the structure elucidation problem. This holds true for strategies involving prediction and classification as well as for computational approaches based on molecular forces and the equations of motion.

Statistical analysis has played a major role in studies of protein sequences and their evolution since the early studies of Ycas and Gamow [195, 575, 555]. Most work has focused on the statistics of local nonrandom patterns with a specific structure or function, while reliable global statistics of entire genomes have been made possible by the vast amounts of data now available.

The universe of protein sequences can be analyzed in its entirety across species, but also in an organism-specific manner where, for example, the length distribution of the polypeptide chains in the largest possible proteome can be identified completely. A key question is whether the protein sequences we see today represent "edited" versions of sequences that were of essentially random composition when evolution started working on them [555]. Alternatively, they could have been created early on with a considerable bias in their composition.

Using the present composition of soluble proteins, one can form on the order of 10^{112} "natural" sequences of length-100 amino acids. Only a very tiny fraction of these potential sequences has been explored by Nature. A "random origin hypothesis," which asserts that proteins originated by stochastic processes according to simple rules, has been put forward by White and Jacobs [556, 555]. This theory can be taken formally as a null hypothesis when examining different aspects of the randomness of protein sequences, in particular to what extent proteins can be distinguished from random sequences.

The evidence for long-range order and regularity in protein primary structure is accumulating. Surprisingly, species-specific regularity exists even at a level below the compositional level: the typical length of prokaryotic proteins is consistently different from the typical length in eukaryotes [64]. This may be linked to the idea that the probability of folding into a compact structure increases more rapidly with length for eukaryotic than for prokarytic sequences [555]. It has been suggested that the observed differences in the sequence lengths can be explained by differences in the concentration of disulfide bonds between cysteine residues and its influence on the optimal domain sizes [304].

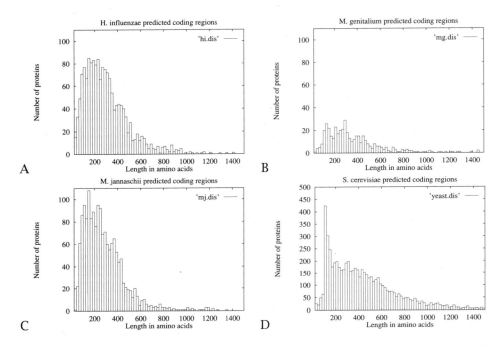

Figure 1.4: Length Distributions for Predicted Protein Coding Regions in Entire Genomes. **A.** *H. influenzae*, among the 1,743 regions, amino acid chains of lengths between 140 and 160 are the most frequent. **B.** *M. genitalium* with 468 regions, and preferred amino acid chains of length between 120 and 140 or 280 and 300. **C.** The archaeon *M. jannaschii* with 1,735 regions; amino acid chains of length between 140 and 160 are the most frequent. **D.** *S. cerevisiae*, among the 6,200 putative protein coding regions, amino acid chains of length between 100 and 120 are the most frequent; this interval is followed by the interval 120 to 140. As described in a 1997 correspondence in *Nature*, the *S. cerevisiae* set clearly contains an overrepresentation (of artifact sequences) in the 100–120 length interval [144].

Several other types of long-range regularities have been investigated, for example, the preference for identical or similar residue partners in beta-sheets [543, 570, 268, 45] and in close contact pairs [273], the long- and short-distance periodicity in packing density [175], and whether mutations in the amino acid sequence are significantly correlated over long distances [515, 485, 214].

The advent of the complete genomes from both prokaryotic and eukaryotic organisms has made it possible to check whether earlier observations based on incomplete and redundant data hold true when single organisms are compared. One quite surprising observation has been that proteins appear to be made out of different sequence units with characteristic length of ≈ 125 amino acids in eukaryotes and ≈ 150 amino acids in prokaryotes [64]. This indicates a possible underlying order in protein sequence organization that is more fundamental than the sequence itself. If such a systematics has indeed been created by evolution, the *length* distributions of the polypeptide chains may be more fundamental than what conventionally is known as the "primary" structure of proteins.

In 1995 the first complete genome of a free living organism, the prokaryote *Haemophilus influenzae*, was published and made available for analysis [183]. This circular genome contains 1,830,137 bp with 1,743 predicted protein coding regions and 76 genes encoding RNA molecules. In figure 1.4 the length distribution of *all* the putative proteins in this organism is shown. For comparison, the figure also shows the length distributions of the ≈ 468 proteins in the complete *Mycoplasma genitalium* genome [189], as well as the $\approx 1,735$ predicted protein coding regions in the complete genome of the archaeon *Methanococcus jannaschii* [105].

By comparing *Saccharomyces cerevisiae* (figure 1.4) against the distributions for the prokaryotes, it is possible by mere inspection to observe that the peaks for the prokaryote *H. influenzae* and the eukaryote *S. cerevisiae* are positioned in what clearly are different intervals: at 140–160 and 100–120, respectively.

Performing *redundancy* reduction together with spectral analysis has led to the conclusion that a eukaryotic distribution from a wide range of species peaks at 125 amino acids and that the distribution displays a periodicity based on this size unit [64]. Figure 1.4D also clearly shows that weaker secondary and tertiary peaks are present around 210 and 330 amino acids. This distribution is based on the entire set of proteins in this organism, and not a redundancy reduced version.

Interestingly, the distribution for the archaeon *M. jannaschii* lies in between the *H. influenzae* and the *S. cerevisiae* distributions. This is in accordance with the emerging view that the archaeon kingdom shares many similarities with eukaryotes rather than representing a special kind of bacteria in the prokaryotic kingdom [564, 105, 197]. This indicates that the universal ancestral progenote has induced conserved features in genomes of bacteria, archaea, and eucaryota:

$$\mathtt{prokaryota(nonucleus)} \neq \mathtt{bacteria}. \qquad (1.2)$$

This classification issue for archaeon organisms has led to confusion in textbooks and in the rational basis for classifying organisms in sequence databases [197].

Annotated protein primary structures also accumulate rapidly in the public databases. Table 1.4 shows the number of protein sequences in the top-scoring organisms in one of the protein sequence databases, SWISS-PROT [24]. Figure

Species	Sequences
Homo sapiens	6,742
Saccharomyces cerevisiae	4,845
Escherichia coli	4,661
Mus musculus	4,269
Rattus norvegicus	2,809
Bacillus subtilis	2,229
Caenorhabditis elegans	2,163
Haemophilus influenzae	1,746
Schizosaccharomyces pombe	1,654
Drosophila melanogaster	1,443
Methanococcus jannaschii	1,429
Arabidopsis thaliana	1,240
Mycobacterium tuberculosi	1,228
Bos bovis	1,202
Gallus gallus	948

Table 1.4: The Number of Sequences for the 15 Most Abundant Organisms in SWISS-PROT rel. 39.16, April 2001.

1.5 shows the development of the size of this database. Like GenBank, it grows exponentially, although at a much slower pace. This illustrates how much more slowly the biologically meaningful interpretation of the predicted genes arises. New techniques are needed, especially for functional annotation of the information stemming from the DNA sequencing projects [513].

Another database which grows even more slowly is the Protein Data Bank (PDB). This reflects naturally the amount of experimental effort that normally is associated with the determination of three dimensional protein structure, whether performed by X-ray crystallography or NMR. Still, as can be seen in Figure 1.6 this database also grows exponentially, and due to the initiation of many structural genomics projects in the US, Japan and Europe it is very likely that this pattern will continue for quite a while.

1.3.3 Protein Function

Many functional aspects of proteins are determined mainly by local sequence characteristics, and do not depend critically on a full 3D structure maintained in part by long-range interactions [149]. In the context of overall functional prediction, these characteristics can provide essential hints toward the precise function of a particular protein, but they can also be of significant value in establishing negative conclusions regarding compartmentalization—for example, that a given protein is nonsecretory or nonnuclear.

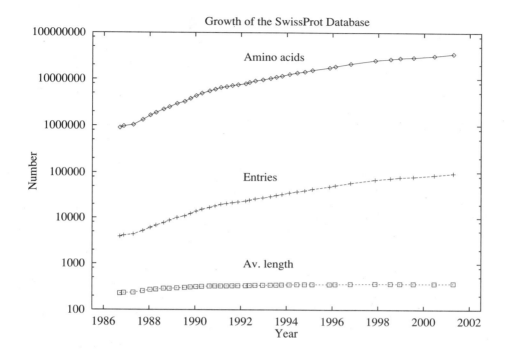

Figure 1.5: The Exponential Growth of the SWISS-PROT Database in the Period 1987–2001. The size of SWISS-PROT rel. 39.16 is in the order of 34,800,000 amino acids from 95,000 entries.

One of the major tasks within bioinformatics in the postgenome era will be to find out what the genes really do in concerted action, either by simultaneous measurement of the activity of arrays of genes or by analyzing the cell's protein complement [408, 360, 413]. It is not unlikely that it will be hard to determine the function of many proteins experimentally, because the function may be related specifically to the native environment in which a particular organism lives. Bakers yeast, *Saccharomyces cerevisiae*, has not by evolution been designed for the purpose of baking bread, but has been shaped to fit as a habitant of plant crops like grapes and figs [215]. Many genes may be included in the genome for the purpose of securing survival in a particular environment, and may have no use in the artificial environment created in the laboratory. It may even, in many cases, be almost impossible to imitate the natural host, with its myriad other microorganisms, and thereby determine the exact function of a gene or gene product by experiment.

The only effective route toward the elucidation of the function of some of

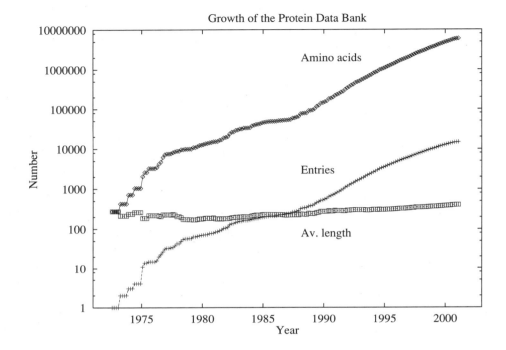

Figure 1.6: The Exponential Growth of the PDB Database in the Period 1972–2001. The size of PDB (April 19, 2001) is in the order of 6,033,000 amino acids from 14,910 entries (average length 405 aa).

these so-called orphan proteins may be computational analysis and prediction, which can produce valuable indirect evidence for their function. Many protein characteristics can be inferred from the sequence. Some sequence features will be related to cotranslational or postfolding modifications; others, to structural regions providing evidence for a particular general three-dimensional topology. Prediction along these lines will give a first hint toward functionality that later can be subjected to experimental verification [288].

In the last couple of years a number of methods that do not rely on direct sequence similarity have been published [380, 162, 271, 378]. One quite successful method has been exploiting gene expression data obtained using DNA array [425] and chip technology (see chapter 12). Genes of unknown function that belong to a cluster of genes displaying similar expression over time, or tissue types, may be assigned the function of the most prevalent gene function in that cluster (provided the cluster has genes with known function as members).

In this way functional information may be transferred between genes with little or no sequence similarity. However, coregulated genes may also in many cases have widely different functions, so often this approach cannot be used alone. Another problem is that as the DNA arrays become larger and larger, covering for example an entire mammalian genome, more and more clusters of genes significantly down- or upregulated will appear, where not a single gene has functional information assigned to it.

Another approach is the so-called "Rosetta stone" method, which is based on patterns of domain fusions [379, 167]. The underlying idea is that if two proteins in one organism exist as one fused multidomain protein in another organism, this may indicate that the two proteins are involved in performing the same function even though they are not directly related in sequence.

A third tool that can be used for linking together proteins of similar function is phylogenetic profiles [423]. In phylogenetic profiles each protein is represented as the organisms in which homologs are observed. If two proteins have identical (or very similar) phylogenetic profiles it indicates that they normally are observed together—an organism encodes either both or neither of the proteins in its genome. One possible explanation for this is that the proteins together perform a similar function. Phylogenetic profiles should be expected to become more powerful as more genomes become available. They have been successfully applied to the yeast genome but until several multicellular organisms have been sequenced they are of limited use for predicting the function of human proteins.

1.3.4 Protein Function and Gene Ontologies

Genomewide assignment of function requires that the functional role of proteins be described in a systematic manner using well defined categories, keywords, and hierachies. A gene ontology is essentially a specification of relevant concepts in molecular biology and the relationships among those concepts. If information in the scientific literature and in databases is to be shared in the most useful way, ontologies must be exchanged in a form that uses standardized syntax and semantics. In practice this means for example that functional categories and systematics must be designed to cover a wide range of organisms, if not all, and that the system is able to incorporate new discoveries as they appear over time.

One of the major developments [21, 22] in this area has been the creation of the *Gene Ontology Consortium*, which has participation from different areas, including fruitfly (FlyBase), budding yeast (Saccharomyces Genome Database), mouse (Mouse Genome and Gene Expression Databases), brassica (The Arabidopsis Information Resource), and nematode (WormBase). The goal of the

Gene Ontology Consortium is to produce a dynamic controlled vocabulary that is based on three organizing principles and functional aspects: (1) molecular function, (2) biological process and (3) cellular component. A protein can represent one or more molecular functions, be used in one or more biological processes, and be associated with one or more cellular components.

Molecular function describes the tasks performed by individual gene products; examples are transcription factor and DNA helicase. Biological process describes broad biological goals, such as mitosis or purine metabolism, that are accomplished by ordered assemblies of molecular functions. Cellular component encompasses subcellular structures, locations, and macromolecular complexes; examples include nucleus, telomere, and origin recognition complex.

There are many ways to construct ontologies, including some with focus on molecular complexes or the immune system; see for example the RiboWeb ontology [123] or the ImMunoGenetics ontology [213]. Another prominent example is the *EcoCyc* ontology [307, 308], which is the ontology used in a database describing the genome and the biochemical machinery of *E. coli*. The database describes pathways, reactions, and enzymes of a variety of organisms, with a microbial focus. *EcoCyc* describes for example each metabolic enzyme of *E. coli*, including its cofactors, activators, inhibitors, and subunit structure. When known, the genes encoding the subunits of an enzyme are also listed, as well as the map position of a gene on the *E. coli* chromosome.

1.4   On the Information Content of Biological Sequences

The concept of information and its quantification is essential for understanding the basic principles of machine-learning approaches in molecular biology (for basic definitions see appendix B, for a review see [577]). Data-driven prediction methods should be able to extract essential features from individual examples and to discard unwanted information when present. These methods should be able to distinguish positive cases from negative ones, also in the common situation where a huge excess of negative, nonfunctional sites and regions are present in a genome. This discrimination problem is of course intimately related to the molecular recognition problem [363, 544, 474] in the cellular environment: How can macromolecules find the sites they are supposed to interact with when similar sites are present in very large numbers?

Machine-learning techniques are excellent for the task of discarding and compacting redundant sequence information. A neural network will, if not unreasonably oversized, use its adjustable parameters for storing common features that apply to many data items, and not allocate individual parameters to individual sequence patterns. The encoding principle behind neural network training procedures superimposes sequences upon one another in a way that transforms a complex topology in the input sequence space into a simpler representation. In this representation, related functional or structural categories end up clustered rather than scattered, as they often are in sequence space.

For example, the set of all amino acid segments of length 13, where the central residue is in a helical conformation, is scattered over a very large part of the sequence space of segments of length 13. The same holds true for other types of protein secondary structures like sheets and turns. In this sequence space, 20^{13} possible segments exist (when excluding the twenty-first amino acid, selenocysteine). The different structural categories are typically *not* found in nicely separated regions of sequence space [297, 244]; rather, islands of sheets are found in sequence regions where segments preferably adopt a helical conformation, and vice versa. Machine-learning techniques are used because of their ability to cope with nonlinearities and to find more complex correlations in sequence spaces that are not functionally segregated into continuous domains.

Some sequence segments may even have ability to attain both the helix and the sheet conformation, depending on the past history of interaction with other macromolecules and the environment. Notably, this may be the case for the prion proteins, which recently have been associated with mad cow disease, and in humans with the Creutzfeldt–Jakob syndrome. In these proteins the same sequence may adopt different very stable conformations: a normal conformation comprising a bundle of helices and a disease-inducing "bad" conformation with a mixture of helices and sheets. The bad-conformation prions even have an autocatalytic effect, and can be responsible for the transformation of normal conformation prions into bad ones [266, 267, 444]. In effect, the protein itself serves as carrier of structural information which can be inherited. To distinguish this pathogen from conventional genetic material, the term "prion" was introduced to emphasize its proteinaceous and infectious nature. The 1997 Nobel Prize for Physiology or Medicine was given to Stanley B. Prusiner for his work on prions. The proposal that proteins alone can transmit an infectious disease has come as a considerable surprise to the scientific community, and the mechanisms underlying their function remain a matter of hot debate.

Based on local sequence information, such conformational conflicts as those in the prion proteins will of course be impossible to settle by any prediction method. However, a local method may be able to report that a piece of sequence may have a higher potential for, say, both helix and sheet as opposed to coil. This has actually been the case for the prion sequences [266, 267] when they are analyzed by one of the very successful machine-learning methods in sequence analysis, the PHD method of Rost and Sander. We return to this and other methods for the prediction of protein secondary structure in chapter 6.

Another issue related to redundancy is the relative importance of individual amino acids in specifying the tertiary structure of a protein [347]. To put it differently: What fraction of a protein's amino acid sequence is sufficient to specify its structure? A prize—the Paracelsus Challenge—has even been put forth to stimulate research into the role of sequence specificity in contrast to protein stability [450, 291, 449]. The task is to convert one protein fold into another, while retaining 50% of the original sequence. Recently, a protein that is predominantly beta-sheet has in this way been transmuted into a native-like, stable, four-helix bundle [143]. These studies clearly show that the residues determine the fold in a highly nonlinear manner. The identification of the minimal requirements to specify a given fold will not only be important for the design of prediction approaches, but also a significant step towards solving the protein folding problem [143].

The analysis of the redundancy and information content of biological sequences has been strongly influenced by linguistics since the late 1950s. Molecular biology came to life at a time when scientific methodology in general was affected by linguistic philosophy [326]. Many influential ideas stemming from the philosophical and mathematical treatment of natural languages were for that reason partly "recycled" for the analysis of "natural" biological sequences—and still are for that matter (see chapter 11). The digital nature of genetic information and the fact that biological sequences are translated from one representation to another in several consecutive steps have also contributed strongly to the links and analogies between the two subjects.

The study of the translation genetic code itself was similarly influenced by the time at which the code was cracked. The assignment of the 20 amino acids and the translation stop signal to the 64 codon triplets took place in the 1960s, when the most essential feature a code could have was its ability to perform error correction. At that time the recovery of messages from spacecraft was a key topic in coding and information theory. Shannon's information-theoretical procedures for the use of redundancy in encoding to transmit data over noisy channels without loss were in focus. In the case of the genetic code, its block structure ensures that the most frequent errors in the codon–anticodon recognition will produce either the same amino acid, as intended, or insert an amino acid with at least some similar physicochemical properties, most notably its hydrophobicity. The importance of other nonerror-correcting properties of the genetic code may have been underestimated, and we shall see in chapter 6 that a neural network trained on the mapping between nucleotide triplets and amino acids is simpler for the standard code, and much more complex when trained on more error-correcting genetic codes that have been suggested as potential alternatives to the code found by evolution [524].

The amount of information in biological sequences is related to their compressibility. Intuitively, simple sequences with many repeats can be represented using a shorter description than complex and random sequences that never repeat themselves. Data-compression algorithms are commonly used in computers for increasing the capacity of disks, CD-ROMs, and magnetic tapes. Conventional text-compression schemes are so constructed that they can recover the original data perfectly without losing a single bit. Text-compression algorithms are designed to provide a shorter description in the form of a less redundant representation—normally called a code—that may be interpreted and converted back into the uncompressed message in a reversible manner [447]. The literature on molecular biology itself is full of such code words, which shortens this particular type of text. The abbreviation DNA, for *deoxyribonucleic acid*, is one example that contributes to the compression of this book [577].

In some text sequences—for example, the source code of a computer program—losing a symbol may change its meaning drastically, while compressed representations of other types of data may be useful even if the original message cannot be recovered completely. One common example is sound data. When sound data is transmitted over telephone lines, it is less critical to reproduce everything, so "lossy" decompression in this case can be acceptable. In lossless compression, the encoded version is a kind of program for computing the original data. In later chapters both implicit and explicit use of compression in connection with machine learning will be described.

In section 1.2 an experimental approach to the analysis of the redundancy of large genomes was described. If large genomes contained just a proportionally increased number of copies of each gene, the kinetics of DNA renaturation experiments would be much faster than observed. Therefore, the extra DNA in voluminous genomes most likely does not code for proteins [116], and consequently algorithmic compression of sequence data becomes a less trivial task.

The study of the statistical properties of repeated segments in biological sequences, and especially their relation to the evolution of genomes, is highly informative. Such analysis provides much evidence for events more complex than the fixation and incorporation of single stochastically generated mutations. Combination of interacting genomes, both between individuals in the same species and by horizontal transfer of genetic information between species, represents intergenome communication, which makes the analysis of evolutionary pathways difficult.

Nature makes seemingly wasteful and extravagant combinations of genomes that become sterile organisms unable to contribute further to the evolution of the gene pool. Mules are well-known sterile crosses of horses and donkeys. Less well known are *ligers*, the offspring of mating male LIons and female tiGERS. *Tigrons* also exist. In contrast to their parents, they are very nervous and uneasy animals; visually they are true blends of the most char-

Figure 1.7: A Photograph of a Liger, the Cross between a Lion and a Tiger. Courtesy of the Los Angeles Wild Animal Way Station (Beverly Setlowe).

acteristic features of lions and tigers. It is unclear whether free-living ligers can be found in the wild; most of their potential parents inhabit different continents[1], but at the Los Angeles Wild Animal Way Station several ligers have been placed by private owners who could no longer keep them on their premises. Figure 1.7 shows this fascinating and intriguing animal.

In biological sequences *repeats* are clearly—from a description length viewpoint—good targets for compaction. Even in naturally occurring sequence without repeats, the statistical biases—for example, skew dipeptide, and skew di- and trinucleotide, distributions—will make it possible to find shorter symbol sequences where the original message can be rewritten using representative words and extended alphabets.

The ratio between the size of an encoded corpus of sequences and the original corpus of sequences yields the compression rate, which quantifies

---

[1]In a few Asian regions, lions and tigers live close to one another, for example, in Gujarat in the northwestern part of India.

globally the degree of regularity in the data:

$$R_C = \frac{S_E}{S_O}. \tag{1.3}$$

One important difference between natural text and DNA is that repeats occur differently. In long natural texts, repeats are often quite small and close to each other, while in DNA, long repeats can be found far from each other [447]. This makes conventional sequential compression schemes [56] less effective on DNA and protein data. Still, significant compression can be obtained even by algorithms designed for other types of data, for example, the compress routine from the UNIX environment, which is based on the Lempel–Ziv algorithm [551]. Not surprisingly, coding regions, with their reading frame and triplet regularity, will normally be more compressible than more random noncoding regions like introns [279]. Functional RNAs are in general considered to be less repetitive than most other sequences [326], but their high potential for folding into secondary structures gives them another kind of inherent structure, reducing their randomness or information content.

Hidden Markov models are powerful means for analyzing the sequential pattern of monomers in sequences [154]. They are generative models that can produce any possible sequence in a given language, each message with its own probability. Since the models normally are trained to embody the regularity in a sequence set, the vast majority of possible sequences end up having a probability very close to 0. If the training is successful, the sequences in the training set (and, hopefully, their homologues) end up having a higher probability. One may think of a hidden Markov model as a tool for parameterizing a distribution over the space of all possible sequences on a given alphabet. A particular family of proteins—globins, for example—will be a cloud of points in sequence space. Training a model on some of these sequences is an attempt to create a distribution on sequence space that is peaked over that cloud.

1.4.1   Information and Information Reduction

Classification and prediction algorithms are in general computational means for *reducing* the amount of information. The input is information-rich sequence data, and the output may be a single number or, in the simplest case, a *yes* or *no* representing a choice between two categories. In the latter case the output holds a maximum of one bit if the two possibilities are equally likely. A segregation of amino acid residues, depending on whether they are in an alpha-helical conformation or not, will be such a dichotomy, where the average output information will be significantly under one bit per residue, because in natural proteins roughly only 30% of the amino acids are found in the helical category. On average less than one yes/no question will then be required to "guess" the conformational categories along the sequences.

The contractive character of these algorithms means that they cannot be inverted; prediction programs cannot be executed backward and thus return the input information. From the output of a neural network that predicts the structural class of an amino acid residue, one cannot tell what particular input amino acid it was, and even less its context of other residues. Similarly, the log-likelihood from a hidden Markov model will not make it possible to reproduce the original sequence to any degree.

In general, computation discards information and proceeds in a logically irreversible fashion. This is true even for simple addition of numbers; the sum does not hold information of the values of the addends. This is also true for much of the sequence-related information processing that takes place in the cell. The genetic code itself provides a most prominent example: the degenerate mapping between the 64 triplets and the 20 amino acids plus the translation stop signal. For all but two amino acids, methionine and tryptophan, the choice between several triplets will make it impossible to retrieve the encoding mRNA sequence from the amino acids in the protein or which of the three possible stop codons actually terminated the translation. The individual probability distribution over the triplets in a given organism—known as its codon usage—determines how much information the translation will discard in practice.

Another very important example is the preceding process, which in eukaryotes produces the mature mRNA from the pre-mRNA transcript of the genomic DNA. The noncoding regions, introns, which interrupt the protein coding part, are removed and spliced out in the cell nucleus (see also sections 1.1.2 and 6.5.4) But from the mature mRNA it seems difficult or impossible to locate with high precision the junctions where the intervening sequences belonged [495, 496], and it will surely be impossible to reproduce the intron sequence from the spliced transcript. Most of the conserved local information at the splice junctions is in the introns. This makes sense because the exons, making up the mature mRNA sequence, then are unconstrained in terms of their protein encoding potential. Interestingly, specific proteins seem to associate with the exon-exon junctions in the mature mRNA only as a consequence of splicing [256], thus making the spliced messenger "remember" where the introns were. The splicing machinery leaves behind such signature proteins at the junctions, perhaps with the purpose of influencing downstream metabolic events in vivo such as mRNA transport, decay and translation.

Among the more exotic examples of clear-cut information reduction are phenomena like RNA editing [59] and the removal of "inteins" from proteins [301, 257]. In RNA editing the original transcript is postprocessed using guide RNA sequences found elsewhere in the genome. Either single nucleotides or longer pieces are changed or skipped. It is clear that the original RNA copy of the gene cannot in any way be recovered from the edited mRNA.

It has also been discovered that polypeptide chains in some cases are spliced, sequence fragments known as inteins are removed, and the chain ends are subsequently ligated together. In the complete genome of the archaeon *Methanococcus jannaschii*, a surprisingly large number of inteins were discovered in the predicted open reading frames. Many other examples of logically and physically irreversible processes exist. This fact is of course related to the irreversible thermodynamic nature of most life processes.

The information reduction inherent in computational classification and prediction makes it easier to see why in general it does not help to add extra input data to a method processing a single data item. If strong and valuable correlations are not present in the extra data added, the method is given the increased burden of discarding even more information on the route toward the output of a single bit or two. Despite the fact that the extra data contain some exploitable features, the result will often be a lower signal-to-noise level and a decreased prediction performance (see chapter 6).

Protein secondary structure prediction normally works better when based on 13 amino acid segments instead of segments of size 23 or higher. This is not due solely to the curse of dimensionality of the input space, with a more sparse coverage of the space by a fixed number of examples [70]. Given the amount of three-dimensional protein structure data that we have, the amount of noise in the context of 10 extra residues exceeds the positive effect of the long-range correlations that are in fact present in the additional sequence data.

Machine-learning approaches may have some advantages over other methods in having a built-in robustness when presented with uncorrelated data features. Weights in neural networks vanish during training unless positive or negative correlations keep them alive and put them into use. This means that the 23-amino-acid context not will be a catastrophe; but it still cannot outperform a method designed to handle an input space where the relation between signal and noise is more balanced.

Information reduction is a key feature in the *understanding* of almost any kind of system. As described above, a machine-learning algorithm will create a simpler representation of a sequence space that can be much more powerful and useful than the original data containing all details.

The author of *Alice in Wonderland*, the mathematician Charles Dodgson (Lewis Carroll), more than 100 years ago wrote about practical issues in relation to maps and mapping. In the story "Sylvie and Bruno Concluded" the character Mein Herr tells about the most profound map one can think of, a map with the scale *one kilometer per kilometer*. He is asked, "Have you used it much?" He answers, "It has not been unfolded yet. The farmers were against it. They said that it would cover all the soil and keep the sunlight out! Now we use the country itself, as its own map. And I can assure you that it is almost as good."

In the perspective of Mein Herr, we should stay with the unstructured, flat-file public databases as they are, and not try to enhance the principal features by using neural networks or hidden Markov models.

1.4.2 Alignment Versus Prediction: When Are Alignments Reliable?

In order to obtain additional functional insights as well as additional hints toward structural and functional relationships, new sequences are normally aligned against all sequences in a number of large databases [79]. The fundamental question is: When is the sequence similarity high enough that one may safely infer either a structural or a functional similarity from the pairwise alignment of two sequences? In other words, given that the alignment method has detected an overlap in a sequence segment, can a similarity threshold be defined that sifts out cases where the inference will be reliable? Below the threshold some pairs will be related and some will not, so subthreshold matches cannot be used to obtain negative conclusions. It is well known that proteins can be structurally very similar even if the sequence similarity is very low. At such low similarity levels, pure chance will produce other pairwise alignments that will mix with those produced by genuinely related pairs.

The nontrivial answer to this question is that it depends entirely on the particular structural or functional aspect one wants to investigate. The necessary and sufficient similarity threshold will be different for each task. Safe structural inference will demand a similarity at one level, and functional inference will in general require a new threshold for each functional aspect. Functional aspects may be related to a sequence as a whole—for example, whether or not a sequence belongs to a given class of enzymes. Many other functional aspects depend entirely on the local sequence composition. For example, does the N-terminal of a protein sequence have a signal peptide cleavage site at a given position or not?

In general, one may say that in the zone of safe inference, alignment should be preferred to prediction. In the best situations, prediction methods should enlarge the regions of safe inference. This can be done by evaluation of the confidence levels that are produced along with the predictions from many methods, a theme treated in more detail in chapter 5.

Sander and Schneider pioneered the algorithmic investigation of the relationship between protein sequence similarity and structural similarity [462]. In a plot of the alignment length against the percentage of identical residues in the overlap, two domains could be discerned: one of exclusively structurally similar pairs, and one containing a mixture of similar and nonsimilar pairs.

Structural similarity was defined by more than 70% secondary structure assignment identity in the overlap. It was observed that this criterion corresponds to a maximum root-mean-square deviation of 2.5Å for a structural alignment of the two fragments in three dimensions. The mixed region reflects the fact that the secondary structure identity may exceed 70% by chance, especially for very short overlaps, even in pairs of completely unrelated sequences.

The border between the two domains, and thereby the threshold for sequence similarity, measured in percentage identity, depends on the length of the aligned region (the overlap). Sander and Schneider defined a length-dependent threshold function: for overlap length $l < 10$, no pairs are above the threshold; for $10 < l < 80$, the threshold is $290.15l^{-0.562}$%; and for $l > 80$, the threshold is 24.8%.

This threshold can be used to answer the question whether alignment is likely to lead to a reliable inference, or whether one is forced to look for prediction methods that may be available for the particular task. *If* the new sequence is superthreshold, alignment or homology building should be the preferred approach; if it is subthreshold, prediction approaches by more advanced pattern-recognition schemes should be employed, possibly in concert with the alignment methods.

In this type of analysis the "safe zone of inference" is of course not 100% *safe* and should be used as a guideline only, for example when constructing test sets for validation of high-throughput prediction algorithms. In many cases the change of a single amino acid is known to lead to a completely different, possibly unfolded and unfunctional protein. Part of the goal in the so-called *single-nucleotide polymorphism* projects is to identify coding SNPs, which may affect protein conformation and thereby for example influence disease susceptibility and/or alter the effect of drugs interacting with a particular protein [394].

1.4.3 Prediction of Functional Features

The sequence identity threshold for structural problems cannot be used directly in sequence prediction problems involving *functionality*. If the aim is safe inference of the exact position of a signal peptide cleavage site in a new sequence from experimentally verified sites in sequences from a database, it is a priori completely unknown what the required degree of similarity should be.

Above, "structurally similar" was defined by quantification of the mean distance in space. In an alignment, *functional* similarity means that any two residues with similar function should match without any shift. Two cleavage sites should line up exactly residue by residue, if a site in one sequence should be positioned unambiguously by the site in the other. In practice, whether a perfect separation between a completely safe zone and a mixed zone can be obtained by alignment alone will depend on the degree of conservation of different types of functional sites.

This binary criterion for successful alignment can, together with a definition of the zone-separating principle, be used to determine a threshold function that gives the best discrimination of functional similarity [405]. The principle for establishing a nonarbitrary threshold is general; the approach may easily be generalized to other types of sequence analysis problems involving, for instance, glycosylation sites, phosphorylation sites, transit peptides for chloroplasts and mitochondria, or cleavage sites of polyproteins, and to nucleotide sequence analysis problems such as intron splice sites in pre-mRNA, ribosome binding sites, and promoters. But for each case a specific threshold must be determined.

For problems such as those involving splice sites in pre-mRNA or glycosylation sites of proteins, there are several sites per sequence. One way of addressing this problem is to split each sequence into a number of subsequences, one for each potential site, and then use the approach on the collection of subsequences. Alternatively, the fraction of aligned sites per alignment may be used as a functional similarity measure, in analogy with the structural similarity used by Sander and Schneider (the percentage of identical secondary structure assignments in the alignment). In this case, a threshold value for functional similarity—analogous to the 70% structural similarity threshold used by Sander and Schneider—must be defined before the similarity threshold can be calculated.

1.4.4 Global and Local Alignments and Substitution Matrix Entropies

The optimality of pairwise alignments between two sequences is not given by some canonical or unique criterion with universal applicability throughout the entire domain of sequences. The matches produced by alignment algorithms depend entirely on the parameters quantitatively defining the similarity of corresponding monomers, the cost of gaps and deletions, and most notably whether the algorithms are designed to optimize a score globally or locally.

Some problems of biological relevance concern an overall, or global, comparison between two sequences, possibly with the exception of the sequence ends, while others would be meaningless unless attacked by a subsequence angle for the localization of segments or sites with similar sequential structure.

Classical alignment algorithms are based on dynamic programming—for optimal global alignments, the Needleman–Wunsch algorithm [401, 481], and for optimal local alignments, the Smith–Waterman algorithm [492] (see chapter

4). Dynamic programming is a computing procedure to manage the combinatorial explosion that would result from an exhaustive evaluation of the scores associated with any conceivable alignment of two sequences. Still, dynamic programming is computationally demanding, and a number of heuristics for further reduction of the resources needed for finding significant alignments have been developed [417, 419]. Other very fast and reliable heuristic schemes do not build on dynamic programming, but interactively extend small subsequences into longer matches [13, 14]. The conventional alignment schemes have been described in detail elsewhere [550, 428]; here we will focus on some of the important aspects related to the preparation of dedicated data sets.

How "local" a local alignment scheme will be in practice is strongly influenced by the choice of substitution matrix. If the score level for matches is much higher than the penalty for mismatches, even local alignment schemes will tend to produce relatively long alignments. If the mismatch score will quickly eat up the match score, short, compact overlaps will result.

A substitution matrix specifies a set of scores s_{ij} for replacing amino acid i by amino acid j. Some matrices are generated from a simplified protein evolution model involving amino acid frequencies, p_i, and pairwise substitution frequencies, q_{ij}, observed in existing alignments of naturally occurring proteins. A match involving a rare amino acid may count more than a match involving a common amino acid, while a mismatch between two interchangeable amino acids contributes a higher score than a mismatch between two functionally unrelated amino acids. A mismatch with a nonnegative score is known as a similarity or a conservative replacement. Other types of substitution matrices are based on the relationships between the amino acids according to the genetic code, or physicochemical properties of amino acids, or simply whether amino acids in alignments are identical or not.

All these different substitution matrices can be compared and brought on an equal footing by the concept of substitution matrix entropy. As shown by Altschul [8], any amino acid substitution matrix is, either implicitly or explicitly, a matrix of logarithms of normalized target frequencies, since the substitution scores may be written as

$$s_{ij} = \frac{1}{\lambda} \left(\ln \frac{q_{ij}}{p_i p_j} \right) \tag{1.4}$$

where λ is a scaling factor. Changing λ will change the absolute value of the scores, but not the relative scores of different local alignments, so it will not affect the alignments [405].

The simplest possible scoring matrices are *identity matrices*, where all the diagonal elements have the same positive value (the match score, s), and all the off-diagonal elements have the same negative value (the mismatch score,

$\bar{s}$). This special case has been treated by Nielsen [405]. An identity matrix may be derived from the simplest possible model for amino acid substitutions, where all 20 amino acids appear with equal probability and the off-diagonal substitution frequencies are equal:

$$p_i = \frac{1}{20} \quad \text{for all } i,$$
$$q_{ij} = \begin{cases} q & \text{for } i = j \\ \bar{q} & \text{for } i \neq j. \end{cases} \tag{1.5}$$

In other words, when an amino acid mutates, it has equal probabilities $\bar{q}$ of changing into any of the 19 other amino acids.

There is a range of different identity matrices, depending on the ratio between the positive and negative scores, $s/\bar{s}$. If $s = -\bar{s}$, a local alignment must necessarily contain more matches than mismatches in order to yield a positive score, resulting in short and strong alignments, while if $s \gg -\bar{s}$, one match can compensate for many mismatches, resulting in long and weak alignments. The percentage identity p in gapfree local identity matrix alignment has a minimum value

$$p > \frac{-\bar{s}}{s - \bar{s}}. \tag{1.6}$$

We define $r = \bar{q}/q$, the mutability or the probability that a given position in the sequence has changed into a random amino acid (including the original one). $r = 0$ corresponds to no changes, while $r = 1$ corresponds to an infinite evolutionary distance.

Since the sum of all q_{ij} must be 1, we use the relation $20q + 380\bar{q} = 1$ to calculate the target frequencies

$$q = \frac{1}{20 + 380r} \quad \text{and} \quad \bar{q} = \frac{r}{20 + 380r} \tag{1.7}$$

and the s_{ij} values may be calculated using (1.4). Since the score ratio, $s/\bar{s}$, is independent of λ and therefore a function of r, we can calculate r numerically from the score ratio.

The *relative entropy* of an amino acid substitution matrix was defined thus by Altschul:

$$\mathcal{H} = \sum_{i,j} q_{ij} s_{ij} \text{bits} \tag{1.8}$$

where the s_{ij}s are normalized so that $\lambda = \ln 2$ (corresponding to using the base-2 logarithm in (1.4)). The relative entropy of a matrix can be interpreted as the amount of information carried by each position in the alignment (see also appendix B for all information-theoretic notions such as entropy and relative entropy).

The shorter the evolutionary distance assumed in the calculation of the matrix, the larger H is. At zero evolutionary distance ($r = 0$), the mismatch penalty $\bar{s}$ is infinite, that is, gaps are completely disallowed, and the relative entropy is equal to the entropy of the amino acid distribution: $\mathcal{H} = -\sum_i p_i \log_2 p_i$. In the identity model case, $\mathcal{H} = \log_2 20 \approx 4.32$ bits, and the local alignment problem is reduced to the problem of finding the longest common substring between two sequences. Conversely, as the evolutionary distance approaches infinity ($r \simeq 1$), all differences between the q_{ij} values disappear and $\mathcal{H}$ approaches 0.

1.4.5 Consensus Sequences and Sequence Logos

When studying the specificity of molecular binding sites, it has been common practice to create consensus sequences from alignments and then to choose the most common nucleotide or amino acid as representative at a given position [474]. Such a procedure throws a lot of information away, and it may be highly misleading when interpreted as a reliable assessment of the molecular specificity of the recognizing protein factors or nucleic acids. A somewhat better alternative is to observe all frequencies at all positions simultaneously.

A graphical visualization technique based on the Shannon information content at each position is the sequence *logo* approach developed by Schneider and coworkers [473]. The idea is to emphasize the deviation from the uniform, or flat, distribution, where all monomers occur with the same probability, p. In that case, $p = 0.25$ for nucleotide sequence alignments and $p = 0.05$ in amino acid sequence alignments.

Most functional sites display a significant degree of deviation from the flat distribution. From the observed frequencies of monomers at a given position, i, the deviation from the random case is computed by

$$D(i) = \log_2 |A| + \sum_{k=1}^{|A|} p_k(i) \log_2 p_k(i), \tag{1.9}$$

where $|A|$ is the length of the alphabet, normally 4 or 20. Since the logarithm used is base 2, $D(i)$ will be measured in bits per monomer. In an amino acid alignment $D(i)$ will be maximal and equal $\log_2 20 \approx 4.32$ when only one fully conserved amino acid is found at a given position. Similarly, the deviation will be two bits maximally in alignments of nucleotide sequences.

With the logo visualization technique a column of symbols is used to display the details of a consensus sequence. The total height of the column is equal to the value of $D(i)$, and the height of each monomer symbol, k, is proportional to its probability at that position, $p_k(i)$. Monomers drawn with different colors can be used to indicate physicochemical properties, such as charge and hydrophobicity, or nucleotide interaction characteristics, such as weak or strong hydrogen bonding potential. Compared with the array of numbers in a weight matrix covering the alignment region, the logo technique is quite powerful and fairly easy to use. When D is summed over the region of the site, one gets a measure of the accumulated information in a given type of site, for example, a binding site. D may indicate the strength of a binding site, and can be compared against the information needed to find true sites in a complete genome or protein sequence [474]. With this information-theoretical formulation of the degree of sequence conservation, the problem of how proteins can find their required binding sites among a huge excess of nonsites can be addressed in a quantitative manner [474, 472].

Figures 1.8 and 1.9 show two examples of alignment frequencies visualized by the logo technique. The first is from an alignment of translation initiation sites in *E. coli*. In the nuclear part of eukaryotic genomes, the initiation triplet—the start codon—is very well conserved and is almost always AUG, representing the amino acid methionine. In prokaryotes several other initiation triplets occur with significant frequencies, and the logo shows to what extent the nucleotides at the three codon positions are conserved [422]. Since the same *E. coli* ribosome complex will recognize *all* translation initiation sites, the logo indicates the specificity of the interaction between ribosomal components and the triplet sequence. The conserved Shine–Dalgarno sequence immediately 5' to the initiation codon is used to position the mRNA on the ribosome by base pairing.

A logo is clearly most informative if only sequences that share a similar signal are included, but it can also be used in the process of identifying different patterns belonging to different parts of the data. In the extremely thermophilic archaeon *Sulfolobus solfataricus*, translation initiation patterns may depend on whether genes lie inside operons or at the start of an operon or single genes. In a recent study [523], a Shine-Dalgarno sequence was found upstream of the genes inside operons, but not for the first gene in an operon or isolated genes. This indicates that two different mechanisms are used for translation initiation in this organism.

Figure 1.9 displays a logo of mammalian amino acid sequence segments aligned at the start of alpha-helices [99]. The logo covers the transition region: to the left, the conformational categories of coil and turn appear most often, and to the right, amino acids frequent in alpha-helices are found at the tops of the columns. Interestingly, at the N-terminus, or the cap of the helix, the distribution of amino acids is more biased than within the helix itself [435]. A logo of the C-terminus helix shows the capping in the other end. Capping residues are presumably an integral part of this type of secondary structure, because their side chain hydrogen bonds stabilize the dipole of the helix [435]. An analogous delimitation of beta-sheets—so-called beta breakers—marks the

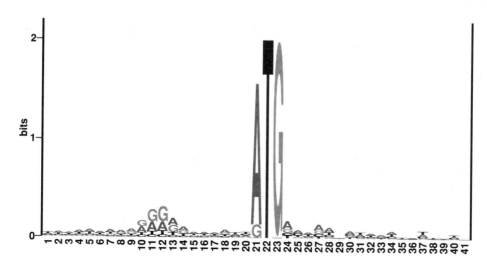

Figure 1.8: Logo Showing an Alignment of Translation Start Triplets That Are Active in *E. coli*. Translation starts at position 21 in the logo. The conventional initiation triplet ATG encoding methionine is by far the most abundant and dominates the logo. The data were obtained from [422].

termini of this chain topology [133].

Sequence logos are useful for a quick examination of the statistics in the context of functional sites or regions, but they can also show the range in which a sequence signal is present. If one aligns a large number of O-glycosylation sites and inspects the logo, the interval where the compositional bias extends will immediately be revealed. Such an analysis can be used not only to shape the architecture of a prediction method but also to consider what should actually be predicted. One may consider lumping O-glycosylated serines and threonines together if their context shares similar properties [235]. If they differ strongly, individual methods handling the two residue types separately should be considered instead. In the cellular environment, such a difference may also indicate that the enzymes that transfer the carbohydrates to the two residues are nonidentical.

Sequence logos using monomers will treat the positions in the context of a site *independently*. The logo will tell nothing about the correlation between the different positions, or whether the individual monomers appear simultaneously at a level beyond what would be expected from the single-position statistics. However, the visualization technique can easily handle the occurrence of, say, dinucleotides or dipeptides, and show pair correlations in the form of stacks of combined symbols. The size of the alphabets, $|A|$, in (1.9)

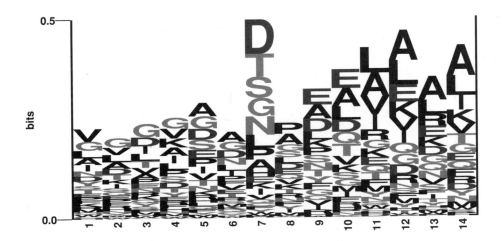

Figure 1.9: Logo Showing an Alignment of Alpha-Helix N-termini. The data comprised a nonredundant set of mammalian proteins with known three-dimensional structure [99]. The helix starts at position 7 in the logo. The secondary structure assignment was performed by the Kabsch and Sander algorithm [297]. The largest compositional bias in this region is observed at the position just before the helix start.

will change accordingly; otherwise, the same formula applies.

Figure 1.10 shows an example of a dinucleotide-based logo of donor splice sites in introns from the plant *Arabidopsis thaliana*. In addition to the well-known consensus dinucleotides GT and GC (almost invisible) at the splice junction in the center of the logo, the logo shows that the GT dinucleotide, which appears inside the intron at the third dinucleotide position, occurs more frequently than expected.

A slight variation of the logo formula (1.9), based on relative entropy (or Kullback–Leibler asymmetric divergence measure [342, 341]), is the following:

$$\mathcal{H}(i) = \mathcal{H}(P(i), Q(i)) = \sum_{k=1}^{|A|} p_k(i) \log \frac{p_k(i)}{q_k(i)}. \tag{1.10}$$

This quantifies the contrast between the observed probabilities $P(i)$ and a reference probability distribution $Q(i)$. Q may, or may not, depend on the position i in the alignment. When displaying the relative entropy, the height of each letter can also, as an alternative to the frequency itself, be computed from the background scaled frequency at that position [219].

In order for the logo to be a reliable description of the specificity, it is essential that the data entering the alignment be nonredundant. If a given site is included in multiple copies, the probability distribution will be biased artificially.

In chapter 6 we will see how neural networks go beyond the positionwise uncorrelated analysis of the sequence, as is the case for the simple logo visualization technique and also for its weight matrix counterpart, where each position in the matrix is treated independently. A weight matrix assigns weights to the positions that are computed from the ratio of the frequencies of monomers in an alignment of some "positive" sites and the frequencies in a reference distribution. A sum of the logarithms of the weights assigned to given monomers in a particular sequence will give a score, and a threshold may be adjusted so that it will give the best recognition of true sites, in terms of either sensitivity or specificity.

Neural networks have the ability to process the sequence data nonlinearly where correlations between different positions can be taken into account. "Nonlinear" means essentially that the network will be able to produce correct predictions in cases where one category is correlated with one of two features, but not both of them simultaneously. A linear method would not be able to handle such a two-feature case correctly.

In more complex situations, many features may be present in a given type of site, with more complex patterns of correlation between them. The ability to handle such cases correctly by definition gives the neural network algorithms great power in the sequence data domain.

An O-glycosylation site may be one case where amino acids of both positive and negative charges may be acceptable and functional, but not both types at the same time. A conventional monomer weight matrix cannot handle this common situation. However, for some prediction problems one can get around the problem by developing weight matrices based on dipeptides or more complex input features. Another strategy may be to divide all the positive cases into two or more classes, each characterized by its own weight matrix. Such changes in the approach can in some cases effectively convert a nonlinear problem into a linear one.

In general, the drawback of linear techniques is that it becomes impossible to *subtract* evidence. In linear methods two types of evidence will combine and add up to produce a high score, even if the biological mechanism can accept only one of them at a time. A nonlinear method can avoid this situation simply by decreasing the score if the combined evidence from many features exceeds a certain level.

A clever change in the input representation will in many cases do part of the job of transforming the topology of the sequence space into a better-connected space in which isolated islands have been merged according to the functional class they belong to. Since the correlations and features in sequences often are largely unknown, at least when one starts the prediction analysis, the nonlinear

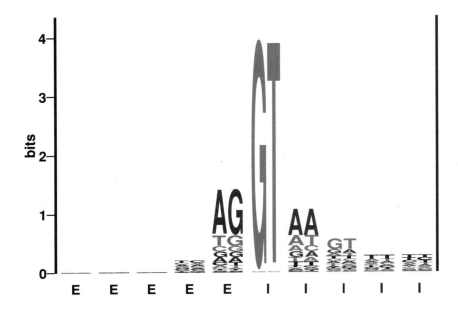

Figure 1.10: A Logo of Donor Splice Sites from the Dicot Plant *A. thaliana* (cress). The logo is based on frequencies of nonoverlapping dinucleotides in the exon/intron transition region, using the standard Shannon information measure entering equation (1.9) with the alphabet size $|A| = 16$. The logo was prepared on a nonredundant data set of sequences extracted from GenBank [327].

potential of neural networks gives them a big advantage in the development phase for many types of tasks.

The issue of which method to use has for many years been a highly dogmatic matter in artificial intelligence. In the data domain of biological sequences, it is clear that many different methods will be able to perform at the same level *if* one knows in advance which features to look for. If an analysis of the weights in a neural network trained on a given task (see chapter 6) shows that the network is being excited (or inhibited) toward a positive (or negative) prediction by specific sequence features, rules can often be constructed that also will have a high discriminatory power. It is the experience of many people that machine-learning methods are *productive* in the sense that near-optimal methods can be developed quite fast, given that the data are relatively clean; it often can be much harder to try to design powerful rules from scratch.

1.5 Prediction of Molecular Function and Structure

The methods and applications described in this book will be targeted toward the agenda formulated by von Heijne in his early book on sequence analysis: "What can you do with your sequence once you have it?" [540]. Applications well suited for treatment by machine-learning approaches will be described in detail in later chapters; here we give an annotated list of some important computational problems that have been tackled within this framework in the analysis of data from DNA, RNA, and protein sequences. In some cases sequences are represented by experimentally determined biochemical characteristics rather than symbols from a finite alphabet of monomers.

1.5.1 Sequence-based Analysis

In most cases, single-stranded sequences are used, no matter whether the object in the cellular environment is DNA or RNA. One exception is the analysis of structural elements of DNA, such as bendability or intrinsic bending potential, which must be based on a true double-stranded interpretation of the double helix.

Intron splice sites and branch points in eukaryotic pre-mRNA. Intervening sequences that interrupt the genes of RNA and proteins are characterized, but not unambiguously defined, by local features at the splice junctions. Introns in protein-encoding genes present the most significant computational challenge. In some organisms, nuclear introns are few and their splice sites are well conserved (as in *S. cerevisiae*), but in many other eukaryotes, including man, it is a major problem to locate the correct transition between coding and noncoding regions, and thus to determine the mature mRNA sequence from the genomic DNA. In yeast, introns occur mainly in genes encoding ribosomal proteins. The fact that genes in many organisms are being spliced differently, depending on tissue type or stage of development, complicates the task considerably. Weight matrices, neural networks, and hidden Markov models have been applied to this problem in a multitude of different versions.

Gene finding in prokaryotes and eukaryotes. Machine-learning techniques have been applied to almost all steps in computational gene finding, including the assignment of translation start and stop, quantification of reading frame potential, frame interruption of splice sites, exon assignment, gene modeling, and assembly. Usually, highly diverse combinations of machine-learning approaches have been incorporated in individual methods.

Recognition of promoters—transcription initiation and termination. Initiation of transcription is the first step in gene expression and constitutes an important point of control in the organism. The initiation event takes place when RNA polymerase—the enzyme that catalyzes production of RNA from the DNA template—recognizes and binds to certain DNA sequences called promoters. This prediction problem is hard due to both the large variable distance between various DNA signals that are the substrate for the recognition by the polymerase, and the many other factors involved in regulation of the expression level. The elastic matching abilities of hidden Markov models have made them ideal for this task, especially in eukaryotes, but neural networks with carefully designed input architecture have also been used.

Gene expression levels. This problem may be addressed by predicting the strength of known promoter signals if the expression levels associated with their genes have been determined experimentally. Alternatively, the expression level of genes may be predicted from the sequence of the coding sequence, where the codon usage and/or in some cases, the corresponding codon adaption indices, have been used to encode the sequence statistics.

Prediction of DNA bending and bendability. Many transactions are influenced and determined by the flexibility of the double helix. Transcription initiation is one of them, and prediction of transcription initiation or curvature/bendability from the sequence would therefore be valuable in the context of understanding a large range of DNA-related phenomena.

Nucleosome positioning signals. Intimately related to the DNA flexibility is the positioning of eukaryotic DNA when wrapped around the histone octamers in chromatin. Detection of the periodicity requires non-integer sensitivity—or an elastic matching ability as in hidden Markov models—because the signals occur every 10.1–10.6 bp, or every full turn of the double-stranded helix.

Sequence clustering and cluster topology. Because sequence data are notoriously redundant, it is important to have clustering techniques that will put sequences into groups, and also to estimate the intergroup distances at the same time. Both neural networks, in the form of self-organizing maps, and hidden Markov models have been very useful for doing this. One advantage over other clustering techniques has been the unproblematic treatment of large data sets comprising thousands of sequences.

Prediction of RNA secondary structure. The most powerful methods for computing and ranking potential secondary structures of mRNA, tRNA, and rRNA are based on the minimization of the free energy in the interaction between base pairs and between pairs of base pairs and their stacking energies [586, 260]. This is nontrivial for many reasons, one being that loop-to-loop interactions are hard to assess without a combinatorial explosion in the number of structures to be evaluated. Neural networks and grammar methods have had some success in handling features at which the more traditional minimization procedures for obtaining the energetically most favored conformation are less successful.

Other functional sites and classes of DNA and RNA. Many different types of sites have been considered for separate prediction, including branch points in introns, ribosome binding sites, motifs in protein–DNA interactions, other regulatory signals, DNA helix categories, restriction sites, DNA melting points, reading frame-interrupting deletions in EST sequences, classification of ribosomal RNAs according to phylogenetic classes, and classification of tRNA sequences according to species.

Protein structure prediction. This area has boosted the application of machine-learning techniques within sequence analysis, most notably through the work on prediction of protein secondary structure of Qian and Sejnowski [437]. Virtually all aspects of protein structure have been tackled by machine learning. Among the specific elements that have been predicted are categories of secondary structure, distance constraints between residues (contacts), fold class, secondary structure class or content, disulfide bridges between cysteine residues, family membership, helical transmembrane regions and topology of the membrane crossing, membrane protein class (number of transmembrane segments), MHC motifs, and solvent accessibility.

Protein function prediction. Functionally related features that have been considered for prediction are intracellular localization, signal peptide cleavage sites (secreted proteins), de novo design of signal peptide cleavage sites (optimized for cleavage efficiency), signal anchors (N-terminal parts of type-II membrane proteins), glycosylation signals for attachment of carbohydrates (the state and type of glycosylation determines the lifetime in circulation; this is strongly involved in recognition phenomena and sorting), phosphorylation and other modifications related to posttranslational modification (the presence of phosphorylation sites indicates that the protein is involved in intracellular signal transduction, cell cycle control, or mediating nutritional and environmental stress signals), various binding sites and active sites in proteins (enzymatic activity).

Protein family classification. The family association has been predicted from a global encoding of the dipeptide frequencies into self-organizing maps and feed-forward neural networks, or local motif-based prediction that may enhance the detection of more distant family relationships.

Protein degradation. In all organisms proteins are degraded and recycled. In organisms with an immune system the specificity of the degradation is essential for its function and the successful discrimination between self and nonself. Different degradation pathways are active; in several of them proteins are unfolded prior to proteolytic cleavage, and therefore the specificity is presuambly strongly related to the pattern in the sequence and not to its 3D structure. This general problem has therefore quite naturally been attacked by machine-learning techniques, the main problem being the limited amount of experimentally characterized data.

Chapter 2

Machine-Learning Foundations: The Probabilistic Framework

2.1 Introduction: Bayesian Modeling

Machine learning is by and large a direct descendant of an older discipline, statistical model fitting. Like its predecessor, the goal in machine learning is to extract useful information from a corpus of data D by building good probabilistic models. The particular twist behind machine learning, however, is to automate this process as much as possible, often by using very flexible models characterized by large numbers of parameters, and to let the machine take care of the rest. Silicon machine learning also finds much of its inspiration in the learning abilities of its biological predecessor: the brain. Hence, a particular vocabulary is required in which "learning" often replaces "fitting."

Clearly, machine learning is driven by rapid technological progress in two areas:

- Sensors and storage devices that lead to large databases and data sets

- Computing power that makes possible the use of more complex models.

As pointed out in [455], machine-learning approaches are best suited for areas where there is a large amount of data but little theory. And this is exactly the situation in computational molecular biology.

While available sequence data are rapidly increasing, our current knowledge of biology constitutes only a small fraction of what remains to be discovered. Thus, in computational biology in particular, and more generally in biology and all other information-rich sciences, one must reason in the presence of a high degree of uncertainty: many facts are missing, and some of the facts are wrong. Computational molecular biologists are, then, constantly faced with induction and *inference* problems: building models from available data. What are the right class of models and the right level of complexity? Which details are important and which should be discarded? How can one compare different models and select the best one, in light of available knowledge and sometimes limited data? In short, how do we know if a model is a good model? These questions are all the more acute in machine-learning approaches, because complex models, with several thousand parameters and more, are routinely used and sequence data, while often abundant, are inherently "noisy."

In situations where few data are available, the models used in machine-learning approaches have sometimes been criticized on the ground that they may be capable of accommodating almost any behavior for a certain setting of their parameters, and that simpler models with fewer parameters should be preferred to avoid overfitting. Machine-learning practitioners know that many *implicit* constraints emerge from the structure of the models and, in fact, render arbitrary behavior very difficult, if not impossible, to reproduce. More important, as pointed out in [397], choosing simpler models because few data are available does not make much sense. While it is a widespread practice and occasionally a useful heuristic, it is clear that the amount of data collected and the complexity of the underlying source are two completely different things. It is not hard to imagine situations characterized by a very complex source and relatively few data. Thus we contend that even in situations where data are scarce, machine-learning approaches should not be ruled out a priori. But in all cases, it is clear that questions of inference and induction are particularly central to machine learning and to computational biology.

When reasoning in the presence of certainty, one uses deduction. This is how the most advanced theories in information-poor sciences, such as physics or mathematics, are presented in an axiomatic fashion. Deduction is not controversial. The overwhelming majority of people agree on how to perform deductions in specific way: if X implies Y, and X is true, then Y must be true. This is the essence of Boole's algebra, and at the root of all our digital computers. When reasoning in the presence of uncertainty, one uses induction and inference: if X implies Y, and Y is true, then X is *more plausible*. An amazing and still poorly known fact is that there is a simple and unique consistent set of rules for induction, model selection, and comparison. It is called Bayesian inference. The Bayesian approach has been known for some time, but only recently has it started to infiltrate different areas of science and technology systematically, with useful results [229, 372, 373]. While machine learning may appear to some as an eclectic collection of models and learning algorithms, we believe the Bayesian framework provides a strong underlying foundation that unifies the different techniques. We now review the Bayesian framework in general. In the following chapters, we apply it to specific classes of models and problems.

The Bayesian point of view has a simple intuitive description. The Bayesian approach assigns a degree of plausibility to any proposition, hypothesis, or model. (Throughout this book, hypothesis and model are essentially synonymous; models tend to be complex hypotheses with many parameters.) More precisely, in order properly to carry out the induction process, one ought to proceed in three steps:

1. Clearly state what the hypotheses or models are, along with *all* the background information and the data.

2. Use the language of probability theory to assign prior probabilities to the hypotheses.

3. Use probability calculus for the inference process, in particular to evaluate posterior probabilities (or degrees of belief) for the hypotheses in light of the available data, and to derive *unique* answers.

Such an approach certainly seems reasonable. Note that the Bayesian approach is not directly concerned with the creative process, how to generate new hypotheses or models. It is concerned only with assessing the value of models with respect to the available knowledge and data. This assessment procedure, however, may be very helpful in generating new ideas.

But why should the Bayesian approach be so compelling? Why use the language of probability theory, as opposed to any other method? The surprising answer to this question is that it can be proved, in a strict mathematical sense, that this is the only consistent way of reasoning in the presence of uncertainty. Specifically, there is a small set of very simple commonsense axioms, the Cox Jaynes axioms, under which it can be shown that the Bayesian approach is the unique consistent approach to inference and induction. Under the Cox Jaynes axioms, degrees of plausibility satisfy all the rules of probabilities exactly. Probability calculus is, then, all the machinery that is required for inference, model selection, and model comparison.

In the next section, we give a brief axiomatic presentation of the Bayesian point of view using the Cox Jaynes axioms. For brevity, we do not present any proofs or any historical background for the Bayesian approach, nor do we discuss any controversial issues regarding the foundations of statistics. All of these can be found in various books and articles, such as [51, 63, 122, 433, 284].

2.2   The Cox Jaynes Axioms

The objects we deal with in inference are propositions about the world. For instance, a typical proposition X is "Letter A appears in position i of sequence O." A proposition is either true or false, and we denote by $\bar{X}$ the complement of a proposition X. A hypothesis H about the world is a proposition, albeit a possibly complex one composed of the conjunction of many more elementary propositions. A model M can also be viewed as a hypothesis. The difference is that models tend to be very complex hypotheses involving a large number of parameters. In discussions where parameters are important, we will consider that $M = M(w)$, where w is the vector of all parameters. A complex model M can easily be reduced to a binary proposition in the form "Model M accounts for data D with an error level ϵ" (this vague statement will be made more precise in the following discussion). But for any purpose, in what follows there is no real distinction between models and hypotheses.

Whereas propositions are either true or false, we wish to reason in the presence of uncertainty. Therefore the next step is to consider that, given a certain amount of information I, we can associate with each hypothesis a degree of plausibility or confidence (also called degree or strength of belief). Let us represent it by the symbol $\pi(X|I)$. While $\pi(X|I)$ is just a symbol for now, it is clear that in order to have a scientific discourse, one should be able to compare degrees of confidence. That is, for any two propositions X and Y, either we believe in X more than in Y, or we believe in Y more than in X, or we believe in both equally. Let us use the symbol $>$ to denote this relationship, so that we write $\pi(X|I) > \pi(Y|I)$ if and only if X is more plausible than Y. It would be very hard not to agree that in order for things to be sensible, the relationship $>$ should be transitive. That is, if X is more plausible than Y, and Y is more plausible than Z, then X must be more plausible than Z. More formally, this is the first axiom,

$$\pi(X|I) > \pi(Y|I) \quad \text{and} \quad \pi(Y|I) > \pi(Z|I) \quad \text{imply} \quad \pi(X|I) > \pi(Z|I). \quad (2.1)$$

This axiom is trivial; it has, however, an important consequence: $>$ is an ordering relationship, and therefore degrees of belief can be expressed by real numbers. That is, from now on, $\pi(X|I)$ represents a number. This of course does not mean that such a number is easy to calculate, but merely that such a number exists, and the ordering among hypotheses is reflected in the ordering of real numbers. To proceed any further and stand a chance of calculating degrees of belief we need additional axioms or rules for relating numbers representing strengths of belief.

The amazing fact is that only two additional axioms are needed to constrain the theory entirely. This axiomatic presentation is usually attributed to

Cox and Jaynes [138, 283]. To better understand these two remaining axioms, the reader may imagine a world of very simple switches, where at each instant in time a given switch can be either on or off. Thus, all the elementary hypotheses or propositions in this world, at a given time, have the simple form "switch X is on" or "switch X is off." (For sequence analysis purposes, the reader may imagine that switch X is responsible for the presence or absence of the letter X, but this is irrelevant for a general understanding.) Clearly, the more confident we are that switch X is on (X), the less confident we are that switch X is off $(\bar{X})$. Thus, for any given proposition X, there should be a relationship between $\pi(X|I)$ and $\pi(\bar{X}|I)$. Without assuming anything about this relationship, it is sensible to consider that, all else equal, the relationship should be the same for all switches and for all types of background information, that is, for all propositions X and I. Thus, in mathematical terms, the second axiom states that there exists a function F such that

$$\pi(\bar{X}|I) = F[\pi(X|I)]. \tag{2.2}$$

The third axiom is only slightly more complicated. Consider this time two switches X and Y and the corresponding four possible joint states. Then our degree of belief that X is on and Y is off, for instance, naturally depends on our degree of belief that switch X is on, and our degree of belief that switch Y is off, *knowing that X is on*. Again, it is sensible that this relationship be independent of the switch considered and the type of background information I. Thus, in mathematical terms, the third axiom states that there exists a function G such that

$$\pi(X, Y|I) = G[\pi(X|I), \pi(Y|X, I)]. \tag{2.3}$$

So far, we have not said much about the information I. I is a proposition corresponding to the conjunction of all the available pieces of information. I can represent background knowledge, such as general structural or functional information about biological macromolecules. I can also include specific experimental or other data. When it is necessary to focus on a particular corpus of data D, we can write $I = (I, D)$. In any case, I is not necessarily fixed and can be augmented with, or replaced by, any number of symbols representing propositions, as already seen in the right-hand side of (2.3). When data are acquired sequentially, for instance, we may write $I = (I, D_1, \ldots, D_n)$. In a discussion where I is well defined and fixed, it can be dropped altogether from the equations.

The three axioms above entirely determine, up to scaling, how to calculate degrees of belief. In particular, one can prove that there is always a rescaling κ of degrees of belief such that $\mathbf{P}(X|I) = \kappa(\pi(X|I))$ is in $[0, 1]$. Furthermore, $\mathbf{P}$ is unique and satisfies all the rules of probability. Specifically, if degrees of belief are restricted to the $[0, 1]$ interval, then the functions F and G must be given by $F(x) = 1 - x$ and $G(x, y) = xy$. The corresponding proof will not be given here and can be found in [138, 284]. As a result, the second axiom can be rewritten as the sum rule of probability,

$$\mathbf{P}(X|I) + \mathbf{P}(\bar{X}|I) = 1, \tag{2.4}$$

and the third axiom as the product rule,

$$\mathbf{P}(X, Y|I) = \mathbf{P}(X|I)\mathbf{P}(Y|X, I). \tag{2.5}$$

From here on, we can then replace degrees of confidence by probabilities. Note that if uncertainties are removed, that is, if $\mathbf{P}(X|I)$ is 0 or 1, then (2.4) and (2.5) yield, as a special case, the two basic rules of deduction or Boolean algebra, for the negation and conjunction of propositions [(1) "X or $\bar{X}$" is always true; (2) "X and Y" is true if and only if both X and Y are true]. By using the symmetry $\mathbf{P}(X, Y|I) = \mathbf{P}(Y, X|I)$ together with (2.5), one obtains the important Bayes theorem,

$$\mathbf{P}(X|Y, I) = \frac{\mathbf{P}(Y|X, I)\mathbf{P}(X|I)}{\mathbf{P}(Y|I)} = \mathbf{P}(X|I)\frac{\mathbf{P}(Y|X, I)}{\mathbf{P}(Y|I)}. \tag{2.6}$$

The Bayes theorem is fundamental because it allows inversion: interchanging conditioning and nonconditioning propositions. In a sense, it embodies inference or learning because it describes exactly how to update our degree of belief $\mathbf{P}(X|I)$ in X, in light of the new piece of information provided by Y, to obtain the new $\mathbf{P}(X|Y, I)$. $\mathbf{P}(X|I)$ is also called the prior probability, and $\mathbf{P}(X|Y, I)$, the posterior probability, with respect to Y. This rule can obviously be iterated as information becomes available. Throughout the book, $\mathbf{P}(X)$ is universally used to denote the probability of X. It should be clear, however, that the probability of X depends on the surrounding context and is not a universal concept. It is affected by the nature of the background information and by the space of alternative hypotheses under consideration.

Finally, one should be aware that there is a more general set of axioms for a more complete theory that encompasses Bayesian probability theory. These are the axioms of decision or utility theory, where the focus is on how to take "optimal" decisions in the presence of uncertainty [238, 63, 431] (see also appendix A). Not surprisingly, the simple axioms of decision theory lead one to construct and estimate Bayesian probabilities associated with the uncertain environment, and to maximize the corresponding expected utility. In fact, an even more general theory is game theory, where the uncertain environment includes other agents or players. Since the focus of the book is on data modeling only, these more general axiomatic theories will not be needed.

2.3 Bayesian Inference and Induction

We can now turn to the type of inference we are most interested in: deriving a parameterized model $M = M(w)$ from a corpus of data D. For simplicity, we will drop the background information I from the following equations. From Bayes theorem we immediately have

$$\mathbf{P}(M|D) = \frac{\mathbf{P}(D|M)\mathbf{P}(M)}{\mathbf{P}(D)} = \mathbf{P}(M)\frac{\mathbf{P}(D|M)}{\mathbf{P}(D)}. \tag{2.7}$$

The prior $\mathbf{P}(M)$ represents our estimate of the probability that model M is correct before we have obtained any data. The posterior $\mathbf{P}(M|D)$ represents our updated belief in the probability that model M is correct given that we have observed the data set D. The term $\mathbf{P}(D|M)$ is referred to as the likelihood.

For data obtained sequentially, one has

$$\mathbf{P}(M|D^1,\ldots,D^t) = \mathbf{P}(M|D^1,\ldots,D^{t-1})\frac{\mathbf{P}(D^t|M,D^1,\ldots,D^{t-1})}{\mathbf{P}(D^t|D^1,\ldots,D^{t-1})}. \tag{2.8}$$

In other words, the old posterior $\mathbf{P}(M|D^1,\ldots,D^{t-1})$ plays the role of the new prior. For technical reasons, probabilities can be very small. It is often easier to work with the corresponding logarithms, so that

$$\log \mathbf{P}(M|D) = \log \mathbf{P}(D|M) + \log \mathbf{P}(M) - \log \mathbf{P}(D). \tag{2.9}$$

To apply (2.9) to any class of models, we will need to specify the prior $\mathbf{P}(M)$ and the data likelihood $\mathbf{P}(D|M)$. Once the prior and data likelihood terms are made explicit, the initial modeling effort is complete. All that is left is cranking the engine of probability theory. But before we do that, let us briefly examine some of the issues behind priors and likelihoods in general.

2.3.1 Priors

The use of priors is a strength of the Bayesian approach, since it allows incorporating prior knowledge and constraints into the modeling process. It is sometimes also considered a weakness, on the ground that priors are subjective and different results can be derived with different priors. To these arguments, Bayesians can offer at least four different answers:

1. In general, the effects of priors diminish as the number of data increases. Formally, this is because the likelihood $-\log \mathbf{P}(D|M)$ typically increases linearly with the number of data points in D, while the prior $-\log \mathbf{P}(M)$ remains constant.

2. There are situations where objective criteria, such as maximum entropy and/or group invariance considerations, can be used to determine non-informative priors (for instance, [228]).

3. Even when priors are not mentioned explicitly, they are used implicitly. The Bayesian approach forces a clarification of one's assumption without sweeping the problem of priors under the rug.

4. Finally, and most important, the effects of different priors, as well as different models and model classes, can be assessed within the Bayesian framework by comparing the corresponding probabilities.

It is a matter of debate within the statistical community whether a general objective principle exists for the determination of priors in all situations, and whether maximum entropy (MaxEnt) is such a principle. It is our opinion that such a general principle does not really exist, as briefly discussed at the end of Appendix B. It is best to adopt a flexible and somewhat opportunistic attitude toward the selection of prior distributions, as long as the choices, as well as their quantitative consequences, are made explicit via the corresponding probabilistic calculations. MaxEnt, however, is useful in certain situations. For completeness, we now briefly review MaxEnt and group-theoretical considerations for priors, as well as three prior distributions widely used in practice.

Maximum Entropy

The MaxEnt principle states that the prior probability assignment should be the one with the maximum entropy consistent with all the prior knowledge or constraints (all information-theoretic notions, such as entropy and relative entropy, are reviewed for completeness in appendix B). Thus the resulting prior distribution is the one that "assumes the least," or is "maximally non-committal," or has the "maximum uncertainty." In the absence of any prior constraints, this leads of course to a uniform distribution corresponding to Laplace's "principle of indifference." Thus, when there is no information available on a parameter w, other than its range, a uniform prior over the range is a natural choice of prior. MaxEnt applies in modeling situations parametrized by a distribution P or by the corresponding histogram. MaxEnt is equivalent to using the entropic prior $\mathbf{P}(P) = e^{-\mathcal{H}(P)}/Z$, where $\mathcal{H}(P)$ is the entropy of P. MaxEnt is applied and further discussed in section 3.2. MaxEnt can also be viewed as a special case of an even more general principle, *minimum relative entropy* [486] (see appendix B).

Group-Theoretic Considerations

In many situations some, if not all, of the constraints on the prior distribution can be expressed in group-theoretical terms, such as invariance with respect to a group of transformations. A typical example is a scale parameter, such as the standard deviation σ of a Gaussian distribution. Suppose that we have only an idea of the range of σ, in the form $e^a < \sigma < e^b$. Then, within such range, the density $f(\sigma)$ of σ should be invariant to scaling of σ, and therefore f should be proportional to $d\sigma/\sigma$. By simple normalization, we find

$$f(\sigma) = \frac{1}{b-a} \frac{d\sigma}{\sigma}. \tag{2.10}$$

This is equivalent to having $\log \sigma$ uniformly distributed on the interval $[a, b]$ or having the densities of σ and σ^m identical. Other examples of group invariance analysis can be found in [282, 228].

Useful Practical Priors: Gaussian, Gamma, and Dirichlet

When prior distributions are not uniform, two useful and standard priors for continuous variables are the Gaussian (or normal) prior and the gamma prior. Gaussian priors with 0 mean are often used for the initialization of the weights between units in neural networks. A Gaussian prior, on a single parameter, has the form

$$\mathcal{N}(w|\mu, \sigma) = \frac{1}{\sqrt{2\pi}\sigma} \exp(-\frac{(w-\mu)^2}{2\sigma^2}). \tag{2.11}$$

In the present context, one of the reasons the Gaussian distribution is preeminent is related to the maximum entropy principle. When the only information available about a continuous density is its mean μ and its variance σ^2, then the Gaussian density $\mathcal{N}(\mu, \sigma)$ is the one achieving maximal entropy [137] (see Appendix B).

The gamma density [177] with parameters α and λ is given by

$$\Gamma(w|\alpha, \lambda) = \frac{\lambda^\alpha}{\Gamma(\alpha)} w^{\alpha-1} e^{-\lambda w} \tag{2.12}$$

for $w > 0$, and 0 otherwise. $\Gamma(\alpha)$ is the gamma function $\Gamma(\alpha) = \int_0^\infty e^{-x} x^{\alpha-1} dx$. By varying α and λ and translating w, the gamma density allows a wide range of priors, with more mass concentrated in one specific region of parameter space. Gamma priors are useful whenever the range of a parameter is bounded on one side—for instance, in the case of a positive parameter such as a standard deviation ($\sigma \geq 0$).

Finally, in the case of multinomial distributions that play an essential role in this book, such as the choice of a letter from an alphabet at a given position in a sequence, an important class of priors are the Dirichlet priors [63, 376]. By definition, a Dirichlet distribution on the probability vector $P = (p_1, \ldots, p_K)$, with parameters α and $Q = (q_1, \ldots, q_K)$, has the form

$$D_{\alpha Q}(P) = \frac{\Gamma(\alpha)}{\prod_i \Gamma(\alpha q_i)} \prod_{i=1}^{K} p_i^{\alpha q_i - 1} = \prod_{i=1}^{K} \frac{p_i^{\alpha q_i - 1}}{Z(i)}, \tag{2.13}$$

with $\alpha, p_i, q_i \geq 0$ and $\sum p_i = \sum q_i = 1$. For such a Dirichlet distribution, $\mathbf{E}(p_i) = q_i$, $\mathbf{Var}(p_i) = q_i(1 - q_i)/(\alpha + 1)$, and $\mathbf{Cov}(p_i p_j) = -q_i q_j/(\alpha + 1)$. Thus Q is the mean of the distribution, and α determines how peaked the distribution is around its mean. Dirichlet priors are important because they are the natural conjugate priors for multinomial distributions, as will be demonstrated in chapter 3. This simply means that the posterior parameter distribution, after having observed some data from a multinomial distribution with Dirichlet prior, also has the form of a Dirichlet distribution. The Dirichlet distribution can be seen as the multivariate generalization of the beta distribution, and can also be interpreted as a maximum entropy distribution over the space of distributions P, with a constraint on the average distance (i.e. relative entropy) to a reference distribution determined by Q and α (see appendix B).

2.3.2   Data Likelihood

In order to define $\mathbf{P}(D|M)$, one must come to grips with how a model M could also give rise to a different observation set D': in a Bayesian framework, sequence models *must* be probabilistic. A deterministic model assigns a probability 0 to all the data except the one it can produce exactly. This is clearly inadequate in biology and perhaps is one of the major lessons to be derived from the Bayesian point of view. Scientific discourse on sequence models—how well they fit the data and how they can be compared with each other—is *impossible* if the likelihood issue is not addressed honestly.

The likelihood question is clearly related to issues of variability and noise. Biological sequences are inherently "noisy," variability resulting in part from random events amplified by evolution. Mismatches and differences between specific individual sequences and the "average" sequence in a family, such as a protein family, are bound to occur and must be quantified. Because the same DNA or amino acid sequence will differ between individuals of the same species, and even more so across species, modelers always need to think in probabilistic terms. Indeed, a number of models used in the past in a more or less heuristic way, without clear reference to probabilities, are suddenly illuminated when the probabilistic aspects are made explicit. Dealing with the probabilistic aspects not only clarifies the issues and allows a rigorous discourse, but often also suggests new modeling avenues.

The computation of the likelihood is of course model-dependent and cannot be addressed in its generality. In section 2.4, we will outline some general principles for the derivation of models where the likelihood can be estimated without too many difficulties. But the reader should be aware that whatever criterion is used to measure the difference or error between a model and the data, such a criterion always comes with an underlying probabilistic model that needs to be clarified and is amenable to Bayesian analysis. Indeed, if the fit of a model $M = M(w)$ with parameters w is measured by some error function $f(w, D) \geq 0$ to be minimized, one can always define the associated likelihood to be

$$\mathbf{P}(D|M(w)) = \frac{e^{-f(w,D)}}{Z},\qquad (2.14)$$

where $Z = \int_w e^{-f(w,D)} dw$ is a normalizing factor (the "partition function" in statistical mechanics) that ensures the probabilities integrate to 1. As a result, minimizing the error function is equivalent to maximum likelihood (ML) estimation, or more generally maximum a posteriori (MAP) estimation. In particular, when the sum of squared differences is used to compare quantities, a rather common practice, this implies an underlying Gaussian model. Thus the Bayesian point of view clarifies the probabilistic assumptions that *must* underlie any criteria for matching models with data.

2.3.3 Parameter Estimation and Model Selection

We now return to the general Bayesian inference machinery. Two specific models M_1 and M_2 can be compared by comparing their probabilities $\mathbf{P}(M_1|D)$ and $\mathbf{P}(M_2|D)$. One objective often is to find or approximate the "best" model within a class—that is, to find the set of parameters w maximizing the posterior $\mathbf{P}(M|D)$, or $\log \mathbf{P}(M|D)$, and the corresponding error bars (see appendix A). This is called MAP estimation. In order to deal with positive quantities, this is also equivalent to minimizing $-\log \mathbf{P}(M|D)$:

$$\mathcal{E} = -\log \mathbf{P}(M|D) = -\log \mathbf{P}(D|M) - \log \mathbf{P}(M) + \log \mathbf{P}(D).\qquad (2.15)$$

From an optimization standpoint, the logarithm of the prior plays the role of a regularizer, that is, of an additional penalty term that can be used to enforce additional constraints, such as smoothness. Note that the term $\mathbf{P}(D)$ in (2.15) plays the role of a normalizing constant that does not depend on the parameters w, and is therefore irrelevant for this optimization. If the prior $\mathbf{P}(M)$ is uniform over all the models considered, then the problem reduces to finding the maximum of $\mathbf{P}(D|M)$, or $\log \mathbf{P}(D|M)$. This is just ML estimation. In summary, a substantial portion of this book and of machine-learning practice is based on MAP estimation, that is, the minimization of

$$\mathcal{E} = -\log \mathbf{P}(D|M) - \log \mathbf{P}(M), \tag{2.16}$$

or even the simpler ML estimation, that is, the minimization of

$$\mathcal{E} = -\log \mathbf{P}(D|M). \tag{2.17}$$

In most interesting models, the function being optimized is complex and its modes cannot be solved analytically. Thus one must resort to iterative and possibly stochastic methods such as gradient descent or simulated annealing, and also settle for approximate or suboptimal solutions.

Bayesian inference, however, is iterative. Finding a highly probable model within a certain class is only its first level. Whereas finding the optimal model is common practice, it is essential to note that this is really useful only if the distribution $\mathbf{P}(M|D)$ is sharply peaked around a unique optimum. In situations characterized by a high degree of uncertainty and relatively small amounts of data available, this is often not the case. Thus a Bayesian is really interested in the function $\mathbf{P}(M|D)$ over the entire space of models rather than in its maxima only, and more precisely in evaluating expectations with respect to $\mathbf{P}(M|D)$. This leads to higher levels of Bayesian inference, as in the case of prediction problems, marginalization of nuisance parameters, and class comparisons.

2.3.4 Prediction, Marginalization of Nuisance Parameters, and Class Comparison

Consider a prediction problem in which we are trying to predict the output value y of an unknown parameterized function f_w, given an input x. It is easy to show that the optimal prediction is given by the expectation

$$\mathbf{E}(y) = \int_w f_w(x)\mathbf{P}(w|D)dw. \tag{2.18}$$

This integral is the average of the predictions made by each possible model f_w, weighted by the plausibility $\mathbf{P}(w|D)$ of each model. Another example is the process of marginalization, where integration of the posterior parameter distribution is carried out only with respect to a subset of the parameters, the so-called nuisance parameters [225]. In a frequentist framework, where probabilities are defined in terms of observed frequencies, the notion of distribution over the parameters is not defined, and therefore nuisance parameters cannot be integrated out easily. Finally, one is often led to the problem of comparing two model classes, C_1 and C_2. To compare C_1 and C_2 in the Bayesian framework, one must compute $\mathbf{P}(C_1|D)$ and $\mathbf{P}(C_2|D)$ using Bayes' theorem: $\mathbf{P}(C|D) = \mathbf{P}(D|C)\mathbf{P}(C)/\mathbf{P}(D)$. In addition to the prior $\mathbf{P}(C)$, one must calculate the *evidence* $\mathbf{P}(D|C)$ by averaging over the entire model class:

$$\mathbf{P}(D|C) = \int_{w \in C} \mathbf{P}(D, w|C)dw = \int_{w \in C} \mathbf{P}(D|w, C)\mathbf{P}(w|C)dw. \qquad (2.19)$$

Similar integrals also arise with hierarchical models and hyperparameters (see below). In cases where the likelihood $\mathbf{P}(D|w, C)$ is very peaked around its maximum, such expectations can be approximated using the mode, that is, the value with the highest probability. But in general, integrals such as (2.18) and (2.19) require better approximations—for instance using Monte Carlo sampling methods [491, 396, 69], as briefly reviewed in chapter 4. Such methods, however, are computationally intensive and not always applicable to the models to be considered. This book is mostly concerned only with likelihood calculations and the first level of Bayesian inference (ML and MAP). The development of methods for handling higher levels of inference is an active area of research, and these should be considered whenever possible. The available computer power is of course an important issue in this context.

2.3.5 Ockham's Razor

As a final point raised in section 2.1, it does not make sense to choose a simple model on the basis that available data are scarce. *Everything else being equal*, however, it is true that one should prefer a simple hypothesis to a complex one. This is Ockham's razor. As pointed out by several authors, Ockham's razor is automatically embodied in the Bayesian framework [285, 373] in at least two different ways. In the first, trivial way, one can introduce priors that penalize complex models. But even without such priors, parameterized complex models will tend to be consistent with a larger volume of data space. Since a likelihood $\mathbf{P}(D|M)$ must sum to 1 over the space of data, if $\mathbf{P}(D|M)$ covers a larger expanse of data space, the likelihood values for given data sets will be smaller on average. Therefore, all else equal, complex models will tend to assign a correspondingly smaller likelihood to the observed data.

2.3.6 Minimum Description Length

An alternative approach to modeling is the *minimum description length* (MDL) [446]. MDL is related to ideas of data compression and information transmission. The goal is to transmit the data over a communication channel. Transmitting the data "as is" is not economical: nonrandom data contains structure and redundancies, and therefore must be amenable to compression. A good model of the data should capture their structure and yield good compression. The optimal model is the one that minimizes the length of the total message required to describe the data. This includes both the length required to specify the model itself and the data given the model. To a first approximation, MDL is closely related to the Bayesian point of view. According to Shannon's theory of communication [483], the length of the message required to communicate an event that has probability p is proportional to $-\log p$. Thus the most probable model has the shortest description. Some subtle differences between MDL and the Bayesian point of view can exist, however, but these will not concern us here.

2.4 Model Structures: Graphical Models and Other Tricks

Clearly, the construction or selection of suitable models is dictated by the data set, as well as by the modeler's experience and ingenuity. It is, however, possible to highlight a small number of very general techniques or tricks that can be used to shape the structure of the models. Most models in the literature can be described in terms of combinations of these simple techniques. Since in machine learning the starting point of any Bayesian analysis is almost always a high-dimensional probability distribution $\mathbf{P}(M, D)$ and the related conditional and marginal distributions (the posterior $\mathbf{P}(M|D)$, the likelihood $\mathbf{P}(D|M)$, the prior $\mathbf{P}(M)$, and the evidence $\mathbf{P}(D)$); these rules can be seen as ways of decomposing, simplifying, and parameterizing such high-dimensional distributions.

2.4.1 Graphical Models and Independence

By far the most common simplifying trick is to assume some independence between the variables or, more precisely, some conditional independence of subsets of variables, conditioned on other subsets of variables. These independence relationships can often be represented by a graph where the variables are associated with the nodes, and a missing edge represents a particular independence relationship (precise definitions can be found in appendix C). See [416, 350, 557, 121, 499, 106, 348, 286] for general reviews, treatments, or pointers to the large literature on this topic.

The independence relationships result in the fundamental fact that the global high-dimensional probability distribution, over all variables, can be factored into a product of simpler local probability distributions over lower-dimensional spaces associated with smaller clusters of variables. The clusters are reflected in the structure of the graph.

Graphical models can be subdivided into two broad categories depending on whether the edges of the associated graph are directed or undirected. Undirected edges are typical in problems where interactions are considered to be symmetric, such as in statistical mechanics or image processing [272, 199, 392]. In the undirected case, in one form or another, these models are called Markov random fields, undirected probabilistic independence networks, Boltzmann machines, Markov networks, and log-linear models.

Directed models are used in cases where interactions are not symmetric and reflect causal relationships or time irreversibility [416, 286, 246]. This is typically the case in expert systems and in all problems based on temporal data. The Kalman filter, a tool widely used in signal processing and control, can be viewed in this framework. In the case of temporal series, the independence assumptions are often those used in Markov models. Not surprisingly, most if not all of the models discussed in this book—NNs and HMMs in particular— are examples of graphical models with directed edges. A systematic treatment of graphical models in bioinformatics is given in chapter 9. Typical names for such models in the literature are Bayesian networks, belief networks, directed probabilistic independence networks, causal networks, and influence diagrams. It is also possible to develop a theory for the mixed case [557], where both directed and undirected edges are present. Such mixed graphs are also called chain independence graphs. The basic theory of graphical models is reviewed in appendix C.

Here we introduce the notation needed in the following chapters. By $G = (V, E)$ we denote a graph G with a set V of vertices and a set E of edges. If the edges are directed, we write $G = (V, \vec{E})$. In an undirected graph, $N(i)$ represents the sets of all the neighbors of vertex i, and $C(i)$ represents the set of all the vertices that are connected to i by a path. So,

$$N(i) = \{j \in V : (i, j) \in E\}. \tag{2.20}$$

In a directed graph, we use the obvious notation $N^-(i)$ and $N^+(i)$ to denote all the parents of i and all the children of i, respectively. Likewise, $C^-(i)$ and $C^+(i)$ denote the ancestors, or the "past," and the descendants of i, or the "future" of i. All these notations are extended in the obvious way to any set of vertices I. So for any $I \subseteq V$,

$$N(I) = \{j \in V : \exists i \in I \quad (i, j) \in E\} - I. \tag{2.21}$$

This is also called the boundary of I.

One fundamental observation is that in most applications the resulting graphs are *sparse*. Thus the global probability distribution factors into a relatively small number of relatively small local distributions. And this is key to the implementation of efficient computational structures for learning and inference, based on the local propagation of information between clusters of variables in the graph. The following techniques are not independent of the general graphical model ideas, but can often be viewed as special cases.

2.4.2 Hidden Variables

In many models, it is typical to assume that the data result in part from the action of hidden or latent variables, or causes, that either are not available in the data gathered or perhaps are fundamentally unobservable [172]. Missing data can also be treated as a hidden variable. The activations of the hidden units of a network, or the state sequence of an HMM, are typical examples of hidden variables. Another example is provided by the coefficients of a mixture (see below). Obviously the parameters of a model, such as the weights of an NN or the emission/transition probabilities of an HMM, could also be regarded as hidden variables in some sense, although this would be an unconventional terminology. Typical inference problems in hidden variable models are the estimation of the probability distribution over the set of hidden variables, its modes, and the corresponding expectations. These often appear as subproblems of the general parameter estimation problem in large parameterized models, such as HMMs. An important algorithm for parameter estimation with missing data or hidden variable is the EM algorithm, described in chapter 4 and further demonstrated in chapter 7 on HMMs.

2.4.3 Hierarchical Modeling

Many problems have a natural hierarchical structure or decomposition. This can result, for instance, from the existence of different time scales or length scales in the problem. The clusters described above in the general section on graphical modeling can also be viewed as nodes of a higher-level graphical model for the data (see, for instance, the notion of junction tree in [350]). In a related but complementary direction, the prior on the parameters of a model can have a hierarchical structure in which parameters at one level of the hierarchy are used to define the prior distribution on the parameters at the next level in a recursive way, with the number of parameters typically decreasing at each level as one ascends the hierarchy. All the parameters above a given level are often called "hyperparameters" with respect to that level.

Hyperparameters are used to provide more flexibility while keeping control over the complexity and structure of the model. Hyperparameters have "high gain" in the sense that small hyperparameter variations can induce large model variations at the level below. Hyperparameters also allow for parameter reduction because the model prior can be calculated from a (usually smaller) number of hyperparameters. In symbolic form,

$$\mathbf{P}(w) = \int_{\alpha} \mathbf{P}(w \mid \alpha)\mathbf{P}(\alpha)d\alpha, \qquad (2.22)$$

where α represents hyperparameters for the parameter w with prior $\mathbf{P}(\alpha)$. As a typical example, consider the connection weights in a neural network. In a given problem, it may be a good idea to model the prior on a weight by using a Gaussian distribution with mean μ and standard deviation σ. Having a different set of hyperparameters μ and σ for each weight may yield a model with too few constraints. All the σs of a given unit, or in an entire layer, can be tied and assumed to be identical. At a higher level, a prior can be defined on the σs, and so on. An example of a hierarchical Dirichlet model is given in appendix D.

2.4.4 Hybrid Modeling/Parameterization

Parameterization issues are important in machine learning, if only because the models used are often quite large. Even when the global probability distribution over the data and the parameters has been factored into a product of simpler distributions, as a result of independence assumptions, one often must still parameterize the component distributions. Two useful general approaches for parameterizing distributions are mixture models and neural networks.

In mixture models, a complex distribution P is parameterized as a linear convex combination of simpler or canonical distributions in the form

$$P = \sum_{i=1}^{n} \lambda_i P_i, \tag{2.23}$$

where the $\lambda_i \geq 0$ are called the mixture coefficients and satisfy $\sum_i \lambda_i = 1$. The distributions P_i are called the components of the mixture and can carry their own parameters (means, standard deviations, etc.). A review of mixture models can be found in [173, 522].

Neural networks are also used to reparameterize models, that is, to compute model parameters as a function of inputs and connection weights. As we shall see, this is in part because neural networks have universal approximation properties and good flexibility, combined with simple learning algorithms. The simplest example is perhaps in regression problems, where a neural network can be used to calculate the mean of the dependent variable as a function of the independent variable, the input. A more subtle example will be given in chapter 9, where neural networks are used to calculate the transition and emission parameters of an HMM. The term "hybrid" is sometimes used to describe situations in which different model classes are combined, although the combination can take different forms.

2.4.5 Exponential Family of Distributions

The exponential family of distributions is briefly reviewed in appendix A. Here it suffices to say that many of the most commonly used distributions (Gaussian, multinomial, etc.) belong to this family, and that using members of the family often leads to computationally efficient algorithms. For a review of the exponential family, with a comprehensive list of references, see [94].

2.5 Summary

We have briefly presented the Bayesian approach to modeling and inference. The main advantage of a Bayesian approach is obvious: it provides a principled and rigorous approach to inference, with a strong foundation in probability theory. In fact, one of the most compelling reasons in favor of Bayesian induction is its uniqueness under a very small set of commonsense axioms. We grant that mathematicians may be more receptive than biologists to such an argument.

The Bayesian framework clarifies a number of issues, on at least three different levels. First, a Bayesian approach forces one to clarify the prior knowledge, the data, and the hypotheses. The Bayesian framework is entirely open to, and actually encourages, questioning any piece of information. It deals with the subjectivity inherent in the modeling process not by sweeping it under the rug but, rather, by incorporating it up front in the modeling process. It is fundamentally an iterative process where models are progressively refined. Second, and this is perhaps the main lesson here, sequence models *must* be probabilistic and come to grips with issues of noise and variability in the data, in a quantifiable way. Without this step it is impossible to have a rigorous scientific discourse on models, to determine how well they fit the data, and ultimately to compare models and hypotheses. Third, the Bayesian approach clarifies how to proceed with inference, that is, how to compare models and quantify errors and uncertainties, basically by cranking the engine of probability. In particular, it provides unambiguous, unique answers to well-posed questions. It defines the set of rules required to play a fair modeling game. The basic step is to compute model plausibilities, with respect to the available data and the associated expectations, using the rules of probability theory and possibly numerical approximations.

The Bayesian approach can lead to a better understanding of the weaknesses of a model, and thereby help in generating better models. In addition, an objective way of comparing models, and of making predictions based on models, will become more important as the number, scope, and complexity of models for biological macromolecules, structure, function, and regulation increase. Issues of model comparison and prediction will become progressively more central as databases grow in size and complexity. New ideas are likely to emerge from the systematic application of Bayesian probabilistic ideas to sequence analysis problems.

The main drawback of the Bayesian approach is that it can be computationally intensive, especially when averages need to be computed over high-dimensional distributions. For the largest sequence models used in this book, one is unlikely to be able to carry out a complete Bayesian integration on currently available computers. But continuing progress in Monte Carlo [491, 69] and other approximation techniques, as well as steady increases in raw computing power in workstations and parallel computers, is encouraging.

Once the general probabilistic framework is established, the next central idea is that of graphical models: to factor high-dimensional probability distributions by exploiting independence assumptions that have a graphical substrate. Most machine-learning models and problems can be represented in terms of recursive sparse graphs, at the levels of both the variables involved, observed or hidden, and the parameters. Sparse recursive graphs appear as a universal underlying language or representational structure for most models and machine-learning applications.

Chapter 3

Probabilistic Modeling and Inference: Examples

What are the implications of a Bayesian approach for modeling? For any type of model class, it is clear that the first step must be to make the likelihood $\mathbf{P}(D|M)$ and the prior $\mathbf{P}(M)$ explicit. In this chapter, we look at a few simple applications of the general probabilistic framework. The first is a very simple sequence model based on die tosses. All other examples in the chapter, including the basic derivation of statistical mechanics, are variations obtained either by increasing the number of dice or by varying the observed data.

3.1 The Simplest Sequence Models

The simplest, but not entirely trivial, modeling situation is that of a single coin flip. This model has a single parameter p and the data consist of a string, containing a single letter, over the alphabet $A = \{H, T\}$, H for head and T for tail. Since we are interested in DNA sequences, we shall move directly to a slightly more complex version with four letters, rather than two, and the possibility of observing longer strings.

3.1.1 The Single-Die Model with Sequence Data

The data D then consist of DNA strings over the four-letter alphabet $A = \{A, C, G, T\}$. The simple model we want to use is to assume that the strings have been obtained by independent tosses of the same four-sided die (figure 3.1).

Figure 3.1: Two Views of the Four-Sided DNA Die Used to Generate of DNA Strings.

Because the tosses are independent and there is a unique underlying die, for likelihood considerations it does not really matter whether we have many strings or a single long string. So we assume that the data consist of a single observation sequence of length N: $D = \{O\}$, with $O = X^1 \ldots X^N$ and $X^i \in A$. Our model M has four parameters p_A, p_C, p_G, p_T satisfying $p_A + p_C + p_G + p_T = 1$. The likelihood is then given by

$$\mathbf{P}(D|M) = \prod_{X \in A} p_X^{n_X} = p_A^{n_A} p_C^{n_C} p_G^{n_G} p_T^{n_T}, \tag{3.1}$$

where n_X is the number of times the letter X appears in the sequence O. The negative log-posterior is then

$$- \log \mathbf{P}(M|D) = - \sum_{X \in A} n_X \log p_X - \log \mathbf{P}(M) + \log \mathbf{P}(D). \tag{3.2}$$

If we assume a uniform prior distribution over the parameters, then the MAP parameter estimation problem is identical to the ML parameter estimation problem and can be solved by optimizing the Lagrangian

$$\mathcal{L} = - \sum_{X \in A} n_X \log p_X - \lambda(1 - \sum_{X \in A} p_X) \tag{3.3}$$

associated with the negative log-likelihood and augmented by the normalizing constraint. Here, and in the rest of the book, positivity constraints are checked directly in the results. Setting the partial derivatives $\partial \mathcal{L}/\partial p_X$ to zero immediately yields $p_X = n_X/\lambda$. Using the normalization constraint gives $\lambda = N$ so that finally, as expected, we get the estimates

$$p_X^* = \frac{n_X}{N} \quad \text{for all} \quad X \in A. \tag{3.4}$$

Note that the value of the negative log-likelihood per letter, for the optimal parameter set P^*, approaches the entropy (see appendix B) $\mathcal{H}(P^*)$ of P^* as $N \to \infty$:

$$\lim_{N \to \infty} -\frac{1}{N} \sum_{X \in A} n_X \log \frac{n_X}{N} = -\sum_{X \in A} p_X^* \log p_X^* = \mathcal{H}(P^*). \quad (3.5)$$

Another way of looking at these results is to say that except for a constant entropy term, the negative log-likelihood is essentially the relative entropy between the fixed die probabilities p_X and the observed frequencies n_X/N. In the section on statistical mechanics below, we will see how this is also related to the concept of free energy.

The observed frequency estimate $p_X = n_X/N$ is of course natural when N is large. The strong law of large numbers tells us that for large enough values of N, the observed frequency will almost surely be very close to the true value of p_X. But what happens if N is small, say $N = 4$? Suppose that in a sequence of length 4 we do not observe the letter A at all? Do we want to set the probability p_A to zero? Probably not, especially if we do not have any reason to suspect that the die is highly biased. In other words, our prior beliefs do not favor model parameters with value 0. As described in chapter 2, the corresponding natural prior in this case is not a uniform prior but rather a Dirichlet prior on the parameter vector P. Indeed, with a Dirichlet prior $\mathcal{D}_{\alpha Q}(P)$ the negative log-posterior becomes

$$-\log \mathbf{P}(M|D) = -\sum_{X \in A} [n_X + \alpha q_X - 1] \log p_X + \log Z + \log \mathbf{P}(D). \quad (3.6)$$

Z is the normalization constant of the Dirichlet distribution that does not depend on the probabilities p_X. Thus the MAP optimization problem is very similar to the one previously solved, except that the counts n_X are replaced by $n_X + \alpha q_X - 1$. We immediately get the estimates

$$p_X^* = \frac{n_X + \alpha q_X - 1}{N + \alpha - |A|} \quad \text{for all} \quad X \in A \quad (3.7)$$

provided this estimate is positive. In particular, the effect of the Dirichlet prior is equivalent to adding pseudocounts to the observed counts. With the proper choice of average distribution Q (for instance, Q uniform) and α, the estimates p_X^* can never be negative or 0. When Q is uniform, we say that the Dirichlet prior is *symmetric*. Notice that the uniform distribution over P is a special case of symmetric Dirichlet prior, with $q_X = 1/\alpha = 1/|A|$. It is also clear from (3.6) that the posterior distribution $\mathbf{P}(M|D)$ is a Dirichlet distribution $\mathcal{D}_{\beta R}$ with $\beta = N + \alpha$ and $r_X = (n_X + \alpha q_X)/(N + \alpha)$.

The expectation of the posterior is the vector r_X which is slightly different from the MAP estimate (3.1). This suggests using an alternative estimate for

p_X, the predictive distribution or MP (mean posterior) estimate

$$p_X^* = \frac{n_X + \alpha q_X}{N + \alpha}.$$ (3.8)

This is in general a better choice. Here in particular the MP estimate minimizes the expected relative entropy distance $f(P^*) = \mathbf{E}(\mathcal{H}(P, P^*))$, where the expectation is taken with respect to the posterior $\mathbf{P}(P|D)$.

The die model with a single Dirichlet prior is simple enough such that one can proceed analytically with higher levels of Bayesian inference. For instance, we can compute the evidence $\mathbf{P}(D)$:

$$\mathbf{P}(D) = \int \mathbf{P}(D|w)\mathbf{P}(w)\,dw = \int_{\sum p_X = 1} \prod_{X \in A} p_X^{n_X + \alpha q_X - 1} \frac{\Gamma(\alpha)}{\Gamma(\alpha q_X)}\,dp_X.$$ (3.9)

This integral is very similar to the integral of a Dirichlet distribution and therefore can be easily calculated, yielding

$$\mathbf{P}(D) = \frac{\Gamma(\alpha)}{\prod_{X \in A} \Gamma(\alpha q_X)} \frac{\prod_{X \in A} \Gamma(\beta r_X)}{\Gamma(\beta)},$$ (3.10)

This evidence is the ratio of the normalizing constants of the prior and posterior distributions.

We leave it as an exercise for the reader to continue playing with the Bayesian machinery. Useful exercises would be to find the values of α and q_X that maximize the evidence, to define a prior on α and q_X using hyperparameters, and to study MAP and MP estimates when the prior distribution is a mixture of Dirichlet distributions

$$\mathbf{P}(P) = \sum_i \lambda_i \mathcal{D}_{\alpha_i Q_i}(P)$$ (3.11)

(see also appendix D and [489]). In the latter case, the posterior is also a mixture of Dirichlet distributions. This is a general result: whenever the prior distribution is a mixture of conjugate distributions, the posterior is also a mixture of conjugate distributions.

3.1.2   The Single-Die Model with Counts Data

With the same die model, we now assume that available data consists of the counts themselves, $D = \{n_X\}$, rather than the actual sequence. A simple combinatorial calculation shows that the likelihood now has the form

$$\mathbf{P}(D|M) = \mathbf{P}(n_X|p_X) = \frac{N!}{\prod_{X \in A} n_X!} \prod_{X \in A} p_X^{n_X}$$ (3.12)

with $\sum_X n_X = N$. This is similar to (3.1), except for the factorial term that counts the number of ways the set of numbers (n_X) can be realized in a sequence of length N. This distribution on the counts n_X generated by a simple die model is also called a *multinomial distribution*, generalizing the notion of binomial distribution associated with coin (that is, two-sided die) flips. With a little abuse, the die model itself will sometimes be called a multinomial model.

With a Dirichlet prior $\mathcal{D}_{\alpha Q}(P)$ on the parameter vector P, a calculation similar to the one above shows that the posterior distribution on P is also a Dirichlet distribution $\mathcal{D}_{\beta R}(P)$ with $\beta = N + \alpha$ and $r_X = (n_X + \alpha q_X)/\beta$. Not surprisingly, the MAP and MP estimates P^* are identical to (3.7) and (3.8).

We now consider the distribution that a fixed vector P induces on the counts n_X. Taking the logarithm of (3.12) and using Stirling's approximation formula for factorials

$$n! \approx (\frac{n}{e})^n \sqrt{2\pi n}, \tag{3.13}$$

we get

$$\log(\mathbf{P}(D|P) \approx C - \mathcal{H}(n_X/N, p_X), \tag{3.14}$$

where C is a constant independent of n_X and $\mathcal{H}$ is the relative entropy between the empirical distribution and P. When P is uniform except for constant terms, the relative entropy above reduces to the entropy of the empirical distribution. Therefore in this case

$$\mathbf{P}(D|P) \approx \frac{e^{\mathcal{H}(n_X/N}}{Z}. \tag{3.15}$$

This is called the *entropic* distribution. In other words, a uniform P induces an entropic distribution over the counts n_X, that is, over the space of all possible histograms. As we will see in section 3.2, this is one of the standard justifications for the MaxEnt principle that amounts to using an entropic prior. Notice the similarities but also the differences between a Dirichlet distribution and an entropic distribution

$$\frac{\exp(-\sum_X p_X \log p_X)}{Z} \tag{3.16}$$

over P. We leave it as an exercise to show that if P has an entropic prior, the posterior after observing n_X is not entropic, nor Dirichlet. The entropic distribution is not the conjugate of a multinomial. With an entropic prior, the MAP estimate is still of the form $p_X^* = n_X/N$.

While the simple die model is of course very crude, it is important to note that this is exactly the model we adopt when we compute first-order statistics, that is, the proportion of each letter in a given family of sequences, such as exons, introns, or a protein family. This can be viewed as a first step in an iterative modeling process, and therefore the performance of subsequent models must be evaluated with respect to the first-order model. The multiple-die model of the next section and, in chapter 7, hidden Markov models (HMMs) are just slightly more complex generalizations of the simple die model. The simple die model can trivially be extended by having strings of letters on each face. This is equivalent to extending the alphabet. For instance, one can use a die with 64 faces to model DNA triplets.

3.1.3   The Multiple-Die Model with Sequence Data

Another simple sequence model is the multiple-die model. Here the data consist of K sequences, each of length N. For instance, the reader could think of a multiple alignment of K sequences in which case the gap symbol "–" could be considered one of the symbols in the alphabet. In the multiple-die model we assume that there are N independent dice, one for each position, and that each sequence is the result of flipping the N dice in a fixed order. Let p_X^i denote the probability of producing the letter X with die number i, and n_X^i the number of times the letter X appears in position i. Because the dice and the sequences are assumed to be independent, the likelihood function is

$$P(D|M) = \prod_{i=1}^{N} \prod_{X \in A} p_X^{n_X^i}. \tag{3.17}$$

With uniform prior across all dice, a calculation identical to the single-die case yields

$$p_X^{i*} = \frac{n_X^i}{K} \quad \text{for all} \quad X \in A. \tag{3.18}$$

Again we leave it as an exercise for the reader to study the effect of Dirichlet priors on this model, and to consider possible generalizations (see also [376]). A well-known class of models used in language modeling is the n-gram models. In an n-gram model, there are $|A|^{n-1}$ dice. Each die is associated with a different prefix of length $n - 1$. Each die is a simple die with $|A|$ faces, one letter per face. Sequences are generated by scanning a window of length n, selecting the die associated with the current prefix, and flipping it at random. Thus the choice of the die to be flipped is not independent of the previous flips. These n-gram models can be viewed as Markov models of order equal to the length of the prefix, also called the "memory" of the model. The single-die model has memory of length 0. There exist also variants with variable memory length (see [448] for an example with application to biological sequences), as well as mixtures of higher-order Markov models, also called interpolated Markov models. Higher-order models are computationally more expensive, with the number of possible prefixes growing very rapidly with the size of the alphabet and the memory length. With the small DNA alphabet, however, Markov models of order 5 or so remain feasible.

3.2   Statistical Mechanics

There are at least five good reasons to understand the rudiments of statistical mechanics in connection with machine learning and computational biology. First, statistical mechanics can be viewed as one of the oldest and best examples of Bayesian reasoning [280, 281], although the presentation often given is slightly flawed in our opinion because of the confusion between MaxEnt and Bayes. Second, statistical mechanics has traditionally been concerned with deriving the statistical macroscopic properties of large ensembles of simple microscopically interacting units—the equilibrium behavior, the phase transitions, and so on. The results and techniques of statistical mechanics are useful in understanding the properties and learning evolution of a number of graphical models used in machine learning [252, 482, 50]. Statistical mechanical models have also been applied directly to biological macromolecules—for instance, in the protein-folding problem (see [151] for a review). Finally, statistical mechanics is useful for understanding several algorithms that are fundamental for machine learning, such as simulated annealing and the EM algorithms described in chapter 4.

Here we give a Bayesian derivation of statistical mechanics from first principles, and develop the basic concepts, especially those of the Boltzmann-Gibbs distribution and free energy, that will be needed in the next chapters. In the basic statistical mechanics framework, one considers a stochastic system that can be in a number of "microscopic" states: $S = \{s_1, \ldots, s_{|S|}\}$, with p_s denoting the probability of being in state s for a distribution $P = (p_s)$. This can be viewed as a die model $M(w)$, with parameters $w = p_s$, although for the time being it is not necessary to assume that the tosses are independent. The key difference from the examples above is in the data. The faces of the die, the microscopic states, are not observable but act as hidden variables. Instead, we assume that there is a function $f(s)$ of the states and that the only "macroscopic" observable quantity, the data, is the expectation or average of f. So, with a slight abuse of notation, in this section we write $D = \mathbf{E}(f) = \sum_s p_s f(s)$.

Very often in statistical mechanics the states have a microscopic structure so that $s = (x_1, \ldots, x_n)$, where the x_i are local variables. For instance, the x_i can be binary spin variables, in which case $|S| = 2^n$. Likewise, f is typically the energy of the system and can be written as a quadratic function in the local variables: $f(s) = f(x_1, \ldots, x_n) = \sum_{ij} w_{ij} x_i x_j + \sum_i w_i x_i$. The interaction parameters w_{ij} can be local, as in the case of spins on a lattice, or long-range, and are related to the underlying graphical model. While such assumptions are important in modeling particular systems and developing a detailed theory, they will not be needed in the following sections. The first question we can ask is: Given the observation of the average of f, what can we say about the state distribution P?

3.2.1 The Boltzmann-Gibbs Distribution

Standard Derivation

Most standard treatments at this point are based on the maximum entropy principle. Without any additional information, one ought to choose the distribution P that satisfies the constraint $\sum_s f(s) p_s = D$ and has the highest entropy, because this is the solution that is the most "spread out" and makes the fewest additional assumptions. This problem can easily be solved by writing down the Lagrangian $\mathcal{L}$, which consists of a linear combination of the function being optimized with the relevant constraints:

$$\mathcal{L} = -\sum_s p_s \log p_s - \lambda(\sum_s p_s f(s) - D) - \mu(\sum_s p_s - 1). \qquad (3.19)$$

By equating the partial derivatives of $\mathcal{L}$ with respect to p_s to 0, we immediately find that the only solution distributions are of the form

$$p_s^*(\lambda) = \frac{e^{-\lambda f(s)}}{Z(\lambda)}, \qquad (3.20)$$

where the normalizing factor $Z(\lambda) = \sum_s e^{-\lambda f(s)}$ is called the partition function. In statistical mechanics, the Lagrange multiplier is related to the temperature T of the system by the definition $\lambda = 1/kT$, where k is the Boltzmann constant. For all our purposes here we will not need to consider the temperature and will work directly with the parameter λ. Note, however, that λ, and therefore the temperature, are entirely determined by the observation D, since we must have

$$\sum_s \frac{e^{-\lambda f(s)}}{Z(\lambda)} f(s) = D. \qquad (3.21)$$

Often, it will even be sufficient to assume that $\lambda = 1$. The optimal distribution P^* is called the Boltzmann-Gibbs distribution of the system. It is important to realize that *any* distribution P can be represented as a Boltzmann-Gibbs distribution, at least at a fixed temperature, by using an energy function proportional to $-\log P$. It is also easy to see that a similar formula is derived when there are multiple linear constraints on the parameters p_s.

While the Boltzmann-Gibbs distribution is very useful, from a Bayesian standpoint the standard derivation is not entirely satisfactory for three reasons: (1) The prior distribution is not explicit. As a result, how would one incorporate additional prior information on the p_s, such as knowing that the first state occurs more frequently than the others? (2) The probabilistic model is not explicit. In particular, how one would calculate the likelihood $\mathbf{P}(D|p_s)$; (3) The justification for the use of MaxEnt is weak. In particular, is there any connection between MaxEnt and ML or MAP estimation? In all fairness, the use of MaxEnt is partially justified by the combinatorial argument given above, which shows that maximizing the entropy is essentially equivalent to maximizing the number of possible realizations $N!/\prod_s n_s!$ when the tosses are independent [282]. In this sense, the MaxEnt solution is the one that can be realized in the largest number of ways. Such an argument, however, is based only on the number of realizations and does not take into account their relative probabilities. We now address these three criticisms.

Bayesian Derivation

The main problem with the standard derivation is that the probabilistic model is not really explicit. In particular, the likelihood function $\mathbf{P}(D|p_s)$ is not clearly defined and little progress can be made in this direction without considering actual runs of the system. Thus we must enlarge the initial setup by assuming that there is a fixed number N that is very large and that the system is observed over such a period. Variable observation times could also be considered but would further complicate the analysis. Accordingly, we decide to parameterize the model using the counts n_s. Note also that what is really observed is $D = (\sum_s n_s f(s))/N \neq \sum_s p_s f(s)$.

Several priors on the counts n_s are possible. As we have seen, a natural prior would be to use a Dirichlet prior on n_s/N. A nonsymmetric Dirichlet prior could easily incorporate any additional information regarding the frequency of occurrence of any particular state. We leave it as an exercise for the reader to calculate the posterior obtained with a Dirichlet prior, but this is obviously not the Boltzmann-Gibbs solution. For instance, if the prior is uniform and $f(s_1) = D$, then the vector $(N, 0, \ldots, 0)$, with the lowest possible entropy, maximizes the probability of the data by rendering it certain! Here we rather decide to use the entropic prior, which is the distribution on n_s obtained when P is uniform. Again, such a prior is best justified when the runs are independent, that is, the underlying probabilistic model is a simple die with $|S|$ faces. Although in what follows we confine ourselves to this zeroth-order Markov model, one could consider higher-order Markov models. A Markov model of order 1, for instance, would include a different set of parameters associated with the transition probabilities from state to state, equivalent to $|S|$ dice. Certain aspects of Markov models of order 1 and Boltzmann-Gibbs distributions are treated in chapter 4.

The likelihood function is then trivial and has value 1 or 0, depending on whether or not $D = \sum_s f(s)n_s/N$. We can finally proceed with the first step of Bayesian inference, and estimate the parameters n_s by MAP estimation. Using the formalism introduced earlier this leads immediately to the Lagrangian

$$\mathcal{L} = -\sum_s \frac{n_s}{N} \log \frac{n_s}{N} - \lambda\left(\sum_s (f(s)\frac{n_s}{N} - D\right) - \mu\left(\sum_s n_s - N\right), \qquad (3.22)$$

where the entropy act as a regularizer. This is of course virtually identical to (3.19) and yields a MAP Boltzmann-Gibbs distribution for n_s/N. A similar result can be derived using the parameters p_s instead of n_s, but in a more cumbersome way in terms of both justifying the entropic prior and calculating the likelihood function, since different values of n_s can be consistent with D.

In conclusion, the Boltzmann-Gibbs distribution corresponds to a first step of Bayesian inference by MAP, with an entropic prior. Therefore MaxEnt is best viewed not as an universal principle but simply as a shortcut for the first level of Bayesian inference in a multinomial setting associated with an entropic prior. Such prior can be challenged and examples can be constructed where MaxEnt leads to the "wrong" solution. We leave it as an exercise for the reader to construct such examples and envision how to proceed again with higher steps of Bayesian inference (hyperparameters, integration over priors).

3.2.2   Thermodynamic Limit and Phase Transitions

The temperature is a good example of an *intensive* quantity, that is, a quantity that by definition is independent of system size. On the other hand, *extensive* quantities, such as the energy, grow with the size of the system. For large systems with local interactions, this growth is typically linear with the size of the system. Thus the value of an extensive quantity per unit of volume tends to a limiting value as the size of the system goes to infinity, the so-called *thermodynamic limit*.

One of the main goals of statistical mechanics is to estimate the thermodynamic limit of macroscopic quantities, that is, to approximate expectations with respect to the Boltzmann-Gibbs distribution. In particular, one of the main goals is to approximate the partition function $Z(\lambda)$, since this function contains most of the relevant information about the system. In particular, it is easy to show that all the moments of the function f can be computed from $Z(\lambda)$, and more precisely from its logarithm. For instance, for the first two moments, the mean and the variance, an elementary calculation gives

$$\mathbf{E}(f) = -\frac{\partial}{\partial \lambda} \log Z(\lambda) \qquad (3.23)$$

$$\mathbf{Var}(f) = -\frac{\partial^2}{\partial \lambda^2} \log Z(\lambda). \qquad (3.24)$$

Likewise, the entropy of the Boltzmann-Gibbs distribution P^* can be expressed as

$$\mathcal{H}(P^*) = -\sum_s P^*(s) \log P^*(s) = \log Z(\lambda) + \lambda E(f). \qquad (3.25)$$

Another central topic of statistical mechanics is the study of phase transitions, that is abrupt changes in the behavior of the system as some of the parameters, especially the temperature T or equivalently λ, are varied. A first-order phase transition is said to occur at a critical value λ_C if $E(f)$ is discontinuous at λ_C. A second-order phase transition occurs at λ_C if $E(f)$ is continuous but **Var** (f) is discontinuous. The study of phase transitions is also important in learning theory [252, 482], but this is beyond the scope of this book.

3.2.3 The Free Energy

The logarithm of the partition function is called the *free energy* because of its important role (see (3.23), (3.24), and (3.25)). More precisely, the free energy $\mathcal{F} = \mathcal{F}(f, \lambda) = \mathcal{F}(\lambda)$ is defined to be

$$\mathcal{F}(\lambda) = -\frac{1}{\lambda} \log Z(\lambda). \qquad (3.26)$$

The above formula can obviously be rewritten in terms of the free energy. For instance,

$$\mathcal{H}(P^*) = -\lambda \mathcal{F}(\lambda) + \lambda E(f). \qquad (3.27)$$

This is equivalent to

$$\mathcal{F}(\lambda) = E(f) - \frac{1}{\lambda} \mathcal{H}(P^*), \qquad (3.28)$$

which is sometimes used as an alternative definition of the free energy. In this definition, the free energy depends on the function f, the parameter λ, and the distribution P^* over states. The definition therefore can be extended to any other distribution $Q(s)$:

$$\mathcal{F}(f, Q, \lambda) = \mathcal{F}(Q, \lambda) = E_Q(f) - \frac{1}{\lambda} \mathcal{H}(Q), \qquad (3.29)$$

where E_Q denotes expectations with respect to the distribution Q. Here we drop the dependency on f, but the choice of f as a negative log-probability is important in statistical applications, such as the derivation of the EM algorithm, as described below and in chapter 4. By comparing this free energy with the Lagrangian above, it is also clear that the Boltzmann-Gibbs distribution is equivalently characterized as the distribution that minimizes the free energy.

Consider now any two distributions $Q(s)$ and $R(s)$. We want to be able to compare their free energies. A simple calculation gives

$$\mathcal{F}(Q,\lambda) - \mathcal{F}(R,\lambda) = \sum_s [Q(s) - R(s)][f(s) + \frac{1}{\lambda}\log R(s)] + \frac{1}{\lambda}\mathcal{H}(Q,R), \quad (3.30)$$

where $\mathcal{H}(Q,R) = \sum_s Q(s)\log(Q(s)/R(s))$ is the relative entropy between Q and R.

It is useful to remark that if we take the energy of s to be the negative likelihood $f(s) = -\log R(s)$, where R is some distribution over the states, then the Boltzmann-Gibbs distribution is proportional to $R^\lambda(s)$. In particular, at $\lambda = 1$ the Boltzmann-Gibbs distribution of the system is R itself: $P^*(s,1) = R$, and the free energy reduces to 0. Furthermore, for any other distribution Q, the difference in free energies is then equal to the relative entropy

$$\mathcal{F}(Q,1) - \mathcal{F}(R,1) = \mathcal{H}(Q,R). \quad (3.31)$$

Since the relative entropy is always nonnegative, then $\mathcal{F}(Q,1) \geq \mathcal{F}(R,1)$, with equality if and only if $Q = R$. Again the Boltzmann-Gibbs distribution minimizes the free energy. It is also important to note that there is nothing special about the $\lambda = 1$ temperature. We could, for instance, define $f(s) = -\log R(s)/\lambda$, and then obtain $\mathcal{F}(Q,\lambda) - \mathcal{F}(R,\lambda) = \mathcal{H}(Q,R)/\lambda$.

3.2.4 The Hidden Variables Case

In many modeling situations there are hidden/unobserved/latent variables or causes denoted by H. If D denotes the data, we assume that there is available a joint distribution on the hidden and observed variables $\mathbf{P}(D,H|w)$, parameterized by w. In the case of interest to us, w as usual denotes the parameters of a model. From a statistical mechanics perspective, we can consider that the states of the system are the values assumed by the hidden variables. If we define f by

$$f(H) = -\log \mathbf{P}(D,H|w), \quad (3.32)$$

then at $\lambda = 1$ the Boltzmann-Gibbs distribution is given by the posterior

$$P^* = P^*(H,1) = \mathbf{P}(H|D,w) \quad (3.33)$$

and the free energy by

$$\mathcal{F}(P^*,1) = -\log \mathbf{P}(D|w), \quad (3.34)$$

which is the negative log-likelihood of the data. Furthermore, for any other distribution Q, the difference in free energies is given by

$$\mathcal{F}(Q,1) - \mathcal{F}(P^*,1) = \mathcal{H}(Q,P^*) \quad (3.35)$$

or

$$\log \mathbf{P}(D|w) = -\mathcal{F}(Q,1) + \mathcal{H}(Q,P^*). \tag{3.36}$$

In order to maximize the data likelihood, when the posterior $\mathbf{P}(H|D,w)$ and the corresponding expectations are difficult to calculate, one can sometimes use a suboptimal strategy based on a different family of distributions Q for which calculations are more tractable, without departing too much from the true posterior. This idea of minimizing the free energy term $\mathcal{F}(Q,\lambda)$ is developed in [146, 255] and in the section on variational methods in appendix A.

Chapter 4

Machine Learning Algorithms

4.1 Introduction

In this chapter we cover the main algorithms for machine-learning applications that will be used thoughout the rest of the book. We briefly describe each of the algorithms and provide pointers to the vast literature on this topic.

Once a parameterized model $M(w)$ for the data has been constructed, we have seen that the next steps are the following:

1. The estimation of the complete distribution $\mathbf{P}(w, D)$ and the posterior $\mathbf{P}(w|D)$

2. The estimation of the optimal set of parameters w by maximizing $\mathbf{P}(w|D)$, the first level of Bayesian inference

3. The estimation of marginals and expectations with respect to the posterior, that is, for instance, of integrals of the form $\mathbf{E}(f) = \int f(w)\mathbf{P}(w|D)dw$, the higher levels of Bayesian inference

Thus the algorithms can be subdivided into three categories, depending on whether the goal is to estimate a probability density, one of its modes, or the corresponding expectations. For practical reasons we shall use this distinction, although it is somewhat arbitrary. Indeed, any problem can be reformulated as an optimization problem, and the probability of an event is the expectation of the corresponding indicator function: $\mathbf{P}(A) = \mathbf{E}(1_A)$. Likewise, dynamic programming, which is often used to estimate sequence data likelihoods, can be viewed as an optimization technique.

In section 4.2, we briefly review dynamic programming, one of the key algorithms in sequence analysis, and its application in the estimations of sequence likelihoods. In the following two sections we look at algorithms for

81

the optimization of $\mathbf{P}(w|D)$, including gradient descent and EM (expectation maximization)/GEM (generalized expectation maximization). The treatment of simulated annealing is postponed to section 4.6, after the treatment in section 4.5 of Monte Carlo Markov chain methods (MCMC) for the stochastic sampling of high-dimensional distributions and the computation of the corresponding expectations. This is because simulated annealing relies heavily on stochastic sampling. In section 4.7 we take a brief look at evolutionary algorithms, and conclude in section 4.8 with several complements and practical aspects.

4.2 Dynamic Programming

Dynamic programming [66] is to a very general optimization technique that can be applied any time a problem can be recursively subdivided into two similar subproblems of smaller size, such that the solution to the larger problem can be obtained by piecing together the solutions to the two subproblems. The prototypical problem to which dynamic programming can be applied is that of finding the shortest path between two nodes in a graph. Clearly the shortest path from node A to node B, going through node C, is the concatenation of the shortest path from A to C with the shortest path from C to B. This is also called the "Bellman principle." A general solution to the original problem is then constructed by recursively piecing together shorter optimal paths.

Dynamic programming and its many variations are ubiquitous in sequence analysis. The Needleman–Wunch and Smith–Waterman algorithms [401, 481, 492], as well as all other sequence-alignment algorithms such as the Viterbi decoding algorithm of electrical engineers, are examples of dynamic programming. Alignment algorithms can be visualized in terms of finding the shortest path in the appropriate graph with the appropriate metric. Aligning two sequences of length of N requires finding a shortest path in a graph with N^2 vertices. Since dynamic programming essentially requires visiting all such vertices once, it is easy to see that its time complexity scales as $O(N^2)$.

In chapters 7 and 8, dynamic programming and the Viterbi algorithm are heavily used to compute likelihoods and align sequences to HMMs during the training and exploitation phases. Accordingly, we give there a detailed derivation of the corresponding algorithms. Other variations on dynamic programming used in other chapters are sketched or left as an exercise. Because dynamic programming is very well known and is at the root of many conventional algorithms for sequence analysis, we refer the reader to the abundant literature on the topic (in particular [550] and references therein). Reinforcement-learning algorithms are also another important class of learning algorithms that can be viewed as generalizations of dynamic programming ideas [298].

4.3 Gradient Descent

Often we are interested in parameter estimation, that is, in finding the best possible model $M(w)$ that minimizes the posterior $f(w) = -\log \mathbf{P}(w|D)$, or possibly the likelihood $-\log \mathbf{P}(D|w)$. Whenever a function $f(w)$ is differentiable, one can try to find its minima by using one of the oldest optimization algorithms, gradient descent. As its name indicates, gradient descent is an iterative procedure that can be expressed vectorially as

$$w^{t+1} = w^t - \eta \frac{\partial f}{\partial w^t}, \qquad (4.1)$$

where η is the step size, or learning rate, which can be fixed or adjusted during the learning process.

While the general gradient-descent principle is simple, in complex parameterized models it can give rise to different implementations, depending on how the gradient is actually computed [26]. In graphical models, this often requires the propagation of information "backwards." As we will see in the next chapters, this is the case for gradient-descent learning applied to neural networks (the backpropagation algorithm) and to hidden Markov models (the forward–backward procedure). Obviously the outcome of a gradient-descent procedure depends on the initial estimate. Furthermore, if the function being optimized has a complex landscape, gradient descent in general will terminate in a local minimum rather than a global one. Whenever feasible, therefore, it is wise to run the procedure several times, with different starting points and learning rates.

It is well known that there are situations where plain gradient descent can be slow and inefficient. To overcome such problems, a number of variations on gradient descent are possible, such as conjugate gradient descent, that use second-order information or more complex directions of descent constructed from the current gradient and the history of previous directions. Additional details and references can be found in [434]. In spite of its relative crudeness, gradient descent remains useful, easy to implement, and widely used.

4.3.1 Random-Direction Descent

There are a number of other descent procedures that do not necessarily follow the line of steepest descent. These can be useful when the gradient is difficult to compute, when the physics of the hardware directly supports such approaches, or when escaping from local minima is important. For instance, one could generate a random perturbation of the current estimate and accept it only if it lies below the current level. If it does not, the opposite perturbation is accepted, or alternatively a new perturbation is tried. In *line search*

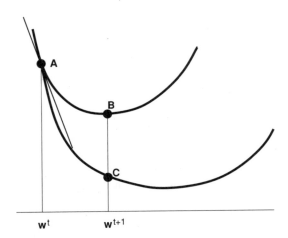

Figure 4.1: Three Consecutive Points of the EM Algorithm. Starting from w^t, in order to minimize the likelihood surface $F(w) = -\log \mathbf{P}(D|w)$, the EM algorithm minimizes a surface $G(w)$, with $G(w^t) = F(w^t) = A$. The surface G dominates the surface F, and the two surfaces have the same gradient at $w = w^t$. w^{t+1} corresponds to point B, the minimum of G. Point C is determined by calculating the new posterior on the hidden variables $\mathbf{P}(H|D, w^{t+1})$.

algorithms, once a direction of descent has been determined, the lowest point along that direction is searched before generating a new direction. Ideas related to line search and random descent are also found in the EM algorithm in the next section, and in evolutionary algorithms toward the end of the chapter.

4.4   EM/GEM Algorithms

Another important class of optimization algorithms is the expectation maximization (EM) and generalized expectation maximization (GEM) algorithms [147, 387]. Such algorithms have been used in many different applications and also in sequence analysis [352, 113]. In the case of HMMs, the EM algorithm is also called the Baum–Welch algorithm [54]. Since the usefulness of these algorithms goes beyond HMMs, we give here a general treatment of EM/GEM algorithms, using the concept of free energy of chapter 3, along the lines suggested in [400].

   The EM algorithm is useful in models and situations with hidden variables. Typical examples of hidden variables are missing or unobservable data, mixture parameters in a mixture model, and hidden node states in graphical models (hidden units in NNs, hidden states in HMMs). If D denotes the data, we assume that there is available a parameterized joint distribution on the hidden and observed variables $P(D, H|w)$, parameterized by w. In the case of main interest to us, w denotes, as usual, the parameters of a model. Let us assume that the objective is to maximize the likelihood $\log P(D|w)$. The same ideas can easily be extended to the case of MAP estimation. Since in general it is difficult to optimize $\log P(D|w)$ directly, the basic idea is to try to optimize the expectation $E(\log P(D|w))$:

$$E(\log P(D|w)) = E(\log P(D, H|w) - \log P(H|D, w)). \qquad (4.2)$$

The EM algorithm is an iterative algorithm that proceeds in two alternating steps, the E (expectation) step and the M (maximization) step. During the E step, the distribution of the hidden variables is computed, given the observed data and the current estimate of w. During the M step, the parameters are updated to their best possible value, given the presumed distribution on the hidden variables. Starting with an estimate w^0 at time 0, the EM algorithm can be written more precisely at time t as follows:

1. E step: Compute the distribution $Q^*(H)$ over H such that $Q^*(H) = P(H|D, w^{t-1})$.

2. M step: Set $w^t = \arg_w \max E_{Q^*}[\log P(D, H|w)]$.

As seen in chapter 3, if we define the energy of a hidden configuration H to be $f(H) = -\log P(D, H|w)$, then the Boltzmann-Gibbs distribution at $\lambda = 1$ is given by the posterior $P(H|D, w)$. In other words, the first step of the EM algorithm is the minimization, with respect to Q, of the free energy

$$\mathcal{F}(f, Q, 1) = \mathcal{F}(w, Q, 1) = \mathcal{F}(w, Q) = E_Q(f) - \mathcal{H}(Q). \qquad (4.3)$$

The second step is a minimization with respect to f, that is, with respect to w. Thus, omitting the constant parameter $\lambda = 1$, the EM algorithm can be rephrased in the following form:

1. E step: Compute the Boltzmann-Gibbs distribution $Q^*(H)$ that minimizes $\mathcal{F}(w^{t-1}, Q)$.

2. M step: Set w^t to minimize $\mathcal{F}(w^{t-1}, Q^*)$.

It is important to note that although Q^* depends on w, Q^* is held *fixed* during the M step. Also from chapter 3, the value of the free energy for the Boltzmann-Gibbs distribution is equal to the negative log-likelihood of the data, $\mathcal{F}(w, Q^*, 1) = -\log P(D|w)$.

In summary, the EM algorithm is an optimization procedure on the free energy $\mathcal{F}$ that proceeds by alternate optimization in the Q and w directions. Hence it produces a sequence of estimates of the form

$$(w^t, Q^t) \to (w^t, Q^{t+1}) \to (w^{t+1}, Q^{t+1}) \to (w^{t+1}, Q^{t+2})\ldots, \qquad (4.4)$$

satisfying, for every t

1. $\mathcal{F}(w^t, Q^t) \geq \mathcal{F}(w^t, Q^{t+1}) \geq \mathcal{F}(w^{t+1}, Q^{t+1}) \geq \mathcal{F}(w^{t+1}, Q^{t+2}) \geq \ldots$

2. $\mathcal{F}(w^t, Q^{t+1}) = -\log \mathbf{P}(D|w^t)$

3. $Q^{t+1} = \mathbf{P}(H|D, w^t)$ and $\mathcal{F}(w^t, Q^t) - \mathcal{F}(w^t, Q^{t+1}) = \mathcal{H}(Q^t, Q^{t+1})$

It is then clear that, except for rare saddle points, the EM algorithm converges to a local minimum of $\mathcal{F}(w, Q)$ which is also a local minimum of $-\log \mathbf{P}(D|M)$, as desired.

It is instructive to look at the EM algorithm from the point of view of w only. Suppose we have an estimate w^t at time t, with the corresponding likelihood $-\log \mathbf{P}(D|w^t)$. Then

$$w^{t+1} = \arg_w \min[-\mathbf{E}_{Q^{t+1}} \log \mathbf{P}(H, D|w)] \qquad (4.5)$$

with $Q^{t+1} = \mathbf{P}(H|D, w^t)$. By writing $\mathbf{P}(H, D|w) = \mathbf{P}(H|D, w)\mathbf{P}(D|w)$ and collecting terms, this is equivalent to

$$w^{t+1} = \arg_w \min[-\log \mathbf{P}(D|w) + \mathcal{H}(Q^{t+1}, \mathbf{P}(H|D, w))]. \qquad (4.6)$$

Thus, starting from w^t, the EM algorithm finds the minimum of the surface $G(w) = -\log \mathbf{P}(D|w) + \mathcal{H}(Q^{t+1}, \mathbf{P}(H|D, w))$ that dominates the surface $F(w) = -\log \mathbf{P}(D|w)$ that one really wants to optimize. Thus the optimization procedure tends to maximize the likelihood, without going too far from the current value of $\mathbf{P}(H|D, w^t)$, to keep the cross-entropy term small. Taking derivatives vectorially yields

$$\frac{\partial G}{\partial w} = -\frac{\partial \log \mathbf{P}(D|w)}{\partial w} - \sum_H Q^{t+1}(H) \frac{\partial \mathbf{P}(H|D, w)/\partial w}{\mathbf{P}(H|D, w)}. \qquad (4.7)$$

The second term in the right-hand side cancels when $w = w^t$. Therefore,

$$\frac{\partial G}{\partial w}\Big|_{w=w^t} = -\frac{\partial \log \mathbf{P}(D|w)}{w}\Big|_{w=w^t}. \qquad (4.8)$$

The tangent to the new surface G is identical to the tangent to the original surface $F(w) = -\log \mathbf{P}(D|w)$. Thus gradient descents on the negative log-likelihood and the EM algorithm are descending in the same directions (figure

4.1). The EM algorithm is further simplified when the distribution $\mathbf{P}(D, H | w)$ belongs to the exponential family. In particular, in this case, the function G is always convex. The particularization of the EM algorithm to exponential distributions is left as an exercise.

Finally, any algorithm that descends the function G (without necessarily finding its minimum), and hence improves the likelihood, is called a GEM (generalized EM) algorithm [147]. The geometric picture above shows that gradient descent on the likelihood can be viewed as a GEM algorithm (see also [400] for a discussion of how the E and M steps can be executed partially, for instance, online).

4.5 Markov-Chain Monte-Carlo Methods

Markov-chain Monte-Carlo (MCMC) methods belong to an important class of stochastic methods that are related to statistical physics and are increasingly used in Bayesian inference and machine learning [578, 202, 396, 520, 69]. Recall that one of the basic goals derived from the general Bayesian framework is to compute expectations with respect to a high-dimensional probability distribution $P(x_1, \ldots, x_n)$, where the x_i can be the values of model parameters or hidden variables, as well as observed data. The two basic ideas behind MCMC are very simple. The first idea (Monte Carlo) is to approximate such expectations by

$$\mathbf{E}(f) = \sum_{x_1, \ldots, x_n} f(x_1, \ldots, x_n) P(x_1, \ldots, x_n) \approx \frac{1}{T} \sum_{t=0}^{T} f(x_1^t, \ldots, x_n^t) \qquad (4.9)$$

for large T, provided $(x_1^t, \ldots, x_n^t)$ are sampled according to their distribution $P(x_1, \ldots, x_n)$. In order to sample from P, the second basic idea is to construct a Markov chain having P as its equilibrium distribution, then simulate the chain and try to sample from its equilibrium distribution.

Before we proceed with the rudiments of Markov chains, it is worth noting a few points. The mean of the estimator on the right-hand side of (4.9) is $\mathbf{E}(f)$. If the samples are independent, its variance is $\mathbf{Var}(f)/T$. In this case, the precision of the estimate does not depend on the dimension of the space being sampled. Importance sampling and rejection sampling are two well-known Monte-Carlo algorithms for generating independent samples that will not be reviewed here. Both algorithms tend to be inefficient in high-dimensional state spaces. The samples created using Markov-chain methods are not independent. But at equilibrium they are still representative of P. The dependence of one sample on the previous one is the key to the better efficiency of MCMC methods with higher-dimensional spaces. After all, if P is differentiable or even just continuous, the probability $P(x_1, \ldots, x_n)$ of a sample provides information about its neighborhood. This remains true even in cases where P can be computed efficiently only up to a constant normalizing factor. Finally, MCMC methods, like any other method based on a single estimator, are at best an approximation to the ideal Bayesian inference process that would rely on the calculation of $\mathbf{P}(\mathbf{E}(f)|D)$ given any sample D.

4.5.1 Markov Chains

The theory of Markov chains is well established [176]. Here we review only the most basic concepts and refer the reader to the textbook literature for more information. As in statistical mechanics, consider a system $S = \{s_1, s_2, \ldots, s_{|S|}\}$ with $|S|$ states. Let $S^0, S^1, \ldots, S^t, \ldots$ be the sequence of variables representing the state of the system at each time. Thus each integer from 1 to $|S|$ is associated with one state of the chain, and at any time the chain is in one particular state. The variables S^t form a *Markov chain* if and only if for any t

$$\mathbf{P}(S^{t+1}|S^0, .., S^t) = \mathbf{P}(S^{t+1}|S^t). \tag{4.10}$$

Intuitively, this can be rephrased by saying that the future depends on the past only through the present. S^t is called the state of the chain at time t. A Markov chain is entirely defined by the initial distribution $P(S^0)$ and the *transition probabilities* $P^t = P(S^{t+1}|S^t)$. Here we will be concerned only with *stationary* Markov chains, where the transition probabilities are constant, that is, independent of time. The transition matrix of the chain is then the matrix $T = (t_{ij})$, where t_{ij} is the probability of moving from state s_j to state s_i. Note that, in relation to (4.9), the state space of the chain is defined by the coordinates $x_1, \ldots, x_n$; that is, each S^t is an n-dimensional variable.

A distribution over the state space of the chain is said to be *stable* if, once reached, it persists forever. Thus a stable distribution Q must satisfy the balance equation

$$Q(s_i) = \sum_{k=1}^{|S|} t_{ik}Q(s_k) = (1 - \sum_{j\neq i} t_{ji})Q(s_i) + \sum_{j\neq i} t_{ij}Q(s_j) \tag{4.11}$$

or equivalently

$$-\sum_{j\neq i} t_{ji}Q(s_i) + \sum_{j\neq i} t_{ij}Q(s_j) = 0. \tag{4.12}$$

Thus, a *sufficient* condition for stability is the *pairwise* balance equation

$$t_{ji}Q(s_i) = t_{ij}Q(s_j) \tag{4.13}$$

for every i and j. This expresses the fact that the average number of transitions from s_i to s_j is equal to the average number of transitions from s_j to s_i, and therefore the overall distribution over states is preserved.

A Markov chain can in general have several stable distributions. Markov chains with finite state space always have at least one stable distribution. Obviously, in MCMC sampling procedures, we will be interested in stable distributions, in fact in the even stronger conditions of *ergodic* distributions. Here, a distribution is defined to be ergodic if and only if the chain always converges to it, regardless of the choice of the initial distribution at time 0. In the case of an ergodic Markov chain, there is only one stable distribution, called the *equilibrium* distribution. Conditions for the ergodicity of a Markov chain, and bounds on the rate of convergence to the equilibrium distribution, are well known [150, 180].

In order to achieve our goal of sampling from $P(x_1, \ldots, x_n)$, we now turn to the two main MCMC algorithms: Gibbs sampling and the Metropolis algorithm.

4.5.2 Gibbs Sampling

Gibbs sampling, also known as the heatbath method, is the simplest MCMC algorithm [199]. It can be applied to a wide range of situations, especially when the conditional distributions $P(x_i | x_j : j \neq i)$ can be computed easily, or when the variables X_i take on values from a small set. In Gibbs sampling, one iteratively samples each single variable, conditioned on the most recent value of all the other variables. Starting from $(x_1^t, \ldots, x_n^t)$,

1. Select x_1^{t+1} according to $P(X_1 | x_2^t, x_3^t, \ldots, x_n^t)$.

2. Select x_2^{t+1} according to $P(X_2 | x_1^{t+1}, x_2^t, \ldots, x_n^t)$.

3. ....

n. Select x_n^{t+1} according to $P(X_n | x_1^{t+1}, x_2^{t+1}, \ldots, x_{n-1}^{t+1})$.

In this version, we cycle through the variables sequentially. It is also possible to cycle through the variables in any order, or to uniformly select the variables at each step. One can even use any other fixed distribution, as long as each variable has a nonzero probability of being visited. It is also possible to sample variables by groups rather than one by one. By applying the definition, it is trivial to check that the Gibbs sampling algorithm leads to a stable distribution. Proofs of ergodicity and further information can be found in the general references on MCMC methods given above and in [209, 191, 490]. An example of specific Gibbs sampling equations for Bayesian networks is given in appendix C. We now turn to another MCMC method, the Metropolis algorithm, of which Gibbs sampling is a special case.

4.5.3 Metropolis Algorithm

Again let us suppose that the goal is to sample from a given distribution $P(s) = P(x_1, \ldots, x_n)$. The Metropolis algorithm [388] randomly generates perturbations of the current state, and accepts or rejects them depending on how the probability of the state is affected.

More precisely, the Metropolis algorithm is defined using two auxiliary families of distributions Q and R. $Q = (q_{ij})$ is the selection distribution; q_{ij} is the probability of selecting state s_i while being in state s_j. $R = (r_{ij})$ is the acceptance distribution; r_{ij} is the probability of accepting state s_i while being in state s_j and having selected s_i as a possible next state. Obviously, we must have $q_{ij} \geq 0$ and $r_{ij} \geq 0$, and $\sum_i q_{ij} = 1$. For the time being, and in most practical cases, one can assume that Q is symmetric, $q_{ij} = q_{ji}$, but this hypothesis can also be relaxed. Starting from a state s_j at time t ($S^t = s_j$), the algorithm proceeds as follows:

1. Randomly select a state s_i according to the distribution q_{ij}.

2. Accept s_i with probability r_{ij}. That is, $S^{t+1} = s_i$ with probability r_{ij} and $S^{t+1} = s_j$ with probability $1 - r_{ij}$.

In the most common version of the Metropolis algorithm, the acceptance distribution is defined by

$$r_{ij} = \min\left(1, \frac{P(s_i)}{P(s_j)}\right). \tag{4.14}$$

We leave it as an exercise to show that Gibbs sampling can be rewritten as a Metropolis algorithm. When P is expressed in terms of an energy function $P(s) = e^{-\mathcal{E}(s)/kT}/Z$, this can be rewritten as

$$r_{ij} = \min(1, e^{-[\mathcal{E}(s_i) - \mathcal{E}(s_j)]/kT}) = \min(1, e^{-\Delta_{ij}\mathcal{E}/kT}). \tag{4.15}$$

Note that only the ratio of the probabilities is needed, not the partition function. As a result, the algorithm can be expressed in its most familiar form:

1. Randomly select a state s_i according to the distribution q_{ij}.

2. If $\mathcal{E}(s_i) \leq \mathcal{E}(s_j)$ accept s_i. If $\mathcal{E}(s_i) > \mathcal{E}(s_j)$, accept s_i only with probability $e^{-\Delta_{ij}\mathcal{E}/kT}$. If s_i is rejected, stay in s_j.

It is easy to see that the distribution P is stable under the Metropolis algorithm. We have $t_{ij} = q_{ij}P(s_i)/P(s_j)$ and $t_{ji} = q_{ji}$. Since Q is symmetric, this immediately gives

$$P(s_j)t_{ij} = P(s_i)t_{ji}. \tag{4.16}$$

In other words, since the pairwise balance equations are satisfied, P is stable.

To ensure ergodicity, it is necessary and sufficient to ensure that there are no absorbing states in the chain, or equivalently that there is always a path of transitions with *nonzero probability* from any s_i to any s_j. This of course depends on the structure of q_{ij}. Several general remarks can be made. We can construct a graph G by connecting two points i and j with an edge if and only if $q_{ij} > 0$. If the resulting graph is complete (or even just very dense), the chain is clearly ergodic. This type of Metropolis algorithm can be termed "global" because there is a nonzero probability of moving from any state i to any state j in one step, or at most very few steps, if the graph is dense but not complete. When the graph is more sparse, one obtains more "local" versions of the Metropolis algorithm. Ergodicity is still preserved, provided any two points are connected by at least one path. An example of this situation is when the algorithm is applied componentwise, perturbing one component at a time. In most practical applications, the selection probability q_{ji} is chosen uniformly over the neighbors j of vertex i. Usually, q_{ii} is also chosen to be 0, although this does not really impact any of the results just described.

Finally, there are several variations and generalizations of the Metropolis algorithm using, for instance, the derivatives of the energy function, other acceptance functions [242, 396], and cluster Monte Carlo algorithms [510, 547]. In particular, it is even possible to remove the condition that Q be symmetric, as long as the balance is preserved by modifying the acceptance function R accordingly:

$$r_{ij} = \min\left(1, \frac{P(s_i)q_{ij}}{P(s_j)q_{ji}}\right). \tag{4.17}$$

4.6 Simulated Annealing

Simulated annealing [321] (see also [67] for a review) is a general-purpose optimization algorithm inspired by statistical mechanics. It combines MCMC ideas such as the Metropolis algorithm with a schedule for lowering the temperature. The name has its origin in metallurgy, where metals that have been annealed (cooled slowly) exhibit strength properties superior to metals that have been quenched (cooled rapidly). The greater macroscopic strength is associated with internal molecular states of lower energy.

Consider the problem of minimizing a function $f(x_1, \ldots, x_n)$. Without any loss of generality, we can assume that $f \geq 0$ everywhere. As usual, we can regard f as representing the energy of a statistical mechanical system with states $s = (x_1, \ldots, x_n)$. We have seen that the probability of being in state s at temperature T is given by the Boltzmann–Gibbs distribution $P(s) = P(x_1, \ldots, x_n) = e^{-f(s)/kT}/Z$. The first key observation in order to understand simulated annealing is that at low temperatures, the Boltzmann–

Gibbs distribution is dominated by the states of lowest energy, which become the most probable. In fact, if there are m states where the minimum of the function f is achieved, we have

$$\lim_{T \to 0} P(s) = \begin{cases} 1/m & \text{if } s \text{ is a ground state} \\ 0 & \text{otherwise.} \end{cases} \tag{4.18}$$

If we could simulate the system at temperatures near 0, we would immediately have the ground states, that is, the minima of f. The catch is that any MCMC method fails in general to reach the Boltzmann–Gibbs equilibrium distribution in a reasonable time, because movement in state space is inhibited by regions of very low probability, that is, by high energy barriers. Simulated annealing attempts to overcome this problem by starting with a high temperature, where the Boltzmann–Gibbs distribution is close to uniform, and progressively lowering it according to some annealing schedule. While simulated annealing is usually used in combination with the Metropolis algorithm, it is in fact applicable to any MCMC method, and in particular to Gibbs sampling.

The annealing schedule of course plays a crucial role. There are a number of theoretical results [199] showing that for a logarithmic annealing schedule of the form

$$T^t = \frac{K}{\log t} \tag{4.19}$$

($t \geq 1$), the algorithm converges almost surely to one of the ground states, for some value of the constant K (see [230] for a lower bound on K). (From the context, no confusion should arise between T the temperature and T the time horizon.) Intuitively, this is easy to see [396]. If we let $s_{\max}$ and $s_{\min}$ denote two states with maximal and minimal energy, then from the Boltzmann–Gibbs distribution we have,

$$\frac{P^t(s_{\max})}{P^t(s_{\min})} = \left(\frac{1}{t}\right)^{\Delta \mathcal{E}/kK}, \tag{4.20}$$

where $\Delta \mathcal{E} = \mathcal{E}(s_{\max}) - \mathcal{E}(s_{\min})$. If we take $K = \Delta \mathcal{E}/k$, we then have $P^t(s_{\max}) = P^t(s_{\min})/t$. Therefore, for any state s,

$$P^t(s) \geq P^t(s_{\max}) = \frac{1}{t} P^t(s_{\min}) \geq \frac{1}{t} P^1(s_{\min}). \tag{4.21}$$

In particular, the number of times any state s is visited during the annealing is lower-bounded by $P^1(s_{\min}) \sum_t 1/t$, which is divergent. Thus, with K scaled with respect to the highest energy barrier, it is impossible for the algorithm to remain trapped in a bad local minimum.

It must be noted, however, that a logarithmic annealing schedule is very slow and generally impractical. A logarithmic schedule suggests that a significant fraction of all possible states is visited, and therefore is essentially equivalent to an exhaustive search. Thus it is not surprising that it is guaranteed to find the global optimum. On the other hand, if an exhaustive search had been an alternative, it would have been used in the first place. Most problems of interest are typically NP complete, with an exponential number of possible states ruling out any possibility of conducting exhaustive searches. In practice, simulated annealing must be used with faster schedules, such as geometric annealing schedules of the form

$$T^t = \mu T^{t-1} \tag{4.22}$$

for some $0 < \mu < 1$. Naturally, the best one can then hope for is to converge in general to approximate solutions corresponding to points of low energy, but not to the global minima.

Other interesting algorithms related to simulated annealing [547, 381] and MCMC basic ideas, such as dynamical and hybrid Monte Carlo methods [152, 396], are discussed in the references.

4.7 Evolutionary and Genetic Algorithms

In the present context, evolutionary algorithms [261, 476] perhaps have a special flavor since their source of inspiration, evolution, is at the heart of our domain. Evolutionary algorithms are a broad class of optimization algorithms that attempt to simulate in some way the inner workings of evolution, as we (think we) understand it. One component common to all these algorithms is the generation of random perturbations, or mutations, and the presence of a fitness function that is used to assess the quality of a given point and filter out mutations that are not useful. In this sense, random descent methods and even simulated annealing can be viewed as special cases of evolutionary algorithms. One of the broadest subclasses of evolutionary algorithms is the genetic algorithms.

Genetic algorithms [328, 330] and the related field of artificial life push the evolutionary analogy one step further by simulating the evolution of populations of points in fitness space. Furthermore, in addition to mutations, new points are generated by a number of other operations mimicking genetic operators and sexual reproduction, such as crossover. While genetic algorithms are particularly flexible and make possible the evolution of complex objects, such as computer programs, they remain quite slow even on current computers, although this is of course subject to yearly improvements. Applications of genetic algorithms to problems in molecular biology can be found in [329, 233, 415]. Other evolutionary algorithms are described in [53] and references therein. Evolutionary algorithms will not be considered any further in this book.

4.8 Learning Algorithms: Miscellaneous Aspects

In connection with learning algorithms, there is a wide range of implementation details, heuristics, and tricks that have significant practical importance. Abundant material on such tricks can be found, for instance, in the annual proceedings of NIPS (Neural Information Processing Conference). Here we cover only a small subset of them from a general standpoint. A few model-specific tricks are presented in the relevant chapters.

4.8.1 Control of Model Complexity

In one form or another, modelers are constantly confronted with the problem of striking a balance between underfitting and overfitting the data, between models that have too few and too many degrees of freedom. One approach to this problem is to regularize the objective likelihood function with a term that takes model complexity into account. The most principled versions of this approach are based on equalities or bounds relating the training error $\mathcal{E}_T$ to the generalization error $\mathcal{E}_G$. These bounds typically state that with high probability $\mathcal{E}_G \leq \mathcal{E}_T + C$, where C is a term reflecting the complexity of the model. Examples of such a formula can be found in [533], using the concept of VC dimension, and in [5, 16], using statistical asymptotic theory. The generalization error is then minimized by minimizing the regularized training error $\mathcal{E}_T + C$. The term $\mathcal{E}_T$ measures the data fit and the term C can often be viewed as a prior favoring simpler models. Such practices can yield good results and have heuristic value. But, as pointed out in chapter 2, from a Bayesian point of view they also have some weaknesses. With complex data, a prior expecting the data to be generated by a simple model does not make much sense. In general, we would recommend instead using powerful flexible models, with many degrees of freedom and strong priors on their parameters and structure, rather than their overall complexity, to control overfitting.

4.8.2 Online/Batch Learning

Training is said to be *online* when some degree of model fitting or parameter adjustment occurs as the data come in, or after the presentation of each example. In *batch* or *offline* learning, on the other hand, parameter values are adjusted only after the presentation of a large number of examples, if not the entire training set. Obviously there is a spectrum of possibilities in between. Online learning can have some advantages in that it does not require holding many training examples in memory, and it is more flexible and easier to implement. It is also closer to the Bayesian spirit of updating one's belief as data become available, and to the way biological systems seem to learn. More important, perhaps, learning after the presentation of each example may introduce a degree of stochasticity that may be useful to explore the space of solutions and avoid certain local minima. It can also be shown, of course, that with sufficiently small learning rates, online learning approximates batch learning (see also [49]). Accordingly, in this book we usually provide online learning equations.

4.8.3 Training/Test/Validation

One of the most widely used practices consists in using only a subset of the data for model fitting and the remaining data, or portions of it, for the validation of the model. It is important to note that such a practice is not entirely Bayesian, since in the general framework of chapter 2 all the data are used for model fitting, without any reference or need for validation. In practice, cross-validation techniques remain very useful because they are generally easy to implement and yield good results, especially when data are abundant. A second remark, of course, is that there are many ways of splitting the data into different subsets and allocating such subsets to training or validation experiments. For instance, different data sets can be used to train different experts that are subsequently combined, or validation sets can be used to determine the values of hyperparameters. Such matters become even more important when data are relatively scarce. Whenever feasible, it is good to have at least three distinct data sets: one for training, one for validation and training adjustments, and one for testing overall performance.

Special additional care is often required in bioinformatics because sequences have a high probability of being related through a common ancestor. In chapter 1 the problem of constructing low-similarity test sets, which may be essential to assess reliably the predictive performance of a method obtained by machine learning, was addressed in detail.

4.8.4 Early Stopping

When a model is too flexible with respect to the available data—because it contains too many parameters—overfitting is observed during training. This means that while the error on the training set decreases monotonically as a function of training epochs, the error on a validation set also decreases at first, then reaches a minimum and begins to increase again. Overfitting is then associated with the model's memorizing the training data or fitting noise in the data to a point that is deleterious for generalization. The correct approach in such a situation of course would be to modify the model. Another widely used but less sound alternative is early stopping, whereby training is stopped as soon as the error rate on the training set reaches a certain threshold, or after a fixed number of training cycles. The threshold itself, or the number of cycles, is not easy to determine. One possibility is to stop training as soon as the error rate begins to increase on a validation set different from the training set. The drawback of such an approach is that data must be sacrificed from the training set for validation. Furthermore, this type of early stopping can still lead to a partial overfitting of the validation data with respect to the test data. In other words, the performance of the model on the validation set used to decide when to stop is typically somewhat better than the overall generalization performance on new data. Early stopping, like other validation methods, is, however, easy to implement and useful in practice, especially with abundant data.

4.8.5 Ensembles

When a complex model is fitted to the data by ML or MAP optimization, different model parameters are derived by varying a number of factors during the learning procedure, such as the initial parameter values, the learning rate, the order of presentation of the examples, the training set, and so on. Furthermore, different classes of models may be tried. It is natural to suspect that better prediction or classification may be achieved by averaging the opinion of different models or experts in some way (appendix A and [223, 237, 277, 568, 426, 340, 339]). A pool of models for a given task is also called an ensemble, in analogy to statistical mechanics (see also the notion of the committee machine in the literature). Mathematically, this intuition is based on the fact that for convex error functions, the error of the ensemble is less than the average error of its members (Jensen's inequality in appendix B). Thus the ensemble performs better than a typical single expert. There are different ways of combining the predictions produced by several models. Uniform averages are widely used, but other schemes are possible, with variable weights, including the possibility of learning the weights during training. Note that in the case of a well-defined class of models within the Bayesian framework of chapter 2, the optimal prediction is obtained by integrating over all possible models (see (2.18)). Thus averaging models can be construed as an approximation to such an integral.

4.8.6 Balancing and Weighting Schemes

An important issue to consider is whether or not training sets are balanced. In binomial classification problems, the number of available positive examples can differ significantly from the number of negative examples. Likewise, in multinomial classification problems, significant variations can exist in the proportions in which each class is represented in the data. This situation can be particularly severe with biological databases where, for instance, certain organisms or certain types of sequences are overrepresented due to a large number of different factors, as described in chapter 1.

Ideally, for the purpose of correct classification, all relevant classes should be equally represented in the training set. In chapter 6 such balanced training strategies will be described. In some cases, underrepresentation of a certain class in the training data has led to a low test prediction performance on that particular class. Such behavior has often been interpreted as evidence for missing information, for example that beta-sheet prediction requires more long-range sequence information than does helix prediction. While any protein structure prediction method will gain from the proper addition of long-range information, beta-sheet performance has been substantially improved just by applying a balanced training scheme [452].

Another possibility is to use weighting schemes to artificially balance training sets, equivalent to effectively duplicating rare exemplars several times over. A number of weighting schemes have been developed for DNA and protein sequences, especially in the context of multiple alignments [10, 536, 487, 201, 249, 337]. The weighting scheme in [337] is particularly interesting, and optimal in a maximum entropy sense.

There is a number of other techniques that we do not cover for lack of space. Again these can easily be found in the literature (NIPS Proceedings) and other standard references on neural network techniques. They include:

- Active sampling.

- Pruning methods. These are methods that perform simplification of models during or after learning. Typically, they consist of finding ways to determine which parameters in a model have little impact on its performance, and then removing them. Redundant parameters will often be equivalent not just to those with small numerical values, but also large weights that inhibit each other may contribute little to the quality of a model.

- Second-order methods. These methods take advantage of second-order information by computing or approximating the Hessian of the likelihood—for instance, to adjust learning rates or compute error bars. The efficient approximation of the Hessian is an interesting problem that must be considered in the context of each model.

Chapter 5

Neural Networks: The Theory

5.1 Introduction

Artificial neural networks (NNs) [456, 252, 70] were originally developed with the goal of modeling information processing and learning in the brain. While the brain metaphor remains a useful source of inspiration, it is clear today that the artificial neurons used in most NNs are quite remote from biological neurons [85]. The development of NNs, however, has led to a number of practical applications in various fields, including computational molecular biology. NNs have become an important tool in the arsenal of machine-learning techniques that can be applied to sequence analysis and pattern recognition problems.

At the most basic level, NNs can be viewed as a broad class of parameterized graphical models consisting of networks with interconnected units evolving in time. In this book we use only pairwise connections but, if desirable, one can use more elaborate connections associated with the interaction of more than two units, leading to the "higher-order" or "sigma-pi" networks [456]. The connection from unit j to unit i usually comes with a weight denoted by w_{ij}. Thus we can represent an NN with a weight-directed graph or "architecture." For simplicity, we do not use any self-interactions, so that we can assume that $w_{ii} = 0$ for all the units.

It is customary to distinguish a number of important architectures, such as recurrent, feed-forward, and layered. A *recurrent* architecture is an architecture that contains directed loops. An architecture devoid of directed loops is said to be *feed-forward*. Recurrent architectures are more complex with richer dynamics and will be considered in chapter 9. An architecture is *layered* if the units are partitioned into classes, also called layers, and the connectivity patterns are defined between the classes. A feed-forward architecture is not necessarily layered.

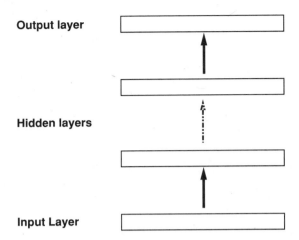

Figure 5.1: Layered Feed-Forward Architecture or Multilayer Perceptron (MLP). Layers may contain different numbers of units. Connectivity patterns between layers also may vary.

In most of this chapter and in many current applications of NNs to molecular biology, the architectures used are layered feed-forward architectures, as in figure 5.1. The units are often partitioned into *visible* units and *hidden* units. The *visible* units are those in contact with the external world, such as input and output units. Most of the time, in simple architectures the input units and the output units are grouped in layers, forming the input layer and the output layer. A layer containing only hidden units is called a hidden layer. The number of layers is often referred to as the "depth" of a network. Naturally NNs can be assembled in modular and hierarchical fashion to create complex overall architectures. The design of the visible part of an NN depends on the input representation chosen to encode the sequence data and the output that may typically represent structural or functional features.

The behavior of each unit in time can be described using either differential equations or discrete update equations (see [26] for a summary). Only the discrete formalism will be used in this book. In a layered feed-forward architecture, all the units in a layer are updated simultaneously, and layers are updated sequentially in the obvious order. Sometimes it is also advantageous to use stochastic units (see appendix C on graphical models and Bayesian networks). In the rest of this chapter, however, we focus on deterministic units. Typically a unit i receives a total input x_i from the units connected to it, and then produces an output $y_i = f_i(x_i)$, where f_i is the transfer function of the unit. In general, all the units in the same layer have the same transfer function, and the total input is a weighted sum of incoming outputs from the previous layer, so that

$$x_i = \sum_{j \in N^-(i)} w_{ij} y_j + w_i, \tag{5.1}$$

$$y_i = f_i(x_i) = f_i \left(\sum_{j \in N^-(i)} w_{ij} y_j + w_i \right), \tag{5.2}$$

where w_i is called the bias, or threshold, of the unit. It can also be viewed as a connection with weight w_i to an additional unit, with constant activity clamped to 1. The weights w_{ij} and w_i are the parameters of the NNs. In more general NNs other parameters are possible, such as time constants, gains, and delays. In the architectures to be considered here, the total number of parameters is determined by the number of layers, the number of units per layer, and the connectivity between layers. A standard form for the connectivity between layers is the "fully connected" one, where each unit in one layer is connected to every unit in the following layer. More local connectivity patterns are obviously more economical. Note, however, that even full connectivity between layers is sparse, compared with complete connectivity among all units. In situations characterized by some kind of translation invariance, it can be useful for each unit in a given layer to perform the same operation on the activity of translated groups of units in the preceding layer. Thus a single pattern of connections can be shared across units in a given layer. In NN jargon this is called "weight sharing." It is routinely used in image-processing problems and has also been used with some success in sequence analysis situations where distinct features are separated by variable distances. The shared pattern of weights defines a filter or a convolution kernel that is used to uniformly process the incoming activity. With weight sharing, the number of free parameters associated with two layers can be small, even if the layers are very large. An example of this technique is given below in section 6.3 on secondary structure prediction.

There are a number of transfer functions that are widely used. Sometimes the transfer function is linear—like the identity function, as in regression problems, in which case the unit is called a linear unit. Most of the time, however, the transfer functions are nonlinear. Bounded activation functions are often called squashing functions. When f is a threshold function,

$$f(x) = \begin{cases} 1 & \text{if } x > 0 \\ 0 & \text{otherwise,} \end{cases} \tag{5.3}$$

the unit is also called a threshold gate. A threshold gate simulates a binary decision based on the weighted "opinion" of the relevant units. Obviously, the bias can be used to offset the location of the threshold. In this book we use a $(0, +1)$ formalism that is equivalent to any other scale or range, such as $(-1, +1)$. Threshold gates are discontinuous. Thus they are often replaced with sigmoidal transfer functions, which have the advantage of being continuous and differentiable. In this book, we use the *logistic* transfer function

$$f(x) = \sigma(x) = \frac{1}{1 + e^{-x}} \tag{5.4}$$

especially to estimate the probability of binary events. But other possible sigmoidal transfer functions lead to essentially equivalent results, such as $f(x) = \tanh(x)$ and $f(x) = \arctan(x)$. It is also possible to introduce a gain λ_i for each unit by writing $y_i = f_i(\lambda_i x_i)$. Another important type of unit in what follows is the *normalized exponential unit*, also called softmax, which is used to compute the probability of an event with n possible outcomes, such as classification into one of n possible classes. Let the index j run over a group of n output units, computing the n membership probabilities, and x_j denote the total input provided by the rest of the NN into each output unit. Then the final activity y_i of each output unit is given by

$$y_i = \frac{e^{-x_i}}{\sum_{k=1}^{n} e^{-x_k}}. \tag{5.5}$$

Obviously, in this case $\sum_{i=1}^{n} y_i = 1$. When $n = 2$, the normalized exponential is equivalent to a logistic function via a simple transformation

$$y_1 = \frac{e^{-x_1}}{e^{-x_1} + e^{-x_2}} = \frac{1}{1 + e^{-(x_2 - x_1)}}. \tag{5.6}$$

It is important to note that any probability distribution $P = (p_i)$ $(1 \leq i \leq n)$ can be represented in normalized exponential form from a set of variables x_j $(1 \leq j \leq m)$,

$$P_i = \frac{e^{-x_i}}{\sum_{k=1}^{m} e^{-x_k}}, \tag{5.7}$$

as long as $m \geq n$. This can be done in infinitely many ways, by fixing a positive constant K and letting $x_i = \log p_i + K$ for $i = 1, \ldots, n$ (and $x_j = -\infty$ for $j > n$ if needed). If $m < n$ there is no exact solution, unless the p_i assume only m distinct values at most.

Another type of widely used functions is the *radial basis functions* (RBFs), where typically f is a bell-shaped function like a Gaussian. Each RBF unit i has a "reference" input x_i^*, and f operates on the distance $d(x_i^*, x_i)$ measured with respect to some metric $y_i = f(d(x_i^*, x_i))$. In spatial problems, d is usually the Euclidean distance.

Clearly a modeler should be able to choose the type of units, connectivity, and transfer functions as needed in relation to the task to be solved. As a result, the reader may be under the impression that the concept of NN is somewhat fuzzy, and rightly so! According to our loose definition, one can take the position that polynomials are NNs. Alternatively, one could of course put further restrictions on the definition of NNs. Historically, the term NN has been used mostly to refer to networks where the inputs satisfy (5.1) and the transfer functions are threshold functions or sigmoids. We do not think that much is to be gained by adopting such a dogmatic position. The current nomenclature of model classes is in part the product of historical accidents. The reality is that there is a continuous spectrum of possible parameterized models without precise boundaries. A modeler should be as free as possible in designing a model and proceeding with Bayesian inference.

In NN applications, it has been customary to distinguish between *regression* and *classification* or recognition problems. In regression problems, the goal is to approximate or fit a given surface. In classification or recognition problems, the goal is to be able to classify a given input into a relatively small number of classes. While useful, this distinction is also somewhat arbitrary since in the limit, classification—for example, into two classes—can be viewed as fitting a usually discontinuous binary function. The problem of learning the genetic code (see chapter 6) is a good example of a problem at the boundary of the two classes of problems. Classification problems have perhaps been slightly more frequent in past applications of NNs to molecular biology, due to the discrete nature of the sequence data and the standard problem of recognizing particular patterns such as alpha helices, fold classes, splice sites, or exons. But continuous data, such as hydrophobicity scales or stacking energies, can also be important. We shall examine both regression and classification NNs more closely in the coming sections.

One of the most important aspects of NNs is that they can learn from examples. Obviously, in the general Bayesian statistical framework this is nothing else than model fitting and parameter estimation. Very often the data D consist of input–output sample pairs $D = (D_1, \ldots, D_K)$, with $D_i = (d_i, t_i)$ (d for data, t for target) from the regression or classification function to be approximated. In practice, the data are often split into *training data* and *validation data* in some way. The training data are used for model fitting, and the validation data in model validation. The validation data can also be split into validation and *test data*, where the validation set is used for early stopping and the test data for assessing the overall performance of the model. These model-fitting tasks, where the target values of the outputs in the fitted data are known, are usually described in the literature as *supervised learning*. When the target values are not known, the terms *unsupervised* or *self-organization* are often used. Again, this historical distinction has its usefulness but should not be taken too dogmatically. As for supervised learning algorithms, one of the main practices in the past has been, starting from a random set of parameters, to define an "error function" by comparing the outputs produced by the network against the target outputs. Then the network parameters are optimized by gradient descent with respect to the error function. As pointed out in chapter 2, such practice is best analyzed in the general Bayesian statistical framework by explicitly stating the underlying probabilistic models and assumptions, and proceeding with the proper Bayesian inductions. Many forms of supervised and unsupervised learning for NNs in the literature can be viewed as ML or MAP estimation.

In the rest of the chapter we shall focus on layered feed-forward NN architectures, the multilayer perceptrons with inputs given by (5.1) and linear/threshold/sigmoidal/normalized exponential transfer functions, and their application within sequence analysis. In the next section, we briefly cover the universal approximation properties of NNs. In particular, we prove that any reasonable function can be approximated to any precision by a shallow, and possibly very large, NN. In section 5.3, we apply the general framework of chapter 2 to NNs. We examine priors and likelihood functions, how to design NN architectures, and how to carry out the first level of Bayesian inference. In section 5.4, we apply the general framework of chapter 4 to learning algorithms and derive the well-known backpropagation algorithm. Many other theoretical results on NNs, beyond the scope of this book, can be found in the references. Computational complexity issues for NNs and machine learning in general are reviewed in [314]. A more complete Bayesian treatment of NNs, including higher levels of Bayesian inference, is given in [373, 398, 517]. In addition to NNs, there are a number of other flexible parameterized models for regression and classification, such as splines [546], Gaussian processes [559, 206, 399] (appendix A), and support vector machines [533, 475].

5.2 Universal Approximation Properties

Perhaps one reassuring property of NNs is that they can approximate any reasonable function to any degree of required precision. The result is trivial[1] for Boolean functions, in the sense that any Boolean function can be built using a combination of threshold gates. This is because any Boolean function can be synthesized using NOT and AND gates, and it is easy to see that AND and NOT gates can be synthetized using threshold gates. For the general regression case, it can be shown that any reasonable real function $f(x)$ can be approximated to any degree of precision by a three-layer network with x in the input layer, a hidden layer of sigmoidal units, and one layer of linear output units,

---

[1]This section concentrates primarily on threshold/sigmoidal units. Obviously the result is also well known if polynomials are included among NNs.

as long as the hidden layer can be arbitrarily large. There are a number of different mathematical variations and proofs of this result (see, e.g., [264, 265]).

Here we give a simple constructive proof of a special case, which can easily be generalized, to illustrate some of the basic ideas. For simplicity, consider a continuous function $y = f(x)$ where both x and y are one-dimensional. Assume without loss of generality that x varies in the interval $[0, 1]$, and that we want to compute the value of $f(x)$ for any x within a precision ϵ. Since f is continuous over the compact interval $[0, 1]$, f is uniformly continuous and there exists an integer n such that

$$|x_2 - x_1| \le \frac{1}{n} \implies |f(x_2) - f(x_1)| \le \epsilon. \tag{5.8}$$

Therefore it is sufficient to approximate f with a function g such that $g(0) = f(0)$, and $g(x) = f(k/n)$ for any x in the interval $((k-1)/n, k/n]$ and any $k = 1, \ldots, n$. The function g can be realized exactly by a NN with one input unit representing x, $n+1$ hidden threshold gate units all receiving connections from the input unit, and one output unit receiving a connection from each hidden unit. The hidden units are numbered from 0 to n. The output has a linear transfer function in order to cover the range of ys (figure 5.2). All the weights from the input unit to the n hidden units are set to 1, and the kth hidden unit has a threshold (bias) of $(k-1)/n$. Thus, for any x in the interval $((k-1)/n, k/n]$, all the hidden unit activations are set to 0 except for the first $k+1$, which take the value 1. Thus the value of the input is directly coded in the number of hidden units that are turned on. The weight of the connection from the kth hidden unit to the output unit is $\Delta_k f = f(k/n) - f(k-1/n)$, with $\Delta_0 f = f(0)$. The output unit is just the identity function, with 0 bias. Thus if $x = 0$, $g(x) = 0$. For any $k = 1, 2, \ldots, n$, if x is in the interval $[(k-1)/n, k/n]$, then $g(x) = f(0) + \sum_{j=1}^{k} f(j/n) - f(j-1/n) = f(k/n)$, as desired.

It should be clear that it is not too difficult to generalize the previous result in several directions, to encompass the following:

1. Multidimensional inputs and outputs

2. Sigmoidal transfer functions and other types

3. Inputs on any compact set

4. Functions f that may have a finite number of discontinuities and more

While it is useful to know that any function can be approximated by an NN, the key point is that the previous proof does not yield very economical architectures. In fact, one can show that for essentially random functions, compact architectures do not exist. It is only for "structured" functions that compact

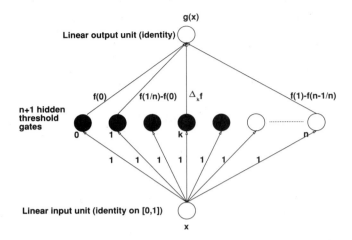

Figure 5.2: Universal Approximation Architecture with One Input Unit, $n + 1$ Hidden Threshold Gate Units, and One Linear Output Unit Computing the Approximation $g(x)$ to $f(x)$.

architectures exist, and in this case the architecture constructed in the universal approximation theorems are far from optimal. Better architectures may exist, with a better allocation of hidden units, and possibly with more than a single hidden layer. It is for these cases that learning approaches become important.

5.3   Priors and Likelihoods

We now apply the general theory of chapter 2. In particular, we show how the theory can be used to determine the choice of an objective function and of the transfer functions of the output units. In this section we shall assume that the data consist of a set of independent input-output pairs $D_i = (d_i, t_i)$. The data are noisy in the sense that for a given d_i, different outputs t_i could be observed. Noise at the level of the input d could also be modeled, but will not be considered here. The operation of the NN itself is considered to be deterministic. We have

$$\mathbf{P}((d_i, t_i)|w) = \mathbf{P}(d_i|w)\mathbf{P}(t_i|d_i, w) = \mathbf{P}(d_i)\mathbf{P}(t_i|d_i, w), \qquad (5.9)$$

the last equality resulting from the fact that in general we can assume that the inputs d are independent of the parameters w. Thus, for a given architecture parameterized by w, we have, using (2.9),

$$-\log \mathbf{P}(w|D) = -\sum_{i=1}^{K} \log \mathbf{P}(t_i|d_i, w) - \sum_{i=1}^{K} \log \mathbf{P}(d_i) - \log \mathbf{P}(w) + \log \mathbf{P}(D), \quad (5.10)$$

where we have used the fact that $\mathbf{P}((d_i, t_i)|w) = \mathbf{P}(d_i)\mathbf{P}(t_i|d_i, w)$, and have taken into account the independence of the different data points. In the first level of Bayesian inference (MAP), we want to minimize the left-hand side. We can ignore $\mathbf{P}(D)$ as well as $\mathbf{P}(d_i)$, since these terms do not depend on w, and concentrate on the prior term and the likelihood.

In order to calculate the likelihood, we shall have to distinguish different cases, such as regression and classification, and further specify the probabilistic model. In doing so, we follow the analysis in [455]. But the basic idea is to consider that, for a given input d_i, the network produces an estimated output $y(d_i)$. The model is entirely defined when we specify how the observed data $t_i = t(d_i)$ can statistically deviate from the network output $y_i = y(d_i)$. If the output layer has many units, we need to write y_{ij} for the output of the jth unit on the ith example. For notational convenience, in what follows we will drop the index that refers to the input. Thus we derive online equations for a generic input–output pair (d, t). Offline equations can easily be derived by summing over inputs, in accordance with (5.10).

5.3.1 Priors

Unless additional information is available, the most natural and widely used priors for NN parameters are zero-mean Gaussian priors. Hyperparameters, such as the standard deviation of the Gaussians, can be chosen differently for connection weights and biases and for units in different layers. If a weight w has a Gaussian prior with standard deviation σ, the corresponding contribution to the negative log-posterior, up to constant factors, is given by $w^2/2\sigma^2$. This can also be viewed as a regularization factor that penalizes large weights often associated with overfitting. In gradient-descent learning, this adds a factor $-w/\sigma^2$ to the update of w. This factor is also called *weight decay*. *Weight sharing* is a different kind of prior obtained when different groups of units in a given layer are assumed to have identical incoming connection weights. Weight sharing is easily enforced during gradient-descent learning. It is useful in problems characterized by some form of translational invariance where the same operation, such as the extraction of characteristic features, needs to be applied to different regions of the input. The pattern of shared units essentially implements a convolution kernel, whence the name *convolutional networks*.

Gaussian and other priors for NN parameters and hyperparameters are studied in detail in [373, 398, 517]. In [373] Laplace approximation techniques are used to determine optimal hyperparameters. In [398] Monte Carlo methods are derived for the integration of priors and Bayesian learning in MLPs. The advantages of Bayesian learning include the automatic determination of regularization parameters without the need for a validation set, the avoidance of overfitting when using large networks, and the quantification of prediction uncertainty. In [398] it is shown that in the limit of a single hidden layer with an infinite number of hidden units, an NN with Gaussian weight priors defines a Gaussian process on the space of input–output functions. Hence the idea of using Gaussian processes directly [559, 399, 206], bypassing any NN implementation. While Gaussian processes provide a very flexible tool for both regression and classification problems, they are computationally demanding and can be applied only to moderate-size problems with currently available technology.

5.3.2   Gaussian Regression

In the case of regression, the range of y can be arbitrary, and therefore the simplest transfer functions in the output layer are linear (actually the identity) functions. It is also natural to assume a Gaussian probabilistic model, that is, $\mathbf{P}(t|d, w) = \mathbf{P}(t|y(d), w) = \mathbf{P}(t|y)$ is Gaussian, with mean vector $y = y(d)$. Assuming further that the covariance matrix is diagonal and that there are n output units indexed by j, we have

$$\mathbf{P}(t|d, w) = \prod_{j=1}^{n} \frac{1}{\sqrt{2\pi}\sigma_j} \exp(-\frac{(t_j - y_j)^2}{2\sigma_j^2}). \tag{5.11}$$

The standard deviations σ_j are additional parameters of this statistical model. If we further assume that they are constant $\sigma_j = \sigma$, then the negative log-likelihood for the current input boils down to

$$\mathcal{E} = \sum_j \left(\frac{(t_j - y_j)^2}{2\sigma^2} - \frac{1}{2}\log 2\pi - \log \sigma \right). \tag{5.12}$$

Again the last two terms are independent of w, and can be ignored while trying to estimate the optimal set of parameters w. The first term of course is the usual least-mean-square (LMS) error, routinely used in many applications, sometimes without explicating the underlying statistical model. The derivative of the negative log-likelihood $\mathcal{E}$ with respect to an output y_j is

$$\frac{\partial \mathcal{E}}{\partial y_j} = \frac{\partial \mathcal{E}}{\partial x_j} = -\frac{t_j - y_j}{\sigma_j} = -\frac{t_j - y_j}{\sigma}, \tag{5.13}$$

the first equality resulting from the assumption that the output transfer function is the identity.

In summary, we see that in the regression case with Gaussian noise, the output transfer function should be linear, the likelihood error function is the LMS error function (possibly scaled by σ_j along each component j), and the derivative of $\mathcal{E}$ with respect to the total input activity into the output layer, for each example, has the simple expression $-(t_j - y_j)/\sigma_j = -(t_j - y_j)/\sigma$.

5.3.3 Binomial Classification

Consider now a classification problem with only two classes, A and $\bar{A}$. For a given input d, the target output t is 0 or 1. The natural probabilistic model is a binomial model. The single output of the network then represents the probability that the input is a member of the class A or $\bar{A}$, that is the expectation of the corresponding indicator function. This can be computed by a sigmoidal transfer function. Thus,

$$y = y(d) = \mathbf{P}(d \in A) = \mathbf{P}(t|d, w) = y^t (1 - y)^{(1-t)} \tag{5.14}$$

and

$$\mathcal{E} = -\log \mathbf{P}(t|d, w) = -t \log y - (1 - t) \log(1 - y). \tag{5.15}$$

This is the relative entropy between the output distribution and the observed distribution, and

$$\frac{\partial \mathcal{E}}{\partial y} = -\frac{t - y}{y(1 - y)}. \tag{5.16}$$

In particular, if the output transfer function is the logistic function, then

$$\frac{\partial \mathcal{E}}{\partial x} = -(t - y). \tag{5.17}$$

Therefore, in the case of binomial classification, the output transfer function should be logistic; the likelihood error function is essentially the relative entropy between the predicted distribution and the target distribution. The derivative of $\mathcal{E}$ with respect to the total input activity into the output unit, for each example, has the simple expression $-(t - y)$.

5.3.4 Multinomial Classification

More generally, consider a classification task with n possible classes $A_1, \ldots, A_n$. For a given input d, the target output t is a vector with a single 1 and $n - 1$ zeros. The most simple probabilistic model is a multinomial model. The corresponding NN has n output units, each one giving the probability of the membership of the input in the corresponding class. Thus

$$\mathbf{P}(t|d, w) = \prod_{j=1}^{n} y_j^{t_j}, \tag{5.18}$$

with, as usual, $t_j = t_j(d)$ and $y_j = y_j(d)$. For each example,

$$\mathcal{E} = -\log \mathbf{P}(t|d, w) = -\sum_{j=1}^{n} t_j \log y_j. \tag{5.19}$$

Again, this is the relative entropy between the output distribution and the observed distribution, and

$$\frac{\partial \mathcal{E}}{\partial y_j} = -\frac{t_j}{y_j}. \tag{5.20}$$

In particular, if the output layer consists of a set of normalized exponentials, then for each input d_i,

$$\frac{\partial \mathcal{E}}{\partial x_j} = -(t_j - y_j), \tag{5.21}$$

where x_j is the total input into the jth normalized exponential.

Thus, in multinomial classification, the output transfer function should be normalized exponentials. The likelihood error function is essentially the relative entropy between the predicted distribution and the target distribution. The derivative of E with respect to the total input activity into the output layer, for each example and each component, has the simple expression $-(t_j - y_j)$.

5.3.5 The General Exponential Family Case

In fact, results similar to the previous cases can be derived every time the likelihood function belongs to the exponential family of distributions (see appendix A and [384, 94]). The exponential family contains many of the most common distributions such as Gaussian, gamma, binomial, multinomial, exponential, beta, Poisson, and negative binomial. For each member of the family, there is an appropriate choice of output transfer function $y = f(x)$ such that the derivative $\partial \mathcal{E}/\partial x_j$ of E with respect to the total input activity into the jth output unit has a simple expression, proportional for each example to $(t_j - y_j)$, the difference between the target output t_j and the actual output y_j.

We have just seen that the proper statistical framework allows one to construct suitable transfer functions for the output layer, as well as suitable error functions to measure network performance. The design of the hidden layers, however, is more problem-dependent, and cannot be dealt with in much

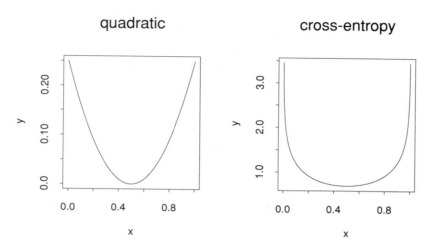

Figure 5.3: Comparison of the One-Dimensional Quadratic and Cross-Entropy Error Functions, with Respect to the Target Value of 0.5. Note the difference in ranges: the cross-entropy is infinite for $x = 0$ and $x = 1$.

generality. The framework described above has emerged only in recent years, and has not always been followed by NN practitioners, including many of the examples to be examined in the next sections. Many authors have used an LMS error function even in binomial classification problems, where a relative entropy error is more appropriate.

The question, then, is: "How have reasonably good results been derived, even when using a somewhat improper framework?" The answer to this question is best understood in the simple example above. Suppose that in a binary classification problem, the probability we wish to learn is, for the sake of argument, $p = 0.5$. For each x in $[0, 1]$ the LMS error is $(0.5 - x)^2$, whereas the relative entropy is $-0.5 \log x - 0.5 \log(1 - x)$. These two functions are plotted in figure 5.3. Both functions are convex ($\cup$), with a a minimum at $p = 0.5$, as desired. The main difference, however, is in the dynamic range: unlike the relative entropy, the LMS error is bounded. The dynamic range difference can be important when the errors of many examples are superimposed, and also during learning.

5.4 Learning Algorithms: Backpropagation

In the majority of applications to be reviewed, MAP or ML estimation of NN parameters is done by gradient descent (see [26] for a general review). The calculations required to obtain the gradient can be organized in a nice fashion that leverages the graphical structure of NN. Using the chain rule, weights are updated sequentially, from the output layer back to the input layer, by propagating an error signal backward along the NN connections (hence the name "backpropagation"). More precisely, in the online version of the algorithm, and for each training pattern, we have for any weight parameter w_{ij}

$$\frac{\partial E}{\partial w_{ij}} = \frac{\partial E}{\partial y_i}\frac{\partial y_i}{\partial w_{ij}} = \frac{\partial E}{\partial y_i}f_i'(x_i)y_j. \tag{5.22}$$

Thus the gradient-descent learning equation is the product of three terms,

$$\Delta w_{ij} = -\eta\frac{\partial E}{\partial w_{ij}} = -\eta\epsilon_i y_j, \tag{5.23}$$

where η is the learning rate, y_j is the output of the unit from which the connection originates (also called the presynaptic activity), and $\epsilon_i = (\partial E/\partial y_i)f_i'(x_i)$ is a postsynaptic term called the backpropagated error. The backpropagated error can be computed recursively by

$$\frac{\partial E}{\partial y_i} = \sum_{k\in N^+(i)}\frac{\partial E}{\partial y_k}f_k'(x_k)w_{ki}. \tag{5.24}$$

The propagation from the children of a node to the node itself is the signature of backpropagation. While backpropagation is the most widely used algorithm for MAP estimation of MLPs, EM and simulated annealing have also been used. Algorithms for learning the architecture itself can also be envisioned, but they remain inefficient on large problems.

We can now review some of the main applications of NNs to molecular biology. Other general surveys of the topics can be found in [432, 571, 572].

Chapter 6

Neural Networks: Applications

The application of neural network algorithms to problems within the field of biological sequence analysis has a fairly long history, taking the age of the whole field into consideration. In 1982 the perceptron was applied to the prediction of ribosome binding sites based on amino acid sequence input [506]. Stormo and coworkers found that the perceptron algorithm was more successful at finding *E. coli* translational initiation sites than a previously developed set of rules [507]. A perceptron without hidden units was able to generalize and could find translational initiation sites within sequences that were not included in the training set.

This linear architecture is clearly insufficient for many sequence recognition tasks. The real boost in the application of neural network techniques first came after the backpropagation training algorithm for the multilayer perceptron was brought into common use in 1986 [456], and especially after Qian and Sejnowski published their seminal paper on prediction of protein secondary structure in 1988 [437]. This and other papers that quickly followed [78, 262] were based on an adaptation of the NetTalk multilayer perceptron architecture [480], which from its input of letters in English text predicted the associated phonemes needed for speech synthesis and for reading the text aloud. This approach could immediately be adapted to tasks within the field of sequence analysis just by changing the input alphabet into alphabets of the amino acids or nucleotides. Likewise, the encoding of the phonemes could easily be transformed into structural classes, like those commonly used for the assignment of protein secondary structure (helices, sheets, and coil), or functional categories representing binding sites, cleavage sites, or residues being posttranslationally modified.

In this chapter we review some of the early work within the application areas of nucleic acids and proteins. We go into detail with some examples of more recent work where the methodologies are advanced in terms of either the training principles applied or the network architectures, especially when networks are combined to produce more powerful prediction schemes. We do not aim to mention and describe the complete spectrum of applications. For recent reviews see, for example, [432, 61, 77, 320, 571, 572].

6.1 Sequence Encoding and Output Interpretation

One important issue, before we can proceed with NN applications to molecular biology, is the encoding of the sequence input. In any type of prediction approach, the input representation is of cardinal importance. If a very clever input representation is chosen, one that reveals exactly the essentials for a particular task, the problem may be more or less solved, or at least can be solved by simple linear methods. In an MLP the activity patterns in the last hidden layer preceding the output unit(s) should represent the transformed input information in linearly separable form. This clearly is much easier if the input representation has not been selected so as further to increase the nonlinearity of the problem.

One would think that a very "realistic" encoding of the monomers in a sequence, using a set of physical-chemical features of potential relevance, should always outperform a more abstract encoding taken from the principles and practice of information theory [137]. However, in line with the contractive nature of most prediction problems (see section 1.4), it does not always help just to add extra information because the network has to discard most of it before it reaches the output level.

During training of an MLP, the network tries to segregate the input space into decision regions using hyperplanes. The numerical representation of the monomers therefore has a large impact on the ease with which the hidden units can position the planes in the space defined by the representation that has been chosen.

In many sequence analysis problems, the input is often associated with a window of size W covering the relevant sequence segment or segments. Typically the window is positioned symmetrically so that the upstream and downstream contexts are of the same size, but in some cases asymmetric windows perform far better than symmetric ones. When the task is to predict signal peptide cleavage sites (section 6.4) or intron splice sites in pre-mRNA (section 6.5.2), asymmetric windows may outperform symmetric ones. Both these sequence types (N-terminal protein sorting signals and noncoding intronic DNA) are eventually removed, and it makes sense to have most of the features needed for their processing in the regions themselves, leaving the mature protein least constrained. Windows with holes where the sequence appears nonconsecutively have been used especially for the prediction of promoters and the exact position of transcriptional initiation in DNA, but also for finding beta-sheet partners in proteins [268, 46] and for the prediction of distance constraints between two amino acids based on the sequence context of both residues [368, 174].

For each position in a window W, there are $|A|$ different possible monomers. The most used representation is the so-called *orthogonal* (also called local, as opposed to distributed) encoding, where the letters $x_1, x_2, \ldots$ are encoded by the orthogonal binary vectors $(1, 0, \ldots, 0)$, $(0, 1, \ldots, 0)$, and so on. Such a representation has the advantage of not introducing any algebraic correlations between the monomers. N- and C-terminal positions in incomplete windows of amino acid sequences are usually encoded using a dedicated character. Sometimes this character is also used to encode unknown monomers in a sequence, but unknown monomers may be handled better using just a string of zeros so that they have no impact on the input layer.

The sparse encoding scheme has the disadvantage of being wasteful because it requires an input layer of size $|A| \times W$. $|A|$ letters could in principle be encoded using as few as $\log_2 |A|$ binary units. Furthermore, using continuous values in the input layer of an MLP, even a single unit could encode all possible letters. Such a compact encoding would in almost all cases give rise to drastically increased nonlinearity in the prediction problem at hand. If all amino acids were encoded using values between, say, 0 and 1, many of the induced correlations between the monomers would have no biological relevance, almost no matter in what order the monomers were mapped to the interval.

Obviously, there are trade-offs between different encodings that involve the complexity of the space in which the input windows live, the network architecture size, and ease of learning. In much of the best work done so far in this field, the orthogonal representation has been the most successful encoding scheme. With a more complex encoding of the sequence, whether orthogonal or not, the network must filter this extra information through a representation as a point in a space with dimensionality according to the number of hidden units, and then further on to a few, often a single, output unit(s). If one includes too much extra information related to the physicochemical properties of the residues in the input layer, possibly information that is not strongly correlated to the output, one makes the network's task harder. In this case, it is best to use more hidden units in order to be able to discard this extra information and find the relevant features in a sea of noise. This situation, with the lack of a better alternative, has contributed to the success of the orthogonal representation.

If one wants to use real-numbered quantification of residue hydrophobicity, volume, charge, and so on, one should be aware of the harmful impact it can have on the input space. Instead of just using a seemingly better representation of the input residues, it may be much better to use preprocessed versions of the original sequence segments. When designing such preprocessed versions, one may exploit the statistics of certain words present in the window, the average hydrophobicity over the window or separately in the left and right parts of a symmetric window, and so on. Another interesting possibility, demonstrated in one of the examples below, is to let an NN learn its own representation. In another example a binary word encoding was shown to have a positive effect on protein secondary structure prediction [313, 548, 17]. In this case, it was possible, from the optimal encoding scheme generated by a simulated annealing approach, to discover physicochemical properties relevant to the formation of secondary structure.

An important strategy for decreasing the nonlinearity of a prediction problem is to switch from a representation based on monomers to one based on dimers or trimers. In the case of nucleotides, 16- and 64-letter alphabets result, and in a large number of biological recognition problems, the pair or triplet correlations are so large that the gain in significant correlations compares favorably with the negative impact of the increased dimensionality of the input space. In DNA, base pair stacking is the most important thermodynamic contribution to helical stability (more important than base pairing). Pair correlations in RNA–RNA recognition interactions, for example, have their physical basis in the stacking energies between adjacent base pairs [112]. In proteins the dipeptide distribution similarly has a strong bias associated with steric hindrance, translation kinetics, and other purely biochemical factors.

If RNA and DNA sequences are encoded by dinucleotides or trinucleotides, there is also the possibility of letting the multimers *overlap*. The sparse encoding of the multimers ensures that no a priori relationship is imprinted on the sequence data. The advantage of the encoding of the sequence as overlapping triplets is that the hidden units directly receive context information for each single nucleotide that they otherwise would have to deduce from the training process.

Yet another strategy for decreasing (or in some cases increasing) the nonlinearity of a prediction problem is to group monomers from one alphabet to form new alphabets in which the pattern that should be detected will have more contrast to the background [306]. The reduced alphabets can then be encoded using the orthogonal vector representation, and at the same time reduce the dimensionality of the input space and thus the number of adjustable parameters in the network. Meaningful groupings can be based on physicochemical properties or on estimated mutation rates found in evolutionary studies of protein families. Table 6.1 lists some of the previously used groupings based on ab initio descriptions of the monomers or on their structural or functional preferences as observed in experimental data.

Molecule	Size	Grouping
DNA	2	Purines vs. pyrimidines: R = A, G; Y = C, T
DNA	2	Strong vs. weak hydrogen bonding: S = C, G; W = A, T
DNA	2	Less physiochemical significance: keto, K = T, G vs. amino, M = A, C
Protein	3	Structural alphabet: ambivalent (Ala, Cys, Gly, Pro, Ser, Thr, Trp, Tyr) external (Arg, Asn, Asp, Gln, Glu, His, Lys) internal (Ile, Leu, Met, Phe, Val)
Protein	8	Chemical alphabet: acidic (Asp, Glu) aliphatic (Ala, Gly, Ile, Leu, Val) amide (Asn, Gln) aromatic (Phe, Trp, Tyr) basic (Arg, His, Lys) hydroxyl (Ser, Thr): imino (Pro) sulfur (Cys, Met)
Protein	4	Functional alphabet: acidic and basic (same as in chemical alphabet) hydrophobic nonpolar (Ala, Ile, Leu, Met, Phe, Pro, Trp, Val) polar uncharged (Asn, Cys, Gln, Gly, Ser, Thr, Tyr)
Protein	3	Charge alphabet: acidic and basic (as in chemical alphabet) neutral (all the other amino acids)
Protein	2	Hydrophobic alphabet: hydrophobic (Ala, Ile, Leu, Met, Phe, Pro, Trp, Val) hydrophilic (Arg, Asn, Asp, Cys, Gln, Glu, Gly, His, Lys, Ser, Thr, Tyr)

Table 6.1: Merged Alphabets of Biomolecular Monomers. Some of these alphabets are based on ab initio descriptions of the monomers, others are derived from statistical properties of the monomers as indicated by structural or functional preferences. Random partition of the amino acids into k classes that maximizes a similarity measure between sequences can also be constructed. Source: [306]. See also references therein.

In one case, it has been shown recently that a protein can largely maintain its folded structure, even if the total number of different amino acids in its composition is reduced from the conventional twenty down to five [443]. Apart from a few positions close to a binding site, fifteen amino acid types were replaced by other residues taken from the smaller, representative group of five (I, K, E, A, and G). Further reduction in the diversity down to three different amino acids did not work. This means that proteins in earlier evolutionary time still may have been able to obtain stable, folded structures with a much smaller repertoire of amino acid monomers. It should be noted that this reduced alphabet is in no way canonical: many proteins will certainly not be able to do without cysteines. While the recoding of sequences using smaller alphabets (table 6.1) at first may seem purely a computational trick, more experimental work on "essential" amino acids can possibly be exploited in bioinformatics approaches to construct simpler sequence spaces that can be better covered by the limited amounts of data available. The simplification strategy arrived at here was also inspired by the phylogenetic variation in this protein. This is exactly the type of information that has been used to improve protein structure prediction methods, as described in the next sections of this chapter.

In other applications the encoding does not preserve the consecutive order of the residues in a sequence but seeks to cast the whole sequence, or large segments of it, into global preprocessed measures that can be used as input information in a network. For example, this is the case when the aim is to predict the fold class or family relationship of a protein from the frequencies of the 400 dipeptides it contains [179, 18]. In the indirect sequence encoding used in one approach to discriminate between exons and introns, 6-mer statistics, GC composition, sequence vocabulary, and several other indicators are included as global measures in the input layer [529].

In the NN applications described below, we also show how important it is to design good strategies for *output interpretation* or postprocessing. In most cases, however, intelligent postprocessing may be as important as, or even more important than, selecting optimal network architectures in terms of the smallest numerical generalization error as quantified by the activities of the output neurons. Often the number of output neurons corresponds directly to the number of output classes, again using sparse encoding by orthogonal vectors of zeros and ones. The output interpretation and postprocessing will always be designed individually for each task, based on features known previously from the biological frame of reference. If it is known a priori that, say, alpha-helices in proteins have a minimum length of four amino acids, small "helices" that are predicted can often be removed and lead to a better overall predictive performance. In cases where a sequence is known to possess a *single* functional site of a given type only—for example, a cleavage site in the N-terminal signal peptide—a carefully designed principle for the numerical threshold used for assignment of sites may lead to much better recognition of true sites and significantly lower rates of false positives. A discussion of the relation between the analog network error and the discrete classification error can be found in [90].

HUMAN

Figure 6.1: English-Reading People Will Normally Interpret the Two Identical Symbols in this Word Differently: the first as an *h* and the second as an *a*. In biological sequences a similar information processing capability is needed as structural and functional features most often result from the cooperativity of the sequence rather than from independent contributions from individual nucleotides or amino acids. The neural network technique has the potential to detect such short- and long-range sequence correlations, and in this way complement what can be obtained by conventional alignment and analysis by hidden Markov models.

6.2 Sequence Correlations and Neural Networks

Many structural or functional aspects of sequences are not conserved in terms of sequence, not even when amino acid similarities are taken into account. It is well known that protein structures, for example, can be highly conserved despite a very low sequence similarity when assessed and quantified by the amino acid identity position by position. What makes up a protein structure, either locally or globally, is the *cooperativity* of the sequence, and not just independent contributions from individual positions in it.

This holds true not only for the protein as a whole but also locally, say for a phosphorylation site motif, which must be recognized by a given kinase. Even for linear motifs that are known to interact with the same kinase, sequence patterns can be very different [331]. When the local structures of such sequence segments are inspected (in proteins for which the structure has been determined and deposited in the Protein Data Bank), they may indeed be conserved structurally despite the high compositional diversity [74].

The neural network technique has the potential of sensing this cooperativity through its ability to correlate the different input values to each other. In fact, the cooperativity in the weights that result from training is supposed to mirror the relevant correlations between the monomers in the input, which again are correlated to the prediction task carried out by the network.

The ability of the artificial neural networks to sense correlations between individual sequence positions is very similar to the ability of the human brain when interpreting letters in natural language differently based on their language!naturalcontext. This is well known from pronunciation where, for example, the four a's in the sentence *Mary had a little lamb* correspond to three different phonemes [480]. Another illustration of this kind of ability is shown in figure 6.1. Here the identical symbol will be interpreted differently *provided* the brain receiving the information that is projected onto the retina has been trained to read the English language, that is, trained to understand the sequential pattern in English language!Englishtext.

It is precisely this ability that has made the neural networks successful in the sequence analysis area, in particular because they complement what one can obtain by weight matrices and to some degree also by hidden Markov models. The power of the neural network technique is not limited to the analysis of local correlations, as the sequence information being encoded in the input layer can come from different parts of a given sequence [368]. However, most applications have focused on local and linear sequence segments, such as those presented in the following sections.

6.3 Prediction of Protein Secondary Structure

When one inspects graphical visualizations of protein backbones on a computer screen, local folding regularities in the form of repeated structures are immediately visible. Two such types of secondary structures, which are maintained by backbone hydrogen bonds, were actually suggested by theoretical considerations before they were found in the first structures to be solved by X-ray crystallography. There is no canonical definition of classes of secondary structure, but Ramachandran plots representing pairs of dihedral angles for each amino acid residue show that certain angular regions tend to be heavily overrepresented in real proteins. One region corresponds to alpha-helices, where backbone hydrogen bonds link residues i and $i + 4$; another, to beta-sheets, where hydrogen bonds link two sequence segments in either a parallel or antiparallel fashion.

The sequence preferences and correlations involved in these structures have made secondary structure prediction one of the classic problems in computational molecular biology [362, 128, 129, 196]. Many different neural network architectures have been applied to this task, from early studies [437, 78, 262, 370, 323] to much more advanced approaches [453, 445].

The assignment of the secondary structure categories to the experimentally determined 3D structure is nontrivial, and has in most of the work been performed by the widely used DSSP program [297]. DSSP works by analysis of the repetitive pattern of potential hydrogen bonds from the 3D coordinates of the backbone atoms. An alternative to this assignment scheme is the program STRIDE, which uses both hydrogen bond energy and backbone dihedral angles rather than hydrogen bonds alone [192]. Yet another is the program DEFINE, whose principal procedure uses difference distance matrices for evaluating the match of interatomic distances in the protein to those from idealized secondary structures [442].

None of these programs can be said to be perfect. The ability to assign what visually appears as a helix or a sheet, in a situation where the coordinate data have limited precision, is not a trivial algorithmic task. Another factor contributing to the difficulty is that quantum chemistry does not deliver a nice analytical expression for the strength of a hydrogen bond. In the prediction context it would be ideal not to focus solely on the visual, or topological, aspects of the assignment problem, but also to try to produce a more predictable assignment scheme. A reduced assignment scheme, which would leave out some of the helices and sheets and thereby make it possible to obtain close to perfect prediction, could be very useful, for example in tertiary structure prediction, which often uses a predicted secondary structure as starting point.

6.3.1 Secondary Structure Prediction Using MLPs

The basic architecture used in the early work of Qian and Sejnowski is a fully connected MLP with a single hidden layer [437]. The input window has an odd length W, with an optimal size typically of 13 amino acids. Orthogonal encoding is used for the input with an alphabet size $|A| = 21$, corresponding to 20 amino acids and one terminator symbol to encode partial windows at the N- or C-terminal. Thus, the input layer has $13 \times 21 = 273$ units. The typical size of the hidden layer consists of 40 sigmoidal units. The total number of parameters of this architecture is then $273 \times 40 + 40 \times 3 + 40 + 3 = 11,083$. The output layer has three sigmoidal units, with orthogonal encoding of the alpha-helix, the beta-sheet, and the coil classes. The output represents the classification, into one of the three classes, of the residue located at the center of the input window. The classification is determined by the output unit with the greatest activity, an interpretation strategy known as the winner-take-all principle. This principle acts as an extra nonlinear feature in the relation between the input and the final output classification. Networks without hidden units will therefore, when interpreted by the winner-take-all principle, not be entirely linear. Another way to put it is that the internal representation in the hidden layer of the sequence input does not need to be perfectly linearly separable. As long as the distance to the separating hyperplane is smallest for the correct output unit, it does not matter that the input representation ends up slightly in the wrong decision region.

The networks are initialized using random uniform weights in the $[-0.3, 0.3]$ interval, and subsequently trained using backpropagation with the LMS error function (note that a normalized exponential output layer with the relative entropy as error function would have been more appropriate). The typical size of a training set is roughly 20,000 residues extracted from the Brookhaven Protein Data Bank (PDB). Thus the ratio of parameters to examples is fairly high, larger than 0.5. Today many more protein structures have been solved experimentally, so that a similar database of secondary structure assignments will be much larger.

When training on protein sequences, a random presentation order of input windows across the training set is used to avoid performance oscillations associated with the use of contiguous windows. With this architecture, performance goes from a 33% chance level to 60%, after which overfitting begins. More precisely, the overall correct percentage is $Q_3 = 62.7\%$, with the correlation coefficients $C_\alpha = 0.35$, $C_\beta = 0.29$, and $C_c = 0.38$ [382]. As a consequence of the imbalance in the amount of helix, sheet, and coil in natural proteins (roughly found in proportions 0.3/0.2/0.5), mere percentages of correctly predicted window configurations can be bad indicators of the predictive performance. A much used alternative measure, which takes into account the relation between correctly predicted positives and negatives as well as false positives and negatives, is the correlation coefficient [382],

$$C_X = \frac{(P_X N_X) - (N_X^f P_X^f)}{\sqrt{(N_X + N_X^f)(N_X + P_X^f)(P_X + N_X^f)(P_X + P_X^f)}},\qquad(6.1)$$

where X can be any of the categories helix, sheet, coil, or two or more of these categories merged as one. P_X and N_X are the correctly predicted positives and negatives, and P_X^f and N_X^f are similarly the incorrectly predicted positives and negatives. A perfect prediction gives $C(X) = 1$, whereas a fully imperfect one gives $C(X) = -1$ (for a more detailed discussion of this and other performance measures, see section 6.7 below).

The authors conducted a number of experiments to test architectural and other variations and concluded that increasing the size of the input beyond 13 or adding additional information, such as amino acid hydrophobicities, does not lead to performance improvement. Likewise, no improvement appears to result from using finer secondary structure classification schemes, higher-order or recurrent networks, or pruning methods.

The main improvement is obtained by cascading the previous architecture with a second network that can take advantage of the analog certainty values present in the three output units and their correlations over adjacent positions. The second network also has an input window of length 13, corresponding to 13 successive outputs of the first network. Thus the input layer of the top network is 13×3. The top network also has a hidden layer with 40 units, and the usual 3 output units. With this cascaded architecture, the overall performance reaches $Q_3 = 64.3\%$, with the correlations $C_\alpha = 0.41$, $C_\beta = 0.31$, and $C_c = 0.41$. After training, the authors observed that the top network ultimately cleans up the output of the lower network, mostly by removing isolated assignments. From these and other results, it was concluded that there appears to be a theoretical limit of slightly above 70% performance for any "local" method, where "local" refers to the size of the input window to the prediction algorithm. In 1988 these overall results appeared to be much better than all previous methods, including the renowned Chou-Fasman method [129]. The subsequent growth in the data material has significantly increased the performance of more advanced NN approaches to this problem, but the increase has not caused a similar improvement in the performance of the Chou-Fasman method [549]. As can be seen below, several secondary structure prediction methods have now exceeded the level of 70% with a comfortable margin—some are even quite close to the level of 80%.

6.3.2 Prediction Based on Evolutionary Information and Amino Acid Composition

Most of the subsequent work on predicting secondary structure using NNs [78, 262, 323, 505, 451, 452, 290, 427] has been based on the architecture described above, sometimes in combination with other methods [582, 377] such as the Chou-Fasman rules [129].

In one interesting case the Chou-Fasman rules were used to initialize a network [377]. This knowledge-based network was born with a performance similar to the one obtained by encoding the rules directly into the weights. Experimental data from PDB could then be used to train extra free connections that had been added. All the exceptions in the relation between input sequence and conformational categories not covered by the rules would then be handled by the extra parameters adjusted by training. This network structure is also interesting because it allows for easy inspection of the weights, although it still performs only slightly better than the Qian–Sejnowski architecture. Compared to the Chou-Fasman rules, the performance was, as expected, greatly improved.

An evaluation of the MLP architecture in comparison with Bayesian methods has also been made [505]. In this work the Bayesian method makes the unphysical assumption that the probability of an amino acid occurring in each position in the protein is independent of the amino acids occurring elsewhere. Still, the predictive accuracy of the Bayesian method was found to be only minimally less than the accuracy of the neural networks previously constructed. A neural formalism in which the output neurons directly represent the conditional probabilities of structural classes was developed. The probabilistic formalism allows introduction of a new objective function, the mutual information, that translates the notion of correlation as a measure of predictive accuracy into a useful training measure. Although an accuracy similar to other approaches (utilizing a mean-square error) is achieved using this new measure, the accuracy on the training set is significantly higher, even though the number of adjustable parameters remains the same. The mutual information measure predicts a greater fraction of helix and sheet structures correctly than the mean-square-error measure, at the expense of coil accuracy.

Although tests made on different data sets can be hard to compare, the most significant performance improvement as compared to previous methods has been achieved by the work of Rost and Sander, which resulted in the PHD prediction server [451, 452, 453]. In the 1996 Asilomar competition CASP2 (Critical Assessment of Techniques for Protein Structure Prediction), this method performed much better than virtually all other methods for making predictions of secondary structure [161]. This unique experiment attempts to gauge the current state of the art in protein structure prediction by means of blind prediction. Sequences of a number of target proteins that are in the process of being solved are made available to predictors before the experimental structures are available. The PHD method reached a performance level of 74% on the unknown test set in the ab initio section of the competition, which contains contact, secondary structure, and molecular simulation predictions. This category is the most prestigious and inherently the most difficult prediction category, where the only prior knowledge is the primary structure in the amino acid sequence.

Prediction of secondary structure in a three-state classification based on single sequences seems to be limited to $< 65\text{--}68\%$ accuracy. In the mid-1980s, prediction accuracy reached 50–55% three-state accuracy, but more advanced neural network algorithms and increased data sets pushed the accuracy to the 65% level, a mark long taken as insurmountable. The key feature in the PHD approach, as well as in other even more powerful methods that have been constructed recently, has been to go beyond the local information contained in stretches of 13–21 consecutive residues by realizing that sequence families contain much more useful information than single sequences. Previously, this conclusion had also been reached in many studies using alignment of multiple sequences; see for example [587, 139, 60].

The use of evolutionary information improved the prediction accuracy to $> 72\%$, with correlation coefficients $C_\alpha = 0.64$ and $C_\beta = 0.53$. The way to use evolutionary information for prediction was the following. First, a database of known sequences was scanned by alignment methods for similar sequences. Second, the list of sequences found was filtered by a length-dependent threshold for significant sequence identity. Third, based on all probable 3D homologues, a profile of amino acid exchanges was compiled. Fourth, this profile was used for prediction.

The first method been proven in a cross-validation experiment based on 250 unique protein chains to predict secondary structure at a sustained level

```
DSSP  E  L  L  L   L  E  E  E  E  E   E  E  E  E  E   E  E  E  H  H  H
SH3   N  S  T  N   K  D  W  W  K  V   E  V  N  D  R   Q  G  F  V  P  A  A  Y
a1    N  K  S  N   P  D  W  W  E  G   E  L  N  G  Q   R  G  V  F  P  A  S  Y
a2    E  E  H  .   G  E  W  W  K  A   K  s  s  K  R   E  G  F  I  P  S  N  Y
a3    R  S  T  .   G  D  W  W  L  A   r  v  T  G  R   E  G  Y  V  P  S  N  F
a4    F  S  .  .   .  .  F  F  G  V   e  v  D  D  L   Q  V  F  V  P  P  A  Y

V     0  0  0  0   0   0  0  0  0 40   0  60  0  0  0  0  20  20 60  0  0  0  0
L     0  0  0  0   0   0  0 20  0  0   0  20  0  0 20  0   0   0 20  0  0  0  0
I     0  0  0  0   0   0  0  0  0  0   0   0  0  0  0  0   0   0 20  0  0  0  0
M     0  0  0  0   0   0  0  0  0  0   0   0  0  0  0  0   0   0  0  0  0  0  0
F    20  0  0  0   0   0 20 20  0  0   0   0  0  0  0  0   0  60 20  0  0  0 20
W     0  0  0  0   0  80 80  0  0  0   0   0  0  0  0  0   0   0  0  0  0  0  0
Y     0  0  0  0   0   0  0  0  0  0   0   0  0  0  0  0   0  20  0  0  0  0 80
G     0  0  0  0  50   0  0  0 20 20   0   0  0 40  0  0  80   0  0  0  0  0  0
A     0  0  0  0   0   0  0  0  0 40   0   0  0  0  0  0   0   0  0 40 40  0  0
P     0  0  0  0  25   0  0  0  0  0   0   0  0  0  0  0   0   0  0 100 20  0  0
S     0 60 25  0   0   0  0  0  0  0   0  20 20  0  0  0   0   0  0  0 40 20  0
T     0  0 50  0   0   0  0  0  0  0   0   0 20  0  0  0   0   0  0  0 40 20  0
C     0  0  0  0   0   0  0  0  0  0   0   0  0  0  0  0   0   0  0  0  0  0  0
H     0  0 25  0   0   0  0  0  0  0   0   0  0  0  0  0   0   0  0  0  0  0  0
R    20  0  0  0   0   0  0  0  0  0  20   0  0  0 60 20   0   0  0  0  0  0  0
K     0 20  0  0  25   0  0  0 40  0  20   0  0 20  0  0   0   0  0  0  0  0  0
Q     0  0  0  0   0   0  0  0  0  0   0   0  0 20 40  0   0   0  0  0  0  0  0
E    20 20  0  0   0   0  0  0 20  0  60   0  0 20 40  0   0   0  0  0  0  0  0
N    40  0  0 100  0   0  0  0  0  0   0   0 40  0  0  0   0   0  0  0  0 40  0
D     0  0  0  0   0  75  0  0  0  0   0   0 20 40  0  0   0   0  0  0  0  0  0

Ndel  0  0  1  3   1   1  0  0  0  0   0   0  0  0  0  0   0   0  0  0  0  0  0
Nins  0  0  0  0   0   0  0  0  0  0   2   3  1  0  0  0   0   0  0  0  0  0  0
CW  1.0 0.8 0.7 0.8 0.6 1.1 1.5 1.5 0.8 0.9 1.0 0.7 0.7 0.9 0.9 0.7 1.5 1.0 1.2 1.5 0.9 0.7 1.5
```

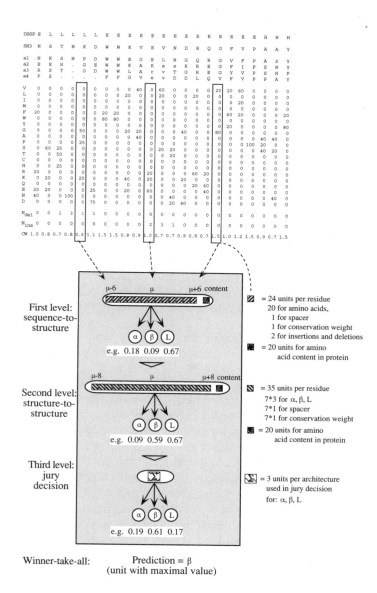

Figure 6.2: The PHD Architecture for Secondary Structure Prediction Developed by Rost and Sander. The input is based not on a conventional orthogonal encoding of the query sequence, but on a profile made from amino acid occurrences in columns of a multiple alignment of sequences with high similarity to the query sequence.

of > 72% three-state accuracy was the PHD neural network scheme [451, 452, 453]. For this method the profiles, along with additional information derived from the multiple sequence alignments and the amino acid content of the protein, were fed as input into a neural network system, as shown in figure 6.2. The input was based not on a conventional orthogonal encoding of a single sequence, but on a profile made from amino acid occurrences in columns of a multiple alignment of sequences with high similarity to the query sequence. In the example shown in figure 6.2 five sequences are included in the profile. The lowercase letters indicate deletions in the aligned sequence. To the resulting 20 values at one particular position in the protein (one column), three values are added: the number of deletions, the number of insertions, and a conservation weight. Thirteen adjacent columns are used as input. The "L" (loop) category is equivalent to the coil category in most other work. The whole network system for secondary structure prediction consists of three layers: two network layers and one layer averaging over independently trained networks.

In this work the profiles were taken from the HSSP database [471]. HSSP is a derived database merging structural and sequence information. For each protein of known 3D structure from PDB, the database has a multiple sequence alignment of all available homologues and a sequence profile characteristic of the family.

The backpropagation training of the networks was either *unbalanced* or *balanced*. In a large, low-similarity database of proteins the distribution over the conformational categories helix, sheet, and coil is, as indicated above, roughly 30%, 20%, and 50%, respectively. In unbalanced training the 13 amino acid-wide profile vectors were presented randomly with the same frequency. In the balanced version, the different categories were presented equally often. This means that the helix and sheet examples were presented about twice as often as the coil. In the final network system a mixture of networks trained by these two approaches was used. Networks trained by the balanced approach allow a much more reliable prediction of the sheet category.

Many other details of the architectures are important in yielding a prediction with a high overall accuracy, a much more accurate prediction of sheets than previously obtained, and a much better prediction of secondary structure segments rather than single residues. For 40% of all residues predicted with *high reliability*, the method reached a value of close to 90%, that is, was as accurate as homology modeling would be, if applicable. Almost 10 percentage points of the improvement in overall accuracy stemmed from using evolutionary information.

Clearly, one of the main dangers of the Qian-Sejnowski architecture is the overfitting problem. Rost and Sander started with the same basic architecture, but used two methods to address the overfitting problem. First, they used early stopping. Second, they used ensemble averages [237, 340] by train-

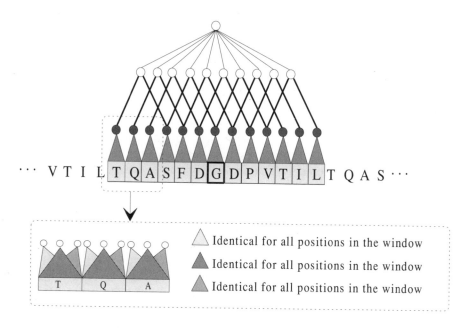

Figure 6.3: Riis and Krogh Network for Predicting Helices. The network uses the local encoding scheme and has a built-in period of three residues. Dark circles symbolize three hidden units, and heavy lines, three weights. In the lower part of the figure, shaded triangles symbolize 20 shared weights, and shaded rectangles, 20 input units. The network has a window size of 13 residues and has one output neuron.

ing different networks independently, using different input information and learning procedures. But the most significant new aspect of their work is the use of multiple alignments, in the sense that profiles (i.e. position-dependent frequency vectors derived from multiple alignments), rather than raw amino acid sequences, are used in the network input. The reasoning behind this is that multiple alignments contain more information about secondary structure than do single sequences, the secondary structure being considerably more conserved than the primary sequence.

6.3.3 Network Ensembles and Adaptive Encoding

Another interesting NN approach to the secondary structure prediction problem is the work of Riis and Krogh [338, 445], who address the overfitting problem by careful design of the NN architecture. Their approach has four main components. First, the main reason underlying the large number of parameters of the previous architectures is the large input layer (13×21). This number is greatly reduced by using an adaptive encoding of amino acids, that is, by letting the NN find an optimal and compressed representation of the input letters. This is achieved by encoding each amino acid using the analog values of M units, that is, with a local or distributed encoding. More precisely, the authors first use an orthogonal encoding with 20 units, the zero vector being used to represent the N- and C-terminal spacer symbols. Thus the input layer has size $W \times 20$. This input layer is connected to a first hidden layer of $M \times W$ units, but with a particular connectivity pattern. Each sequence position in the input layer is connected to a set of M sigmoidal units, and such connections are forced to be translation-invariant, that is, identical across sequence positions. This technique is also called weight-sharing in the NN literature. In an image-processing problem, the fixed set of connections would equivalently define the kernel of a convolution filter. The weight-sharing property is easily enforced during training by an obvious modification of the backpropagation algorithm, where weight updates are summed for weights sharing the same value. Thus each letter of the alphabet is encoded into the analog values of M units. In pattern-recognition problems, it is also common to think of the M units as feature detectors. Note that the features useful in solving the problems are discovered and optimized during learning, and not hardwired in advance. The number of free connections, including biases, between the full input layer and this representation layer is only $21 \times M$, regardless of the window size W. This leads to a great reduction from the over 10,000 parameters typically used in the first layer of the previous architectures. In their work, the authors use the values $M = 3$ and $W = 15$.

Second, Riis and Krogh design a different network for each of the three classes. In the case of alpha-helices, they exploit the helix periodicity by building a three-residue periodicity between the first and second hidden layers (see figure 6.3). The second hidden layer is fully interconnected to the output layer. In the case of beta-sheets and coils, the first hidden layer is fully interconnected to the second hidden layer, which has a typical size of 5–10 units. The second hidden layer is fully connected to the corresponding output unit. Thus a typical alpha-helix network has a total of 160 adjustable parameters, and a typical beta-sheet or coil network contains 300–500 adjustable parameters. The authors used balanced training sets, with the same number of positive and negative examples, when training these architectures in isolation.

Third, Riis and Krogh use *ensembles* of networks and filtering to improve the prediction. Specifically, they use five different networks for each type of structure at each position. The networks in each ensemble differ, for instance, in the number of hidden units used. The combining network takes a window of 15 consecutive single predictions. Thus the input layer to the combining network has size $15 \times 3 \times 5 = 225$ (figure 6.4). In order to keep the number of parameters within a reasonable range, the connectivity is restricted by having one hidden unit per position and per ensemble class (α, β, or coil). Thus the input is locally connected to a hidden layer with $3 \times 15 = 45$ units. Finally, the hidden layer is fully connected to three softmax (normalized exponentials) output units, computing the probability of membership in each class for the central residue. Consistent with the theory presented above, the error measure used is the negative log-likelihood, which in this case is the relative entropy between the true assignments and the predicted probabilities.

Finally, Riis and Krogh use multiple alignments together with a weighting scheme. Instead of profiles, for which the correlations between amino acids in the window are lost, predictions are made first from single sequences and are then combined using multiple alignments. This strategy is also used elsewhere [587, 457, 358], and can be applied to any method for secondary structure prediction from primary sequences, in combination with any alignment method. The final prediction is made by combining all the single-sequence predictions in a given column of the multiple alignment, using a weighting scheme. The weighting scheme used to compensate for database biases is the maximum-entropy weighting scheme [337]. The individual score in a given column can be combined by weighted average or weighted majority, depending on whether the averaging operates on the soft probability values produced by the single-sequence prediction algorithm, or on the corresponding hard decisions. One may expect soft averaging to perform better, since information is preserved until the very last decision; this is confirmed by the authors' observations, although the results of weighted average and weighted majority are similar. A small network with a single hidden layer of five units is then applied to filter the consensus secondary structure prediction derived, using the multiple alignment (see [445] for more detail). The small network also uses the fact that coil regions are less conserved and therefore have higher per-column entropy in a multiple alignment.

A number of experiments and tests are presented showing that (1) the architecture, with its local encoding, avoids the overfitting problem; (2) the performance is not improved by using a number of additional inputs, such as the normalized length of the protein or its average amino acid composition; (3) the improvement resulting from each algorithmic component is quantified—for instance, multiple alignments lead to roughly a 5% overall improvement, mostly associated with improvement in the prediction of the more conserved α and β structures; (4) the network outputs can be interpreted as classification probabilities. Most important, perhaps, the basic accuracy achieved is $Q_3 = 66.3\%$ when using sevenfold cross-validation on the same database of 126 nonhomologous proteins used by Rost and Sander. In combination with multiple alignments, the method reaches an overall accuracy of $Q_3 = 71.3\%$, with correlation coefficients $C_\alpha = 0.59$, $C_\beta = 0.50$, and $C_c = 0.41$. Thus, in

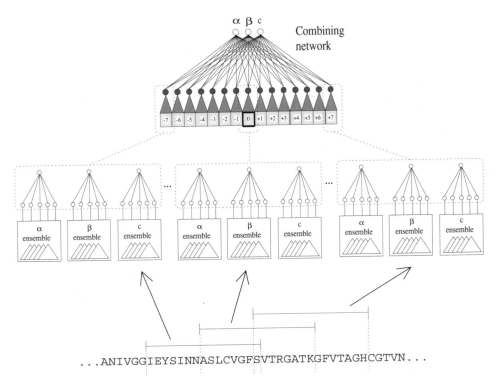

Figure 6.4: The Ensemble Method in the Riis and Krogh Prediction Scheme for Combining and Filtering Ensembles of Networks. The combining network (top of figure) takes a window of $3 \times 5 \times 15$ predictions from the ensembles of the dedicated secondary structures. In the combining network, the ensembles for each of the three structures are weighted separately by position-specific weights for each window position.

spite of a considerable amount of architectural design, the final performance is practically identical to [453]. This of course adds evidence to the consensus of an accuracy upper bound slightly above 70-75% on any prediction method based on local information only.

6.3.4 Secondary Structure Prediction Based on Profiles Made by Position-Specific Scoring Matrices

The key contribution of the PHD method was the use of sequence profiles that contain more structural information for extraction by the neural network. Profiles are based on sequences identified by alignment, and the profile quality obviously depends on the alignment approach used to select the sequences behind the profile.

The PSI-BLAST method [12] is an iterative approach where the sequences found in an initial scan of a database (typically Swiss-Prot) based on a single sequence are used to generate a new search profile, which in turn is used to pick up additional sequences. This type of "sequence walking" will normally reach more family members, even if it is also associated with risk of picking up unrelated sequences, weakening the structurally conserved, family-specific bias in the profile.

In the PSIPRED method [290, 386] Jones used this iterative approach as a clever way of generating profiles for use as improved input to the network scheme. These profiles were based on so-called *position-specific* scoring matrices and did significantly increase the predictive power of the neural network. When obtaining the profiles, the initial database scan was performed using the Blosum62 substitution matrix, while in subsequent scans substitution scores were calculated from the multiple alignment position by position.

Replacing the HSSP profiles used in the PHD method by this more sophisticated approach led to an increase in predictive performance of several percentage points, up to 76.5% for the prediction based on three categories, helix (DSSP H/G/I), sheet (DSSP E/B) and coil. If the G and I helix categories are included in the coil category, the percentage increases further to 78.3%. Thus, depending on the precise definition of observed secondary structure, the overall percent correct varies 1-2%. This variation is essentially the same for most of the neural network methods, and is in fact observed also for other methods as well. In the 1998 Asilomar CASP3 competition (Critical Assessment of Techniques for Protein Structure Prediction), the PSIPRED method was indeed the best for secondary structure, reaching a performance of 77% on one set of sequences and 73% on a subset of diffucult targets [324], which is comparable to the level reported for a larger set of test sequences consisting of 187 unique folds.

6.3.5 Prediction by Averaging over 800 Different Networks

Although helices and sheets have preferred lengths, as observed in wildtype proteins, the length distributions for both types of structure are quite broad. If only a single neural network is used to provide the prediction, the window size will have to be selected as a compromise that can best find the transition from coil to noncoil and from noncoil to coil as measured on a large data set. However, larger windows can benefit from the additional signal in long secondary structures, while short windows often will perform better on structures of minimal length that do not overlap with the previous or next secondary structures, and so on. As single networks, the large and small windows will perform worse, but in individual cases they will typically be more confident, i.e., output values are closer to the saturated values of zero and one.

When combining many different networks, the critical issue is therefore how to benefit from those networks that overall are suboptimal, but in fact are more reliable on a smaller part of the data. When the number of networks becomes large, simple averaging will make the noise from the suboptimal networks become very destructive—in one case an upper limit for the productive number of networks to be combined has been suggested to be around eight [118]. In this work, approximate performance values for the networks were at the level of 73.63% (one network), 74.70% (two), 74.73% (four), and 74.76% (eight) for a three-category prediction scheme.

However, Petersen and coworkers showed recently [427] that it is possible to benefit from as many as 800 networks in an ensemble with strong architectural diversity: different window sizes, different numbers of hidden units, etc. The key element in the procedure is to identify, from the 800 networks, those predictions that are likely to be of high confidence for a given amino acid residue in the test data. By averaging over the highly confident predictions only, it becomes possible to exploit many networks and prevent the noise from the suboptimal networks from eradicating the signal from the confident true positive (and true negative) predictions.

Using this scheme, it was possible to increase the prediction level above what could be obtained with the PSIPRED method. When measured on the two different ways of merging the DSSP categories into categories of helix, sheet, and coil, the improvement ranged from 77.2% (standard merging) to 80.2% as measured as the mean at the per-amino acid level. The percentages are slightly higher when reported as mean per-chain (77.9%-80.6%).

Output Expansion

In this study the performance was improved by introducing another new feature in the output layer. The Petersen scheme was designed to incorporate so-called *output expansion* where the networks provide a prediction not only for the secondary structure category corresponding to a single (central) amino acid in the input window, but simultaneous predictions for the neighboring residues as well.

This idea is related to earlier ideas of constructing networks by training using *hints* that essentially further constrain the network weights, thereby leading to improved generalization.

Networks that are trained to predict currency exchange rates, e.g. dollar versus yen, may be improved if they also are forced to predict the American budget deficit, or similar features that are somehow related to the original output [1]. This idea must also be formulated as the learning-of-many-related-tasks-at-the-same-time approach, or multitask learning [115]. A network learning many related tasks at the same time can use these tasks as inductive bias for one another and thus learn better.

In protein secondary structure, it is certainly true that the conformational categories for the adjacent residues represent information that is correlated to the category one wants to predict. Other hints could be, for example, the surface exposure of the residue (as calculated from the structure in PDB), or the hydrophobicity as taken from a particular hydrophobicity scale.

6.4 Prediction of Signal Peptides and Their Cleavage Sites

Signal peptides control the entry of virtually all proteins to the secretory pathway in both eukaryotes and prokaryotes [542, 207, 440]. They comprise the N–terminal part of the amino acid chain, and are cleaved off while the protein is translocated through the membrane.

Strong interest in automated identification of signal peptides and prediction of their cleavage sites has been evoked not only by the huge amount of unprocessed data available but also by the commercial need for more effective vehicles for production of proteins in recombinant systems. The mechanism for targeting a protein to the secretory pathway is believed to be similar in all organisms and for many different kinds of proteins [296]. But the identification problem is to some extent organism-specific, and NN-based prediction methods have therefore been most successful when Gram-positive and Gram-negative bacteria, and eukaryotes have been treated separately [404, 131]. Signal peptides from different proteins do not share a strict consensus sequence—in fact, the sequence similarity between them is rather low. However, they do share a common structure with a central stretch of 7–15 hydrophobic amino acids (the hydrophobic core), an often positively charged region in the N-terminal of the preprotein, and three to seven polar, but mostly uncharged, amino acids just before the cleavage site.

This (and many other sequence analysis problems involving "sites") can be tackled from two independent angles: either by prediction of the site itself or by classifying the amino acids in the two types of regions into two different categories. Here this would mean classifying all amino acids in the sequence as cleavage sites or noncleavage sites; since most signal peptides are below 40 amino acids in length, it makes sense to include only the first 60–80 amino acids in the analysis. Alternatively, the amino acids could be classified as belonging to the signal sequence or the mature protein. In the approach described below, the two strategies have been combined and found to contribute complementary information. While the prediction of functional sites often is fairly local and therefore works best using small windows, larger windows are often needed to obtain good prediction of regional functional assignment.

6.4.1   SignalP

In the SignalP prediction scheme [404], two types of networks provide different scores between 0 and 1 for each amino acid in a sequence. The output from the signal peptide/nonsignal peptide networks, the *S-score*, can be interpreted as an estimate of the probability of the position's belonging to the signal peptide, while the output from the cleavage site/noncleavage site networks, the *C-score*, can be interpreted as an estimate of the probability of the position's being the first in the mature protein (position +1 relative to the cleavage site).

In figure 6.5, two examples of the values of C- and S-scores for signal peptides are shown. A typical signal peptide with a typical cleavage site will yield curves like those shown in figure 6.5A, where the C-score has one sharp peak that corresponds to an abrupt change in S-score. In other words, the example has 100% correctly predicted positions, according to both C-score and S-score. Less typical examples may look like figure 6.5B, where the C-score has several peaks.

In this work the data were divided into five subsets, and five independent networks were selected based on cross-validation for each task (and for each organism class). The individual C- and S-scores were therefore obtained by averaging over these five networks. In the final implementation for the three classes of organisms, 15 networks are included for each score. The work on signal peptide prediction provides another example of the importance of postprocessing of the network outputs, and of how "intelligent" interpretation can significantly improve the overall performance.

The C-score problem was best solved by networks with asymmetric windows, that is, windows including more positions upstream than downstream of the cleavage site: 15 and 2–4 amino acids, respectively. This corresponds well with the location of the cleavage site pattern information when viewed as a signal peptide sequence logo [404]. The S-score problem, on the other hand, was overall best solved by symmetric windows, which not surprisingly are better at identifying the contrast between the compositional differences of signal peptides and of mature protein. For human and *E. coli* sequences, these

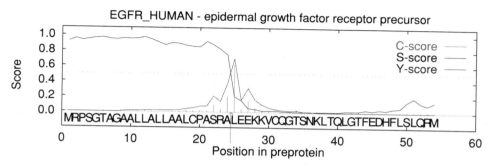

A

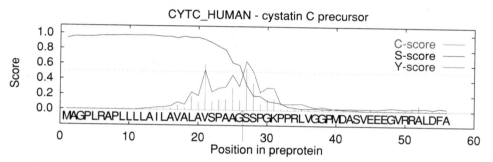

B

Figure 6.5: Examples of Predictions for Sequences with Verified Cleavable Signal Peptides. The values of the C-score (output from cleavage site networks), S-score (output from signal peptide networks), and Y-score (combined cleavage site score, $Y_i = \sqrt{C_i \Delta_d S_i}$) are shown for each position in the sequences. The C- and S-scores are averages over five networks trained on different parts of the data. The C-score is trained to be high for the position immediately *after* the cleavage site, that is, the first position in the mature protein. The true cleavage sites are marked with arrows. **A** is a sequence with all positions correctly predicted according to both C-score and S-score. **B** has two positions with C-score higher than 0.5—the true cleavage site would be incorrectly predicted when relying on the maximal value of the C-score alone, but the combined Y-score is able to predict it correctly.

windows were larger: 27 and 39 amino acids, respectively.

Since the sequences in most cases have only one cleavage site, it is not necessary to use as assignment criterion a fixed cutoff of, say, 0.5 when interpreting the C-score for single positions. The C-score networks may also be evaluated at the *sequence* level by assigning the cleavage site of each signal peptide to the position in the sequence with the maximal C-score and calculating the percentage of sequences with the cleavage site correctly predicted by this assignment. This is how the performance of the earlier weight matrix method [539] was calculated. Evaluating the network output at the sequence level improved the performance; even when the C-score had no peaks or several peaks above the cutoff value, the true cleavage site was often found at the position where the C-score was highest.

If there are several C-score peaks of comparable strength, the true cleavage site may often be found by inspecting the S-score curve in order to see which of the C-score peaks coincides best with the transition from the signal peptide to the nonsignal peptide region. The best way of combining the scores turned out to be a simple geometric average of the C-score and a smoothed derivative of the S-score. This combined measure has been termed the *Y-score*:

$$Y_i = \sqrt{C_i \Delta_d S_i}, \tag{6.2}$$

where $\Delta_d S_i$ is the difference between the average S-score of d positions before and d positions after position i:

$$\Delta_d S_i = \frac{1}{d} \left(\sum_{j=1}^{d} S_{i-j} - \sum_{j=0}^{d-1} S_{i+j} \right). \tag{6.3}$$

The Y-score gives a certain improvement in sequence level performance (percent correct) relative to the C-score, but the single-position performance (C_C) is not improved. An example in which the C-score alone gives a wrong prediction while the Y-score is correct is shown in figure 6.5B.

It is interesting that this method also can be used for detection of seemingly wrong assignments of the initiation methionine. Inspection of a number of long signal peptides deposited in SWISS-PROT has shown that such sequences often contain a second methionine 5–15 amino acids from the annotated N-terminus [422]. Figure 6.6 shows a SignalP prediction for the sequence of human angiotensinogen. In the N-terminal, this sequence has a surprisingly low S-score, but after the second methionine in the sequence it increases to a more reasonable level. The prediction strongly indicates that the translation initiation has been wrongly assigned for this sequence.

6.5 Applications for DNA and RNA Nucleotide Sequences

6.5.1 The Structure and Origin of the Genetic Code

Since the genetic code was first elucidated [407], numerous attempts have been made to unravel its potential underlying symmetries [216, 6, 509, 514, 125] and evolutionary history [168, 563, 294, 569]. The properties of the 20 amino acids and the similarities among them have played a key role in this type of

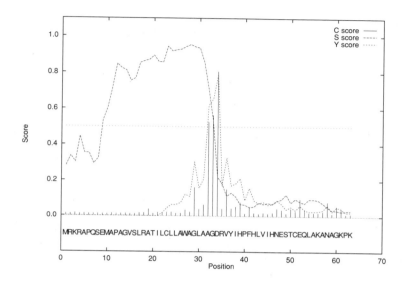

Figure 6.6: SignalP Prediction of the Sequence of ANGT_HUMAN, human angiotensinogen. The S-score (signal peptide score) has a high value for residues within signal peptides, while the C- and Y-scores (cleavage site scores) are high at position +1 immediately after possible cleavage sites. Note that the S-score is comparatively low for the region between the first Met and the second Met.

analysis. The codon assignments are correlated to the physical properties of the amino acids in a systematic and error-correcting manner. The three positions in the triplets associate to widely different features of the amino acids. The first codon position is correlated to amino acid biosynthetic pathways [569, 514], and to their evolution evaluated by synthetic "primordial soup" experiments [159, 478]. The second position is correlated to the hydrophatic properties of the amino acids [140, 566], and the degeneracy of the third position is related to the molecular weight or size of the amino acids [240, 514]. These features are used for error correction in two ways. First, the degeneration is correlated to the abundance of the amino acids in proteins, which lowers the chance that a mutation changes the amino acid [371]. Second, similar amino acids have similar codons, which lowers the chance that a mutation has a hazardous effect on the resulting protein structure [140, 216, 6].

In the neural network approach to studying the structure of the genetic code, the analysis is new and special in that it is unbiased and completely data-driven [524]. The neural network infers the structure directly from the mapping between codons and amino acids as it is given in the standard genetic code (figure 6.7). Hence, no a priori relationships are introduced between the

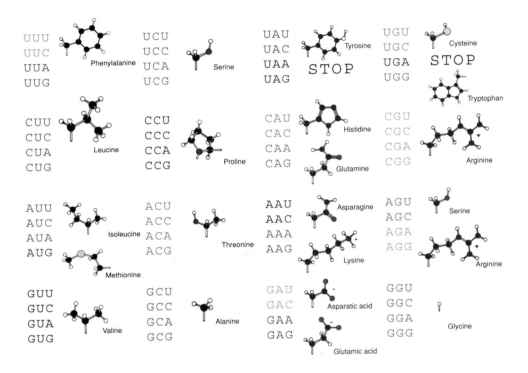

Figure 6.7: The Standard Genetic Code. Triplets encoding the same amino acid are shown in the same shade of gray.

nucleotides or amino acids.

In the network that learns the genetic code, the input layer receives a nucleotide triplet and outputs the corresponding amino acid. Thus the 64 different triplets are possible as input, and in the output layer the 20 different amino acids appear (see figure 6.8). Inputs and outputs are sparsely encoded; 12 units encode the input and 20 units encode the output.

Networks with three and four intermediate units were relatively easy to train; it was harder to obtain perfect networks with two intermediate units. The only way minimal networks (with two intermediates) could be found was by an adaptive training procedure [524]. For this task, at least, it was observed that the conventional backpropagation training scheme treating all training examples equally fails to find a minimal network, which is known to exist.

The standard technique for training feed-forward architectures is backpropagation; the aim is to get a low analog network error E but not necessarily

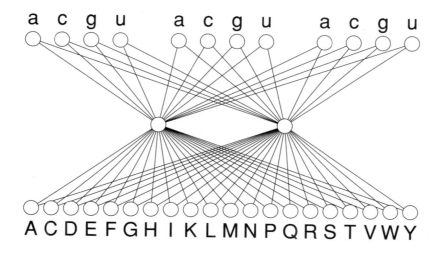

Figure 6.8: Architecture of the Neural Network Trained to Learn the Standard Genetic Code. The network had 12 input units, two (or more) intermediate units, and 20 output units. The input layer encoded the nucleotide triplets as a binary string comprising three blocks of four bits, with adenine as 0001, cytosine as 0010, guanine as 0100, and uracil as 1000. The output layer encoded the amino acids with alanine as 10000000000000000000, cysteine as 01000000000000000000, ... Intermediate and output units had real-valued activities in the range between 0.0 and 1.0. The network parameters ($12 \cdot 2 + 2 \cdot 20 = 64$ weights and $2 + 20 = 22$ thresholds) were adjusted using the backpropagation algorithm [456] in a balanced form, where for each codon the training cycle was repeated in inverse proportion to the number of codons associated with the amino acid. Thus each of the leucine codons received on the average six times less training than the single methionine codon. During training, the criterion for successful learning was that the activity of the corresponding output unit should be larger than all others (the winner-take-all principle). In each training epoch the codons were presented to the network in random order.

a low classification error $\mathcal{E}_C$. This often makes it difficult to train networks down to $\mathcal{E}_C = 0.0$. In the literature, several training strategies have been pursued in order to obtain low classification errors. First, a simple but effective modification is to use a high learning rate for wrongly classified examples and a low learning rate for correctly classified examples. In the first phase of training, most examples are wrongly classified. This results in a high learning rate and therefore a fast decrease in network error $\mathcal{E}$. Later in training only the hard cases have a high learning rate. Thereby noise is introduced and jumps in the network error level to lower plateaus are favored.

Second, another effective procedure is to modify the presentation frequencies for the different categories so that a more balanced situation results. In the case of the genetic code this means that the same number of codons should be presented for each amino acid, no matter how many appear in the original code. Thus the single methionine codon should be included in the set six times and each cysteine codon should appear three times. The training set is then enlarged from 61 to 186 codons, tripling the training time for each epoch.

Third, an even more powerful strategy for obtaining a low classification error will be to have an adaptive training set, where the training examples are included or excluded after determining whether they are classified correctly by the current network. Such a scheme may introduce more noise in the learning process, which helps to avoid local minima. Introducing noise in the training is usually done by updating the network after each example rather than after each epoch. The next step is to shuffle the examples within each epoch prior to presentation. Using the adaptive procedure makes the epoch concept disappear, and each example is chosen at random from a pool with subsequent updating of the network. To increase the frequency of a hard-to-learn example, each example misclassified is put into the pool of examples, replacing one in the pool. To ensure that no examples are lost, only part of the pool is open for exchange. In the long run this procedure ensures that every example is shown and hard-to-learn examples are shown more often. In summary, the procedure is as follows:

1. Initialize the first and second parts of the pool with the training examples.

2. Choose an example randomly from the pool and present it to the network.

3. Train the network by backpropagation.

4. If the example is classified correctly, then go to 2.

5. If the example is misclassified, put it in the second part of the pool, thus replacing a randomly chosen example.

6. Repeat until $\mathcal{E}_C = 0$.

A network with two hidden units was successfully trained using this adaptive training scheme. During training, the network develops an internal representation of the genetic code mapping. The internal representation of the structure of the code is given by the activities of the two intermediate units, which may easily be visualized in the plane. The network transforms the 61 12-component vectors representing the amino acid encoding codons into 61 points in the plane, which, provided the network has learned the code, may be separated linearly by the 20 output units.

Figure 6.9 shows how the network arrives at the internal representation by adaptive backpropagation training. Each codon is mapped into a point (x, y)

in the plane indicated by the one-letter abbreviation for the matching amino acid. During training, the 61 points follow trajectories emerging from their prelearning positions close to the center ($x \approx 0.5, y \approx 0.5$) and ending at their final locations on the edge of a slightly distorted circular region.

The network identifies three groups of codons corresponding to three parts of the circular region (figure 6.9). Subsequently it was discovered that these groups divide the GES scale of transfer free energies [166] into three energy intervals, $[-3.7 : -2.6]$, $[-2.0 : 0.2]$, and $[0.7 : 12.3]$ (kcal/mol), respectively (see table 6.2). The only case that does not conform to the network grouping is the extremely hydrophilic amino acid arginine, which is known to be an exception in the context of the genetic code [319, 509, 514]. The number of arginine codons is in conflict with its abundance in naturally occurring proteins [470]. Arginine has been suggested as a late addition to the genetic code [294]. In alpha-helices it has a surprising tendency to be at the same side as hydrophobic residues [136]. The network locates arginine in the intermediate group. The trained network maps the three stop codons to (x, y) positions in the vicinity of adjacent codons in the code: UAA, UAG close to Tyr (Y), and UGA close to Trp (W) (points not shown).

The fact that the network needs at least two intermediate units to learn the genetic code mapping means that the code is inherently nonlinear. In classification terms this means that the genetic code is nonlinearly separable. This holds true for the (otherwise sensible) sparse encoding of the nucleotides used by most workers. Computerized analysis of DNA or pre-mRNA striving to relate patterns in the nucleotides to amino acids [100, 102] will therefore be a nonlinear problem regardless of the algorithm applied. It is quite easy to prove that the genetic code is indeed nonlinear, since all serine codons cannot be separated linearly from the other codons.

The weights of the trained network have, unlike many other neural networks, a fairly comprehensible structure (figure 6.10). The size of the weights connecting the input units to the intermediates reflects the importance of particular nucleotides at specific codon positions. Interestingly, the second codon position has by far the largest weights, followed by the first and third positions, in agreement with earlier observations [424]. The two intermediate units to a large extent share the discrimination tasks between them; the unit to the left is strongly influenced by A or G at the second codon position, and the unit to the right, by C or U. At the first codon position A and C, and G and U, influence the two units, respectively. In the genetic code C and U are equivalent at the third codon position for all amino acids, and similarly for A and G with the exception of three amino acids (Ile, Met, and Trp). The network handles this equivalence by having positive and negative weights at the third codon position for the two pairs.

The rationale behind the correlation between the second position and the

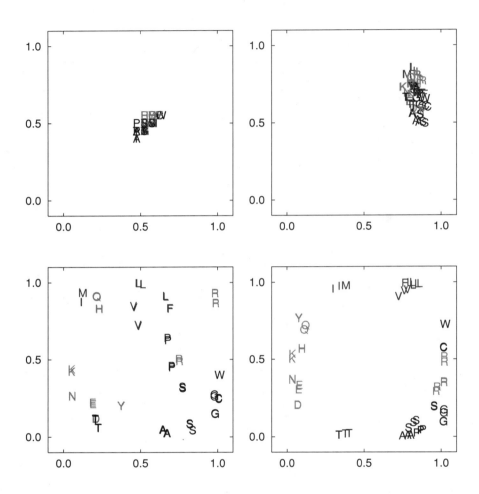

Figure 6.9: Hidden Unit Activities in the Genetic Code Neural Network. Each plot shows the two real-valued activities for all 61 amino acid encoding triplets in the code. In the untrained network with randomly assigned weights, all 61 points are located near the center of the square; after seven epochs the points have moved into a transient local minimum, where the activities of the intermediate units are close to 1 and the activities of all the output units are close to 0; at 30 epochs the groups have started to segregate but are still mixed; finally, at 13,000 epochs the network positions the 61 codons in groups on the edge of the circular region. After the four epochs shown, the number of correctly classified codons was 2, 6, 26, and 61, respectively.

Amino acid	Water-oil	Codons					
Phe	−3.7	UUU	UUC				
Met	−3.4	AUG					
Ile	−3.1	AUU	AUC	AUA			
Leu	−2.8	UUA	UUG	CUU	CUC	CUA	CUG
Val	−2.6	GUU	GUC	GUA	GUG		
Cys	−2.0	UGU	UGC				
Trp	−1.9	UGG					
Ala	−1.6	GCU	GCC	GCA	GCG		
Thr	−1.2	ACU	ACC	ACA	ACG		
Gly	−1.0	GGU	GGC	GGA	GGG		
Ser	−0.6	UCU	UCC	UCA	UCG	AGU	AGC
Pro	0.2	CCU	CCC	CCA	CCG		
Tyr	0.7	UAU	UAC				
His	3.0	CAU	CAC				
Gln	4.1	CAA	CAG				
Asn	4.8	AAU	AAC				
Glu	8.2	GAA	GAG				
Lys	8.8	AAA	AAG				
Asp	9.2	GAU	GAC				
Arg	12.3	CGU	CGC	CGA	CGG	AGA	AGG

Table 6.2: The amino acids and their transfer free energies in kcal/mol as given by the GES scale [166]. The GES scale separates codons with uracil and adenine at the second codon position from each other, leaving as an intermediate class amino acids with cytosine and guanine. The transfer free energy values are computed by considering a hydrophobic term based on the surface area of the groups involved, and two hydrophilic terms accounting for polar contributions arising from hydrogen bond interactions and the energy required to convert the charged side chains to neutral species at pH 7.

hydrophobicity of the amino acids may, in addition to the obvious advantage of minimizing the likelihood of mutation or mistranslation events changing a hydrophobic amino acid into a hydrophilic one [538, 409, 87], be more fundamental. In the early version of the genetic code, classes of codons coded for classes of amino acids [562]. Mostly these classes were purely related to the problem of folding a polypeptide chain in an aqueous environment. Lipid membranes, which may be phylogenetically older than the cytoplasm [316, 73, 117, 76], have not played a major role in the literature on the early protein synthesis apparatus. The problem of understanding the origin of cells is often dismissed by stating that "somehow" primitive ribosomes and genes became enclosed by a lipid membrane [117]. In scenarios described by Blobel and Cavalier-Smith [73, 117], genes and ribosomes associated with the surface of liposome-like vesicles where a mechanism for the cotranslational in-

Figure 6.10: A Graphical Representation of the Input Unit Weights in the Trained Genetic Code Network. For each of the three codon positions the height of the letters indicates the size of the sum of the two weights connecting an input unit to the two intermediate units. If the sum is negative, the letters are upside down.

sertion of membrane proteins evolved. A segregation into genetic code classes founded on the amino acid properties in their relation to lipid environments may therefore also have been a basic necessity.

6.5.2 Eukaryotic Gene Finding and Intron Splice Site Prediction

Since the beginning of the 1980s a highly diverse set of methods has been developed for the problem of identifying protein-coding regions in newly sequenced eukaryotic DNA. Correct exon assignments may in principle be obtained by two independent approaches: prediction of the location of the alternating sequence of donor and acceptor sites, or classification of nucleotides—or continuous segments of nucleotides—as belonging to either the coding or the noncoding category.

Intron splice sites have a relatively confined local pattern spanning the range of 15–60 nucleotides; protein-coding regions (exons) are often much larger, having typical lengths of 100–150 nucleotides, an interval that is quite stable across a wide range of eukaryotic species. For both types of objects, the pattern strength or regularity is the major factor influencing the potential accuracy of their detection.

Some intron splice site sequences are very close to the "center of gravity" in a sequence space [344], while others deviate considerably from the consensus pattern normally described in textbooks on the subject (see Figure 1.10 for a sequence logo of donor sites from the plant *Arabidopsis thaliana*). Likewise, exon sequence may conform strongly or weakly to the prevailing reading frame pattern in a particular organism. The strength of the coding region pattern may be correlated, for example, to the gene expression level or the amino acid composition of the protein. The codon usage specific to a given organism and a given gene in most cases creates a fairly strong 3-periodicity with biased frequencies at the three codon positions [525, 305]. In some organisms, such as bacteria, the bias is largest on the first position, while in mammals the bias is strongest on the third position (see figure 6.11). Proteins rich in proline, serine, and arginine residues will often be associated with bad reading frames because they have codons that deviate from the prevailing choices on the first and second codon positions. However, in the context of the mRNA translation by the ribosome, the strength of a reading frame should be quantified by inspecting the three different possibilities, not just the average codon usage statistics [525]. Figure 6.11 shows the overall bias in the nucleotide distribution on the three codon positions in triplets from coding regions in genes from *Enterobacteria*, mammals, *Caenorhabditis elegans*, and the plant *A. thaliana*, respectively.

In a study using neural networks for the prediction of intron splice sites, it was observed [102] that there is a kind of compensating relationship between the strength of the donor and acceptor site pattern and the strength of the pattern present in the associated coding region. Easily detectable exons may allow weaker splice sites, and vice versa. In particular, very short exons, which usually carry a weak signal as coding regions, are associated with strong splice

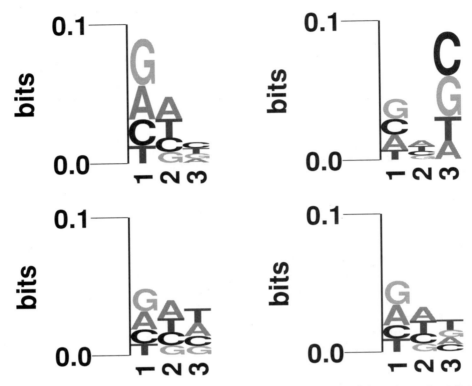

Figure 6.11: Sequence Logos of Codons from Four Different Types of Organisms: (top) Enterobacteria and Mammals; (bottom) *C. elegans* and *A. thaliana.* While bacterial genes have a strong bias on the first codon position, the bias is strongest on the third codon position in mammals.

sites. This relation is also moderated by the distribution for the intron length, which varies considerably from organism to organism.

The correlation between splice site *strength* and "exonness" has been exploited in the artificial neural network-based prediction scheme known as Net-Gene [102], where two local splice site networks are used jointly with an exon prediction network equipped with a large window of 301 nucleotides. This scheme considerably reduces the number of false positive predictions and, at the same time, enhances the detection of weak splice sites by lowering the prediction threshold when the signal from the exon prediction network is sharp in the transition region between coding and noncoding sequence segments (see section 6.5.4).

6.5.3 Examples of Gene Structure Prediction by Sensor Integration

The use of a combination of sensors for detection of various signals related to a complex object has a long history in the theory of pattern recognition. Several schemes have been developed in which NN components play a major role, earliest the GRAIL and GeneParser systems.

The GRAIL system is an NN-based example of sensor integration used for coding-region recognition. The first network, from 1991, combined into a joint prediction seven measures known to provide a nontrivial indication of the presence of a coding region [528]. The later GRAIL II coding system considers discrete coding-region candidates, rather than using a fixed-size sliding window for evaluation of the coding potential, as in the earlier system [529]. As one of the input features, the network is provided with a measure of the length of the coding-region candidate, and can therefore correlate the other measures specifically to known differences between short and long exons.

The performance of the GRAIL system has evolved over the years primarily by the development of more complex sensor indicators, and not by more sophisticated neural networks. The MLP with one hidden layer trained by backpropagation remains the same. Among the most advanced indicators is a fifth-order nonhomogeneous Markov chain for 6-mer based evaluation of the coding potential in DNA [529]. The GRAIL system not only performs recognition of coding-region candidates, but also gene modeling (exon assembly), detection of indel errors and suggestion of likely corrections, detection of CpG islands, and recognition of PolII promoters and polyadenylation sites.

In the GeneParser scheme [494] intron/exon and splice site indicators are weighted by a neural network to approximate the log-likelihood that a sequence segment exactly represents an intron or exon (first, internal, or last). A dynamic programming algorithm is then applied to this data to find the combination of introns and exons that maximizes the likelihood function. Using this method, suboptimal solutions can be generated rapidly, each of them the optimum solution containing a given intron–exon junction. The authors also quantified the robustness of the method to substitution and frame-shift errors and showed how the system can be optimized for performance on sequences with known levels of sequencing errors.

Dynamic programming (DP) is applied to the problem of precisely identifying internal exons and introns in genomic DNA sequences. The GeneParser program first scores the sequence of interest for splice sites and for the following intron- and exon-specific content measures: codon usage, local compositional complexity, 6-tuple frequency, length distribution, and periodic asymmetry. This information is then organized for interpretation by DP. GeneParser employs the DP algorithm to enforce the constraints that introns and exons must be adjacent and nonoverlapping, and finds the highest-scoring combination of introns and exons subject to these constraints. Weights for the various classification procedures are determined by training a simple feed-forward neural network to maximize the number of correct predictions. In a pilot study, the system has been trained on a set of 56 human gene fragments containing 150 internal exons in a total of 158,691 bps of genomic sequence. When tested against the training data, GeneParser precisely identifies 75% of the exons and correctly predicts 86% of coding nucleotides as coding, while only 13% of non-exon bps were predicted to be coding. This corresponds to a correlation coefficient for exon prediction of 0.85. Because of the simplicity of the network weighting scheme, generalized performance is nearly as good as with the training set.

6.5.4   Prediction of Intron Splice Sites by Combining Local and Global Sequence Information

The complementarity of the splice site strength and coding region intensity was discovered in an NN study where prediction of sites was combined with a coding/noncoding prediction in the NetGene method [102]. The first Net-Gene program from 1991 was trained exclusively on human sequences, and has been available on the Internet since 1992 (netgene@cbs.dtu.dk). In this method three separate networks work together: the assignment thresholds of two local donor and acceptor sites' networks are regulated by a global network performing a coding/noncoding prediction. The three networks use windows of 15, 41, and 301 bp, respectively. Instead of a fixed threshold for splice site assignment in the local networks, the sharpness of the transition of the global exon-to-intron signal regulates the actual threshold. The aim was to improve the ratio between true and false donor and acceptor sites assigned. In regions with abruptly decreasing exon activity, donor sites should be "promoted" and acceptor sites suppressed, and vice versa in regions with abruptly increasing exon activity. In regions with only small changes in exon activity—that is, where the level was constantly high (inside exons) and where it was constantly low (inside introns, in untranslated exons and in the intergenic DNA)—a rather high confidence level in the splice site assignment should be demanded in order to suppress false positives.

To detect edges in the coding/noncoding output neuron levels, essentially the first derivative of the coding output neuron activity was computed by summing activities to the right of a given point and subtracting the corresponding sum for the left side, then dividing this difference by the number of addends. In order to reduce the number of cases where the individual sums covered both intron and exon regions, half the average length of the internal exons in the training set, 75 bp, was used as the scope when summing, giving derivatives close to +1 in the 3' end of introns and close to −1 in the 5' end for perfect coding/noncoding assignments.

In figure 6.12 an average-quality example of the coding/noncoding signal, the derivative Δ, and the forest of donor and acceptor site signals exceeding an activity of 0.25 are given for the GenBank entry HUMOPS, taken from the test set used in the study [102]. Note that some regions inside introns and in the nontranscribed part of the sequences show exonlike behavior.

In compiling algorithms that regulate the splice site assignment levels, the following expressions were used to assess possible weightings between the strength of the exon signal and the output, O, from the separate splice site networks: if

$$O_{\text{donor}} > e_D \Delta + c_D \tag{6.4}$$

assign splicing donor site, and if

$$O_{\text{acceptor}} > e_A \Delta + c_A \tag{6.5}$$

assign splicing acceptor site, where Δ was computed as described above. The constants c_D and c_A are equivalent to the ordinary cutoff assignment parameters, whereas e_D and e_A control the impact of the exon signal. Together the four constants control the relative strengths between the donor site and the coding/noncoding network on one side, and between the acceptor site and the coding/noncoding network on the other.

The four constants were optimized in terms of correlation coefficients and the percentage of true splice sites detected [102]. Compared with other methods, the number of false positives assigned was much lower—by a factor between 2 and 30, depending on the required level of detection of true sites—when the cutoff assignment level was controlled by the exon signal.

The general picture concerning the confidence levels on the splice site prediction and the coding/noncoding classification (as measured by the output neuron activities) was that exons smaller than 75 bp had rather weak exon output neuron levels (0.3–0.6) but relatively strong donor and acceptor site output neuron levels (0.7–1.0). Conversely, longer internal exons in general had rather sharp edges in the output neuron activities, with donor and acceptor site activities being somewhat weaker.

A similar method has been developed for prediction of splice sites in the plant *Arabidopsis thaliana*, NetPlantGene [245]. This plant model organism was the first for which the complete genome was sequenced, as the size of its genome (400Mbp) is very moderate compared with many other plants (see figure 1.2).

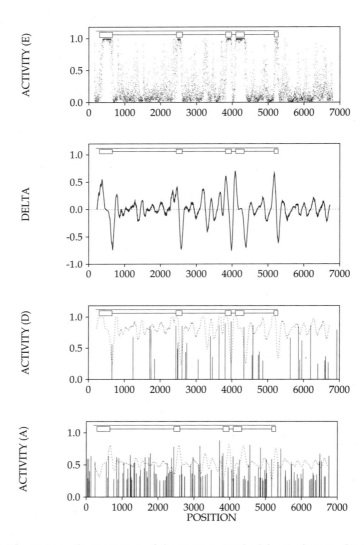

Figure 6.12: The Steps in the Operation of the NetGene Method for Prediction of Splice Sites on the Test Gene with GenBank Locus HUMOPS. A. (Top) Analog output from the output neuron in the coding/noncoding network, showing strong exon signals from the correct exons. Inside the introns and in the terminal nontranscribed part of the sequence, a number of regions show exonlike behavior. The boxes correspond to correct exons and the joining lines to introns, whereas the top line gives the extension of the transcript. B. The derivative of the analog coding/noncoding output. C. The donor site activities (≥ 0.25) from the donor site assignment network. D. (Bottom) The acceptor site activities (≥ 0.25) from the acceptor site assignment network. The variable cutoff assignment level for a 90% detection of true splice sites is shown as a dashed curve on the pin diagrams (3 and 4).

6.5.5 Doing Sequence Analysis by Inspecting the Order in Which Neural Networks Learn

Neural networks are well known for their ability to generalize from a set of examples to new cases. Recently another ability of the method has been recognized: important information on the internal structure of the training material can be obtained if the learning process is monitored carefully. A network does not learn the examples in random order; depending on the number of adjustable parameters, it will learn the linearly separable part of the data first and outliers that deviate from the prevailing patterns later. This was clear from the early work of Qian and Sejnowski [437] and from other work on alpha-helix prediction in proteins [244]. The training proceeds in two phases: a linearly separable part of the data is learned fast, while other examples are correctly classified by the network more slowly. In this later phase the network will often unlearn some of the examples learned in the first phase. It is obvious from the work on the genetic code described above that a similar, but more complex, picture emerges here.

The order in which a set of examples is learned first by a network reveals information on the relative nonlinearity of each single example, and hence on the pattern of regularity present in the complete set [97, 98]. This in turn can be used to identify abnormal examples that deviate strongly from the prevailing patterns, either due to the application of unnatural classification strategies or simply due to classification errors introduced randomly, without systematics. The neural network method provides a means for obtaining a high-quality feedback on low-quality data with a sound balance between abilities to model complex systematics and to detect deviations from ill-defined rules.

The ability to find errors has been exploited in many different projects, not only in the area of sequence analysis but also in other cases where input data may be assigned to an incorrect category. In the work using networks to predict intron splice sites, it was described in detail how to find errors produced by very different sources [100, 101]. During a training session the success of the learning was monitored in two different ways, one taking the training set as a whole and the other inspecting each window configuration separately. The performance on the training set as a whole is quantified by monitoring the decrease in the total network error E. If E remains constant for a large number of presentations of the training set, it indicates that no improvement can be gained from further training. The network has learned a single window configuration if the real–numbered activity of the output neuron fell on the same side of a cutoff value as the training target of the window configuration in question. The cutoff value separating the two output category assignments was mostly chosen to be 0.5. Thus, at any moment during training, an objective criterion for successful learning points uniquely to those inputs not being

Epoch	GenBank Locus	Sequence
1	HUMA1ATP	TACATCTTCTTTAAAGGTAAGGTTGCTCAACCA
1	HUMA1ATP	CCTGAAGCTCTCCAAGGTGAGATCACCCTGACG
1	HUMACCYBA	CCACACCCGCCGCCAGGTAAGCCCGGCCAGCCG
1	HUMACCYBA	CGAGAAGATGACCCAGGTGAGTGGCCCGCTACC
1	HUMACTGA	GCGCCCCAGACACCAGGTGAGTGGATGGCGCCG
1	HUMACTGA	AGAGAAGATGACTCAGGTGAGGCTCGGCCGACG
1	HUMACTGA	CACCATGAAGATCAAGGTGAGTCGAGGGGTTGG
1	HUMADAG	TCTTATACTATGGCAGGTAAGTCCATACAGAAG
1	HUMALPHA	CGTGGCTCTGTCCAAGGTAAGTGCTGGGCTACC
1	HUMALPI	CCTGGCTCTGTCCAAGGTAAGGGCTGGGCCACC
1	HUMALPPD	TGTGGCTCTGTCCAAGGTAAGTGCTGGGCTACC
1	HUMAPRTA	CCTGGAGTACGGGAAGGTAAGAGGGCTGGGGTG
1	HUMCAPG	GAAGGCTGCCTTCAAGGTAAGGCATGGGCATTG
1	HUMCFVII	GGAGTGTCCATGGCAGGTAAGGCTTCCCCTGGC
1	HUMCP21OH	CACCTTGGGCTGCAAGGTGAGAGGCTGATCTCG
1	HUMCP21OHC	CACCTTGGGCTGCAAGGTGAGAGGCTGATCTCG
1	HUMCS1	GTGGCAATGGCTCCAGGTAAGCGCCCCTAAAAT
1	HUMCSFGMA	AATGTTTGACCTCCAGGTAAGATGCTTCTCTCT
1	HUMCSPB	AAAGACTTCCTTTAAGGTAAGACTATGCACCTG
1	HUMCYC1A	GCTACGGACACCTCAGGTGAGCGCTGGGCCGGG
...	...	...
2	HUMA1ATP	CCTGGGACAGTGAATCGTAAGTATGCCTTTCAC
2	HUMA1ATP	AAAATGAAGACAGAAGGTGATTCCCCAACCTGA
2	HUMA1GLY2	CGCCACCCTGGACCGGGTGAGTGCCTGGGCTAG
2	HUMA1GLY2	GAGAGTACCAGACCCGGTGAGAGCCCCCATTCC
2	HUMA1GLY2	ACCGTCTCCAGATACGGTGAGGGCCAGCCCTCA
2	HUMA1GLY2	GGGCTGTCTTTCTATGGTAGGCATGCTTAGCAG
2	HUMA1GLY2	CACCGACTGGAAAAAGGTAAACGCAAGGGATTG
2	HUMACCYBA	GCGCCCCAGGCACCAGGTAGGGGAGCTGGCTGG
2	HUMACCYBA	CAGCCTTCCTTCCTGGGTGAGTGGAGACTGTCT
2	HUMACCYBA	CACAATGAAGATCAAGGTGGGTGTCTTTCCTGC
2	HUMACTGA	TCGCGTTTCTCTGCCGGTGAGCGCCCCGCCCCG
2	HUMADAG	CTTCGACAAGCCCAAAGTGAGCGCGCGCGGGGG
2	HUMADAG	TGTCCAGGCCTACCAGGTGGGTCCTGTGAGAAG
2	HUMADAG	CGAAGTAGTAAAAGAGGTGAGGGCCTGGGCTGG
...	...	...
11	HUMCS1	AACGCAACAGAAATCCGTGAGTGGATGCCGTCT
11	HUMGHN	AACACAACAGAAATCCGTGAGTGGATGCCTTCT
52	HUMHSP90B	CTCTAATGCTTCTGATGTAGGTGCTCTGGTTTC
80	HUMMETIF1	ACCTCCTGCAAGAAGAGTGAGTGTGAGGCCATC
112	HUMHSP90B	ATACCAGAGTATCTCAGTGAGTATCTCCTTGGC
113	HUMHST	GCGGACACCCGCGACAGTGAGTGGCGCGGCCAG
113	HUMLACTA	GACATCTCCTGTGACAGTGAGTAGCCCCTATAA
151	HUMKAL2	ATCGAACCAGAGGAGTGTACGCCTGGGCCAGAT
157	HUMCS1	CACCTACCAGGAGTTTGTAAGTTCTTGGGGAAT
157	HUMGHN	CACCTACCAGGAGTTTGTAAGCTCTTGGGGAAT
164	HUMALPHA	CAACATGGACATTGATGTGCCGACCCCCGGGCCA
622	HUMCFVII	CTGATCGCGGTGCTGGGTGGGTACCACTCTCCC
636	HUMADAG	CCTGGAACCAGGCTGAGTGAGTGATGGGCCTGG
895	HUMAPOCIB	TCCAGCAAGGATTCAGGTTGTTGAGTGCTTGGG
970	HUMALPHA	CGGGCCAAGAAAGCAGGTGGAGCTGGGGCCCGG
2114	HUMAPRTA	ATCGACTACATCGCAGGCGAGTGCCAGTGGCCG

Table 6.3: Donor Site Window Configurations Learned Early and Late in the Course of Training. The applied network was small (nine nucleotides in the window, two hidden units, and one output unit), and it was trained on small 33bp segments surrounding the 331 splice sites in part I of the data set. Shown is the training epoch at which a configuration was assigned that spliced donor correctly by the network, its GenBank locus, and the nucleotide context surrounding the central G. Segments with large deviations from the standard donor site consensus sequence, $\frac{C}{A}$AG/GT$\frac{G}{A}$AGT, were learned only after a relatively large number of presentations.

classified correctly.

Table 6.3 shows how a small network with limited resources learns the donor sites. Many of them are learned quickly, while others require a considerable number of epochs. By examining the unlearnable window configurations, it was shown that a surprisingly large number of wrongly assigned donor sites could be detected. They appear in the public databases due to insufficient proofreading of the entries, but also due to experimental errors and erroneous interpretation of experiments. Information about the degree of regularity of, for example, donor site window configurations could be obtained by monitoring the course of the training. For the donor site assignment problem, window configurations learned early in the training process showed stronger conformity to the standard 5' consensus sequence ^C_AAG/GT^G_AAGT than those learned late.

6.6   Prediction Performance Evaluation

Over the years different means for evaluating the accuracy of a particular prediction algorithm have been developed [31]. Some prediction methods are optimized so as to produce very few false positives, others to produce very few false negatives, and so on. Normally it is of prime interest to ensure, for any type of prediction algorithm, that the method will be able to perform well on novel data that have not been used in the process of constructing the algorithm. That is, the method should be able to generalize to new examples from the same data domain.

It is often relevant to measure accuracy of prediction at different levels. In signal peptide prediction, for example, accuracy may be measured by counting how many *sequences* are correctly classified as signal peptides or nonsecretory proteins, instead of counting how many residues are correctly predicted to belong to a signal peptide. Similarly, protein secondary structure may be evaluated at the mean per-chain level, or at the per-amino acid level.

At higher levels, however, the measures tend to be more complicated and problem-specific. In the signal peptide example, it is also relevant to ask how many signal peptide sequences have the position of the cleavage site correctly predicted. In gene finding, a predicted exon can have have both ends correct, or only overlap to some extent. Burset and Guigo [110] have defined four simple measures of gene-finding accuracy at the exon level—sensitivity, specificity, "missing exons", and "wrong exons"—counting only predictions that are completely correct or completely wrong. For secondary structure prediction, this approach would be too crude, since the borders of structure elements (helices and sheets) are not precisely defined. Instead, the segment overlap measure (SOV) can be applied [454, 580]. This is a set of segment-based heuristic evaluation measures in which a correctly predicted segment position can give maximal score even though the prediction is not identical to the assigned segment. The score punishes broken predictions strongly, such as two predicted helices where only one is observed compared to one too small unbroken helix. In this manner the uncertainty of the assignment's exact borders is reflected in the evaluation measure. As this example illustrates, a high-level accuracy measure can become rather *ad hoc* when the precise nature of the prediction problem is taken into consideration.

For the sake of generality, we will therefore focus our attention on single residue/nucleotide assessment measures. For the secondary structure problem, consider an amino acid sequence of length N. The structural data **D** available for the comparison is the secondary structure assignments **D** = $d_1, \ldots, d_N$. For simplicity, we will first consider the dichotomy problem of two alternative classes, for instance α-helix versus non-α-helix. In this case, the d_is are in general equal to 0 or 1. We can also consider the case where d_i has a value between 0 and 1, for example representing the surface exposure of amino acids, or the probability or degree of confidence, reflecting the uncertainty of our knowledge of the correct assignment at the corresponding position. The analysis for the multiple-class case, corresponding for example to three states, α-helices, β-sheets, and coil, is very similar. We now assume that our prediction algorithm or model, outputs a prediction of the form **M** = $m_1, \ldots, m_N$. In general, m_i is a probability between 0 and 1 reflecting our degree of confidence in the prediction. Discrete 0/1 outputs, obtained for instance by thresholding or "winner-take-all" approaches, are also possible and fall within the theory considered here. The fundamental and general question we address is: How do we assess the accuracy of **M**, or how do we compare **M** to **D**?

A variety of approaches have been suggested in different contexts and at different times and this may have created some confusion. The issue of prediction accuracy is strongly related to the frequency of occurrence of each class. In protein secondary structure prediction the non-helix class covers roughly 70% of the cases in natural proteins, while only 30% belong to the helix class. Thus a constant prediction of "non-helix" is bound to be correct 70% of the time, although it is highly non-informative and useless.

Below we review different approaches and clarify the connections among them and their respective advantages and disadvantages.

A fundamental simplifying assumption underlying all these approaches is that the amino acid positions are weighted and treated equally (the independence and equivalence assumption). Thus, we assume e.g. that there is no weighting scheme reducing the influence of positions near the N- or C-termini, or no built-in mechanism that takes into account the fact that particular predictions must vary somewhat "smoothly" (for instance, if a residue belongs to the α-helix category, its neighbors have a slightly higher chance of also being in the α-helix category). Conversely, when predicting functional sites such as intron splice sites, translation start sites, glycosylation, or phosphorylation sites, we assume the prediction of a site is either true or false, so that there is no reward for almost correctly placed sites.

Under the independence and equivalence assumption, if both **D** and **M** are binary, it is clear that their comparison can be entirely summarized by four numbers

- TP = number of times d_i is helix, m_i is helix (true positive)

- TN = the number of times d_i is non-helix, m_i is non-helix (true negative)

- FP = the number of times d_i is non-helix, m_i is helix (false positive)

- FN = the number of times d_i is helix, m_i is non-helix (false negative)

satisfying $TP + TN + FP + FN = N$. When **D** and/or **M** are not binary, then of course the situation is more complex and four numbers do not suffice to summarize the situation. When **M** is not binary, binary predictions can still be obtained by using cutoff thresholds. The numbers TP, TN, FP, and FN will then vary with the threshold choice. The numbers TP, TN, FP, and FN are often arranged into a 2×2 contingency matrix,

	M	**M̄**
D	TP	FN
D̄	FP	TN

Even with four numbers alone, it is not immediately clear how a given prediction method fares. This is why many of the comparison methods aim at constructing a single number measuring the "distance" between **D** and **M**. But it must be clear from the outset that information is always lost in such a process, even in the binary case, i.e. when going from the four numbers above to a single one. In general, several different vectors (TP, TN, FP, FN) will yield the same distance. We now review several ways of measuring the performance of **M** and their merits and pitfalls.

6.7 Different Performance Measures

6.7.1 Percentages

The first obvious approach is to use percentages derived from TP, TN, FP, and FN. For instance, Chou and Fasman [128, 129] used the percentage of correctly predicted helices

$$PCP(\mathbf{D},\mathbf{M}) = 100\frac{TP}{TP + FN}, \tag{6.6}$$

which is the same as the sensitivity (see section 6.7.9) expressed as a percentage. This number alone provides no information whatsoever about false positives. It can be complemented by the percentage of correctly predicted non-helices

$$PCN(\mathbf{D},\mathbf{M}) = 100\frac{TN}{TN + FP}. \tag{6.7}$$

The average of the previous two numbers has been used in the literature [128, 129] and is often called Q_α. While Q_α is a useful indicator, it can be misleading [549] and can be computed only if both $\mathbf{D}$ and $\mathbf{M}$ are binary. Intuitively, any single number that is constructed using only two numbers out of the four (TP, TN, FP, FN) is bound to be highly biased in some trivial way. If the two numbers are TP and FP, for instance, then any two situations (TP, TN, FP, FN) and (TP, TN', FP, FN') lead to the same score regardless of how different they may be.

6.7.2 Hamming Distance

In the binary case, the Hamming distance between $\mathbf{D}$ and $\mathbf{M}$ is defined by

$$HD(\mathbf{D},\mathbf{M}) = \sum_i |d_i - m_i|. \tag{6.8}$$

This sum is obviously equal to the total number of errors $FP + FN$. Thus it is equivalent to a single percentage measure. This distance does not take into account the proportion of examples that belong to a given class. It becomes less and less useful as this proportion moves away from 50%. In the non purely binary case, the Hamming distance is called the L^1 distance.

6.7.3 Quadratic "Distance"

The quadratic or Euclidean or LMS (least mean square) "distance" is defined by

$$Q(\mathbf{D},\mathbf{M}) = (\mathbf{D} - \mathbf{M})^2 = \sum_i (d_i - m_i)^2. \tag{6.9}$$

Strictly speaking, a proper distance is defined by taking the square root of the above quantity (see the L^2 distance in the next section). In the purely binary case, the quadratic distance reduces to the Hamming distance and is again equal to $FP + FN$. This quantity has the advantage of being defined for non-binary variables, and it is often associated with a negative log-likelihood approach for a Gaussian model of the form

$$P(d_i|m_i) = \frac{1}{\sigma\sqrt{2\pi}} \exp(-(d_i - m_i)^2/2\sigma^2) \qquad (6.10)$$

where σ acts as a scaling factor with respect to $Q(\mathbf{D}, \mathbf{M})$. For binary variables, the quadratic distance is identical to the Hamming distance. The main drawback is that the Gaussian model is often not relevant for prediction problems and the value of the quadratic distance again poorly reflects the proportion of positions that belongs to a given class. Another problem is that the LMS distance has a limited dynamic range due to the fact that m_i and d_i are between 0 and 1. This is not ideal for learning algorithms where large error signals can be used to accelerate the learning process. A logarithmic variation on the LMS distance that obviates this problem is given by

$$LQ(\mathbf{D}, \mathbf{M}) = -\sum_i \log[1 - (d_i - m_i)^2]. \qquad (6.11)$$

This modified error function has been used in several neural network implementations; see for example [99, 245, 236].

6.7.4 L^p Distances

More generally, the L^P distance is defined by

$$LP(\mathbf{D}, \mathbf{M}) = [\sum_i |d_i - m_i|^p]^{1/p}. \qquad (6.12)$$

Such a distance applies of course to any numerical values. When $p = 1$ we find the Hamming distance, and when $p = 2$ we find the proper Euclidean distance. When $p \to \infty$, the L^∞ distance is the sup distance: $\max_i |d_i - m_i|$. This distance provides an upper bound associated with the worst case, but is not very useful in assessing the performance of a protein secondary structure prediction algorithm. Other values of p are rarely used in practice, and are of little help for assessing prediction performance in this context. In the binary case, the L^p distance reduces to $(FP + FN)^{1/p}$. For $p = 1$, this reduces again to the Hamming distance.

6.7.5 Correlation

One of the standard measures used by statisticians is the correlation coefficient, also called the Pearson correlation coefficient:

$$C(\mathbf{D}, \mathbf{M}) = \sum_i \frac{(d_i - \bar{d})(m_i - \bar{m})}{\sigma_{\mathbf{D}} \sigma_{\mathbf{M}}}, \tag{6.13}$$

where $\bar{d} = \sum d_i / N$ and $\bar{m} = \sum m_i / N$ are the averages and $\sigma_{\mathbf{D}}, \sigma_{\mathbf{M}}$ the corresponding standard deviations. In the context of secondary structure prediction, this is also known as the Matthews correlation coefficient in the literature since it was first used in [382]. The correlation coefficient is always between -1 and $+1$ and can be used with non-binary variables. It is a measure of how strongly the normalized variables $(d_i - \bar{d})/\sigma_{\mathbf{D}}$ and $(m_i - \bar{m})/\sigma_{\mathbf{M}}$ tend to have the same sign and magnitude. A value of -1 indicates total disagreement and $+1$ total agreement. The correlation coefficient is 0 for completely random predictions. Therefore it yields easy comparison with respect to a random baseline. If two variables are independent, then their correlation coefficient is 0. The converse in general is not true.

In vector form, the correlation coefficient can be rewritten as a dot product between normalized vectors

$$C(\mathbf{D}, \mathbf{M}) = \frac{(\mathbf{D} - \bar{d}\mathbf{1})(\mathbf{M} - \bar{m}\mathbf{1})}{\sqrt{(\mathbf{D} - \bar{d}\mathbf{1})^2}\sqrt{(\mathbf{M} - \bar{m}\mathbf{1})^2}} = \frac{\mathbf{DM} - N\bar{d}\bar{m}}{\sqrt{(\mathbf{D}^2 - N\bar{d}^2)(\mathbf{M}^2 - N\bar{m}^2)}}, \tag{6.14}$$

where $\mathbf{1}$ denotes the N-dimensional vector of all ones. As such, $C(\mathbf{D}, \mathbf{M})$ is related to the L^2 distance, but is not a distance itself since it can assume negative values. If the vectors $\mathbf{D}$ and $\mathbf{M}$ are normalized, then clearly $Q(\mathbf{D}, \mathbf{M}) = (\mathbf{D} - \mathbf{M})^2 = 2 - 2\mathbf{DM} = 2 - 2C(\mathbf{D}, \mathbf{M})$. Unlike some of the previous measures, the correlation coefficient has a global form rather than being a sum of local terms.

In the case where $\mathbf{D}$ and $\mathbf{M}$ consist of binary 0/1 vectors, we have $\mathbf{D}^2 = TP + FN$, $\mathbf{M}^2 = TP + FP$, $\mathbf{DM} = TP$, etc. With some algebra the sum above can be written as

$$C(\mathbf{D}, \mathbf{M}) = \frac{TP - N\bar{d}\bar{m}}{N\sqrt{\bar{d}\bar{m}(1 - \bar{d})(1 - \bar{m})}}. \tag{6.15}$$

Here the average number of residues in the helix class satisfies $\bar{d} = (TP + FN)/N$, and similarly for the predictions $\bar{m} = (TP + FP)/N$. Therefore

$$\begin{aligned}
C(\mathbf{D}, \mathbf{M}) &= \frac{N \times TP - (TP + FN)(TP + FP)}{\sqrt{(TP + FN)(TP + FP)(TN + FP)(TN + FN)}} \\
&= \frac{TP \times TN - FP \times FN}{\sqrt{(TP + FN)(TP + FP)(TN + FP)(TN + FN)}}. \tag{6.16}
\end{aligned}$$

The correlation coefficient uses all four numbers (TP, TN, FP, FN) and may often provide a much more balanced evaluation of the prediction than for instance the percentages. There are situations, however, where even the correlation coefficient is unable to provide a completely fair assessment. The correlation coefficient will, for example, be relatively high in cases where a prediction algorithm gives very few or no false positives, but at the same time very few true positives. One simple observation that will be useful in a later section is that C is symmetric with respect to FP and FN.

One interesting property of the correlation coefficient is that there is a simple approximate statistical test for deciding whether it is significantly better than zero, i.e. whether the prediction is significantly more correlated with the data than a random guess with the same $\bar{m}$ would be. If the chi-squared test is applied to the 2×2 contingency matrix containing TP, TN, FP, and FN, it is easy to show that the test statistic is $\chi^2 = N \times C^2(\mathbf{D}, \mathbf{M})$.

6.7.6 Approximate Correlation

Burset and Guigo [110] defined an "approximate correlation" measure to compensate for an alleged problem with the Matthews correlation coefficient: that it is not defined when any of the sums $TP + FN$, $TP + FP$, $TN + FP$, or $TN + FN$ reaches zero, e.g. if there are no positive predictions. Instead, they use the Average Conditional Probability (ACP), which is defined as

$$ACP = \frac{1}{4} \left[\frac{TP}{TP + FN} + \frac{TP}{TP + FP} + \frac{TN}{TN + FP} + \frac{TN}{TN + FN} \right] \qquad (6.17)$$

if all the sums are nonzero; otherwise, it is the average over only those conditional probabilities that are defined. The Approximate Correlation (AC) is a simple transformation of the ACP:

$$AC = 2 \times (ACP - 0.5). \qquad (6.18)$$

Like C, AC gives 1, 0, and -1 for perfect, random, and all-false predictions, respectively, and Burset and Guigó observe that it is close to the real correlation value.

However, the problem they intend to solve does not exist, since it is easy to show that C approaches 0 if any of the sums approaches 0. This also makes intuitive sense, since a prediction containing only one category is meaningless and does not convey any information about the data. On the contrary, it can be shown that the AC approach introduces an unfortunate discontinuity in this limit because of the deletion of undefined probabilities from the expression for ACP, so it does *not* give 0 for meaningless predictions. Since there is furthermore no simple geometrical interpretation for AC, it is an unnecessary approximation and we see no reason to encourage its use.

6.7.7 Relative Entropy

The relative entropy, or cross entropy, or KL (Kullback-Leibler) contrast between two probability vectors $\mathbf{X} = (x_1, \ldots, x_M)$ and $\mathbf{Y} = (y_1, \ldots, y_M)$ with $x_i, y_i \geq 0$ and $\sum x_i = \sum y_i = 1$ is defined as

$$H(\mathbf{X}, \mathbf{Y}) = \sum_{i=1}^{M} x_i \log \frac{x_i}{y_i} = -H(\mathbf{X}) - \sum_i x_i \log y_i \tag{6.19}$$

where $H(\mathbf{X}) = -\sum x_i \log x_i$ is the usual entropy. It has its roots in information theory [342, 341]. It is well known that $H(\mathbf{X}, \mathbf{Y})$ is always positive, convex in both its variables, and equal to 0 if and only if $\mathbf{X} = \mathbf{Y}$. Strictly speaking, it is not a distance, for instance because it is not symmetric. It is easy to construct a distance using a symmetrized version. In practice, however, this is rarely necessary and the form above is sufficient. If $\mathbf{Y} = \mathbf{X} + \epsilon$ is close to $\mathbf{X}$, then a simple Taylor expansion shows that

$$H(\mathbf{X}, \mathbf{X} + \epsilon) = -\sum_i x_i \left[\log(1 + \frac{\epsilon_i}{x_i}) \right] \approx \sum_i \frac{\epsilon_i^2}{x_i}. \tag{6.20}$$

In particular, if $\mathbf{X}$ is uniform, then in its neighborhood the relative entropy behaves like the LMS error.

Returning to the secondary structure prediction problem, we can then assess the performance of the prediction $\mathbf{M}$ by the quantity:

$$H(\mathbf{D}, \mathbf{M}) = \sum_{i=1}^{N} \left[d_i \log \frac{d_i}{m_i} + (1 - d_i) \log \frac{(1 - d_i)}{(1 - m_i)} \right]. \tag{6.21}$$

This is just the sum of the relative entropies at each position i. This form of course works perfectly well on non-binary data (for example, binding affinities), or when $\mathbf{D}$ alone is binary. When $\mathbf{M}$ is also binary, then the relative entropy has $FP + FN$ components that are infinite (it behaves like $H(\mathbf{D}, \mathbf{M}) \approx (FP + FN)\infty$) and cannot really be used.

6.7.8 Mutual Information

Consider two random variables X and Y with probability vectors $\mathbf{X} = (x_1, \ldots, x_M)$ and $\mathbf{Y} = (y_1, \ldots, y_K)$. Let Z be the joint random variable $Z = (X, Y)$ over the cartesian product with probability vector $\mathbf{Z}$. The mutual information $I(X, Y)$ or $I(\mathbf{X}, \mathbf{Y})$ between X and Y is defined as the relative entropy between Z and the product XY:

$$I(X, Y) = H(Z, XY). \tag{6.22}$$

As such it is always positive. It is easy to understand the mutual information in Bayesian terms: it represents the reduction in uncertainty of one variable when the other is observed, that is between the *prior* and *posterior distributions*. The uncertainty in X is measured by the entropy of its prior $H(X) = \sum x_i \log x_i$. Once we observe $y = y$, the uncertainty in X is the entropy of the posterior distribution, $H(X|y = y) = \sum_x P(X = x|y = y) \log P(X = x|y = y)$. This is a random variable that depends on the observation y. Its average over the possible ys is called the *conditional entropy*:

$$H(X|y) = \sum_y P(y)H(X|y = y).$$
(6.23)

Therefore the difference between the entropy and the conditional entropy measures the average information that an observation of y brings about X. It is straightforward to check that

$$I(X,y) = H(X) - H(X|y) = H(y) - H(y|X) = H(X) + H(y) - H(Z) = I(y,X)$$
(6.24)

or, using the corresponding distributions,

$$I(\mathbf{X},\mathbf{Y}) = H(\mathbf{X}) - H(\mathbf{X}|\mathbf{Y}) = H(\mathbf{Y}) - H(\mathbf{Y}|\mathbf{X}) = H(\mathbf{X}) + H(\mathbf{Y}) - H(\mathbf{Z}) = I(\mathbf{Y},\mathbf{X}).$$
(6.25)

Going back to the secondary structure problem, when $\mathbf{D}$ and $\mathbf{M}$ are both binary, the mutual information is measured by

$$
\begin{aligned}
I(\mathbf{D},\mathbf{M}) =\ & -H\left(\frac{TP}{N}, \frac{TN}{N}, \frac{FP}{N}, \frac{FN}{N}\right) \\
& - \frac{TP}{N} \log\left[\frac{TP + FP}{N}\frac{TP + FN}{N}\right] - \frac{FN}{N} \log\left[\frac{TP + FN}{N}\frac{TN + FN}{N}\right] \\
& - \frac{FP}{N} \log\left[\frac{TP + FP}{N}\frac{TN + FP}{N}\right] - \frac{TN}{N} \log\left[\frac{TN + FN}{N}\frac{TN + FP}{N}\right]
\end{aligned}
$$
(6.26)

or

$$
\begin{aligned}
I(\mathbf{D},\mathbf{M}) =\ & -H\left(\frac{TP}{N}, \frac{TN}{N}, \frac{FP}{N}, \frac{FN}{N}\right) \\
& - \frac{TP}{N} \log[\bar{d}\bar{m}] - \frac{FN}{N} \log[\bar{d}(1 - \bar{m})] \\
& - \frac{FP}{N} \log[(1 - \bar{d})\bar{m}] - \frac{TN}{N} \log[(1 - \bar{d})(1 - \bar{m})]
\end{aligned}
$$
(6.27)

(see also [549]), where $\bar{d} = (TP + FN)/N$ and $\bar{m} = (TP + FP)/N$ (as before), and

$$H(\frac{TP}{N}, \frac{TN}{N}, \frac{FP}{N}, \frac{FN}{N}) = -\frac{TP}{N}\log\frac{TP}{N} - \frac{TN}{N}\log\frac{TN}{N} - \frac{FP}{N}\log\frac{FP}{N} - \frac{FN}{N}\log\frac{FN}{N} \tag{6.28}$$

is the usual entropy. Like the correlation, the mutual information is a global measure rather than a sum of local terms. It is clear that the mutual information always satisfies $0 \le I(\mathbf{D}, \mathbf{M}) \le H(\mathbf{D})$. Thus in the assessment of prediction performance, it is customary to use the normalized mutual information [452, 454] coefficient

$$IC(\mathbf{D}, \mathbf{M}) = \frac{I(\mathbf{D}, \mathbf{M})}{H(\mathbf{D})} \tag{6.29}$$

with

$$H(\mathbf{D}) = -\frac{TP + FN}{N}\log\left[\frac{TP + FN}{N}\right] - \frac{TN + FP}{N}\log\left[\frac{TN + FP}{N}\right] \tag{6.30}$$

or, more briefly expressed, $H(\mathbf{D}) = -\bar{m}\log\bar{m} - (1 - \bar{m})\log(1 - \bar{m})$. The normalized mutual information satisfies $0 \le IC(\mathbf{D}, \mathbf{M}) \le 1$. When $IC(\mathbf{D}, \mathbf{M}) = 0$, then $I(\mathbf{D}, \mathbf{M}) = 0$ and the prediction is totally random ($\mathbf{D}$ and $\mathbf{M}$ are independent). When $IC(\mathbf{D}, \mathbf{M}) = 1$, then $I(\mathbf{D}, \mathbf{M}) = H(\mathbf{D}) = H(\mathbf{M})$ and the prediction is perfect. Like the correlation coefficient, the mutual information coefficient is a global measure rather than a sum of local terms. The mutual information is symmetric in FP and FN, but the mutual information coefficient is *not* symmetric because of its denominator.

6.7.9   Sensitivity and Specificity

In a two-class prediction case where the output of the prediction algorithm is continuous, the numbers TP, TN, FP, and FN depend on how the threshold is selected. Generally, there is a tradeoff between the number of false positives and the number of false negatives produced by the algorithm.

In a ROC curve (receiver operating characteristics) one may summarize such results by displaying for threshold values within a certain range the "hit rate" (sensitivity, $TP/(TP + FN)$) versus the "false alarm rate" (also known as false positive rate, $FP/(FP + TN)$). Typically the hit rate increases with the false alarm rate (see figure 8.10). Alternatively, one can also display the sensitivity ($TP/(TP + FN)$) versus the specificity ($TP/(TP + FP)$) in a similar plot or separately as a function of threshold in two different plots.

While the sensitivity is the probability of correctly predicting a positive example, the specificity as defined above is the probability that a positive prediction is correct. In medical statistics, the word "specificity" is sometimes used in a different sense, meaning the chance of correctly predicting a negative example: $TN/(FP + TN)$, or 1 minus the false positive rate. We prefer to refer to this as the sensitivity of the negative category.

If we write $x = TP/(TP + FN)$ for the sensitivity and $y = TP/(TP + FP)$ for the specificity, then

$$TP + FP = \frac{TP}{y} \qquad TP + FN = \frac{TP}{x}$$

$$TN + FP = N - (TP + FN) = \frac{Nx - TP}{x}$$

$$TN + FN = N - (TP + FP) = \frac{Ny - TP}{y} \tag{6.31}$$

provided $x \neq 0$ and $y \neq 0$, which is equivalent to $TP \neq 0$, a rather trivial case. In other words, we just reparameterize (TP, TN, FP, FN) using (TP, x, y, N). In this form, it is clear that we can substitute these values in (6.16) to derive, after some algebra, an expression for the correlation coefficient as a function of the specificity and the sensitivity:

$$C(\mathbf{D}, \mathbf{M}) = \frac{Nxy - TP}{\sqrt{(Nx - TP)(Ny - TP)}}. \tag{6.32}$$

Notice that this expression is entirely symmetric in x and y, i.e. in the specificity and sensitivity, or equivalently also in FP and FN, the number of false positives and false negatives. In fact, for a given TP, exchanging FP and FN is equivalent to exchanging x and y. A similar calculation can be done in order to re-express the mutual information of (6.27) or the mutual information coefficient of (6.29) in terms of TP, x, y, and N. The mutual information is entirely symmetric in x and y, or FP and FN (this is not true of the mutual information coefficient).

6.7.10 Summary

In summary, under the equivalence and independence assumption, if both $\mathbf{D}$ and $\mathbf{M}$ are binary, then all the performance information is contained in the numbers TP, TN, FP, and FN. Any measure of performance using a single number discards some information. The Hamming distance and the quadratic distance are identical. These distances, as well as the percentages and the L^p distances, are based on only two out of the four numbers TP, TN, FP, and FN. The correlation coefficient and the mutual information coefficient are based on all four parameters and provide a better summary of performance in this case. In the continuous case, the recommended measures are the correlation coefficient and the relative entropy.

Chapter 7

Hidden Markov Models: The Theory

7.1 Introduction

In the 1990s, only roughly a third of the newly predicted protein sequences show convincing similarity to other known sequences [80, 224, 155], using pairwise comparisons [11, 418]. This situation is even more unfortunate in the case of new, incomplete sequences or fragments. Large databases of fragments are becoming available as a result of various genome, cDNA, and other sequencing projects, especially those producing ESTs (expressed sequences tags) [200]. At the beginning of 1997, approximately half of GenBank consisted of fragment data. Such data cover a substantial fraction, if not all, of the expressed human genome. It is of course of great interest to recognize and classify such fragments, and recover any additional useful information.

A promising approach to improve the sensitivity and speed of current database-searching techniques has been to use consensus models built from multiple alignments of protein families [23, 52, 250, 334, 41, 38]. Unlike conventional pairwise comparisons, a consensus model can in principle exploit additional information, such as the position and identity of residues that are more or less conserved throughout the family, as well as variable insertion and deletion probabilities. All descriptions of sequence consensus, such as profiles [226], flexible patterns [52], and blocks [250], can be seen as special cases of the hidden Markov model (HMM) approach.

HMMs form another useful class of probabilistic graphical models used, over the past few decades, to model a variety of time series, especially in speech recognition [359, 439] but also in a number of other areas, such as ion channel recordings [48] and optical character recognition [357]. HMMs have also earlier been applied to problems in computational biology, including the modeling of coding/noncoding regions in DNA [130], of protein binding sites in DNA [352], and of protein superfamilies [553] (see also [351]). Only since the mid-1990s [334, 41], though, have HMMs been applied systematically to model, align, and analyze entire protein families and DNA regions, in combination with machine-learning techniques.

HMMs are closely related to, or special cases of, neural networks, stochastic grammars, and Bayesian networks. In this chapter we introduce HMMs directly and show how they can be viewed as a generalization of the multiple dice model of chapter 3. We develop the theory of HMMs—in particular the main propagation and machine-learning algorithms—along the lines of chapter 4. The algorithms are used in the following sections where we outline how to apply HMMs to biological sequences. Specific applications are treated in chapter 8, while relationships to other model classes are left for later chapters.

7.1.1 HMM Definition

A first-order discrete HMM is a stochastic generative model for time series defined by a finite set S of states, a discrete alphabet A of symbols, a probability transition matrix $T = (t_{ji})$, and a probability emission matrix $E = (e_{iX})$. The system randomly evolves from state to state while emitting symbols from the alphabet. When the system is in a given state i, it has a probability t_{ji} of moving to state j and a probability e_{iX} of emitting symbol X. Thus an HMM can be visualized by imagining that two different dice are associated with each state: an emission die and a transition die. The essential first-order Markov assumption of course is that the emissions and transitions depend on the current state only, and not on the past. Only the symbols emitted by the system are observable, not the underlying random walk between states; hence the qualification "hidden." The hidden random walks can be viewed as hidden or latent variables underlying the observations.

As in the case of neural networks, the directed graph associated with nonzero t_{ji} connections is also called the architecture of the HMM. Although this is not necessary, we will always consider that there are two special states, the *start* state and the *end* state. At time 0, the system is always in the start state. Alternatively, one can use a distribution over all states at time 0. The transition and emission probabilities are the parameters of the model. An equivalent theory can be developed by associating emissions with transitions, rather than with states. HMMs with continuous alphabets are also possible, but will not be considered here because of our focus on the discrete aspects of biological sequences.

A very simple example of an HMM is given in figure 7.1. In this example, we can imagine that there are two "DNA dice." The first die has an emission probability vector of ($e_{1A} = 0.25, e_{1C} = 0.25, e_{1G} = 0.25, e_{1T} = 0.25$). The second die has an emission probability vector of ($e_{2A} = 0.1, e_{2C} = 0.1, e_{2G} = 0.1, e_{2T} = 0.7$). The transition probabilities are given in the figure. Suppose that we now observe a sequence such as ATCCTTTTTTTCA. There are at least three questions that one can ask immediately: How likely is this sequence for this particular HMM? (This is the likelihood question.) What is the most probable sequence of transitions and emissions through the HMM underlying the production of this particular sequence? (This is the decoding question.) And finally, assuming that the transition and emission parameters are not known with certainty, how should their values be revised in light of the observed sequence? (This is the learning question.) We recommend that the reader try to answer these questions on the simple example above. Precise algorithmic answers for all three problems in the general case will be given in the following sections. We now consider different types of HMM architectures for biological applications.

7.1.2 HMMs for Biological Sequences

In biological sequence applications, the main HMM alphabets are of course the 20-letter amino acid alphabet for proteins and the four-letter nucleotide alphabet for DNA/RNA problems. Depending on the task, however, a number of other alphabets can be used, such as a 64-letter alphabet of triplets, a three-letter alphabet (α, β, coil) for secondary structure, and Cartesian products of alphabets (see table 6.1). If necessary, a space symbol can be added to any of these alphabets. In this chapter and chapter 8, we use the protein and DNA alphabets only.

In the simple HMM example above, there are only two hidden states, with a fully interconnected architecture between them. In real applications we need to consider more complex HMM architectures, with many more states and typically sparser connectivity. The design or selection of an architecture is highly problem-dependent. In biological sequences, as in speech recognition, the linear aspects of the sequences are often well captured by the so-called left–right architectures. An architecture is left–right if it prevents returning to any state once a transition from that state to any other state has occurred. We first review the most basic and widely used left–right architecture for biological sequences, the standard linear architecture (figure 7.2).

To begin with, consider the problem of modeling a family of related sequences, such as a family of proteins. As in the application of HMMs to speech recognition, a family of proteins can be seen as a set of different utterances of the same word, generated by a common underlying HMM. The standard ar-

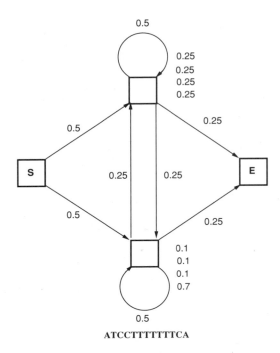

Figure 7.1: A Simple Example of an HMM, with Two States in Addition to the *Start* and *End* States.

chitecture can be seen as a very simple variation of the multiple-die model of chapter 3. The multiple-die model is in fact a trivial HMM with a linear sequence of states, one for each die. Transition probabilities from one state to the next are all set to 1. The emission probability of each die is associated with the composition of the family in the corresponding column. The main problem with such a model, of course, is that there are insertions and deletions: the sequences in the family in general do not have the same length N. Even if a gap symbol is added to the die alphabet, a preexisting multiple alignment is required to determine the emission probabilities of each die. The standard architecture is a simple but fundamental variation of the simple die model, where special states for insertions and deletions are added at all possible positions.

In the standard architecture, in addition to *start* and *end*, there are three other classes of states: the *main* states, the *delete* states, and the *insert* states, with $S = \{\text{start}, m_1, \ldots, m_N, i_1, \ldots, i_{N+1}, d_1, \ldots, d_N, \text{end}\}$. Delete states are

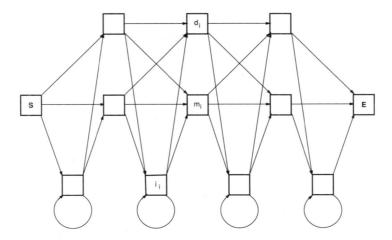

Figure 7.2: The Standard HMM Architecture. S is the start state, E is the end state, and d_i, m_i, and i_i denote delete, main, and insert states, respectively.

also called gap or skip states. N is the length of the model, typically equal to the average length of the sequences in the family. The main and insert states always emit an amino acid symbol, whereas the delete states are mute. This is of course equivalent to adding a space symbol to the alphabet and forcing the emission of the delete states to be concentrated on this symbol. The linear sequence of state transitions, start $\rightarrow m_1 \rightarrow m_2 \ldots \rightarrow m_N \rightarrow$ end, is the backbone of the model. These are the states corresponding to a multiple-die model. For each main state, corresponding insert and delete states are needed to model insertions and deletions. More precisely, there is a 1:1 correspondence between main states and delete states, and a 1:1 correspondence between backbone transitions and insert states. The self-loop on the insert states allows for multiple insertions at a given site. With an alphabet of size $|A|$, the standard architecture has approximately $2N|A|$ emission parameters and $9N$ transition parameters, without taking into account small boundary effects (the exact numbers are $(2N + 1)|A|$ emissions and $9N + 3$ transitions). Thus, for large N, the number of parameters is of the order of $49N$ for protein models and $17N$ for DNA models. Of course, neglecting boundary effects, there are also $2N$ normalization emission constraints and $3N$ normalization transition constraints.

7.2   Prior Information and Initialization

There are a number of ways in which prior information can be incorporated in the design of an HMM and its parameters. In the following sections we will give examples of different architectures. Once the architecture is selected, one can further restrain the freedom of the parameters in some of its portions, if the corresponding information is available in advance. Examples of such situations could include highly conserved motifs and hydrophobic regions. Linking the parameters of different portions is also possible, as in the weight-sharing procedure of NNs. Because of the multinomial models associated with HMM emissions and transitions, the natural probabilistic priors on HMM parameters are Dirichlet distributions (see chapter 2).

7.2.1   Dirichlet Priors on Transitions

In the standard architecture, for the vector of transitions t_{ji} out of a state i, a Dirichlet distribution $\mathcal{D}_{\alpha_i Q_i}(t_{ji})$ works well. One can use the same Dirichlet distribution for all the states of the same type—for instance, for all the main states, except the last one because of boundary effects. Thus three basic priors—$\mathcal{D}_{\alpha_m Q_m}$, $\mathcal{D}_{\alpha_i Q_i}$, and $\mathcal{D}_{\alpha_d Q_d}$—can be used for the transitions out of main, insert, and delete states. The hyperparameters' αs can be further reduced, if desirable, by having $\alpha_m = \alpha_i = \alpha_d$. Notice that the Dirichlet vectors Qs are usually not uniform, and are different for each state type. This is because transitions toward main states are expected to be predominant.

7.2.2   Dirichlet Priors on Emissions

The situation for emissions $\mathcal{D}_{\alpha_i Q_i}(e_{iX})$ is similar. A simple option is to use the same Dirichlet distribution for all the insert states and all the main states. The vector Q can be chosen as the uniform vector. Another possibility is to have Q equal to the average composition frequency of the training set. In [334] Dirichlet mixtures are also used.

7.2.3   Initialization

The transition parameters are typically initialized uniformly or at random. In the standard architecture, uniform initialization without a prior that favors transitions toward the main states is not, in general, a good idea. Since all transitions have the same costs, emissions from main states and insert states also have roughly the same cost. As a result, insert states may end up being

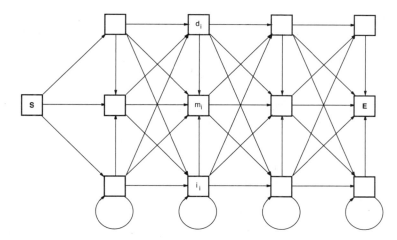

Figure 7.3: Variation on the Standard HMM Architecture. S is the start state, E is the end state, and d_i, m_i, and i_i denote delete, main, and insert states, respectively.

used very frequently, obviously not a very desirable solution. In [41], this problem was circumvented by introducing a slightly different architecture (figure 7.3), where main states have a lower fan-out (3) than insert or delete states (4), and therefore are less costly around the point where transitions out of each state are uniformly distributed. In a similar way, emissions can be initialized uniformly, at random, or sometimes even with the average composition. Any initialization that significantly deviates from uniform can introduce undesirable biases if Viterbi learning (see 7.4.3) is used.

Initialization from Multiple Alignments

Finally, it is important to realize that if a multiple alignment of a training set is available, it can be used to determine the parameters of the corresponding standard architecture, or at least to initialize them prior to learning. In the latter situation, the hope of course is that by starting closer to the optimal solutions, learning might be faster and/or yield a better solution. From a multiple alignment, we can assign a main state to any column of the alignment that contains less than 50% gaps. A column with more than 50% gaps is assigned to a corresponding insert state. Delete states are associated with the gaps in the columns with less than 50% gaps. Emissions of main and insert states can be initialized from the frequency counts of the corresponding columns, although these need to be regularized (with Dirichlet distributions and/or their mixtures) to avoid emission biases associated with 0 counts. A similar approach can be taken to determine the transition parameters.

7.3 Likelihood and Basic Algorithms

In this section, we study the basic HMM algorithms needed to answer the first two questions raised above. In particular, we study how to compute the likelihood, and the most probable sequence of state transitions and emissions, associated with an observation sequence. These algorithms are recursive and can be viewed as forms of dynamic programming or as propagation algorithms in the directed graph associated with the HMM [439]. All these algorithms are essential building blocks for the learning algorithms of the following section. The presence of delete states here slightly complicates the equations.

First, consider the problem of computing the likelihood $\mathbf{P}(O|w)$ of a sequence $O = \mathsf{X}^1 \ldots \mathsf{X}^t \ldots \mathsf{X}^T$ according to an HMM $M = M(w)$ with parameter w. We define a *path* π in M to be a sequence of consecutive states of M starting with the *start* state and ending with the *end* state, together with the choice of an emission letter for each of the emitting states along the path. If the sequence of emission letters along the path coincides with O, then

$$\mathbf{P}(O, \pi | w) = \prod_{start}^{end} t_{ji} \prod_{t=1}^{T} e_{i\mathsf{X}^t}, \tag{7.1}$$

where the first product is taken over all transitions along the path π, and the second product over the corresponding emitting states i in π. If the sequence of emission letters along the path does not coincide with O, then obviously $\mathbf{P}(O, \pi | w) = 0$. The likelihood of a sequence can then be expressed by

$$\mathbf{P}(O|w) = \sum_{\pi} \mathbf{P}(O, \pi | w). \tag{7.2}$$

This expression, however, does not lead to an efficient computation of the likelihood or its derivatives, because the number of paths in an architecture is typically exponential. Luckily, there is a more efficient way of organizing the computation of the likelihood, known as the forward algorithm. All the other algorithms in this section are similar and can be seen as ways of organizing calculations using an iterative propagation mechanism through the architecture, in order to avoid looking at all possible hidden paths.

7.3.1 The Forward Algorithm

Let us define

$$\alpha_i(t) = \mathbf{P}(S^t = i, \mathsf{X}^1 \ldots \mathsf{X}^t | w), \tag{7.3}$$

the probability of being in state i at time t, having observed the letters $X^1 \ldots X^t$ in the model $M(w)$. We can initialize

$$\alpha_{start}(0) = 1. \tag{7.4}$$

Without a *start* state, we would use an initial probability over all states. What we want to compute is $\mathbf{P}(O|w) = \alpha_{end}(T)$. The $\alpha_i(t)$ can be computed recursively by simple propagation:

$$\alpha_i(t+1) = \sum_{j \in S} \alpha_j(t) t_{ij} e_{iX^{t+1}} = \sum_{j \in N^-(i)} \alpha_j(t) t_{ij} e_{iX^{t+1}}. \tag{7.5}$$

The neighborhood notation is used again to stress the advantage of general sparse connectivity. This equation is true for any emitting state. For *delete* states, it must be modified slightly

$$\alpha_i(t+1) = \sum_{j \in N^-(i)} \alpha_j(t+1) t_{ij}. \tag{7.6}$$

At first sight, (7.5) and (7.6) do not define a proper propagation mechanism because in (7.6) the time $t+1$ appears on both sides of the equation. It is easy to see, however, that iterations of (7.5) and (7.6) must converge to a stable set of values $\alpha_i(t+1)$. This is obvious when there are no directed loops in the architecture going through delete states only, as in the case of the standard architecture. In this case (7.6) must be iterated N times at most. But even when there are loops through delete states in the architecture, (7.6) is in general convergent, since the propagation of probabilities through a silent loop gives rise to a geometric series with ratio equal to the product of the transitions along the loop. This ratio is typically less than 1 (see appendix D for more details).

A directed path from j to i in an HMM is said to be *silent* if the only internal nodes it contains correspond to delete (silent) states. The probability of such a path is the product of the probabilities of the transitions it contains. We denote by t_{ij}^D the probability of moving from j to i silently. Thus t_{ij}^D is the sum of the probabilities of all the silent paths joining j to i. In the standard architecture, t_{ij}^D is trivial to compute since there is at most one silent path from j to i. With this notation, the forward propagation can also be expressed by first computing $\alpha_i(t+1)$ for all the emitting states, using (7.5). The forward variables for the delete states can then be computed by

$$\alpha_i(t+1) = \sum_{j \in E} \alpha_j(t+1) t_{ij}^D, \tag{7.7}$$

where E denotes the set of all emitting states. Note that the propagation in (7.5) and (7.6) can be seen as the propagation in a linear neural network with

T layers, one per time step, and M units in each layer, one for each HMM state. All the units are linear. The unit corresponding to emitting states i in layer $t + 1$ has a linear transfer function with slope $e_{iX^{t+1}}$. In this sense, the computation of likelihoods in an HMM is equivalent to forward propagation in a linear network with roughly N layers and $|S|$ units per layer. The presence of delete states adds connections within a layer. In the case of the standard architecture, in spite of these intralayer connections, the NN architecture remains feed-forward: hence the simple convergence of (7.6) during propagation. Because the algorithm consists essentially in updating T layers of M units each, the forward algorithm scales as $O(MT)$ operations. In the standard architecture, both M and T are of the same order as N ($M \approx 3N$), so the forward propagation scales as $O(N^2)$ operations.

Finally, one should also observe that using the forward variables as HMMs can be viewed as a dynamic mixture model. This is because the probability of emitting the letter X^t can be decomposed as $\sum_i \alpha_i(t) e_{iX^t}$.

7.3.2   The Backward Algorithm

As in the case of neural networks, during learning we will need to propagate probabilities backward. The backward algorithm is the reverse of the forward algorithm. Let us define the backward variables by

$$\beta_i(t) = \mathbf{P}(X^{t+1} \ldots X^T | S^t = i, w), \tag{7.8}$$

the probability of being in state i at time t, with a partial observation of the sequence from X^{t+1} until the end. Obviously,

$$\beta_{end}(T) = 1. \tag{7.9}$$

The propagation equation to compute the βs recursively is given by

$$\beta_i(t) = \sum_{j \in N^+(i)} \beta_j(t+1) t_{ji} e_{jX^{t+1}} \tag{7.10}$$

for the emitting states. For the delete states,

$$\beta_i(t) = \sum_{j \in N^+(i)} \beta_j(t) t_{ji}. \tag{7.11}$$

After updating the emitting states, this can be rewritten as

$$\beta_i(t) = \sum_{j \in E} \beta_j(t) t_{ji}^D. \tag{7.12}$$

The remarks made above about the forward algorithm also apply to the backward algorithm. In particular, in the standard architecture, the complexity of the backward algorithm also scales as $O(N^2)$.

Using the forward and backward variables, we can easily compute the probability of being in state i at time t, given the observation sequence O and the model w, by

$$\gamma_i(t) = \mathbf{P}(S^t = i | O, w) = \frac{\alpha_i(t)\beta_i(t)}{\mathbf{P}(O|w)} = \frac{\alpha_i(t)\beta_i(t)}{\sum_{j \in S} \alpha_j(t)\beta_j(t)}, \tag{7.13}$$

or the probability $\gamma_{ji}(t)$ of using the $i \to j$ transition at time t by

$$\mathbf{P}(S^{t+1} = j, S^t = i | O, w) = \begin{cases} \alpha_i(t)t_{ji}e_{jX^{t+1}}\beta_j(t+1)/\mathbf{P}(O|w) & \text{if } j \in E \\ \alpha_i(t)t_{ji}\beta_j(t)/\mathbf{P}(O|w) & \text{if } j \in D \end{cases} \tag{7.14}$$

where D represents the set of delete states. Obviously, we also have

$$\gamma_i(t) = \mathbf{P}(S^t = i | O, w) = \sum_{j \in S} \gamma_{ji}(t). \tag{7.15}$$

By maximizing $\gamma_i(t)$ we can find the most likely state at time t. In the decoding question, however, we are interested in the most likely path. The most likely path will also be useful for learning and for aligning sequences to the model. The most probable path can be computed using the so-called Viterbi algorithm, which is another application of dynamic programming and, in essence, is the same algorithm one uses for pairwise alignments. It is also very similar to the forward algorithm.

7.3.3 The Viterbi Algorithm

For the Viterbi algorithm, we need to define the variables

$$\delta_i(t) = \max_{\pi_i(t)} \mathbf{P}(\pi_i(t)|w), \tag{7.16}$$

where $\pi_i(t)$ represents a "prefix" path, with emissions $X^1 \ldots X^t$ ending in state i. Thus, $\delta_i(t)$ is the probability associated with the most probable path that accounts for the first t symbols of O and terminates in state i. These variables can be updated using a propagation mechanism similar to the forward algorithm, where sums are replaced by maximization operations:

$$\delta_i(t+1) = [\max_j \delta_j(t)t_{ij}]e_{iX^{t+1}} \tag{7.17}$$

for the emitting states, and

$$\delta_i(t+1) = [\max_j \delta_j(t+1)t_{ij}] \tag{7.18}$$

for the delete states. The convergence is even more obvious than in the case of the forward algorithm; a cycle of delete states can never belong to an optimal path, because it decreases the overall probability without producing any letters. In order to recover the optimal path itself one must at each time keep track of the previous optimal state. The resulting Viterbi path will be used below both for learning and multiple alignments.

7.3.4 Computing Expectations

For a given set of parameters w and a given sequence O, $\mathbf{P}(\pi|O,w)$ defines a posterior probability distribution $Q(\pi)$ on the hidden variables, that is, the paths' πs. We have seen in chapters 3 and 4 that Q plays an important role. In particular, during learning, we will need to compute expectations with respect to Q, such as the expected number of times the state i is visited, the expected number of times the letter X is emitted from i, and the expected number of times the $i \to j$ transition is used. Because of the factorial nature of HMMs, Q is easy to compute and the associated expectations can be obtained from the forward–backward variables. Let

- $n(i, \pi, O)$ be the number of times i is visited, given π and O;

- $n(i, \mathsf{X}, \pi, O)$ be the number of times the letter X is emitted from i, given π and O;

- $n(j, i, \pi, O)$ be the number of times the $i \to j$ transition is used, given π and O.

Then the respective expectations are given by

$$n_i = \sum_{\pi} n(i, \pi, O)\mathbf{P}(\pi|O,w) = \sum_{t=0}^{T} y_i(t), \qquad (7.19)$$

$$n_{i\mathsf{X}} = \sum_{\pi} n(i, \mathsf{X}, \pi, O)\mathbf{P}(\pi|O,w) = \sum_{t=0,\mathsf{X}^t=\mathsf{X}}^{T} y_i(t) \qquad (7.20)$$

and, similarly, for the transitions

$$n_{ji} = \sum_{\pi} n(j, i, \pi, O)\mathbf{P}(\pi|O,w) = \sum_{t=0}^{T} y_{ji}(t). \qquad (7.21)$$

We now have all the tools in place to tackle the HMM learning problem.

7.4 Learning Algorithms

Various algorithms are available for HMM training, including the Baum–Welch or EM (expectation maximization) algorithm, as well as different forms of gradient-descent and other GEM (generalized EM) [147, 439, 39] algorithms. Obviously, one could also use simulated annealing, although this remains impractical for large models. As usual, we concentrate on the first level of Bayesian inference: finding the optimal parameters by MAP estimation. We begin with ML estimation, concentrating on emission parameters; the calculations for transition parameters are similar. We also assume first that the data consist of a single sequence O. For each learning algorithm, we thus derive ML online learning equations first. We then briefly indicate how these equations should be modified for batch learning with multiple sequences and when priors are included (MAP). In the case of K training sequences, these can be considered as independent and the overall likelihood is equal to the product of the individual likelihoods. In the case of HMMs, higher levels of Bayesian inference have been used very little so far, even less than with neural networks. These will be discussed only very briefly.

Consider again the likelihood $P(O|w) = \sum_\pi P(O, \pi|w)$. In ML, we would like to optimize the Lagrangian

$$\mathcal{L} = -\log P(O|w) - \sum_{i \in E} \lambda_i (1 - \sum_X e_{iX}) - \sum_{i \in S} \mu_i (1 - \sum_j t_{ji}), \qquad (7.22)$$

where the λs and μs are positive Lagrange multipliers. From (7.1), we have

$$\frac{\partial P(O, \pi|w)}{\partial e_{iX}} = \frac{n(i, X, \pi, O)}{e_{iX}} P(O, \pi|w). \qquad (7.23)$$

By setting the partial derivatives of the Lagrangian to 0, at the optimum we must have

$$\lambda_i e_{iX} = \sum_\pi n(i, X, \pi, O) Q(\pi) = n_{iX}, \qquad (7.24)$$

and similarly for transition parameters. Recall that Q is the posterior probability $P(\pi|O, w)$. By summing over all alphabet letters, we find

$$\lambda_i = \sum_\pi \sum_X n(i, X, \pi, O) Q(\pi) = \sum_\pi n(i, \pi, O) Q(\pi) = n_i. \qquad (7.25)$$

Thus, at the optimum, we must have

$$e_{iX} = \frac{\sum_\pi n(i, X, \pi, O) Q(\pi)}{\sum_\pi n(i, \pi, O) Q(\pi)} = \frac{\sum_\pi P(\pi|O, w) n(i, X, \pi, O)}{\sum_\pi P(\pi|O, w) n(i, \pi, O)}. \qquad (7.26)$$

The ML equations cannot be solved directly because in (7.26) the posterior distribution Q depends on the values of e_{iX}. However, (7.26) suggests a simple iterative algorithm whereby Q is first estimated as $Q(\pi) = \mathbf{P}(\pi|O, w)$, and then the parameters are updated using (7.26). It turns out that this is exactly the EM algorithm for HMMs.

7.4.1 EM Algorithm (Baum–Welch)

Recall that in the EM algorithm we define the energy over hidden configurations, $f(\pi) = -\log \mathbf{P}(O, \pi|w)$. The EM algorithm can be defined as an iterative double minimization process of the function (free energy at temperature 1) $\mathcal{F}(w, Q) = \mathbf{E}_Q(f) - \mathcal{H}(Q)$ with respect first to Q and then to w. The first minimization step yields the posterior $Q(\pi) = \mathbf{P}(\pi|O, w) = \mathbf{P}(\pi, O|w)/\mathbf{P}(O|w)$, which we know how to calculate. For the second minimization step, we must minimize $\mathcal{F}$, with respect to w, under the probability normalization constraints. Since the entropy term is independent of w, we must finally minimize the Lagrangian

$$\mathcal{L} = \mathbf{E}_Q(f) - \sum_{i \in E} \lambda_i \Big(1 - \sum_X e_{iX}\Big) + \sum_{i \in S} \mu_i \Big(1 - \sum_j t_{ji}\Big), \qquad (7.27)$$

with $Q(\pi) = \mathbf{P}(\pi|O, w)$ *fixed*. Using (7.23), we get

$$\lambda_i e_{iX} = \sum_\pi n(i, X, \pi, O) Q(\pi) = n_{iX} \qquad (7.28)$$

and, by summing over all alphabet letters,

$$\lambda_i = \sum_\pi \sum_X n(i, X, \pi, O) Q(\pi) = \sum_\pi n(i, \pi, O) Q(\pi) = n_i. \qquad (7.29)$$

These equations are identical to (7.24) and (7.25). It can be checked that they correspond to a minimum, so that the EM reestimation equations are

$$e_{iX}^+ = \frac{\sum_\pi n(i, X, \pi, O) Q(\pi)}{\sum_\pi n(i, \pi, O) Q(\pi)} = \frac{\sum_{t=0, X^t = X}^{T} y_i(t)}{\sum_{t=0}^{T} y_i(t)} = \frac{n_{iX}}{n_i}. \qquad (7.30)$$

In the case of transition parameters, one similarly obtains

$$t_{ji}^+ = \frac{\sum_\pi n(j, i, \pi, O) Q(\pi)}{\sum_\pi n(i, \pi, O) Q(\pi)} = \frac{\sum_{t=0}^{T} y_{ji}(t)}{\sum_{t=0}^{T} y_i(t)} = \frac{n_{ji}}{n_i}. \qquad (7.31)$$

Thus the EM equations are implemented using the forward and backward procedures. In fact, the EM algorithm for HMMs is sometimes called the forward–backward algorithm. e_{iX}^+ is the expected number of times in state i observing symbol X, divided by the expected number of times in state i, and t_{ji}^+ is the expected number of transitions from i to j, divided by the expected number of transitions from state i. These are exactly the same iteration equations obtained by setting the derivatives of the Lagrangian associated with the likelihood (7.22) to 0. This is a particular property of HMMs and factorial distributions, and *not* a general rule.

In the case of K sequences $O_1, \ldots, O_K$, a similar calculation shows that we have

$$e_{iX}^+ = \frac{\sum_{j=1}^{K} \sum_{\pi} n(i, X, \pi, O_j) \mathbf{P}(\pi|O_j, w)}{\sum_{j=1}^{K} \sum_{\pi} n(i, \pi, O_j) \mathbf{P}(\pi|O_j, w)}. \tag{7.32}$$

It should also be clear how to modify the present equations in the case of MAP estimation by EM. Each training sequence requires one forward and one backward propagation. Thus the EM algorithm scales as $O(KN^2)$ operations.

The batch EM algorithm is widely used for HMMs. It must be noted, however, that the online use of the EM algorithm can be problematic. This is because the EM algorithm, unlike gradient descent, does not have a learning rate. The EM algorithm can take large steps in the descent direction generated by each training example in isolation, converging toward poor local minima of $\mathcal{E}$. This "carpet-jumping" effect can be avoided with gradient-descent learning, as long as the learning rate is small.

7.4.2   Gradient Descent

The gradient-descent equations on the negative log-likelihood can be derived by exploiting the relationship between HMMs and NNs, and using the back-propagation equations. Here we derive them directly. Instead of using the Lagrangian with the normalization constraints, as above, we use an equivalent useful reparameterization. We reparameterize the HMM using normalized exponentials, in the form

$$e_{iX} = \frac{e^{w_{iX}}}{\sum_Y e^{w_{iY}}} \quad \text{and} \quad t_{ji} = \frac{e^{w_{ji}}}{\sum_k e^{w_{ki}}}, \tag{7.33}$$

with w_{iX} and w_{ij} as the new variables. This reparameterization has two advantages: (1) modification of the ws automatically preserves normalization constraints on emission and transition distributions; (2) transition and emission probabilities can never reach the value 0. A simple calculation gives

$$\frac{\partial e_{iX}}{\partial w_{iX}} = e_{iX}(1 - e_{iX}) \quad \text{and} \quad \frac{\partial e_{iX}}{\partial w_{iY}} = -e_{iX}e_{iY}, \tag{7.34}$$

and similarly for the transition parameters. By the chain rule,

$$\frac{\partial \log \mathbf{P}(O|w)}{w_{i\mathsf{X}}} = \sum_{\mathsf{Y}} \frac{\partial \log \mathbf{P}(O|w)}{e_{i\mathsf{Y}}} \frac{\partial e_{i\mathsf{Y}}}{w_{i\mathsf{X}}}. \tag{7.35}$$

Therefore, applying (7.2), (7.23), and (7.33) to (7.35), the online gradient-descent equations on the negative log-likelihood are

$$\Delta w_{i\mathsf{X}} = \eta(n_{i\mathsf{X}} - n_i e_{i\mathsf{X}}) \quad \text{and} \quad \Delta w_{ji} = \eta(n_{ji} - n_i t_{ji}), \tag{7.36}$$

where η is the learning rate. $n_{i\mathsf{X}}$ and n_{ji} are again the expected counts derived by the forward–backward procedure for each single sequence if the algorithm is to be used online. Batch gradient-descent equations can easily be derived by summing over all training sequences. For MAP estimation, one needs to add the derivative of the log prior, with respect to the ws, to the online gradient-descent learning equations. For instance, a Gaussian prior on each parameter would add a weight decay term to (7.36).

Just like EM, the gradient-descent equations require one forward and one backward propagation. Therefore $O(KN^2)$ operations must be performed per training cycle. Some care must be taken in the implementation, however, to minimize the overhead introduced by the normalized exponential parameterization. Unlike EM, online gradient descent is a smooth algorithm. A number of other related smooth algorithms are discussed in [39]. A useful aspect of smooth algorithms is that unlearning is easy. If a sequence happens to be in the training set by error (that is, if it does not belong to the family being modeled), it is easy to remove its antagonistic impact from the model by reversing the effect of the gradient-descent equations.

7.4.3 Viterbi Learning

Both the EM and the gradient-descent update equations are based on the calculation of expectations over all possible hidden paths. The general Viterbi learning idea is to replace calculations involving all possible paths with calculations involving only a small number of likely paths, typically only the most likely one, associated with each sequence. Thus an emission count such as $n(i, \mathsf{X}, \pi, O)$ averaged over all paths is replaced by a single number $n(i, \mathsf{X}, \pi^*(O))$, the number of times X is emitted from i along the most probable path $\pi^*(O)$. In the standard architecture, $n(i, \mathsf{X}, \pi^*(O))$ is always 0 or 1, except for the insert states, where it can occasionally be higher as a result of repeated insertions of the same letter. For this reason, a plain online Viterbi EM makes little sense because parameters would mostly be updated to 0 or 1. For online Viterbi gradient descent, at each step along a Viterbi path, and for any state i on the path, the parameters of the model are updated according to

$$\Delta w_{ix} = \eta(E_{ix} - e_{ix}) \quad \text{and} \quad \Delta w_{ji} = \eta(T_{ji} - t_{ji}). \tag{7.37}$$

$E_{ix} = 1$ (resp. $T_{ji} = 1$) if the emission of X from i (resp. $i \to j$ transition) is used, and 0 otherwise. The new parameters are therefore updated incrementally, using the discrepancy between the frequencies induced by the training data and the probability parameters of the model.

In the literature, Viterbi learning is sometimes presented as a quick approximation to the corresponding non-Viterbi version. The speed advantage is only relatively minor, and of the order of a factor of 2, since computing $\pi^*(O)$ does not require the backward propagation. As far as approximations are concerned, Viterbi learning is somewhat crude, since sequence likelihoods in general are not sharply peaked around a single optimal path. Thus it is not uncommon to observe significant differences between Viterbi and non-Viterbi learning both during the training phase and at the end. In our experience, we have often observed that Viterbi learning yields good results when modeling protein families, but not when modeling general DNA elements, such as exon or promoter regions, where non-Viterbi learning performs better. This probably is partially due to the fact that optimal paths play a particular role in the case of proteins.

In fact, a complementary view of Viterbi learning is that it constitutes an algorithm per se, trying to optimize a different objective function. We can define a new probability measure P^V, and hence a new model (hidden Viterbi model) on the space of sequences, by

$$P^V(O|w) = \frac{\mathbf{P}(\pi^*(O)|w)}{\sum_O \mathbf{P}(\pi^*(O)|w)}. \tag{7.38}$$

Viterbi learning then is an attempt at minimizing

$$\mathcal{E} = \sum_{k=1}^{K} -\log P^V(O_k|w). \tag{7.39}$$

It is important to note that as the parameters w evolve, the optimal paths π^* can change abruptly, and therefore $\mathcal{E}$ can be discontinuous. Obviously, regularizer terms can be added to (7.39) for a Viterbi version of MAP.

7.4.4 Other Aspects

As usual, many other issues can be raised regarding learning improvements, such as balancing the training set [157, 337], varying the learning rate, or using second-order information by estimating the Hessian of the likelihood. These issues are discussed in the literature and cannot be covered here in detail for lack of space. We wish, however, briefly to discuss scaling, architecture selection or learning, and ambiguous symbols, since these are of particular practical importance.

Scaling

The probabilities $\mathbf{P}(\pi|O, w)$ are typically very small, since they are equal to the product of many transition and emission probabilities, each less than 1. For most models, this will easily exceed the precision of any machine, even in double precision. Therefore, in the implementation of the learning algorithms, and in particular of the forward and backward procedures, one is faced with precision issues. These can be addressed by using a scaling procedure, where forward and backward variables are scaled during the propagation in order to avoid underflow. The scaling procedure is somewhat technical and is described in appendix D. In Viterbi learning, the precision problem is easily addressed by working with the logarithm of the path probabilities.

Learning the architecture

A natural question to raise is whether the HMM architecture itself can be learned from the data. Algorithms for learning HMM architectures have indeed been developed for general HMMs—for instance, in [504]—and even in the context of biological sequences [193]. The basic idea in [504] is to start with a very complex model, essentially one state per data letter, and then iteratively merge states. The choice of states to merge and the stopping criterion are guided by an evaluation of the posterior probability. In [193], on the other hand, the starting point is a small, fully interconnected HMM. The algorithm in this case proceeds by iteratively deleting transitions with very low probability and duplicating the most connected states, until the likelihood or posterior reaches a sufficient level. In both cases, good results are reported on small test cases associated with HMMs having fewer than 50 states. While these methods may be useful in some instances, they are slow and unlikely to be practical, on current computers, for most of the large HMMs envisioned in chapter 8 without leveraging any available prior knowledge. The number of all possible architectures with $|S|$ states is of course very large. A much more tractable special case of architecture learning is whether the length N of the standard HMM architecture can be learned.

Adaptable model length

The approach described so far for the standard architecture is to fix N to the average length of the sequences being modeled. In practice, this simple approach seems to work quite well. Naturally, after training, if such a value of N does not seem to be optimal, a new value can be selected and the training procedure restarted.

In [334] a "surgery" algorithm is presented for the *dynamic* adjustment of the HMM length during learning. The idea is to add or remove states wherever needed along the architecture, while respecting the overall connectivity pattern. If an insert state is used by more than 50% of the family of sequences being modeled, meaning that the insert state is present in more than 50% of the corresponding Viterbi paths, then a new main state is created at the corresponding position, together with corresponding new delete and insert states. The new state emission and transition probabilities can be initialized uniformly. Likewise, if a delete state is used by more than 50% of the sequences, it can be removed together with the corresponding main and insert states. The rest of the architecture is left untouched, and the training proceeds. Although this approach has not been shown to converge always to a stable length, in practice it seems to do so.

Architectural variations

As already pointed out, a number of other architectures, often related to the standard architecture, have been used in molecular biology applications. These include the multiple HMM architecture (figure 8.5) for classification, and the loop (figure 8.16) and wheel (figure 8.17) architectures for periodic patterns. The standard architecture has also been used to model protein secondary structure [187] and build libraries of secondary structure consensus patterns for proteins with similar fold and function. Several other architectures have been developed for gene finding both in prokaryotes [336] and eukaryotes [107]. Examples of specific applications will be given in chapter 8.

Ambiguous symbols

Because sequencing techniques are not perfect, ambiguous symbols are occasionally present. For instance, X represents A or C or G or T in DNA sequences, and B represents asparagine or aspartic acid in protein sequences. Such symbols can easily be handled in a number of ways in conjunction with HMMs. In database searches, it is prudent practice to use the "benefit of the doubt" approach, in which an ambiguous symbol is replaced by its most likely alternative in the computation of sequence likelihoods and Viterbi paths. Additional care must be used with sequences having an unusually high proportion of ambiguous symbols, since these are likely to generate false positive responses.

7.5 Applications of HMMs: General Aspects

Regardless of the design and training method, once an HMM has been successfully derived from a family of sequences, it can be used in a number of different tasks, including

1. Multiple alignments

2. Database mining and classification of sequences and fragments

3. Structural analysis and pattern discovery.

All these tasks are based on the computation, for any given sequence, of its probability according to the model as well as its most likely associated path, and on the analysis of the model structure itself. In most cases, HMMs have performed well on all tasks, yielding, for example, multiple alignments that are comparable with those derived by human experts. Specific examples and details on proteins and DNA applications of HMMs will be given in chapter 8. HMM libraries of models can also be combined in a hierarchical and modular fashion to yield increasingly refined probabilistic models of sequence space regions. HMMs could in principle be used in generative mode also to produce *de novo* sequences having a high likelihood with respect to a target family, although this property has not been exploited.

7.5.1 Multiple Alignments

Computing the Viterbi path of a sequence is also called, for obvious reasons, "aligning a sequence to the model." Multiple alignments can be derived, in an efficient way, by aligning the Viterbi paths to each other [334, 41]. While training a model may sometimes be lengthy, it can be done offline. Once the training phase is completed, the multiple alignment of K sequences requires the computation of K Viterbi paths, and therefore scales only as $O(KN^2)$. This is linear in K, and should be contrasted with the $O(N^K)$ scaling of multidimensional dynamic programming alignment, which is exponential in K. The multiple alignments derived by HMMs are in some sense richer than conventional alignments. Indeed, consider a conventional alignment of two sequences and assume that, at a given position, the second sequence has a gap with respect to the first sequence. This gap could be the result of a deletion in the second sequence or an insertion in the first sequence. These are two distinct sets of Viterbi paths in an HMM that are not distinguished in a conventional alignment.

Another way of looking at this issue is to consider that a conventional multiple alignment could be derived by training an HMM architecture that is similar to the standard architecture, but where the length of the model is fixed to the length of the longest sequence being aligned and all insert states are removed, leaving only main and delete states. Thus, all the Viterbi paths consist only of main-state emissions or gaps with respect to main states. But in any case, it should be clear that the multiple alignments derived by an HMM with both insert and delete states are potentially richer and in fact should be plotted in three dimensions, rather than the two used by conventional multiple alignments (the third dimension being reserved for emissions occurring on HMM insert states). Because this is both graphically difficult and unconventional, HMM alignments are still plotted in two dimensions like conventional ones. Lowercase letters are then often reserved for letters produced by HMM insert states.

The insert and delete states of an HMM represent formal operations on sequences. One important question is whether and how they can be related to evolutionary events. This issue is also related, of course, to the construction of phylogenetic trees, and their relation to HMMs and multiple alignments. The standard architecture by itself does not provide a good probabilistic model of the evolutionary process because it lacks the required tree structure as well as a clear notion of substitution (in addition to insertion and deletion). Probabilistic models of evolution are addressed in chapter 10.

The reader should perhaps be reminded one more time that the treatment of HMM multiple alignments we have just presented is based on a single HMM, and therefore corresponds only to the first step of a full Bayesian treatment. Even for a simple question, such as whether two amino acids in two different sequences should be aligned to each other, a full Bayesian treatment would require integration of the answer across all HMMs with respect to the proper posterior probability measure. To the best of our knowledge, such integrals have not been computed in the case of HMMs for biological sequences (but see [583]). It is difficult to guess whether much could be gained through such a computationally intensive extension of current practice.

Finally, HMMs could also be used in conjunction with substitution matrices [27]. HMM emission distributions could be used to calculate substitution matrices, and substitution matrices could be used to influence HMMs during or after training. In the case of large training sets, one might expect that most substitution information is already present in the data itself, and no major gains would be derived from an external infusion of such knowledge.

7.5.2   Database Mining and Classification

Given a trained model, the likelihood of any given sequence (as well as the likelihood of the associated Viterbi path) can be computed. These scores can be used in discrimination tests and in database searches [334, 38] to separate sequences associated with the training family from the rest. This is applicable to both complete sequences and fragments [42]. One important aspect to be examined in chapter 8 is that such scores must be calibrated as a function of sequence length.

HMMs can also be used in classification problems, for instance, across protein families or across subfamilies of a single protein family. This can be done by training a model for each class, if class-specific training sets are available. We have used this approach to build two HMMs that can reliably discriminate between tyrosine and serine/threonine kinase subfamilies. Otherwise, unsupervised algorithms related to clustering can be used in combination with HMMs to generate classifications. An example here is the discrimination of globin subfamilies (see [334] and chapter 8). It is believed that the total number of protein superfamilies is relatively small, on the order of 1000 [127, 93]. A global protein classification system, with roughly one HMM per family, is becoming a feasible goal, from both an algorithmic and a computational standpoint. Global classification projects of this sort are currently under way, and should become useful auxiliary tools in a number of tasks, such as gene finding, protein classification, and structure/function prediction (see [497]).

7.5.3   Structural Analysis and Pattern Discovery

Information can also be derived, and new patterns discovered, by examining the structure of a trained HMM. The parameters of an HMM can be studied in the same way as the connections of an NN. High emission or transition probabilities are usually associated with conserved regions or consensus patterns that may have structural/functional significance. One convenient way of detecting such patterns is to plot the entropy of the emission distributions along the backbone of the model. Any other function of position, such as hydrophobicity or bendability, can also be averaged and plotted using the HMM probabilities. Patterns that are characteristic of a given family, such as features of secondary structure in proteins (hydrophobicity in alpha-helices) and regions of high bendability in DNA, are often easier to detect in such plots. This is because the variability of individual sequences is smoothed out by the expectations. There are other patterns, such as periodicities, that can be revealed by analyzing the structure of a model. The initial weak detection of such a pattern with the standard architecture can guide the design of more specialized architectures, such as wheel and loop architectures, to enhance the periodic signal. The ability to detect weak patterns from raw unaligned data is a very useful feature of HMMs. Several examples will be given in chapter 8.

Chapter 8

Hidden Markov Models: Applications

8.1 Protein Applications

In the case of proteins, HMMs have been successfully applied to many families, such as globins, immunoglobulins, kinases, and G-protein-coupled receptors (see, e.g., [334, 41, 38]). HMMs have also been used to model secondary structure elements, such as alpha-helices, as well as secondary structure consensus patterns of protein superfamilies [187]. In fact, by the end of 1997, HMM data bases of protein families (Pfam) [497] and protein family secondary structures (FORESST) [187] became available. Multiple alignments derived from such HMMs have been reported and discussed in the literature. Large multiple alignments are typically too bulky to be reproduced here. But in most cases, HMM alignments are found to be very good, within the limits of variability found in multiple alignments produced by human experts resulting from diverse degrees of emphasis on structural or phylogenetic information. In the rest of this first half of the chapter, we concentrate on the application of HMMs to a specific protein family, the G-protein-coupled receptors (GCRs or GPCRs), along the lines of [38, 42]. Additional details can be found in these references.

8.1.1 G-Protein-Coupled Receptors

G-protein-coupled receptors are a rich family of transmembrane proteins capable of transducing a variety of extracellular signals carried by hormones, neurotransmitters, odorants, and light (see [436, 325, 508, 227, 552] for recent reviews). Although the detailed biophysical mechanisms underlying the transduction have not been worked out for all members of the family, in most cases stimulation of the receptor leads to the activation of a guanine nucleotide-binding (G) protein [402]. All the receptors in the family are believed to have similar structure, characterized by seven hydrophobic membrane-spanning alpha-helices. The seven transmembrane regions are connected by three extracellular and three intracellular loops. The amino termini are extracellular and often glycosylated, whereas the carboxyl termini are cytoplasmic and usually phosphorylated. The exact three-dimensional packing of the helices, and more generally the complete tertiary structure, are only partially known [47, 420].

The family is usually divided into subclasses on the basis of transmitter types, such as muscarinic receptors, catecholamine receptors, odorant receptors, and so forth. From a methodological standpoint, the GPCR family is particularly challenging. Its members have very variable lengths and, on average, are fairly long: the length of known GPCRs varies from roughly 200 to 1200 amino acids. The family is highly variable and some of its members have less than 20% residues in common.

8.1.2 Structural Properties

In [38], 142 GPCR sequences extracted from the PROSITE database [23] were used to train an HMM architecture of length $N = 430$, the average length of the training sequences, using on-line Viterbi learning during 12 cycles of iterations through the entire training set.

As an example of a structural property, the entropy of the emission distribution of the main states of the corresponding model is given in figure 8.1. The amplitude profile of the entropy contains seven major oscillations directly related to the seven transmembrane domains. To a first approximation, the hydrophobic domains tend to be less variable, and therefore associated with regions of lower entropy. This structural feature was discovered by the HMM without any prior knowledge of alpha-helices or hydrophobicity.

8.1.3 Raw Score Statistics

To test the discrimination abilities of the model, 1600 random sequences were generated with the same average composition as the GCPRs in the training set, with lengths 300, 350, 400, 450, 500, 550, 600, 650, 700, 750, 800, 1000 (100 sequences at each length), and 1500 and 2000 (200 sequences at each length). For any sequence, random or not, its raw score according to the model is calculated. Here, the raw score of a sequence O is the negative log-likelihood of the corresponding Viterbi path. The raw scores of all the random sequences

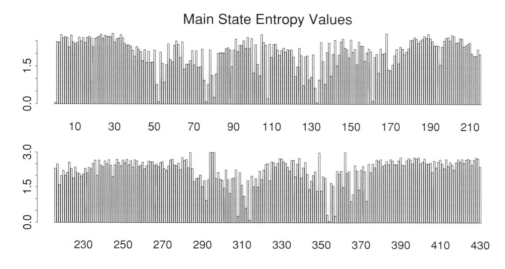

Figure 8.1: Entropy Profile of the Emission Probability Distributions Associated with the Main States of the HMM After 12 Cycles of Training.

are plotted in figure 8.2, together with the scores of the GPCRs in the training set and the scores of all the sequences in the SWISS-PROT database.

The model clearly discriminates random sequences with similar average composition from true GPCRs. Consistent with previous experiments [41, 334], the scores of the random sequences and of the SWISS-PROT sequences cluster along two similar lines. The clustering along a line indicates that the cost of adding one amino acid is roughly constant on average. The linearity is not preserved for very short sequences, since these can have more irregular Viterbi paths. For very long sequences (above model length) the linearity becomes increasingly precise. This is because the Viterbi paths of very long sequences, with a fixed average composition, must rely heavily on insert states and in fact are forced to loop many times in a particular insert state that becomes predominant as the length goes to infinity. The predominant insert state is the most cost-effective one. It is easy to see that the cost-effectiveness of an insert state k depends equally on two factors: its self-transition probability t_{kk} and the cross-entropy between its emission probability vector e_{kx} and the fixed probability distribution associated with the sequences under consideration. More precisely, if we look at the scores of long random sequences generated using a fixed source $P = (p_x)$ as a function of sequence length, the corresponding

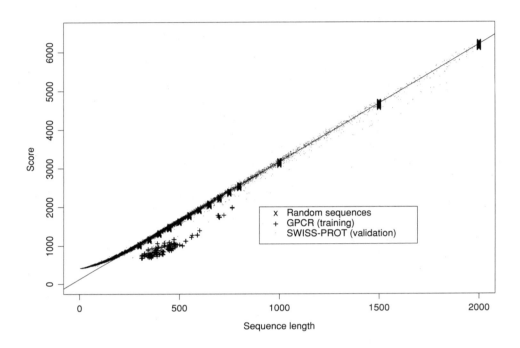

Figure 8.2: Scores (Negative Log-likelihoods of Optimal Viterbi Paths). Represented sequences consist of 142 GPCR training sequences, all sequences from the SWISS-PROT database of length less than or equal to 2000, and 220 randomly generated sequences with same average composition as the GPCRs of length 300, 350, 400, 450, 500, 550, 600, 650, 700, 750, 800 (20 at each length). The regression line was obtained from the 220 random sequences.

scores cluster along a regression line with slope

$$\min_k [-\log t_{kk} - \sum_X p_X \log e_{kX}]. \tag{8.1}$$

Furthermore, for a large fixed length l, the scores are approximately normally distributed (Central Limit Theorem) with variance

$$l\,[\mathbf{E}_P(\log^2 e_{kX}) - \mathbf{E}_P(\log e_{kX})] = l\,\mathbf{Var}_P[\log e_{kX}]. \tag{8.2}$$

In particular, the standard deviation of the scores increases as the square root of the length l. Proof of these results and additional details can be found in [38].

Random sequence length l	Number of sequences	Empirical average score (AS)	Predicted AS $3.038l + 122.11$	Empirical SD $0.66\sqrt{l}$	Predicted SD
300	100	1041.4	1033.5	13.24	11.43
350	100	1187.1	1185.4	13.12	12.34
400	100	1337.6	1337.3	12.50	13.20
450	100	1487.6	1489.2	16.85	14.00
500	100	1638.5	1641.1	13.74	14.75
550	100	1790.3	1793.0	15.26	15.47
600	100	1944.4	1944.9	16.70	16.16
650	100	2093.3	2096.8	16.54	16.82
700	100	2250.6	2248.7	18.65	17.46
750	100	2397.9	2400.6	16.96	18.07
800	100	2552.5	2552.5	19.66	18.66
1000	100	3160.2	3160.1	21.62	20.87
1500	200	4678.9	4679.1	25.51	25.56
2000	200	6199.1	6198.1	29.59	29.51

Table 8.1: Statistics of the Scores of Randomly Generated Sequences with Similar Average Composition as the GPCRs (8.2).

The formula derived for the slope is true asymptotically and does not necessarily apply for relatively small lengths, although this is the case for the present model. For the model under consideration, the optimal insert state for average composition identical to GPCRs is insert state 20. The equation of the empirical regression line is $y = 3.038l + 122.11$, whereas the approximation in (8.1) yields a slope prediction of 3.039. From the estimate in (8.2), the standard deviation should increase as $\sigma \approx 0.66\sqrt{l}$. An empirical regression of the standard deviation on the square root of the length gives $\sigma \approx 0.63\sqrt{l} + 1.22$. There is good agreement between the theoretical estimates and the empirical results, as can be seen in table 8.1. Generally, of course, the quality of the fit improves with the length of the sequences, and this is most evident for the standard deviation. In the present case, however, (8.1) and (8.2) are quite accurate even for relatively short sequences, with length comparable to or even less than the length of the model. Similar results are obtained if we use a different random source based on the average composition of the SWISS-PROT sequences.

8.1.4 Score Normalization, Database Searches, and Discrimination Tests

Having done this statistical analysis, we can now address the obvious question of how to conduct discrimination tests, that is, how to decide algorithmically whether a sequence belongs to the GPCR family or not. Clearly, one would like to use the scores produced by the model to discriminate between GPCR and non-GPCR sequences. However, the raw scores cannot be used directly because (a) the scores tend to grow linearly with the length and (b) the dispersion of the scores varies with the length and, at least in the case of long, randomly generated sequences, increases in proportion to the square root of the length. Therefore the raw scores need to be centered and scaled first.

This normalization procedure can be done in several ways. For centering, one can use empirical averages calculated at each length, or averages derived from empirical regression lines, or average estimates derived from (8.1) and (8.2). Depending on the final goal, the base level can be calculated with respect to random sequences of similar composition or with respect to an actual database, such as SWISS-PROT. In the present case, the two are similar but not identical. For scaling, one can use empirical standard deviations or theoretical estimates and these can be calculated again on different sources such as SWISS-PROT or random sequences of similar composition. Each method has its advantages and drawbacks, and in practical situations one may try several of them. In general, empirical estimates may be more accurate but also more costly, especially for long sequences, since the calculation of the corresponding scores grows with the square of the length $O(l^2)$.

When using an actual database for centering or scaling, problems can arise if few sequences are present in the database from a given length interval of interest; it also may not be possible to remove the sequences belonging to the family being modeled from the database if these are not known a priori. This is particularly dangerous in the estimation of standard deviations. Here, it may be necessary to use an iterative algorithm where at each step a new standard deviation is calculated by ignoring the sequences in the database that are detected as members of the family at the corresponding step. The new standard deviation is used to generate a new set of normalized scores, as well as a new set of putative members of the family. Another general problem is that of short sequences, which often behave differently from very long ones. In certain cases, it may be practical to use a different normalization procedure for short sequences. Finally, in the case of an HMM library, a fixed set of randomly generated sequences, with the same average composition as SWISS-PROT, could be used across different models.

In the GPCR example, for any sequence O of length l, we use the normalized score $\mathcal{E}_S(O)$ based on the residual with respect to the empirical regression line of the random sequences of similar average composition, divided by the approximate standard deviation derived from (8.2):

$$\mathcal{E}_S(O) = \frac{[3.038l + 122.11 - \mathcal{E}(O)]}{0.66\sqrt{l}}, \qquad (8.3)$$

where $\mathcal{E}(O)$ is the negative log-likelihood of the Viterbi path. One obvious issue is the setting of the detection threshold. Here, the smallest score on the training set is 16.03 for the sequence labeled UK33_HCMVA. This low score is isolated because there are no other scores smaller than 18. Thus the threshold can be set at 16 or a little higher. By removing very long sequences exceeding the maximal GPCR length as well as sequences containing ambiguous amino acids, the search algorithm presented here yields no false negatives and two false positives (threshold 16) or one false negative and no false positives (threshold 18). At short lengths (below the length of the model), (8.2) is not necessarily a good approximation, so that it may be worthwhile to try a mixed scheme where a normalization factor is calculated empirically at short lengths ($l < N$) and (8.2) is used for larger lengths ($l > N$). Finally, thresholds may be set using the fact that the extreme score of a set of random sequences of fixed length follows an extreme value distribution [550].

8.1.5 Hydropathy Plots

Because of the particular structure of the GPCRs, one may reasonably conclude that it should be possible to detect easily whether a given sequence belongs to this class by drawing its hydropathy plot according to one of the well-known hydropathy scales [166]. If this was the case, it would render the HMM approach much less attractive for detection experiments, at least for this particular family. To check this point, hydropathy plots of a number of sequences were constructed, using a 20-amino-acid window. Examples of plots obtained for three sequences are given in figure 8.3. As can be seen, these plots can be very noisy and ambiguous. Therefore it seems very unlikely that one could achieve good detection rates based on hydropathy plots alone. Consensus patterns, hydropathy plots, and HMMs should rather be viewed as complementary techniques.

One can also compute a hydropathy plot from the HMM probabilities, as explained in chapter 7. Such a plot, shown in figure 8.4, displays the expected hydropathy at each position, rather than the hydropathy observed in any individual sequence. As a result, the signal is amplified and the seven transmembrane regions are clearly identifiable.

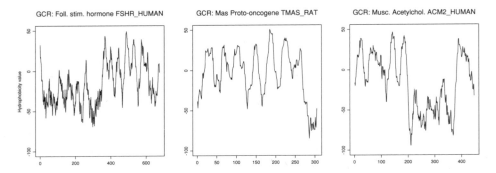

Figure 8.3: Hydropathy Plots for Three GPCRs of Length Less Than 1000, Using a Window of 20 Amino Acids. The vertical axis represents free energy for transferring a hypothetical alpha-helix of length 20, at the corresponding location, from the membrane interior to water. A peak of 20 kcal/mol or more usually signals the possible presence of a transmembrane alpha-helix.

8.1.6 Bacteriorhodopsin

Bacteriorhodopsin (see [317] for a brief review and [248] for a structural model) is a seven-transmembrane-domain protein that functions as a light-driven proton pump in *Halobacterium halobium*. Although it is functionally related to rhodopsin, it is not a GPCR. Structural and evolutionary relation-ships between bacteriorhodopsin and the GPCRs are not entirely clear at the moment. The raw score given by the HMM to bacteriorhodopsin is 852.27 for the primary sequence given in [411], and 851.62 for the slightly different se-quence in [318]. Since the length of bacteriorhodopsin is $l = 248$, these scores are in fact close to the regression line constructed on the random sequences of similar average composition, and slightly below it. The residual of the first sequence, for instance, is 23.26 and its normalized score is 2.23, according to (8.3). This confirms that bacteriorhodopsin is not a GPCR and is consistent with the lack of a significant degree of homology between bacteriorhodopsin and GPCRs.

In [414] it is suggested that a higher degree of homology can be obtained by changing the linear order of the helices, and that the sequences may be evo-lutionarily related via exon shuffling. We thus constructed a new sequence by moving the seven helices of bacteriorhodopsin into the order (5,6,7,2,3,4,1), as suggested by these authors. Intracellular and extracellular domains were left untouched. The raw HMM score of this artificial sequence is 840.98. Although it is closer to the GPCR scores, the difference does not appear to be particularly significant. The HMM scores therefore do not seem to provide much support

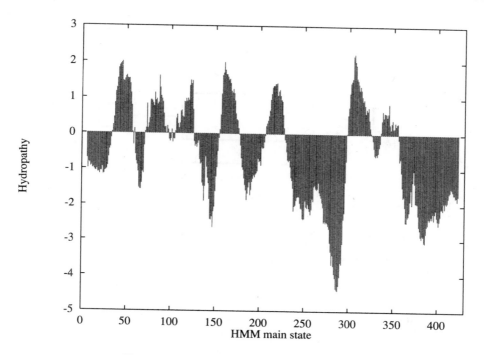

Figure 8.4: Hydropathy Plot for the GPCR HMM.

for the hypothesis presented in [414]. This point, however, requires further work because of the relatively short length of bacteriorhodopsin and the role the nonhelical domain may play in the scores.

8.1.7 Classification

By "classification" we mean the organization of a family of sequences into subclasses. This can be useful, for instance, in phylogenetic reconstruction. Classification using HMMs can be achieved in at least two different ways: (1) by training several models in parallel (figure 8.5) and using some form of competitive learning [334], or (2) by looking at how likelihoods and paths cluster within a single model. The first approach is not suitable here: the total number of sequences we have, especially for some receptor classes, is too small to train—for, say, 15 models in parallel. This experiment would require further algorithmic developments, such as the inclusion of prior information in the models, as well as new versions of the databases with more sequences.

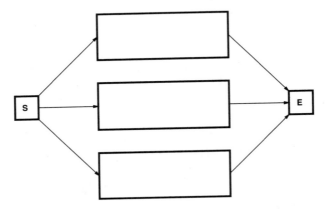

Figure 8.5: Classification HMM. Schematic representation of the type of multiple HMM architecture used in [334] for detecting subfamilies within a protein family. Each "box" between the start and end states corresponds to a single standard HMM.

For the second approach, it is clear from visual inspection of the multiple alignment that there are clusterings and interesting relationships among the Viterbi paths corresponding to different receptor subgroups. For instance, all the thyrotropin receptor precursors (TSHR) have a long initial loop on insert state 20, the same state that is optimal for (8.1). Interestingly, the same is true for the lutropin-gonadotropic hormone receptor precursor (LSHR). Here, we shall not attempt to exploit these relationships systematically to classify GPCRs from scratch, but rather shall analyze the behavior of the HMM scores with respect to the preexisting classification into major receptor classes.

For this purpose, we first extract all receptor classes for which we have at least seven representative sequences in order to avoid major bias effects. The classes and the number of corresponding sequences are olfactory (11), adenosine (9), opsin (31), serotonin (18), angiotensin (7), dopamine (12), acetylcholine (18), and adrenergic (26), for a total of 132 sequences representing 62% of the extended database obtained after searching SWISS-PROT. The histogram of the distances or normalized scores to the random regression line of the sequences in the eight classes selected in this way is plotted in figure 8.6. The normalized scores extend from 20 to 44 and are collected in bins of size 2.

The clustering of all the sequences in a given receptor subclass around a particular distance is striking. Olfactory receptors are the closest to being random. This is perhaps not too surprising, since these receptors must interact with a very large space of possible odorants. Adrenergic receptors are the most distant from the random regression line, and hence appear to be the most con-

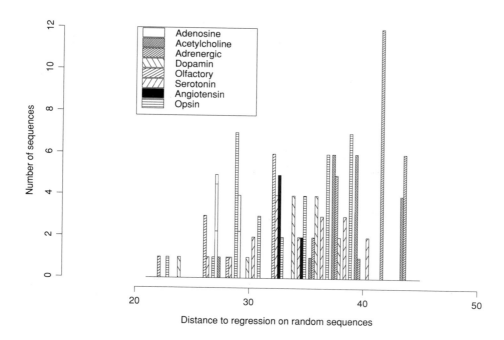

Figure 8.6: Histogram of the Distances (Normalized Scores) to the Randomly Generated Sequences for Different Classes of GPCRs. Olfactory receptors are closest to being random. Adrenergic receptors appear to be the most constrained and the most distant from the line. Different classes of receptors tend to cluster at different distances. Angiotensin receptors have a particularly narrow distribution of distances.

strained. There are also apparent differences on the standard deviation of each class. For instance, the angiotensin receptors occupy a narrow band, and only one angiotensin receptor type is known, whereas the opsin receptors are more spread out. Most classes seem to have a bell-shaped distribution, but there are exceptions. The opsins appear to have a bimodal distribution. This could be the result of the existence of subclasses within the opsins. The second peak corresponds mostly to rhodopsin (OPSD) sequences and a few red-sensitive opsins (OPSR). The presence of two peaks does not seem to result from differences between vertebrate and invertebrate opsins. With future database releases, it may be possible to improve the resolution and reduce sampling effects. But even so, these results suggest a strong relationship between the score assigned to a sequence by the HMM model and the sequence's membership in a given receptor class. On the other hand, it must also be noted that it would be very difficult to recover the underlying class structure from the histogram of scores alone, without any a priori knowledge of receptor types. A detailed classification of the entire GPCR family together with a complete phylogenetic reconstruction is beyond our scope here.

8.1.8   Fragment Detection from ESTs and cDNA

As a result of EST and cDNA sequencing efforts over the past few years, there are several databases of DNA sequences corresponding to protein fragments. It is naturally of interest to be able to recognize and classify such fragments, and to be able to recover any new useful information. HMMs could be tailored to such tasks in several ways. One obvious possibility is, for a given protein family, to train different HMMs to recognize different portions of the protein. Here we conducted a number of preliminary tests using the GPCR family and artificially generated fragments. While the typical length of interest to us was around $l = 150$, we also investigated what happens at smaller lengths, and when sequencing noise is taken into account. Sequencing noise was approximated by converting amino acid sequences to DNA and introducing random independent changes in the DNA with a fixed noise probability p. We concentrated on three length levels: $l = 150$, 100, and 50, and three noise percentage levels: $p = 0$, 5, and 10.

We first constructed five data sets, all containing fragments of fixed length 150. In the first set the fragments were extracted at random locations from the training data set of 142 GPCRs. In the second set, 200 fragments were extracted randomly from a larger database of GPCRs [325]. In the third set, we generated 200 random sequences of fixed length 150 with average composition identical to the GPCRs. In the fourth set, we randomly extracted segments of length 150 from a database of kinase sequences. Finally, in the fifth set we did the same but using the SWISS-PROT database.

As with pairwise sequence alignments, HMMs can be used to produce both local or global alignments. Here we analyze the scores associated with global alignments to the model, that is with the negative log-likelihoods of the complete Viterbi paths. The histograms of the corresponding scores are plotted in figure 8.7. These results show in particular that with a raw score threshold of about 625, such a search can eliminate a lot of the false positives while producing only a reasonable number of false negatives. The same results are plotted in figure 8.8, but with a length $l = 50$ and a noise $p = 10\%$. As can be seen, the overlap between the distributions is now more significant. This of course requires a more careful analysis of how performance deteriorates as a function of fragment length and noise across the entire SWISS-PROT database.

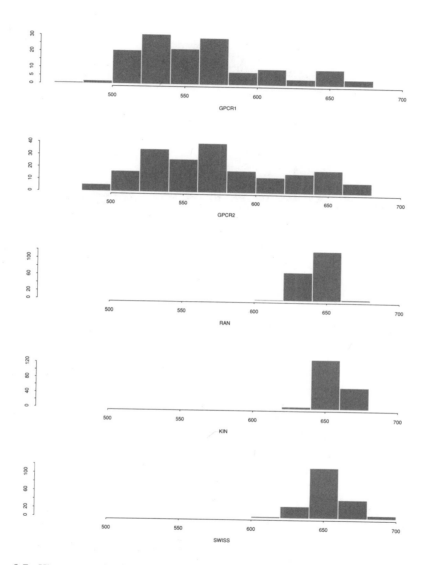

Figure 8.7: Histogram of Scores of Different Fragment Sequences of Length 150. The first histogram is constructed from 142 random fragments taken from the training set. All other histograms are based on 200 fragment sequences taken, in a random fashion, from a larger database of GPCRs, from randomly generated sequences with similar average composition, from a database of kinases, and from SWISS-PROT, respectively.

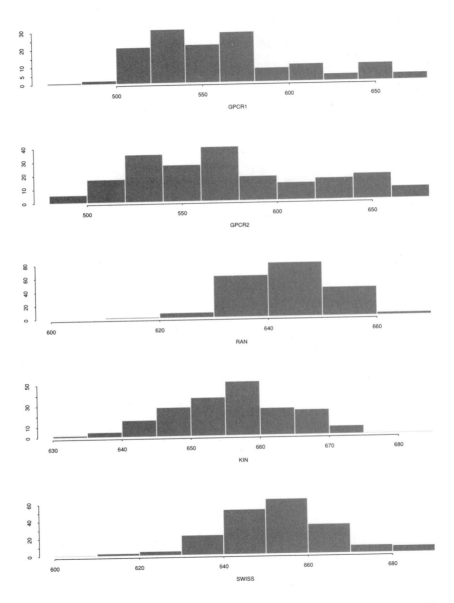

Figure 8.8: As Figure 8.7, with Fragments of Length 50 and $p = 10\%$ Noise Level.

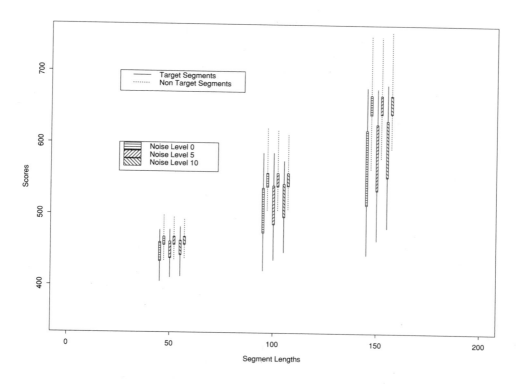

Figure 8.9: Summary of Scores on Entire SWISS-PROT Database. Segment lengths are shown on the horizontal axis, segment scores on the vertical axis. The figure depicts the standard deviations (striped columns), and the ranges (thin lines) of the scores, for both target (GPCR) sequences and non-target sequences, for all three segment lengths (50, 100, and 150) and noise levels (0, 5, and 10).

Summary of Results

The overall results are summarized in figure 8.9. Segment lengths are shown on the horizontal axis. Segment scores are shown on the vertical axis. The figure depicts the standard deviations (striped columns) and the ranges (thin lines) of the scores, for both target (GPCR) sequences and nontarget sequences, for all three fragment lengths (50, 100, and 150) and noise levels (0, 5, and 10). For each fragment length, the lines represent the ranges for all noise levels for target (GPCR) and nontarget sequences. To make all possible ranges for all noise levels visible, the lines representing the score ranges are slightly displaced with respect to the real fragment length.

At a given fragment length (e.g., 50), six lines represent, from left to right, noise level 0 for targets, noise level 0 for nontargets, noise level 5 for targets, noise level 5 for nontargets, noise level 10 for targets and noise level 10 for nontargets. Regression lines can be computed for all scores for all target and all nontarget fragments and each noise level:

- Target sequences

    Noise level 0: $y = 387.4 + 1.199\,l$

    Noise level 5: $y = 384.0 + 1.314\,l$

    Noise level 10: $y = 382.3 + 1.401\,l$

- Non-target sequences

    Noise level 0: $y = 364.7 + 1.909\,l$

    Noise level 5: $y = 364.8 + 1.910\,l$

    Noise level 10: $y = 364.8 + 1.911\,l$

These regression lines are obtained from only three fragment lengths. Therefore they constitute only an approximation to the scores at all intermediary lengths. The lines intercept for a fragment length of about 35. This means that 35 is the approximate length limit for nonzero discrimination based on scores alone.

As expected, for the target sequences the slopes of the regression lines substantially increase with noise. Intercepts do not vary much. The slopes and intercepts for the nontarget sequences are stable; the noise level does not have a strong influence on nontarget sequences. The approximate regression line for all nontarget sequences is $y \approx 364.8 + 1.91l$. Consistent with the results in [38], this slope is inferior to the slope of the similar line that can be derived at greater lengths. The standard deviations of the scores can be studied similarly, as a function of length and noise level.

ROC results

After scoring the entire database, one can compute, for each length and each noise level, the number of true and false positives and the number of true and false negatives, for a given score threshold. These sensitivity/selectivity results can be summarized by drawing the corresponding ROCs (receiver operating characteristics), as in figure 8.10.

ROC curves are obtained by computing, for threshold values scanned within a given range, the sensitivity or hit rate (proportion of true positives) and the selectivity or false alarm rate (proportion of false positives) from the

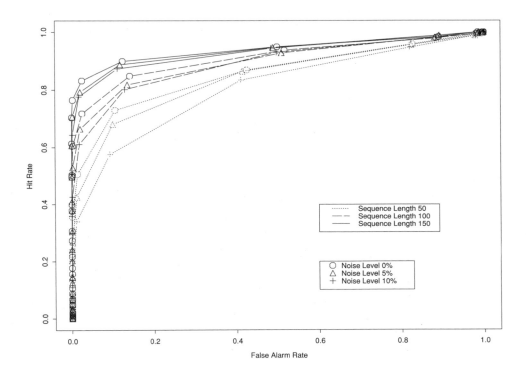

Figure 8.10: ROCs for All Scores of All SWISS-PROT Fragments at Lengths 50, 100, and 150 and Noise Levels 0, 5, and 10. Sequences with ambiguous symbols are filtered out.

number of true/false positives and negatives. Threshold range is a function of fragment length. For each segment length, the minimum threshold is a (rounded) value where no non-GPCR fragment is classified as positive across noise levels; the maximum threshold is a (rounded) value where no known GPCR (from PROSITE) is classified negative across noise levels. These curves provide a convenient means for setting thresholds as a function of desirable goals. As can be seen, there is a nice progressive ordering of the curves as a function of noise and length. The curves tend to "stick" to the vertical axes. This clearly shows that very low false alarm rates are obtained even for high hit rates: there is very good detection of a large number of target sequences. However, the curves do not "stick" to the horizontal axes. This shows that to detect the higher percentage of target sequences, the number of false positives must increase substantially. This is certainly due to the fact

	0	5	10
50	1.16	1.18	1.03
100	1.63	1.49	1.50
150	2.41	2.14	1.96

Table 8.2: Imperfect "Summary" of All Results that Make Possible Estimation of the Performance of Intermediate Length Fragments and Noise Levels.

that GPCRs comprise both relatively conserved and highly variable regions. It is virtually impossible to distinguish a short fragment, extracted from a highly variable region, from the general SWISS-PROT background. Likewise, longer fragments that include more conserved regions are easier to separate from the background. For short fragment lengths and high noise levels, these curves suggest that additional filters should be constructed to improve performance.

Detection analysis with the d' measure

Given the scores of two populations to be discriminated, and assuming that these two distributions are Gaussians with the same standard deviation equal to 1, the d' measure gives the distance between the centers of the two Gaussians for a certain level of false positives and negatives.

A preliminary detection analysis of the SWISS-PROT scores with a d' measure shows that d' varies widely with the classification threshold. This indicates that the score distribution curves are not Gaussian (as can observed from the histograms). Because it would be interesting to give a single measure of performance for each noise level and fragment length, the following method is used. A linear interpolation measure of false alarm rates is computed for a hit rate of 0.9 at each noise level and fragment length. The d' measure is then computed for the resulting pair $(0.9, x)$, where x is the linearly interpolated false alarm value. Table 8.2 gives the results for each noise level and fragment length.

Improving Detection Rates

So far we have examined only the raw scores produced by the HMM, that is, the negative likelihood of the Viterbi paths. HMMs, however, contain considerable additional information that could be used in principle to improve database mining performance. In fact, for each fragment, a number of additional indicators can be built and combined—for instance, in a Bayesian network—to improve performance. Most notably, the structure of the paths themselves can be used. As one might expect, there is a clear difference between the paths of

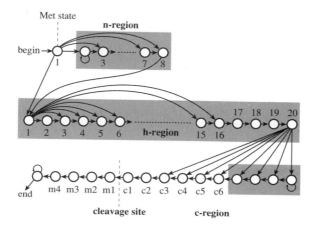

Figure 8.11: The HMM Used for Signal Peptide Discrimination. The model [406] is designed so that it implements an explicit modeling of the length distribution in the various regions. The states in a shaded box are tied to one another.

true and false positives. The path of a false positive is on average more discontinuous and contains a larger number of gaps. Several measures of path discontinuity can be constructed. One can use (1) the number of transitions out of delete states in a path; (2) the length of the longest contiguous block of emitting states in a path; or (3) the logarithm of the probability of the path itself (transitions only/no emissions). In one test, the combination of such measures with raw scores improves the detection of true positives by 15–20%. Other directions for improving detection rates are explored in [42].

8.1.9   Signal Peptide and Signal Anchor Prediction by HMMs

In section 6.4.1 the problem of finding signal peptides in the N-terminal part of prokaryotic and eukaryotic sequences was introduced. The window-based neural network approach [404] can exploit the correlations among the amino acids, in particular around the cleavage site, but without extra input units, it cannot benefit from the pattern in the entire sequence and the different length distributions that characterize signal peptides.

The length properties of signal peptides are in fact known to differ between various types of organisms: bacterial signal peptides are longer than their eukaryotic counterparts, and those of Gram-positive bacteria are longer than those of Gram-negative bacteria. In addition, there are compositional differences that correlate with the position in the signal peptide and also in the first few residues of the mature protein.

Combined model

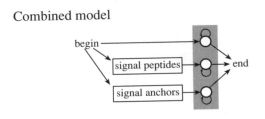

Signal anchor model

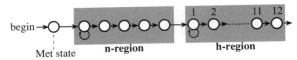

Figure 8.12: The HMM Designed to Discriminate Between Signal Peptides and Signal Anchors. The block diagram (top) shows how the combined model [406] is put together from the signal peptide model and the anchor model. The final states shown in the shaded box are tied to one another, and model all residues not in a signal peptide or an anchor. The model of signal anchors (bottom) has only two types of states (grouped by the shaded boxes) apart from the Met state.

Another important and difficult problem is that some proteins have N-terminal sequences that initiate translocation in the same way as signal peptides do, but are not cleaved by signal peptidase [541, 406]. The uncleaved signal peptide is known as a signal anchor, a special type of membrane protein. Signal anchors typically have hydrophobic regions longer than those of cleaved signal peptides, and other regions differ also in their compositional features.

Nielsen and Krogh [406] constructed a hidden Markov model designed both to discriminate between signal peptides and nonsignal peptides and to locate the cleavage site. The HMM was designed so that it took known signal peptide features into account, in particular the different regions described in section 6.4.1. In their scheme a signal peptide model was combined with a model of signal anchors, in order to obtain a prediction tool that was able to discriminate between signal peptides and anchors.

The signal peptide model is shown in figure 8.11. It implements an explicit modeling of the length distribution in the various regions using *tied* states that have the same amino acid distribution in the emission and transition probabilities associated with them.

To discriminate among signal peptides, signal anchors, and soluble nonsecretory proteins, the model was augmented by a model of anchors as shown in figure 8.12. The whole model was trained using all types of sequences (known signal peptides and known anchor sequences, as well as cytoplasmic and nuclear sequences). The most likely path through the combined model yields a prediction of which of the three classes the protein belongs to.

In terms of predictive performance in relation to discrimination between signal peptide sequences and nonsignal peptide sequences, the combination of C-score and S-score neural networks (see section 6.4.1) had a discrimination level comparable to that of the HMM. For eukaryotes the networks were slightly better, while for Gram-negative bacteria the HMM was slightly better [406]. For discrimination between cleaved signal peptides and uncleaved signal anchors, the HMM had a correlation coefficient of 0.74, corresponding to a sensitivity of 71% and a specificity of 81%—while the S-score from the neural network could be used to obtain a performance on this task not exceeding 0.4 for the correlation coefficient. The HMM is much better at recognizing signal anchor and therefore at detecting this type of membrane-associated protein.

However, these results should not be taken as a claim that the neural network method is unable to solve the signal anchor problem, since the signal anchors were not included as training data in the neural network model, as was the case for the HMM [406].

A similar approach in the form of a structured HMM has been used to model and predict transmembrane protein toplogy in the TMHMM method [335]. TMHMM can discriminate between soluble and membrane proteins with both specificity and sensitivity better than 99%, although the accuracy drops when signal peptides are present. Due to the high degree of accuracy the method is excellent for scanning entire genomes for detection of integral membrane proteins [335].

8.2   DNA and RNA Applications

Multiple alignments of nucleotide sequences are harder to make than alignments of protein sequences. One reason is that parameters in amino acid substitution matrices can be estimated by means of evolutionary and biochemical analysis, while it is hard to obtain good measures of general mutation and deletion costs of individual nucleotides in nucleic acids. The "twilight zone" of dubious alignment significance is reached faster for sequences from a shorter alphabet, and fewer evolutionary events are therefore needed to get into the twilight zone when aligning DNA.

HMMs do not a priori require an explicit definition of the substitution costs. The HMM approach avoids the computationally hard many-to-many multiple-sequence alignment problem by recasting it as a many-to-one sequence-to-HMM alignment problem [155]. The different positions in a model can in practice have individual implicit substitution costs associated with them. These features have contributed to the fact that in several cases HMMs applied to nucleic acids have led to the discovery of new patterns not previously revealed by other methods. In protein-related applications, HMMs have more often led to improvements of earlier methods.

8.2.1   Gene Finding in Prokaryotes and Eukaryotes

Gene finding requires the integration of many different signals: promoter regions, translation start and stop context sequences, reading frame periodicities, polyadenylation signals, and, for eukaryotes, intron splicing signals, compositional contrast between exons and introns, potential differences in nucleosome positioning signals, and sequence determinants of topological domains. The last involves the matrix (or scaffold) attachment regions (MARs or SARs), which are associated with higher-order chromosomal organization. The attachment signals may be involved in promoting transcriptional activity in vivo, and have recently been reported to be present between genes. For prokaryotes the DNA sequence also needs to allow strong compaction in a chromatin-like structure. The length of the extended DNA from a single operon corresponds to the diameter of the cell. Since all these signals to a large extent complement each other, in the sense that some may be weak when others are strong, a probabilistic approach for their integration is the natural way to handle the complexity of the problem.

In prokaryotes, gene finding is made simpler by the fact that coding regions are not interrupted by intervening sequences. Still, especially for relatively short open reading frames, it is nontrivial to distinguish between sequences that represent true genes and those that do not. In the highly successful gene finder GeneMark [81, 83, 82], which in its first version was based on frame dependent nonhomogeneous Markov models, a key feature strongly improving the performance is a clever detection of the "shadow" of a true coding region on the non-coding strand (for further detail see chapter 9).

A hidden Markov model has also been developed to find protein-coding genes in *E. coli* DNA [336] (work done before the complete *E. coli* genome became available). This HMM includes states that model the codons and their frequencies in *E. coli* genes, as well as the patterns found in the intergenic region, including repetitive extragenic palindromic sequences and the Shine–Dalgarno motif. To take into account potential sequencing errors and/or frameshifts in a raw genomic DNA sequence, it allows for the (very unlikely) possibility of insertions and deletions of individual nucleotides within a codon. The parameters of the HMM are estimated using approximately 1 million nucleotides of annotated DNA, and the model is tested on a disjoint set of contigs containing about 325,000 nucleotides. The HMM finds the exact locations of about 80% of the known *E. coli* genes, and approximate locations for about 10%. It also finds several potentially new genes and locates several places where insertion or deletion errors and/or frameshifts may be present in the contigs.

A number of powerful HMMs and other probabilistic models for gene finding in eukaryotes had been developed (see chapter 9 and [343, 107] and references therein). Eukaryotic gene models are typically built by assembling a number of components, such as submodels for splice sites, exons, and introns to take advantage of the corresponding weak consensus signals and compositional differences. The individual submodels must remain relatively small if the goal is to scan entire genomes in reasonable time. Other key elements include the use of three exon submodels in parallel in order to take into account the three possible ways introns may interrupt the reading frame, as well as features to incorporate exon and intron length distributions, promoters, poly-adenylation signals, intergenic sequences, and strand asymmetry. It is often better to train the entire recognition system at once, rather than each of its components separately. In particular, the standard HMM algorithms can be modified in order to optimize the global gene parse produced by the system rather than the sequence likelihoods [333]. The best gene recognition is achieved by some of these models [107], with complete exon recognition rates in the 75 to 80% range (with exact splice sites). Additional work is required to improve the detection rates further. Such improvements may come from the incorporation of new, better submodels of promoters or initial and terminal exons, as well as other physical properties and signals present in the DNA, such as bendability or nucleosome positioning. Such compactification signals, which have been completely neglected so far, are likely to play an important role in the biological gene-finding machinery as well. In the rest of this chapter, we build relatively large models of gene components and describe such possible signals.

8.2.2   HMMs of Human Splice Sites, Exons, and Introns

Strong research efforts have been directed toward the understanding of the molecular mechanism responsible for intron splicing ever since it was discovered that eukaryotic genes contain intervening sequences that are removed from the mRNA molecules before they leave the nucleus to be translated. Since the necessary and sufficient sequence determinants for proper splicing are still largely unknown, probabilistic models in the form of HMMs have been used to characterize the splicing signals found experimentally.

Unlike the case of protein families, it is essential to remark that all exons and their associated splice site junctions are neither directly nor closely related by evolution. However, they still form a "family" in the sense of sharing certain general characteristics. For example, in a multiple alignment of a set of flanked exons, the consensus sequences of the splice sites should stand out as highly conserved regions in the model, exactly like a protein motif in the case of a protein family. As a result, one should be particularly careful to regard insertions and deletions in the HMM model as formal string operations rather than evolutionary events.

To see whether an HMM would pick up easily known features of human acceptor and donor sites, a model with the standard architecture as shown in figure 7.2 was trained on 1000 randomly selected flanked donor and acceptor sites [32, 33, 35]. By close inspection of the parameters of the HMM trained specifically on the flanked acceptor sites, it was observed that the model learns the acceptor consensus sequence perfectly: ([TC] ... [TC] [N] [CT] [A] [G] [G]). The pyrimidine tract is clearly visible, as are a number of other known weak signals, such as a branching (lariat) signal with a high A in the 3' end of the intron. (See figure 8.13.)

Similarly, the donor sites are clearly visible in a model trained on flanked donor sites but are harder to learn than the acceptor sites. The consensus sequence of the donor site is learned perfectly: ([CA] [A] [G] [G] [T] [AG] [A] [G]). The same is true for the G-rich region [164], extending roughly 75 bases downstream from the human donor sites (figure 8.13). The fact that the acceptor site is easier to learn is most likely explained by the more extended nature of acceptor site regions as opposed to donor sites. However, it could also result from the fact that exons in the training sequences are always flanked by *exactly* 100 nucleotides upstream. To test this hypothesis, a similar model using the same sequences, but in *reverse* order, is trained. Surprisingly, the model still learns the acceptor site much better than the donor site (which is now downstream from the acceptor site). The random order of the nucleotides in the polypyrimidine tract region downstream from the acceptor site presumably contributes to this situation. In contrast, the G-rich region in the 5' intron end has some global structure that can be identified by the HMM.

8.2.3 Discovering Periodic Patterns in Exons and Introns by Means of New HMM Architectures

In another set of experiments a standard HMM was trained on human exons flanked by intron sequence. A set of 500 randomly selected flanked internal exons, with the length of the exons restricted to between 100 and 200 nucleotides, was used (internal human exons have an average length of ≈ 150 nucleotides).

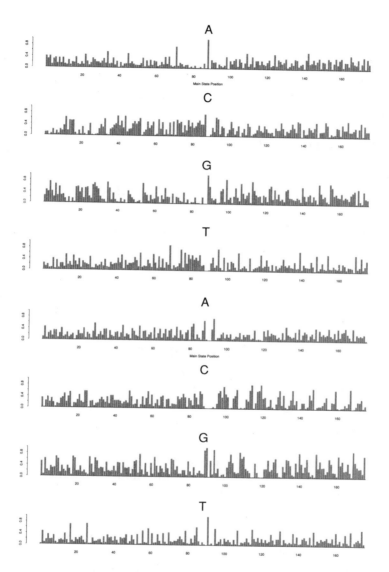

Figure 8.13: Emission Distribution from Main States of an HMM Model Trained on 1000 Acceptor (top) and 1000 Donor Sites (bottom). The flanking sequence is kept constant with 100 nucleotides on each side; the model, however, has length 175. For the acceptor sites, the characteristic consensus sequence is easily recognizable ([TC]...[TC][N][CT][A][G][G]). Note the high A probability associated with the branch point downstream from the acceptor site. The characteristic consensus sequence of the donor site is also easily recognizable ([CA][A][G][G][T][AG][A][G]). Learning is achieved using the standard architecture (figure 7.2) initialized uniformly, and by adding a regularizer term to the objective function that favors the backbone transition path.

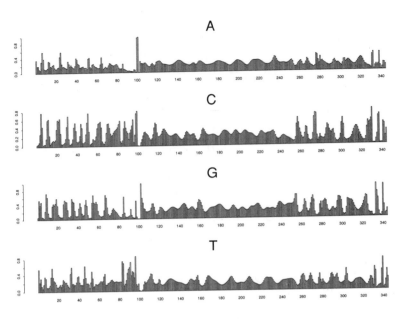

Figure 8.14: Emission Distribution from Main States of an HMM Model Trained on 500 Flanked Internal Exons. The length of the exons was constrained to the interval between 100 and 200 nucleotides, with average of 142, and fixed intron flanking of 100 on each side. The number of main states in the model was 342. Note the oscillatory pattern in the exon region and outside.

The probability of emitting each of the four nucleotides, across the main states of the trained model, is plotted in figure 8.14. We see striking periodic patterns, especially in the exon region, characterized by a minimal period of 10 nucleotides with A and G in phase, and C and T in antiphase. A periodic pattern in the parameters of the models of the form [AT][CG] (or [AT]G), with a periodicity of roughly 10 base pairs, can be seen at positions 10, 19, 28, 37, 46, 55, 72, 81, 90, 99, 105, 114, 123, 132 and 141. The emission profile of the backbone was also compared for two nucleotides jointly. The plots of A+G and C+T are considerably smoother than those of A+T and C+G on both the intron side and the exon side. The 10 periodicity is visible both in the smooth phase/antiphase pattern of A+G and C+T and in the sharp contrast of high A+T followed by high C+G. There is also a rough three-base pair periodicity, especially visible in C+G, where every third emission corresponds to a local minimum. This is consistent with the reading frame features of human genes [525], which are especially strong on the third codon position ($\approx$30% C and $\approx$26% G; see figure 6.11).

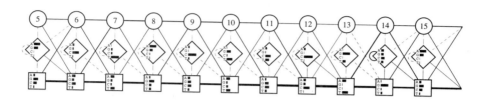

Figure 8.15: The Repeated Segment of the Tied Model. Rectangles represent main states and circles represent delete states. Histograms represent emission distributions from main and insert states. Thickness of connections is proportional to corresponding transition distribution. Position 15 is identical to position 5.

In order further to characterize the periodicity, a wide range of different HMM architectures were trained on nonflanked *internal* exons, in order to separate features from the special gradients in the nucleotide composition known to be present in initial and terminal exons [164]. When training on the bulk of the internal exons in the length interval between 100 and 200 nucleotides, a clear and consistent pattern emerged in the emission probabilities, no matter which architecture was applied. The architectural variation included conventional left–right HMM models, left–right models with identical segments "tied" together, and loop or "wheel" models with better ability to reveal periodic patterns in the presence of noise. Although the conventional type of left–right architecture is not the ideal model of an exon, due to the large length variations, it still identifies the periodic pattern quite well.

To test the periodicity yet further, a "tied" exon model with a hardwired periodicity of 10 was trained [33]. The tied model consists of 14 identical segments of length 10 and five additional positions in the beginning and the end of the model, making a total length of 150. During training the segments are kept identical by *tying* the parameters—that is, the parameters are constrained to be exactly the same throughout learning, as in the weight-sharing procedure for neural networks. The model was trained on 800 internal exon sequences of length between 100 and 200, and it was tested on 262 different sequences. The parameters of the repeated segment after training are shown in figure 8.15. Emission probabilities are represented by horizontal bars of corresponding proportional length. There is a lot of structure in this segment. The most prominent feature is the regular expression [^T][AT]G at positions 12–14. The same pattern was often found at positions with very low entropy in the standard models described above. In order to test the significance, the tied model was compared with a standard model of the same length. By comparing the average negative log-likelihood they both assign to the exon sequences and

Loop states	A	C	G	T
I1	0.1957	0.4808	0.1986	0.1249
M1	0.3207	0.0615	0.0619	0.5559
I2	0.0062	0.0381	0.5079	0.4478
M2	0.1246	0.2982	0.5150	0.0622
I3	0.4412	0.1474	0.2377	0.1737
M3	0.2208	0.6519	0.1159	0.0114
I4	0.2743	0.5893	0.0676	0.0689
M4	0.3709	0.0113	0.0603	0.5575
I5	0.1389	0.2946	0.0378	0.5287
M5	0.0219	0.0121	0.9179	0.0481
I6	0.0153	0.9519	0.0052	0.0277
M6	0.0905	0.1492	0.7017	0.0586
I7	0.1862	0.3703	0.3037	0.1399
M7	0.3992	0.2835	0.3119	0.0055
I8	0.2500	0.4381	0.2968	0.0151
M8	0.4665	0.0043	0.1400	0.3891
I9	0.6892	0.0156	0.2912	0.0040
M9	0.0121	0.2000	0.7759	0.0120
I10	0.2028	0.3701	0.0117	0.4155
M10	0.3503	0.3459	0.2701	0.0787
I11	0.1446	0.6859	0.0861	0.0834

Table 8.3: Emission Distributions for the Main and Insert States of a Loop Model (Figure 8.16) After Training on 500 Exon Sequences of Length 100-200.

to random sequences of similar composition, it was clear that the tied model achieves a level of performance comparable with the standard model, but with significantly fewer free parameters. Therefore a period of around 10 in the exons seems to be a strong hypothesis.

As the left–right architectures are not the ideal model of exons, it would be desirable to have a model with a loop structure, possibly such that the segment can be entered as many times as necessary for any given exon. See [336] for a loop structure used for *E. coli* DNA. One example of such a true loop model is shown schematically in figure 8.16. In the actual exon experiment the loop had length 10, with two flanks of length 4. This model was trained using gradient descent and the Dirichlet regularization for the backbone transitions to favor main states. Additional regularization must be used for the anchor state as a result of its particular role and connectivity. The Dirichlet vector used for the anchor state is (0.1689 0.1656 0.1656 0.1689 0.1656 0.1656). The emission distribution of the main and insert states inside the loop is shown in table 8.3. Again the results are remarkably consistent with those obtained with the tied model. The pattern [^T][AT]G is clearly visible, starting at main state 3 (M3).

Table 8.4 compares the temporal evolution of the cumulative negative log-likelihood of the training set in an experiment involving three models: a free model, a tied model, and a loop model. Although, as can be expected, the free model achieves the best scores after 12 cycles, this seems to be the result of

Cycle	NLL free model	NLL tied model	NLL loop model
1	1.013e+05	1.001e+05	9.993e+04
2	1.008e+05	9.902e+04	9.886e+04
3	9.965e+04	9.884e+04	9.873e+04
4	9.886e+04	9.875e+04	9.859e+04
5	9.868e+04	9.869e+04	9.855e+04
6	9.854e+04	9.865e+04	9.849e+04
7	9.842e+04	9.862e+04	9.848e+04
8	9.830e+04	9.861e+04	9.852e+04
9	9.821e+04	9.860e+04	9.845e+04
10	9.810e+04	9.859e+04	9.842e+04
11	9.803e+04	9.859e+04	9.844e+04
12	9.799e+04	9.859e+04	9.843e+04

Table 8.4: Evolution of the NLL Scores over 12 Cycles of Gradient Descent, with $\eta = 0.01$, for a Free Model (Figure 7.2), a Tied Model (Figure 8.15), and a Loop Model (Figure 8.16). All models are trained on 500 exons of length between 100 and 200 in all reading frames.

some degree of overfitting. The loop model, and to a lesser extent the tied model, outperform the free model during the first learning cycles. The loop model performs better than the tied models at all cycles. The free model has a better score than the loop model only after cycle 7. This is also an indication that the loop model is a better model for the data.

Finally, a different sort of loop model was trained on both exon and intron sequences. This HMM architecture has the form of a "wheel" with a given number of main states, without flanking states arranged linearly or any distinction between main and insert states, and without delete states. Thus there are no problems associated with potential silent loops. Sequences can enter the wheel at any point. The point of entry can of course be determined by dynamic programming. By using wheels with different numbers of states and comparing the cumulative negative log-likelihood of the training set, the most likely periodicity can be revealed. If wheels of nine states perform better than wheels of 10 states, the periodicity can be assumed to be related to the triplet reading frame rather than to structural aspects of the DNA (see below).

Figure 8.17 displays wheel model architectures (in this case of length 10 nucleotides) where sequences can enter the wheel at any point. The thickness of the arrows from "outside" represents the probability of starting from the corresponding state. After training, the emission parameters in the wheel model showed a periodic pattern [^T][AT]G in a clearly recognizable form in states 8, 9, and 10 of the exon model (top), and in states 7, 8, and 9 in the intron model (bottom). By training wheels of many different lengths, it was found that models of length 10 yielded the best fit. Implicitly, this is also confirmed by the fact that the skip probabilities are not strong in these models. In other words, if the data were nine-periodic, a wheel model with a loop of length 10 should be able to fit the data, by heavy use of the possibility of skipping a state in the

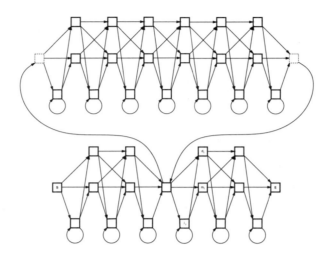

Figure 8.16: A Loop HMM Model Comprising Two Flanks and a Loop Anchored on a Silent State. The flanks and the loop are similar to the standard architecture.

wheel. State repeating in a nine-state wheel is nonequivalent to state skipping in a 10-state wheel. These wheel models do not contain independent *insert states* (as the linear left–right HMM architectures do). A repeat of the same state does not give the same freedom in terms of likelihood as if independent inserts were allowed. Moreover, in analogy to gap penalties in conventional multiple alignments, the HMM training procedure uses a regularization term favoring main states over skip states.

All the experiments were repeated using several subsets of exons starting in the one of the three codon positions in the reading frame, without any significant change in the observed patterns of the emission probabilities. For comparison, figure 8.18 shows the emission probabilities from a nine-state wheel model trained on the coding part of complete mRNA sequences of concatenated exons. This model clearly recognizes the triplet reading frame (compare to figure 6.11). The fact that the pattern is present in intron sequences provides additional evidence against a reading-frame-associated origin for the pattern in the exons.

The experiments indicate that the periodicity is strongest in exons, and possibly also in the immediate flanking intron sequence, but on the average somewhat weaker in arbitrarily selected deep intron segments. In none of the experiments using simple linear left–right HMM architectures was a clear regular oscillation pattern detected in the noncoding sequence. By using the wheel model to estimate the average negative log-likelihood per nucleotide for various types of sequence—different types of exons, introns, and intragenic regions—it was found that the periodic pattern is strongest in exons. The period in the alignments (average distance between state 9 nucleotides) is on the order of 10.1–10.2 nucleotides.

It is well known that "bent DNA" requires a number of small individual bends that are in phase [488]. Only when bends are phased at $\approx$ 10.5 bp (corresponding to one full turn of the double helix) can stable long-range curvature be obtained. Using the wheel model to perform alignments of introns and exons, it was found that the sequence periodicity has a potential structural implication because the $\approx$ 10-periodic bending potential of the aligned sequences displays the same periodicity. The bendability of the sequences was assessed using parameters for trinucleotide sequence-dependent bendability deduced from DNaseI digestion data [96]. DNaseI interacts with the surface of the minor groove, and bends the DNA molecule away from the enzyme. The experiments [96] therefore quantitatively reveal bendability parameters on a scale where low values indicate no bending potential and high values correspond to large bending or bendability toward the major groove, for the 32 double-stranded triplets: AAA/ATT, AAA/TTT, CCA/TGG, and so on. The profiles of the bending potentials of exons and introns have been related to nucleosome positioning [34]. These differences in the strength of the signals in coding and noncoding regions have possible implications for the recognition of genes by the transcriptional machinery.

8.2.4 HMMs of Human Promoter Regions

We have also trained a number of HMMs using DNA sequences from human promoter regions. In one experiment, promoter data were extracted from the GenBank [62]. Specifically, all human sequences that contained at least 250 nucleotides upstream and downstream from an experimentally determined transcriptional start point were extracted. Sequences containing non-nucleotide symbols were excluded. The redundancy was carefully reduced using the second Hobohm algorithm [259] and a novel method for finding a similarity cutoff, described in [422]. Briefly, this method is based on performing all pairwise alignments for a data set, fitting the resulting Smith-Waterman scores to an extreme value distribution [9, 550], and choosing a value above which there are more observations than expected from the distribution. A standard linear architecture with length N = 500 was trained using the remaining 625 sequences, all with length 501 (see [421] for details). The training was facilitated by initializing the main state emissions associated with the TATA-box using consensus probabilities from promoters with experimentally verified TATA-boxes.

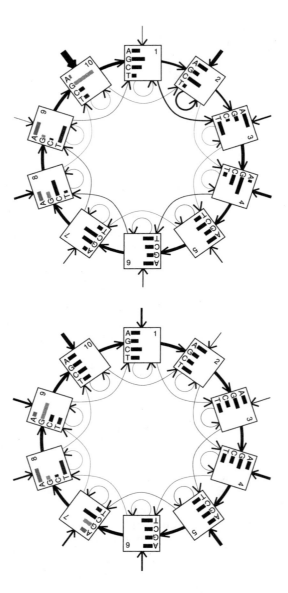

Figure 8.17: Wheel HMMs Used for Identifying Periodic Patterns. A. 10-state wheel trained on 500 internal exons of length between 100 and 200 nucleotides. Nonperfect alignment and interference with the reading frame cause features of the pattern to appear in states 2, 3, and 4 as well as 8, 9, and 10. B. 10-state wheel trained on 2000 human introns. 25 nucleotides were removed at the 5' and 3' ends in order to avoid effects of the conserved sequence patterns at the splice sites.

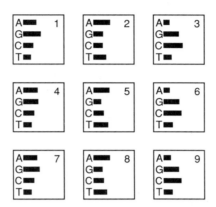

Figure 8.18: The Emission Probabilities from a Nine-State Wheel Model Trained on Complete mRNA Sequences Without the Skip and Loop Arrows. The three-periodic reading frame pattern is clearly visible, with higher frequencies of A and G, A and T, and C and G on the first, second, and third codon positions, respectively.

A bendability profile can be computed directly from the trained HMM (see Appendix D), or from the HMM-derived multiple alignment. A profile derived from a multiple alignment is shown in figure 8.19. The most striking feature is a significant increase in bendability in the region immediately *downstream* of the transcriptional start point. As promoters most often have been characterized by a number of upstream patterns and compositional tendencies, it is interesting that the HMM alignment corresponds to structurally similarity in the downstream region of these otherwise unrelated promoter sequences. They are not biased towards genes related to a specific function, etc. From a careful analysis of the sequence periodicities, we conjecture that the increase in downstream bendability is related to nucleosome positioning and/or facilitation of interaction with other factors involved in transcriptional initiation. We have also computed similar profiles from the HMM backbone probabilities using different physical scales such as stacking energies [410], nucleosome positioning [218], and propeller twist [241]. All profiles consistently show a large signal around the transcriptional start point with differences between the upstream and downstream regions. Additional results, including the periodic patterns, are discussed in [421] (see also [30] for a general treatment on how to apply additive, structural, or other scales to sequence analysis problems).

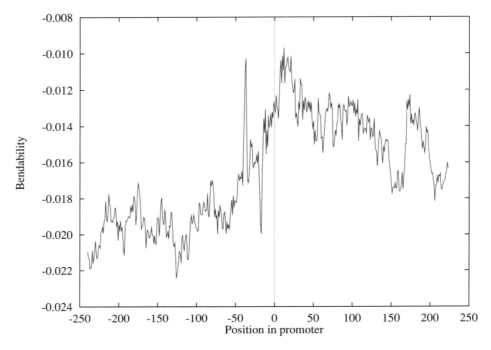

Figure 8.19: The Bendability Profile of Human Promoter Regions. The initiation site is roughly in the middle. The overall bendability is significantly increased downstream from the initiation site. This average profile was made from a multiple sequence alignment. A profile computed from the emission probabilities, instead of the actual triplet frequencies, produced a very similar pattern for the bendability.

8.3 Advantages and Limitations of HMMs

8.3.1 Advantages of HMMs

The numerous advantages of HMMs in computational molecular biology should be obvious by now. HMMs come with a solid statistical foundation and with efficient learning algorithms. They allow a consistent treatment of insertions and deletion penalties, in the form of locally learnable probabilities. Learning can take place directly from raw sequence data. Unlike conventional supervised NNs, HMMs can accommodate inputs of variable length and they do not require a teacher. They are the most flexible generalization of sequence profiles. They can be used efficiently in a number of tasks ranging from multiple alignments, to data mining and classification, to structural analysis and pattern discovery. HMMs are also easy to combine into libraries and in modular and hierarchical ways.

8.3.2 Limitations of HMMs

In spite of their success, HMMs can suffer in particular from two weaknesses. First, they often have a large number of unstructured parameters. In the case of protein models, the architecture of figure 7.2 has a total of approximately $49N$ parameters ($40N$ emission parameters and $9N$ transition parameters). For a typical protein family, N is on the order of a few hundred, resulting immediately in models with over 10,000 free parameters. This can be a problem when only a few sequences are available in a family, not an uncommon situation in early stages of genome projects. It should be noted, however, that a typical sequence provides on the order of 2N constraints, and 25 sequences or so provide a number of examples in the same range as the number of HMM parameters.

Second, first-order HMMs are limited by their first-order Markov property: they cannot express dependencies between hidden states. Proteins fold into complex 3D shapes determining their function. Subtle long-range correlations in their polypeptide chains may exist that are not accessible to a single HMM. For instance, assume that whenever X is found at position i, it is generally followed by Y at position j, and whenever X′ is found at position i, it tends to be followed by Y′ at j. A single HMM typically has two fixed emission vectors associated with the i and j positions. Therefore, it cannot capture such correlations. Only a small fraction of distributions over the space of possible sequences can be represented by a reasonably constrained HMM.[1] It must be noted, however, that HMMs can easily capture long-range correlations that are expressed in a constant way across a family of sequences, even when such correlations are the result of 3D interactions. This is the case, for example, for two linearly distant regions in a protein family that must share the same hydropathy as a result of 3D closeness. The same hydropathy pattern will be present in all the members of the family and is likely to be reflected in the corresponding HMM emission parameters after training.

Chapters 9 to 11 can be viewed as attempts to go beyond HMMs by combining them with NNs to form hybrid models (chapter 9), by modeling the evolutionary process (chapter 10), and by enlarging the set of HMM production rules (chapter 11).

---

[1] Any distribution can be represented by a single exponential-size HMM, with a start state connected to different sequences of deterministic states, one for each possible alphabet sequence, with a transition probability equal to the probability of the sequence itself.

Chapter 9

Probabilistic Graphical Models in Bioinformatics

9.1 The Zoo of Graphical Models in Bioinformatics

High-dimensional probability distributions are one of the fist obstacles one encounters when applying the Bayesian framework to typical real-life problems. This is because the data is high-dimensional, and so are the models we use, often with many thousand parameters and up. High-dimensionality comes also with other so called hidden variables. In general, the resulting global distribution $\mathbf{P}(D, M, H)$ is mathematically intractable and this is where the theory of graphical models comes into play. Using the fact that to a large extent the bulk of the dependencies in the real world are usually local, the high-dimensional distribution is approximated by a product of distributions over smaller clusters of variables defined over smaller spaces and which are tractable [348, 292]. In standard Markovian models, for instance, phenomena at time $t + 1$ may be linked to the past only through what happens in the present at time t. As a result, the global probability distribution $\mathbf{P}(X_1, \ldots, X_N)$ can be factored as a product of local probability distributions of the form $\mathbf{P}(X_{t+1}|X_t)$.

To be more specific, let us concentrate on a particular class of graphical models, namely Bayesian networks [416] (a more formal treatment of graphical models is given in appendix C). A Bayesian network consists of a directed acyclic graph with N nodes. To each node i is associated a random variable X_i. The parameters of the model are the local conditional probabilities, or characteristics, of each random variable given the random variables associated with the parent nodes $\mathbf{P}(X_i|X_j : j \in N^-(i))$, where $N^-(i)$ denotes all the parents of vertex i. The"Markovian" independence assumptions of a Bayesian network

225

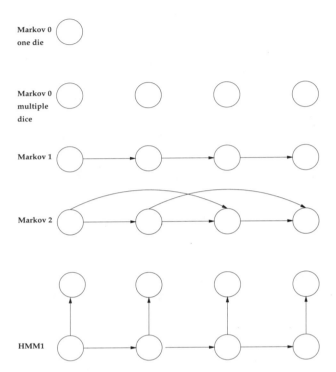

Figure 9.1:   Bayesian Network Representation of Markov Models of Increasing Complexity. Markov models of order 0 correspond to a single die or a collection of independent dice. Markov models of order 1 correspond to the standard notion of first order Markov chain. In Markov models of order 2, the present depends on the two previous time steps. All HMMs of order 1 have the same Bayesian network representation given here.

are equivalent to the global factorization property

$$\mathbf{P}(X_1, \ldots, X_N) = \prod_i \mathbf{P}(X_i | X_j : j \in N^-(i)). \tag{9.1}$$

In other words, the global probability distribution is the product of all the local characteristics. In practical applications, the directed nature of the edges of a Bayesian network is used to represent causality or temporal succession. Thus it should come as no surprise that Bayesian networks are being intensively used to model biological sequences, in the same way as they have been used to model speech or other sequential domains, and to construct expert systems.

In fact, the Bayesian framework allows us to build an increasingly complex suite of Bayesian network models for biological (and other) sequences. This hi-

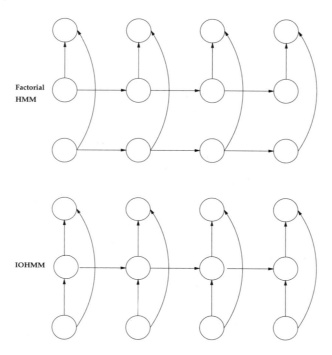

Figure 9.2: Bayesian Network Representation of Factorial HMMs and IOHMMs.

erarchy of models stems from the fact that, at some level, biological sequences have a sequential primary structure. The simplest probabilistic model for biological sequences we can think of is the single-die model of chapter 3, with four (nucleotides for DNA) or 20 (amino acid for proteins) faces, shown in figure 3.1. Such a model is represented by a Bayesian network with a single node or better with multiple identical disconnected nodes, one for each position in a sequence or in a family of sequences. The die model is trivial and remote from actual biological sequences but it serves as a first step and is often used as a background model against which to compare more sophisticated approaches.

At the next level, we can imagine a sequence of distinct dice, one for each position. This is essentially the model used when making profiles, abstracted for instance from pre-existing multiple alignments. If we connect the nodes of this model in a left-right chain, we get a standard first-order Markov model. Second- and higher-order Markov models, where the present may depend on several steps in the immediate past, are also possible. Their Bayesian network representation is obvious as well as their main weakness: a combinatorial ex-

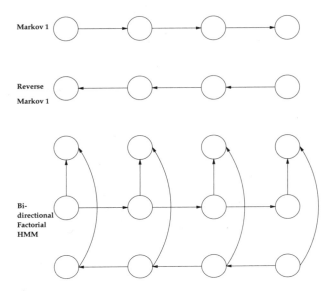

Figure 9.3: Bayesian Networks with Backward Markov Chains. All the backward chains in this figure can be replaced by forward chains via a simple change of variables.

plosion of the parameter space as the degree of the chain increases. For a small alphabet size such as DNA, however, Markov models of order up to six are possible and are commonly used in the literature, for instance in gene finding algorithms (see figure 9.1).

Simple left-right Markov models, however, do not directly capture insertions and deletions. We have seen that such events can be taken into account by using hidden Markov models (HMMs). HMMs can easily be represented as Bayesian networks. As such, their representation is similar to that of other models, such as Kalman filters. The Bayesian network representation of HMMs clarifies their probabilistic structures and the corresponding evidence propagation and learning algorithms, such as the well-known forward-backward algorithms and several other EM/gradient-descent variants [493].

More complex Markovian models have been used in artificial intelligence, for instance, factorial HMMs where the output depends on two or more forward Markov chains. In the speech domain, for instance, one chain can represent audio information and the other video information about lip configuration [203, 205]. Another set of models described in [40, 58] and discussed in a later section are the IOHMMs (input-output HMMs) (see figure 9.2). These models can be used to translate a given input sequence into an output sequence over

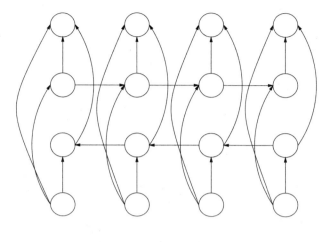

BIOHMM

Figure 9.4: Bayesian Network Representation of a BIOHMM. Note the presence of numerous undirected cycles.

a possibly different alphabet.

One important observation about biological sequences is that in reality they have a spatial rather than temporal structure. In particular, information from the "future" could be used to interpret the present without breaking any causality constraint. As a minimum, this suggests introducing backward Markovian chains in the previous models. Yet one must be careful, for it is easy to show that a simple backward Markov chain is entirely equivalent to a forward chain by a change of variables. The parameters of the two corresponding Bayesian network models are related by Bayes's rule. Likewise, if we reverse the direction of one of the chains of a factorial HMM, we obtain another factorial HMM that is entirely identical to the first one, and hence there is little to be gained (see figure 9.3). If we introduce a backward chain in an IOHMM, however, we obtain a new class of models we call BIOHMM (bi-directional IOHMM) [36] (see figure 9.4).

In the last section of this chapter, we will look at the applications of BIOHMMs and related models to the prediction of protein secondary structure. But first, we turn to other applications of probabilistic graphical models to sequence analysis problems, and in particular to DNA symmetries, gene finding, and gene parsing, and to general techniques for combining artificial NNs with graphical models.

9.2 Markov Models and DNA Symmetries

In a piece of double-helical DNA, the number of As is equal to the number of Ts, and the number of Cs is equal to the number of Gs. What appears today as a trivial property in fact was essential in guiding Watson and Crick towards the discovery of the double-helix model in the early 1950s. This property is also known as Chargaff's first parity rule [119]. Chargaff's second parity rule, however, is less known and states that the same thing is approximately true for a piece of *single-stranded* DNA of reasonable size. This rule, first stated in the 1960s [303, 120], has received some recognition in the recent years [430, 185, 231].

The validity of Chargaff's second parity rule can be studied across different organisms, across different kinds of DNA such as coding versus non-coding, and across different length scales. For simplicity, here we look only at genomic DNA in yeast. If we measure the DNA composition of the W and C strands of each chromosome of yeast we find that this composition is remarkably stable and follows Chargaff's second parity rule with approximately 30% for A and T, and 20% for C and G (table 9.1). Notably, the same symmetry is observed in yeast mitochondrial DNA but with a different composition. Likewise, single-stranded genomic DNA in other organisms has a different but still symmetric average composition.

To study the symmetries of double-stranded DNA we count how often each nucleotide occurs on each strand over a given length. These frequencies correspond to a probabilistic Markov model of order 1. It is then natural also to look at Markov models of higher orders (order N) by looking at the statistics of the corresponding N-mers. In particular, we can ask whether Chargaff's second parity rule holds for orders beyond the first, for instance for dinucleotides, equivalent to second-order Markov models.

A DNA Markov model of order N has 4^N parameters associated with the transition probabilities $P(X_N|X_1, \ldots, X_{N-1})$, also denoted $P(X_1, \ldots, X_{N-1} \rightarrow X_N)$, for all possible $X_1, \ldots, X_N$ in the alphabet together with a starting distribution of the form $\pi(X_1, \ldots, X_{N-1})$. Because the number of parameters grows exponentially, only models up to a certain order can be determined from a finite data set. A DNA Markov model of order 5, for instance, has 1,024 parameters and a DNA Markov model of order 10 has slightly over one million parameters. Conversely, the higher the order, the larger the data set needed to properly fit the model.

Because of the complementarity between the strands, a Markov model of order N of one strand immediately defines a Markov model of order N on the reverse complement. We say that a Markov model of order N is *symmetric* if it is identical to the Markov model of order N of the reverse complement. Thus a Markov model is symmetric if and only if $P(X_1 \ldots X_N) = P(\overline{X_N} \ldots \overline{X_1})$.

	A	C	G	T	Total bp
Chr. 1	69,830	44,641	45,763	69,969	230,203
	30.33%	19.39%	19.88%	30.39%	
Chr. 2	249,640	157,415	154,385	251,700	813,140
	30.70%	19.36%	18.99%	30.95%	
Chr. 3	98,210	62,129	59,441	95,559	315,339
	31.14%	19.70%	18.85%	30.30%	
Chr. 4	476,752	289,343	291,354	474,480	1,531,929
	31.12%	18.89%	19.02%	30.97%	
Chr. 5	176,531	109,828	112,314	178,197	576,870
	30.60%	19.04%	19.47%	30.89%	
Chr. 6	82,928	52,201	52,435	82,584	270,148
	30.70%	19.32%	19.41%	30.57%	
Chr. 7	338,319	207,764	207,450	337,403	1,090,936
	31.01%	19.04%	19.02%	30.93%	
Chr. 8	174,022	109,094	107,486	172,036	562,638
	30.93%	19.39%	19.10%	30.58%	
Chr. 9	134,340	85,461	85,661	134,423	439,885
	30.54%	19.43%	19.47%	30.56%	
Chr. 10	231,097	142,211	143,803	228,329	745440
	31.00%	19.08%	19.29%	30.63%	
Chr. 11	206,055	127,713	126,005	206,672	666,445
	30.92%	19.16%	18.91%	31.01%	
Chr. 12	330,586	207,777	207,064	332,745	1,078,172
	30.66%	19.27%	19.21%	30.86%	
Chr. 13	286,296	176,735	176,433	284,966	924,430
	30.97%	19.12%	19.09%	30.83%	
Chr. 14	241,561	151,651	151,388	239,728	784,328
	30.80%	19.34%	19.30%	30.56%	
Chr. 15	339,396	209,022	207,416	335,449	1,091,283
	31.10%	19.15%	19.01%	30.74%	
Chr. 16	293,947	180,364	180,507	293,243	948,061
	31.01%	19.02%	19.04%	30.93%	
Chr. mt	36,169	6,863	7,813	34,934	85,779
	42.17%	8.00%	9.11%	40.73%	
16 nuclear Chr.	3,729,510	2,313,349	2,308,905	3,717,483	12,069,247
	30.90%	19.17%	19.13%	30.80%	
All Chr.	3,765,679	2,320,212	2,316,718	3,752,417	12,155,026
	30.98%	19.09%	19.06%	30.87%	

Table 9.1: First-order Distribution of Yeast Genomic and Mitochondrial DNA per Chromosome.

A → A	0.3643	AA	0.1154
A → T	0.2806	AT	0.0889
A → G	0.1858	AG	0.0589
A → C	0.1684	AC	0.0533
T → A	0.2602	TA	0.0814
T → T	0.3662	TT	0.1146
T → G	0.1858	TG	0.0581
T → C	0.1882	TC	0.0589
G → A	0.3166	GA	0.0581
G → T	0.2784	GT	0.0511
G → G	0.1945	GG	0.0357
G → C	0.2106	GC	0.0387
C → A	0.3304	CA	0.0619
C → T	0.3116	CT	0.0583
C → G	0.1639	CG	0.0307
C → C	0.1941	CC	0.0364

Table 9.2: Second-order Transition Parameters and Dinucleotide Distribution of Yeast 500 bp Upstream Regions.

If we look at genomic DNA in yeast, for instance, we find a very high degree of symmetry in all the higher-order Markov models with orders up to at least 9, even within various subregions of DNA (table 9.2). Some have suggested that this symmetry could easily be explained from the first-order symmetry. Indeed, if $\mathbf{P}(A) = \mathbf{P}(T)$ *and if* $\mathbf{P}(AA) = \mathbf{P}(A)\mathbf{P}(A)$ then automatically $\mathbf{P}(AA) = \mathbf{P}(TT)$. The question then is precisely whether the higher order Markov models are *factorial*, i.e., entirely determined by the products resulting from the lower-order models.

More formally, a Markov model of order N induces a distribution over lower-order M-mers called the restriction or projection of the orginal distribution. This projection is easily obtained for instance by generating a long string with the Markov model of order N and measuring the statistics of the M-mers. In particular, a Markov model of order N induces a first-order equilibrium distribution that must satisfy the balance equation

$$P(X_2, \ldots, X_N) = \sum_Y P(X_N | Y, X_2 \ldots, X_{N-1})$$
$$P(Y, X_2, \ldots, X_{N-1}) \tag{9.2}$$

If a Markov model of order N is symmetric, its restrictions or projections to lower orders are also symmetric. The converse, however is not true. In gen-

	2	3	4	5	6	7	8	9
0	1.0	.99	.99	.99	.99	.99	.97	.95
1	.98	.97	.97	.97	.95	.90	.77	.55
2		.94	.95	.94	.91	.83	.66	.45
3			.97	.94	.89	.77	.57	.36
4				.82	.73	.58	.39	.24
5					.60	.46	.29	.18
6						.34	.21	.14
7							.12	.10
8								.09

Table 9.3: Counts and Symmetry Effects. Row 0 represents the correlation for the counts C of N-mers ($N = 2, \ldots, 9$) between the direct upstream strand and its reverse complement. In rows $M = 1$ to 9, similar correlations are computed but using the ratio $C/E(C)$, where $E(C)$ is the *expected* number of counts produced by a Markov model of order M fitted to the upstream regions. Horizontal = N-mers, vertical = model order.

eral, a symmetric Markov model of order N can have multiple not necessarily symmetric extensions to a Markov model of order M, $M > N$. Thus the fact that the first-order distribution of yeast, for instance, is symmetric does not necessarily imply that the second order distribution is also symmetric. But this is precisely the case. A given Markov model of order N, however, has a unique *factorial extension* to Markov models of order $M > N$. For instance, a first-order Markov model defined by the parameters p_X (p_A, p_C, p_G, p_T) has a second-order factorial extension with parameters $p_{XY} = p_X p_Y$.

For a given Markov model of order N, we can factor out the symmetry effects due to any Markov model of lower order M. For each N-mer and its reverse complement we can get the ratio (or the difference) between the number of expected counts according to the model of order N and to the model of order M used factorially. The residual symmetry can be measured by looking at the correlation of the ratios between N-mers and their respective reverse complements. If we use this approach in yeast, we find a considerable amount of residual symmetry in the higher-order models that cannot be entirely explained, for instance, by the symmetry of the first-order composition (table 9.3).

Thus higher-order Markov models allow us to study Chargaff's second parity rule in great detail. Chargaff's second parity rule is of course not true locally, and it is also violated in some viral genomes. There are also well-known compositional biases around the origin of replication in prokaryotic genomes. But by and large it is remarkably valid and probably results from a complex mixture of influences operating at different scales. It is clear that because of

DNA	W ORFs	C ORFs	Total
Chr. 1	56	51	107
Chr. 2	200	226	426
Chr. 3	75	99	174
Chr. 4	400	419	819
Chr. 5	146	141	287
Chr. 6	67	67	134
Chr. 7	298	273	571
Chr. 8	153	131	284
Chr. 9	106	118	224
Chr. 10	201	186	387
Chr. 11	175	161	336
Chr. 12	261	286	547
Chr. 13	246	244	490
Chr. 14	219	201	420
Chr. 15	295	278	573
Chr. 16	256	244	500
Total	3154	3125	6279

Table 9.4: Number of ORFs of Length Greater than 100 per Strand and per Chromosome in Yeast, Excluding tRNA and rRNA Genes. The total excludes the mitochondrial chromosome.

Chargaff's first parity rule, any force operating on DNA that does not distinguish between the two strands will contribute to Chargaff's second parity rule. Mutations induced for instance by radiation are likely to fall in this class. Likewise, the replication machinery of the cell must be optimized for producing the same number of complementary base pairs, and this also should favor the first-order version of Chargaff's second parity rule. Other effects under study may be more long-ranged, such as the approximately symmetric distribution of genes on each strand (table 9.4). This distribution could also be modeled using probabilistic Markov models.

9.3 Markov Models and Gene Finders

One the most important applications of Markov and graphical models to sequence analysis has been the construction of various gene finders and gene parsers such as GeneMark and GeneMark.hmm [81, 82, 367], GLIMMER [461], GRAIL [529], GenScan [107] and now GenomeScan, and Genie [441]. Our goal here is not to give an exhaustive list of all gene finders, nor to describe each one of them in detail, nor to compare their respective merits and drawbacks,

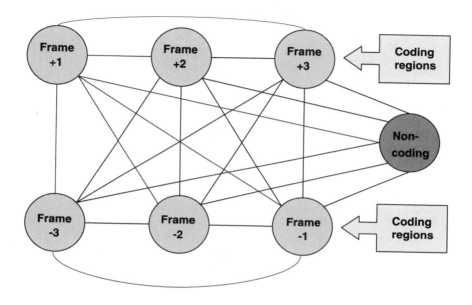

Figure 9.5: Graphical Representation of GeneMark for Prokaryotic Genomes. For prokaryotic genomes, typical high-level modules include modules for coding region and non-coding regions.

but to provide a synthetic overview showing how they can be constructed and understood in terms of probabilistic graphical models.

Integrated gene finders and gene parsers typically have a modular architecture and often share the same basic strategies. They comprise two basic kinds of elementary modules aimed at detecting boundary elements or variable length regions. Examples of boundary modules associated with localized signals include splice sites, start and stop codons, various transcription factor and other protein binding sites (such as the TATA-box), transcription start points, branch points, terminators of transcription, polyadenylation sites, ribosomal binding sites, topoisomerase I cleavage sites, and topoisomerase II binding sites. Region modules instead are usually associated with exons, introns, and intergenic regions. Exon models in turn are often subdivided into initial, internal, and terminal exons due to the well-known statistical dif-

GeneMark.hmm

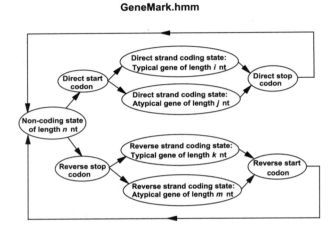

Figure 9.6: Graphical Representation of GeneMark.hmm for Prokaryotic Genomes.

ferences among these elements. Ultimately, computational models of entire genomes must include also other regions, including various kinds of repetitive regions, such as Alu sequences.

High-level graphical representations of several genefinders are displayed in figures 9.5, 9.6, 9.7, and 9.8. reprinted here with permission from the authors. The high-level representations and the underlying graphical models are of course significantly more complex for eukaryotic gene finders than for prokaryotic ones, due for instance to the presence of exons and introns. It is important to observe that the graphs in these figures do not directly represent Bayesian networks but rather transition state diagrams, in the same way the standard HMM architectures of chapter 7 do not correspond to the Bayesian network representation of HMMs that we saw in the first section of this chapter. In fact, most genefinders can be viewed as HMMs, or variations of HMMs, at least at some level.

The high-level nodes in these graphs represent boundary or region modules. There are some differences between the gene finders in the choice of modules and in how the modules are implemented and trained. In the case of boundary modules, early implementations used simple consensus sequences. These have evolved into profiles or weight matrix schemes, which are special cases of first-order Markov models in which scores are interpreted as log-likelihoods or log ratios, and Markov models. Because the DNA alphabet has only four letters, higher-order Markov models can be used when sufficient training data is available. Neural networks, which algebraically can be viewed

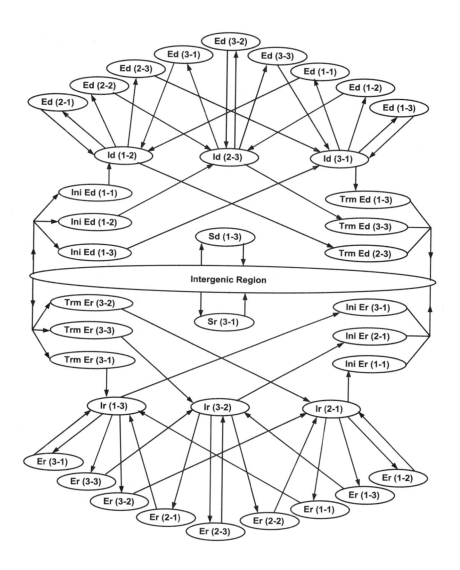

Figure 9.7:   Graphical Representation of High-level States of GeneMark.hmm for Eukaryotic Genomes. The model include states corresponding to initial and terminal exons, internal exons, introns, in all reading frames and for the direct and reverse strand.

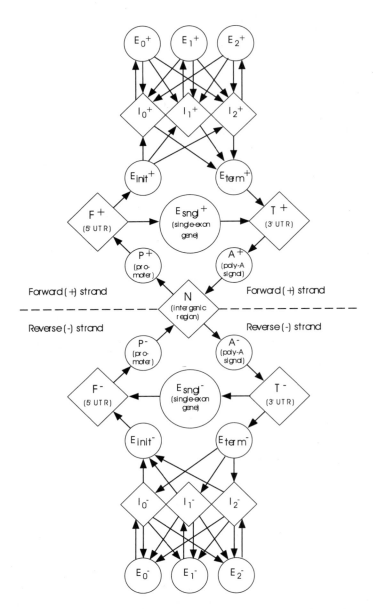

Figure 9.8: Graphical Representation of Hidden States in GenScan. Similar to figure 9.7. Notice the additional states, for instance, for poly-A signals.

as generalization of weight matrices, are also used in some boundary modules.

Variable length regions are usually modeled with Markov models of order up to 6. In particular, coding regions have well known 3- and 6-periodicities that can easily be incorporated into Markov models of order 3 or 6. Exon models must take into account reading frames and knowledge of reading frame must somehow propagate through the intervening sequence to the next exon. The state connectivity can be used to model the different reading frames but also the length distribution of each component, i.e. how long the system ought to remain in each state. Such durations can also be modeled or adjusted using empirical distributions extracted from the available data, or by fitting theoretical distributions to the training data (see also [154]). Because genes can occur on either strand in the 5' to 3' orientation, gene finders must be able to model both situations in mirror fashion. A gene casts a "shadow" on the opposite strand and therefore a single strand can be scanned to find genes located on either strand.

The resulting models can be used to "scan" and parse large genomic regions using dynamic programming and Viterbi paths (maximum likelihood, maximum a posteriori, or even conditional maximum likelihood as in [339]), which, depending on the size of the regions, can be computationally demanding. The "hits" can be further filtered and improved by leveraging the information about coding regions contained in large ESTs and protein databases, including databases of HMM models such as Pfam, using alignments. The parameters of the various boundary or region models can be fitted to different organisms, or even different genomic regions with different compositional biases or different gene classes, resulting in different specialized gene finders and gene parsers.

Although the performance of gene finders is not easy to measure and compare, overall it has significantly improved over the past few years. These programs now play an important role in genome annotation projects. Several significant challenges remain, however, such as creating better models of regulatory regions and of alternative splicing.

9.4 Hybrid Models and Neural Network Parameterization of Graphical Models

9.4.1 The General Framework

In order to overcome the limitations of HMMs, we shall look here at the possibility of combining HMMs and NNs to form hybrid models that contain the expressive power of artificial NNs with the sequential time series aspect of HMMs. In this section we largely follow the derivation in [40]. There are a

number of ways in which HMMs and NNs can be combined. Hybrid architectures have been used in both speech and cursive handwriting recognition
[84, 126]. In many of these applications, NNs are used as front-end proces-
sors to extract features, such as strokes, characters, and phonemes. HMMs
are then used in higher processing stages for word and language modeling[1].
The HMM and NN components are often trained separately, although there are
some exceptions [57]. In a different type of hybrid architecture, described in
[126], the NN component is used to classify the pattern of likelihoods produced by several HMMs. Here, in contrast, we will cover hybrid architectures
[40] where the HMM and NN components are inseparable. In these architectures, the NN component is used to reparameterize and modulate the HMM
component. Both components are trained using unified algorithms in which
the HMM dynamic programming and the NN backpropagation blend together.
But before we proceed with the architectural details, it is useful to view the
hybrid approach from the general probabilistic standpoint of chapter 2 and of
graphical models.

The General Hybrid Framework

From Chapter 2, we know that the fundamental objects we are interested in
are probabilistic models $M(\theta)$ of our data, parameterized here by θ. Problems
arise, however, whenever there is a mismatch between the complexity of the
model and the data. Overly complex models result in overfitting, overly simple
models in underfitting.

The general hybrid modeling approach attempts to address both problems.
When the model is too complex, it is reparameterized as a function of a simpler
parameter vector w, so that $\theta = f(w)$. This is the single-model case. When
the data are too complex, the only solution, short of resorting to a different
model class, is to model the data with several $M(\theta)$s, with θ varying discretely
or continuously as $M(\theta)$ covers different regions of data space. Thus the parameters must be modulated as a function of the input, or context, in the
form $\theta = f(I)$. This is the multiple-model case. In the general case, both may
be desirable, so that $\theta = f(w, I)$. This approach is hybrid in the sense that
the function f can belong to a different model class. Since neural networks
have well-known universal approximation properties (see chapter 5), a natural
approach is to compute f with an NN, but other representations are possible.
This approach is hierarchical because model reparameterizations can easily be
nested at several levels. Here, for simplicity, we confine ourselves to a single
level of reparameterization.

---

[1]In molecular biology applications, NNs could conceivably be used to interpret the analog
output of various sequencing machines, although this is not our focus here.

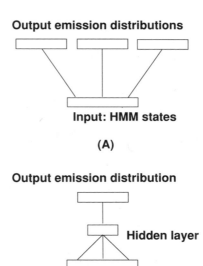

Output emission distributions

Input: HMM states

(A)

Output emission distribution

Hidden layer

Input: HMM states

(B)

Figure 9.9:   From HMM to hybrid HMM/NN. A: Schematic representation of simple HMM/NN hybrid architecture used in [41]. Each HMM state has its own NN. Here, the NNs are extremely simple, with no hidden layer and an output layer of softmax units computing the state emission or transition parameters. For simplicity only output emissions are represented. B: Schematic representation of an HMM/NN architecture where the NNs associated with different states (or different groups of states) are connected via one or several hidden layers.

9.5   The Single-Model Case

Basic Idea

In a general HMM, an emission or transition vector θ is a function of the state i only: $\theta = f(i)$. The first basic idea is to have a NN on top of the HMM for the computation of the HMM parameters, that is, for the computation of the function f. NNs are universal approximators, and therefore can represent any f. More important perhaps, NN representations of the parameters make possible the flexible introduction of many possible constraints. For simplicity, we discuss emission parameters only in a protein context, but the approach extends immediately to transition parameters as well, and to all other alphabets.

In the reparameterization of (7.33), we can consider that each of the HMM emission parameters is calculated by a small NN, with one input set to 1 (bias), no hidden layers, and 20 softmax output units (figure 9.9A). The connections between the input and the outputs are the w_{iX} parameters. This can be generalized immediately by having arbitrarily complex NNs for the computation of the HMM parameters. The NNs associated with different states can also be linked with one or several common hidden layers, the overall architecture being dictated by the problem at hand (figure 9.9B). In the case of a discrete alphabet, however, such as for proteins, the emission of each state is a multinomial distribution, and therefore the output of the corresponding network should consist of $|A|$ normalized exponential units.

Example

As a simple example, consider the hybrid HMM/NN architecture of figure 9.10, consisting of the following

1. Input layer: one unit for each state i. At each time, all units are set to 0, except one that is set to 1. If unit i is set to 1, the network computes e_{iX}, the emission distribution of state i.

2. Hidden layer: $|H|$ hidden units indexed by h, each with transfer function f_h (logistic by default) and bias b_h ($|H| < |A|$).

3. Output layer: $|A|$ softmax units or normalized exponentials, indexed by X, with bias b_X.

4. Connections: $\alpha = (\alpha_{hi}$ connects input position i to hidden unit h). $\beta = (\beta_{Xh}$ connects hidden unit h to output unit X). No confusion with the HMM forward or backward variable should be possible.

For input i, the activity in the hth unit in the hidden layer is given by

$$f_h(\alpha_{hi} + b_h). \tag{9.3}$$

The corresponding activity in the output layer is

$$e_{iX} = \frac{e^{-[\sum_h \beta_{Xh} f_h(\alpha_{hi}+b_h)+b_X]}}{\sum_Y e^{-[\sum_h \beta_{Yh} f_h(\alpha_{hi}+b_h)+b_Y]}}. \tag{9.4}$$

Remarks

For hybrid HMM/NN architectures, a number of points are worth noting:

- The HMM states can be partitioned into groups, with different networks for different groups. In protein applications one can use different NNs for insert states and for main states, or for different groups of states along the protein sequence corresponding to different regions (hydrophobic, hydrophilic, alpha-helical, etc.).

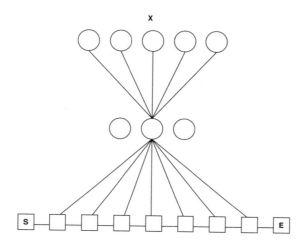

Figure 9.10: Simple Hybrid Architecture. Schematic representation of HMM states. Each state is fully interconnected to the common hidden layer. Each unit in the hidden layer is fully interconnected to each normalized exponential output unit. Each output unit calculates the emission probability e_{iX}.

- HMM parameter reduction can easily be achieved using small hidden layers with $|H|$ hidden units and $|H|$ small compared with N or $|A|$. In figure 9.10, with $|H|$ hidden units and considering only main states, the number of parameters is $|H|(N + |A|)$ in the HMM/NN architecture, versus $N|A|$ in the corresponding simple HMM. For protein models, this yields roughly $|H|N$ parameters for the HMM/NN architecture, versus $20N$ for the simple HMM. $|H| = |A|$ is roughly equivalent to (7.33).

- The number of parameters can be adaptively adjusted to variable training set sizes by changing the number of hidden units. This is useful in environments with large variations in database sizes, as in current molecular biology applications.

- The entire bag of NN techniques—such as radial basis functions, multiple hidden layers, sparse connectivity, weight sharing, Gaussian priors, and hyperparameters—can be brought to bear on these architectures. Several initializations and structures can be implemented in a flexible way. By allocating different numbers of hidden units to different subsets of emissions or transitions, it is easy to favor certain classes of paths in the models when necessary. In the HMM of figure 7.2 one must in general introduce a bias favoring main states over insert states prior to any learning. It is easy also to link different regions of a protein that may have similar properties by weight sharing and other types of long-range correlations. By setting the output bias to the proper values, the model can be initialized to the average composition of the training sequences or any other useful distribution.

- Classical prior information in the form of substitution matrices is easily incorporated. Substitution matrices ([8]; see also chapters 1 and 10) can be computed from databases, and essentially produce a background probability matrix $P = (p_{XY})$, where p_{XY} is the probability that X will be changed into Y over a certain evolutionary time. P can be implemented as a linear transformation in the emission NN.

- Although HMMs with continuous emission distributions are outside the scope of this book, they can also be incorporated in the HMM/NN framework. The output emission distributions can be represented in the form of samples, moments, and/or mixture coefficients. In the classical mixture of Gaussians case, means, covariances, and mixture coefficients can be computed by the NN. Likewise, additional HMM parameters, such as exponential parameters to model the duration of stay in any given state, can be calculated by an NN.

Representation in Simple HMM/NN Architectures

Consider the particular HMM/NN described above (figure 9.10), where a subset of the HMM states is fully connected to $|H|$ hidden units, and the hidden units are fully connected to $|A|$ softmax output units. The hidden unit bias is not really necessary in the sense that for any HMM state i, any vector of biases b_h, and any vector of connections α_{hi}, there is a new vector of connections α'_{hi} that produces the same vector of hidden unit activations with 0 bias. This is not true in the general case—for example, as soon as there are multiple hidden layers, or if the input units are not fully interconnected to the hidden layer. We have retained the biases for the sake of generality, and also because even if they do not enlarge the space of possible representations, they may still facilitate the learning procedure. Similar remarks hold more generally for the transfer functions. With an input layer fully connected to a single hidden layer, the same hidden layer activation can be achieved with different activation functions by modifying the weights.

A natural question to ask is "What is the representation used in the hidden layer, and what is the space of emission distributions achievable in this fashion?" Each HMM state in the network can be represented by a point in the $[-1, 1]^{|H|}$ hypercube. The coordinates of a point are the activities of the $|H|$ hidden units. By changing its connections to the hidden units, an HMM state can occupy any position in the hypercube. Thus, the space of emission distributions that can be achieved is entirely determined by the connections from the hidden layer to the output layer. If these connections are held fixed, then each HMM state can select a corresponding optimal position in the hypercube where its emission distribution, generated by the NN weights, is as close as possible to the truly optimal distribution—for instance, in cross-entropy distance. During on-line learning, all parameters are learned at the same time, so this may introduce additional effects.

Further to understand the space of achievable distributions, consider the transformation from hidden to output units. For notational convenience, we introduce one additional hidden unit numbered 0, always set to 1, to express the output biases in the form $b_X = \beta_{X0}$. If, in this extended hidden layer, we turn single hidden units to 1, one at a time, we obtain $|H|+1$ different emission distributions in the output layer $P^h = (p_X^h)$ $(0 \le h \le |H|)$, with

$$p_X^h = \frac{e^{-\beta_{Xh}}}{\sum_{Y \in A} e^{-\beta_{Yh}}}. \tag{9.5}$$

Consider now a general pattern of activity in the hidden layer of the form $(1, \mu_1, \ldots, \mu_{|H|})$. By using (9.4) and (9.5), the emission distribution in the output layer is then

$$e_{iX} = \frac{e^{-\sum_{h=0}^{|H|} \beta_{Xh} \mu_h}}{\sum_{Y \in A} e^{-\sum_{h=0}^{|H|} \beta_{Yh} \mu_h}} = \frac{\prod_{h \in H} [p_X^h]^{\mu_h} [\sum_{Y \in A} e^{-\beta_{Yh}}]^{\mu_h}}{\sum_{Y \in A} \prod_{h \in H} [p_Y^h]^{\mu_h} [\sum_{Z \in A} e^{-\beta_{Zh}}]^{\mu_h}}. \tag{9.6}$$

After simplification, this yields

$$e_{iX} = \frac{\prod_{h \in H} [p_X^h]^{\mu_h}}{\sum_{Y \in A} \prod_{h \in H} [p_Y^h]^{\mu_h}}. \tag{9.7}$$

Therefore, all the emission distributions achievable by the NN have the form of (9.7), and can be viewed as "combinations" of $|H|+1$ fundamental distributions P^h associated with each single hidden unit. In general, this combination is different from a convex linear combination of the P^hs. It consists of three operations: (1) raising each component of P^h to the power μ_h, the activity of the hth hidden unit; (2) multiplying all the corresponding vectors componentwise; (3) normalizing. In this form, the hybrid HMM/NN approach is different from a mixture of Dirichlet distributions approach.

Learning

HMM/NN architectures can be optimized according to ML or MAP estimation. Unlike HMMs, for hybrid HMM/NN architectures the M step of the EM algorithm cannot, in general, be carried out analytically. However, one can still use some form of gradient descent using the chain rule, by computing the derivatives of the likelihood function with respect to the HMM parameters, and then the derivatives of the HMM parameters with respect to the NN parameters. The derivatives of the prior term, when present, can easily be incorporated. It is also possible to use a Viterbi learning approach by using only the most likely paths. The derivation of the learning equations is left as an exercise and can also be found in [40]. In the resulting learning equations the HMM dynamic programming and the NN backpropagation components are intimately fused. These algorithms can also be seen as GEM (generalized EM) algorithms [147].

9.5.1   The Multiple-Model Case

The hybrid HMM/NN architectures described above address the first limitation of HMMs: the control of model structure and complexity. No matter how complex the NN component, however, the final model so far remains a single HMM. Therefore the second limitation of HMMs, long-range dependencies, remains. This obstacle cannot be overcome simply by resorting to higher-order HMMs. Most often these are computationally intractable. A possible approach is to try to build Markov models with variable memory length by introducing a new state for each relevant context. This requires a systematic method for determining relevant contexts of variable lengths directly from the data. Furthermore, one must hope the number of relevant contexts remains small. An interesting approach along these lines can be found in [448], where English is modeled as a Markov process with variable memory length of up to ten letters or so.

To address the second limitation without resorting to a different model class, one must consider more general HMM/NN hybrid architectures, where the underlying statistical model is a *set* of HMMs. To see this, consider again the $X - Y/X' - Y'$ problem mentioned at the end of chapter 8. Capturing such dependencies requires *variable* emission vectors at the corresponding locations, together with a linking mechanism. In this simple case, four different emission vectors are needed: e_i, e_j, e_i' and e_j'. Each one of these vectors must assign a high probability to the letters X, Y, X', and Y', respectively. More important, there must be some kind of memory, that is, a mechanism to link the distributions at i and j, so that e_i and e_j are used for sequence O and e_i' and e_j' are used for sequence O'. The combination of e_i and e_j' (or e_i' and e_j) should be rare or not allowed, unless required by the data. Thus e_i and e_j must belong to a first HMM and e_i' and e_j' to a second HMM, with the possibility of switching from one HMM to the other as a function of input sequence. Alternatively, there must be a single HMM but with variable emission distributions, again modulated by some input.

In both cases, then, we consider that the emission distribution of a given state depends not only on the state itself but also on an additional stream of information I. That is now $\theta = f(i, I)$. Again, in a multiple-HMM/NN hybrid architecture this more complex function f can be computed by an NN. Depending on the problem, the input I can assume different forms, and may be called a "context" or "latent" variable. When feasible, I may even be equal to the currently observed sequence O. Other inputs are possible, however, over different alphabets. An obvious candidate in protein modeling tasks would be the secondary structure of the protein (alpha-helices, beta-sheets and coils). In general, I could also be any other array of numbers representing latent variables for the HMM modulation [374]. We briefly consider two examples.

Mixtures of HMM Experts

A first possible approach is to consider a model M that is a mixture distribution (2.23) of n simpler HMMs' $M_1, \ldots, M_n$. For any sequence O, then,

$$\mathbf{P}(O|M) = \sum_{i=1}^{n} \lambda_i \mathbf{P}(O|M_i), \tag{9.8}$$

where the mixture coefficients λ_i satisfy $\lambda_i \geq 0$ and $\sum_i \lambda_i = 1$. In generative mode, sequences are produced at random by each individual HMM, and M_i is selected with probability λ_i. Such a system can be viewed as a larger single HMM, with a starting state connected to each one of the HMMs' M_i, with transition probability λ_i (figure 8.5). As we have seen in chapter 8, this type of model is used in [334] for unsupervised classification of globin protein sequences. Note that the parameters of each submodel can be computed by an NN to create an HMM/NN hybrid architecture. Since the HMM experts form a larger single HMM, the corresponding hybrid architecture is identical to what we saw in section 9.2. The only peculiarity is that states have been replicated, or grouped, to form different submodels. One further step is to have variable mixture coefficients that depend on the input sequence or some other relevant information. These mixture coefficients can be computed as softmax outputs of an NN, as in the mixture-of-experts architecture of [277].

Mixtures of Emission Experts

A different approach is to modulate a single HMM by considering that the emission parameters e_{iX} should also be a function of the additional input I. Thus $e_{iX} = P(i, X, I)$. Without any loss of generality, we can assume that P is a

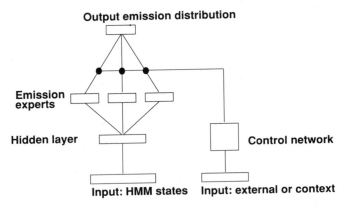

Figure 9.11: Schematic Representation of a General HMM/NN Architecture in Which the HMM Parameters Are Computed by an NN of Arbitrary Complexity That Operates on State Information, but Also on Input or Context. The input or context is used to modulate the HMM parameters, for instance, by switching or mixing different parameter experts. For simplicity, only emission parameters are represented, with three emission experts and a single hidden layer. Connections from the HMM states to the control network, and from the input to the hidden layer, are also possible.

mixture of n emission experts P_j

$$P(i,\mathsf{X},I) = \sum_{j=1}^{n} \lambda_j(i,\mathsf{X},I)P_j(i,\mathsf{X},I). \tag{9.9}$$

In many interesting cases, λ_j is independent of X, resulting in the probability vector equation over the alphabet

$$P(i,I) = \sum_{j=1}^{n} \lambda_j(i,I)P_j(i,I). \tag{9.10}$$

If $n = 1$ and $P(i,I) = P(i)$, we are back to a single HMM. An important special case is derived by further assuming that λ_j does not depend on i, and $P_j(i,\mathsf{X},I)$ does not depend on I explicitly. Then

$$P(i,I) = \sum_{j=1}^{n} \lambda_j(I)P_j(i). \tag{9.11}$$

This provides a principled way to design the top layers of general hybrid HMM/NN architectures, such as the one depicted in figure 9.11.

The components P_j are computed by an NN, and the mixture coefficients by another gating NN. Naturally, many variations are possible and, in the most general case, the switching network can depend on the state i, and the distributions P_j on the input I. In the case of protein modeling, if the switching depends on position i, the emission experts could correspond to different types of regions, such as hydrophobic and hydrophilic, rather than different subclasses within a protein family.

Learning

For a given setting of all the parameters, a given observation sequence, and a given input vector I, the general HMM/NN hybrid architectures reduce to a single HMM. The likelihood of a sequence, or some other measure of its fitness, with respect to such an HMM can be computed by dynamic programming. As long as it is differentiable in the model parameters, we can then backpropagate the gradient through the NN, including the portion of the network depending on I, such as the control network of figure 9.11. With minor modifications, this leads to learning algorithms similar to those described above. This form of learning encourages cooperation between the emission experts of figure 9.11. As in the usual mixture-of-experts architecture [277], it may be useful to introduce some degree of competition among the experts, so that each of them specializes on a different subclass of sequences.

When the input space has been selected but the value of the relevant input I is not known, it is possible to learn its values together with the model parameters using Bayesian inversion. Consider the case where there is an input I associated with each observation sequence O, and a hybrid model with parameters w, so that we can compute $\mathbf{P}(O|I, w)$. Let $\mathbf{P}(I)$ and $\mathbf{P}(w)$ denote our priors on I and w. Then

$$\mathbf{P}(I|O, w) = \frac{\mathbf{P}(O|I, w)\mathbf{P}(I)}{\mathbf{P}(O|w)}, \tag{9.12}$$

with

$$\mathbf{P}(O|w) = \int_I \mathbf{P}(O|I, w)\mathbf{P}(I)dI. \tag{9.13}$$

The probability of the model parameters, given the data, can then be calculated, again using Bayes's theorem:

$$\mathbf{P}(w|D) = \frac{\mathbf{P}(D|w)\mathbf{P}(w)}{\mathbf{P}(D)} = \frac{[\prod_O \mathbf{P}(O|w)]\mathbf{P}(w)}{\mathbf{P}(D)}, \tag{9.14}$$

assuming the observations are independent. These parameters can be optimized by gradient descent on $-\log \mathbf{P}(w|D)$. The main step is the evaluation

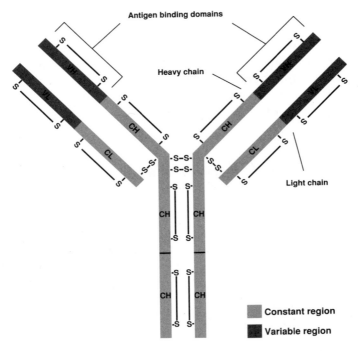

Figure 9.12: A Schematic Model of the Structure of a Typical Human Antibody Molecule Composed of Two Light (L) and Two Heavy (H) Polypeptide Chains. Interchain and intrachain disulfide bonds are indicated (S). Cysteine residues are associated with the bonds. two identical active sites for antigen binding, corresponding to the variable regions, are located in the arms of the molecule.

of the likelihood $\mathbf{P}(O|w)$ and its derivatives with respect to w, which can be done by Monte Carlo sampling. The distribution on the latent variables I is calculated by (9.12). The work in [374] is an example of such a learning approach. The density network used for protein modeling can be viewed essentially as a special case of HMM/NN hybrid architecture where each emission vector acts as a softmax transformation on a low-dimensional, real "hidden" input I, with independent Gaussian priors on I and w. The input I modulates the emission vectors, and therefore the underlying HMM, as a function of sequence.

9.5.2   Simulation Results

We now review a simple application of the principles behind HMM/NN single-model hybrid architectures, demonstrated in [40], on the immunoglobulin protein family. Immunoglobulins, or antibodies, are proteins produced by B cells that bind with specificity to foreign antigens in order to neutralize them or target their destruction by other effector cells. The various classes of immunoglobulins are defined by pairs of light and heavy chains that are held together principally by disulfide bonds. Each light and heavy chain molecule contains one variable (V) region and one (light) or several (heavy) constant (C) regions (figure 9.12). The V regions differ among immunoglobulins, and provide the specificity of the antigen recognition. About one third of the amino acids of the V regions form the hypervariable sites, responsible for the diversity of the vertebrate immune response. The database is the same as that used in [41], and consists of human and mouse heavy chain immunoglobulin V region sequences from the Protein Identification Resources (PIR) database. It corresponds to 224 sequences with minimum length 90, average length $N = 117$, and maximum length 254.

The immunoglobulin V regions were first modeled using a single HMM [41], similar to the one in figure 7.3, containing a total of $52N + 23 = 6107$ adjustable parameters. Here we consider a hybrid HMM/NN architecture with the following characteristics. The basic model is an HMM with the architecture of figure 7.3. All the main-state emissions are calculated by a common NN with two hidden units. Likewise, all the insert-state emissions are calculated by a common NN with one hidden unit. Each state transition distribution is calculated by a different softmax network. Neglecting edge effects, the total number of parameters of this HMM/NN architecture is 1507: $(117 \times 3 \times 3) = 1053$ for the transitions and $(117 \times 3 + 3 + 3 \times 20 + 40) = 454$ for the emissions, including biases. This architecture is used for demonstration purposes and is not optimized. We suspect that the number of parameters could be further reduced.

The hybrid architecture is then trained online, using both gradient descent and the corresponding Viterbi version. The training set consists of a random subset of 150 sequences identical to the training set used in the experiments with a simple HMM. All weights from the input to the hidden layer are initialized with independent Gaussians, with mean 0 and standard deviation 1. All the weights from the hidden layer to the output layer are initialized to 1. This yields a uniform emission probability distribution on all the emitting states.[2] Note that if all the weights are initialized to 1, including those from input layer to hidden layer, then the hidden units cannot differentiate from one another. The transition probabilities out of insert or delete states are initialized uniformly to 1/3. We introduce, however, a small bias along the backbone that

---

[2]With Viterbi learning, this is probably better than a nonuniform initialization, such as the average composition, since a nonuniform initialization may introduce distortions in the Viterbi paths.

```
                                     1                24
F37262    -------------------------AELM--KPGASVKISCKATG--YKFSS----Y--------WIEWVKQRPGHGLEWIGENL-
B27563    ------------------------LQQPGAELV--KPGASVKLSCKASG--YTFTN----Y--------WIHWVKQRPGRGLEWIGRID-
C30560    ------------------QVHLQQSGAELV--KPGASVKISCKASG--YTFTS----Y--------WMNWVKQRPGQGLEWIGEID-
G1HUDW    ------------------QVTLRESGPALV--RPTQTLTLTCTFSG--FSLSGetmc---------VAWIRQPPGEALEWLAWDI-
S09711    mkhlwffllvraprwclsQVQLQESGPGLV--KPSETLSVTCTVSG-----------gsvssglYWSWIRQPPGKGPEWIGYIY-
B36006    --------------------------------KISCKGSG--YSFTS----Y--------WIGWVRQMPGKGLEWMGIIY-
F36005    ------------------QVQLVESGGGVV--QPGRSLRLSCAASG--FTFSS----Y--------AMHWVRQAPGKGLEWVAVIS-
A36194    mgwsfiflfllsvtagvhsEVQLQQSGAELV--RAGSSVKMSCKASG--YTFTN----Y--------GINWVKQRPGQGLEWIGYQS-
A31485    ------------------EVKLDETGGGLV--QPGRPMKLSCVASG--FTFSD----Y--------WMNWVRQSPEKGLEWVAQIRN
D33548    ------------------QVQLVQSGAEVK--KPGASVKVSCEASG--YTFTG----H--------YMHWVRQAPGQGLEWMGWIN-
AVMSJ5    ------------------EVKLLESGGGLV--QPGGSLKLSCAASG--FDFSK----Y--------GVHWVRQSPGKGLEWLGVIW-
D30560    ------------------QVQLKQSGPSLV--QPSQSLSITCTVSD--FSLTN----F--------AMHWVRQAPGKGLEWVSGIS-
S11239    melglswifllailkgvqcEVQLVESGGGLV--QPGRSLRLSCAASG--FTFND----Y--------ELYWVRQAPGQGLEDLGYIS-
G1MSAA    ------------------EVQLVESGGGLV--KAGSSVKMSCKATG--YTFSS----Y--------ELYWVRQAPGQGLEDLGYIS-
I27888    -----------------QLQESGSGLV--KPSQTLSLTCAVSGgsISSGG----Y--------SWSWIRQPPGKGLEWIGYIY-
PL0118    ------------------EVQLVESGGGLV--QPGGSLKLSCAASG--FTFSG----S--------AMHWVRQASGKGLEWVGRIRS
PL0122    ------------------EVQLVESGGGLV--KPGGSLKLSCTASG--FTFSS----Y--------WMSWVRQAPGKGLEWVSRISS
A33989    ------------------DVQLDQSESVVI--KPGGSLKLSCAASG--DTFTS----S--------VMHWVKQKPGQGLEWIGYIN-
A30502    ------------------EVQLQQSGPELV--KPGASVKMSCKASG--FTFSS----Y--------IMSWVRQTPEKRLEWVATIS-
PH0097    ------------------DVKLVESGGGLV--KPGGSLKLSCAASG--FTFSS----Y--------IMSWVRQTPEKRLEWVATIS-
```

```
             60        70        80        90       100
F37262    -P-G-SDSTKYNEKFKGKATFTADTSSNTAYMQLSSLTSEDSAVYYCARnyygssnlfay-----------------------
B27563    -P-N-SGGTKYNEKFKNKATLTINKPSNTAYMQLSSLTSDDSAVYYCARgydysyya------------MDYWGQGTsvtvss---
C30560    -P-S-NSYTNNNQKFKNKATLTVDKSSNTAYMQLSSLTSEDSAVYYCARscgsq---------------YFDYWGQGJlvtvss---
G1HUDW    ----1NDDKYYGASLETRLAVSKDTSKNQVVLSMNTVGPGDTATYYCARvlvsrtsisqysy-------YMDVWGKGTsvtvss---
S09711    ---Y-SGSTNYNPSLRSRVTISVDTSKNQFSLKLGSVTAADTAVYYCARrlvsrtsisqysy-------FDIWGQGTmvtvss---
B36006    -P-G-DSDTRYSPSFQGQVTISADKSISTAYLQWSSLKASDTAMYYCARrymgygdqa----------DRKASDAFDIWGQGTmvtvss---
F36005    -Y-D-GSNKYYADSVKGRFTISRDNSKNTLYLQMNSLRAEDTAVYYCAR------------------FDYWGQGTtltvss---
A36194    -T-G-SFYSTYNEKVKGKTTLTVDKSSSTAYMQLRGLTSEDSAVYFCARsnyyggsys---------MDYWGQGTsvtvss---
A31485    KP-Y-NYETYYSDSVKGRFTISRDDSKSSVYLQMNNLRVEDMGIYYCTGsyyg---------------FFDYWGQGTlvtvss---
D33548    -P-N-SGGTNYAEKFQGRVTITRDTSINTAYMELSRLRSDDTAVYYCARasycgydcyy----------AYWGQGTlvtvsae---
AVMSJ5    -P-D-SGTINYTPSLKDKFIISRDNAKNSLYLQMSKVRSEDTALYYCAR1hyygyn-----------------MDYWGQGTsvtvss---
D30560    -P-R-GGNTDYNAAFMSRLSITKDNSKSQVFFKMNSLQADDTAIYYCTKegyfgnydya----------FDIWGQGTmvtvss---
S11239    --wD-SSSIGYADSVKGRFTISRDNAKNSLYLQMNSLRAEDMALYYCVKgrdyydsggyftva-------FDIWGQGTmvtvss---
G1MSAA    -S-S-SAYPNYAQKFQGRVTIADESTNTAYMELSSLRSEDTAVYFCAVrvisryfdg-----------WGQGTlv-----
I27888    -S-G-GSFTYYPDTVTGRFTISRDDAQNTLYLEMNSLRSEDTAIYYCTRdeedpttlvapfa--------MDYWGQGTsvtvs----
PL0118    ---H-SGSTYNPSLKSRVTISVDRSKNQFSLKLSSVTAADTAVYYCTR---------------------------------
PL0122    KA-N-SYATAYAASVKGRFTISRDDSKNTLYLQMNNLQTEDTAVYYCTRearwggw-------------YFEHWGQGTmvtvts---
A33989    KA-D-GGSTYYADSVKGRFTISRDNNNNKLYLQMNNLQTEDTAVYYCARgg----------------FAYWGQGTlvtv-----
A30502    -P-Y-NDGTKYNEKFKGKATLTSDKSSSTAYMELSSLTSEDSAVYYCARgg----------------FAYWGQGTlvtv-----
PH0097    -S-G-GRYTYYSDSVKGRFTISRDNAKNTLYLQMSSLRSEDTAMYYSTAsgds------------FDYWGQGTtltvssak-
```

Figure 9.13: Multiple Alignment of 20 Immunoglobulin Sequences, Randomly Extracted from the Training and Validation Data Sets. Validation sequences: F37262, G1HUDW, A36194, A31485, D33548, S11239, I27888, A33989, A30502. Alignment is obtained with a hybrid HMM/NN architecture trained for 10 cycles, with two hidden units for the main-state emissions and one hidden unit for the insert-state emissions. Lowercase letters correspond to emissions from insert states. Note that the signal peptide on some of the sequences is captured as repeated transitions through the first insert state in the model.

favors main-to-main transitions, in the form of a nonsymmetric Dirichlet prior. This prior is equivalent to introducing a regularization term in the objective function that is equal to the logarithm of the backbone transition path. The regularization constant is set to 0.01 and the learning rate to 0.1. Typically, 10 training cycles are more than sufficient to reach equilibrium.

In figure 9.13, we display the multiple alignment of 20 immunoglobulin sequences, selected randomly from both the training and the validation sets. The validation set consists of the remaining 74 sequences. This alignment is very stable between 5 and 10 epochs. It corresponds to a model trained using Viterbi learning for 10 epochs. This alignment is similar to the multiple alignment previously derived with a simple HMM, having more than four times as many parameters. The algorithm has been able to detect most of the salient features of the family. Most important, the cysteine residues (C) toward the beginning and the end of the region (positions 24 and 100 in this multiple alignment), which are responsible for the disulfide bonds that hold the chains, are perfectly aligned. The only exception is the last sequence (PH0097), which has a serine (S) residue in its terminal portion. This is a rare but recognized exception to the conservation of this position. A fraction of the sequences in the data set came with a signal peptide sequence in the N-terminal (see section 6.4). We did not remove them prior to training. The model is capable of detecting and accommodating these signal peptides by treating them as initial repeated inserts, as can be seen from the alignment of three of the sequences (S09711, A36194, S11239). This multiple alignment also contains a few isolated problems, related in part to the overuse of gaps and insert sates. Interestingly, this is most evident in the hypervariable regions, for instance, at positions 30–35 and 50–55. These problems should be eliminated with a more careful selection of hybrid architecture and/or regularization. Alignments in this case did not seem to improve with use of gradient descent and/or a larger number of hidden units, up to four.

In figure 9.14, we display the activity of the two hidden units associated with each main state. For most states, at least one of the activities is saturated. The activities associated with the cysteine residues responsible for the disulfide bridges (main states 24 and 100) are all saturated and are in the same corner $(-1, +1)$. Points close to the center $(0, 0)$ correspond to emission distributions determined by the bias only.

9.5.3 Summary

A large class of hybrid HMM/NN architectures has been described. These architectures improve on single HMMs in two complementary directions. First, the NN reparameterization provides a flexible tool for the control of model complexity, the introduction of priors, and the construction of an input-dependent mechanism for the modulation of the final model. Second, modeling a data set with multiple HMMs allows the coverage of a larger set of distributions and the expression of nonstationarity and correlations inaccessible to single HMMs. Similar ideas have been introduced in [58] using the notion of input/output HMMs (IOHMMs). The HMM/NN approach is meant to complement rather than replace many of the existing techniques for incorporating prior information in sequence models.

Two important issues for the success of a hybrid HMM/NN architecture on a real problem are the design of the NN architecture and the selection of the external input or context. These issues are problem-dependent and cannot

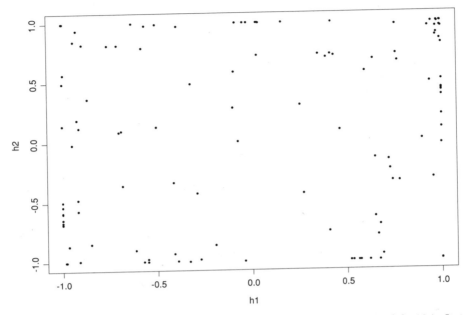

Figure 9.14: Activity of the Two Hidden Units Associated with the Emission of the Main States. The two activities associated with the cysteines (C) are in the upper left corner, almost overlapping, with coordinates $(-1,+1)$.

be handled with generality. We have described some examples of architectures, using mixture ideas for the design of the NN component. Different input choices are possible, such as contextual information, sequences over a different alphabet, or continuous parameterization variables [374].

The methods described in this section are not limited to HMMs, but can be applied to any class of probabilistic models. The basic idea is to calculate and possibly modulate the parameters of the models using NNs (or any other flexible reparameterization). Several implicit examples of hybrid architectures can be found in the literature (for example [395]). In fact, the NN architectures of chapter 5 can be viewed as hybrid architectures. In the standard regression case, a Gaussian model is used for each point in input space. Each Gaussian model is parameterized by its mean. The standard NN architecture simply computes the mean at each point. Although the principle of hybrid modeling is not new, by exploiting it systematically in the case of HMMs, we have generated new classes of models. In other classes the principle has not yet been applied systematically, for example, probabilistic models of evolution (chapter 10) and stochastic grammars (chapter 11). In the next section, we closely follow [37] and apply similar techniques to a larger class of probabilistic models, namely to BIOHMMs and the problem of predicting protein secondary structure.

9.6 Bidirectional Recurrent Neural Networks for Protein Secondary Structure Prediction

Protein secondary structure prediction (see also section 6.3) can be formulated as the problem of learning a synchronous sequential translation from strings in the amino acid alphabet to strings written in the alphabet of structural categories. Because biological sequences are spatial rather than temporal, we have seen that BIOHMMs are an interesting new class of graphical models for this problem. In particular, they offer a sensible alternative to methods based on a fixed-width input window. The expressive power of these models enables them to capture distant information in the form of contextual knowledge stored into hidden state variables. In this way, they can potentially overcome the main disadvantage of feedforward networks, namely the linear growth of the number of parameters with the window size. Intuitively, these models are parsimonious because of the implicit weight sharing resulting from their stationarity; i.e., parameters do not vary over time.

We have used BIOHMMs directly to predict protein secondary structure with some success [36]. As graphical models, however, BIOHMMs contain undirected loops and therefore require a computationally intensive evidence-propagation algorithm (the junction tree algorithm [287]), rather than the simpler Pearl's algorithm for loopless graphs such as HMMs (see also appendix C). Thus to speed up the algorithm, we can use the technique of the previous section and use neural networks, both feedforward and recurrent, to reparameterize the graphical model.

9.6.1 Bidirectional Recurrent Neural Nets

Letting t denote position within a protein sequence, the overall model can be viewed as a probabilistic model that outputs, for each t, a vector $O_t = (o_{1,t}, o_{2,t}, o_{3,t})$ with $o_{i,t} \geq 0$ and $\sum_i o_{i,t} = 1$. The $o_{i,t}$s are the secondary structure class membership probabilities. The output prediction has the functional form

$$O_t = \eta(F_t, B_t, I_t) \tag{9.15}$$

and depends on the forward (upstream) context F_t, the backward (downstream context) B_t, and the input I_t at time t. The vector $I_t \in \mathbf{R}^k$ encodes the external input at time t. In the most simple case, where the input is limited to a single amino acid, $k = 20$, by using the orthogonal binary encoding (see section 6.1). In this case, it is not necessary to include an extra input symbol to represent the terminal portions of the protein. Larger input windows extending over several amino acids are of course also possible. The function η is realized by a neural network $\mathcal{N}_\eta$ (see center and top connections in figure 9.15). Thus to guarantee a consistent probabilistic interpretation, the three output units of network $\mathcal{N}_\eta$ are obtained as normalized exponentials (or *softmax*)

$$o_{i,t} = \frac{\exp(net_{i,t})}{\sum_{l=1}^{3} \exp(net_{l,t})} i = 1, 2, 3; \tag{9.16}$$

where $net_{i,t}$ is the activation of the ith output unit at position t. The performance of the model can be assessed using the usual relative entropy between the estimated and the target distribution.

The novelty of the model is in the contextual information contained in the vectors $F_t \in \mathbf{R}^n$ and especially in $B_t \in \mathbf{R}^m$. These satisfy the recurrent bidirectional equations

$$\begin{aligned} F_t &= \phi(F_{t-1}, I_t) \\ B_t &= \beta(B_{t+1}, I_t) \end{aligned} \tag{9.17}$$

Here $\phi(\cdot)$ and $\beta(\cdot)$ are learnable nonlinear state transition functions. They can be implemented in different forms, but here we assume that they are realized by two NNs, $\mathcal{N}_\phi$ and $\mathcal{N}_\beta$ (left and right subnetworks in figure 9.15), with n and m logistic output units, respectively. Thus, $\mathcal{N}_\phi$ and $\mathcal{N}_\beta$ are fed by $n + k$ and $m + k$ inputs, respectively. Here also larger input windows are possible, especially in combination with the weight-sharing approach described in [445], and different inputs could be used for the computation of F_t, B_t, and O_t. The *forward* chain F_t stores contextual information contained to the left of time t and plays the same role as the internal state in standard RNNs. The novel part of the model is the presence of an additional *backward* chain B_t, in charge of storing contextual information contained to the right of time t, i.e. in the future. The actual form of the bidirectional dynamics is controlled by the connection weights in the subnetworks $\mathcal{N}_\phi$ and $\mathcal{N}_\beta$. As we shall see, these weights can be adjusted using a maximum-likelihood approach. Since (9.17) involves two recurrences, two corresponding boundary conditions must be specified, at the beginning and the end of the sequence. For simplicity, here we use $F_0 = B_{N+1} = 0$, but it is also possible to adapt the boundaries to the data, extending the technique suggested in [184] for standard RNNs.

The discrete time index t ranges from 1 to N, the total length of the protein sequence being examined. Hence the probabilistic output O_t is parameterized by a RNN and depends on the input I_t and on the contextual information, from the *entire* protein, summarized into the pair (F_t, B_t). In contrast, in a conventional NN approach this probability distribution depends only on a relatively short subsequence of amino acids. Intuitively, we can think of F_t and B_t as "wheels" that can be "rolled" along the protein. To predict the class at position t, we roll the wheels in opposite directions from the N and C terminus up

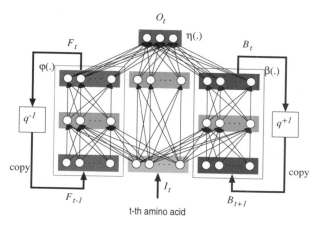

Figure 9.15: Bidirectional Recursive Neural Network Architecture. Inputs correspond to amino acid letters in a given protein sequence. Outputs correspond to secondary structure classification into alpha-helices, beta-sheets, and coils.

to position t and then combine what is read on the wheels with I_t to calculate the proper output using η.

The global mapping from the input amino acid sequence to the sequence of output categories can be described by the graphical model shown in figure 9.16. The network represents the direct dependencies among the variables I_t, F_t, B_t, O_t, unrolled over time for $t = 1, \ldots, N$. Each node is labeled by one of the variables and arcs represent direct functional dependencies. This graph represents the underlying Bayesian network BIOHMMs except that the internal relationships amongst I_t, F_t, B_t, O_t here are deterministic((9.15) and (9.17)), rather than probabilistic. The overall BRNN model, however, is a probabilistic model. As we have seen, inference in the BIOHMMs is tractable but requires time complexity of $O(n^3)$ for each time step (here n is the typical number of states in the chains), limiting their practical applicability to the secondary structure prediction task [36].

An architecture resulting from (9.15) and (9.17) is shown in figure 9.15 where, for simplicity, all the NNs have a single hidden layer. The hidden state F_t is copied back to the input. This is graphically represented in figure 9.15 using the causal *shift operator* q^{-1} that operates on a generic temporal variable X_t and is symbolically defined as $X_{t-1} = q^{-1}X_t$. Similarly, q, the inverse (or noncausal) shift operator is defined $X_{t+1} = qX_t$ and $q^{-1}q = 1$. As shown in Figure 9.15, a noncausal copy is performed on the hidden state B_t. Clearly, removal of $\{B_t\}$ would result in a standard causal RNN.

The number of degrees of freedom of the model depends on two factors: (1) the dimensions n and m of the forward and backward state vectors; (2) the number of hidden units in the three feedforward networks realizing the state transition and the output functions (see figure 9.15). It is important to remark that the BRNN has been defined as a stationary model; that is, the connection weights in the networks realizing $\beta(\cdot)$, $\phi(\cdot)$ and $\eta(\cdot)$ do not change over time, i.e. with respect to position along the protein. This is a form of weight sharing that reduces the number of free parameters and the risk of overfitting, without necessarily sacrificing the capability to capture distant information.

9.6.2 Inference and Learning

Since the graph shown in figure 9.16 is acyclic, nodes can be topologically sorted, defining unambiguously the global processing scheme. Using the network unrolled through time, the BRNN prediction algorithm updates all the states F_t from left to right, starting from $F_0 = 0$. Similarly, states B_t are updated from right to left. After forward and backward propagations have taken place, the predictions O_t can be computed. The forward and backward propagations need to be computed from end to end only once per protein sequence. As a result, the time complexity of the algorithm is $O(NW)$, where W is the number of weights and N the protein length. This is the same complexity as feedforward networks fed by a fixed-size window. In the case of BRNNs, W typically grows as $O(n^2)$ and the actual number of weights can be reduced by limiting the number of hidden units in the subnetworks for $\phi(\cdot)$ and $\beta(\cdot)$. Thus, inference in BRNNs is more efficient than in bidirectional IOHMMs, where the complexity is $O(Nn^3)$ [36].

Learning can be formulated as a maximum likelihood estimation problem, where the log-likelihood is essentially the relative entropy function between the predicted and the true conditional distribution of the secondary structure sequence given the input amino acid sequence

$$\ell = \sum_{\text{sequences}} \sum_{t=1}^{N} z_{i,t} \log o_{i,t}, \tag{9.18}$$

with $z_{i,t} = 1$ if the secondary structure at position t is i and $z_{i,t} = 0$ otherwise. The optimization problem can be solved by gradient ascent. The only difference with respect to standard RNNs is that gradients must be computed by taking into account noncausal temporal dependencies. Because the unrolled network is acyclic, the generalized backpropagation algorithm can be derived as a special case of the backpropagation through structure algorithm [188]. Intuitively, the error signal is first injected into the leaf nodes, corresponding to the output variables O_t. The error is then propagated through time in both

output: sequence of secondary structure symbols

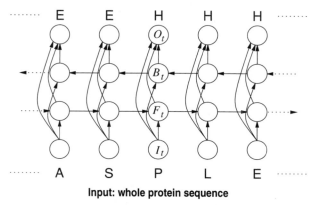

Input: whole protein sequence

Figure 9.16:   Direct Dependencies Among the Variables Involved in a Bidirectional BRNN. The boundary conditions are provided by $F_0 = B_{N+1} = 0$ and by the inputs associated with the current protein sequence.

directions, by following any reverse topological sort of the unrolled network (see figure 9.16). Obviously, this step also involves backpropagation through the hidden layers of the NNs. Since the model is stationary, weights are shared among the different replicas of the NNs at different time steps. Hence, the total gradient is simply obtained by summing all the contributions associated with different time steps.

To speedup convergence, it was found convenient to adopt an online weight-updating strategy. Once gradients relative to a single protein have been computed, weights are immediately updated. This scheme was enriched also with a heuristic adaptive learning rate algorithm that progressively reduces the learning rate if the average error reduction within a fixed number of epochs falls below a given threshold.

9.6.3   Long-range Dependencies

One of the principal difficulties in training standard RNNs is the problem of vanishing gradients [57]. Intuitively, in order to contribute to the output at position or time t, the input signal at time $t - \tau$ must be propagated in the forward chain through τ replicas of the NN that implements the state transition function. However, during gradient computation, error signals must be propagated backward along the same path. Each propagation can be interpreted as the product between the error vector and the Jacobian matrix associated with the transition function. Unfortunately, when the dynamics develop attractors that allow the system to store past information reliably, the norm of the Jacobian is < 1. Hence, when τ is large, gradients of the error at time t with respect to inputs at time $t - \tau$ tend to vanish exponentially. Similarly, in the case of BRNNs, error propagation in both the forward and the backward chains is subject to exponential decay. Thus, although the model has in principle the capability of storing remote information, such information cannot be learnt effectively. Clearly, this is a theoretical argument and its practical impact needs to be evaluated on a per-case basis.

In practice, in the case of proteins, the BRNN can reliably utilize input information located within about ±15 amino acids (i.e., the total effective window size is about 31). This was empirically evaluated by feeding the model with increasingly long protein fragments. We observed that the average predictions at the central residues did not significantly change if fragments were extended beyond 41 amino acids. This is an improvement over standard NNs with input window sizes ranging from 11 to 17 amino acids [453, 445, 290]. Yet there is presumably relevant information located at longer distances that these models have not been able to discover so far.

To limit this problem, a remedy was proposed motivated by recent studies [364] suggesting that the vanishing-gradients problem can be mitigated by the use of an explicit delay line applied to the output, which provides shorter paths for the effective propagation of error signals. Unfortunately, this idea cannot be applied directly to BRNNs since output feedback, combined with bidirectional propagation, would generate cycles in the unrolled network. A similar mechanism, however, can be implemented using the following modified dynamics:

$$
\begin{aligned}
F_t &= \phi(F_{t-1}, F_{t-2}, \ldots, F_{t-s}, I_t) \\
B_t &= \beta(B_{t+1}, B_{t+2}, \ldots, B_{t+s}, I_t).
\end{aligned}
\tag{9.19}
$$

The explicit dependence on forward or backward states introduces *shortcut* connections in the graphical model, forming shorter paths along which gradients can be propagated. This is akin to introducing higher-order Markov chains in the probabilistic version. However, unlike Markov chains where the number of parameters would grow exponentially with s, in the present case the number of parameters grows only linearly with s. To reduce the number of parameters, a simplified version of (9.19) limits the dependencies to state vectors located s residues away from t:

$$
\begin{aligned}
F_t &= \phi(F_{t-1}, F_{t-s}, I_t) \\
B_t &= \beta(B_{t+1}, B_{t+s}, I_t).
\end{aligned}
\tag{9.20}
$$

Another variant of the basic architecture that also lets us increase the effective window size consists in feeding the output networks with a window in the

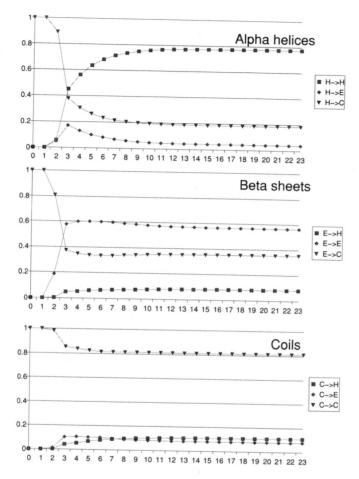

Figure 9.17: Distant Information Exploited by the BRNN. The horizontal axis represents τ, the distance from a given position beyond which all entries are set to null values. Each curve represents a normalized row of the test-set confusion matrix.

forward and backward state chains. In this case, the prediction is computed as

$$O_t = \eta(F_{t-s},\ldots,F_{t+s},B_{t-s},\ldots,B_{t+s},I_t). \qquad (9.21)$$

Notice that the window can extend in the past and the future of t on both vectors F_t and B_t.

9.6.4 Implementation and Results

BRNNs have been used to implement SSpro, a secondary structure prediction server available through the Internet[3]. In addition to BRNNs, SSpro uses other features that over the years have proved to be useful for secondary structure prediction, such as ensembles and profiles (see section 6.3). Profiles, in particular, are most useful when used at the input level. Details of experiments and performance analysis of the first version of SSpro which used BLAST-generated profiles are given in [37]. The most recent version of SSpro uses PSIBLAST profiles and achieves a performance of about 80% correct prediction. SSpro has been ranked among the top predictors both at the 2000 CASP blind prediction competition and through the independent automatic evaluation server EVA of Rost (http://dodo.bioc.columbia.edu/~eva/), based on the new sequences that are deposited each week in the PDB.

Beyond the performance results, to study the capabilities of BRNNs models to capture long-ranged information a number of experiments were performed. For each protein and for each amino acid position t, we fed the BRNN mixture described above with a sequence obtained by replacing all inputs outside the range $[t - \tau, t + \tau]$ with null values. The experiment was repeated for different values of τ from 0 to 23. Figure 9.17 shows the results. Each diagram is a normalized row of the test set confusion table, for the semi-window size τ ranging from 0 to 23. So for example the line labeled $H \rightarrow C$ in the first diagram is the percentage of helices classified as coils, as a function of τ. The curves are almost stable for $\tau > 15$. Although the model is not sensitive to *very* distant information, it should be remarked that typical feedforward nets reported in the literature do not exploit information beyond $\tau = 8$.

Given the large number of protein sequences available through genome and other sequencing projects, even small percentage improvements in secondary structure prediction are significant for structural genomics. Machine learning algorithms combined with graphical models and their NN parameterizations are one of the best approaches so far in this area. BRNNs and the related ideas presented here begin to address problems of long-ranged dependencies. As a result, BRNNs have now been developed to predict a number of other structural features including amino acid partners in beta sheets, number of residue contacts, and solvent accessibility [45, 429]. These structural modules are part of a broader strategy towards 3D prediction based on the intermediary prediction of contact maps, with both low (secondary structure) and high (amino acid) resolution, starting from the primary sequence and the predicted structural features. Indeed, prediction of the arrangement of secondary structure elements with respect to each other in three-dimensions would go a long way

---

[3]SSpro is accessible through http://promoter.ics.uci.edu/BRNN-PRED/.

towards the prediction of protein topology and three-dimensional structure.

There are several directions in which this work could be extended including many architectural variations. In addition to the use of larger input windows for I_t, one may consider non-symmetrical chains for the past and the future, and the use of priors on the parameters and/or the architecture together with a maximum a posteriori learning approach. It may also be advantageous to use an array of "wheels," instead of just two wheels, of various memory capacity, rolling in different directions along the protein and possibly over shorter distances. It is also worth noting that using multi-layered perceptrons for implementing $\beta(.)$ and $\phi(.)$ is just one of the available options. For example, recurrent radial basis functions or a generalization of second-order RNN [208] are easily conceivable alternative parameterization. Finally, the ideas described in this section can be applied to other problems in bioinformatics, as well as other domains, where non-causal dynamical approaches are suitable. Obvious candidates for further tests of the general method include the prediction of protein functional features, such as signal peptides.

Chapter 10

Probabilistic Models of Evolution: Phylogenetic Trees

10.1 Introduction to Probabilistic Models of Evolution

This chapter deals with evolution and the inference of phylogenetic trees from sequence data. It is included of course because sequence evolution is a central topic in computational molecular biology, but also because the ideas and algorithms used are again a perfect illustration of the general probabilistic inference framework of chapter 2.

Evolutionary relationships between organisms—existing or extinct—have been inferred using morphological and/or biochemical characteristics since the time of Darwin. Today, phylogenetic trees are commonly derived from DNA and protein sequences [182]. Due to the extreme stability of the DNA molecule, it can be extracted in large intact pieces even from organisms that have been dead for many years [251]. The extinct elephant-like mammoth has been phylogenetically mapped by its DNA, and for deceased humans precise family relationships can also be established. Among the most recent examples are the proof of the identity of the last Russian tsar, Nicholas II [211, 274], and the disproof of the story of Anna Anderson, who claimed she was the tsar's missing daughter Anastasia [212, 477]. The bones (and the DNA) of the tsar had been lying in the soil since 1918.

The literature contains a number of methods for inferring phylogenetic trees from sequence data. Most of the approaches are variations on two major methods: parsimony methods [181] and likelihood methods [178, 519, 269]. Not surprisingly, likelihood methods are based on a probabilistic model of the evolutionary process (see also [295]). Actually, the term "likelihood methods" is typically used in this field in connection with a particular class of probabilistic models. Although parsimony methods are often described independently of any underlying model of evolution, we will show that they can be viewed as approximations to likelihood methods.

From the general Bayesian framework and the Cox–Jaynes axioms, we know that in order to infer a phylogenetic tree from a set of sequences, we *must* begin with a probabilistic model of evolution. Maximum likelihood (ML) is then the most basic inference step we can perform with respect to such a model. ML encompasses all the other approaches currently found in the literature, including the ML approach in [178] with respect to a particular model class. As we have seen, HMMs are not a complete model of the evolutionary process. Evolution can proceed at the molecular level not only by insertions and deletions but also by substitutions, inversions, and transpositions. Therefore different models must be used. But first we need some elementary background and notation for trees.

10.1.1 Trees

A tree T is a connected acyclic graph. In a tree every two points are joined by a unique path, and the number of vertices always exceeds the number of edges by exactly 1. A tree is *binary* if each vertex has either one or three neighbors. A tree is *rooted* if a node r has been selected and termed the root. In phylogenetic trees, the root is intended to represent an ancestral sequence from which all the others descend. Two important aspects of phylogenetic trees, both rooted and unrooted, are the topology and the branch length. The topology refers to the branching pattern of the tree associated with the times of divergence. The branch length is often used to represent in some way the time distance between events (figure 10.1).

10.1.2 Probabilistic Models

The most basic but still useful probabilistic model of evolution is again a variation of the simple dice model. We can imagine that starting from an ancestral sequence, evolution proceeds randomly, using position-independent substitutions only. If we look at a given fixed position i in the sequences, and if we let $\chi^i(t)$ denote the letter at position i at time t, we can make the usual Markov process assumption that the probability

$$p^i_{YX}(t) = \mathbf{P}(\chi^i(t+s) = Y | \chi^i(s) = X) \tag{10.1}$$

is independent of $s \geq 0$ for $t > 0$. Thus, for each position i, there is a probability $p^i_{YX}(t)$ that X is substituted into Y over an evolutionary period of time

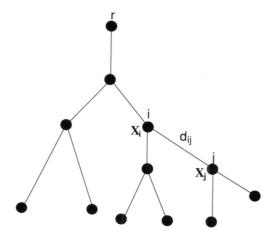

Figure 10.1: A Simple Binary Phylogenetic Tree. r is the root; d_{ji} is the time distance between i and j; X_i is the letter assigned to the hidden vertex i. The observed letters are at the leaves at the bottom. The probability of the substitution from vertex i to vertex j is $p_{X_j X_i}(d_{ji})$.

t. Thus for each t and each position i we have a collection of $|A|$ dice. To simplify the model further, we shall, for now, make the additional approximation that the substitution probabilities are identical at all positions, so that $p_{YX}^i(t) = p_{YX}(t)$. Obviously, we must have $p_{YX}(t) \geq 0$ for any X, Y and any t, and furthermore $\sum_Y p_{YX}(t) = 1$. From (10.1), one must also have the Chapman-Kolmogorov relation,

$$p_{YX}(t + s) = \sum_{Z \in A} p_{YZ}(t) p_{ZX}(s), \qquad (10.2)$$

due to the independence of the events at time t and time s.

10.2 Substitution Probabilities and Evolutionary Rates

All that remains to specify the model entirely is to determine the substitution probabilities $p_{YX}(t)$. These are related to the substitution matrices, such as PAM matrices, discussed in chapter 1. It is sensible to make the further assumption that

$$\lim_{t \to 0^+} p_{YX}(t) = \delta(Y, X) = \begin{cases} 1 & \text{if } Y = X \\ 0 & \text{otherwise} \end{cases}. \qquad (10.3)$$

If we let $P(t)$ denote the matrix $P(t) = (p_{YX}(t))$, from (10.3) we can define $P(0) = Id$, where Id is the $|A| \times |A|$ identity matrix. One can then show that each component of $P(t)$ is differentiable, so that we can write $P'(t) = (p'_{YX}(t))$. The process is now entirely specified by its right derivative at 0,

$$Q = P'(0) = \lim_{t \to 0^+} \frac{P(t) - Id}{t}. \tag{10.4}$$

This is because (10.4) implies that

$$P'(t) = QP(t) = P(t)Q. \tag{10.5}$$

To see this rapidly, just write $P(t + dt) = P(t)P(dt) = P(t)(P(0) + Qdt) = P(t)(Id + Qdt)$, the first equality resulting from (10.2) and the second from (10.4), so that $P(t + dt) - P(t) = P(t)Qdt$. If we let $Q = (q_{YX})$, from (10.5) the final solution is given by

$$P(t) = e^{Q(t)} = Id + \sum_{n=1}^{\infty} \frac{Q^n t^n}{n!}. \tag{10.6}$$

Note that if Q is symmetric, so is P, and vice versa. Such an assumption may simplify calculations, but it is not biologically realistic and will not be used here. Finally, a distribution column vector $p = (p_X)$ is *stationary* if $P(t)p = p$ for all times t. Thus, once in a stationary distribution, the process remains in it forever. From (10.4), this implies that p is in the kernel of Q: $Qp = 0$. And from (10.6) the two statements are in fact equivalent. If we assume that the observed sequences have been produced with the system in its stationary distribution, then p is easily estimated from the average composition of the observed sequences.

   To summarize, we have defined a class of probabilistic models for the evolution of sequences. Such models are characterized by four assumptions:

1. At each site, evolution operates by substitution only, and therefore without indels (insertions and deletions). All observed sequences must have the same length.

2. Substitutions at each position are independent of one another.

3. Substitution probabilities depend only on the current state, and not on the past history (Markov property).

4. The Markov process is the same for all positions.

None of these assumptions are satisfied by real DNA, where the sequence length can change as a result of indels; evolution of different positions is not independent; evolution rates are not uniform both in time and as a function of position; and, last, real DNA is subjected to recombination. But this constitutes a useful first approximation. Many current research efforts concentrate on relaxing some of these assumptions. The first two assumptions are probably the most difficult to relax. For indels, one can easily add a gap symbol to the alphabet A within the present framework, although this is not entirely satisfactory. In any case, to specify a model further within the class described above, one must provide the matrix of rates Q.

10.3 Rates of Evolution

First note that the rate matrix Q is defined up to a multiplicative factor because $P(t) = \exp(Qt) = \exp[(\lambda Q)(t/\lambda)]$ for any $\lambda \neq 0$. In one simple subclass of models, we assume that λdt is the probability that a substitution occurs at a given position over a small time interval dt. Thus λ is the rate of substitution per unit time. Furthermore, when a substitution occurs, a letter is chosen with probability $p = (p_X)$. Thus we have

$$p_{YX}(dt) = (1 - \lambda dt)\delta(Y, X) + \lambda dt p_Y. \qquad (10.7)$$

This is equivalent to specifying the matrix Q by

$$q_{XX} = \lambda(p_X - 1) \quad \text{and} \quad q_{YX} = \lambda p_Y \qquad (10.8)$$

for any X and Y. From (10.8) and (10.6), or directly from (10.7) by noting that $e^{-\lambda t}$ is the probability of not having any substitutions at all over a period of length t, we have

$$p_{YX}(t) = e^{-\lambda t}\delta(Y, X) + (1 - e^{-\lambda t})p_Y. \qquad (10.9)$$

It is useful to note that the distribution p used in (10.7) can be chosen arbitrarily. However, once chosen, it can be shown that it is the stationary distribution of (10.9); hence the common notation used above. As above, p can be obtained directly from the data if we assume that the data are at equilibrium.

Again, $p_{YX}(t)$ depends on t via the product λt only. In the absence of any other evidence, we can choose $\lambda = 1$ and thus measure t in units of expected numbers of substitutions. If λ is allowed to vary along each branch of the tree, this is equivalent to measuring time with clocks running at different rates on different branches. Thus the total length from the root to the leaves of the tree need not be constant along all possible paths.

Another useful property of the process defined by (10.9) is that it is *reversible* in the sense that the substitution process looks the same forward and backward in time. This is easily seen from the fact that (10.9) yields the balance equations

$$p_{YX}(t)p_X = p_{XY}(t)p_Y. \qquad (10.10)$$

Reversibility is also satisfied by other probabilistic models of evolution [302].

10.4   Data Likelihood

Given a set of sequences and an evolutionary probabilistic model, we can try to find the most likely tree topology as well as the most likely lengths for the branches [178, 519]. This explains the use of the expression "ML methods for phylogeny."

We first assume that we have K sequences over the alphabet A, all with the same length N, and a corresponding given phylogenetic tree T with root r and time lengths d_{ji} between adjacent vertices i and j. The first goal is to compute the likelihood $\mathbf{P}(O_1, \ldots, O_K | T)$ according to the evolutionary Markovian models described above. Because of the independence assumption across column positions, we have

$$\mathbf{P}(O_1, \ldots, O_K | T) = \prod_{k=1}^{N} \mathbf{P}(O_1^k, \ldots, O_K^k | T), \tag{10.11}$$

where O_j^k represents the kth letter observed in the jth sequence. Therefore we need to study only the term $\mathbf{P}(O_1^k, \ldots, O_K^k | T)$ associated with the column k and with the letters O_j^k at the K leaves of the tree. In what follows, we will use the generic notation O to denote the set of observed letters at a fixed position. We can consider that at each vertex i of the tree there is a *hidden* random variable χ_i representing the letter associated with vertex i. Thus a phylogenetic tree can be viewed as a simple Bayesian network (appendix C) with a tree structure in which the conditional probability of a node j, given its parent i, is parameterized by the time distance d_{ji} in the form

$$\mathbf{P}(\chi_j = \mathsf{Y} | \chi_i = \mathsf{X}) = p_{\mathsf{YX}}(d_{ji}). \tag{10.12}$$

Thus all the well-known algorithms for Bayesian networks can be applied in this simple case. In particular, the likelihood $\mathbf{P}(O|T) = \mathbf{P}(O_1^k, \ldots, O_K^k | T)$ can be computed in two ways: starting from the root or starting from the leaves.

Starting from the root, let (X_i) denote an assignment of letters to the internal nodes I other than the leaves, and including the root r. The letters assigned to the internal nodes play of course the role of hidden variables, similar to the HMM paths in chapter 7. In this notation, X_i is assigned to vertex i and the notation is extended to include the letters observed at the leaves. The probability of such a global assignment is easily computed:

$$\mathbf{P}(O, (\mathsf{X}_i) | T) = \mathbf{P}((\mathsf{X}_i) | T) = p_r(\mathsf{X}_r) \prod_{i \in I} \prod_{j \in N^+(i)} p_{\mathsf{Y}_j \mathsf{X}_i}(d_{ji}), \tag{10.13}$$

where p_r is the prior probability distribution for the letters at the root node. $N^+(i)$ denotes the set of children of vertex i, the edges being oriented from the root to the leaves. Assuming that the process is at equilibrium, p_r is the stationary distribution $p = p_r$ and thus can be estimated from the average composition. The observation likelihood is computed by summing over all possible assignments:

$$\mathbf{P}(O|T) = \sum_{(X_i)} p_r(X_r) \prod_{I-\{r\}} \prod_{j \in N^+(i)} p_{Y_j X_i}(d_{ji}). \tag{10.14}$$

The sum above contains $|A|^{|T|-K}$ terms and is computationally not efficient. $|T|$ is the number of trees.

The likelihood is computed more efficiently by recursively propagating the evidence from the observed leaves to the root. Let $O^+(i)$ denote the portion of evidence contained in the subtree rooted at vertex i, that is, the letters observed on the leaves that are descendants of i. Then if i is a leaf of the tree,

$$\mathbf{P}(O^+(i)|X_i = X, T) = \begin{cases} 1 & \text{if X is observed at } i \\ 0 & \text{otherwise} \end{cases}. \tag{10.15}$$

A different distribution can be used when the letter associated with a leaf is known only with some ambiguity. If i is any internal node,

$$\mathbf{P}(O^+(i)|X_i = X, T) = \sum_{Y \in A} \sum_{j \in N^+(i)} p_{YX}(d_{ji})\mathbf{P}((O^+(j)|X_j = Y, T). \tag{10.16}$$

The evidence O can be propagated in this way all the way to the root r. The complete likelihood is then easily shown to be

$$\mathbf{P}(O|T) = \sum_{X \in A} p_r(X)\mathbf{P}(O^+(r)|X_r = X, T) = \sum_{X \in A} p_r(X)\mathbf{P}(O|X_r = X, T). \tag{10.17}$$

This algorithm, which again is a propagation algorithm for Bayesian networks, is sometimes called the "peeling" or "pruning" algorithm. Note that the average composition for p_r and the $p_{YX}^k(d_{ji})$ probabilities can be chosen differently for each column position without changing the structure of the previous calculations. Thus the evolutionary models on each site are similar but need not be identical. It is also worth noting that, instead of integrating over all possible assignments of the internal nodes, one could compute an optimal (most probable) assignment of letters for the internal node. This is the equivalent of the Viterbi path computations we have seen for HMMs.

One useful observation is that if the evolutionary model is reversible and if there are no external constraints on the position of the root (e.g., a requirement that all the leaves be contemporaneous), then the likelihood is independent of the position of the root. The process being the same forward or backward, the root can be moved arbitrarily along any edge of the tree and therefore over the

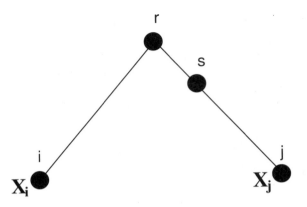

Figure 10.2: Tree Rooted at r with Possible Alternative Root s on the r-to-j Branch.

entire tree. More formally, consider a tree starting with a root r, two children i and j, and an alternative root s on the branch from r to j (figure 10.2). From (10.16) and (10.17), we have

$$\mathbf{P}(O|T) = \sum_{X,Y,Z\in A} p_r(X)p_{YX}(d_{ir})\mathbf{P}(O^+(i)|\chi_i = Y, T)p_{ZX}(d_{sr})\mathbf{P}(O^+(s)|\chi_s = Z, T).$$
(10.18)

Taking into account the reversibility and assuming the system at equilibrium: $p = p_r = p_s$ and $p_r(X)p_{ZX}(d_{sr}) = p_s(Z)p_{XZ}(d_{rs})$. Now

$$\sum_{Y\in A} p_{YX}(d_{ir})\mathbf{P}(O^+(i)|\chi_i = Y, T) = \mathbf{P}(O^{++}(r)|\chi_r = X, T), \qquad (10.19)$$

where the $++$ notation denotes evidence of a tree rooted at s rather than r. Likewise,

$$\mathbf{P}(O^+(s)|\chi_s = Z, T) = \sum_{W\in A} \mathbf{P}(O^{++}(j)|\chi_j = W, T)p_{WZ}(d_{js}). \qquad (10.20)$$

Collecting terms, we finally have

$$\mathbf{P}(O|T) = \sum_{X\in A} p_s(X)\mathbf{P}(O^{++}(s)|\chi_s = X, T). \qquad (10.21)$$

Thus we are free to position the root anywhere on the tree without altering the likelihood, or we can speak of the likelihood of the equivalence class associated with the unrooted tree.

10.5   Optimal Trees and Learning

Little work has been done so far to define prior distributions on the space of phylogenetic trees, in terms of both the branching process and the branching lengths. We thus omit the topic of priors and proceed with the first Bayesian inferential step: estimating ML trees. Section 10.4 computed the likelihood for a given tree topology and branching length. For a given topology, the lengths d_{ji} can be viewed as the parameters of the models and therefore can be optimized by ML. As for HMMs, in general the ML estimate cannot be determined analytically but can be approximated using, for example, gradient descent, EM, or perhaps some form of Viterbi learning. We leave it as an exercise for the reader to find EM or gradient-descent equations for the optimization of the branch length [178].

10.5.1   Optimal Topologies

The optimization of the topology is a second problem that requires approximations. The number of possible trees, even unrooted, is exponentially large and the space of topologies cannot be searched exhaustively. Heuristic algorithms for navigating in this space toward good topologies are described in the literature [178] and will not be reviewed here in detail. One widely used heuristic algorithm consists of progressively adding species (i.e., observation sequences) one by one, starting with a two-species tree. At each step, a new species is selected and all its possible positions with respect to the current tree are considered. The most likely is selected before proceeding to the next step. One serious caveat with a search algorithm of this sort is that the final tree topology depends on the order of presentation of the observation sequences.

   In any case, it is clear that the ML approach to phylogenetic trees is rather computationally intensive. A complete Bayesian treatment of phylogeny is even more intensive since, in addition to priors, it requires integrating across trees in order, for instance, to estimate the probability that a given substitution has or has not occurred in the past. Parsimony methods can be viewed as fast approximations to ML.

10.6   Parsimony

The basic idea behind parsimony is that the optimal tree is the one requiring the smallest number of substitutions along its branches. In this sense, it is somewhat related to MDL (minimum description length) ideas. More formally, consider again an assignment (X_i) to the internal nodes of the tree, the notation being extended to the leaves. The letters at the leaves are fixed and determined by the observations. Then the parsimony cost (error) of the assignment is defined to be

$$\mathcal{E}_P((\mathsf{X}_i)|T) = \sum_{i \in I} \sum_{j \in N^+(i)} \delta(\mathsf{X}_i, \mathsf{X}_j). \tag{10.22}$$

In other words, a fixed cost is introduced for any nonidentical substitution, and the goal is to find an assignment and then a tree with minimal cost. For a given tree, a minimal assignment is also called a minimum mutation fit.

To see the connection with ML methods, recall that for a given tree, the probability of an assignment (X_i) is given by

$$\mathbf{P}((\mathsf{X}_i)|T) = p_r(\mathsf{X}_r) \prod_{i \in I} \prod_{j \in N^+(i)} p_{\mathsf{X}_j \mathsf{X}_i}(d_{ji}), \tag{10.23}$$

and the negative log-probability by

$$\mathcal{E}((\mathsf{X}_i)|T) = -\log p_r(\mathsf{X}_r) - \sum_{i \in I} \sum_{j \in N^+(i)} \log p_{\mathsf{X}_j \mathsf{X}_i}(d_{ji}). \tag{10.24}$$

If we let

$$p_{\mathsf{X}_j \mathsf{X}_i}(d_{ji}) = \begin{cases} a & \text{if } \mathsf{X}_j = \mathsf{X}_i \\ (1-a)/(|A|-1) & \text{if } \mathsf{X}_j \neq \mathsf{X}_i \end{cases}, \tag{10.25}$$

with $1/|A| < a < 1$, then it is easy to check that there exist two constants $\alpha > 0$ and β such that

$$\mathcal{E} = \alpha \mathcal{E}^P + \beta. \tag{10.26}$$

In fact, $\alpha = \log[a(|A|-1)/(1-a)]$ and $\beta = -|E|\log a + \log|A|$, where $|E|$ is the number of edges in the tree T. In other words, a minimum mutation fit for a given tree is equivalent to a Viterbi (most likely) assignment in an ML phylogeny model defined by (10.25) on the same tree topology. Thus parsimony can be viewed as an approximation to an ML approach to phylogeny. It implicitly assumes that changes are rare, uniform across the alphabet and across time. Thus, if the amount of change is small over the evolutionary times being considered, parsimony methods are statistically justified. Recursive algorithms for parsimony are well known [181]. In weighted parsimony [464], one can relax the assumption of uniform substitutions across the alphabet by introducing different weights $w(\mathsf{Y},\mathsf{X})$ for each type of substitution. Again, it is easy to see that this can be viewed in a special ML context by letting, for any Y in A,

$$p_{\mathsf{Y}\mathsf{X}}(d_{ji}) = \frac{e^{-\alpha w(\mathsf{Y},\mathsf{X})}}{\sum_{\mathsf{Z} \in A} e^{-\alpha w(\mathsf{Z},\mathsf{X})}}. \tag{10.27}$$

Parsimony methods are computationally faster than ML methods, and probably this is one of the reasons for their wider use. Parsimony methods, however, can lead to wrong answers when evolution is rapid. Comparison tests between ML and parsimony can be conducted on artificial data generated by a probabilistic evolutionary model. For small samples, obviously both ML and parsimony methods can lead to the wrong phylogeny. In the case of large samples, however, phylogenetic trees are usually correctly reconstructed by ML, but not always by parsimony.

10.7 Extensions

In summary, we have reviewed the basic methodology for constructing phylogenies. The key point is that phylogenetic reconstruction is another application of Bayesian inference methods. The first step required is the construction of tractable probabilistic models of the evolutionary process. Markov substitution models form such a class. We have shown that the main algorithms for phylogenetic reconstruction currently in use, including parsimony methods, are special cases or approximations to ML inference within such a class. Algorithms for phylogenetic reconstruction are computationally intensive, especially when exploration of a large number of possible trees is required.

HMMs and probabilistic tree models of evolution have some complementary strengths and weaknesses. HMMs are needed to produce multiple alignments that are the starting point of evolutionary reconstruction algorithms. Evolutionary models are needed to regularize HMMs, that is to post-process the raw counts of multiple alignment columns to produce emission probabilities that are finely tuned for homology searches in large data bases. It is clear that one direction of research is to try to combine them, that is, to combine trees and alignments, phylogeny, and structure [247, 519], and come up with probabilistic models of the evolutionary process that allow insertions and deletions while *remaining computationally tractable* (see also tree-structured HMMs in appendix C).

A single Markovian substitution process is a bad model of evolution for all the reasons discussed in this chapter, and also because over large evolutionary times it produces a single equilibrium distribution. This is inconsistent with what we observe and, for instance, with the use of a mixture of Dirichlet distributions (Appendix D) as a prior for HMM emission probabilities. Past its relaxation time, a simple Markov model cannot give rise to clusters of distributions and to the different components of a Dirichlet mixture. To account for possible clusters, we must use the simple model over relatively short transient periods, or move to a higher class of evolutionary models.

What would a higher-level model of evolution look like? Imagine that we could observe multiple alignments produced at different times in the course of evolution, say every hundred million years. At each observation epoch, the alignment columns would represent a sample from a complex distribution over possible columns. It is this distribution that evolves over time. Thus in this class of higher-level models, evolution takes place on the distribution over distributions. A simple example of a model in this class can be constructed as follows. We can imagine that the original ($t = 0$) distribution on emission distributions is a Dirichlet mixture $\mathbf{P}(P) = \sum_i \lambda_i \mathcal{D}_{\alpha_i Q_i}(P)$ and that we have a simple Markovian substitution process *operating on the Qs* (and possibly additional processes operating on the αs and λs). At time t, the distribution becomes $\mathbf{P}(P) = \sum_i \lambda_i^t \mathcal{D}_{\alpha_i^t Q_i^t}(P)$. For instance, with a PAM matrix substitution model, if Q_i is chosen equal to the binary unit vector with a single 1 in position i (representing the letter X), then Q_i^t at time t is associated with the ith column of the corresponding PAM matrix (representing $p_{.X}(t)$). Such a model is consistent with regularizing HMM emissions using Dirichlet mixtures associated with PAM matrix columns [497].

Chapter 11

Stochastic Grammars and Linguistics

11.1 Introduction to Formal Grammars

In this chapter we explore one final class of probabilistic models for sequences, stochastic grammars. The basic idea behind stochastic grammars is a direct extension of the simple dice model of chapter 3 and of HMMs.

As briefly mentioned in chapter 1, formal grammars were originally developed to model natural languages, around the same time that the double-helical structure of DNA was elucidated by Watson and Crick. Since then, grammars have been used extensively in the analysis and design of computer languages and compilers [3]. Grammars are natural tools for modeling strings of letters and, more recently, they have been applied to biological sequences. In fact, many problems in computational molecular biology can be cast in terms of formal languages [91, 479]. Here, language!formalthe basic goal again is to produce, by machine learning, the corresponding grammars from the data.

Next, we review the rudiments of the theory of formal grammars, including different classes of grammars, their properties, the Chomsky hierarchy, and the connection to HMMs. In section 11.3, we demonstrate how stochastic grammars can be applied to biological sequences, and especially the application of context-free grammars to RNA molecules. In the subsequent three sections we consider priors, likelihoods, and learning algorithms. Finally, in the last two sections we cover the main applications.

11.2 Formal Grammars and the Chomsky Hierarchy

11.2.1 Formal Languages

We begin with an alphabet A of letters. The set of all finite strings over A is denoted by A^*. $\varnothing$ denotes the empty string. A *language* is a subset of A^*. In this trivial sense, we can say that promoters or acceptor sites in intervening sequences form a language over the DNA alphabet. Such a definition by itself is not very useful unless we define simple ways of generating, recognizing, and classifying languages. A grammar can be seen as a compact set of rules for generating a language. language!formal

11.2.2 Formal Grammars

A formal grammar is a set of rules for producing all the strings that are syntactically correct, and only those strings. A *formal grammar* G consists of an alphabet A of letters, called the terminal symbols; a second alphabet V of variables, also called nonterminal symbols; and a set R of production rules. Among the nonterminal symbols, there is a special $s = start$ variable. Each production rule in R consists of a pair (α, β), more commonly denoted $\alpha \rightarrow \beta$, where α and β are elements of $(A \cup V)^*$. The arrow in $\alpha \rightarrow \beta$ can be read as "produces" or "expands into." We use Greek letters to denote strings that could be combinations of nonterminal and terminal symbols. Thus, in the most general case, α and β are strings made up of letters and variables. In addition, we will assume that α contains at least one nonterminal symbol. Given G and two strings γ and δ over $(A \cup V)$, we say that δ can be *derived* from γ if there is a finite sequence of strings $\pi = \alpha_1, \ldots, \alpha_n$ such that $\gamma \rightarrow \alpha_1 \rightarrow \ldots \rightarrow \alpha_n \rightarrow \delta$ (also denoted $\gamma \rightarrow_\pi \delta$), each step corresponding to an application of a production rule in R. The language $L = L(G)$ *generated* by the grammar G is the set of all terminal strings that can be derived from the start state s.

As an example, let us consider the grammar defined by $A = \{X, Y\}$, $V = \{s\}$, and $R = \{s \rightarrow XsX, s \rightarrow YsY, s \rightarrow X, s \rightarrow Y, s \rightarrow \varnothing\}$. The string XYYX can be derived from the string s: $s \rightarrow XsX \rightarrow XYsYX \rightarrow XYYX$, by applying the first, second, and fourth production rules in succession. More generally, it is easy to show that G generates the set of all palindromes over A. Palindromes are strings that can be read identically in the forward and backward directions. We can now define several different types of grammars and the Chomsky hierarchy. The Chomsky hierarchy is a classification of grammars by increasing degrees of complexity and expressive power.

11.2.3   The Chomsky Hierarchy

The Chomsky hierarchy and its properties are summarized in table 11.1.

Regular Grammars

One of the simplest classes of grammars is the regular grammars (RGs). In a regular grammar, the left-hand side of a production rule is a single variable, and the right-hand side is typically a single letter of the alphabet followed by at most a single variable. Thus strings can grow in only one direction. More precisely, a grammar G is *regular* (or right-linear) if all the production rules are of the form $u \to Xv$, or $u \to X$, or $u \to \varnothing$, where u and v are single nonterminal symbols. A language is regular if it can be generated by a regular grammar. language!regularRegular languages can also be described by other means—for instance, in terms of regular expressions. Regular languages can be recognized very efficiently, although their expressive power is limited.

Context-free Grammars

Regular grammars are special cases of context-free grammars (CFGs), that is, grammars where the replacement of a variable by an expression does not depend on the context surrounding the variable being replaced. More precisely, a grammar G is *context-free* if all the production rules in R are of the form $u \to \beta$, where u is a single nonterminal symbol. A language is language!context-freecontext-free if it can be generated by a context-free grammar. Context free-grammars can be expressed in canonical forms, also called normal forms, such as the "Chomsky normal form" or the "Greibach normal form." A context-free grammar is said to be in Chomsky normal form if each production rule has one of the following three forms: (1) $s \to \varnothing$; (2) $u \to vw$, where u, v, and w are nonterminal symbols; (3) $u \to X$. In addition, if $s \to \varnothing$ is in R, then v and w in (2) must be different from s.

The palindrome grammar above is context-free but not regular. Context-free grammars are often used to specify the syntax of computer languages and to build compilers. As can be expected, not all languages are context-free. For example, copy languages are not context-free. A *copy* language consists of all the strings where the second half is a copy of the first half. XXYXXY belongs to a copy language (corresponding to direct repeats in DNA). Although copy languages may appear similar to palindromes, they really require a more complex class of grammars. Context-free grammars have also been used to model natural languages, but with limited success because natural languages are not context-free.

	Regular	Context-free	Context-sensitive	Recursively enumerable
Production rules	$u \to Xv$ $u \to X$	$u \to vw$ $u \to X$	$\alpha Xy \to \alpha \beta y$	All
Closure properties	$\cup, ., \star$ $\cap, ^-$	$\cup, ., \star$ no $\cap$, no $^-$	$\cup, ., \star$	All
Automata equivalence	Finite-state automata	Pushdown automata	Bounded tape Turing machine	Turing machine
Characteristic language		Palindromes	Copy language	All
Characteristic dependencies	No long-range	Nested	Crossing	All

Table 11.1: The Zoo of Grammars and Their Associated Production Rules and Equivalence Relations.

Context-sensitive Grammars

Within the grammars that are not context-free, we can define the subclass of context-sensitive grammars (CSGs). A grammar G is *context-sensitive* if all the production rules are of the form $\alpha Xy \to \alpha \beta y$ for X in A, $\beta \neq \emptyset$. (X can be replaced by β in the context $\alpha - y$.) In addition, the single rule $s \to \emptyset$ is allowed, provided s does not appear on the right-hand side of any other production rule. A language is context-sensitive if it can be generated by a context-sensitive grammar. It can be shown that copy languages are context-sensitive but not context-free. Context-sensitive languages are characterized by grammars in which the right-hand side of the production rules is at least as long as the left-hand side.

Recursively Enumerable Grammars

These are the most general grammars, without any of the restrictions above. Recursively enumerable refers to the fact that if a word is in the corresponding language, its derivation can always be obtained on a Turing machine in finite time, simply by listing all possible (countable) derivations. Recursively enumerable is weaker than recursive: in general membership of a word in a language cannot be established in finite time, as in the classical halting problem. The term "Chomsky hierarchy" refers to the theorem that the main classes of grammars we have seen so far form a strictly increasing sequence. That is,

$$RGs \subset CFGs \subset CSGs \subset REGs, \tag{11.1}$$

where all the inclusions are strict and RGs = regular grammars, CFGs = context-free grammars, CSGs = context-sensitive grammars and REGs = recursively enumerable grammars. Going up the Chomsky hierarchy allows one to have more general rules, but also more restrictions on the language by excluding more strings.

11.2.4 Ambiguity and Parsing

A derivation can be arranged in a tree structure, called a *parse tree*, that reflects the syntactic structure of a sequence. Parsing can be done top down or bottom up. A sequence is *ambiguous* if it admits more than one parse tree. The notion of ambiguity is important for compilers. Ambiguity introduces complexity in parsing, both in the parsing algorithm and because the number of parse trees may grow exponentially with the length of the string being parsed. There are algorithms and complexity results for parsing specific grammars. A grammar is said to be *linear* if the right-hand sides of all the production rules contain at most one nonterminal symbol. Fast parsing algorithms exist for linear context-free grammars. In general, language recognition and sequence parsing become more computationally demanding as one ascends the Chomsky hierarchy.

11.2.5 Closure Properties

Each of the grammar classes in the Chomsky hierarchy is closed or stable under a number of language operations, such as union ($L_1 \cup L_2$), concatenation ($L_1.L_2$), and iteration (L_1^*). Regular languages are also closed under complement ($\bar{L}_1$) and intersection ($L_1 \cap L_2$). Context-free languages are not closed under complement or intersection.

11.2.6 Dependencies

Two additional ways of looking at grammars are in terms of the patterns they can generate and in terms of automata. Regular grammars can generate overall patterns, such as alternating strings like XYXYXYXY. Like HMMs, regular grammars cannot handle long-range dependencies in a string. Context-free grammars can model certain simple long-range dependencies, that is, *nested* dependencies. A pattern of dependencies is *nested* if it can be drawn without having two lines cross each other. Nested dependencies are characteristic of context-free languages such as palindromes, where the first letter must match the last one, the second must match the second to last, and so on. When dependencies cross, as in a copy language, a context-sensitive language is necessary because crossing dependencies can be implemented only with the freedom of movement that nonterminals enjoy during context-sensitive derivation.

11.2.7 Automata

A final way of understanding the Chomsky hierarchy is to look at the automata associated with each language. Without going into details, regular languages correspond to finite state automata (FSA), with typically one state per nonterminal symbol in the grammar, as in HMMs. In such automata, there is no storage facility apart from the states themselves: everything must be hardwired. Context-free languages correspond to pushdown automata (PDA), which are like finite-state automata but with a memory stack. Only the top of the stack is accessible at any one time. This one-place memory holder is used for palindromes by pushing in, and popping off, one symbol at a time. Such automata cannot handle crossing dependencies because they can access only the top of the stack at any one time. Context-sensitive languages are associated with Turing machines with a linearly bounded tape, that is, with tape length proportional to the I/O strings. Left and right movements along the tape are needed for copying and for handling crossing dependencies. Finally, general languages, that is recursively enumerable languages, correspond to Turing machines (TMs) with unbounded tape, that is, the standard model of universal computers.

11.2.8   Stochastic Grammars and HMMs

So far we have considered deterministic grammars. Stochastic grammars are obtained by superimposing a probability structure on the production rules. Specifically, each production rule $\alpha \rightarrow \beta$ is assigned a probability $\mathbf{P}(\alpha \rightarrow \beta)$, so that $\sum_{\beta} \mathbf{P}(\alpha \rightarrow \beta) = 1$. A stochastic grammar is therefore characterized by a set of parameters w and can be viewed as a probabilistic generative model for the corresponding language (i.e., the language associated with the underlying deterministic grammar).

By now, it should be clear to the reader that HMMs can be viewed exactly as stochastic regular grammars (SRGs). To see this, it suffices to replace the transition from a state s_j to a state s_i in an HMM, together with the emission of the alphabet letter X, with the SRG production rule $s_j \rightarrow Xs_i$ with associated probability $t_{ij}e_{iX}$. Stochastic context-free grammars (SCFGs) then form a more general class of models. They are used in the following sections to model the structure of RNA sequences, and can also be viewed as further generalizations of the dice models of chapter 3. SCFGs include a type of die that has two letters on each face. In the simplest RNA models, the two letters reflect base complementarity. Thus some of the RNA dice have four faces, just like a simple DNA die, but the letters on the faces are AU, UA, CG, and GC (excluding GU, UG pairs) (see figure 11.1).

Figure 11.1: Illustration of the Complementarity in the Watson–Crick Base Paring in DNA. In RNA uracil (U) replaces thymine (T).

11.2.9 Graph Grammars

So far we have considered grammars over alphabets of letters. It is possible, however, to consider more general alphabets where the "letters" are graphs or pixel configurations in image processing. In the case of graph grammars (see [165, 158] and other papers in the same volume), one must carefully specify how graphs are to be joined to each other during the derivation process. Graph grammars have considerable expressive power, and could be a natural candidate for modeling secondary and tertiary structures of biological macromolecules. Little work, however, has been done in this direction so far; a key problem is the lack of efficient learning algorithms for general (or even restricted) graph grammars.

11.3   Applications of Grammars to Biological Sequences

Ultimately, one would like to derive grammar models all the way up to the scale of genes, chromosomes, and even genomes. After all, genomes represent only a very small fraction of all the possible DNA sequences of comparable length. But to begin with, one must consider simpler examples, associated with smaller grammars, such as RNA secondary structure and palindromes.

11.3.1   RNA Secondary Structure and Biological Palindromes

RNA Secondary Structure

Many components in biological macromolecules consist of RNA. Important RNA families include transfer RNA (tRNA), ribosomal RNA (rRNA), small nuclear RNA in the spliceosome (snRNA), messenger RNA (mRNA), and various classes of introns. New phylogenies of small RNA molecules can also be selected in vitro for particular functions, such as protein binding or catalysis [109, 356, 469, 55].

Although RNA normally is single-stranded, helices formed by complementary base pairing strongly control how the RNA folds to form a distinctive 3D structure. The folding of an RNA chain into a functional molecule is largely determined by the Watson–Crick pairs A–U and G–C, but also to some extent by G–U and, more rarely, G–A pairs. RNA nucleotides interact to form secondary structure motifs such as stems, loops, bulges, and pseudoknots where otherwise unpaired nucleotides far from each other in the sequence interact [573]. These pairings often have a nested structure and cannot be modeled efficiently using a regular language or HMMs. We first consider the case of biological palindromes in RNA and other molecules.

Biological Palindromes

There are many examples of RNA/DNA palindromes associated, for example, with protein binding sites. Biological palindromes are slightly different from the ones described above because the letters are not identical when they are matched pairwise, starting from both ends, but complementary. For example, AGAUUUCGAAAUCU is an RNA palindrome. In DNA such palindromes are called inverted repeats.

Because of the complementary double-helix structure of DNA, each half of the palindrome on one side of the helix has a mirror image on the other strand. Thus, if a palindrome string is read from left to right on one strand, the same string can be read from right to left on the opposite strand. RNA palindromes can have arbitrary lengths, and therefore it is likely that they need to be modeled by context-free or more complex grammars (technically, palindromes with a fixed upper length can be modeled by a regular grammar). RNA palindromes are typically folded so that they create hairpin (stem-loop) structures.

A grammar for RNA palindromes is given by

$$s \rightarrow AsU \mid UsA \mid CsG \mid GsC \mid \varnothing, \tag{11.2}$$

where we have listed all the alternative production rules in one line separated by a "|". A palindrome can be generated by: $s \rightarrow AsU \rightarrow AGsCU \rightarrow AGUsACU$, etc. The parse tree produced can be drawn to reflect the base pairing (see also figure 11.2). Real RNA palindromes are not as perfect, but an occasional mismatched pair does not destroy the secondary structure. Some alternative pairings, such as UG, are more tolerated than others; hence also the need to introduce probabilities. It is also common for the stem of a hairpin to have bulges of unpaired bases. RNA is usually not flexible enough to make a 180° turn at the tip of the hairpin. There is often a loop of at least three to four unpaired bases, and sometimes the loop is much longer. Likewise, in DNA palindromes the two halves of the relevant palindrome can be separated by significant distances. All such features can be incorporated into a grammar but complicate the rules.

The previous grammar can generate strings corresponding to single palindromes. Both DNA and RNA are rich in compound palindromes, that is, sequential and recursive ones. Sequential palindromes occur when two or more palindromes follow each other side by side. Recursive palindromes occur when one palindrome is nested within another. The secondary RNA structure associated with a recursive palindrome is a stem with another stem budding from its side. Obtaining simple recursive palindromes is surprisingly easy: one needs only to add the production rule of the form $s \rightarrow ss$. Duplicating the variable s allows for the start of a new palindrome anywhere within an existing one. The corresponding grammar generates structures of branched stems, known as orthodox secondary structures. The best-known example is perhaps the cloverleaf structure of transfer RNA. There are many other examples, especially in ribosomal RNA, of structures consisting of combinations of loops and nested stems. The grammar of recursive palindromes is context-free but, unlike the grammar of simple palindromes, it is ambiguous. The double inverted repeat UGAUCA–UGAUCA can be parsed as a single hairpin, but also as two or more side-by-side stems, not necessarily of equal length. The alternative parse tree corresponds to alternative secondary structures. There are known cases where structural ambiguity seems to be used to confer different roles on the same RNA element. Other examples of ambiguity in DNA linguistics include overlapping genes—in HIV viruses, where some segments of the genome can encode more than one gene, using ambiguous starting points and reading frames.

11.3.2 Context-free Grammars for RNA

More generally, the types of rules needed for an SCFG for RNA are the following:

1. Pair emission rules, for Watson–Crick pairs

$$u \to AvU \mid UvA \mid CvG \mid GvC, \tag{11.3}$$

   but also for rarer pairs (in order of rarity)

$$u \to GvU \mid GvA. \tag{11.4}$$

2. Single-letter left emissions (unpaired bases)

$$u \to Av \mid Cv \mid Gv \mid Uv. \tag{11.5}$$

3. Single-letter right emissions (unpaired bases)

$$u \to vA \mid vC \mid vG \mid vU. \tag{11.6}$$

4. Single-letter emissions (unpaired bases)

$$u \to A \mid C \mid G \mid U. \tag{11.7}$$

5. Branching (or bifurcation)

$$u \to vw. \tag{11.8}$$

6. Deletions (or skips)

$$u \to v. \tag{11.9}$$

The nonterminal variables on the left-hand side of the production rules, such as u, play the role of HMM states and must be numbered $u_1, u_2, \ldots$. As with HMMs, these nonterminal variables can be partitioned into three classes: match, insert, and delete or skip, each with different distributions. *Match* corresponds to important columns in RNA multiple alignments. The main difference from HMMs is the possibility for some states to emit two paired symbols. For a nonterminal u associated with an insert state, a production rule of the form $u \to Xu$ allows multiple insertions. These are needed in loop regions to adjust the loop length. An example of CFG RNA grammar adapted from [460]

a. Productions

$$P = \{ \quad s \rightarrow u_1, \qquad u_7 \rightarrow G\, u_8,$$
$$u_1 \rightarrow C\, u_2\, G, \qquad u_8 \rightarrow G,$$
$$u_1 \rightarrow A\, u_2\, U, \qquad u_8 \rightarrow U,$$
$$u_2 \rightarrow A\, u_3\, U, \qquad u_9 \rightarrow A\, u_{10}\, U,$$
$$u_3 \rightarrow u_4\, u_9, \qquad u_{10} \rightarrow C\, u_{10}\, G,$$
$$u_4 \rightarrow U\, u_5\, A, \qquad u_{10} \rightarrow G\, u_{11}\, C,$$
$$u_5 \rightarrow C\, u_6\, G, \qquad u_{11} \rightarrow A\, u_{12}\, U,$$
$$u_6 \rightarrow A\, u_7, \qquad u_{12} \rightarrow U\, u_{13},$$
$$u_7 \rightarrow U\, u_7, \qquad u_{13} \rightarrow C \qquad \}$$

b. Derivation

$$s \Rightarrow u_1 \Rightarrow Cu_2G \Rightarrow CAu_3UG \Rightarrow CAu_4u_9UG$$
$$\Rightarrow CAu_5Au_9UG \Rightarrow CAUCu_6Gau_9UG$$
$$\Rightarrow CAUCAu_7GAu_9UG \Rightarrow CAUCAGu_8GAu_9UG$$
$$\Rightarrow CAUCAGGGAu_9UG$$
$$\Rightarrow CAUCAGGGAAu_{10}UUG$$
$$\Rightarrow CAUCAGGGAAGu_{11}CUUG$$
$$\Rightarrow CAUCAGGGAAGAu_{12}UCUUG$$
$$\Rightarrow CAUCAGGGAAGAUu_{13}UCUUG$$
$$\Rightarrow CAUCAGGGAAGAUCUCUUG$$

c. Parse tree

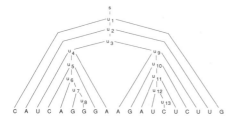

d. Secondary Structure

Figure 11.2: The Simple Context-free Grammar and the Derivation of the Particular Sequence CAUCAGGGAAGAUCUCUUG. A. Set of production rules of the grammar, where s is the start symbol and u_1 to u_{13} are nonterminals. B. Derivation. C. Parse tree associated with the derivation. D. Secondary structure reflecting the parse tree. Adapted from [460].

is given in figure 11.2, with the derivation of a sequence, its parse tree, and secondary structure.

The list of rule types given above is of course redundant, and not all combinations of rule types and nonterminal classes are needed to model RNA. In spite of their different name, the RNA covariance models of [156] are essentially equivalent to the SCFG models. The models in [156] use only the following:

- Match states with pair, single left, and single right emissions

- Insert states with single left and single right emissions

- Delete and branching states.

There are of course trade-offs among the richness of a grammar, the time it takes to train it, and whether it underfits or overfits the data.

11.3.3 Beyond Context-free Grammars

So far we have remained in the realm of context-free grammars, pushdown automata, and nested dependencies. Many of the simple evolutionary operations, such as insertions, deletions, and substitutions, can be expressed in isolation by context-free production rules. There are, however, other genetic operations on blocks of nucleic acid strings—such as duplications, inversions, translocations, and transpositions—that lead to the crossing of dependencies and therefore cannot be accounted for properly in a context-free style. Direct repeats in DNA are fairly common, and essentially form a copy language. As such, they can be modeled by context-sensitive grammars. Crossing of dependencies is also seen in the secondary and tertiary structures of biological molecules. One example here is the pseudoknots occurring in RNA structures.

As already mentioned, pseudoknots occur when a single-stranded loop region forms Watson–Crick base pairs with a complementary sequence outside the loop. Pseudoknots can be viewed as palindromes that are interleaved rather than nested. For instance, AACCGGUU can be regarded as the nesting of two palindromes: AAUU and CCGG. On the other hand, AACCUUGG is a pseudoknot because the complementary pairings must cross each other. Features such as pseudoknots are referred to as non-orthodox secondary structures. The previous context-free grammars are not sufficient to model pseudoknots. Pseudoknots, like direct repeats, can be described using context-sensitive grammars. Finally, it must be noted that the language of DNA may be viewed as the superposition or intersection of several other languages—for instance, for transcription, splicing, and translation. Even if each individual language were context-free, we have seen that there is no reason for the intersection to be context-free.

11.4   Prior Information and Initialization

11.4.1   Learning the Grammar Rules and Initialization from Multiple Alignments

All the rules in an SCFG, as well as their probabilities, can easily be derived from a multiple alignment when one is available, as in the case of HMMs, and with the same caveats. In [156], an algorithm is reported by which the production rules themselves are derived from a set of unaligned sequences. For large RNA molecules, the process of constructing the grammar can also be hierarchically decomposed, whereby a high-level grammar (called metagrammar in [460]) is first constructed on the basis of secondary-structure large-scale motifs [502], such as helices and loops. Each motif is then separately represented by a set of SCFG rules.

		3' A	3' C	3' G	3' U
5'	A	0.160097	0.135167	0.192695	1.590683
5'	C	0.176532	0.134879	3.403940	0.162931
5'	G	0.219045	1.718997	0.246768	0.533199
5'	U	2.615720	0.152039	0.249152	0.249152

Table 11.2: Helix Pseudocounts Are Added to Actual Observed Frequencies to Reflect Prior Information. The 16 parameters in the Dirichlet prior were computed from distributions of basepaired positions in a large alignment of 16S rRNA sequences [346]. From the alignment a four-parameter Dirichlet prior for nucleotide distributions in loop regions was made as well: A (0.26); C (0.21); G (0.18); U (0.20).

11.4.2 Dirichlet Priors

Dirichlet priors are the natural choice for the production rules of stochastic grammars. In the list in section 11.3.2, there are two main different types of rules that need to be considered: the pair emission rules $u \rightarrow XvY$ and the singlet emission rules of the form $u \rightarrow Xv$ for loop regions. In the case of RNA, there are 16 (resp. 4) possible versions of the first (resp. second) type of rule. Because of Watson–Crick base pairing, the corresponding Dirichlet vectors are not uniform. They can easily be derived from a database of aligned RNA structures, such as [346] (table 11.2).

The other rules, such as branch production, can also be Dirichlet-regularized if necessary.

11.5 Likelihood

First, consider the problem of computing the likelihood $\mathbf{P}(O|w)$ of a sequence $O = X^1 \ldots X^t \ldots X^T$ according to a grammar $M = M(w)$ with parameter w. Recalling that SCFGs are ambiguous, let $\pi = \alpha_1, \ldots, \alpha_n$ be a derivation of O from the start state s. Then

$$\mathbf{P}(s \rightarrow_\pi O|w) = \mathbf{P}(s \rightarrow \alpha_1|w)\mathbf{P}(\alpha_1 \rightarrow \alpha_2|w)\ldots\mathbf{P}(\alpha_n \rightarrow O|w), \quad (11.10)$$

$$\mathbf{P}(O|w) = \sum_\pi \mathbf{P}(s \rightarrow_\pi O|w). \quad (11.11)$$

These expressions are of course very similar to the ones obtained in the case of HMMs, where HMM paths are replaced by grammar derivations. Again, this expression for the likelihood is not directly practical because the number of possible parse trees is exponential in the length of the sequence. Again, this problem can be circumvented by using dynamic programming. In the case of nonstochastic context-free grammars in Chomsky normal form, this algorithm is known as the Cocke–Kasami–Younger algorithm [393]. The derivation of a slightly more general version for stochastic context-free grammars is similar to the forward propagation algorithm for HMMs, and is left as an exercise (it is also called the "inside" algorithm). The most probable parse tree of a sequence according to an SCFG can be found by a similar version of dynamic programming that generalizes the Viterbi algorithm of HMMs. By analogy, we will use the term *Viterbi parse tree* or *Viterbi derivation*. One important point to consider is that the additional complexity of SCFGs with respect to HMMs results in three-dimensional forms of dynamic programming that scale as $O(N^3)$ rather than $O(N^2)$ (see [460, 156] for additional details).

11.6   Learning Algorithms

Learning algorithms for SCFGs of one sort or the other are described in [25, 345, 459, 460, 156]. As in the case of HMMs, the basic idea at the first level of Bayesian inference is to estimate model parameters by maximizing the likelihood or the posterior through some iterative algorithm. In most of the examples cited above, this is done by some form of the EM algorithm, although one could also use other methods, such as gradient descent. The derivation of each learning rule is only sketched because it closely parallels what has been described in detail in the case of HMMs. For the sake of simplicity, we begin with ML estimation with a single training sequence O and an SCFG with known rules and parameters w. Extensions to MAP estimation and/or multiple training sequences are straightforward. Let us consider a generic production rule of the form $u \rightarrow \beta$. For any derivation π of O, we can define $n(\beta, u, \pi, O)$ to be the number of times the rule $u \rightarrow \beta$ is used in π. Similarly, let $n(u, \pi, O) = \sum_\beta n(\beta, u, \pi, O)$.

11.6.1   The EM Algorithm

For the E step of the algorithm, we let $Q(\pi) = \mathbf{P}(\pi | O, w)$. If $P_{u \rightarrow \beta}$ denotes the probability parameter associated with the rule, then the EM reestimation equations are given by

$$P_{u \rightarrow \beta}^+ = \frac{\sum_\pi Q(\pi) n(\beta, u, \pi, O)}{\sum_\pi Q(\pi) n(u, \pi, O)} = \frac{\sum_\pi \mathbf{P}(\pi | O, w) n(\beta, u, \pi, O)}{\sum_\pi \mathbf{P}(\pi | O, w) n(u, \pi, O)} = \frac{n_{u \rightarrow \beta}}{n_u}.$$
$$(11.12)$$

This reestimation formula is simple: all the complexity is hidden in the calculation of the numerator and the denominator. These can be calculated by a dynamic programming procedure similar to the one discussed in section 11.5,

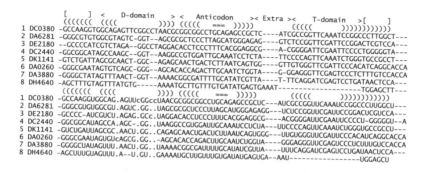

Figure 11.3: Comparison of Multiple Alignments of Several Representative tRNAs in the Data Set (top) [502] with That Produced by the Trained Grammar **RandomTRNA618** (bottom). Parentheses indicate base paired positions; = = =, the anticodon; '[]', the 5' and 3' sides of the acceptor helix. For **RandomTRNA618**, capital letters correspond to nucleotides aligned to the match nonterminals of the grammar; lowercase letters to insertions; -, to deletions by skip productions; and ., to fill characters required for insertions. The sequences are taken from the seven groups above and are denoted by their database section codes: 1. ARCHAE (*Halobacterium cutirubrum*), 2. CY (*Saccharomyces cerevisiae*), 3. CYANELCHLORO (*Cyanophora paradoxa*), 4. CYANELCHLORO (*Chlamydomonas reinhardtii*), 5. EUBACT (*Mycoplasma capricolum*), 6. VIRUS (*Phage T5*), 7. MT (*Aspergillus nidulans*), 8. PART III (*Ascaris suum*).

and to the forward–backward algorithm of HMMs, which scales as $O(N^3)$ instead of $O(N^2)$ for HMMs, where N is the average sequence length. When the grammar is in Chomsky normal form, this is known also as the inside–outside algorithm [345]. In the case of K training sequences $O_1, \ldots, O_K$, the EM reestimation formula becomes

$$P_{u \to \beta}^+ = \frac{\sum_{j=1}^K \sum_\pi \mathbf{P}(\pi | O_j, w) n(\beta, u, \pi, O_j)}{\sum_{j=1}^K \sum_\pi \mathbf{P}(\pi | O_j, w) n(u, \pi, O_j)}. \tag{11.13}$$

A version of the EM algorithm for SCFGs, called tree-grammar EM, is developed in [460]. It has the advantage of scaling as $O(N^2)$, but requires *folded* RNA as training samples. The folding structure provides more information than the raw sequence but less information than a complete parse. If a complete parse is available, one could just count the number of occurrences of each production rule. The folding structure, on the other hand, provides a skeleton tree where the leaves are labeled with the letters of the sequence, but not the interior nodes. From the skeleton one can tell which nucleotides are base paired, but one cannot directly tell whether a letter was emitted by a match or insert nonterminal symbol. The tree-grammar EM estimates the probabilities associated with the nonterminal symbols.

It is also possible to consider a global iterative training algorithm, as in [460], where at each step (1) the current grammar is used to fold the train-

Data set	Type of tRNA	Total	Zero	MT10CY10	MT100	Random
ARCHAE	archaea	103	0	0	0	50
CY	cytoplasm	230	0	10	0	100
CYANELCHLORO	cyanelle and chloroplast	184	0	0	0	100
EUBACT	eubacteria	201	0	0	0	100
VIRUS	viruses	24	0	0	0	10
MT	mitochondria	422	0	10	100	200
PART III	part III	58	0	0	0	58
Total		1222	0	20	100	618

Table 11.3: Validation Results for SCFG RNA Models of tRNA Families.

ing sequences, then (2) the folded sequences are used to optimize the grammar parameters—for instance, using tree-grammar EM. Production rules can be added or removed from the grammar, as in the algorithms for adjusting the length of a standard HMM architecture.

11.6.2 Gradient Descent and Viterbi Learning

While to the best of our knowledge only the EM algorithm has been used in the SCFG literature, it is clear that one could use other learning algorithms, such as gradient descent and Viterbi learning (simulated annealing remains too expensive for complex SCFGs).

As with HMMs, we can reparameterize a SCFG by

$$P_{u\to\beta} = \frac{e^{w_{u\to\beta}}}{\sum_\gamma e^{w_{u\to\gamma}}}. \tag{11.14}$$

The online gradient-descent learning equation is then

$$\Delta w_{u\to\beta} = \eta(n_{u\to\beta} - n_u P_{u\to\beta}), \tag{11.15}$$

where η is the learning rate. In the case of Viterbi learning for SCFGs, all counts of the form $n(\beta, u, \pi, O)$, which are averaged over all derivations π, are replaced by the counts $n(\beta, u, \pi^*, O)$ associated with the most likely derivation only. Most of the other remarks on gradient descent and Viterbi learning made in the case of HMMs apply to SCFGs, with the proper modifications. Viterbi learning from folded sequences is essentially equivalent to initializing an SCFG from a preexisting multiple alignment.

11.7 Applications of SCFGs

A trained SCFG can be used in much the same way as we used HMMs in chapters 7 and 8. For each example sequence, we can compute its Viterbi parse

Data set	ZeroTrain	MT10CY10	MT100	RandomTRNA618
ARCHAE	94.87	100.00	100.00	100.00
CY	98.28	99.76	99.89	99.87
CYANELCHLORO	96.22	99.64	99.64	99.79
EUBACT	99.69	99.86	99.86	99.86
VIRUS	96.83	100.00	100.00	100.00
MT	89.19	98.33	98.91	98.93
PART III	55.98	81.10	83.21	83.00

Table 11.4: Percentages of Base Pairs in the Original Alignment That Are Also Present in the Secondary Structure Predicted by Each of the Four Grammars.

tree. For RNA sequences, the syntactic structure or the equivalent parse tree provide a candidate for optimal folding that can be used to predict secondary structure. This approach complements previous methods for RNA secondary structure prediction based on phylogenetic analysis or thermodynamic considerations. The parse trees can also be used to derive multiple alignments where aligned columns or pairs of columns are associated with nonterminal main states. Gaps must be added in the obvious way. This is useful to determine common consensus patterns. Negative log-likelihood (or log-posterior) scores can be computed for any sequence. As in the case of HMMs, the score of a sequence depends on its length and must be normalized, as discussed in chapter 8. These scores in turn can be used to discriminate members of the family from non-members, to search databases, and possibly to discover new members of the family. In generative mode, SCFG could be used to generate new putative members of a given family, although this has not been tested. Finally, SCFGs can also be combined in modular ways. An example is discussed in [156] in which a tRNA SCFG grammar is combined with an intron grammar to search for tRNA genes.

11.8 Experiments

Here we report the validation results in [460] for SCFG RNA models of tRNA families. Similar results are described in [156]. The original data set consists of the sequences and alignments of 1222 unique tRNAs extracted from the database described in [502]. The length varies between 51 and 93 bases, and the sequences are subdivided into seven disjoint sets corresponding to different tRNA types (table 11.3).

For discrimination experiments, 2016 non-tRNA test sequences are generated from the non-tRNA features (including mRNA, rRNA, and protein coding

Data Set	Above 5 σ				Between 4 and 5 σ				Below 4 σ			
	ZT	MT10	MT100	R618	ZT	MT10	MT100	R618	ZT	MT10	MT100	R618
ARCHAE	66	103	103	103	19	0	0	0	18	0	0	0
CY	135	230	230	230	53	0	0	0	42	0	0	0
CYANELCH	61	184	184	184	52	0	0	0	71	0	0	0
EUBACT	160	201	201	201	30	0	0	0	11	0	0	0
VIRUS	16	24	24	24	4	0	0	0	4	0	0	0
MT (train)	N/A	10	99	193	N/A	0	1	6	N/A	0	0	1
MT (test)	64	389	313	218	89	10	7	3	269	13	2	1
PART III	0	9	7	29	1	15	14	8	57	34	37	21
NON-TRNA	0	0	0	0	0	0	1	1	2016	2016	2015	2015
Totals	502	1150	1161	1182	248	25	23	18	2488	2063	2054	2038

Table 11.5: Number of tRNAs in Each Family That Are Successfully Discriminated from the Non-tRNAs Using a Threshold on the Discrimination Score.

regions) in GenBank. Roughly 20 non-tRNA sequences are created for each length in the interval between 20 and 120. Four different grammars are then created. The first grammar (**ZeroTrain**) is a control that is not trained on any sequence and contains only prior information on tRNA. The other three grammars (**MT10CY10**, **MT100**, and **RandomTRNA618**) are trained from different sets as shown in table 11.3, using the tree-grammar EM algorithm. The four grammars are compared on three tasks: multiple alignments, secondary structure prediction, and discrimination.

11.8.1   Multiple Alignments

All 1222 tRNA sequences in the data set are aligned using each of the four grammars. The best multiple alignment is obtained with **RandomTRNA618**. The predicted alignment agrees substantially with the original data set alignment (figure 11.3). Boundaries of helices and loops are the same. The major difference is the extra arm, which is highly variable in both length and sequence. There are also cases [460] where the grammar alignments suggest small improvements over the original alignment.

11.8.2   RNA Secondary Structure Prediction

As for secondary structure, in most cases the Viterbi parse tree gives the correct secondary structure. Table 11.4 gives the percentages of base pairs in the original alignment that are also present in the secondary structure predicted by each grammar. For ARCHAE and VIRUS, all three trained grammars achieve 100% recognition. For CY, CYANELCHLORO, and EUBACT the agreement is also very good. In the case of PART III, it is substantially weaker.

11.8.3   Discrimination

Discrimination for each of the four grammars is tested by computing the normalized scores of all 2016 non-tRNA sequences and comparing them against the scores of the 1222 tRNA sequences in the data set. Non-tRNA rarely have a normalized score above 4, so that a discrimination threshold is set at 5. Table 11.5 summarizes the results by displaying the number of tRNAs in each family that are successfully discriminated from the non-tRNAs in this way. Some of the respective histograms are given in figure 11.4.

Training with as few as 20 sequences significantly improves the detection rates, as seen by comparing the results of **MT10CY10** and **ZeroTrain**. **MT10CY10** perfectly discriminates tRNAs from non-tRNA sequences, except for the subsets MT and PART III, where the **ZeroTrain** grammar fails. **MT10CY10** discriminates reasonably well on the MT subset but not on PART III. Setting aside PART III sequences, **MT10CY10** discriminates 399 out of 422 mitochondrial sequences, performing almost as well as the grammars trained on many more tRNA sequences. None of the grammars achieves good discrimination on PART III sequences, not even **RandomTRNA618**, which is trained in part on such sequences. Training on PART III sequences improves performance on some of these sequences, but half of them remain with a normalized score below the threshold of 5.

11.9   Future Directions

We have reviewed the basic theory of formal languages and grammars. We have seen how stochastic grammars can be applied to biological sequences by generalizing the dice model and the HMM ideas. SCFGs, in particular, and the corresponding learning algorithms have been used to derive statistical models of tRNA. The trained grammars have been used to align, fold, and discriminate tRNA sequences with good results. The SCFG approach is a viable method for determining tRNA secondary structure. It complements the two preexisting methods, one based on phylogenetic analysis of homologous sequences [186, 565, 278] and the other on thermodynamic considerations [521, 222, 527, 585]. SCFGs for RNA, however, have been less thoroughly tested than HMMs for protein families and additional work is required to establish this approach further. Whereas the SCFGs are capable of finding global structural alignments of RNA, a new dynamical programming algorithm for obtaining local structural alignments has recently been giving good results [220, 221]. This local method is an extension of the Smith–Waterman alignment scheme combined with another dynamical programming technique for finding the maximal number of complementary nucleotide pairs.

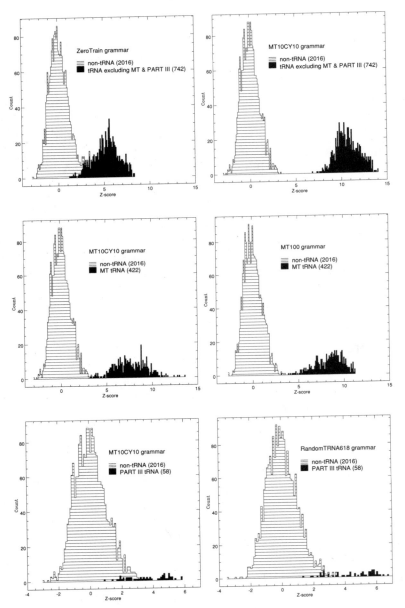

Figure 11.4: Some of the Normalized Score Histograms Showing Results of Discrimination Tests with Various Grammars.

The grammar methods described in this chapter have some limitations. First, they are computationally intensive, so that, in their present form, they become somewhat impractical for long sequences, typically above $N = 200$ or so. Second, not all RNA structures can be captured by an SCFG. The associated parse trees cannot capture tertiary interactions such as pseudoknots and non-pairwise interactions, which so far have been ignored. Third, the method as described in this chapter does not include a model for introns that are present in some tRNA genes. Such limitations point to a few obvious directions for future work, including the following:

- Algorithmic and perhaps hardware speed improvements

- Development of grammars, perhaps graph grammars, or other models, and the corresponding training algorithms to incorporate RNA tertiary structures, and possibly the tertiary structure of other molecules

- Combination of SCFGs in modular ways, as for HMMs, to model more complex RNA sequences, including the corresponding introns—work in this direction is reported in [156]

- Modeling larger and more challenging RNA sequences, such as rRNA

- Finally, along the lines of chapter 9, developing hybrid SCFG/NN architectures (or SG/NN), where an NN is used to compute the parameters of a SCFG and/or to modulate or mix different SCFGs.

Chapter 12

Microarrays and Gene Expression

12.1 Introduction to Microarray Data

A number of new microarray-based technologies have been developed over the last few years, and technological development in this area is likely to continue at a brisk pace. These technologies include DNA hybridization arrays (gene expression arrays, oligonucleotide arrays for sequencing and polymorphism), protein arrays, tissue arrays, and combinatorial chemistry arrays. By making possible the combinatorial interaction of a large number of molecules with a large library, these high-throughput approaches are rapidly generating terabytes of information that are overwhelming conventional methods of biological analysis. In this chapter, we focus primarily on DNA gene expression microarrays. We closely follow the derivation in [44] and show how the general probabilistic framework can be applied systematically to array data. A more complete treatment of DNA microarrays can be found in [43].

DNA gene expression microarrays allow biologists to study genome-wide patterns of gene expression [148, 160, 263] in any given cell type, at any given time, and under any given set of conditions. In these arrays, total RNA is reverse-transcribed to create either radioactive- or fluorescent-labeled cDNA that is hybridized with a large DNA library of gene fragments attached to a glass or membrane support. Phosphorimaging or other imaging techniques are used to produce expression measurements for thousands of genes under various experimental conditions. Use of these arrays is producing large amounts of data, potentially capable of providing fundamental insights into biological processes ranging from gene function to development, cancer, and aging, and pharmacology [498, 567, 7, 217, 354, 511, 7, 554, 369, 169, 171]. Even partial understanding of the available information can provide valuable clues. For instance, co-expression of novel genes may provide leads to the functions of many genes for which information is not available currently. Data analysis techniques for microarray data, however, are still at an early stage of development [581].

Gene expression array data can be analyzed on at least three levels of increasing complexity. The first level is that of single genes, where one seeks to establish whether each gene in isolation behaves differently in a control versus a treatment situation. The second level is multiple genes, where clusters of genes are analyzed in terms of common functionalities, interactions, co-regulation, etc. The third level attempts to infer the underlying gene and protein networks that ultimately are responsible for the patterns observed.

To begin with, we assume for simplicity that for each gene X the data consists of a set of measurements $x_1^c, \ldots, x_{n_c}^c$ and $x_1^t, \ldots, x_{n_t}^t$ representing expression levels, or rather their logarithms, in both a control and treatment situation. Treatment is of course taken in a broad sense to mean any condition different from the control. For each gene, the fundamental question we wish to address is whether the level of expression is significantly different in the two situations. While it might seem that standard statistical techniques could easily address such a problem, this is in fact not the case.

One approach commonly used in the literature is a simple-minded fold approach, in which a gene is declared to have significantly changed if its average expression level varies by more than a constant factor, typically 2, between the treatment and control conditions. Inspection of gene expression data suggests, however, that such a simple "2-fold rule" is unlikely to yield optimal results, since a factor of 2 can have quite different significance in different regions of the spectrum of expression levels.

A related approach to the same question is the use of a t-test, for instance on the logarithm of the expression levels. This is similar to the fold approach because the difference between two logarithms is the logarithm of their ratio. This approach is not necessarily identical to the first because the logarithm of the mean is not equal to the mean of the logarithms; in fact, it is always strictly greater by convexity of the logarithm function. But with a reasonable degree of approximation, a test of the significance of the difference between the log expression levels of two genes is equivalent to a test of whether or not their fold change is significantly different from 1.

In a t-test, the empirical means m_c and m_t and variances s_c^2 and s_t^2 are used to compute a normalized distance between the two populations in the form

$$t = (m_c - m_t) / \sqrt{\frac{s_c^2}{n_c} + \frac{s_t^2}{n_t}} \tag{12.1}$$

where, for each population, $m = \sum_i x_i/n$ and $s^2 = \sum_i (x_i - m)^2/(n-1)$ are the well-known estimates for the mean and standard deviation. It is well known from the statistics literature that t follows approximately a Student distribution (appendix A), with

$$f = \frac{[(s_c^2/n_c) + (s_t^2/n_t)]^2}{\frac{(s_c^2/n_c)^2}{n_c-1} + \frac{(s_t^2/n_t)^2}{n_t-1}} \tag{12.2}$$

degrees of freedom. When t exceeds a certain threshold depending on the confidence level selected, the two populations are considered to be different. Because in the t-test the distance between the population means is normalized by the empirical standard deviations, this has the potential for addressing some of the shortcomings of the fixed fold-threshold approach. The fundamental problem with the t-test for microarray data, however, is that the repetition numbers n_c and/or n_t are often small because experiments remain costly or tedious to repeat, even with current technology. Small populations of size $n = 1, 2$, or 3 are still very common and lead, for instance, to significant underestimates of the variances. Thus a better framework is needed to address these shortcomings.

12.2   Probabilistic Modeling of Array Data

12.2.1   Gaussian Model

Array data requires a probabilistic approach because it is highly noisy and variable, and many relevant variables remain unobserved behind the massive data sets. In order to develop a probabilistic approach for array data, the lessons learnt with sequence data are worth remembering. In sequence data, we saw in chapter 3 that the simplest probabilistic model is that of a die associated with the average composition of the family of DNA, RNA, or protein sequences under study. The next level of modeling complexity is a first-order Markov model with one die per position or per column in a multiple alignment. We have seen how, in spite of their simplicity, these models are still useful as a background, for instance, against which the performances of more sophisticated models are assessed.

In array data, the simplest model would assume that all data points are independent from one another and extracted from a single continuous distribution, for instance a Gaussian distribution. While trivial, this "Gaussian die" model still requires the computation of interesting quantities, such as the average level of activity and its standard deviation, that can be useful to calibrate or assess global properties of the data. The next equivalent level of modeling is a set of independent distributions, one for each dimension, for instance each gene. While it is obvious that genes interact with one another in complex ways and therefore are not independent, the independence approximation is still useful and underlies *any* attempt, probabilistic or other, to determine whether expression-level differences are significant on a *gene-by-gene* basis.

Here we first assume that the expression-level measurements of a gene in a given situation have a roughly Gaussian distribution. In our experience, with common technologies this assumption is reasonable, especially for the logarithm of the expression levels, corresponding to lognormal raw expression levels. To the best of our knowledge, large-scale replicate experiments have not yet been carried out to make more precise assessments. It is clear, however, that other distributions, such as gammas or mixtures of Gaussians/gammas, could be introduced at this stage. These would impact the details of the analysis (see also [558, 403]), but not the general Bayesian probabilistic framework.

Thus, in what follows we assume that the data has been pre-processed—including taking logarithms if needed—to the point that we can model the corresponding measurements of each gene in each situation (treatment or control) with a normal distribution $\mathcal{N}(x; \mu, \sigma^2)$. For each gene and each condition, we have a two-parameter model $w = (\mu, \sigma^2)$, and by focusing on one such model we can omit indices identifying the gene or the condition. Assuming that the observations are independent, the likelihood is given by

$$
\begin{aligned}
\mathbf{P}(D|\mu, \sigma^2) &\approx \prod_i \mathcal{N}(x_i; \mu, \sigma^2) \\
&= C(\sigma^2)^{-n/2} \exp(-\sum_i (x_i - \mu)^2 / 2\sigma^2) \\
&= C(\sigma^2)^{-n/2} \exp(-(n(m - \mu)^2 + (n-1)s^2)/2\sigma^2) \quad (12.3)
\end{aligned}
$$

where i ranges over replicate measurements. In this chapter, we write C to denote the normalizing constant of any distribution ($C = 1/Z$). The likelihood depends only on the sufficient statistics n, m, and s^2. In other words, all the information about the sample that is relevant for the likelihood is summarized in these three numbers. The case in which either the mean or the variance of the Gaussian model is supposed to be known is of course easier and is well studied in the literature [86, 431].

A full Bayesian treatment requires introducing a prior $\mathbf{P}(\mu, \sigma^2)$. The choice of a prior is part of the modeling process, and several alternatives [86, 431] are possible, a sign of the flexibility of the Bayesian approach rather than its arbitrariness. Here a conjugate prior is convenient and adequately captures several properties of DNA microarray data including, as we shall see, the fact that μ and σ^2 are generally *not* independent.

12.2.2 The Conjugate Prior

Recall that when both the prior and the posterior have the same functional form, the prior is said to be a conjugate prior. When estimating the mean alone for a normal model of known variance, the obvious conjugate prior is also a normal distribution. In the case of dice models for biological sequences, we have seen that the standard conjugate prior is a Dirichlet distribution. The form of the likelihood in (12.3) shows that the conjugate prior density must also have the form $P(\mu|\sigma^2)P(\sigma^2)$, where the marginal $P(\sigma^2)$ correponds to a scaled inverse gamma distribution (equivalent to $1/\sigma^2$ having a gamma distribution, see appendix A), and the conditional distribution $P(\mu|\sigma^2)$ is normal.

This leads to a hierarchical model with a vector of four hyperparameters for the prior $\alpha = (\mu_0, \lambda_0, \nu_0$ and $\sigma_0^2)$ with the densities

$$\mathbf{P}(\mu|\sigma^2) = \mathcal{N}(\mu; \mu_0, \sigma^2/\lambda_0) \tag{12.4}$$

and

$$\mathbf{P}(\sigma^2) = \mathcal{I}(\sigma^2; \nu_0, \sigma_0^2). \tag{12.5}$$

The expectation of the prior is finite if and only if $\nu_0 > 2$. The prior $\mathbf{P}(\mu, \sigma^2) = \mathbf{P}(\mu, \sigma^2|\alpha)$ is given by

$$C\sigma^{-1}(\sigma^2)^{-(\nu_0/2+1)} \exp\left[-\frac{\nu_0}{2\sigma^2}\sigma_0^2 - \frac{\lambda_0}{2\sigma^2}(\mu_0 - \mu)^2\right]. \tag{12.6}$$

Notice that it makes perfect sense with array data to assume a priori that μ and σ^2 are *dependent*, as suggested immediately by visual inspection of typical microarray data sets (figure 12.1). The hyperparameters μ_0 and σ^2/λ_0 can be interpreted as the location and scale of μ, and the hyperparameters ν_0 and σ_0^2 as the degrees of freedom and scale of σ^2. After some algebra, the posterior has the same functional form as the prior:

$$\mathbf{P}(\mu, \sigma^2|D, \alpha) = \mathcal{N}(\mu; \mu_n, \sigma^2/\lambda_n)\mathcal{I}(\sigma^2; \nu_n, \sigma_n^2) \tag{12.7}$$

with

$$\mu_n = \frac{\lambda_0}{\lambda_0 + n}\mu_0 + \frac{n}{\lambda_0 + n}m \tag{12.8}$$

$$\lambda_n = \lambda_0 + n \tag{12.9}$$

$$\nu_n = \nu_0 + n \tag{12.10}$$

$$\nu_n\sigma_n^2 = \nu_0\sigma_0^2 + (n-1)s^2 + \frac{\lambda_0 n}{\lambda_0 + n}(m - \mu_0)^2. \tag{12.11}$$

The parameters of the posterior combine information from the prior and the data in a sensible way. The mean μ_n is a convex weighted average of the prior mean and the sample mean. The posterior degree of freedom v_n is the prior degree of freedom plus the sample size. The posterior sum of squares $v_n \sigma_n^2$ is the sum of the prior sum of squares $v_0 \sigma_0^2$, the sample sum of squares $(n-1)s^2$, and the residual uncertainty provided by the discrepancy between the prior mean and the sample mean.

While it is possible to use a prior mean μ_0 for gene expression data, in many situations it is sufficient to use $\mu_0 = m$. The posterior sum of squares is then obtained precisely as if one had v_0 additional observations all associated with deviation σ_0^2. While superficially this may seem like setting the prior after having observed the data [372], a similar effect is obtained using a preset value μ_0 with $\lambda_0 \to 0$, i.e., with a very broad standard deviation so that the prior belief about the location of the mean is essentially uniform and vanishingly small. The selection of the hyperparameters for the prior is discussed in more detail below.

It is not difficult to check that the conditional posterior distribution $P(\mu|\sigma^2, D, \alpha)$ of the mean is normal $\mathcal{N}(\mu_n, \sigma^2/\lambda_n)$. The marginal posterior $P(\mu|D, \alpha)$ of the mean is Student $t(v_n, \mu_n, \sigma_n^2/\lambda_n)$, and the marginal posterior $P(\sigma^2|D, \alpha)$ of the variance is scaled inverse gamma $\mathcal{I}(v_n, \sigma_n^2)$.

In the literature, semi-conjugate prior distributions also are used where the functional form of the prior distributions on μ and σ^2 are the same as in the conjugate case (normal and scaled inverse gamma, respectively) but independent of each other, i.e. $\mathbf{P}(\mu, \sigma^2) = \mathbf{P}(\mu)\mathbf{P}(\sigma^2)$. However, as previously discussed, this assumption of independence is unlikely to be suitable for DNA microarray data. More complex priors also could be constructed using mixtures, mixture of conjugate priors leading to mixtures of conjugate posteriors.

12.2.3   Parameter Point Estimates

The posterior distribution $\mathbf{P}(\mu, \sigma^2|D, \alpha)$ is the fundamental object of Bayesian analysis and contains the relevant information about *all* possible values of μ and σ^2. However, in order to perform the t-test described above, for instance, we need to collapse this information-rich distribution into single point estimates of the mean and variance of the expression level of a gene in a given situation. This can be done in a number of ways. In general, the most robust answer is obtained using the mean of the posterior (MP) estimate. An alternative is to use the mode of the posterior, or MAP (maximum a posteriori) estimate. For completeness, we derive both kinds of estimates.

By integration, the MP estimate is given by

$$\mu = \mu_n \quad \text{and} \quad \sigma^2 = \frac{v_n}{v_n - 2}\sigma_n^2 \tag{12.12}$$

provided $v_n > 2$. If we take $\mu_0 = m$, we then get the following MP estimate

$$\mu = m \quad \text{and} \quad \sigma^2 = \frac{v_n \sigma_n^2}{v_n - 2} = \frac{v_0 \sigma_0^2 + (n-1)s^2}{v_0 + n - 2} \qquad (12.13)$$

provided $v_0 + n > 2$. This is the default estimate implemented in the Cyber-T software described below. From (12.7), the MAP estimates are

$$\mu = \mu_n \quad \text{and} \quad \sigma^2 = \frac{v_n \sigma_n^2}{v_n - 1} \qquad (12.14)$$

If we use $\mu_0 = m$, these reduce to

$$\mu = m \quad \text{and} \quad \sigma^2 = \frac{v_n \sigma_n^2}{v_n - 1} = \frac{v_0 \sigma_0^2 + (n-1)s^2}{v_0 + n - 1}. \qquad (12.15)$$

Here the modes of the marginal posterior are given by

$$\mu = \mu_n \quad \text{and} \quad \sigma^2 = \frac{v_n \sigma_n^2}{v_n + 2}. \qquad (12.16)$$

In practice, (12.13) and (12.15) give similar results and can be used with gene expression arrays. The slight differences between the two closely parallel what is seen with Dirichlet priors on sequence data in chapter 3, (12.13) being generally a slightly better choice. The Dirichlet prior is equivalent to the introduction of pseudo-counts to avoid setting the probability of any amino acid or nucleotide to zero. In array data, few observation points are likely to result in a poor estimate of the variance. With a single point ($n = 1$), for instance, we certainly want to refrain from setting the corresponding variance to zero; hence the need for regularization, which is achieved by the conjugate prior. In the MP estimate, the empirical variance is modulated by v_0 "pseudo-observations" associated with a background variance σ_0^2.

12.2.4 Full Bayesian Treatment and Hyperparameter Point Estimates

At this stage of modeling, each gene is associated with two models $w_c = (\mu_c, \sigma_c^2)$ and $w_t = (\mu_t, \sigma_t^2)$, two sets of hyperparameters α_c and α_t, and two posterior distributions $\mathbf{P}(w_c|D, \alpha_c)$ and $\mathbf{P}(w_t|D, \alpha_t)$. A full probabilistic treatment would require introducing prior distributions over the hyperparameters. These could be integrated out to obtain the true posterior probabilities $\mathbf{P}(w_c|D)$ and $\mathbf{P}(w_t|D)$, which then could be integrated over all values of w_t and w_c to determine whether or not the two models are different. Notice that this approach is significantly more general than the plain t-test and could in principle detect interesting changes that are beyond the scope of the t-test.

For instance, a gene with the same mean but a very different variance between the control and treatment situations goes undetected by a t-test, although the change in variance might be biologically relevant. Even if we restrict ourselves to only the means μ_c and μ_t and these have a Gaussian posterior distribution, the probability $\mathbf{P}(|\mu_c - \mu_t| < \epsilon)$ must be estimated numerically. While the latter is not difficult to perform with today's computers, it is also possible to use simpler and more approximate strategies to the full Bayesian treatment that rely solely on point estimates.

Point estimates, however, entail hyperparameters that can be addressed in a number of ways [372, 375]. Here, again, one possibility is to define a prior on the hyperparameters and try to integrate them out in order to compute the true posterior $\mathbf{P}(w|D)$ and determine the location of its mode, leading to true MAP estimates of w. More precisely, this requires integrating $\mathbf{P}(w|\alpha)$ and $\mathbf{P}(w|\alpha|D)$ with respect to the hyperparameter vector α. An alternative that avoids the integration of the hyperparameters is the evidence framework described in [372]. In the evidence framework, we compute point estimates of the hyperparameters by MAP estimation (MP would again require integrating over hyperparameters) over the posterior

$$\mathbf{P}(\alpha|D) = \frac{\mathbf{P}(D|\alpha)\mathbf{P}(\alpha)}{\mathbf{P}(D)}. \tag{12.17}$$

If we take a uniform prior $\mathbf{P}(\alpha)$, then this is equivalent to maximizing the evidence $\mathbf{P}(D|\alpha)$

$$\begin{aligned}
\mathbf{P}(D|\alpha) &= \mathbf{P}(D|w,\alpha)\mathbf{P}(w|\alpha)/\mathbf{P}(w|D,\alpha) \\
&= \mathbf{P}(D|w)\mathbf{P}(w|\alpha)/\mathbf{P}(w|D,\alpha). \tag{12.18}
\end{aligned}$$

In principle, computing the evidence requires integrating out the parameters w of the model. Using the expression for the likelihood and the conjugate prior and posterior, however, we can obtain the evidence without integration, directly from (12.18):

$$\mathbf{P}(D|\alpha) = (2\pi)^{-n/2} \frac{\sqrt{\lambda_0}}{\sqrt{\lambda_n}} \frac{(\nu_0/2)^{\nu_0/2}}{(\nu_n/2)^{\nu_n/2}} \frac{\sigma_0^{\nu_0}}{\sigma_n^{\nu_n}} \frac{\Gamma(\nu_n/2)}{\Gamma(\nu_0/2)}. \tag{12.19}$$

The partial derivatives and critical points of the evidence are discussed in [44] where it is shown, for instance, that the mode is achieved for $\mu_0 = m$.

12.2.5 Bayesian Hypothesis Testing

In essence so far we have modeled the log-expression level of each gene in each situation using a Gaussian model. If all we care about is whether a given gene has changed or not, we could model directly the difference between the log-expression levels in the control and treatment cases. These differences can be considered pairwise or in paired fashion, as is more likely the case with current microarray technology where the logarithm of the ratio between the expression levels in the treatment and control situations is measured along two different channels (red and green).

We can model again the differences $x^t - x^c$ with a Gaussian $\mathcal{N}(\mu, \sigma^2)$. Then the null hypothesis H, given the data, is that $\mu = 0$ (no change). To avoid assigning a probability of 0 to the null hypothesis, a Bayesian approach here must begin by giving a non-zero prior probability for $\mu = 0$, which may appear a little contrived. In any case, following the lines of the previous derivation for the conjugate prior, we can set $\mathbf{P}(\sigma^2) = \mathcal{I}(\sigma^2; \nu_0, \sigma_0^2)$. For the mean μ, we use the mixture

$$\mu = \begin{cases} 0 & : \quad \text{with probability} \quad p \\ \mathcal{N}(0, \sigma^2/\lambda) & : \quad \text{with probability} \quad 1 - p \end{cases} \tag{12.20}$$

The parameter p could be fixed from previous experiments, or treated as an hyperparameter with, for instance, a Dirichlet prior. We leave as an exercise for the reader to compute the relevant statistics $\log[\mathbf{P}(\bar{H})/\mathbf{P}(H)]$.

12.2.6 Implementation

For efficiency, an intermediate solution has been implemented in a Web server called Cyber-T[1] [44, 366]. In this approach, we use the t-test with the regularized standard deviation of (12.13) and the number of degrees of freedom associated with the corresponding augmented populations of points, which incidentally can be fractional. In Cyber-T, plain and Bayesian versions of the t-test can be performed on both the raw data and the log-transformed data.

In the simplest case, where we use $\mu_0 = m$, one must select the values of the background standard deviation σ_0^2, and its strength ν_0. The parameter ν_0 represents the degree of confidence in the background variance σ_0^2 versus the empirical variance. The value of ν_0 can be set by the user. The smaller n, the larger ν_0 ought to be. A simple rule of thumb is to assume that $l > 2$ points are needed to estimate the standard deviation properly and keep $n + \nu_0 = l$. This allows a flexible treatment of situations in which the number n of available data points varies from gene to gene. A reasonable default is to use $l = 10$. A special case can be made for genes with activity levels close to the minimal detection level of the technology being used. The measurements for these genes being particularly unreliable, it may be wise to use a stronger prior for them with a higher value of ν_0.

---

[1]Accessible at: http://128.200.5.223/CyberT/.

For σ_0, one could use the standard deviation of the entire set of observations or, depending on the situation, of particular categories of genes. In a flexible implementation, the background standard deviation is estimated by pooling together all the neighboring genes contained in a window of size ws. Cyber-T automatically ranks the expression levels of all the genes and lets the user choose this window size. The default is $ws = 101$, corresponding to 50 genes immediately above and below the gene under consideration. Adaptive window sizes and regression estimates for σ_0^2 can also be considered.

12.2.7 Simulations

We have used the Bayesian approach and Cyber-T to analyze a number of published and unpublished data sets. In every high density array experiments we have analyzed, we have observed a strong scaling of the expression variance over replicated experiments with the average expression level (on both a log-transformed and raw scale). As a result, a threshold for significance based solely on fold changes is likely to be too liberal for genes expressed at low levels and too conservative for highly expressed genes. While several biologically relevant results are reported elsewhere, we have found that the Bayesian approach compares favorably to a simple fold approach or a straight t-test and partially overcomes deficiencies related to low replication in a statistically consistent way [366].

One particularly informative data set for comparing the Bayesian approach to simple t-test or fold change is the high density array experiment reported in [19] comparing wild type *Escherichia coli* cells to mutant cells for the global regulatory protein IHF (integration host factor). The main advantage of this data set is its four-fold replication for both wild type and mutant alleles. The regularizing effect of the prior based on the background standard deviation is shown for this data in Figure 12.1 and in the simulation described below. The figure clearly shows that standard deviations vary substantially over the range of expression levels, in this case roughly in a monotonic decreasing fashion, although other behaviors also have been observed. Interestingly, in these plots the variance in log-transformed expression levels is higher for genes expressed at lower levels rather than at higher ones. These plots confirm that genes expressed at low or near background levels may require a stronger value of ν_0, or alternatively could be ignored in expression analyses. The variance in the measurement of genes expressed at a low level is large enough that in many cases it will be difficult to detect significant changes in expression for this class of loci.

In analyzing the data we found that large fold changes in expression were often associated with p-values not indicative of statistical change in the Bayesian analysis, and conversely subtle fold changes were often highly significant as judged by the Bayesian analysis. In these two situations, the conclusions drawn using the Bayesian approach appear robust relative to those drawn from fold change alone, as large non-statistically significant fold changes were often associated with large measurement errors, and statistically significant genes showing less than two fold changes were often measured very accurately. As a result of the level of experimental replication seen in [19], we were able to look at the consistency of the Bayesian estimator relative to the t-test. We found that in independent samples of size 2 drawn from the IHF data set (i.e., two experiments versus two controls) the set of 120 most significant genes identified using the Bayesian approach had approximately 50% of their members in common, whereas the set of 120 most significant genes identified using the t-test had only approximately 25% of their members in common. This suggests that for two fold replication the Bayesian approach is approximately twice as consistent as a simple t-test at identifying genes as up- or down-regulated, although with only two fold replication there is a great deal of uncertainty associated with high density array experiments.

To further assess the Bayesian approach, an artificial data set can be generated assuming Gaussian distribution of log expressions, with means and variances in ranges similar to those encountered in the data set of [19], with 1000 replicates for each parameter combination. Selected means for the log data and associated standard deviations (in brackets) are as follows: -6 (0.1), -8 (0.2), -10 (0.4), -11 (0.7), -12 (1.0). On this artificially generated data, we can compare the behavior of a simple ratio (2-fold and 5-fold) approach, with a simple t-test, with the Bayesian t-test using the default settings of Cyber-T. The main results, reported in Table 12.1, can be summarized as follows:

- By 5 replications (5 control and 5 treatment) the Bayesian approach and t-test give similar results.

- When the number of replicates is "low" (2 or 3), the Bayesian approach performs better than the t-test.

- The false positive rate for the Bayesian and t-test approach are as expected (0.05 and 0.01 respectively) except for the Bayesian with very small replication (i.e., 2) where it appears elevated.

- The false positive rate on the ratios is a function of expression level and is much higher at lower expression levels. At low expression levels the false positive rate on the ratios is unacceptably high.

- For a given level of replication the Bayesian approach at $p < 0.01$ detects more differences than a 2-fold change except for the case of low expression levels (where the false positive rate from ratios is elevated).

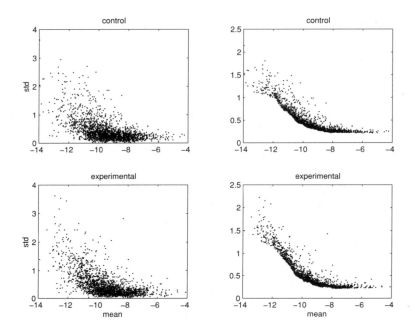

Figure 12.1: DNA Microarray Experiment on *Escherichia coli*. Data obtained from reverse transcribed P[33] labeled RNA hybridized to commercially available nylon arrays (Sigma Genosys) containing each of the 4,290 predicted *E. coli* genes. The sample included a wild-type strain (control) and an otherwise isogenic strain lacking the gene for the global regulatory gene, integration host factor (IHF) (treatment). $n = 4$ for both control and experimental situations. The horizontal axis represents the mean μ of the logarithm of the expression levels, and the vertical axis shows the corresponding standard deviations (std=σ). The left column corresponds to raw data, the right column to regularized standard deviations using Equation (12.13). Window size is $ws = 101$ and $l = 10$ (see main text). Data are from [19].

- The Bayesian approach with 2 replicates outperforms the t-test with 3 replicates (or 2 versus 4 replicates).

- The Bayesian approach has a similar level of performance when comparing 3 treatments to 3 controls, or 2 treatments to 4 controls. This suggests an experimental strategy where the controls are highly replicated and a number of treatments less highly replicated.

n	Log expression from	to	Ratio 2-fold	5-fold	Plain t-test $p < 0.05$	$p < 0.01$	Bayes $p < 0.05$	$p < 0.01$
2	−8	−8	1	0	38	7	73	9
2	−10	−10	13	0	39	11	60	11
2	−12	−12	509	108	65	10	74	16
2	−6	−6.1	0	0	91	20	185	45
2	−8	−8.5	167	0	276	71	730	419
2	−10	−11	680	129	202	47	441	195
3	−8	−8	0	0	42	9	39	4
3	−10	−10	36	0	51	11	39	6
3	−12	−12	406	88	44	5	45	4
3	−6	−6.1	0	0	172	36	224	60
3	−8	−8.5	127	0	640	248	831	587
3	−10	−11	674	62	296	139	550	261
5	−8	−8	0	0	53	13	39	8
5	−10	−10	9	0	35	6	31	3
5	−12	−12	354	36	65	11	54	4
5	−6	−6.1	0	0	300	102	321	109
5	−8	−8.5	70	0	936	708	966	866
5	−10	−11	695	24	688	357	752	441
2v4	−8	−8	0	0	35	4	39	6
2v4	−10	−10	38	0	36	9	40	3
2v4	−12	−12	446	85	46	17	43	5
2v4	−6	−6.1	0	0	126	32	213	56
2v4	−8	−8.5	123	0	475	184	788	509
2v4	−10	−11	635	53	233	60	339	74

Table 12.1: Number of Positives Detected out of 1000 Genes. Data was generated using normal distribution on a log scale in the range of Arfin et al. 2000 [19], with 1000 replicates for each parameter combination. Means of the log data and associated standard deviations (in brackets) are as follows: −6 (0.1), −8 (0.2), −10 (0.4), −11 (0.7), −12 (1.0). For each value of n, the first three experiments correspond to the case of no change and therefore yield false positive rates. Analysis was carried out using Cyber-T with default settings ($ws = 101, l = 10$) and degrees of freedom $n + v_0 - 2$.

12.2.8 More Complex Probabilistic Models

We have developed a probabilistic framework for array data analysis to address a number of current approach shortcomings related to small sample bias and the fact that fold differences have different significance at different expression levels. The framework is a form of hierarchical Bayesian modeling with Gausssian gene-independent models. Although the Gaussian representation requires further testing, other distributions can easily be incorporated in a similar framework. While there can be no perfect substitute for experimental replication (see also [355]), in simulations and controlled replicated experiments [366] it has been shown that the approach has a regularizing effect on the data, that it compares favorably to a conventional t-test, or simple fold-approach and that it can partially compensate for the absence of replication.

Depending on goals and implementation constraints, the method can be extended in a number of directions. For instance, regression functions could be computed off-line to establish the relationship between standard deviation and expression levels and used to produce background standard deviations. Another possibility is to use adaptive window sizes to compute the local background variance, where the size of the window could depend, for instance, on the derivative of the regression function. In an expression range in which the standard deviation is relatively flat (i.e. between -8 and -4 in figure 12.1), the size of the window is less relevant than in a region where the standard deviation varies rapidly (i.e., between -12 and -10 in figure 12.1). A more complete Bayesian approach could also be implemented, for instance integrating the marginal posterior distributions, which in the case considered here are Student distributions, to estimate the probability $\mathbf{P}(\mu_c \approx \mu_t | D, \alpha_t, \alpha_c)$.

The approach also can be extended to more complex designs and/or designs involving gradients of an experimental variable and/or time series designs. Examples would include a design in which cells are grown in the presence of different stressors (urea, ammonia, oxygen peroxide), or when the molarity of a single stressor is varied (0, 5, 10 mM). Generalized linear and nonlinear models can be used in this context. The most challenging problem, however, is to extend the probabilistic framework towards the second level of analysis, taking into account possible interactions and correlations amongst genes. If two or more genes have similar behavior in a given treatment situation, decisions regarding their expression changes can be made more robustly at the level of the corresponding cluster. Multivariate normal models and Gaussian processes (appendix E) could provide the starting probabilistic models for this level of analysis.

With a multivariate normal model, for instance, μ is a vector of means and Σ is a symmetric positive definite covariance matrix with determinant $|\Sigma|$. The likelihood has the form

$$C|\Sigma|^{-n/2} \exp[-\frac{1}{2}\sum_{i=1}^{n}(X_i - \mu)^t \Sigma^{-1}(X_i - \mu)]. \tag{12.21}$$

The conjugate prior, generalizing the normal-scaled-inverse-gamma distribution, is based on the inverse Wishart distribution (appendix A), which generalizes the scaled inverse gamma distribution and provides a prior on Σ. In analogy with the one-dimensional case, the conjugate prior is parameterized by $(\mu_0, \Lambda_0/\lambda_0, \nu_0, \Lambda_0)$. Σ has an inverse Wishart distribution with parameters ν_0 and Λ_0^{-1}. Conditioned on Σ, μ has a multivariate normal prior $\mathcal{N}(\mu; \mu_0, \Sigma/\lambda_0)$. The posterior then has the same form, a product of a multivariate normal with an inverse Wishart, parameterized by $(\mu_n, \Lambda_n/\lambda_n, \nu_n, \Lambda_n)$. The parameters satisfy

$$\mu_n = \frac{\lambda_0}{\lambda_0 + n}\mu_0 + \frac{n}{\lambda_0 + n}m$$

$$\lambda_n = \lambda_0 + n$$
$$\nu_n = \nu_0 + n$$
$$\Lambda_n = \Lambda_0 + \sum_1^n (X_i - m)(X_i - m)^t$$
$$+ \frac{\lambda_0 n}{\lambda_0 + n}(m - \mu_0)(m - \mu_0)^t. \tag{12.22}$$

Estimates similar to (12.13) can be derived for the multidimensional case.

While multivariate normal and other related models may provide a good starting point, good probabilistic models for higher-order effects influencing array data are still at an early stage of development. Most approaches so far have concentrated on more or less *ad hoc* applications of clustering methods.

12.3 Clustering

12.3.1 Overview

At the next level of complexity, we want to remove the simplistic assumption that, for instance, all the genes are independent. This is where we want to begin to look at the covariance matrix of the genes, whether there exist particular clusters of related genes, and so forth. Besides array data, clustering can be applied to many other problems in bioinformatics, including several sequence-analysis problems. Therefore here we also try to provide a brief but broad perspective on clustering that extends somewhat beyond the analysis of array data.

Clustering is a fundamental technique in exploratory data analysis and pattern discovery, aimed at extracting underlying cluster structures. Clustering, however, is a "fuzzy" notion without a single precise definition. Dozens of clustering algorithms exist in the literature and a number of *ad hoc* clustering procedures, ranging from hierarchical clustering to k-means, have been applied to DNA microarray data [160, 7, 253, 511, 484, 124, 194], without any clear emerging consensus. Because of the variety and "open" nature of clustering problems, it is unlikely that a systematic exhaustive treatment of clustering can be given. There are a number of important issues to consider in clustering and clustering algorithms, especially in the context of gene expression.

Data Types

At the highest level, clustering algorithms can be distinguished depending on the nature of the data being clustered. The standard case is when the data points are vectors in Euclidean space. But this is by no means the only possibility. In addition to vectorial data, or numerical data expressed in absolute coordinates, there is the case of relational data, where data is represented in relative coordinates by giving the pairwise distance between any two points. In many cases the data is expressed in terms of a pairwise similarity (or dissimilarity) measure that often does not satisfy the three axioms of a distance (positivity, symmetry, and triangle inequality). There exist situations where data configurations are expressed in terms of ternary or higher-order relationships or where only a subset of all the possible pairwise similarities is given. More importantly, there are cases where the data is not vectorial or relational in nature, but essentially qualitative, as in the case of answers to a multiple-choice questionnaire. This is sometimes also called nominal data. While at the present time gene expression array data is predominantly numerical, this is bound to change in the future. Indeed, the dimension "orthogonal to the genes" covering different experiments, different patients, different tissues, different times, and so forth is at least in part non-numerical. As databases of array data grow, in many cases the data will be mixed with both vectorial and nominal components.

Supervised/Unsupervised

One important distinction amongst clustering algorithms is supervised versus unsupervised. In supervised clustering, clustering is based on a set of given reference vectors or classes. In unsupervised clustering, no predefined set of vectors or classes is used. Hybrid methods are also possible in which an unsupervised approach is followed by a supervised one. At the current early stage of gene expression array experiments, unsupervised methods such as k-means and self-organizing maps [511] are most commonly used. However supervised methods have also been tried [194], in which clusters are predetermined using functional information or unsupervised clustering methods, and then new genes are classified in the various clusters using a classifier, such as a neural network or a support vector machines (appendix E), that can learn the decision boundaries between the data classes.

Similarity

The starting point of several clustering algorithms, including several forms of hierarchical clustering, is a matrix of pairwise similarities between the objects to be clustered. The precise definition of similarity is crucial and can of course greatly impact the output of the clustering algorithm. In sequence analysis, for instance, similarity can be defined using a score matrix for gaps and substitutions and an alignment algorithm. In gene expression analysis, different measures of similarity can be used. Two obvious examples are Euclidean distance (or more generally L^p distances) and correlation between the vectors of expression levels. The Pearson correlation coefficient is just the dot product of two normalized vectors, or the cosine of their angle. It can be measured on each pair of genes across, for instance, different experiments or different time steps. Each measure of similarity comes with its own advantages and drawbacks depending on the situation, and may be more or less suitable to a given analysis. The correlation, for instance, captures similarity in shape but places no emphasis on the magnitude of the two series of measurements and is quite sensitive to outliers. Consider, for instance, measuring the activity of two unrelated genes that are fluctuating close to the background level. Such genes are very similar in Euclidean distance (distance close to 0), but dissimilar in terms of correlation (correlation close to 0). Likewise, consider the two vectors 1000000000 and 0000000001. In a sense they are similar since they are almost always identical and equal to 0. On the other hand, their correlation is close to 0 because of the two "outliers" in the first and last position.

The Number of Clusters

The choice of the number K of clusters is a particularly thorny issue that depends, among other things, on the scale at which one looks at the data. While there have been attempts to develop methods for the automatic determination of the number of clusters [484], it is safe to say that an educated semi-manual trial-and-error approach still remains one of the most efficient techniques, and this is particularly true at the present stage for array data.

Cost Function and Probabilistic Interpretation

Any rigorous discussion of clustering on a given data set presupposes a principled way of comparing different ways of clustering the same data, hence the need for some kind of global cost/error function that can easily be computed. The goal of clustering then is to try to minimize such a function. This is also called parametric clustering in the literature, as opposed to nonparametric clustering, where only local functions are available [72].

In general, at least for numerical data, this function will depend on quantities such as the centers of the clusters, the distance from each point in a cluster to the corresponding center, the average degree of similarity of the points in a given cluster, and so forth. Such a function is often discontinuous with respect to the underlying clustering of the data. Here again there are no universally accepted functions and the cost function must be tailored to the problem, since different cost functions can lead to different answers.

Because of the advantages of probabilistic methods and modeling, it is tempting to associate the clustering cost function with the negative log-likelihood of an underlying probabilistic model. While this is formally always possible, it is of most interest when the structure of the underlying probabilistic model and the associated independence assumptions are clear. This is when the additive terms of the cost function reflect the factorial structure of the underlying probabilities and variables. As we shall see, this is the case with mixture models, where the k-means clustering algorithm can be viewed as a form of EM.

In the rest of this section, we describe in more detail two basic clustering algorithms that can be applied to DNA microarray data, hierarchical clustering, and k-means. Many other related approaches, including vector quantization [104, 484], principal component analysis, factorial analysis, self-organizing maps, NNs, and SVMs, can be found in the references.

12.3.2 Hierarchical Clustering

Clusters can result from a hierarchical branching process. Thus there exist methods for automatically building a tree from data given in the form of pairwise similarities. In the case of gene expression, this is the approach used in [160]. The output of such a method is a tree and not a set of clusters. In particular, it is usually not obvious how to define clusters from the tree since clusters are derived by cutting the branches of the tree at more or less arbitrary points.

The standard algorithm used in [160] recursively computes a dendrogram that assembles all the elements into a tree, starting from the correlation (pr distance or similarity) matrix C. At each step of the algorithm,

- The two most similar elements of the current matrix (highest correlation) are computed and a node joining these two elements is created.

- An expression profile (or vector) is created for the node by averaging the two expression profiles (or vectors) associated with the two points (missing data can be ignored and the average can be weighted by the number of elements in the vectors). Alternatively, a weighted average of the distances is used to estimate the new distance between centers without actually computing the profile.

- A new, smaller correlation matrix is computed using the newly computed expression profile or vector and replacing the two joined elements with the new node.

- With N starting points, the process is repeated at most $N - 1$ times, until a single node remains.

This algorithm is familiar to biologists and has been used in sequence analysis, phylogenetic trees, and average-linkage cluster analysis. As already pointed out, after the construction of such a dendogram there is still a problem in how to display the result and which clusters to choose. At each node, either of the two elements joined by the node can be ordered to the left or the right of the other. Since there are $N - 1$ joining steps, the number of linear orderings consistent with the structure of the tree is 2^{N-1}. An optimal linear ordering maximizing the combined similarity of all neighboring pairs in the ordering cannot general be computed efficiently. A heuristic approximation is used in [160] by weighting genes using average expression level, chromosome position, and time of maximal induction. The main clusters obtained on a set of gene expression data are shown indeed to have biological relevance.

12.3.3   K-Means, Mixture Models, and EM

K-Means

Of all clustering algorithms, k-means [153] has probably the cleanest probabilistic interpretation as a form of EM (expectation maximization) on the underlying mixture model. In a typical implementation of the k-means algorithm, the number of clusters is fixed to some value K. K representative points or centers are initially chosen for each cluster more or less arbitrarily. These are also called centroids or prototypes. Then at each step,

- Each point in the data is assigned to the cluster associated with the closest representative.

- After the assignment, new representative points are computed, for instance by averaging or taking the center of gravity of each computed cluster.

- The two procedures above are repeated until the system converges or fluctuations remain small.

Hence notice that k-means requires choosing the number of clusters and also being able to compute a distance or similarity between points and compute a representative for each cluster given its members.

When the cost function corresponds to an underlying probabilistic mixture model [172, 522], k-means is an online approximation to the classical EM algorithm, and as such in general is bound to converge towards a solution that is at least a local ML or MAP solution. A classical case is when Euclidean distances are used in conjunction with a mixture of Gaussian models. A related application to a sequence clustering algorithm is described in [28].

Mixtures Models and EM

To see this in more detail, imagine a data set $D = (d_1, \ldots, d_N)$ and an underlying mixture model with K components of the form

$$\mathbf{P}(d) = \sum_{k=1}^{K} \mathbf{P}(M_k)\mathbf{P}(d|M_k) = \sum_{k=1}^{K} \lambda_k \mathbf{P}(d|M_k), \tag{12.23}$$

where $\lambda_k \geq 0$ and $\sum_k \lambda_k = 1$ and M_k is the model for cluster k. The Lagrangian associated with the log-likelihood and the normalization constraints on the mixing coefficients is given by

$$\mathcal{L} = \sum_{i=1}^{N} \log\left(\sum_{k=1}^{K} \lambda_k \mathbf{P}(d_i|M_k)\right) - \mu\left(\sum_{k=1}^{K} \lambda_k - 1\right) \tag{12.24}$$

with the corresponding critical equation

$$\frac{\partial \mathcal{L}}{\partial \lambda_k} = \sum_{i=1}^{N} \frac{\mathbf{P}(d_i|M_k)}{\mathbf{P}(d_i)} - \mu = 0. \tag{12.25}$$

Multiplying each critical equation by λ_k and summing over k immediately yields the value of the Lagrange multiplier $\mu = N$. Multiplying again the critical equation across by $\mathbf{P}(M_k) = \lambda_k$, and using Bayes's theorem in the form

$$\mathbf{P}(M_k|d_i) = \mathbf{P}(d_i|M_k)\mathbf{P}(M_k)/\mathbf{P}(d_i) \tag{12.26}$$

yields

$$\lambda_k^* = \frac{1}{N} \sum_{i=1}^{N} \mathbf{P}(M_k|d_i). \tag{12.27}$$

Thus the ML estimate of the mixing coefficients for class k is the sample mean of the conditional probabilities that d_i comes from model k. Consider now that each model M_k has its own vector of parameters (w_{kj}). Differentiating the Lagrangian with respect to w_{kj} gives

$$\frac{\partial \mathcal{L}}{\partial w_{kj}} = \sum_{i=1}^{N} \frac{\lambda_k}{\mathbf{P}(d_i)} \frac{\partial \mathbf{P}(d_i|M_k)}{\partial w_{kj}}. \tag{12.28}$$

Substituting (12.26) in (12.28) finally provides the critical equation

$$\sum_{i=1}^{N} \mathbf{P}(M_k|d_i) \frac{\partial \log \mathbf{P}(d_i|M_k)}{\partial w_{kj}} = 0 \tag{12.29}$$

for each k and j. The ML equations for estimating the parameters are weighted averages of the ML equations $\partial \log \mathbf{P}(d_i|M_k))/\partial w_{kj} = 0$ arising from each point separately. As in (12.27), the weights are the probabilities of membership of the d_i in each class.

As was precisely the case for HMMs, the ML equations (12.27) and (12.29) can be used iteratively to search for ML estimates, yielding also another instance of the EM algorithm. In the E step, the membership probabilities (hidden variables) of each data point are estimated for each mixture component. The M step is equivalent to K separate estimation problems with each data point contributing to the log-likelihood associated with each of the K components with a weight given by the estimated membership probabilities. Different flavors of the same algorithm are possible depending on whether the membership probabilities $\mathbf{P}(M|d)$ are estimated in hard or soft fashion during the E step. The description of k-means given above correspond to the hard version where these membership probabilities are either 0 or 1, each point being assigned to only one cluster. This is analogous to the use of the Viterbi version of the EM algorithm for HMMs, where only the optimal path associated with a sequence is used, rather than the family of all possible paths. Different variations are also possible during the M step of the algorithms depending, for instance, on whether the parameters w_{kj} are estimated by gradient descent or by solving (12.29) exactly. It is well known that the center of gravity of a set of points minimizes its average quadratic distance to any fixed point. Therefore in the case of a mixture of spherical Gaussians, the M step of the k-means algorithm described above maximizes the corresponding quadratic log-likelihood and provides an ML estimate for the center of each Gaussian component.

It is also possible to introduce priors on the parameters of each cluster in the form

$$\mathbf{P}(d) = \sum_{k=1}^{K} \mathbf{P}(d|M_k, w_k)\mathbf{P}(w_k|M_k)\mathbf{P}(M_k) \qquad (12.30)$$

and/or on the mixture coefficients. This leads to more complex hierarchical probabilistic models that may prove useful for DNA array data, or even sequence data. In sequence data, for instance, this could amount to having sequences produced by different dice, the dice coming from different factories, the factories coming from different countries, and so forth, with probabilistic distributions at each level of the hierarchy and on the corresponding properties. To the best of our knowledge, these hierarchical mixture models have not yet been explored systematically in this context.

12.4 Gene Regulation

Finally, at the third level of analysis DNA microarray expression data naturally leads to many questions of gene regulation. Understanding gene regulation at the system level is one of the most interesting and challenging problems in biology, but one where most of the principles remain to be discovered. Here, we mention only some of the main directions of research and provide a few pointers to the literature.

One direction of analysis consists in mining regulatory regions, searching, for instance, for transcription factor DNA binding sites and other regulatory motifs. To some extent, such searches can be done on a genomic scale using purely computational tools [530, 531, 232]. The basic idea is to compute the number of occurrences of each N-mer, typically for values of N in the range of 3 to 10, within an entire genome or within a particular subset of a genome, such as all gene-upstream regions. N-mers that are overrepresented are of particular interest and have been shown to comprise a number of known regulatory motifs. Distribution patterns of overreprsented N-mers can also be very informative [232]. In any case, overrepresentation of course must be assessed with respect to a good statistical background model, which can be a Markov model of some order derived from the actual counts. When in addition gene-expression data becomes available, further tuning of these mining procedures becomes possible by looking, for instance, at overrepresentation in upstream regions of genes that appear to be up-regulated (or down-regulated) under a given condition [89, 231, 535, 111, 270]. Probabilistic algorithms such as EM and Gibbs sampling naturally play an essential role in motif finding, due to both the structural and positional variability of motifs (see programs such as MEME and CONSENSUS). In any case, only a small subset of the motifs found nowadays by these techniques are typically found also in the TRANSFAC [560] database or in the current literature, and most must await future experimental verification.

A second, more ambitious direction is to attempt to model and infer regulatory networks on a global scale, or along more specific subcomponents [532, 190, 584] such as a pathway or a set of coregulated genes. One of the major obstacles here is that we do not yet understand all the details of transcription at the molecular level. For instance, we do not entirely understand the role that noise plays in gene regulation [383, 243]. Furthermore, there are very few examples of regulatory circuits for which detailed information is available, and they all appear to be very complex [579]. On the theoretical side, several mathematical formalisms have been applied to model genetic networks. These range from discrete models, such as Boolean networks, as in the pioneering work of Kauffman [310, 311, 312] to continuous models based on differential equations, such as continuous recurrent neural networks [391] or power-law formalism [537, 466, 258], probabilistic graphical models, and Bayesian networks [190]. None of these formalisms appear to capture all the dimensions of gene regulation, and most of the work in this area remains to be done. Additional references in this active area of research can be found in the proceedings of the ISMB, PSB, and RECOMB conferences of the last few years. Understanding biology at the system level (for instance [88, 309, 239, 289, 576]), not only gene networks, but also protein networks, signaling networks, metabolic networks, and specific systems, such as the immune system or neuronal networks, is likely to remain at the center of the bioinformatics efforts of the next few decades.

Chapter 13

Internet Resources and Public Databases

13.1 A Rapidly Changing Set of Resources

It is well known that resources available on the Internet are changing faster than almost everything else in the world of information processing. This also holds true for the dedicated tools available for biological sequence analysis. New tools are constantly becoming available, while others that are still available are getting obsolete. It is not easy to follow the state of the art in the many specialized areas of bioinformatics, where computational analysis is a powerful alternative to significant parts of the experimental investigation one may carry out.

Many of the tools offered the Internet are made available not by large organizations and research groups but by individual researchers many of whom may be actively involved in the field for only a shorter period. The funding situation, even for some of the major computational services, may change from year to year. This means that links are not updated regularly and that many servers may not be kept running 24 hours per day. If a service gets popular, the server behind it often will be upgraded sufficiently only after some delay. However, in many cases this is counterbalanced by mirror servers established by federal organizations, such as the NCBI in Washington, D.C., the EBI in Hinxton, U.K., and DDJB in Japan.

One highly confusing feature of the "open bioinformatics market" is that the same type of service can be available from many different sites based on different implementations. This is, for example, the case for protein secondary structure prediction, gene finding, and intron splice site prediction. The assignment of solvent exposure to amino acids in proteins is another type of prediction that is available from numerous sources. Since these methods most often have been constructed and tested with different sets of data, it can be hard even for specialists to assess objectively which method one should prefer. Often it may be disadvantageous to try to single out one particular method; instead following the statement from statistics that "averaging is better than voting" and using many methods in concert may lead to a more robust and reliable result.

It is notoriously hard to make benchmarks because benchmark sets of sequences often will overlap strongly with the sequences that went into the construction of some of the algorithms. Some approaches will be created with an inherent ability to "remember" the training data, while others are designed to extract only the average and generalizable features. For such methods the performance on the training set will only about reach the performance on a test set.

As described in Chapter 1 (Section 1.2), the amount of sequence data grows exponentially. Fortunately, the computing power in a typical PC or workstation also grows exponentially and, moreover, is available at ever-decreasing cost. For a long time computers have been getting twice as fast whenever the cost has been reduced roughly by a factor of two. This means that every six to ten months it gets twice as expensive, in terms of the economical cost, to perform the same search against the public databases using a query sequence or a regular expression. This means also that algorithms should constantly be redesigned in order to maintain the status quo.

13.2 Databases over Databases and Tools

In the area of biological sequence analysis there is a long tradition of creating databases over databases as a means for establishing an overview as well as for managing access to the vast number of resources. One of the earliest ones was the LiMB database (Listing of Molecular Biology databases), which has been published in hard copy [353]. Today, the only reasonable medium is the more flexible World Wide Web (WWW). Links can be followed and updated instantly. LiMB contains information about the contents and details of maintenance of databases related to molecular biology. It was created to facilitate the process of locating and accessing data sets upon which the research community depends.

The following sections contain lists of links to databases over databases, to major public sequence databases, and to selected prediction servers. Realistically, these lists should be updated on a daily basis, and the goal has not been to provide a nearly complete guide to the WWW. Rather, this material

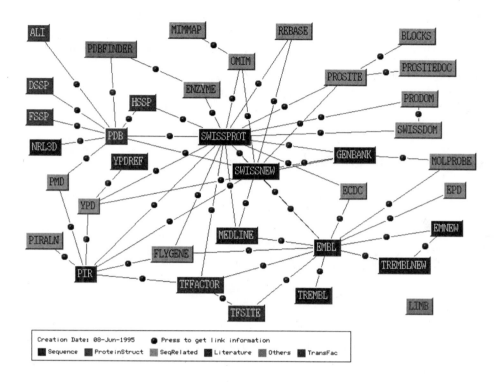

Figure 13.1: Some of the Databases Available over the World Wide Web.

should be seen as examples of the kinds of tools that can be useful for serious analysis of experimental data. It is recommended that the metadatabases be browsed regularly and that the common WWW search engines be used to spot the most recent material. Most of the links listed below come from the page started by Jan Hansen (http://www.cbs.dtu.dk/biolink.html) at the Center for Biological Sequence Analysis in Denmark. The links indicated below focus on sequence and annotation retrieval. Dedicated sites for sequence submission have not been included.

13.3   Databases over Databases in Molecular Biology

SRS Sequence Retrieval System (network browser for databanks in molecular biology)
    http://www.embl-heidelberg.de/srs5/

Survey of Molecular Biology Databases and Servers
   http://www.ai.sri.com/people/pkarp/mimbd/rsmith.html

BioMedNet Library
   http://biomednet.com

DBGET Database Links
   http://www.genome.ad.jp/dbget/dbget.links.html

Harvard Genome Research Databases and Selected Servers
   http://golgi.harvard.edu

Johns Hopkins Univ. OWL Web Server
   http://www.gdb.org/Dan/proteins/owl.html

Index of Biology Internet Servers, USGS
   http://info.er.usgs.gov/network/science/biology/index.html

Listing of Molecular Biology Databases (LiMB)
   gopher://gopher.nih.gov/11/molbio/other

WWW Server for Virology, UW-Madison
   http://www.bocklabs.wisc.edu/Welcome.html

UK MRC Human Genome Mapping Project Resource Centre
   http://www.hgmp.mrc.ac.uk/

WWW for the Molecular Biologists and Biochemists
   http://www.yk.rim.or.jp/~aisoai/index.html

Links to other Bio-Web servers
   http://www.gdb.org/biolinks.html

Molecular Modelling Servers and Databases
   http://www.rsc.org/lap/rsccom/dab/ind006links.htm

EMBO Practical Structural Databases
   http://xray.bmc.uu.se/embo/structdb/links.html

Web Resources for Protein Scientists
   http://www.faseb.org/protein/ProSciDocs/WWWResources.html

ExPASy Molecular Biology Server
   http://expasy.hcuge.ch/cgi-bin/listdoc

The Antibody Resource Page
http://www.antibodyresource.com

Bioinformatics WWW Sites
http://biochem.kaist.ac.kr/bioinformatics.html

Bioinformatics and Computational Biology at George Mason University
http://www.science.gmu.edu/~michaels/Bioinformatics/

INFOBIOGEN Catalog of Databases
http://www.infobiogen.fr/services/dbcat/

National Biotechnology Information Facility
http://www.nbif.org/data/data.html

Human Genome Project Information
http://www.ornl.gov/TechResources/Human_Genome

Archives for biological software and databases
http://www.gdb.org/Dan/software/biol-links.html

Proteome Research: New Frontiers in Functional Genomics (book contents)
http://expasy.hcuge.ch/ch2d/LivreTOC.html

13.4   Sequence and Structure Databases

13.4.1   Major Public Sequence Databases

EMBL WWW Services
http://www.EMBL-heidelberg.de/Services/index.html

GenBank Database Query Form (get a GenBank entry)
http://ncbi.nlm.nih.gov/genbank/query_form.html

Protein Data Bank WWW Server (get a PDB structure)
http://www.rcsb.org

European Bioinformatics Institute (EBI)
http://www.ebi.ac.uk/

EBI Industry support
http://industry.ebi.ac.uk/

SWISS-PROT (protein sequences)
    http://www.expasy.ch/sprot/sprot-top.html

PROSITE (functional protein sites)
    http://expasy.hcuge.ch/sprot/prosite.html

Macromolecular Structures Database
    http://BioMedNet.com/cgi-bin/members1/shwtoc.pl?J:mms

Molecules R Us (search and view a protein molecule)
    http://cmm.info.nih.gov/modeling/net_services.html

PIR-International Protein Sequence Database
    http://www.gdb.org/Dan/proteins/pir.html

SCOP (structural classification of proteins), MRC
    http://scop.mrc-lmb.cam.ac.uk/scop/data/scop.1.html

HIV Sequence Database, Los Alamos
    http://hiv-web.lanl.gov/

HIV Molecular Immunology Database, Los Alamos
    http://hiv-web.lanl.gov/immuno/index.html

TIGR Database
    http://www.tigr.org/tdb/tdb.html

The NCBI WWW Entrez Browser
    http://www.ncbi.nlm.nih.gov/Entrez/index.html

Cambridge Structural Database (small-molecule organic and
    organometallic crystal structures)
    http://www.ccdc.cam.ac.uk

Gene Ontology Consortium
    http://genome-www.stanford.edu/GO/

13.4.2 Specialized Databases

ANU Bioinformatics Hypermedia Server
    (virus databases, classification and nomenclature of viruses)
    http://life.anu.edu.au/

O-GLYCBASE (a revised database of O-glycosylated proteins)
http://www.cbs.dtu.dk/OGLYCBASE/cbsoglycbase.html

Genome Sequence Database (GSDB) (relational database of annotated DNA sequences)
http://www.ncgr.org

EBI Protein topology atlas
http://www3.ebi.ac.uk/tops/ServerIntermed.html

Database of Enzymes and Metabolic Pathways (EMP)
http://www.empproject.com/

MAGPIE (multipurpose automated genome project investigation environment)
http://www.mcs.anl.gov/home/gaasterl/magpie.html

E.coli database collection (ECDC) (compilation of DNA sequences of *E. coli* K12)
http://susi.bio.uni-giessen.de/ecdc.html

Haemophilus influenzae database (HIDC) (genetic map, contigs, searchable index)
http://susi.bio.uni-giessen.de/hidc.htm

EcoCyc: Encyclopedia of *Escherichia coli* Genes and Metabolism
http://www.ai.sri.com/ecocyc/ecocyc.html

Eddy Lab snoRNA Database
http://rna.wustl.edu/snoRNAdb/

GenProtEc (genes and proteins of *Escherichia coli*)
http://www.mbl.edu/html/ecoli.html

NRSub (non-redundant database for Bacillus subtilis)
http://pbil.univ-lyon1.fr/nrsub/nrsub.html

YPD (proteins from *Saccharomyces cerevisiae*)
http://www.proteome.com/YPDhome.html

Saccharomyces Genome Database
http://genome-www.stanford.edu/Saccharomyces/

LISTA, LISTA-HOP and LISTA-HON (compilation of homology databases from yeast)
http://www.ch.embnet.org/

FlyBase (*Drosophila* database)
http://flybase.bio.indiana.edu/

MPDB (molecular probe database)
   http://www.biotech.ist.unige.it/interlab/mpdb.html

Compilation of tRNA sequences and sequences of tRNA genes
   http://www.uni-bayreuth.de/departments/biochemie/trna/index.html

Small RNA database, Baylor College of Medicine
   http://mbcr.bcm.tmc.edu/smallRNA/smallrna.html

SRPDB (signal recognition particle database)
   http://psyche.uthct.edu/dbs/SRPDB/SRPDB.html

RDP (the Ribosomal Database Project)
   http://rdpwww.life.uiuc.edu/

Structure of small ribosomal subunit RNA
   http://rrna.uia.ac.be/ssu/index.html

Structure of large ribosomal subunit RNA
   http://rrna.uia.ac.be/lsu/index.html

RNA modification database
   http://medlib.med.utah.edu/RNAmods/

HAMSTeRS (haemophilia A mutation database) and factor VIII mutation database
   http://europium.csc.mrc.ac.uk/usr/WWW/WebPages/main.dir/main.htm

Haemophilia B (point mutations and short additions and deletions)
   ftp://ftp.ebi.ac.uk/pub/databases/haemb/

Human p53, hprt and lacZ genes and mutations
   http://sunsite.unc.edu/dnam/mainpage.html

PAH mutation analysis (disease-producing human PAH loci)
   http://www.mcgill.ca/pahdb

ESTHER (cholinesterase gene server)
   http://www.ensam.inra.fr/cgi-bin/ace/index

IMGT (immunogenetics database)
   http://www.ebi.ac.uk/imgt/

p53 mutations in human tumors and cell lines
   ftp://ftp.ebi.ac.uk/pub/databases/p53/

Androgen receptor gene mutations database
   ftp://www.ebi.ac.uk/pub/databases/androgen/

Glucocorticoid receptor resource
   http://nrr.georgetown.edu/GRR/GRR.html

Thyroid hormone receptor resource
   http://xanadu.mgh.harvard.edu//receptor/trrfront.html

16SMDB and 23SMDB (16S and 23S ribosomal RNA mutation database)
   http://www.fandm.edu/Departments/Biology/Databases/RNA.html

MITOMAP (human mitochondrial genome database)
   http://www.gen.emory.edu/mitomap.html

SWISS-2DPAGE (database of two-dimensional polyacrylamide gel electrophoresis)
   http://expasy.hcuge.ch/ch2d/ch2d-top.html

PRINTS (protein fingerprint database)
   http://www.biochem.ucl.ac.uk/bsm/dbbrowser/PRINTS/PRINTS.html

KabatMan (database of antibody structure and sequence information)
   http://www.bioinf.org.uk/abs/

ALIGN (compendium of protein sequence alignments)
   http://www.biochem.ucl.ac.uk/bsm/dbbrowser/ALIGN/ALIGN.html

CATH (protein structure classification system)
   http://www.biochem.ucl.ac.uk/bsm/cath/

ProDom (protein domain database)
   http://protein.toulouse.inra.fr/

Blocks database (system for protein classification)
   http://blocks.fhcrc.org/

HSSP (homology-derived secondary structure of proteins)
   http://www.sander.embl-heidelberg.de/hssp/

FSSP (fold classification based on structure-structure alignment of proteins)
   http://www2.ebi.ac.uk/dali/fssp/fssp.html

SBASE protein domains (annotated protein sequence segments)
   http://www.icgeb.trieste.it/~sbasesrv/

TransTerm (database of translational signals)
http://uther.otago.ac.nz/Transterm.html

GRBase (database linking information on proteins involved in gene regulation)
http://www.access.digex.net/~regulate/trevgrb.html

ENZYME (nomenclature of enzymes)
http://www.expasy.ch/enzyme/

REBASE (database of restriction enzymes and methylases)
http://www.neb.com/rebase/

RNaseP database
http://jwbrown.mbio.ncsu.edu/RNaseP/home.html

REGULONDB (database on transcriptional regulation in E. coli)
http://www.cifn.unam.mx/Computational_Biology/regulondb/

TRANSFAC (database on transcription factors and their DNA binding sites)
http://transfac.gbf.de/

MHCPEP (database of MHC-binding peptides)
http://wehih.wehi.edu.au/mhcpep/

Mouse genome database
http://www.informatics.jax.org/mgd.html

Mouse knockout database
http://BioMedNet.com/cgi-bin/mko/mkobrwse.pl

ATCC (American type culture collection)
http://www.atcc.org/

Histone sequence database of highly conserved nucleoprotein sequences
http://www.ncbi.nlm.nih.gov/Baxevani/HISTONES

3Dee (database of protein structure domain definitions)
http://barton.ebi.ac.uk/servers/3Dee.html

InterPro (integrated resource of protein domains and functional sites)
http://www.ebi.ac.uk/interpro/

NRL_3D (sequence-structure database derived from PDB, pictures and searches)
http://www.gdb.org/Dan/proteins/nrl3d.html

VBASE human variable immunoglulin gene sequences
    http://www.mrc-cpe.cam.ac.uk/imt-doc/public/INTRO.html

GPCRD (G protein-coupled receptor data)
    http://www.gpcr.org/7tm/

Human Cytogenetics (chromosomes and karyotypes)
    http://www.selu.com/bio/cyto/human/index.html

Protein Kinase resource
    http://www.sdsc.edu/projects/Kinases/pkr/pk_info.html#Format

Carbohydrate databases
    http://www.boc.chem.ruu.nl/sugabase/databases.html

Borrelia Molecular Biology Home Page
    http://www.pasteur.fr/Bio/borrelia/Welcome.html

Human papillomaviruses database
    http://HPV-web.lanl.gov/

Human 2-D PAGE databases for proteome analysis in health and disease
    http://biobase.dk/cgi-bin/celis

DBA mammalian genome size database
    http://www.unipv.it/~webbio/dbagsh.htm

DOGS database Of Genome Sizes
    http://www.cbs.dtu.dk/databases/DOGS/index.html

U.S. patent citation database
    http://cos.gdb.org/repos/pat/

13.5 Sequence Similarity Searches

Sequence similarity search page at EBI
    http://www.ebi.ac.uk/searches/searches.html

NCBI: BLAST notebook
    http://www.ncbi.nlm.nih.gov/BLAST/

BLITZ ULTRA Fast Search at EMBL
    http://www.ebi.ac.uk/searches/blitz_input.html

EMBL WWW services
   http://www.embl-heidelberg.de/Services/index.html#5

Pattern scan of proteins or nucleotides
   http://www.mcs.anl.gov/compbio/PatScan/HTML/patscan.html

MEME (motif discovery and search)
   http://meme.sdsc.edu/meme/website/

CoreSearch (dentification of consensus elements in DNA sequences)
   http://www.gsf.de/biodv/coresearch.html

The PRINTS/PROSITE scanner (search motif databases with query sequence)
   http://www.biochem.ucl.ac.uk/cgi-bin/attwood/SearchPrintsForm.pl

DARWIN system at ETH Zurich
   http://cbrg.inf.ethz.ch/

PimaII find sequence similarity using dynamic programming
   http://bmerc-www.bu.edu/protein-seq/pimaII-new.html

DashPat find sequence similarity using a hashcode comparison with a pattern library
   http://bmerc-www.bu.edu/protein-seq/dashPat-new.html

PROPSEARCH (search based on amino acid composition, EMBL)
   http://www.embl-heidelberg.de/aaa.html

Sequence search protocol (integrated pattern search)
   http://www.biochem.ucl.ac.uk/bsm/dbbrowser/protocol.html

ProtoMap (automatic hierarchical classification of all swissprot proteins)
   http://www.protomap.cs.huji.ac.il/

GenQuest (Fasta, Blast, Smith Waterman; search in any database)
   http://www.gdb.org/Dan/gq/gq.form.html

SSearch (searches against a specified database)
   http://watson.genes.nig.ac.jp/homology/ssearch-e_help.html

Peer Bork search list (motif/pattern/profile searches)
   http://www.embl-heidelberg.de/~bork/pattern.html

PROSITE Database Searches (search for functional sites in your sequence)
   http://www.ebi.ac.uk/searches/prosite.html

PROWL—Protein Information Retrieval at Skirball Institute
   http://mcphar04.med.nyu.edu/index.html

CEPH genotype database
   http://www.cephb.fr/cephdb/

13.6   Alignment

13.6.1   Pairwise Sequence and Structure Alignment

Pairwise protein alignment (SIM)
   http://expasy.hcuge.ch/sprot/sim-prot.html

LALNVIEW alignment viewer program
   ftp://expasy.hcuge.ch/pub/lalnview

BCM Search Launcher (pairwise sequence alignment)
   http://searchlauncher.bcm.tmc.edu/seq-search/alignment.html

DALI compare protein structures in 3D
   http://www2.ebi.ac.uk/dali/

DIALIGN (aligment program without explicit gap penalties)
   http://www.gsf.de/biodv/dialign.html

13.6.2   Multiple Alignment and Phylogeny

ClustalW (multiple sequence alignment at BCM)
   http://searchlauncher.bcm.tmc.edu/multi-align/multi-align.html

PHYLIP (programs for inferring phylogenies)
   http://evolution.genetics.washington.edu/phylip.html

Other phylogeny programs, a complication from PHYLIP documentation
   http://expasy.hcuge.ch/info/phylogen.sof

Tree of Life Home Page (information about phylogeny and biodiversity)
   http://phylogeny.arizona.edu/tree/phylogeny.html

Links for Palaeobotanists
   http://www.uni-wuerzburg.de/mineralogie/palbot1.html

Phylogenetic analysis programs (the tree of life list)
    http://phylogeny.arizona.edu/tree/programs/programs.html

Cladistics
    http://www.kheper.auz.com/gaia/biosphere/systematics/cladistics.htm

Cladistic software (a list from the Willi Hennig Society)
    http://www.cladistics.org/education.html

BCM search launcher for multiple sequence alignments
    http://searchlauncher.bcm.tmc.edu/multi-align/multi-align.html

AMAS (analyse multiply aligned sequences)
    http://barton.ebi.ac.uk/servers/amas_server.html

Vienna RNA Secondary Structure Package
    http://www.tbi.univie.ac.at/~ivo/RNA/

WebLogo (sequence logo)
    http://www.bio.cam.ac.uk/cgi-bin/seqlogo/logo.cgi

Protein sequence logos using relative entropy
    http://www.cbs.dtu.dk/gorodkin/appl/plogo.html

RNA structure-sequence logo
    http://www.cbs.dtu.dk/gorodkin/appl/slogo.html

RNA mutual information plots
    http://www/gorodkin/appl/MatrixPlot/mutRNA/

13.7   Selected Prediction Servers

13.7.1   Prediction of Protein Structure from Sequence

PHD PredictProtein server for secondary structure, solvent accesibility,
    and transmembrane segments
    http://www.embl-heidelberg.de/predictprotein/predictprotein.html

PhdThreader (fold recognition by prediction-based threading)
    http://www.embl-heidelberg.de/predictprotein/phd_help.html

PSIpred (protein strcuture prediction server)
    http://insulin.brunel.ac.uk/psipred/

THREADER (David Jones)
   http://www.biochem.ucl.ac.uk/~jones/threader.html

TMHMM (prediction of transmembrane helices in proteins)
   http://wwwcbs.dtu.dk/services/TMHMM/

Protein structural analysis, BMERC
   http://bmerc-www.bu.edu/protein-seq/protein-struct.html

Submission form for protein domain and foldclass prediction
   http://genome.dkfz-heidelberg.de/nnga/def-query.html

NNSSP (prediction of protein secondary sturcture by nearest-neighbor algorithms)
   http://genomic.sanger.ac.uk/pss/pss.html

Swiss-Model (automated knowledge-based protein homology modeling server)
   http://www.expasy.ch/swissmod/SWISS-MODEL.html

SSPRED (secondary structure prediction with multiple alignment)
   http://www.mrc-cpe.cam.ac.uk/jong/predict/sspred.htm

SSCP (secondary structure prediction content with amino acid composition)
   http://www.mrc-cpe.cam.ac.uk/jong/predict/sscp.htm

SOPM (Self Optimized Prediction Method, secondary structure) at IBCP, France.
   http://pbil.ibcp.fr/cgi-bin/npsa_automat.pl?page=/NPSA/npsa_sopm.html

NNPREDICT (neural network for residue-by-residue prediction)
   http://www.cmpharm.ucsf.edu/~nomi/nnpredict.html

SSpro (secondary structure in 3 classes)
   http://promoter.ics.uci.edu/BRNN-PRED/

SSpro8 (secondary structure in 8 classes)
   http://promoter.ics.uci.edu/BRNN-PRED/

ACCpro (solvent accessibility)
   http://promoter.ics.uci.edu/BRNN-PRED/

CONpro (contact number)
   http://promoter.ics.uci.edu/BRNN-PRED/

TMAP (service predicting transmembrane segments in proteins)
   http://www.embl-heidelberg.de/tmap/tmap_info.html

TMpred (prediction of transmembrane regions and orientation)
  http://www.ch.embnet.org/software/TMPRED_form.html

MultPredict (secondary structure of multiply aligned sequences)
  http://kestrel.ludwig.ucl.ac.uk/zpred.html

NIH Molecular Modeling Homepage (modelling homepage with links)
  http://cmm.info.nih.gov/modeling/

BCM Search Launcher (protein secondary structure prediction)
  http://searchlauncher.bcm.tmc.edu/seq-search/struc-predict.html

COILS (prediction of coiled coil regions in proteins)
  http://www.ch.embnet.org/software/coils/COILS_doc.html

Coiled Coils
  http://www.york.ac.uk/depts/biol/units/coils/coilcoil.html

Paircoil (location of coiled coil regions in amino acid sequences)
  http://theory.lcs.mit.edu/ bab/webcoil.html

PREDATOR (protein secondary structure prediction from single sequence)
  http://www.embl-heidelberg.de/argos/predator/predator_info.html

DAS (Dense Alignment Surface; prediction of transmembrane regions in proteins)
  http://www.biokemi.su.se/~server/DAS/

Fold-recognition at UCLA-DOE structure prediction server
  http://www.doe-mbi.ucla.edu/people/frsvr/frsvr.html

Molecular Modelling Servers and Databases
  http://bionmr5.bham.ac.uk/modelling/model.html

EVA (automatic evaluation of protein structure prediction servers)
  http://cubic.bioc.columbia.edu/eva/

13.7.2   Gene Finding and Intron Splice Site Prediction

NetGene (prediction of intron splice sites in human genes)
  http://www.cbs.dtu.dk/services/NetGene2/

NetPlantGene (prediction of intron splice sites in *Arabidopsis thaliana*)
  http://www.cbs.dtu.dk/services/NetPGene

GeneQuiz (automated analysis of genomes)
   http://www.sander.embl-heidelberg.de/genequiz/

GRAIL interface (protein coding regions and functional sites)
   http://avalon.epm.ornl.gov/Grail-bin/EmptyGrailForm

GENEMARK (WWW system for predicting protein coding regions)
   http://genemark.biology.gatech.edu/GeneMark

GENSCAN Web Server: Complete gene structures in genomic DNA
   http://gnomic.stanford.edu/~chris/GENSCANW.html

FGENEH Genefinder: Prediction of gene structure in human DNA sequences
   http://mbcr.bcm.tmc.edu/Guide/Genefinder/fgeneh.html

GRAIL and GENQUEST (E-mail sequence analysis, gene assembly,
   and sequence comparison)
   http://avalon.epm.ornl.gov/manuals/grail-genquest.9407.html

CpG islands finder
   http://www.ebi.ac.uk/cpg/

Eukaryotic Pol II promoter prediction
   http://biosci.umn.edu/software/proscan.html

Promoter prediction input form
   http://www-hgc.lbl.gov/projects/promoter.html

Web Signal Scan Service (scan DNA sequences for eukaryotic transcriptional elements)
   http://bimas.dcrt.nih.gov/molbio/signal/

Gene Discovery Page
   http://konops.imbb.forth.gr/~topalis/mirror/gdp.html

List of genome sequencing projects
   http://www.mcs.anl.gov/home/gaasterl/genomes.html

13.7.3 DNA Microarray Data and Methods

Cyber-T (DNA microarray data analysis server)
   http://128.200.5.223/CyberT/

Brown Lab guide to microarraying
   http://cmgm.stanford.edu/pbrown

Stanford Microarray Database
http://genome-www4.stanford.edu/MicroArray/SMD/

Stanford MicroArray Forum
http://cmgm.stanford.edu/cgi-bin/cgiwrap/taebshin/dcforum/dcboard.cgi

Brazma microarray page at EBI
http://industry.ebi.ac.uk/~brazma/Data-mining/microarray.html

Web resources on gene expression and DNA microarray technologies
http://industry.ebi.ac.uk/~alan/MicroArray/

Gene-X (array data management and analysis system)
http://www.ncgr.org/research/genex/

UCI functional genomics array tools and software
http://www.genomics.uci.edu/

Matern's DNA Microarray Page
http://barinth.tripod.com/chips.html

Public source for microarraying information, tools, and protocols
http://www.microarrays.org/

Weisshaar's listing of DNA microarray links
http://www.mpiz-koeln.mpg.de/~weisshaa/Adis/DNA-array-links.html

DNA microarray technology to identify genes controlling spermatogenesis
http://www.mcb.arizona.edu/wardlab/microarray.html

13.7.4 Other Prediction Servers

NetStart (translation start in vertebrate and A. thaliana DNA)
http://www.cbs.dtu.dk/services/NetStart/

NetOGlyc (O-glycosylation sites in mammalian proteins)
http://www.cbs.dtu.dk/services/NetOGlyc/

YinOYang (O-β-GlcNAc sites in eukaryotic protein sequences)
http://www.cbs.dtu.dk/services/YinOYang/

SignalP
(signal peptide and cleavage sites in gram+, gram-, and eukaryotic proteins)
http://www.cbs.dtu.dk/services/SignalP/

NetChop (cleavage sites of the human proteasome)
   http://www.cbs.dtu.dk/services/NetChop/

NetPhos (serine, threonine and tyrosine phosphorylation sites in eukaryotic proteins)
   http://www.cbs.dtu.dk/services/NetPhos/

TargetP (prediction of subcellular location)
   http://www.cbs.dtu.dk/services/TargetP/

ChloroP (chloroplast pransit peptide prediction)
   http://www.cbs.dtu.dk/services/SignalP/

PSORT (prediction of protein-sorting signals and localization from sequence)
   http://psort.nibb.ac.jp/

PEDANT (prtein extraction, description, and analalysis tool)
   http://pedant.mips.biochem.mpg.de/

Compare your sequence to COG database
   http://www.ncbi.nlm.nih.gov/COG/cognitor.html

Prediction of HLA-binding peptides from sequences
   http://www-bimas.dcrt.nih.gov/molbio/hla_bind/index.html

13.8   Molecular Biology Software Links

Visualization for bioinformatics
   http://industry.ebi.ac.uk/ alan/VisSupp/

The EBI molecular biology software archive
   http://www.ebi.ac.uk/software/software.html

The BioCatalog
   http://www.ebi.ac.uk/biocat/e-mail_Server_ANALYSIS.html

Archives for biological software and databases
   http://www.gdb.org/Dan/softsearch/biol-links.html

Barton group software (ALSCRIPT, AMPS, AMAS, STAMP, ASSP, JNET, and SCANPS)
   http://barton.ebi.ac.uk/new/software.html

Cohen group software rotamer library, BLoop, QPack, FOLD, Match,
    http://www.cmpharm.ucsf.edu/cohen/pub/

Bayesian bioinformatics at Wadsworth Center
    http://www.wadsworth.org/res&res/bioinfo/

Rasmol software and script documentation
    http://scop.mrc-lmb.cam.ac.uk/std/rs/

MolScript
    http://ind1.mrc-lmb.cam.ac.uk/external-file-copies/molscript.html

WHAT IF
    http://www.hgmp.mrc.ac.uk/Registered/Option/whatif.html

Biosym (Discover)
    http://ind1.mrc-lmb.cam.ac.uk/external-file-copies/biosym/
        discover/html/Disco_Home.html

SAM software for sequence consensus HMMs at UC Santa Cruz
    http://www.cse.ucsc.edu/research/compbio/sam.html

HMMER (source code for hidden Markov model software)
    http://hmmer.wustl.edu/

ClustalW
    http://www.ebi.ac.uk/clustalw/

DSSP program
    http://www.sander.embl-heidelberg.de/dssp/

Bootscanning for viral recombinations
    http://www.bio.net//hypermail/RECOMBINATION/recom.199607/0004.html

Blocking Gibbs sampling for linkage analysis in very large pedigrees
    http://www.cs.auc.dk/~claus/block.html

ProMSED (protein multiple sequences editor for Windows)
    ftp://ftp.ebi.ac.uk/pub/software/dos/promsed/

DBWatcher for Sun/Solaris
    http://www-igbmc.u-strasbg.fr/BioInfo/LocalDoc/DBWatcher/

ProFit (protein least squares fitting software)
   http://www.bioinf.org.uk/software/

Indiana University IUBIO software and data
   http://iubio.bio.indiana.edu/

Molecular biology software list at NIH
   http://bimas.dcrt.nih.gov/sw.html

ProAnalyst software for protein/peptide analysis
   ftp://ftp.ebi.ac.uk/pub/software/dos/proanalyst/

DRAGON protein modelling tool using distance geometry
   http://www.nimr.mrc.ac.uk/~mathbio/a-aszodi/dragon.html

Molecular Surface Package
   http://www.best.com/~connolly/

Biotechnological Software and Internet Journal
   http://www.orst.edu/~ahernk/bsj.html

MCell (Monte Carlo simulator of cellular microphysiology)
   http://www.mcell.cnl.salk.edu/

HHMpro (HMM simulator for sequence analysis with graphical interface)
   http://www.netid.com/html/hmmpro.html

13.9   Ph.D. Courses over the Internet

Biocomputing course resource list: course syllabi
   http://www.techfak.uni-bielefeld.de/bcd/Curric/syllabi.html

Ph.D. course in biological sequence analysis and protein modeling
   http://www.cbs.dtu.dk/phdcourse/programme.html

The Virtual School of Molecular Sciences
   http://www.ccc.nottingham.ac.uk/vsms/sbdd/

EMBnet Biocomputing Tutorials
   http://biobase.dk/Embnetut/Universl/embnettu.html

Collaborative course in protein structure
     http://www.cryst.bbk.ac.uk/PPS/index.html

GNA's Virtual School of Natural Sciences
     http://www.techfak.uni-bielefeld.de/bcd/Vsns/index.html

Algorithms in molecular biology
     http://www.cs.washington.edu/education/courses/590bi/

ISCB education working group
     http://www.sdsc.edu/pb/iscb/iscb-edu.html

13.10   Bioinformatics Societies

International Society for Computational Biology (ISCB)
     http://www.iscb.org/

Society for Bioinformatics in the Nordic countries
     http://www.socbin.org/

Japanese Society for Bioinformatics
     http://www.jsbi.org/

13.11   HMM/NN simulator

A number of projects described in the book have been carried using the machine learning software environment for biological sequence analysis developed in collaboration by Net-ID, Inc. and employees at the Danish Center for Biological Sequence Analysis in Copenhagen.

The foundation for the software environment is based on NetLibs, an object-oriented library of C++ classes for graphical modeling, machine learning, and inference developed by Net-ID. The library supports the hierarchical and recursive implementation of any graphical model (NNs, HMMs, Bayesian Networks, etc.) together with general local message-passing algorithms for the propagation of information, errors, and evidence during inferential/learning processes and dynamic programming.

Net-Libs provides, among other things, the foundation, for an HMM simulator and an NN simulator for biological sequence analysis. The easy-to-use graphical interface for both simulators is in Java. The software environment runs both under Unix and NT platforms.

In addition, the software environment contains facilities for manipulating input/output sequences, databases, and files, as well as libraries of trained models. The libraries include HMMs for a number of protein families and DNA elements (promoters, splice sites, exons, etc.) and a number of NNs for the detection of particular structural or functional signals, both in protein and DNA sequences.

For more information please contact: admin@netid.com.

Appendix A

Statistics

A.1 Decision Theory and Loss Functions

In any decision problem [238, 63, 431], one is led to define a loss function (or equivalently a reward function) to measure the effect of one's action on a given state of the environment. The fundamental theorem of decision theory is that under a small set of sensible axioms used to describe rational behavior, the optimal strategy is the one that minimizes the expected loss, where expectation is defined with respect to a Bayesian probabilistic analysis of the uncertain environment, given the available knowledge. Note that several of the tasks undertaken in purely scientific data analysis endeavors—such as data compression, reconstruction, or clustering—are decision-theoretic in nature and therefore require the definition of a loss function. Even prediction falls into this category, and this is why in regression, $E(y|x)$ is the best predictor of y given x, when the loss is quadratic (see below).

When one of the goals is to pick the "best" model, as is often the case throughout this book, the expected loss function is equal to the negative log-likelihood (or log-prior). But in general the two functions are distinct. In principle, for instance, one could even have Gaussian data with quadratic negative log-likelihood, but use a quartic loss function.

Two loss functions f_1 and f_2 can be equivalent in terms of minimization properties. This is the case if there is an order-preserving transformation g (if $u \leq v$, then $g(u) \leq g(v)$) such that $f_2 = gf_1$. Then f_1 and f_2 have the same minima. This of course does not imply that minimization (i.e., learning) algorithms applied to f_1 or f_2 behave in the same way, nor that f_1 and f_2 have the same curvature around their minima. As briefly mentioned in chapter 5, a good example is provided by the quadratic function $f_1(y) = \sum_1^K (p_i - y_i)^2/2$ and the cross-entropic function $f_2(y) = -\sum_1^K p_i \log y_i$, when $\sum p_i = 1$. Both functions are convex in y, and have a unique global minimum at $y_i = p_i$, provided f_2 is restricted to $\sum y_i = 1$. In fact, by Taylor-expanding f_2 around p_i, we have

$$f_2(y) = -\sum_1^K p_i \log(p_i + \epsilon_i) \approx \mathcal{H}(p) + \sum_1^K \frac{\epsilon_i^2}{2p_i} \tag{A.1}$$

with $y_i = p_i + \epsilon_i$ and $\sum \epsilon_i = 0$. Therefore, when $p_i = 1/K$ is uniform, one has the even stronger result that $f_2 \approx \mathcal{H}(p) + Kf_1$. Therefore, apart from constant terms, the quadratic and cross-entropy loss f_1 and f_2 coincide around the same optimum and have the same curvature. In the rest of this appendix, we concentrate on the most common quadratic loss functions (or Gaussian likelihoods), but many of the results can be extended to other loss functions, using the remarks above.

A.2 Quadratic Loss Functions

A.2.1 Fundamental Decomposition

To begin, consider a sequence of numbers $y_1, \ldots, y_K$ and the quadratic form $f(y) = \sum_1^K (y - y_i)^2 / K$, that is the average square loss. Then f has a unique minimum at the average $y^* = E(y) = \sum_1^K y_i / K$. This is easily seen by using Jensen's inequality (appendix B), or more directly by writing

$$
\begin{aligned}
f(y) &= \frac{1}{K} \sum_1^K (y - y^* + y^* - y_i)^2 \\
&= (y - y^*)^2 + \frac{1}{K} \sum_1^K (y^* - y_i)^2 + \frac{2}{K} \sum_1^K (y - y^*)(y^* - y_i) \\
&= (y - y^*)^2 + \frac{1}{K} \sum_1^K (y^* - y_i)^2 \geq f(y^*). \tag{A.2}
\end{aligned}
$$

Thus f can be decomposed into the sum of the bias $(y - y^*)^2$ and the variance $\sum_1^K (y^* - y_i)^2$. The bias measures the distance from y to the optimum average, and the variance measures the dispersion of the y_is around the average. This decomposition of quadratic loss functions into the sum of two quadratic terms (Pythagoras' theorem) with the cancellation of any cross-product terms is essential, and will be used repeatedly below in slightly different forms. The above result remains true if the y_i occur with different frequencies or strengths $p_i \geq 0$, with $\sum p_i = 1$. The expected quadratic loss is again minimized by the the weighted average $y^* = E(y) = \sum p_i y_i$ with the decomposition

$$\mathbf{E}\left[(y - y_i)^2\right] = \sum_1^K p_i(y - y_i)^2 = (y - y^*)^2 + \sum_1^K p_i(y^* - y_i)^2. \qquad (A.3)$$

We now show how this simple decomposition can be applied to regression problems, and in several directions, by using slightly different expectation operators, including averaging over different training sets or different estimators.

A.2.2 Application to Regression

Consider a regression problem in which we are trying to estimate a target function $f(x)$ and in which the x, y data are characterized by a distribution $P(x, y)$. For simplicity, as in chapter 5, we shall assume that as a result of "noise," different possible values of y can be observed for any single x. For any x, the expected error or loss $\mathbf{E}[(y - f(x))^2 | x]$ is minimized by the conditional expectations $y^* = \mathbf{E}(y|x)$, where now all expectations are taken with respect to the distribution P, or approximated from corresponding samples. Again this is easily seen by writing

$$\mathbf{E}\left[(y - f(x))^2|x\right] = \mathbf{E}\left[(y - \mathbf{E}(y|x) + \mathbf{E}(y|x) - f(x))^2|x\right] \qquad (A.4)$$

and expanding the square. The cross-product term disappears, leaving the bias/variance decomposition

$$\mathbf{E}\left[(y - f(x))^2|x\right] = [\mathbf{E}(y|x) - f(x)]^2 + \mathbf{E}\left[(y - \mathbf{E}(y|x))^2|x\right]. \qquad (A.5)$$

A.3 The Bias/Variance Trade-off

Consider the same regression framework as above, but where different training sets D are available. For each training set D, the learning algorithm produces a different estimate $f(x, D)$. The performance of such an estimator can be measured by the expected loss $\mathbf{E}[(y - f(x, D))^2 | x, D]$, the expectation again being with respect to the distribution P. The usual calculation shows that

$$\mathbf{E}\left[(y - f(x, D))^2|x, D\right] =$$

$$[f(x, D) - \mathbf{E}(y|x)]^2 + \mathbf{E}\left[(y - \mathbf{E}(y|x))^2|x, D\right]. \qquad (A.6)$$

The variance term does not depend on the training sample D. Thus, for any x, the effectiveness of the estimator $f(x, D)$ is measured by the bias $[f(x, D) - \mathbf{E}(y|x)]^2$, that is, by how it deviates from the optimal predictor $\mathbf{E}(y|x)$. We can now look at the average of such error over all training sets D of a given size. Again writing

$$\mathbf{E}_D\left[(f(x,D) - \mathbf{E}(y|x))^2\right] =$$

$$\mathbf{E}_D\left[(f(x,D) - \mathbf{E}_D(f(x,D)) + \mathbf{E}_D(f(x,D)) - \mathbf{E}(y|x))^2\right], \quad \text{(A.7)}$$

cancellation of the cross-product term leaves the bias-variance decomposition

$$\mathbf{E}_D\left[(f(x,D) - \mathbf{E}(y|x))^2\right] =$$

$$\left[\mathbf{E}_D(f(x,D)) - \mathbf{E}(y|x)\right]^2 + \mathbf{E}_D\left[(f(x,D) - \mathbf{E}_D(f(x,D)))^2\right]. \quad \text{(A.8)}$$

The bias/variance decomposition corresponds to a sort of uncertainty principle in machine learning: it is always difficult to try to decrease one of the terms without increasing the other. This is also the basic trade-off between underfitting and overfitting the data. A flexible machine with a large number of parameters that can cover a large functional space typically achieves a small bias. The machine, however, must be sensitive to the data and therefore the variance associated with overfitting the data tends to be large. A simple machine has typically a smaller variance, but the price to pay is a larger underfitting bias.

A.4   Combining Estimators

As mentioned in chapter 4, it can be useful at times to combine different estimators $f(x,w)$, using a discrete (or even continuous) distribution $p_w \geq 0$, ($\sum_w p_w = 1$) over parameters w associated with each estimator. As in (A.8), the different estimators could, for example, correspond to different training sets. By taking expectations with respect to w, (A.8) can be generalized immediately to

$$\mathbf{E}_w\left[(f(x,w) - \mathbf{E}(y|x))^2\right] =$$

$$\left[\mathbf{E}_w(f(x,w) - \mathbf{E}(y|x))\right]^2 + \mathbf{E}_w\left[(f(x,w) - \mathbf{E}_w(f(x,w)))^2\right]. \quad \text{(A.9)}$$

Thus the loss for the weighted average predictor $f^*(x) = \mathbf{E}_w(f(x,w))$, sometimes also called ensemble average, is always less than the average loss:

$$\mathbf{E}_w\left[(f(x,w) - \mathbf{E}(y|x))^2\right] \geq \left[f^*(x) - \mathbf{E}(y|x)\right]^2. \quad \text{(A.10)}$$

In fact, we can average (A.9) over all possible xs, using the distribution P to obtain "generalization" errors:

$$\mathbf{E}_X\left[f^*(x) - \mathbf{E}(y|x)\right]^2 =$$

$$\mathbf{E}_X\mathbf{E}_w\left[(f(x,w) - \mathbf{E}(y|x))^2\right] - \mathbf{E}_X\mathbf{E}_w\left[(f(x,w) - f^*(x))^2\right]. \quad \text{(A.11)}$$

This is the relation used in [340, 339]. The left-hand term is the expected loss of the ensemble. The first term on the right-hand side is the expected loss across estimators, and the second term is called the ambiguity. Clearly, combining identical estimators is useless. Thus a necessary condition for the ensemble approach to be useful is that the individual estimators have a substantial level of disagreement. All else equal, the ambiguity should be large. One way to achieve this is to use different training sets for each estimator (see [340], where algorithms for obtaining optimal weighting schemes p_w—for instance, by quadratic programming—are also discussed). One important point is that all the correlations between estimators are contained in the ambiguity term. The ambiguity term does not depend on any target values, and therefore can be estimated from unlabeled data.

A.5 Error Bars

For illustration, consider a modeling situation with one parameter w, and a uniform prior. Let $f(w) = -\log\mathbf{P}(D|w)$ be the negative log-likelihood of the data. Under mild differentiability conditions, a maximum likelihood estimator w^* satisfies $f'(w^*) = 0$. Therefore, in the neighborhood of w^*, we can expand $f(w^*)$ in a Taylor series:

$$f(w) \approx f(w^*) + \frac{1}{2}f''(w^*)(w - w^*)^2 \quad \text{(A.12)}$$

or

$$\mathbf{P}(D|w) = e^{-f(w)} \approx Ce^{-\frac{1}{2}f''(w^*)(w-w^*)^2}, \quad \text{(A.13)}$$

where $C = e^{-f(w^*)}$. Thus the likelihood and the posterior $\mathbf{P}(w|M)$ locally behave like a Gaussian, with a standard deviation $1/\sqrt{f''(w^*)}$, associated with the curvature of f. In the multidimensional case, the matrix of second-order partial derivatives is called the Hessian. Thus the Hessian of the log-likelihood has a geometric interpretation and plays an important role in a number of different questions. It is also called the Fisher information matrix (see also [5, 16, 373]).

A.6   Sufficient Statistics

Many statistical problems can be simplified through the use of *sufficient statistics*. A sufficient statistic for a parameter w is a function of the data that summarize all the available information about w. More formally, consider a random variable X with a distribution parameterized by w. A function S of X is a sufficient statistic for w if the conditional distribution $P(X = x|S(X) = s)$ is independent of w with probability 1. Thus $P(X = x|S(X) = s)$ does not vary with w, or

$$\mathbf{P}(X = x|S = s, w) = \mathbf{P}(X = x|S = s). \tag{A.14}$$

This equality remains true if we replace X by any statistics $H = h(X)$. Equivalently, this equality yields $\mathbf{P}(w|X, S) = \mathbf{P}(w|S)$. All information about w is conveyed by S, and any other statistic is redundant. In particular, sufficient statistics preserve the mutual information I (see appendix B): $I(w, X) = I(w, S(X))$.

As an example, consider a sample $X = (X_1, \ldots, X_N)$ drawn from a random variable $\mathcal{N}(\mu, \sigma^2)$, so that $w = (\mu, \sigma)$. Then (m, s) is a sufficient statistic for w, with $m = \sum_i X_i/N$ and $s^2 = \sum_i (X_i - m)^2/(N - 1)$. In other words, all the information about μ contained in the sample is contained in the sample mean m, and similarly for the variance.

A.7   Exponential Family

The *exponential family* [94] is the most important family of probability distributions. It has a wide range of applications and unique computational properties: many fast algorithms for data analysis have some version of the exponential family at their core. Many general theorems in statistics can be proved for this particular family of parameterized distributions. The density in the one-parameter exponential family has the form

$$\mathbf{P}(x|w) = c(w)h(x)e^{q(w)S(x)}. \tag{A.15}$$

Most common distributions belong to the exponential family, including the normal (with either mean or variance fixed), chi square, binomial and multinomial, geometric and negative binomial, exponential and gamma, beta, Poisson, and Dirichlet distributions. All the distributions used in this book are in the exponential family. Among the important general properties of the exponential family is the fact that a random sample from a distribution in the one-parameter exponential family always has a sufficient statistic S. Furthermore, the sufficient statistic itself has a distribution that belongs to the exponential family.

A.8 Additional Useful Distributions

Here we briefly review three additional continuous distributions used in chapter 12.

A.8.1 The Scaled Inverse Gamma Distribution

The scaled inverse gamma distribution $I(x; \nu, s^2)$ with $\nu > 0$ degrees of freedom and scale $s > 0$ is given by:

$$\frac{(\nu/2)^{\nu/2}}{\Gamma(\nu/2)} s^\nu x^{-(\nu/2+1)} e^{-\nu s^2/(2x)} \tag{A.16}$$

for $x > 0$. The expectation is $(\nu/\nu - 2)s^2$ when $\nu > 2$, otherwise it is infinite. The mode is always $(\nu/\nu + 2)s^2$.

A.8.2 The Student Distribution

The Student-t distribution $t(x; \nu, m, \sigma^2)$ with $\nu > 0$ degrees of freedom, location m and scale $\sigma > 0$ is given by:

$$\frac{\Gamma((\nu+1)/2)}{\Gamma(\nu/2)\sqrt{\nu \pi}\sigma} (1 + \frac{1}{\nu}(\frac{x-m}{\sigma})^2)^{-(\nu+1)/2}. \tag{A.17}$$

The mean and the mode are equal to m.

A.8.3 The Inverse Wishart Distribution

The inverse Wishart distribution $I(W; \nu, S^{-1})$, where ν represents the degrees of freedom and S is a $k \times k$ symmetric, positive definite scale matrix, is given by

$$(2^{\nu k/2}\pi^{k(k-1)/4} \prod_{i=1}^{k} \Gamma(\frac{\nu+1-i}{2}))^{-1}|S|^{\nu/2}|W|^{-(\nu+k+1)/2}$$
$$\exp(-\frac{1}{2}tr(SW^{-1})) \tag{A.18}$$

where W is also positive definite. The expectation of W is $E(W) = (\nu - k - 1)^{-1}S$.

A.9   Variational Methods

To understand this section one must be familiar with the notion of relative entropy (appendix B) . In the Bayesian framework, we are often faced with high–dimensional probability distributions $P(x) = P(x_1,...,x_n)$ that are intractable, in the sense that they are too complex to be estimated exactly. The basic idea in variational methods is to approximate $P(x)$ by constructing a tractable family $Q(x,\theta)$ of distributions parameterized by the vector θ and choosing the element in the family closest to P. This requires a way of measuring distances between probability distributions. In variational methods this is generally done using the relative entropy or KL distance $\mathcal{H}(Q,P)$. Thus we try to minimize

$$\mathcal{H}(Q,P) = \sum Q \log \frac{Q}{P} = -\mathcal{H}(Q) + \mathbf{E}_Q(-\log P). \qquad (A.19)$$

When P is represented as a Boltzmann–Gibbs distribution $P = e^{-\lambda \mathcal{E}}/Z(\lambda)$, then

$$\mathcal{H}(Q,P) = -\mathcal{H}(Q) + \lambda \mathbf{E}_Q(\mathcal{E}) + \log Z(\lambda) = \lambda \mathcal{F} + \log Z(\lambda) \qquad (A.20)$$

where $\mathcal{F}$ is the free energy defined in chapter 3. Since the partition function Z does not depend on θ, minimizing $\mathcal{H}$ is equivalent to minimizing $\mathcal{F}$. From Jensen's inequality in appendix B, we know that, for any approximating Q, $\mathcal{H} \geq 0$ or, equivalently, $\mathcal{F} \geq -\log Z(\lambda)/\lambda$. Equality at the optimum can be achieved only if $Q^* = P$.

In modeling situations we often have a family of models parameterized by w and P is the posterior $\mathbf{P}(w|D)$. Using Bayes' theorem and the equation above, we then have

$$\mathcal{H}(Q,P) = -\mathcal{H}(Q) + \mathbf{E}_Q[-\log \mathbf{P}(D|w) - \log \mathbf{P}(w)] + \log \mathbf{P}(D) \qquad (A.21)$$

with $\lambda = 1$ and $E = -\log \mathbf{P}(D|w) - \log \mathbf{P}(w)$. Again, the approximating distributions must satisfy $\mathcal{H} \geq 0$ or $\mathcal{F} \geq -\log \mathbf{P}(D)$.

In a sense, variational methods are close to higher levels of Bayesian inference since they attempt to approximate the entire distribution $\mathbf{P}(w|D)$ rather than focusing on its mode, as in MAP estimation. At an even higher level, we could look at a distribution over the space Q rather than its optimum Q^*. We leave as an exercise for the reader to study further the position of variational methods within the Bayesian framework and to ask, for instance, whether variational methods themselves can be seen as a form of MAP estimation.

But the fundamental problem in the variational approach is of course the choice of the approximating family $Q(x,\theta)$ or $Q(w,\theta)$. The family must satisfy two conflicting requirements: it must be simple enough to be computationally tractable, but not too simple or else the distance $\mathcal{H}(Q,P)$ remains too large. By computationally tractable we mean that one ought to be able to estimate, for instance, $\mathcal{F}$ and $\partial \mathcal{F}/\partial \theta$. A simple case is when the family Q is factorial. Q is a factorial distribution if and only if it has the functional form $Q(x_1,\ldots,x_n) = Q(x_1)\ldots Q(x_n)$. Mean field theory in statistical mechanics is a special case of variational method with factorial approximation (see also [582]). More generally, the construction of a suitable approximating family Q is problem–dependent and remains an art more than a science. In constructing Q, however, it is often useful to use:

- Mixture distributions

- Exponential distributions

- Independence assumptions and the corresponding factorizations (appendix C).

For instance, Q can be written as a mixture of factorial distributions, where each factor belongs to the exponential family. The parameters to be optimized can then be the mixture coefficients and/or the parameters (mean, variance) of each exponential member.

Appendix B

Information Theory, Entropy, and Relative Entropy

Here we briefly review the most basic concepts of information theory used in this book and in many other machine learning applications. For more in-depth treatments, the reader should consult [483], [71], [137], and [577]. The three most basic concepts and measures of information are the entropy, the mutual information, and the relative entropy. These concepts are essential for the study of how information is transformed through a variety of operations such as information coding, transmission, and compression. The relative entropy is the most general concept, from which the other two can be derived. As in most presentations of information theory, we begin here with the slightly simpler concept of entropy.

B.1 Entropy

The entropy $\mathcal{H}(P)$ of a probability distribution $P = (p_1, \ldots, p_n)$ is defined by

$$\mathcal{H}(P) = \mathbf{E}(-\log P) = -\sum_{i=1}^{n} p_i \log p_i. \tag{B.1}$$

The units used to measure entropy depend on the base used for the logarithms. When the base is 2, the entropy is measured in bits. The entropy measures the prior uncertainty in the outcome of a random experiment described by P, or the information gained when the outcome is observed. It is also the minimum average number of bits (when the logarithms are taken base 2) needed to transmit the outcome in the absence of noise.

357

The concept of entropy can be derived axiomatically. Indeed, consider a random variable X that can assume the values $x_1, \ldots, x_n$ with probabilities $p_1, \ldots, p_n$. The goal is to define a quantity $\mathcal{H}(P) = \mathcal{H}(X) = \mathcal{H}(p_1, \ldots, p_n)$ that measures, in a unique way, the amount of uncertainty represented in this distribution. It is a remarkable fact that three commonsense axioms, really amounting to only one composition law, are sufficient to determine $\mathcal{H}$ uniquely, up to a constant factor corresponding to a choice of scale. The three axioms are as follows:

1. $\mathcal{H}$ is a continuous function of the p_i.

2. If all p_is are equal, then $\mathcal{H}(P) = \mathcal{H}(n) = \mathcal{H}(1/n, \ldots, 1/n)$ is a monotonic increasing function of n.

3. Composition law: Group all the events x_i into k disjoint classes. Let A_i represent the indices of the events associated with the ith class, so that $q_i = \sum_{j \in A_i} p_j$ represents the corresponding probability. Then

$$\mathcal{H}(P) = \mathcal{H}(Q) + \sum_{i=1}^{k} q_i \mathcal{H}\left(\frac{\bar{P}_i}{q_i}\right), \tag{B.2}$$

where $\bar{P}_i$ denotes the set of probabilities p_j for $j \in A_i$. Thus, for example, the composition law states that by grouping the first two events into one,

$$\mathcal{H}(1/3, 1/6, 1/2) = \mathcal{H}(1/2, 1/2) + \frac{1}{2}\mathcal{H}(2/3, 1/3). \tag{B.3}$$

From the first condition, it is sufficient to determine $\mathcal{H}$ for all rational cases where $p_i = n_i/n$, $i = 1, \ldots, n$. But from the second and third conditions,

$$\mathcal{H}\left(\sum_{i=1}^{n} n_i\right) = \mathcal{H}(p_1, \ldots, p_n) + \sum_{i=1}^{n} p_i \mathcal{H}(n_i). \tag{B.4}$$

For example,

$$\mathcal{H}(9) = \mathcal{H}(3/9, 4/9, 2/9) + \frac{3}{9}\mathcal{H}(3) + \frac{4}{9}\mathcal{H}(4) + \frac{2}{9}\mathcal{H}(2). \tag{B.5}$$

In particular, by setting all n_i equal to m, from (B.4) we get

$$\mathcal{H}(m) + \mathcal{H}(n) = \mathcal{H}(mn). \tag{B.6}$$

This yields the unique solution

$$\mathcal{H}(n) = C \ln n, \tag{B.7}$$

with $C > 0$. By substituting in (B.4), we finally have

$$\mathcal{H}(P) = -C \sum_{i=1}^{n} p_i \log p_i. \tag{B.8}$$

The constant C determines the base of the logarithm. Base-2 logarithms lead to a measure of entropy and information in bits. For most mathematical calculations, however, we use natural logarithms so that $C = 1$.

It is not very difficult to verify that the entropy has the following properties:

- $\mathcal{H}(P) \geq 0$.

- $\mathcal{H}P|Q) \leq \mathcal{H}(P)$ with equality if and only if P and Q are independent.

- $\mathcal{H}(P_1, \ldots, P_n) \leq \sum_{i=1}^{n} \mathcal{H}(P_i)$ with equality if and only if P and Q are independent.

- $\mathcal{H}(P)$ is convex ($\cap$) in P.

- $\mathcal{H}(P_1, \ldots, P_n) = \sum_{i=1}^{n} \mathcal{H}(P_i|P_{i-1}, \ldots, P_1)$.

- $\mathcal{H}(P) \leq \mathcal{H}(n)$ with equality if and only if P is uniform.

B.2   Relative Entropy

The relative entropy between two distributions $P = (p_1, \ldots, p_n)$ and $Q = (q_1, \ldots, q_n)$, or the associated random variables X and Y, is defined by

$$\mathcal{H}(P, Q) = \mathcal{H}(X, Y) = \sum_{i=1}^{n} p_i \log \frac{p_i}{q_i}. \tag{B.9}$$

The relative entropy is also called cross-entropy, or Kullback–Liebler distance, or discrimination (see [486], and references therein, for an axiomatic presentation of the relative entropy). It is viewed as a measure of the distance between P and Q. The more dissimilar P and Q are, the larger the relative entropy. The relative entropy is also the amount of information that a measurement gives about the truth of a hypothesis compared with an alternative hypothesis. It is also the expected value of the log-likelihood ratio. Strictly speaking, the relative entropy is not symmetric and therefore is not a distance. It can be made symmetric by using the divergence $\mathcal{H}(P, Q) + \mathcal{H}(Q, P)$. But in most cases, the symmetric version is not needed. If $U = (1/n, \ldots, 1/n)$ denotes the uniform density, then $\mathcal{H}(P, U) = \log n - \mathcal{H}(P)$. In this sense, the entropy is a special case of cross-entropy.

By using the Jensen inequality (see section B.4), it is easy to verify the following two important properties of relative entropies:

- $\mathcal{H}(P,Q) \geq 0$ with equality if and only if $P = Q$.

- $\mathcal{H}(P,Q)$ is convex ($\cap$) in P and Q.

These properties are used throughout the sections on free energy in statistical mechanics and the EM algorithm in chapters 3 and 4.

B.3 Mutual Information

The third concept for measuring information is the mutual information. Consider two distributions P and Q associated with a joint distribution R over the product space. The mutual information $\mathcal{I}(P,Q)$ is the relative entropy between the joint distribution R and the product of the marginals P and Q:

$$\mathcal{I}(P,Q) = \mathcal{H}(R,PQ). \tag{B.10}$$

As such, it is always positive. When R is factorial, i.e. equal to the product of the marginals, the mutual information is 0. The mutual information is a special case of relative entropy. Likewise, the entropy (or self-entropy) is a special case of mutual information because $\mathcal{H}(P) = \mathcal{I}(P,P)$. Furthermore, the mutual information satisfies the following properties:

- $\mathcal{I}(P,Q) = 0$ if and only if P and Q are independent.

- $\mathcal{I}(P_1,\ldots,P_n,Q) = \sum_{i=1}^{n} \mathcal{I}(P_i,Q|P_1,\ldots,P_{i-1})$.

It is easy to understand mutual information in Bayesian terms: it represents the reduction in uncertainty of one variable when the other is observed, that is between the *prior* and *posterior distributions*. If we denote two random variables by X and Y, the uncertainty in X is measured by the entropy of its prior $\mathcal{H}(X) = \sum_x \mathbf{P}(X = x) \log \mathbf{P}(X = x)$. Once we observe $Y = y$, the uncertainty in X is the entropy of the posterior distribution, $\mathcal{H}(X|Y = y) = \sum_x \mathbf{P}(X = x|Y = y) \log \mathbf{P}(X = x|Y = y)$. This is a random variable that depends on the observation y. Its average over the possible ys is called the *conditional entropy*:

$$\mathcal{H}(X|Y) = \sum_y P(y)\mathcal{H}(X|Y = y). \tag{B.11}$$

Therefore the difference between the entropy and the conditional entropy measures the average information that an observation of Y brings about X. It is straightforward to check that

$$\mathcal{I}(X,Y) = \mathcal{H}(X) - \mathcal{H}(X|Y) =$$

$$\mathcal{H}(Y) - \mathcal{H}(Y|X) = \mathcal{H}(X) + \mathcal{H}(Y) - \mathcal{H}(Z) = \mathcal{I}(Y,X) \qquad \text{(B.12)}$$

where $\mathcal{H}(Z)$ is the entropy of the joint variable $Z = (X,Y)$. or, using the corresponding distributions,

$$\mathcal{I}(P,Q) = \mathcal{H}(P) - \mathcal{H}(P|Q) =$$

$$\mathcal{H}(Q) - \mathcal{H}(Q|P) = \mathcal{H}(P) + \mathcal{H}(Q) - \mathcal{H}(R) = \mathcal{I}(Q,P). \qquad \text{(B.13)}$$

We leave for the reader to draw the classical Venn diagram associated with these relations.

B.4 Jensen's Inequality

The Jensen inequality is used many times throughout this book. If a function f is convex ($\cap$) and X is a random variable, then

$$\mathbf{E}f(X) \le f\mathbf{E}(X). \qquad \text{(B.14)}$$

Furthermore, if f is strictly convex, equality implies that X is constant. This inequality becomes graphically obvious if one thinks in terms of center of gravity. The center of gravity of $f(x_1),\dots,f(x_n)$ is below $f(x^*)$, where x^* is the center of gravity of $x_1,\dots,x_n$. As a special important case, $\mathbf{E}\log X \le \log \mathbf{E}(X)$. This immediately yields the properties of the relative entropy.

B.5 Maximum Entropy

The maximum entropy principle was discussed in chapters 2 and 3 for the case of discrete distributions. The precise statement of the maximum entropy principle in the continuous case requires some care [282]. But in any case, if we define the *differential entropy* of a random variable X with density P to be

$$\mathcal{H}(X) = - \int_{-\infty}^{+\infty} P(x) \log P(x) dx, \qquad \text{(B.15)}$$

then of all the densities with variance σ^2, the Gaussian $\mathcal{N}(\mu,\sigma)$ is the one with the largest differential entropy. The differential entropy of a Gaussian distribution with any mean and variance σ^2 is given by $[\log 2\pi e\sigma^2]/2$. In n dimensions, consider a random vector X with vector mean μ, covariance matrix C, and density P. Then the differential entropy of P satisfies

$$\mathcal{H}(P) \le \frac{1}{2} \log(2\pi e)^n |C| = \mathcal{H}(\mathcal{N}(\mu,C)) \qquad \text{(B.16)}$$

with equality if and only if X is distributed according to $\mathcal{N}(\mu, C)$ almost everywhere. Here $|C|$ denotes the determinant of C.

These results have a very simple proof using the derivation of the Boltzmann–Gibbs distribution in statistical mechanics. For instance, in the one-dimensional case, a Gaussian distribution can be seen as a Boltzmann–Gibbs distribution with energy $\mathcal{E}(x) = (x - \mu)^2 / 2\sigma^2$ and partition function $\sqrt{2\pi}\sigma$, at temperature 1. Thus the Gaussian distribution must have maximum entropy, given that the only constraint is the observation of the expectation of the energy. The mean of the energy is given by $\int (x - \mu)^2 / 2\sigma^2 P(x)dx$, which is constant, equivalent to the statement that the standard deviation is constant and equal to σ.

This can be generalized to the members of the exponential family of distributions. In the case of the Dirichlet distributions, consider the space of all n-dimensional distributions $P = (p_1, \ldots, p_n)$. Suppose that we are given a fixed distribution $R = (r_1, \ldots, r_n)$, and define the energy of a distributions by its distance, measured in relative entropy, from R:

$$\mathcal{E}(P) = \mathcal{H}(R, P) = \sum_i r_i \log r_i - \sum_i r_i \log p_i. \tag{B.17}$$

If all we observe is the average D of $\mathcal{E}$, then the corresponding maximum entropy distribution for P is the Boltzmann–Gibbs distribution

$$\mathbf{P}(P) = \frac{e^{-\lambda \mathcal{E}}}{Z} = \frac{e^{-\lambda \mathcal{H}(R,P)}}{Z} = \frac{e^{\lambda \mathcal{H}(R)} \prod_i p_i^{\lambda r_i}}{Z(\lambda, R)}, \tag{B.18}$$

where λ is the temperature, which depends on the value D of the average energy. Now, if we let $\alpha = \lambda + n$ and $q_i = (\lambda r_i + 1)/(\lambda + n)$, this distribution is in fact the Dirichlet distribution $\mathcal{D}_{\alpha Q}(P)$ with parameters α and Q (note that $\alpha \geq 0$, $q_i \geq 0$, and $\sum_i q_i = 1$). If r_i is uniform, then q_i is also uniform. Thus any Dirichlet distribution can be seen as the result of a MaxEnt calculation.

B.6 Minimum Relative Entropy

The minimum relative entropy principle [486] states that if a prior distribution Q is given, then one should choose a distribution P that satisfies all the constraints of the problem and minimizes the relative entropy $\mathcal{H}(P, Q)$. The MaxEnt principle is obviously a special case of the minimum relative entropy principle, when Q is uniform. As stated, the minimum relative entropy principle is a principle for finding posterior distributions, or for selecting a praticular class of priors. But the proper theory for finding posterior distributions is the Bayesian theory, and therefore the minimum relative entropy principle (or

MaxEnt) cannot have any universal value. In fact, there are known examples where MaxEnt seems to give the "wrong" answer [229]. Thus, in our view, it is unlikely that a general principle exists for the determination of priors. Or if such a principle is really desirable, it should be that the most basic prior of any model should be uniform. In other words, in any modeling effort there is an underlying hierarchy of priors, and priors at the zero level of the hierarchy should always be uniform in a canonical way. It is instructive to look in detail at the cases where the minimum relative entropy principle yields the same result as a Bayesian MAP estimation (see chapter 3).

Appendix C

Probabilistic Graphical Models

C.1 Notation and Preliminaries

In this appendix, we review the basic theory of probabilistic graphical models [557, 348] and the corresponding factorization of high-dimensional probability distributions. First, a point of notation. If X and Y are two independent random variables, we write $X \perp Y$. Conditional independence on Z is denoted by $X \perp Y | Z$. This means that $\mathbf{P}(X, Y | Z) = \mathbf{P}(X | Z)\mathbf{P}(Y | Z)$. It is important to note that conditional independence implies neither marginal independence nor the converse. By $G = (V, E)$ denote a graph with a set V of vertices and a set E of edges. The vertices are numbered $V = \{1, 2, ..., n\}$. If the edges are directed, we write $G = (V, \vec{E})$. In all the graphs to be considered, there is at most one edge between any two vertices, and there are no edges from a vertex to itself. In an undirected graph, $N(i)$ represents the sets of all the neighbors of vertex i and $C(i)$ represents the set of all the vertices that are connected to i by a path. So,

$$N(i) = \{j \in V : (i, j) \in E\}. \tag{C.1}$$

If there is an edge between any pair of vertices, a graph is said to be *complete*. The *cliques* of G are the subgraphs of G that are both complete and maximal. The *clique graph* G^C of a graph G is the graph consisting of a vertex for each clique in G, and an edge between two vertices, if and only if the corresponding cliques have a nonempty intersection.

In a directed graph, the direction of the edges will often represent causality or time irreversibility. We use the obvious notation $N^-(i)$ and $N^+(i)$ to denote all the parents of i and all the children of i, respectively. Likewise, $C^-(i)$ and $C^+(i)$ denote the ancestors, or the "past," and the descendants of i, or the "future," of i. All these notations are extended in the obvious way to any set of vertices I. So for any $I \in V$,

$$N(I) = \{j \in V : i \in I \quad \text{and} \quad (i, j) \in E\} - I. \tag{C.2}$$

This is also called the boundary of I. In an undirected graph, a set of vertices I is *separated* from a set J by a set K if and only if I and J are disjoint and any path from any vertex in I to any vertex in J contains a vertex in K.

We are interested in high-dimensional probability distributions of the form $\mathbf{P}(X_1, ..., X_n)$, where the X variables represent both hidden and observed variables. In particular, we are interested in the factorization of such distributions into products of simpler distributions, such as conditionals and marginals. Obviously, it is possible to describe the joint distribution using the marginals

$$\mathbf{P}(X_1, ..., X_n) = \prod_{i=0}^{n-1} \mathbf{P}(X_{i+1} | X_1, ..., X_i). \tag{C.3}$$

The set of complete conditional distributions $\mathbf{P}(X_i | X_j : j \neq i)$ also defines the joint distribution in a unique way, *provided they are consistent* (or else no joint distribution can be defined) [68, 20]. The complete set of marginals $\mathbf{P}(X_i)$ is in general highly insufficient to define the joint distribution, except in special cases (see factorial distributions below). The problem of determining a multivariate joint distribution uniquely from an arbitrary set of marginal and conditional distributions is examined in [198]. As we shall see, graphical models correspond to joint distributions that can be expressed economically in terms of local conditionals, or joint distributions over small clusters of variables. Probabilistic inference in such models allows one to approximate useful probabilities, such as posteriors. A number of techniques are typically used to carry inference approximations, including probability propagation, Monte Carlo methods, statistical mechanics, variational methods, and inverse models.

For technical reasons [557], we assume that $\mathbf{P}(X_1, ..., X_n)$ is positive everywhere, which is not restrictive for practical applications because rare events can be assigned very small but nonzero probabilities. We consider graphs of the form $G = (V, E)$, or $G = (V, \vec{E})$, where each variable X_i is associated with the corresponding vertex i. We let X_I denote the set of variables $X_i : i \in I$, associated with a set I of indices. For a fixed graph G, we will denote by $\mathcal{P}(G)$ a family of probability distributions satisfying a set of independence assumptions embodied in the connectivity of G. Roughly speaking, the absence of an edge signifies the existence of an independence relationship. These independence relationships are defined precisely in the next two sections, in the two main cases of undirected and directed graphs. In modeling situations, the real probability distribution may not belong to the set $\mathcal{P}(G)$, for any G. The goal then is to find a G and a member of $\mathcal{P}(G)$ as close as possible to the real distribution—for instance, in terms of relative entropy.

C.2 The Undirected Case: Markov Random Fields

In the undirected case, the family $\mathcal{P}(G)$ corresponds to the notion of Markov random field, or Markov network, or probabilistic independence network, or, in a slightly different context, Boltzmann machine [272, 2]. Symmetric interaction models are typically used in statistical mechanics—for example, Ising models and image processing [199, 392], where associations are considered to be more correlational than causal.

C.2.1 Markov Properties

A Markov random field on a graph G is characterized by any one of the following three equivalent Markov independence properties. The equivalence of these properties is remarkable, and its proof is left as an exercise.

1. **Pairwise Markov Property.** Nonneighboring pairs X_i and X_j are independent, conditional on all the other variables. That is, for any $(i, j) \notin E$,

$$X_i \perp X_j | X_{V-\{i,j\}}. \tag{C.4}$$

2. **Local Markov Property.** Conditional on its neighbors, any variable X_i is independent of all the other variables. That is, for any i in V,

$$X_i \perp X_{V-N(i)\cup\{i\}} | X_{N(i)}. \tag{C.5}$$

3. **Global Markov Property.** If I and J are two disjoint sets of vertices, separated by K, the corresponding set of variables is independent conditional on the variables in the third set:

$$X_I \perp X_J | X_K. \tag{C.6}$$

These independence properties are equivalent to the statement

$$\mathbf{P}(X_i | X_{V-\{i\}}) = \mathbf{P}(X_i | X_{N(i)}). \tag{C.7}$$

C.2.2 Factorization Properties

The functions $\mathbf{P}(X_i | X_j : j \in N(i))$ are called the *local characteristics* of the Markov random field. It can be shown that they uniquely determine the global distribution $\mathbf{P}(X_1, ..., X_n)$, although in a complex way. In particular, and unlike what happens in the directed case, the global distribution is not the product of all the local characteristics. There is, however, an important theorem that relates Markov random fields to Boltzmann–Gibbs distributions. It can be shown that, as a result of the local independence property, the global distribution of a Markov random field has the functional form

$$\mathbf{P}(X_1, ..., X_n) = \frac{e^{-f(X_1, ..., X_n)}}{Z} = \frac{e^{-\sum_C f_C(X_C)}}{Z}, \tag{C.8}$$

where Z is the usual normalizing factor. C runs over all the cliques of G, and f_C is called the *potential* or clique function of clique C. It depends only on the variables X_C occurring in the corresponding clique. f is also called the energy. In fact, $\mathbf{P}$ and G determine a Markov random field if and only if (C.8) holds [500].

It is easy to derive the local characteristics and marginals from the potential clique functions by applying the definition in combination with the Boltzmann–Gibbs representation. The potential functions, on the other hand, are not unique. The determination of a set of potential functions in the general case is more elaborate. But there are formulas to derive the potential functions from the local characteristics. There is an important special case that is particularly simple. This is when the graph G is *triangulated*. A graph G is triangulated if any cycle of length greater than or equal to 4 contains at least one chord. A singly connected graph (i.e. a tree) is an important special case of a triangulated graph. A graph is triangulated if and only if its clique graph has a special property called the *running intersection* property, which states that if a vertex of G belongs to two cliques C_1 and C_2 of G, it must also belong to all the other cliques on a path from C_1 to C_2 in the clique graph G^C. The intersection of two neighboring cliques C_1 and C_2 of G—that is, two adjacent nodes of G^C—is called a *separator*. In a triangulated graph, a separator of C_1 and C_2 separates them in the probabilistic independence sense defined above.

Another important characterization of triangulated graphs is in terms of *perfect numbering*. A numbering of the nodes in V is perfect if for all i, $N(i) \cap \{1, 2, ..., i-1\}$ is complete. A graph is triangulated if and only if it admits a perfect numbering (see [512], [350], and references therein).] The key point here is that for Markov random fields associated with a triangulated graph, the global distribution has the form

$$\mathbf{P}(X_1, ..., X_n) = \frac{\prod_C \mathbf{P}(X_C)}{\prod_S \mathbf{P}(X_S)}, \tag{C.9}$$

where C runs over the cliques and S runs over the separators, occurring in a *junction tree*, that is, a maximal spanning tree of G^C. $\prod_C \mathbf{P}(X_C)$ is the marginal joint distribution of X_C. The clique potential functions are then obvious.

A very special case of the Markov random field is when the graph G has no edges. This is the case when all the variables X_i are independent and $\mathbf{P}(X_1, ..., X_n) = \prod_{i=1}^n \mathbf{P}(X_i)$. Such joint distributions or Markov random fields are called *factorial*. Given a multivariate joint distribution P, it is easy to see that among all factorial distributions, the one that is closest to P in relative entropy is the product of the marginals of P.

C.3   The Directed Case: Bayesian Networks

In the directed case, the family $\mathcal{P}(G)$ corresponds to the notions of Bayesian networks, belief networks, directed independence probabilistic networks, directed Markov fields, causal networks, influence diagrams, and even Markov meshes [416, 557, 121, 106, 286, 246] (see [322] for a simple molecular biology illustration). As already mentioned, the direction on the edges usually represents causality or time irreversibility. Such models are common, for instance, in the design of expert systems.

In the directed case, we have a directed graph $G = (V, \vec{E})$. The graph is also assumed to be *acyclic*, that is, with no directed cycles. This is because it is not possible to consistently define the joint probability of the variables in a cycle from the product of the local conditioning probabilities. That is, in general the product $\mathbf{P}(X_2|X_1)\mathbf{P}(X_3|X_2)\mathbf{P}(X_1|X_3)$ does not consistently define a distribution on X_1, X_2, X_3. An acyclic directed graph represents a partial ordering. In particular, it is possible to number its vertices so that if there is an edge from i to j, then $i < j$. In other words, the partial ordering associated with the edges is consistent with the numbering. This ordering is also called a topological sort. We will assume that such an ordering has been chosen whenever necessary, so that, the past of i $C^-(i)$ is included in $\{1, 2, ..., i - 1\}$, and the future $C^+(i)$ is included in $\{i + 1, ..., n\}$. The *moral* of $G = (V, \vec{E})$ is the undirected graph $G^M = (V, E + M)$ obtained by removing the direction on the edges of G and by adding an edge between any two nodes that are parents of the same child in G (if they are not already connected, of course). The term "moral" was introduced in [350] and refers to the fact that all parents are "married." We can now describe the Markov independence properties of graphical models with an underlying acyclic directed graph.

C.3.1   Markov Properties

A Bayesian network on a directed acyclic graph G is characterized by any one of a number of equivalent independence properties. In all cases, the basic

Markov idea in the directed case is that, conditioned on the present, the future is independent of the past or, equivalently, that in order to predict the future, all the relevant information is assumed to be in the present.

Pairwise Markov Property

Nonneighboring pairs X_i and X_j with $i < j$ are independent, conditional on all the other variables in the past of j. That is, for any $(i, j) \notin \vec{E}$ and $i < j$,

$$X_i \perp X_j | X_{C^-(j)-\{i\}}. \tag{C.10}$$

In fact, one can replace $C^-(j)$ with the larger set $\{1, ..., j-1\}$. Another equivalent statement is that, conditional on a set of nodes I, X_i is independent of X_j if and only if i and j are *d-separated*, that is, if there is no d-connecting path from i to j [121]. A d-connecting path from i to j is defined as follows. Consider a node k on a path from i to j. The node k is called linear, divergent, or convergent, depending on whether the two edges adjacent to it on the path are incoming and outgoing, both outgoing, or both incoming. The path from i to j is d-connecting with respect to I if and only if every interior node k on the path is either (1) linear or diverging and not a member of I, or (2) converging, and $[k \cup C^+(k)] \cap I \neq \varnothing$. Intuitively, i and j are d-connected if and only if either (1) there is a causal path between them or (2) there is evidence in I that renders the two nodes correlated with each other.

Local Markov Property

Conditional on its parents, a variable X_i is independent of all other nodes, except for its descendants. Thus

$$X_i \perp X_j | X_{N^-(i)}, \tag{C.11}$$

as long as $j \notin C^+(i)$ and $j \neq i$.

Global Markov Property

If I and J are two disjoint sets of vertices, we say that K separates I and J in the directed graph G if and only if K separates I and J in the moral undirected graph of the smallest ancestral set containing I, J, and K [349]. With this notion of separation, the global Markov property is the same—that is, if K separates I and J,

$$X_I \perp X_J | X_K. \tag{C.12}$$

It can be also be shown [557] that the directed graph G satisfies all the Markov independence relationships of the associated moral graph G^M. The converse is not true in general, unless G^M is obtained from G by removing edge orientation only, that is, without any marriages. Finally, any one of the three Markov independence properties is equivalent to the statement

$$\mathbf{P}(X_i|X_{C^-(i)}) = \mathbf{P}(X_i|X_{N^-(i)}).\qquad\text{(C.13)}$$

In fact, $C^-(i)$ can be replaced by the larger set $\{1,...,i-1\}$.

C.3.2 Factorization Properties

It is not difficult to see, as a result, that the unilateral local characteristics $\mathbf{P}(X_i|X_{N^-(i)})$ are consistent with one another, and in fact uniquely determine a Bayesian network on a given graph. Indeed, we have

$$\mathbf{P}(X_1,...,X_n) = \prod_i \mathbf{P}(X_i|X_{N^-(i)}).\qquad\text{(C.14)}$$

This property is fundamental. The local conditional probabilities can be specified in terms of lookup tables, although this is often impractical due to the size of the tables. A number of more compact but also less general representations are often used, such as noisy OR- [416] or NN-style representations, such as sigmoidal belief networks [395] for binary variables, where the characteristics are defined by local connection weights and sigmoidal functions, or the obvious generalization to multivalued variables using normalized exponentials. Having a local NN at each vertex to compute the local characteristics is another example of hybrid model parameterization.

C.3.3 Learning and Propagation

There are several levels of learning in graphical models in general and Bayesian networks in particular, from learning the graph structure itself to learning the local conditional distributions from the data. With the exception of section C.3.6, these will not be discussed here; reviews and pointers to the literature can be found in [106, 246]. Another fundamental operation with Bayesian networks is the propagation of evidence, that is, the updating of the probabilities of each X_i conditioned on the observed node variables. Evidence propagation is NP-complete in the general case [135]. But for singly connected graphs (no more than one path between any two nodes in the underlying undirected graph), propagation can be executed in time linear with n, the number of nodes, using a simple message-passing approach [416, 4]. In the general case, all known exact algorithms for multiply connected networks rely on the construction of an equivalent singly connected network, the junction tree, by clustering the original variables, according to the cliques of the corresponding triangulated moral graph ([416, 350, 467], with refinements in [287]).

A similar algorithm for the estimation of the most probable configuration of the variables X_i is given in [145]. Schachter et al. [468] show that all the known exact inference algorithms are equivalent in some sense to the algorithms in [287] and [145]. An important conjecture, supported both by emprirical evidence and results in coding theory, is that the simple message-passing algorithm of [416] yields reasonably good approximations in the multiply connected case (see [385] for details).

C.3.4   Generality

It is worth noting that the majority of models used in this book can be viewed as instances of Bayesian networks. Artificial feed-forward NNs are Bayesian networks in which the local conditional probability functions are delta functions. Likewise, HMMs and Markov systems in general have a very simple Bayesian network representation. In fact, HMMs are a special case of both Markov random fields and Bayesian networks. We leave as a useful exercise for the reader to derive these representations, as well as the Bayesian network representation of many other concepts such as mixtures, hierarchical priors, Kalman filters and other state space models, and so on. The generality of the Bayesian network representation is at the root of many new classes of models currently under investigation. This is the case for several generalizations of HMMs, such as input-output HMMs (see chapter 9), tree-structured HMMs [293], and factorial HMMs [205].

When the general Bayesian network propagation algorithms are applied in special cases, one "rediscovers" well-known algorithms. For instance, in the case of HMMs, one obtains the usual forward–backward and Viterbi algorithms directly from Pearl's algorithm [493]. The same is true of several algorithms in coding theory (turbo codes, Gallager–Tanner–Wiberg decoding) and in the theory of Kalman filters (the Rauch–Tung–Streibel smoother), and even of certain combinatorial algorithms (fast Fourier transform) [4, 204]. We suspect that the inside–outside algorithm for context-free grammar is also a special case, although we have not checked carefully. While belief propagation in general remains NP-complete, approximate algorithms can often be derived using Monte Carlo methods such as Gibbs sampling [210, 578], and variational methods such as mean field theory (appendix A and [465, 276, 204]), sometimes leveraging the particular structure of a network. Gibbs sampling is particularly attractive for Bayesian networks because of its simplicity and generality.

C.3.5 Gibbs Sampling

Assuming that we observe the values of the variables associated with some of the visible nodes, we want to sample the value of any other node i according to its conditional probability, given all the other variables. From the factorization (C.14), we have

$$\mathbf{P}(X_i|X_{V-\{i\}}) = \frac{\mathbf{P}(X_V)}{\mathbf{P}(X_{V-\{i\}})} = \frac{\prod_j \mathbf{P}(X_j|X_{N^-(j)})}{\sum_{x_i} \mathbf{P}(X_1,\ldots,X_i = x_i,\ldots,X_n)}, \tag{C.15}$$

which yields, after simplifications of common numerator and denominator terms,

$$\mathbf{P}(X_i|X_{V-\{i\}}) = \frac{\mathbf{P}(X_i|X_{N^-(i)}) \prod_{j\in N^+(i)} \mathbf{P}(X_j|X_{N^-(j)})}{\sum_{x_i} \mathbf{P}(X_i = x_i|N^-(i)) \prod_{j\in N^+(i)} \mathbf{P}(X_j|X_{N^-(j)})}. \tag{C.16}$$

As expected, the conditional distributions needed for Gibbs sampling are local and depend only on i, its parents, and its children. Posterior estimates can then be obtained by averaging simple counts at each node, which requires very little memory. Additional precision may be obtained by averaging the *probabilities* at each node (see [396] for a partial discussion). As in any Gibbs sampling situation, important issues are the duration of the procedure (or repeated procedure, if the sampler is used for multiple runs) and the discarding of the initial samples ("burn-in"), which can be nonrepresentative of the equilibrium distribution.

C.3.6 Sleep–Wake Algorithm and Helmholtz Machines

A theoretically interesting, but not necessarily practical, learning algorithm for the conditional distributions of a particular class of Bayesian networks is described in [255, 146]. These Bayesian networks consist of two inverse models: the recognition network and the generative network. Starting from the input layer, the recognition network has a feed-forward layered architecture. The nodes in all the hidden layers correspond to stochastic binary variables, but more general versions—for instance, with multivalued units—are possible. The local conditional distributions are implemented in NN style, using combinational weights and sigmoidal logistic functions. The probability that unit i is on is given by

$$\mathbf{P}(X_i = 1) = \frac{1}{1 + e^{-\sum_{k\in N^-(i)} w_{ik}x_k + b_i^l}}, \tag{C.17}$$

where x_k denotes the states of the nodes in the previous layer. The generative network mirrors the recognition network. It is a feed-forward layered network that begins with the top hidden layer of the recognition network and ends up with the input layer. It uses the same units but with a reverse set of connections. These reverse connections introduce local loops so the combined architecture is not acyclic. This is not significant, however, because the networks are used in alternation rather than simultaneously.

The sleep–wake algorithm, named after its putative biological interpretation, is an unsupervised learning algorithm for the forward and backward connection weights. The algorithm alternates between two phases. During each phase, the unit activities in one of the networks are used as local targets to train the weights in the opposite network, using the delta rule. During the wake phase, the recognition network is activated and each generative weight w_{jk} is updated by

$$\Delta w_{jk} = \eta x_k (x_j - p_j), \tag{C.18}$$

where x_j represents the state of unit j in the recognition network and p_j the corresponding probability calculated as in (C.17), using the generative connections. A symmetric update rule is used during the sleep phase, where the fantasies (dreams) produced by the generative network are used to modify the recognition weights [255, 574].

Appendix D

HMM Technicalities, Scaling, Periodic Architectures, State Functions, and Dirichlet Mixtures

D.1   Scaling

As already pointed out, the probabilities $\mathbf{P}(\pi|O, w)$ are typically very small, beyond machine precision, and so are the forward variables $\alpha_i(t)$, as t increases. A similar observation can be made for the backward variables $\beta_i(t)$, as t decreases. One solution for this problem is to scale the forward and backward variables at time t by a suitable coefficient that depends only on t. The scalings on the αs and βs are defined in a complementary way so that the learning equations remain essentially invariant under scaling. We now give the exact equations for scaling the forward and backward variables, along the lines described in [439].[1] For simplicity, throughout this section, we consider an HMM with emitting states only. We leave as an exercise for the reader to adapt the equations to the general case where delete states are also present.

---

[1] The scaling equations in [439] contain a few errors. A correction sheet is available from the author.

D.1.1 Scaling of Forward Variables

More precisely, we define the scaled variables thus:

$$\hat{\alpha}_i(t) = \frac{\alpha_i(t)}{\sum_j \alpha_j(t)}. \tag{D.1}$$

At time 0, for any state i, we have $\alpha_i(0) = \hat{\alpha}_i(0)$. The scaled variables $\hat{\alpha}_i(t)$ can be computed recursively by alternating a propagation step with a scaling step. Let $\hat{\hat{\alpha}}_i(t)$ represent the propagated $\hat{\alpha}_i(t)$ before scaling. Assuming that all variables have been computed up to time $t - 1$, we first propagate $\hat{\alpha}_i$ by (7.5):

$$\hat{\hat{\alpha}}_i(t) = \sum_{j \in N^-(i)} \hat{\alpha}_j(t-1) t_{ij} e_{iX^t}, \tag{D.2}$$

with $\hat{\hat{\alpha}}_i(0) = \alpha_i(0)$. The same remarks as for the propagation of the $\alpha_i(t)$ apply here. Therefore, using (D.1),

$$\hat{\hat{\alpha}}_i(t) = \frac{\alpha_i(t)}{\sum_j \alpha_j(t-1)}. \tag{D.3}$$

We then scale the $\hat{\hat{\alpha}}(t)$s, which by (D.3) is equivalent to scaling the αs:

$$\frac{\hat{\hat{\alpha}}_i(t)}{\sum_j \hat{\hat{\alpha}}_j(t)} = \frac{\alpha_i(t)}{\sum_j \alpha_j(t)} = \hat{\alpha}_i(t). \tag{D.4}$$

This requires computing at each time step the scaling coefficient $c(t) = \sum_i \hat{\hat{\alpha}}_i(t)$. From (D.3), the relation between $c(t)$ and the scaling coefficent $C(t) = \sum_i \alpha_i(t)$ of the αs is given by:

$$C(t) = \prod_{\tau=1}^{t} c(\tau). \tag{D.5}$$

D.1.2 Scaling of Backward Variables

The scaling of the backward variables is slightly different, in that the scaling factors are computed from the forward propagation rather than from the βs. In particular, this implies that the forward propagation must be completed in order for the backward propagation to begin. Specifically, we define the scaled

$$\hat{\beta}_i(t) = \frac{\beta_i(t)}{D(t)}. \tag{D.6}$$

The scaling coefficient is defined to be

$$D(t) = \prod_{\tau=t}^{T} c(\tau). \tag{D.7}$$

The reason for this choice will become apparent below. Assuming all variables have been computed backward to time $t + 1$, the $\hat{\beta}$s are first propagated backward using (7.10) to yield the variables

$$\hat{\hat{\beta}}_i(t) = \sum_{j \in N^+(i)} \hat{\beta}_j(t + 1) t_{ji} e_{jx^{t+1}}. \tag{D.8}$$

The $\hat{\hat{\beta}}_i(t)$ are then scaled by $c(t)$, to yield

$$\hat{\beta}_i(t) = \frac{\hat{\hat{\beta}}_i(t)}{c(t)} = \frac{\beta_i(t)}{D(t)} \tag{D.9}$$

as required by (D.6).

D.1.3 Learning

Consider now any learning equation, such as the EM equation for the transition parameters (7.31):

$$t_{ji}^+ = \frac{\sum_{t=0}^{T} y_{ji}(t)}{\sum_{t=0}^{T} y_i(t)} = \frac{\sum_{t=0}^{T} \alpha_i(t) t_{ji} e_{jx^{t+1}} \beta_j(t + 1)}{\sum_{t=0}^{T} \sum_{j \in S} \alpha_i(t) t_{ji} e_{jx^{t+1}} \beta_j(t + 1)}. \tag{D.10}$$

Any product of the form $\alpha_i(t)\beta_j(t + 1)$ is equal to $C\hat{\alpha}_i(t)\hat{\beta}_j(t + 1)$, with $C = C(t)D(t+1) = \prod_1^T c(t)$ independent of t. The constant C cancels out from the numerator and the denominator. Therefore the same learning equation can be used by simply replacing the αs and βs with the corresponding scaled $\hat{\alpha}$s and $\hat{\beta}$s. Similar remarks apply to the other learning equations.

D.2 Periodic Architectures

D.2.1 Wheel Architecture

In the wheel architecture of chapter 8, we can consider that there is a *start* state connected to all the states in the wheel. Likewise, we can consider that all the states along the wheel are connected to an *end* state. The wheel architecture contains no delete states, and therefore all the algorithms (forward, backward, Viterbi, and scaling) are simplified, in the sense that there is no need to distinguish between emitting and delete states.

D.2.2 Loop Architecture

The loop architecture is more general than the wheel architecture because it contains delete states, and even the possibility of looping through delete states. We introduce the following notation:

- h is the anchor state of the loop. The anchor state is a delete (silent) state, although it is not associated with any main state.

- L denotes the set of states in the loop.

- κ denotes the probability of going once around the loop silently. It is the product of all the t_{ji} associated with consecutive delete states in the loop.

- t_{ji}^d is the probability of the shortest direct silent path from i to j in the architecture.

- t_{ji}^D is the probability of moving silently from i to j. For any two states connected by at least one path containing the anchor, we have $t_{ji}^D = t_{ji}^d(1 + \kappa + (\kappa^2)\ldots) = t_{ji}^d/(1 - \kappa)$.

Forward Propagation Equations

Forward propagation equations are true both for instantaneous propagation and at equilibrium. For any emitting state $i \in E$,

$$\alpha_i(t + 1) = \sum_{j \in N^-(i)} \alpha_j(t)t_{ij}e_{iX^{t+1}}. \tag{D.11}$$

For any silent state i, including the anchor state,

$$\alpha_i(t + 1) = \sum_{j \in N^-(i)} \alpha_j(t + 1)t_{ij}. \tag{D.12}$$

For the anchor state, one may separate the contribution from the loop and from the flanks as

$$\alpha_h(t + 1) = \sum_{j \in N^-(h)-L} \alpha_j(t + 1)t_{hj} + \sum_{j \in N^-(h)\cap L} \alpha_j(t + 1)t_{hj}. \tag{D.13}$$

Implementations

There are three possible ways of implementing the propagation. First, iterate instantaneous propagation equations until equilibrium is reached. Second, iterate the equilibrium equations only once through the loop, for the anchor state. That is, write $x = \alpha_h(t + 1)$, forward-propagate the above equations once through the loop as a function of x, and solve for x at the end. Once the loop is completed, this yields an equation of the form $x = ax + b$ and so $x = b/(1 - a)$. Then replace x by its newly found value in the expression of $\alpha_i(t + 1)$ for all $i \in L$.

Third, solve analytically for x. That is, directly find the equilibrium value of $x = \alpha_h(t + 1)$ (i.e., a and b above). For this, note that the paths leading to the expression of $\alpha_h(t + 1)$ can be partitioned into two classes depending on whether X^{t+1} is emitted inside or outside the loop:

$$\alpha_h(t + 1) = \sum_{j \in N^-(h) - L} \alpha_j(t + 1)t_{hj}(1 + \kappa + \kappa^2 + \dots) + \sum_{j \in E \cap L} \alpha_j(t + 1)t_{hj}^D. \tag{D.14}$$

Thus the second term in the right-hand side accounts for the case where the emission of X^{t+1} inside the loop is followed by any number of silent revolutions terminating with the anchor state. This term contains unknown quantities such as $\alpha_j(t + 1)$. These are easy to calculate, however, using the values of $\alpha_j(t)$ that are known from the previous epoch of the propagation algorithm. So finally,

$$\alpha_h(t+1) = \frac{1}{1 - \kappa} \sum_{j \in N^-(h) - L} \alpha_j(t+1)t_{hj} + \sum_{j \in E \cap L} \sum_{k \in N^-(j)} \alpha_k(t)a_{jk}e_{jX^{t+1}}t_{hj}^D. \tag{D.15}$$

For the specific calculation of the last sum above, we consider the following implementation, where we forward-propagate two quantities, $\alpha_i(t)$ and $\alpha_i^L(t)$. $\alpha_i^L(t)$ is to be interpreted as the probability of being in state i at time t while having emitted symbol t *in the loop and not having traversed the anchor state yet again*. For any emitting state i in the loop, the propagation equations are

$$\alpha_i(t + 1) = \alpha_i^L(t + 1) = \sum_{j \in N^-(i)} \alpha_j(t)t_{ij}e_{iX^{t+1}}. \tag{D.16}$$

For any mute state (delete states and anchor) i in the loop, the propagation equations are

$$\alpha_i^L(t + 1) = \sum_{j \in N^-(i) \cap L} \alpha_j^L(t + 1)t_{ij}. \tag{D.17}$$

These equations should be initialized with $\alpha_h^L(t + 1) = 0$ and propagated all the way once through the loop to yield, at the end, a new value for $\alpha_h^L(t + 1)$.

We then have

$$\alpha_h(t+1) = \frac{1}{1-\kappa}[\sum_{j\in N^-(h)-L} \alpha_j(t+1)t_{hj} + \alpha_h^L(t+1)]. \qquad (D.18)$$

At time 0, initialization is as follows:

- $\alpha_i(0) = 0$ for any emitting state

- $\alpha_i^L(0) = 0$ for any state, including the anchor

- $\alpha_h(0) = \sum_{j\in N^-(h)-L} \alpha_j(0)t_{hj}/(1-\kappa)$

- $\alpha_i(0) = \sum_{j\in N^-(i)} \alpha_j(0)t_{ij}$ for any mute state in the loop exept the anchor

All variables can be computed with one pass through the loop by using propagating $\alpha(t)$ and $\alpha^L(t)$ simultaneously through the loop, in the following order. At step t, assume that $\alpha_i(t)$ is known for the anchor state and all emitting states. Then:

- Set $\alpha_h^L(t+1)$ to 0.

- Forward-propagate simultaneously through the loop the quantities $\alpha_i(t)$ for mute states (D.12), $\alpha_i(t+1) = \alpha_i^L(t+1)$ for emitting states (D.16), and $\alpha_i^L(t+1)$ for all mute states (D.17).

- Calculate $\alpha_h(t+1)$ by (D.18).

Backward propagation and scaling equations for the loop architecture can be derived along the same lines.

D.3 State Functions: Bendability

As discussed in chapters 7 and 8, any function that depends on the local amino acid or nucleotide composition of a family, such as entropy, hydrophobicity, or bendability, can be studied with HMMs. In particular, the expectation of such a function computed from the HMM backbone probabilities enhances patterns that are not always clearly present in individual members of the family. This expectation is straightforward to compute when the corresponding function or scale is defined over single alphabet letters (entropy, hydrophobicity). A little more care is needed when the function depends on adjacent pair or triplet of letters, usually DNA dinucleotides or trinucleotides (bendability, nucleosome positioning, stacking energies, propeller twist). Convolving several functions with the HMM backbone can help determine structural and functional properties of the corresponding family. Over 50 different functions are available in our current HMM simulator. Here we show how to compute such expectations in the case of bendability, which is a little harder because of its dependence on triplets rather than single letters.

D.3.1 Motivation

Average bending profiles can be computed directly from a multiple alignment of the available sequences to avoid the risk of introducing exogenous artifacts. It is useful, however, to be able to define and compute bending profiles directly from an HMM, for several reasons.

- The computation is faster because it can be executed as soon as the HMM is trained, without having to align all the sequences to the model.

- In many of the cases we have tried, the profiles derived from the HMM and the multiple alignment have very similar characteristics. Consistency of the two bending profiles can be taken as further evidence that the HMM is a good model of the data. Discrepant cases may yield additional insights.

- In certain cases—for example, when few data are available—a well-regularized HMM may yield better bending profiles.

D.3.2 Definition of HMM Bending Profiles

We assume a standard linear HMM architecture, but similar calculations can be done with the loop or wheel architectures. In the definition of an HMM bending profile, it is natural to consider only HMM main states $m_0, \ldots, m_{N+1}$, where m_0 is the *start* state and m_{N+1} is the *end* state (unless there are particularly strong transitions to insert states or delete states, in which case such states should be included in the calculation). The bendability $B(i, O)$ of a sequence $O = (X_O^1, \ldots, X_O^N)$ at a position i, away from the boundary, can be defined by averaging triplet bendabilities over a window of length $W = 2l + 1$:

$$B(i, O) = \frac{1}{W} \sum_{j=i-l}^{i+l-2} b(X_O^j, \ldots, X_O^{j+2}),$$
(D.19)

where $b(X, Y, Z)$ denotes the bendability of the XYZ triplet according to some scale ([96] and references therein). The bendability $B(i)$ of the family at position i is then naturally defined by taking the average over all possible backbone sequences:

$$B(i) = \sum_O B(i, O) \mathbf{P}(O).$$
(D.20)

This approach, however, is not efficient because the number of possible sequences is exponential in N. Fortunately, there exists a better way of organizing this calculation.

D.3.3   Efficient Computation of Bendability Profiles

From (D.20), we find

$$B(i) = \sum_O B(i,O) \prod_{k=1}^{N} e_{kX_O^k} \prod_{k=0}^{N+1} t_{m_k m_{k+1}}. \tag{D.21}$$

The last product is the product of all HMM backbone transitions and is equal to some constant C. Substituting (D.19) in (D.21), we have

$$B(i) = \frac{C}{W} \sum_O \sum_{j=i-l}^{i+l-2} b(X_O^j, \ldots, X_O^{j+2}) \prod_{k=1}^{N} e_{kX_O^k}. \tag{D.22}$$

Interchanging the sums yields

$$B(i) = \frac{C}{W} \sum_{j=i-l}^{i+l-2} \sum_O b(X_O^j, \ldots, X_O^{j+2}) \prod_{k=1}^{N} e_{kX_O^k}. \tag{D.23}$$

To sum over all sequences, we can partition the sequences into different groups according to the letters X, Y, and Z appearing at positions $j, j+1$, and $j+2$. After simplifications, this finally yields

$$B(i) = \frac{C}{W} \sum_{j=i-l}^{i+l-2} \sum_{X,Y,Z} b(X,Y,Z) e_{jX} e_{j+1Y} e_{j+2Z}. \tag{D.24}$$

Thus the definition in (D.20) is equivalent to the definition in (D.24), where summations within a window occur over all possible alphabet triplets weighted by the product of the corresponding emission probabilities at the corresponding locations. Definition (D.24) is of course the easiest to implement and we have used it to compute bending profiles from trained HMMs, usually omitting the constant scaling factor C/W. In general, boundary effects for the first and last l states are not relevant.

D.4   Dirichlet Mixtures

First recall from chapters 2 and 3 that the mean of a Dirichlet distribution $\mathcal{D}_{\alpha Q}(P)$ is Q, and the maximum is reached for $p_X = (\alpha q_X - 1)/(\alpha - |A|)$

provided $p_X \geq 0$ for all X. A mixture of Dirichlet distributions is defined by $\mathbf{P}(P) = \sum_1^n \lambda_i \mathcal{D}_{\alpha_i Q_i}(P)$, where the mixture coefficients must satisfy $\lambda_i \geq 0$ and $\sum_i \lambda_i = 1$. The expectation of the mixture is $\sum_i \lambda_i Q_i$, by linearity of the expectation. For a Dirichlet mixture, the maximum in general cannot be determined analytically.

D.4.1 Dirichlet Mixture Prior

Now consider the problem of choosing a prior for the emission distribution $P = (p_X)$ associated with an HMM emitting state or, equivalently, the dice model associated with a column of an alignment. Thus here p_X are the parameters of the model. The data D consists of the letters observed in the column with the corresponding counts $D = (n_X)$, with $\sum_X n_X = N$. The likelihood function for the data is given by

$$\mathbf{P}(D|M) = \mathbf{P}(n_X|p_X) = \prod_X p_X^{n_X}. \tag{D.25}$$

We have seen that a natural prior is to use a single Dirichlet distribution. The flexibility of such a prior may sometimes be too limited, especially if the same Dirichlet is used for all columns or all emitting states. A more flexible prior is a Dirichlet mixture

$$\mathbf{P}(P) = \sum_{i=1}^n \lambda_i \mathcal{D}_{\alpha_i Q_i}(P) \tag{D.26}$$

as in [489], where again the same mixture is used for all possible columns, to reflect the general distribution of amino acid in proteins. The mixture components $\mathcal{D}_{\alpha_i Q_i}$, their number, and the mixture coefficients can be found by clustering methods. An alternative for protein models is to use the vectors Q_i associated with the columns of a PAM matrix (see chapter 10 and [497]). Note that the present mixture model is different from having a different set of mixing coefficients for each column prior. It is also different from parameterizing each P as a mixture in order to reduce the number of HMM emission parameters, provided $n < |A|$ ($n = 9$ is considered optimal in [489]), in a way similar to the hybrid HMM/NN models of chapter 9. We leave it as an exercise for the reader to explore such alternatives.

Now, from the single Dirichlet mixture prior and the likelihood, the posterior is easily computed using Bayes' theorem as usual

$$\mathbf{P}(P|D) = \frac{1}{\mathbf{P}(D)} \sum_{i=1}^n \lambda_i \frac{B(\beta_i, R_i)}{B(\alpha_i, Q_i)} \mathcal{D}_{\beta_i R_i}(P). \tag{D.27}$$

The new mixture components are given by

$$\beta_i = N + \alpha_i \quad \text{and} \quad r_{iX} = \frac{n_X + \alpha_i q_{iX}}{N + \alpha_i}. \tag{D.28}$$

The beta function B is defined as

$$B(\alpha, Q) = \frac{\prod_X \Gamma(\alpha q_X)}{\Gamma(\alpha)}, \tag{D.29}$$

as usual with $\alpha \geq 0$, $q_X \geq 0$, and $\sum_X q_X = 1$. The posterior of a mixture of conjugate distributions is also a mixture of conjugate distributions. In this case, the posterior is also a Dirchlet mixture, but with different mixture components and mixture coefficients. Since the integral of the posterior over P must be equal to one, we immediately have the evidence

$$\mathbf{P}(D) = \sum_{i=1}^{n} \lambda_i \frac{B(\beta_i, R_i)}{B(\alpha_i, Q_i)}. \tag{D.30}$$

As pointed out above, the MAP estimate cannot be determined analytically, although it could be approximated by some iterative procedure. The MP estimate, however, is trivial since it corresponds to the average of the posterior

$$p_X^* = \frac{1}{\mathbf{P}(D)} \sum_{i=1}^{n} \lambda_i \frac{B(\beta_i, R_i)}{B(\alpha_i, Q_i)} r_{iX}. \tag{D.31}$$

This provides a formula for the estimation of optimal model parameters in this framework. Numerical implementation issues are discussed in [489].

D.4.2   Hierarchical Dirichlet Model

In hierarchical modeling, we introduce a higher level of priors, for instance with a Dirichlet prior on the mixture coefficients of the previous model. This two-level model is also a mixture model in the sense that $\mathbf{P}(P|\lambda) = \sum \lambda_i \mathcal{D}_{\alpha_i Q_i}(P)$ but with

$$\mathbf{P}(\lambda) = \mathcal{D}_{\beta Q}(\lambda) = \frac{\Gamma(\beta)}{\prod_i \Gamma(\beta q_i)} \prod_{i=1}^{n} \lambda_i^{\beta q_i - 1}. \tag{D.32}$$

We then have

$$\mathbf{P}(P) = \int_\lambda \mathbf{P}(P|\lambda)\mathbf{P}(\lambda)d\lambda. \tag{D.33}$$

Interchanging sums and integrals yields

$$\mathbf{P}(P) = \sum_{i=1}^{n} \mathcal{D}_{\alpha_i Q_i}(P) \left[\int_{\lambda} \lambda_i \mathcal{D}_{\beta Q}(\lambda) d\lambda \right] = \sum_{i=1}^{n} q_i \mathcal{D}_{\alpha_i Q_i}(P), \qquad \text{(D.34)}$$

the second equality resulting from the Dirichlet expectation formula. Thus this two-level hierarchical model is in fact equivalent to a one-level Dirichlet mixture model, where the mixture coefficients q_i are the expectation of the second-level Dirichlet prior in the hierarchical model.

Appendix E

Gaussian Processes, Kernel Methods, and Support Vector Machines

In this appendix we briefly review several important classes of machine learning methods: Gaussian processes, kernel methods, and support vector machines [533, 141].

E.1 Gaussian Process Models

Consider a regression problem consisting of K input-output training pairs $(x_1, y_1), ..., (x_K, y_K)$ drawn from some unknown distribution. The inputs x are n-dimensional vectors. For simplicity, we assume that y is one-dimensional, but the extension to the multidimensional case is straightforward. The goal in regression is to learn the functional relationship between x and y from the given examples. The Gaussian process modeling approach [559, 206, 399], also known as "kriging," provides a flexible probabilistic framework for regression and classification problems. A number of nonparametric regression models, including neural networks with a single infinite hidden layer and Gaussian weight priors, are equivalent to Gaussian processes [398]. Gaussian processes can be used to define probability distributions over spaces of functions directly, without any need for an underlying neural architecture.

A Gaussian process is a collection of variables $Y = (y(x_1), y(x_2), ...)$, with a joint Gaussian distribution of the form

$$\mathbf{P}(Y|C, \{x_i\}) = \frac{1}{Z} \exp(-\frac{1}{2}(Y - \mu)^T C^{-1}(Y - \mu)) \qquad \text{(E.1)}$$

for any sequence $\{x_i\}$, where μ is the mean vector and $C_{ij} = C(x_i, x_j)$ is the covariance of x_i and x_j. For simplicity, we shall assume in what follows that $\mu = 0$. Priors on the noise and the modeling function are combined into the covariance matrix C. Different sensible parameterizations for C are described below. From (E.1), the predictive distribution for the variable y associated with a test case x is obtained by conditioning on the observed training examples. In other words, a simple calculation shows that y has a Gaussian distribution

$$\mathbf{P}(y|\{y_1, ..., y_K\}, C(x_i, x_j), \{x_1, ..., x_K, x\}) = \frac{1}{\sqrt{2\pi}\sigma} \exp(-\frac{(y - y^*)^2}{2\sigma^2}) \qquad \text{(E.2)}$$

with

$$y^* = k(x)^T C_K^{-1}(y_1, ..., y_K) \quad \text{and} \quad \sigma = C(x, x) - k(x)^T C_K^{-1}k(x) \qquad \text{(E.3)}$$

where $k(x) = (C(x_1, x), ..., C(x_K, x))$ and C_K denotes the covariance matrix based on the K training samples.

E.1.1 Covariance Parameterization

A Gaussian process model is defined by its covariance function. The only constraint on the covariance function $C(x_i, x_j)$ is that it should yield positive semidefinite matrices for any input sample. In the stationary case, the Bochner theorem in harmonic analysis ([177] and given below for completeness) provides a complete characterization of such functions in terms of Fourier transforms. It is well known that the sum of two positive matrices (resp. positive definite) is positive (resp. positive definite). Therefore the covariance can be conveniently parameterized as a sum of different positive components. Useful components have the following forms:

- Noise variance: $\delta_{ij}\theta_1^2$ or, more generally, $\delta_{ij}f(x_i)$ for an input-dependent noise model

- Smooth covariance: $C(x_i, x_j) = \theta_2^2 \exp(-\sum_{u=1}^n \rho_u^2(x_{iu} - x_{ju})^2)$

- And more generally: $C(x_i, x_j) = \theta_2^2 \exp(-\sum_{u=1}^n \rho_u^2|x_{iu} - x_{ju}|^r)$

- Periodic covariance: $C(x_i, x_j) = \theta_3^2 \exp(-\sum_{u=1}^n \rho_u^2 \sin^2[\pi(x_{iu} - x_{ju})/y_u]$

Notice that a small value of ρ_u characterizes components u that are largely irrelevant for the output in a way closely related to the automatic relevance determination framework [398]. For simplicity, we write θ to denote the vector of hyperparameters of the model. Short of conducting lengthy Monte Carlo integrations over the space of hyperparameters, a single value θ can be estimated by minimizing the negative log-likelihood

$$\mathcal{E}(\theta) = \frac{1}{2} \log \det C_K + \frac{1}{2} Y_K^T C_K^{-1} Y_K + \frac{K}{2} \log 2\pi. \tag{E.4}$$

Without any specific shortcuts, this requires inverting the covariance matrix and is likely to require $O(N^3)$ computations. Prediction or classification can then be carried based on (E.3). A binary classification model, for instance is readily obtained by defining a Gaussian process on a latent variable Z as above and letting

$$\mathbf{P}(y_i = 1) = \frac{1}{1 + e^{-z_i}}. \tag{E.5}$$

More generally, when there are more than two classes, one can use normalized exponentials instead of sigmoidal functions.

E.2 Kernel Methods and Support Vector Machines

Kernel methods and support vector machines (SVMs) are related to Gaussian processes and can be applied to both classification and regression problems. For simplicity, we consider here a binary classification problem characterized by a set of labeled training example pairs of the form (x_i, y_i) where x_i is an input vector and $y_i = \pm 1$ is the corresponding classification in one of two classes H^+ and H^-. A a (0,1) formalism is equivalent but leads to more cumbersome notation. As an example, consider the problem of deciding whether a given protein (resp. a given gene) belongs to a certain family, given the amino acid sequences (resp. expression levels) of members within (positive examples) and outside (negative examples) the family [275, 95]. In particular, the length of x_i can vary with i. The label y for a new example x is determined by a discriminant function $\mathcal{D}(x; \{x_i, y_i\})$, which depends on the training examples, in the form $y = \text{sign}(\mathcal{D}(x; \{x_i, y_i\}))$. In a proper probabilistic setting,

$$y = \text{sign}(\mathcal{D}(x; \{x_i, y_i\})) = \text{sign}(\log \frac{\mathbf{P}(H^+|x)}{\mathbf{P}(H^-|x)}) \tag{E.6}$$

In kernel methods, the discriminant function is expanded in the form

$$\mathcal{D}(x) = \sum_i y_i \lambda_i K(x_i, x) = \sum_{H^+} \lambda_i K(x_i, x) - \sum_{H^-} \lambda_i K(x_i, x) \tag{E.7}$$

so that, up to trivial constants, $\log \mathbf{P}(H^+|x) = \sum_{H^+} \lambda_i K(x_i, x)$ and similarly for the negative examples. K is called the kernel function. The intuitive idea is to base our classification of the new example on all the previous examples weighted by two factors: a coefficient $\lambda_i \geq 0$ measuring the importance of example i, and the kernel $K(x_i, x)$ measuring how similar x is to example x_i. Therefore the expression for the discrimination depends *directly* on the training examples. This is different from the case of neural networks, for instance, where the decision depends indirectly on the training examples via the trained neural network parameters. Thus in an application of kernel methods two fundamental choices must be made regarding (a) the kernel K; and (b) the weights λ_i. Variations on these choices lead to a spectrum of different methods, including generalized linear models and SVMs.

E.2.1 Kernel Selection

To a first approximation, from the mathematical theory of kernels, a kernel must be positive definite. By Mercer's theorem of functional analysis (given later in the section E.3.2 for completeness), K can be represented as an inner product of the form

$$K_{ij} = K(x_i, x_j) = \phi(x_i)\phi(x_j). \tag{E.8}$$

Thus another way of looking at kernel methods is to consider that the original x vectors are mapped to a "feature" space via the function $\phi(x)$. Note that the feature space can have very high (even infinite) dimension and that the vectors $\phi(x)$ have the same length even when the input vectors x do not. The similiarity of two vectors is assessed by taking their inner product in feature space. In fact we can compute the euclidean distance $||\phi(x_i) - \phi(x_j)||^2 = K_{ii} - 2K_{ij} + K_{jj}$ which also defines a pseudodistance on the original vectors.

The fundamental idea in kernel methods is to define a linear or nonlinear decision surface in feature space rather than the original space. The feature space does not need to be constructed explicitly since all decisions can be made through the kernel and the training examples. In addition, as we are about to see, the decision surface depends *directly* on a *subset* of the training examples, the support vectors.

Notice that a dot product kernel provides a way of comparing vectors in feature space. When used directly in the discrimination function, it corresponds to looking for linear separating hyperplanes in feature space. However more complex decision boundaries in feature spaces (quadratic or higher order) can easily be implemented using more complex kernels K' derived from the inner product kernel K, such as:

- Polynomial kernels: $K'(x_i, x_j) = (1 + K(x_i, x_j))^m$

- Radial basis kernels: $K'(x_i, x_j) = \exp -\frac{1}{2\sigma^2}(\phi(x_i) - \phi(x_j))^t(\phi(x_i) - \phi(x_j))$

- Neural network kernels: $K'(x_i, x_j) = \tanh(\mu x_i^t x_j + \kappa)$

E.2.2 Fisher Kernels

In [275] a general technique is presented for combining kernel methods with probabilistic generative models. The basic idea is that a generative model, such as an HMM, is typically trained from positive examples only and therefore may not be always optimal for discrimination tasks. A discriminative model, however, can be built from a generative model using both positive and negative examples and a kernel of the form $K(x_i, x_j) = U^t(x_i)F^{-1}U(x_j)$, where the vector U is the gradient of the log-likelihood of the generative model with respect to the model parameters $U(x) = \partial \log P(x|w)/\partial w$. This gradient describes how a given value of w contributes to the generation of example x. For the exponential family of distributions, the gradient forms essentially a sufficient statistics. Notice again that $U(x)$ has fixed length even when x has variable length. For instance, in the case of an HMM trained on a protein family, $U(x)$ is the vector of derivatives that was computed in chapter 7. F is the Fisher information matrix $F = E(U(x)U^t(x))$ with respect to $P(x|w)$, and this type of kernel is called a *Fisher kernel*. The Fisher matrix consists of the second-order derivatives of the log-likelihood and is therefore associated with the local curvature of the corresponding manifold (see, for instance, [15]). F defines the Riemannian metric of the underlying manifold. In particular, the local distance between two nearby models parameterized by w and $w + \epsilon$ is $\epsilon^t F \epsilon/2$. This distance also approximates the relative entropy between the two models. In many cases, at least asymptotically with many examples, the Fisher kernel can be approximated by the simpler dot product $K(x_i, x_j) = U_{x_i}^t U_{x_j}$. The Fisher kernel can also be modified using the transformations described above, for example in the form $K(x_i, x_j) = \exp -\frac{1}{2\sigma^2}(U(x_i) - U(x_j))^t(U(x_i) - U(x_j))$.

It can be shown that, at least asymptotically, the Fisher kernel classifier is never inferior to the MAP decision rule associated with the generative probabilistic model. An application of Fisher kernel methods to the detection of remote protein homologies is described in [275].

E.2.3 Weight Selection

The weights λ are typically obtained through an iterative optimization procedure on an objective function (classification loss). In general, this corresponds to a quadratic optimization problem. Often the weights can be viewed as Lagrange multipliers, or dual weights with respect to the original parameters of the problem (see section E.2.4 below). With large training sets, at the optimum many of the weights are equal to 0. The only training vectors that matter in a given decision are those with nonzero weights and these are called the support vectors.

To see this, consider an example x_i with target classification y_i. Since our decision is based on the sign of $\mathcal{D}(x_i)$, ideally we would like $y_i\mathcal{D}(x_i)$, the margin for example i, to be as large as possible. Because the margin can be rescaled by rescaling the λs, it is natural to introduce additional constraints such as $0 \leq \lambda_i \leq 1$ for every λ_i. In the case where an exact separating manifold exists in feature space, a reasonable criterion is to maximize the margin in the worst case. This is also called risk minimization and corresponds to $\max_\lambda \min_i y_i\mathcal{D}(x_i)$. SVMs can be defined as a class of kernel methods based on structural risk minimization (see section E.2.4 below). Substituting the expression for $\mathcal{D}$ in terms of the kernel yields $\max_\lambda \min_i \sum_j \lambda_j y_i y_j K_{ij}$. This can be rewritten as $\max_\lambda \min_i \sum_j A_{ij}\lambda_j$, with $A_{ij} = y_i y_j K_{ij}$ and $0 \leq \lambda_i \leq 1$. It is clear that in each minimization procedure all weights λ_j associated with a nonzero coefficient A_{ij} will either be 0 or 1. With a large training set, many of them will be zero for each i and this will remain true at the optimum. When the margins are violated, as in most real-life examples, we can use a similar strategy (an alternative also is to use slack variables as in the example given in section E.2.5 below). For instance, we can try to maximize the average margin, the average being taken with respect to the weights λ_i themselves, which are intended to reflect the relevance of each example. Thus in general we want to maximize a quadratic expression of the form $\sum_i \lambda_i y_i \mathcal{D}(x_i)$ under a set of linear constraints on the λ_i. Standard techniques exist to carry out such optimizations. For example, a typical function used for minimization in the literature is:

$$\mathcal{E}(\lambda_i) = -\sum_i [y_i\lambda_i\mathcal{D}(x_i) + 2\lambda_i]. \qquad (E.9)$$

The solution to this constrained optimization problem is unique provided that for any finite set of examples the corresponding kernel matrix K_{ij} is positive definite. The solution can be found with standard iterative methods, although the convergence can sometimes be slow. To accommodate training errors or biases in the training set, the kernel matrix K can be replaced by $K + \mu D$, where D is a diagonal matrix whose entries are either d^+ or d^- in locations corresponding to positive and negative examples [533, 108, 141]. An example of application of SVMs to gene expression data can be found in [95].

In summary, kernel methods and SVMs have several attractive features. As presented, these are supervised learning methods that can leverage labeled data. These methods can build flexible decision surfaces in high-dimensional feature spaces. The flexibility is related to the flexibility in the choice of the kernel function. Overfitting can be controlled through some form of margin

additive constants, the negative log-posterior of the training set is

$$\mathcal{E}(w) = -\sum_i \log \sigma(y_i w^t x_i) + \frac{1}{2} w^t C^{-1} w. \tag{E.15}$$

It is easy to check that at the optimum the solution must satisfy

$$w^* = -\sum_i y_i \lambda_i C x_i \tag{E.16}$$

with $\lambda_i = \partial \log \sigma(z)/\partial z$ taken at $z = y_i w^{*t} x_i$. Thus we obtain a solution with the general form of (E.7) with the kernel $K(x_i, x_j) = x_i^t C x_j$.

E.3 Theorems for Gaussian Processes and SVMs

For completeness, here we state two useful theorems underlying the theory of kernel methods, SVMs, and Gaussian processes: Bochner's theorem in probability and harmonic analysis and Mercer's theorem in functional analysis.

E.3.1 Bochner's Theorem

Bochner's theorem provides a complete characterization of characteristic functions in terms of Fourier transforms, and as a byproduct establishes the equivalence between characteristic functions and covariance functions of continuous stationary processes.

Consider a complex process, that is, a family of complex random variables $\{X_t = U_t + iV_t\}$, with $-\infty < t < +\infty$. For simplicity, assume that $E(X_t) = 0$ and define the covariance by $\mathbf{Cov}(X_u, X_v) = E(X_u, \bar{X}_v)$. We will assume that the process X_t is stationary and continuous, which means that the covariance function is continuous and satisfies

$$\mathbf{Cov}(X_s, X_{s+t}) = f(t). \tag{E.17}$$

Thus it depends only on the distance between variables. Under these assumptions, Bochner's theorem asserts that f satisfies

$$f(t) = \int_{-\infty}^{+\infty} e^{i\lambda t} \mu(d\lambda) \tag{E.18}$$

where μ is a measure on the real line with total mass $f(0)$. That is, f is positive definite and is the Fourier transform of a finite measure. If the variables X_t are real, then the measure μ is symmetric and

$$f(t) = \int_{-\infty}^{+\infty} \cos \lambda t \mu(d\lambda). \tag{E.19}$$

The measure μ is called the spectral measure of the process. Conversely, given any finite measure μ on the real line, it can be shown that there exists a stationary process X_t with spectral measure μ. The measure $\mu/f(0)$ is a probability measure and therefore the function f in (E.18) is a characteristic function. In other words, an equivalent theorem is that a continuous function $g(t)$ is the characteristic function of a probability distribution if and only if it is positive definite (i.e., it satisfies a relation similar to (E.18)) and also satisfies the normalization $g(0) = 1$. Thus up to a normalisation factor, a continuous characteristic function is equivalent to the covariance function of a stationary process. Additional details can be found in [177].

E.3.2   Mercer's Theorem

Mercer's theorem provides the connection between symmetric positive definite kernels and dot products in "feature space". Consider an integral operator $\kappa : L_2 \to L_2$, between two L_2 (square-integrable) spaces, with continuous symmetric kernel K, so that

$$(\kappa f)y = \int K(x,y)f(x)dx. \tag{E.20}$$

Assume that K is also positive definite, i.e.

$$\int f(x)K(x,y)f(y)dxdy > 0 \tag{E.21}$$

if $f \neq 0$. Then there exists an orthonormal set of basis of functions $\xi_i(x)$ such that K can be expanded in the form

$$K(x,y) = \sum_{i=1}^{\infty} \lambda_i \xi_i(x) \xi_i(y) \tag{E.22}$$

with $\lambda_i \geq 0$, and the scalar product product $(\xi_i \xi_j)_{L_2} = \delta_{ij}$ (orthonormality), for any pair of integers i and j. From (E.20) and the orthonormality condition, we have

$$(\kappa \xi_i)y = \int \sum_{j=1}^{\infty} \lambda_j \xi_j(x) \xi_j(y) \xi_i(x)dx = \lambda_i \xi_i(y). \tag{E.23}$$

In other words, κ is a compact operator with an eigenvector decomposition with eigenvectors ξ_i and nonnegative eigenvalues λ_i. If we define the function $\phi(x)$ by

$$\phi(x) = \sum_{i=1}^{\infty} \sqrt{\lambda_i} \xi_i(x), \tag{E.24}$$

then using the orthonormality conditions again yields

$$K(x,y) = \phi(x)\phi(y), \tag{E.25}$$

which is the decomposition required in (E.8). Conversely, if we start with a continuous embedding $\phi(x)$ of x into a feature space of dimension M, we can then define a continuous kernel $K(x,y)$ using (E.25). The corresponding operator is positive definite since

$$\int f(x)K(x,y)f(y)dxdy = \int f(x)(\phi(x)\phi(y))f(y)dxdy =$$

$$\sum_{i=1}^{M} \int f(x)\phi_i(x)\phi_i(y)f(y)dxdy = \sum_{i=1}^{M} (\int f(x)\phi_i(x)dx)^2 \geq 0.$$

$$\tag{E.26}$$

Appendix F

Symbols and Abbreviations

Probabilities

- π: Unscaled degree of confidence or belief

- $\mathbf{P}(P, Q, R \dots)$: Probability (actual probability distributions)

- $\mathbf{E}$ ($\mathbf{E}_Q$): Expectation (expectation with respect to Q)

- **Var**: Variance

- **Cov**: Covariance

- X_i, Y_i (x_i, y_i): Propositions or random variables (x_i actual value of X_i)

- $\bar{X}$: Complement or negation of X

- $X \perp Y$ ($X \perp Y | Z$): X and Y are independent (independent conditionally on Z)

- $\mathbf{P}(x_1, \dots, x_n)$: Probability that $X_1 = x_1, \dots, X_n = x_n$. When the context is clear, this is also written as $\mathbf{P}(X_1, \dots, X_n)$. Likewise, for a specific density Q, we write $Q(x_1, \dots, x_n)$ or $Q(X_1, \dots, X_n)$

- $\mathbf{P}(X|Y)$ ($\mathbf{E}(X|Y)$): Conditional probability (conditional expectation)

- $\mathcal{N}(\mu, \sigma), \mathcal{N}(\mu, C), \mathcal{N}(\mu, \sigma^2), \mathcal{N}(x; \mu, \sigma^2)$: Normal (or Gaussian) density with mean μ and variance σ^2, or covariance matrix C

- $\Gamma(w | \alpha, \lambda)$: Gamma density with parameters α and λ

- $\mathcal{D}_{\alpha Q}$: Dirichlet distribution with parameters α and Q

- $t(x; \nu, m, \sigma^2)$, $t(\nu, m, \sigma^2)$: Student distribution with ν degrees of freedom, location m, and scale σ

- $\mathcal{I}(x; \nu, \sigma^2)$, $\mathcal{I}(\nu, \sigma^2)$: scaled inverse gamma distribution with ν degrees of freedom and scale σ

Functions

- $\mathcal{E}$: Energy, error, negative log-likelihood or log-posterior (depending on context)

- $\mathcal{E}_T$, $\mathcal{E}_G$, $\mathcal{E}_C$: Training error, generalization error, classification error

- $\mathcal{E}_P$: Parsimony error

- $\mathcal{F}$: Free energy

- $\mathcal{L}$: Lagrangian

- $\mathcal{D}$: Decision function

- $\mathcal{R}$: Risk function

- $\mathcal{R}_K$: Empirical risk function

- $\mathcal{H}(P)$, $\mathcal{H}(X)$: Entropy of the distribution P, or the random variable X/differential entropy in continuous case

- $\mathcal{H}(P, Q)$, $\mathcal{H}(X, Y)$: Relative entropy between the distributions P and Q or between the random variables X and Y

- $\mathcal{I}(P, Q)$, $\mathcal{I}(X, Y)$: Mutual information between the distributions P and Q, or the random variables X and Y

- Z: Partition function or normalizing factor (sometimes also C)

- C: Constant or normalizing factor

- $\delta(x, y)$: Kronecker function equal to 1 if $x = y$ and 0 otherwise

- f, f': Generic function and derivative of f

- $\Gamma(x)$: Gamma function

- $B(\alpha, Q)$: Beta function (appendix D)

- We also use convex ($\cup$) to denote upward convexity (positive second derivative), and convex ($\cap$) to denote downward convexity (negative second derivative), rather than the more confusing "convex" and "concave" expressions

Models, Alphabets, and Sequences

- M ($M = M(w)$): Model (model with parameters w)

- D: Data

- I: Background information

- H: Hidden or latent variables or causes

- $S = \{s_1, s_2, \ldots, s_{|S|}\}$: Set of states of a system

- s: Generic state

- A (X): Alphabet (generic letter)

- $A = \{A, C, G, T\}$: DNA alphabet

- $A = \{A, C, G, U\}$: RNA alphabet

- $A = \{A, C, D, \ldots\}$: Amino acid alphabet

- A^*: Set of finite strings over $\mathbf{A}$

- $O = (X^1 \ldots X^t \ldots)$: Generic sequence ("O" stands for "observation" or "ordered")

- $\varnothing$: Empty sequence

- $O_1, \ldots, O_K$: Set of training sequences

- O_k^j: jth letter of kth sequence

Graphs and Sets

- $G = (V, E)$: Undirected graph with vertex set V and edge set E

- $G = (V, \vec{E})$: Directed graph with vertex set V and edge set E

- T: Tree

- $N(i)$: Neighbors of vertex i

- $N^+(i)$: Children of vertex i in a directed graph

- $N^-(i)$: Parents of vertex i in a directed graph

- $C^+(i)$: The future, or descendants, of vertex i in a directed graph

- $C^-(i)$: The past, or ancestors, of vertex i in a directed graph

- $N(I)$: Neighbors or boundary of a set I of vertices

- $\mathcal{P}(G)$: Family of probability distributions satisfying the conditional independence assumptions described by G

- G^C: Clique graph of G

- G^M: Moral graph of G

- $\cup, \cap, \bar{\ }$: Union, intersection, complement of sets

- $\varnothing$: Empty set

Dimensions

- $|A|$: Number of alphabet symbols

- $|S|$: Number of states

- $|H|$: Number of hidden units in HMM/NN hybrid models

- N: Length of sequences (average length)

- K: Number of sequences or examples (e.g., in a training set)

- T: Time horizon (sometimes also temperature when no confusion is possible)

General Parameters

- w : Generic vector of parameters

- t_{ji}: Transition probability from i to j, for instance in a Markov chain

- ^{t} (w_{ij}^t, X^t): Time index, in algorithmic iterations or in sequences

- $^+, ^-$ (w_{ij}^+): Relative time index, in algorithmic iterations

- * (w_{ij}^*): Optimal solutions

- η: Learning rate

Neural Networks

- w_{ij}: Connection weight from unit j to unit i

- w_i, λ_i: Bias of unit i, gain of unit i

- $D_j = (d_j, t_j)$: Training example; d_j is the input vector and t_j is the corresponding target ouput vector

- $y_i = f_i(x_i)$: Input-output relation for unit i: x_i is the total input into the unit, f_i is the transfer function, and y_i is the output

- $y(d_i)$: Output activity of NN with input vector d_i

- $y_j(d_i)$: Activity of the jth ouput unit of NN with input vector d_i

- $t_j(d_i)$: Target value for the jth ouput unit of NN with input vector d_i

Hidden Markov Models

- m, d, i, h: Main, delete, insert, and anchor states. Most of the time, i is just an index

- *start, end:* Start state and end state of an HMM (also denoted S and E in figures)

- E: Set of emitting states of a model

- D: Set of delete (silent) states of a model

- L: In appendix D only, L denotes the set of states in the loop of an HMM loop architecture

- t_{ij} (w_{ij}): Transition probability from state j to state i (normalized exponential representation)

- e_{iX} (w_{iX}): Emission probability for letter X from state i (normalized exponential representation)

- t_{ij}^D: Silent transition probability from state j to state i

- π: Path variables

- $n(i, X, \pi, O)$: Number of times the letter X is produced from state i along a path π for a sequence O in a given HMM

- $\alpha_i(t)$: Forward variables
- $\alpha_i^L(t)$: Forward variables in the HMM loop architecture
- $\beta_i(t)$: Backward variables
- $\hat{\alpha}_i(t)$: Scaled forward variables
- $\hat{\beta}_i(t)$: Scaled backward variables
- $\gamma_i(t)$: Probability of being in state i at time t in an HMM for a given observation sequence
- $\gamma_{ji}(t)$: Probability of using the i to j transition at time t in an HMM for a given observation sequence
- $\delta_i(t)$: Variables used in the recursion of the Viterbi algorithms
- κ: Probability of going around an HMM loop silently
- $b(\mathsf{X}, \mathsf{Y}, \mathsf{Z})$: Bendability of triplet XYZ
- $B(i, O)$: Bendability of sequence O at position i
- $B(i)$: Bendability of a family of sequences at position i
- W: Length of averaging window in bendability calculations

Bidirectional Architectures

- W: Total number of parameters
- O_t: Output probability vector
- B_t: Backward context vector
- F_t: Forward context vector
- I_t: Input vector
- $\eta(.)$: Output function
- $\beta(.)$: Backward transition function
- $\phi(.)$: Forward transition function
- n: Typical number of states in the chains
- q: Shift operator

Grammars

- L: Language

- G: Grammar

- $L(G)$: Language generated by grammar G

- R: Production rules of a grammar

- V: Alphabet of variables

- $s = start$: Start variable

- $\alpha \rightarrow \beta$: Grammar production rule: α "produces" or "expands to" β

- $\pi_i(t)$: Derivation variable in grammars

- $n(\beta, u, \pi, O)$: Number of times the rule $u \rightarrow \beta$ is used in the derivation π of a sequence O in a given grammar

- $P_{\alpha \rightarrow \beta}$ $(w_{\alpha \rightarrow \beta})$: Probability of the production rule $\alpha \rightarrow \beta$ in a stochastic grammar (normalized exponential representation)

Phylogenetic Trees

- r: Root node

- X_i: Letter assigned to vertex i

- d_{ji}: Time distance from node i to node j

- $p_{X_j X_i}(d_{ji})$: Probability that X_i is substituted by X_j over a time d_{ji}

- $\chi^i(t)$: Random variable associated with letter at position i in a sequence at time t

- $p_{YX}^i(t)$: Probability that X is substituted by Y over a time t at position i in a sequence

- $P(t) = (p_{YX}(t))$: Matrix of substitution probabilities for time t

- $Q = (q_{YX})$: Derivative matrix of P at time 0 $(Q = P'(0))$

- $p = (p_X)$: Stationary distribution

- χ_i: Random variable associated with letter at node i in a tree

- I: Set of internal nodes of a tree

- $O^+(i)$: Evidence contained in subtree rooted at note i

Microarrays

- n (n_c, n_t): Number of expression measurements of a gene (in the control and treatment cases)

- $x_1^c, \ldots, x_{n_c}^c$ ($x_1^t, \ldots, x_{n_t}^t$): Expression measurements of a gene in the control case (and treatment case)

- m (m_c, m_t): Empirical means of measurements of a gene (in the control and treatment cases)

- s^2 (s_c^2, s_t^2): Empirical variances of measurements of a gene (in the control and treatment cases)

- $d_1, \ldots, d_N$: N data points to be clustered

- K: Number of clusters

Kernel Methods and Support Vector Machines

- w: Vector of model parameters

- λ_i: Weights

- ξ_i: Slack variables

- $K_{ij} = K(x_i, x_j)$: Kernel function

- F: Fisher information matrix

- $\phi(x)$: Feature vector

- $U(x)$: Gradient vector of the log-likelihood with respect to model parameters

- h: VC dimension

Abbreviations

- CFG: Context-free grammar

- CSG: Context-sensitive grammar

- BIOHMM: Bidirectional IOHMM

- BRNN: Bidirectional RNN

- EM: Expectation maximization

- HMM: Hidden Markov model

- IOHMM: Input-output HMM

- LMS: Least mean square

- MAP: Maximum a posteriori

- MaxEnt: Maximum entropy

- MCMC: Markov chain Monte Carlo

- ML: Maximum likelihood

- MLP: Multilayer perceptron

- MP: Mean posterior

- NN: Neural network

- RNN: Recursive NN

- RG: Regular grammar

- REG: Recursively enumerable grammar

- SG: Stochastic grammar

- SCFG: Stochastic context-free grammar

- SS: Secondary structure

- SVM: Support vector machine

- VC: Vapnik-Chervonenkis

References

[1] Y. Abu-Mustafa. Machines that learn from hints. *Sci. American*, 272:64–69, 1995.

[2] D. H. Ackley, G. E. Hinton, and T. J. Sejnowski. A learning algorithm for Boltzmann machines. *Cognitive Science*, 9:147–169, 1985.

[3] A. V. Aho, R. Sethi, and J. D. Ullman. *Compilers. Principles, Techniques, and Tools.* Addison-Wesley, Reading, MA, 1986.

[4] S. M. Aji and R. J. McEliece. The generalized distributive law. Technical Report, Department of Electrical Engineering, California Institute of Technology, 1997.

[5] H. Akaike. A new look at the statistical model identification. *IEEE Trans. Aut. Control*, 19:716–723, 1974.

[6] C. Alff-Steinberger. The genetic code and error transmission. *Proc. Natl. Acad. Sci. USA*, 64:584–591, 1969.

[7] U. Alon, N. Barkai, D. A. Notterman, K. Gish, S. Ybarra, D. Mack, and A. J. Levine. Broad patterns of gene expression revealed by clustering analysis of tumor and normal colon tissues probed by oligonucleotide arrays. *Proc. Natl. Acad. Sci. USA*, 96:6745–6750, 1999.

[8] S. F. Altschul. Amino acid substitution matrices from an information theoretic perspective. *J. Mol. Biol.*, 219:555–565, 1991.

[9] S. F. Altschul, M. S. Boguski, W. Gish, and J. C. Wootton. Issues in searching molecular sequence databases. *Nat. Genet.*, 6:119–129, 1994.

[10] S. F. Altschul, R. Carrol, and D. J. Lipman. Weights for data related by a tree. *J. Mol. Biol.*, 207:647–653, 1989.

[11] S. F. Altschul, W. Gish, W. Miller, E. W. Myers, and D. J. Lipman. Basic local alignment search tool. *J. Mol. Biol.*, 215:403–410, 1990.

[12] S. F. Altschul, T. L. Madden, A. A. Schaffer, J. Zhang, Z. Zhang, W. Miller, and L. J. Lipman. Gapped BLAST and PSI-BLAST: a new generation of protein database search programs. *Nucl. Acids Res.*, 25:3389–3402, 1997.

[13] S.F. Altschul. A protein alignment scoring system sensitive at all evolutionary distances. *J. Mol. Evol.*, 36:290–300, 1993.

[14] S.F. Altschul. Local alignment statistics. *Meth. Enzymol.*, 274:460–480, 1996.

[15] S. Amari. Natural gradient works efficiently in learning. *Neural Comp.*, 10:251–276, 1998.

[16] S. Amari and N. Murata. Statistical theory of learning curves under entropic loss criterion. *Neural Comp.*, 5:140–153, 1993.

[17] C. A. F. Andersen and S. Brunak. Amino acid subalphabets can improve protein structure prediction. *Submitted*, 2001.

[18] M. A. Andrade, G. Casari, C. Sander, and A. Valencia. Classification of protein families and detection of the determinant residues with an improved self-organizing map. *Biol. Cybern.*, 76:441–450, 1997.

[19] S. M. Arfin, A. D. Long, E. T. Ito, L. Tolleri, M. M. Riehle, E. S. Paegle, and G. W. Hatfield. Global gene expression profiling in *escherichia coli* K12: the effects of integration host factor. *J. Biol. Chem.*, 275:29672–29684, 2000.

[20] B. C. Arnold and S. J. Press. Compatible conditional distributions. *J. Amer. Statist. Assn.*, 84:152–156, 1989.

[21] M. Ashburner. On the representation of gene function in genetic databases. *ISMB*, 6, 1998.

[22] M. Ashburner, C. A. Ball, J. A. Blake, D. Botstein, H. Butler, J. M. Cherry, A. P. Davis K. Dolinski, S. S. Dwight, J. T. Eppig, M. A. Harris, D. P. Hill, L. Issel-Tarver, A. Kasarskis, S. Lewis, J. C. Matese, J. E. Richardson, M. Ringwald, G. M. Rubin, and G. Sherlock. Gene ontology: tool for the unification of biology. *Nature Genet.*, 25:25–29, 2000.

[23] A. Bairoch. The PROSITE dictionary of sites and patterns in proteins, its current status. *Nucl. Acids Res.*, 21:3097–3103, 1993.

[24] A. Bairoch and R. Apweiler. The SWISS-PROT protein sequence data bank and its supplement TrEMBL. *Nucl. Acids Res.*, 25:31–36, 1997.

[25] J. K. Baker. Trainable grammars for speech recognition. In J. J. Wolf and D. H. Klat, editors, *Speech Communication Papers for the 97th Meeting of the Acoustical Society of America*, pages 547–550, 1979.

[26] P. Baldi. Gradient descent learning algorithms overview: A general dynamical systems perspective. *IEEE Trans. on Neural Networks*, 6:182–195, 1995.

[27] P. Baldi. Substitution matrices and hidden Markov models. *J. Comput. Biol.*, 2:497–501, 1995.

[28] P. Baldi. On the convergence of a clustering algorithm for protein-coding regions in microbial genomes. *Bioinformatics*, 16:367–371, 2000.

[29] P. Baldi. *The Shattered Self-the End of Natural Evolution.* MIT Press, Cambridge, MA, 2001.

[30] P. Baldi and Pierre-Francois Baisnee. Sequence analysis by additive scales: DNA structure for sequences and repeats of all lengths. *Bioinformatics*, 16:865–889, 2000.

[31] P. Baldi, S. Brunak, Y. Chauvin, C. A. F. Andersen, and H. Nielsen. Assessing the accuracy of prediction algorithms for classification: an overview. *Bioinformatics*, 16:412–424, 2000.

[32] P. Baldi, S. Brunak, Y. Chauvin, J. Engelbrecht, and A. Krogh. Hidden Markov models for human genes. In G. Tesauro J. D. Cowan and J. Alspector, editors, *Advances in Neural Information Processing Systems*, volume 6, pages 761–768. Morgan Kaufmann, San Francisco, 1994.

[33] P. Baldi, S. Brunak, Y. Chauvin, J. Engelbrecht, and A. Krogh. Periodic sequence patterns in human exons. In *Proceedings of the 1995 Conference on Intelligent Systems for Molecular Biology (ISMB95)*. AAAI Press, Menlo Park, CA, 1995.

[34] P. Baldi, S. Brunak, Y. Chauvin, and A. Krogh. Naturally occurring nucleosome positioning signals in human exons and introns. *J. Mol. Biol.*, 263:503–510, 1996.

[35] P. Baldi, S. Brunak, Y. Chauvin, and A. Krogh. Hidden Markov models for human genes: periodic patterns in exon sequences. In S. Suhai, editor, *Theoretical and Computational Methods in Genome Research*, pages 15–32, New York, 1997. Plenum Press.

[36] P. Baldi, S. Brunak, P. Frasconi, G. Pollastri, and G. Soda. Bidirectional dynamics for protein secondary structure prediction. In R. Sun and C. L. Giles, editors, *Sequence Learning: Paradigms, Algorithms, and Applications*, pages 99–120. Springer Verlag, New York, 2000.

[37] P. Baldi, S. Brunak, P. Frasconi, G. Soda, and G. Pollastri. Exploiting the past and the future in protein secondary structure prediction. *Bioinformatics*, 15:937–946, 1999.

[38] P. Baldi and Y. Chauvin. Hidden Markov models of the G-protein-coupled receptor family. *J. Comput. Biol.*, 1:311–335, 1994.

[39] P. Baldi and Y. Chauvin. Smooth on-line learning algorithms for hidden Markov models. *Neural Comp.*, 6:305–316, 1994.

[40] P. Baldi and Y. Chauvin. Hybrid modeling, HMM/NN architectures, and protein applications. *Neural Comp.*, 8:1541–1565, 1996.

[41] P. Baldi, Y. Chauvin, T. Hunkapillar, and M. McClure. Hidden Markov models of biological primary sequence information. *Proc. Natl. Acad. Sci. USA*, 91:1059–1063, 1994.

[42] P. Baldi, Y. Chauvin, F. Tobin, and A. Williams. Mining data bases of partial protein sequences using hidden Markov models. Net-ID/SmithKline Beecham Technical Report, 1996.

[43] P. Baldi and G. Wesley Hatfield. *Microarrays and Gene Expression*. Cambridge University Press, Cambridge, UK, 2001.

[44] P. Baldi and A. D. Long. A Bayesian framework for the analysis of microarray expression data: regularized *t*-test and statistical inferences of gene changes. *Bioinformatics*, 17(6):509–519, 2001.

[45] P. Baldi, G. Pollastri, C. A. F. Andersen, and S. Brunak. Matching protein β-sheet partners by feedforward and recurrent neural networks. In *Proceedings of the 2000 Conference on Intelligent Systems for Molecular Biology (ISMB00), La Jolla, CA*, pages 25–36. AAAI Press, Menlo Park, CA, 2000.

[46] P. Baldi, G. Pollastri, C. A. F. Andersen, and S. Brunak. Matching protein beta-sheet partners by feedforward and recurrent neural networks. *ISMB*, 8:25–36, 2000.

[47] J. M. Baldwin. The probable arrangement of the helices in G protein coupled receptors. *EMBO J.*, 12:1693–1703, 1993.

[48] F. G. Ball and J. A. Rice. Stochastic models for ion channels: Introduction and bibliography. *Mathemat. Biosci.*, 112:189–206, 1992.

[49] N. Barkai, H. S. Seung, and H. Sompolinsky. Local and global convergence of online learning. *Phys. Rev. L*, 75:1415–1418, 1995.

[50] N. Barkai and H. Sompolinsky. Statistical mechanics of the maximum-likelihood density-estimation. *Phys. Rev. E*, 50:1766–1769, 1994.

[51] V. Barnett. *Comparative Statistical Inference*. John Wiley, New York, 1982.

[52] G. J. Barton. Protein multiple sequence alignment and flexible pattern matching. *Meth. Enzymol.*, 183:403–427, 1990.

[53] E. B. Baum. Toward a model of mind as a laissez-faire economy of idiots. Preprint, 1997.

[54] L. E. Baum. An inequality and associated maximization technique in statistical estimation for probabilistic functions of Markov processes. *Inequalities*, 3:1–8, 1972.

[55] A. A. Beaudry and G. F. Joyce. Directed evolution of an RNA enzyme. *Science*, 257:635–641, 1992.

[56] T. C. Bell, J. G. Cleary, and I. H. Witten. *Text Compression*. Prentice-Hall, Englewood Cliffs, NJ, 1990.

[57] Y. Bengio, Y. Le Cunn, and D. Henderson. Globally trained handwritten word recognizer using spatial representation, convolutional neural networks and hidden Markov models. In J. D. Cowan, G. Tesauro, and J. Alspector, editors, *Advances in Neural Information Processing Systems*, volume 6, pages 937–944. Morgan Kaufmann, San Francisco, CA, 1994.

[58] Y. Bengio and P. Frasconi. An input-output HMM architecture. In J. D. Cowan, G. Tesauro, and J. Alspector, editors, *Advances in Neural Information Processing Systems*, volume 7, pages 427–434. Morgan Kaufmann, San Francisco, 1995.

[59] R. Benne. RNA editing. The long and the short of it. *Nature*, 380:391–392, 1996.

[60] S. A. Benner. Patterns of divergence in homologous proteins as indicators of tertiary and quaternary structure. *Adv. Enzyme Regul.*, 28:219–236, 1989.

[61] S. A. Benner. Predicting the conformation of proteins from sequences. Progress and future progress. *J. Mol. Recog.*, 8:9–28, 1995.

[62] D. A. Benson, M. S. Boguski, D. J. Lipman, and J. Ostell. GenBank. *Nucl. Acids Res.*, 25:1-6, 1997.

[63] J. O. Berger. *Statistical Decision Theory and Bayesian Analysis.* Springer-Verlag, New York, 1985.

[64] A. L. Berman, E. Kolker, and E. N. Trifonov. Underlying order in protein sequence organization. *Proc. Natl. Acad. Sci. USA.*, 91:4044-4047, 1994.

[65] G. Bernardi. The human genome: Organization and evolutionary history. *Ann. Rev. Genetics*, 29:445-476, 1995.

[66] D. Bertsekas. *Dynamic Programming and Optimal Control.* Athena Scientific, Belmont, MA, 1995.

[67] D. Bertsimas and J. Tsitsiklis. Simulated annealing. *Statis. Sci.*, 8:10-15, 1993.

[68] J. Besag. Spatial interaction and the statistical analysis of lattice systems. *J. R. Statis. Soc. B*, 36:192-225, 1974.

[69] J. Besag, P. Green, D. Higdon, and K. Mengersen. Bayesian computation and stochastic systems. *Statis. Sci.*, 10:3-66, 1995.

[70] C. M. Bishop. *Neural Networks for Pattern Recognition.* Clarendon Press, Oxford, 1995.

[71] R. E. Blahut. *Principles and Practice of Information Theory.* Addison-Wesley, Reading, MA, 1987.

[72] M. Blatt, S. Wiseman, and E. Domany. Super-paramagnetic clustering of data. *Phys. Review Lett.*, 76:3251-3254, 1996.

[73] G. Blobel. Intracellular membrane topogenesis. *Proc. Natl. Acad. Sci. USA*, 77:1496, 1980.

[74] N. Blom, S. Gammeltoft, and S. Brunak. Sequence and structure-based prediction of eukaryotic protein phosphorylation sites. *J. Mol. Biol.*, 294:1351-1362, 1999.

[75] N. Blom, J. Hansen, D. Blaas, and S. Brunak. Cleavage site analysis in picornaviral polyproteins by neural networks. *Protein Sci.*, 5:2203-2216, 1996.

[76] M. Bloom and O. G. Mouritsen. The evolution of membranes. In R. Lipowsky and E. Sackmann, editors, *Handbook of Biological Physics vol. 1*, pages 65-95, Amsterdam, 1995. Elsevier Science.

[77] G. Bohm. New approaches in molecular structure prediction. *Biophys. Chem.*, 59:1-32, 1996.

[78] H. Bohr, J. Bohr, S. Brunak, R. M. J. Cotterill, B. Lautrup, L. Nørskov, O. H. Olsen, and S. B. Petersen. Protein secondary structures and homology by neural networks: The α-helices in rhodopsin. *FEBS Letters*, 241:223-228, 1988.

[79] P. Bork, C. Ouzounis, and C. Sander. From genome sequences to protein function. *Curr. Opin. Struct. Biol.*, 4:393-403, 1994.

[80] P. Bork, C. Ouzounis, C. Sander, M. Scharf, R. Schneider, and E. Sonnhammer. Comprehensive sequence analysis of the 182 predicted open reading frames of yeast chromosome iii. *Protein Sci.*, 1:1677-1690, 1992.

[81] M. Borodovsky and J. McIninch. Genmark: Parallel gene recognition for both DNA strands. *Computers Chem.*, 17:123–133, 1993.

[82] M. Borodovsky, J. D. McIninch, E. V. Koonin, K. E. Rudd, C. Medigue, and A. Danchin. Detection of new genes in a bacterial genome using Markov models for three gene classes. *Nucl. Acids Res.*, 23:3554–3562, 1995.

[83] M. Borodovsky, K. E. Rudd, and E. V. Koonin. Intrinsic and extrinsic approaches for detecting genes in a bacterial genome. *Nucl. Acids Res.*, 22:4756–4767, 1994.

[84] H. Bourlard and N. Morgan. *Connectionist Speech Recognition: A Hybrid Approach*. Kluwer Academic, Boston, 1994.

[85] J. M. Bower and D. Beeman. *The Book of Genesis: Exploring Realistic Neural Models with the GEneral NEural SImulations System*. Telos/Springer-Verlag, New York, 1995.

[86] G. E. P. Box and G. C. Tiao. *Bayesian Inference in Statistical Analysis*. Addison-Wesley, Reading, MA, 1973.

[87] A. Brack and L. E. Orgel. Beta structures of alternating polypeptides and their possible prebiotic significance. *Nature*, 256:383–387, 1975.

[88] D. Bray. Protein molecules as computational elements in living cells. *Nature*, 376:307–312, 1995.

[89] A. Brazma, I. J. Jonassen, J. Vilo, and E. Ukkonen. Predicting gene regulatory elements in silico on a genomic scale. *Genome Res.*, 8:1202–1215, 1998.

[90] L. Breiman. Discussion of neural networks and related methods for classification. *J. R. Statis. Soc. B*, 56:409–456, 1994.

[91] V. Brendel and H. G. Busse. Genome structure described by formal languages. *Nucl. Acids Res.*, 12:2561–2568, 1984.

[92] S. Brenner, G. Elgar, R. Sandford, A. Macrae, B. Venkatesh, and S. Aparicio. Characterization of the pufferfish (Fugu) genome as a compact model vertebrate genome. *Nature*, 366:265–268, 1993.

[93] S. E. Brenner, C. Chothia, and T. J. P. Hubbard. Population statistics of protein structures: lessons from structural classification. *Curr. Opin. Struct. Biol.*, 7:369–376, 1997.

[94] L. D. Brown. *Fundamentals of Statistical Exponential Families*. Institute of Mathematical Statistics, Hayward, CA, 1986.

[95] M. P. S. Brown, W. N. Grundy, D. Lin, N. Cristianini, C. Walsh Sugnet, T. S. Furey, M. Ares, and D. Haussler. Knowledge-based analysis of microarray gene expression data by using support vector machines. *Proc. Natl. Acad. Sci. USA*, 97:262–267, 2000.

[96] I. Brukner, R. Sánchez, D. Suck, and S. Pongor. Sequence-dependent bending propensity of DNA as revealed by DNase I: parameters for trinucleotides. *EMBO J.*, 14:1812–1818, 1995.

[97] S. Brunak. Non-linearities in training sets identified by inspecting the order in which neural networks learn. In O. Benhar, C. Bosio, P. Del Giudice, and E. Tabet, editors, *Neural Networks: From Biology to High Energy Physics*, pages 277–288, Pisa, 1991. ETS Editrice.

[98] S. Brunak. Doing sequence analysis by inspecting the order in which neural networks learn. In D. M. Soumpasis and T. M. Jovin, editors, *Computation of Biomolecular Structures — Achievements, Problems and Perspectives*, pages 43–54, Berlin, 1993. Springer-Verlag.

[99] S. Brunak and J. Engelbrecht. Correlation between protein secondary structure and the mRNA nucleotide sequence. *Proteins*, 25:237–252, 1996.

[100] S. Brunak, J. Engelbrecht, and S. Knudsen. Cleaning up gene databases. *Nature*, 343:123, 1990.

[101] S. Brunak, J. Engelbrecht, and S. Knudsen. Neural network detects errors in the assignment of pre-mRNA splice site. *Nucl. Acids Res.*, 18:4797–4801, 1990.

[102] S. Brunak, J. Engelbrecht, and S. Knudsen. Prediction of human mRNA donor and acceptor sites from the DNA sequence. *J. Mol. Biol.*, 220:49–65, 1991.

[103] S. Brunak and B. Lautrup. *Neural Networks—Computers with Intuition.* World Scientific Pub., Singapore, 1990.

[104] J. Buhmann and H. Kuhnel. Vector quantization with complexity costs. *IEEE Trans. Information Theory*, 39:1133–1145, 1993.

[105] C. J. Bult, O. White, G. J. Olsen, L. Zhou, R. D. Fleischmann, G. G. Sutton, J. A. Blake, L. M. FitzGerald, R. A. Clayton, J. D. Gocayne, A. R. Kerlavage, B. A. Dougherty, J. F. Tomb, M. D. Adams, C. I. Reich, R. Overbeek, E. F. Kirkness, K. G. Weinstock, J. M. Merrick, A. Glodek, J. L. Scott, N. S. M. Geoghagen, and J. C. Venter. Complete genome sequence of the methanogenic archaeon, *Methanococcus jannaschii. Science*, 273:1058–1073, 1996.

[106] W. Buntine. A guide to the literature on learning probabilistic networks from data. *IEEE Trans. Knowledge Data Eng.*, 8:195–210, 1996.

[107] C. Burge and S. Karlin. Prediction of complete gene structures in human genomic dna. *J. Mol. Biol.*, 268:78–94, 1997.

[108] C. J. C. Burges. A tutorial on support vector machines for pattern recognition. *Data Mining and Knowledge Discovery*, 2:121–167, 1998.

[109] J. M. Burke and A. Berzal-Herranz. In vitro selection and evolution of RNA: Applications for catalytic RNA, molecular recognition, and drug discovery. *Faseb J.*, 7:106–112, 1993.

[110] M. Burset and R. Guigó. Evaluation of gene structure prediction programs. *Genomics*, 34:353–367, 1996.

[111] H. J. Bussemaker, H. Li, and E. D. Siggia. Building a dictionary for genomes: identification of presumptive regulatory sites by statistical analysis. *Proc. Natl. Acad. Sci. USA*, 97:10096–10100, 2000.

[112] C. R. Calladine and H. R. Drew. *Understanding DNA—The Molecule and How it Works*. Academic Press, London, 1992.

[113] L. R. Cardon and G. D. Stormo. Expectation-maximization algorithm for identifying protein-binding sites with variable lengths from unaligned DNA fragments. *J. Mol. Biol.*, 223:159-170, 1992.

[114] C. R. Carlson and A. B. Kolsto. A small (2.4 mb) bacillus cereus chromosome corresponds to a conserved region of a larger (5.3 mb) bacillus cereus chromosome. *Mol. Microbiol.*, 13:161-169, 1994.

[115] R. Caruana. Learning many related tasks at the same time with backpropagation. In J. D. Cowan, G. Tesauro, and J. Alspector, editors, *Advances in Neural Information Processing Systems 7*, pages 657-664, San Mateo, CA, 1995. Morgan Kaufmann.

[116] T. Cavalier-Smith. Introduction: The evolutionary significance of genome size. In T. Cavalier-Smith, editor, *The Evolution of Genome Size*, pages 1-36. John Wiley & Sons, Chichester, UK, 1985.

[117] T. Cavalier-Smith. The origin of cells: A symbiosis between genes, catalysts, and membranes. *Cold Spring Harbor Symp. Quant. Biol.*, 52:805-824, 1987.

[118] J. M. Chandonia and M. Karplus. New methods for accurate prediction of protein secondary structure. *Proteins*, 35:293-306, 1999.

[119] E. Chargaff. Structure and function of nucleic acids as cell constituents. *Fed. Proc.*, 10:654-659, 1951.

[120] E. Chargaff. How genetics got a chemical education. *Ann. N. Y. Acad. Sci.*, 325:345-360, 1979.

[121] E. Charniak. Bayesian networks without tears. *AI Mag.*, 12:50-63, 1991.

[122] P. Cheeseman. An inquiry into computer understanding. *Comput. Intell.*, 4:57-142, 1988. With discussion.

[123] R. O. Chen, R. Felciano, and R. B. Altman. RIBOWEB: linking structural computations to a knowledge base of published experimental data. *ISMB*, 5:84-87, 1997.

[124] Y. Cheng and G. M. Church. Biclustering of expression data. In *Proceedings of the 2000 Conference on Intelligent Systems for Molecular Biology (ISMB00), La Jolla, CA*, pages 93-103. AAAI Press, Menlo Park, CA, 2000.

[125] G. I. Chipens, Y. U. I. Balodis, and L. E. Gnilomedova. Polarity and hydropathic properties of natural amino acids. *Ukrain. Biokhim. Zh.*, 63:20-29, 1991.

[126] Sung-Bae Cho and Jin H. Kim. An HMM/MLP architecture for sequence recognition. *Neural Comp.*, 7:358-369, 1995.

[127] C. Chotia. One thousand families for the molecular biologist. *Nature*, 357:543-544, 1992.

[128] P. Y. Chou and G. D. Fasman. Empirical predictions of protein conformations. *Ann. Rev. Biochem.*, 47:251-276, 1978.

[129] P.Y. Chou and G.D. Fasman. Prediction of the secondary structure of proteins from their amino acid sequence. *Adv. Enzymol. Relat. Areas Mol. Biol.*, 47:45–148, 1978.

[130] G. A. Churchill. Stochastic models for heterogeneous DNA sequences. *Bull. Mathem. Biol.*, 51:79–94, 1989.

[131] M. G. Claros, S. Brunak, and G. von Heijne. Prediction of n-terminal protein sorting signals. *Curr. Opin. Struct. Biol.*, 7:394–398, 1997.

[132] J-M. Claverie. What if there are only 30,000 human genes. *Science*, 291:1255–1257, 2001.

[133] N. Colloc'h and F. E. Cohen. Beta-breakers: An aperiodic secondary structure. *J. Mol. Biol.*, 221:603–613, 1991.

[134] Int. Human Genome Sequencing Consortium. Initial sequencing and analysis of the human genome. *Nature*, 409:860–921, 2001.

[135] G. F. Cooper. The computational complexity of probabilistic inference using Bayesian belief networks. *Art. Intell.*, 42:393–405, 1990.

[136] J. L. Cornette, K. B. Cease, H. Margalit, J. L. Spouge, J. A. Berzofsky, and C. DeLisi. Hydrophobicity scales and computational techniques for detecting amphiphatic structures in proteins. *J. Mol. Biol.*, 195:659–685, 1987.

[137] T. M. Cover and J. A. Thomas. *Elements of Information Theory.* John Wiley, New York, 1991.

[138] R. T. Cox. Probability, frequency and reasonable expectation. *Am. J. Phys.*, 14:1–13, 1964.

[139] I. P. Crawford, T. Niermann, and K. Kirschner. Prediction of secondary structure by evolutionary comparison: application to the alpha subunit of tryptophan synthase. *Proteins*, 2:118–129, 1987.

[140] F. H. C. Crick. The origin of the genetic code. *J. Mol. Biol.*, 38:367–379, 1968.

[141] N. Cristianini and J. Shawe-Taylor. *An Introduction to Support Vector Machines.* Cambridge University Press, Cambridge, UK, 2000.

[142] L. Croft, S. Schandorff, F. Clark, K. Burrage, P. Arctander, and J. S. Mattick. ISIS, the intron information system, reveals the high frequency of alternative splicing in the human genome. *Nature Genet.*, 24:340–341, 2000.

[143] S. Dalal, S. Balasubramanian, and L. Regan. Protein alchemy: Changing beta-sheet into alpha-helix. *Nat. Struct. Biol.*, 4:548–552, 1997.

[144] S. Das, L. Yu, C. Gaitatzes, R. Rogers, J. Freeman, J. Bienkowska, R. M. Adams, T. F. Smith, and J. Lindelien. Biology's new Rosetta Stone. *Nature*, 385:29–30, 1997.

[145] A. P. Dawid. Applications of a general propagation algorithm for probabilistic expert systems. *Stat. Comp.*, 2:25–36, 1992.

[146] P. Dayan, G. E. Hinton, R. M. Neal, and R. S. Zemel. The Helmholtz machine. *Neural Comp.*, 7:889–904, 1995.

[147] A. P. Dempster, N. M. Laird, and D. B. Rubin. Maximum likelihood from incomplete data via the EM algorithm. *J. R. Statis. Soc.*, B39:1–22, 1977.

[148] J. L. DeRisi, V. R. Iyer, and P. O. Brown. Exploring the metabolic and genetic control of gene expression on a genomic scale. *Science*, 278:680–686, 1997.

[149] D. Devos and A. Valencia. Practical limits of function prediction. *Proteins*, 41:98–107, 2000.

[150] P. Diaconis and D. Stroock. Geometric bounds for eigenvalues of Markov chains. *Ann. Appl. Prob.*, 1:36–61, 1991.

[151] K. A. Dill, S. Bromberg, K. Yue, K. M. Fiebig, D. P. Yee, P. D. Thomas, and H. S. Chan. Principles of protein folding—a perspective from simple exact models. *Protein Sci.*, 4:561–602, 1995.

[152] S. Duane, A. D. Kennedy, B. J. Pendleton, and D. Roweth. Hybrid Monte Carlo. *Phys. Lett. B*, 195:216–222, 1987.

[153] R. O. Duda and P. E. Hart. *Pattern Classification and Scene Analysis.* John Wiley and Sons, 1973.

[154] R. Durbin, S. R. Eddy, A. Krogh, and G. Mitchison. *Biological Sequence Analysis: Probabilistic Models of Proteins and Nucleic Acids.* Cambridge University Press, Cambridge, 1998.

[155] S. R. Eddy. Hidden Markov models. *Curr. Opin. Struct. Biol.*, 6:361–365, 1996.

[156] S. R. Eddy and R. Durbin. RNA sequence analysis using covariance models. *Nucl. Acids Res.*, 22:2079–2088, 1994.

[157] S. R. Eddy, G. Mitchinson, and R. Durbin. Maximum discrimination hidden Markov models of sequence consensus. *J. Comp. Biol.*, 2:9–23, 1995.

[158] H. Ehrig, M. Korff, and M. Lowe. Tutorial introduction to the algebraic approach of graph grammars based on double and single pushouts. In H. Ehrig, H. J. Kreowski, and G. Rozenberg, editors, *Lecture Notes in Computer Science*, volume 532, pages 24–37. Springer-Verlag, 1991.

[159] M. Eigen. The hypercycle. A principle of natural self-organization. Part A: Emergence of the hypercycle. *Naturwissenschaften*, 64:541–565, 1977.

[160] M. B. Eisen, P. T. Spellman, P. O. Brown, and D. Botstein. Cluster analysis and display of genome-wide expression patterns. *Proc. Natl. Acad. Sci USA*, 95:14863–14868, 1998.

[161] D. Eisenberg. Into the black night. *Nat. Struct. Biol.*, 4:95–97, 1997.

[162] D. Eisenberg, E. M. Marcotte, and I. Xenarios T. O. Yeates. Protein function in the post-genomic era. *Nature*, 405:823–826, 2000.

[163] G. Elgar, R. Sandford, S. Aparicio, A. Macrae, B. Venkatesh, and S. Brenner. Small is beautiful: Comparative genomics with the pufferfish (*Fugu rubripes*). *Trends Genet.*, 12:145–150, 1996.

[164] J. Engelbrecht, S. Knudsen, and S. Brunak. G/C rich tract in the 5' end of human introns. *J. Mol. Biol.*, 227:108–113, 1992.

[165] J. Engelfriet and G. Rozenberg. Graph grammars based on node rewriting: An introduction to NLC graph grammars. In H. Ehrig, H. J. Kreowski, and G. Rozenberg, editors, *Lecture Notes in Computer Science*, volume 532, pages 12-23. Springer-Verlag, 1991.

[166] D. M. Engelman, T. A. Steitz, and A. Goldman. Identifying nonpolar transbilayer helices in amino acid sequences of membrane proteins. *Ann. Rev. Biophys. Biophys. Chem.*, 15:321-353, 1986.

[167] A. J. Enright, I. Iliopoulos, N. C. Kyrpides, and C. A. Ouzounis. Protein interaction maps for complete genomes based on gene fusion events. *Nature*, 402:86-90, 1999.

[168] C. J. Epstein. Role of the amino-acid "code" and of selection for conformation in the evolution of proteins. *Nature*, 210:25-28, 1966.

[169] D. T. Ross et al. Systematic variation in gene expression patterns in human cancer cell lines. *Nat. Genet.*, 24:227-235, 2000.

[170] J. C. Venter et al. The sequence of the human genome. *Science*, 291:1304-1351, 2001.

[171] U. Scherf et al. A gene expression database for the molecular pharmacology of cancer. *Nat. Genet.*, 24:236-244, 2000.

[172] B. S. Everitt. *An Introduction to Latent Variable Models*. Chapman and Hall, London, 1984.

[173] B. S. Everitt and D. J. Hand. *Finite Mixture Distributions*. Chapman and Hall, London and New York, 1981.

[174] P. Fariselli and R. Casadio. Prediction of the number of residue contacts in proteins. *ISMB*, 8:146-151, 19.

[175] B. A. Fedorov. Long-range order in globular proteins. *FEBS Lett.*, 62:139-141, 1976.

[176] W. Feller. *An Introduction to Probability Theory and its Applications*, volume 1. John Wiley & Sons, New York, 3rd edition, 1968.

[177] W. Feller. *An Introduction to Probability Theory and its Applications*, volume 2. John Wiley & Sons, New York, 2nd edition, 1971.

[178] J. Felsenstein. Evolutionary trees from DNA sequences: A maximum likelihood approach. *J. Mol. Evol.*, 17:368-376, 1981.

[179] E. A. Ferran, B. Pflugfelder, and P. Ferrara. Self-organized neural maps of human protein sequences. *Protein Sci.*, 3:507-521, 1994.

[180] J. A. Fill. Eigenvalue bounds on convergence to stationarity for nonreversible Markov chains with an application to an exclusion process. *Ann. Appl. Prob.*, 1:62-87, 1991.

[181] W. M. Fitch. Towards defining the course of evolution: Minimum change for a specific tree topology. *Syst. Zool.*, 20:406-416, 1971.

[182] W. M. Fitch and E. Margoliash. Construction of phylogenetic trees. *Science*, 155:279–284, 1967.

[183] R. D. Fleischmann, M. D. Adams, O. White, R. A. Clayton, E. F. Kirkness, A. R. Kerlavage, C. J. Bult, J. F. Tomb, B. A. Dougherty, and J. M. Merrick. Whole-genome random sequencing and assembly of Haemophilus influenzae Rd. *Science*, 269:496–512, 1995.

[184] M. L. Forcada and R. C. Carrasco. Learning the initial state of a second-order recurrent neural network during regular-language inference. *Neural Comp.*, 7:923–930, 1995.

[185] D. R. Forsdyke. Relative roles of primary sequence and (G+C)% in determining the hierarchy of frequencies of complementary trinucleotide pairs in dnas of different species. *J. Mol. Evol.*, 41:573–581, 1995.

[186] G. E. Fox and C. R. Woese. The architecture of 5S rRNA and its relation to function. *J. Mol. Evol.*, 6:61–76, 1975.

[187] V. Di Francesco, J. Garnier, and P. J. Munson. Protein topology recognition from secondary structure sequences—Applications of the hidden Markov models to the alpha class proteins. *J. Mol. Biol.*, 267:446–463, 1997.

[188] P. Frasconi, M. Gori, and A. Sperduti. A general framework for adaptive processing of data structures. *IEEE Trans. Neural Networks*, 9:768–786, 1998.

[189] C. M. Fraser, J. D. Gocayne, O. White, M. D. Adams, R. A. Clayton, R. D. Fleischmann, C. J. Bult, A. R. Kerlavage, G. Sutton, and J. M. Kelley. The minimal gene complement of *Mycoplasma genitalium*. *Science*, 270:397–403, 1995.

[190] N. Friedman, M. Linial, I. Nachman, and D. Pe'er. Using Bayesian networks to analyze expression data. *J. Comp. Biol.*, 7:601–620, 2000.

[191] A. Frigessi, P. Di Stefano, C. R. Hwang, and S. J. Sheu. Convergence rate of the Gibbs sampler, the Metropolis algorithm and other single-site updating dynamics. *J. R. Stat. Soc.*, 55:205–219, 1993.

[192] D. Frishman and P. Argos. Knowledge-based secondary structure assignment. *Proteins*, 23:566–579, 1995.

[193] Y. Fujiwara, M. Asogawa, and A. Konagaya. Stochastic motif extraction using hidden Markov models. In *Proceedings of Second International Conference on Intelligent Systems for Molecular Biology*, pages 138–146, Menlo Park, CA, 1994. AAAI/MIT Press.

[194] T. S. Furey, N. Cristianini, N. Duffy, D. W. Bednarski, M. Schummer, and D. Haussler. Support vector machine classification and validation of cancer tissue samples using microarray expression data. *Bioinformatics*, 16:906–914, 2000.

[195] G. Gamow. Possible relation between deoxyribonucleic acid and protein structures. *Nature*, 173:318, 1954.

[196] J. Garnier, D. J. Osguthorpe, and B. Robson. Analysis of the accuracy and implications of simple methods for predicting the secondary structure of globular proteins. *J. Mol. Biol.*, 120:97–120, 1978.

[197] R. A. Garrett. Genomes: *Methanococcus jannaschii* and the golden fleece. *Curr. Biol.*, 6:1376-1377, 1996.

[198] A. Gelman and T. P. Speed. Characterizing a joint probability distribution by conditionals. *J. R. Statis. Soc. B*, 55:185-188, 1993.

[199] S. Geman and D. Geman. Stochastic relaxation, Gibbs distributions and the Bayesian restoration of images. *IEEE Trans. Pattern Anal. Machine Intell.*, 6:721-741, 1984.

[200] D. Gerhold and C. T. Caskey. It's the genes! EST access to human genome content. *Bioessays*, 18:973-981, 1996.

[201] M. Gerstein, E. Sonnhammer, and C. Chotia. Volume changes in protein evolution. *J. Mol. Biol.*, 236:1067-1078, 1994.

[202] C. J. Geyer. Practical Markov chain Monte Carlo. *Statis. Sci.*, 7:473-511, 1992.

[203] Z. Ghahramani. Learning dynamic Bayesian networks. *Adap. Proc. Seq. Data Struct.*, 1387:168-197, 1998.

[204] Z. Ghahramani. Learning dynamic Bayesian networks. In M. Gori and C. L. Giles, editors, *Adaptive Processing of Temporal Information. Lecture Notes in Artifical Intelligence*. Springer Verlag, Heidelberg, 1998.

[205] Z. Ghahramani and M. I. Jordan. Factorial hidden Markov models. *Machine Learning*, 1997.

[206] M. Gibbs and D. J. C. MacKay. Efficient implementation of Gaussian processes. Technical report, Cavendish Laboratory, Cambridge, UK, 1997.

[207] L. M. Gierasch. Signal sequences. *Biochemistry*, 28:923-930, 1989.

[208] C. L. Giles, C. B. Miller, D. Chen, H. H. Chen, G. Z. Sun, and Y. C. Lee. Learning and extracting finite state automata with second-order recurrent neural networks. *Neural Comp.*, 4:393-405, 1992.

[209] W. R. Gilks, D. G. Clayton, D. J. Spiegelhalter, N. G. Best, A. J. McNeil, L. D. Sharples, and A. J. Kirby. Modelling complexity: Applications of Gibbs sampling in medicine. *J. R. Statis. Soc.*, 55:39-52, 1993.

[210] W. R. Gilks, A. Thomas, and D. J. Spiegelhalter. A language and program for complex Bayesian modelling. *The Statistician*, 43:69-78, 1994.

[211] P. Gill, P. L. Ivanov, C. Kimpton, R. Piercy, N. Benson, G. Tully, I. Evett, E. Hagelberg, and K. Sullivan. Identification of the remains of the Romanov family by DNA analysis. *Nat. Genet.*, 6:130-135, 1994.

[212] P. Gill, C. Kimpton, R. Aliston-Greiner, K. Sullivan, M. Stoneking, T. Melton, J. Nott, S. Barritt, R. Roby, and M. Holland. Establishing the identity of Anna Anderson Manahan. *Nat. Genet.*, 9:9-10, 1995.

[213] V. Giudicelli and M.-P. Lefranc. Ontology for Immunogenetics: IMGT-ONTOLOGY. *Bioinformatics*, 12:1047-1054, 1999.

[214] U. Gobel, C. Sander, R. Schneider, and A. Valencia. Correlated mutations and residue contacts in proteins. *Proteins*, 18:309-317, 1994.

[215] A. Goffeau. Life with 6000 genes. *Science*, 274:546, 1996.

[216] A. L. Goldberg and R. E. Wittes. Genetic code: Aspects of organization. *Science*, 153:420–424, 1966.

[217] T. R. Golub, D. K. Slonim, P. Tamayo, C. Huard, M. Gaasenbeek, J. P. Mesirov, H. Coller, M. L. Loh, J. R. Downing, M. A. Caligiuri, C. D. Bloomfield, and E. S. Lander. Molecular classification of cancer: class discovery and class prediction by gene expression monitoring. *Science*, 286:531–537, 1999.

[218] D. S. Goodsell and R. E. Dickerson. Bending and curvature calculations in B-DNA. *Nucl. Acids Res.*, 22:5497–5503, 1994.

[219] J. Gorodkin, L. J. Heyer, S. Brunak, and G. D. Stormo. Displaying the information contents of structural RNA alignments: the structure logos. *CABIOS*, 13:583–586, 1997.

[220] J. Gorodkin, L. J. Heyer, and G. D. Stormo. Finding common sequence and structure motifs in a set of RNA sequences. In T. Gaasterland, P. Karp, K. Karplus, C. Ouzounis, C. Sander, and A. Valencia, editors, *Proceedings of the Fifth International Conference on Intellelligent Systems for Molecular Biology*, pages 120–123, Menlo Park, California, 1997. AAAI/MIT Press.

[221] J. Gorodkin, L. J. Heyer, and G. D. Stormo. Finding the most significant common sequence and structure motifs in a set of RNA sequences. *Nucl. Acids Res.*, 25:3724–3732, 1997.

[222] M. Gouy, P. Marliere, C. Papanicolaou, and J. Ninio. Prediction of secondary structures of nucleic acids: Algorithmic and physical aspects. *Biochimie*, 67:523–531, 1985.

[223] C. W. J. Granger. Combining forecasts—twenty years later. *J. Forecasting*, 8:167–173, 1989.

[224] P. Green, D. Lipman, L. Hillier, R. Waterson, D. States, and J. M. Claverie. Ancient conserved regions in new gene sequences and the protein databases. *Science*, 259:1711–1716, 1993.

[225] P. C. Gregory and T. J. Loredo. A new method for the detection of a periodic signal of unknown shape and period. *Astrophys. J.*, 398:146–168, 1992.

[226] M. Gribskov, A. D. McLachlan, and D. Eisenberg. Profile analysis: Detection of distantly related proteins. *Proc. Natl. Acad. Sci. USA*, 84:4355–4358, 1987.

[227] T. Gudermann, T. Schoneberg, and G. Schultz. Functional and structural complexity of signal transduction via g-protein-coupled receptors. *Annu. Rev. Neurosci.*, 20:399–427, 1997.

[228] S. F. Gull. Bayesian inductive inference and maximum entropy. In G. J. Erickson and C. R. Smith, editors, *Maximum entropy and Bayesian methods in science and engineering*, pages 53–74. Kluwer, Dordrecht, 1988.

[229] S.F. Gull. Developments in maximum entropy data analysis. In J. Skilling, editor, *Maximum entropy and Bayesian methods*, pages 53–71. Kluwer, Dordrecht, 1989.

[230] B. Hajeck. Cooling schedules for optimal annealing. *Math. of Operation Res.*, 13:311–329, 1988.

[231] S. Hampson, P. Baldi, D. Kibler, and S. Sandmeyer. Analysis of yeast's ORFs upstream regions by parallel processing, microarrays, and computational methods. In *Proceedings of the 2000 Conference on Intelligent Systems for Molecular Biology (ISMB00), La Jolla, CA*, pages 190–201. AAAI Press, Menlo Park, CA, 2000.

[232] S. Hampson, D. Kibler, and P. Baldi. Distribution patterns of locally over-represented *k*-mers in non-coding yeast DNA. 2001. Submitted.

[233] S. Handley. Classifying nucleic acid sub-sequences as introns or exons using genetic programming. In C. Rawlings, D. Clark, R. Altman, L. Hunter, T. Lengauer, and S. Wodak, editors, *Proceedings of the Third International Conference on Intelligent Systems for Molecular Biology*, pages 162–169. AAAI Press, Menlo Park, CA, 1995.

[234] J. Hanke, D. Brett, I. Zastrow, A. Aydin, S. Delbruck, G. Lehmann, F. Luft, J. Reich, and P. Bork. Alternative splicing of human genes: more the rule than the exception? *Trends Genet.*, 15:389–390, 1999.

[235] J. E. Hansen, O. Lund, J. Engelbrecht, H. Bohr, J. O. Nielsen, J. E.-S. Hansen, and S. Brunak. Prediction of O-glycosylation of mammalian proteins: Specificity patterns of UDP-GalNAc:polypeptide n-acetylgalactosaminyltransferase. *J. Biochem. Biol.*, 307:801–813, 1995.

[236] J. E. Hansen, O. Lund, N. Tolstrup, A. A. Gooley, K. L. Williams, and S. Brunak. NetOglyc: prediction of mucin type O-glycosylation sites based on sequence context and surface accessibility. *Glycocon. J.*, 15:115–130, 1998.

[237] L. Hansen and P. Salamon. Neural network ensembles. *IEEE Trans. Pattern Anal. and Machine Intell.*, 12:993–1001, 1990.

[238] J. C. Harsanyi. *Rational behaviour and bargaining equilibrium in games and social situations.* Cambridge University Press, Cambridge, UK, 1977.

[239] L. H. Hartwell, J. J. Hopfield, S. Leibler, and A. W. Murray. From molecular to modular cell biology. *Nature*, 402, Supp.:C47–C52, 1999.

[240] M. Hasegawa and T. Miyata. On the antisymmetry of the amino acid code table. *Orig. Life*, 10:265–270, 1980.

[241] M. A. El Hassan and C. R. Calladine. Propeller-twisting of base-pairs and the conformational mobility of dinucleotide steps in DNA. *J. Mol. Biol.*, 259:95–103, 1996.

[242] W. K. Hastings. Monte Carlo sampling methods using Markov chains and their applications. *Biometrika*, 57:97–109, 1970.

[243] J. Hasty, J. Pradines, M. Dolnik, and J. J. Collins. Noise-based switches and amplifiers for gene expression. *Proc. Natl. Acad. Sci. USA*, 97:2075–2080, 2000.

[244] S. Hayward and J. F. Collins. Limits on α-helix prediction with neural network models. *Proteins*, 14:372–381, 1992.

[245] S. M. Hebsgaard, P. G. Korning, N. Tolstrup, J. Engelbrecht, P. Rouzé, and S. Brunak. Splice site prediction in *Arabidopsis thaliana* pre-mRNA by combining local and global sequence information. *Nucl. Acids Res.*, 24:3439–3452, 1996.

[246] D. Heckerman. Bayesian networks for data mining. *Data Mining and Knowl. Discov.*, 1:79–119, 1997.

[247] J. Hein. Unified approach to alignment and phylogenies. *Meth. Enzymol.*, 183:626–645, 1990.

[248] R. Henderson, J. M. Baldwin, T. A. Ceska, F. Zemlin, E. Beckmann, and K. H. Downing. Model for the structure of bacteriorhodopsin based on high-resolution electron cryo-microscopy. *J. Mol. Biol.*, 213:899–929, 1990.

[249] S. Henikoff and J. Henikoff. Position-based sequence weights. *J. Mol. Biol.*, 243:574–578, 1994.

[250] S. Henikoff and J. G. Henikoff. Protein family classification based on searching a database of blocks. *Genomics*, 19:97–107, 1994.

[251] B. Hermann and S. Hummel, editors. *Ancient DNA.* Springer-Verlag, New York, 1994.

[252] J. Hertz, A. Krogh, and R.G. Palmer. *Introduction to the theory of neural computation.* Addison-Wesley, Redwood City, CA, 1991.

[253] L. J. Heyer, S. Kruglyak, and S. Yooseph. Exploring expression data: identification and analysis of co-expressed genes. *Genome Res.*, 9:1106–1115, 1999.

[254] R. Hinegardner. Evolution of cellular DNA content in teleost fishes. *Am. Nat.*, 102:517–523, 1968.

[255] G. E. Hinton, P. Dayan, B. J. Frey, and R. M. Neal. The wake-sleep algorithm for unsupervised neural networks. *Science*, 268:1158–1161, 1995.

[256] H. Le Hir, M. J. Moore, and L. E. Maquat. Pre-mrna splicing alters mRNP composition: evidence for stable association of proteins at exon-exon junctions. *Genes Dev.*, 14:1098–1108, 2000.

[257] R. Hirata, Y. Ohsumk, A. Nakano, H. Kawasaki, K. Suzuki, and Y. Anraku. Molecular structure of a gene, vma1, encoding the catalytic subunit of H(+)- translocating adenosine triphosphatase from vacuolar membranes of *Saccharomyces cerevisiae. J. Biol. Chem.*, 265:6726–6733, 1990.

[258] W. S. Hlavacek and M. S. Savageau. Completely uncoupled and perfectly coupled gene expression in repressible systems. *J. Mol. Biol.*, 266:538–558, 1997.

[259] U. Hobohm, M. Scharf, R. Schneider, and C. Sander. Selection of representative protein data sets. *Protein Sci.*, 1:409–417, 1992.

[260] I. L. Hofacker, W. Fontana, P. F. Stadler, S. Bonherffer, M. Tacker, and P. Schuster. Fast folding and comparison of RNA secondary structures. *Monatshefte f. Chemie*, 125:167–188, 1994.

[261] J. H. Holland. *Adaptation in Natural and Artificial Systems: An Introductory Analysis with Applications to Biology, Control, and Artificial Intelligence.* MIT Press, Cambridge, MA, 1992.

[262] L. H. Holley and M. Karplus. Protein secondary structure prediction with a neural network. *Proc. Nat. Acad. Sci. USA*, 86:152-156, 1989.

[263] F. C. P. Holstege, E. G. Jennings, J. J. Wyrick, T. I. Lee, C. J. Hengartner, M. R. Green, T. R. Golub, E. S. Lander, and R. A. Young. Dissecting the regulatory circuitry of a eukaryotic genome. *Cell*, 95:717-728, 1998.

[264] K. Hornik, M. Stinchcombe, and H. White. Universal approximation of an unknown function and its derivatives using multilayer feedforward networks. *Neural Networks*, 3:551-560, 1990.

[265] K. Hornik, M. Stinchcombe, H. White, and P. Auer. Degree of approximation results for feedforward networks approximating unknown mappings and their derivatives. *Neural Comp.*, 6:1262-1275, 1994.

[266] Z. Huang, S. B. Prusiner, and F. E. Cohen. Scrapie prions: A three-dimensional model of an infectious fragment. *Folding & Design*, 1:13-19, 1996.

[267] Z. Huang, S. B. Prusiner, and F. E. Cohen. Structures of prion proteins and conformational models for prion diseases. *Curr. Top. Microbiol. Immunol.*, 207:49-67, 1996.

[268] T. J. Hubbard and J. Park. Fold recognition and ab initio structure predictions using hidden Markov models and beta-strand pair potentials. *Proteins*, 25:398-402, 1995.

[269] J. P. Huelsenbeck and B. Rannala. Phylogenetic methods come of age: Testing hypotheses in an evoutionary context. *Science*, 276:227-232, 1997.

[270] J. D. Hughes, P. W. Estep, S. Tavazole, and G. M. Church. Computational identification of *cis*-regulatory elements associated with groups of functionally related genes in *saccharomyces cerevisiae*. *J. Mol. Biol.*, 296:1205-1214, 2000.

[271] T. R. Hughes, M. J. Marton, A. R. Jones, C. J. Roberts, R. Stoughton, C. D. Armour, H. A. Bennett, E. Coffey, H. Dai, Y. D. He, K. J. Kidd, A. M. King, M. R. Meyer, D. Slade, P. Y. Lum, S. B. Stepaniants, D. D. Shoemaker, D. Gachotte, K. Chakraburtty, J. Simon, M. Bard, and S. H. Friend. Functional discovery via a compendium of expression profiles. *Cell*, 102:109-126, 2000.

[272] V. Isham. An introduction to spatial point processes and Markov random fields. *Internat. Statist. Rev.*, 49:21-43, 1981.

[273] O. C. Ivanov and B. Förtsch. Universal regularities in protein primary structure: preference in bonding and periodicity. *Orig. Life Evol. Biosph.*, 17:35-49, 1986.

[274] P. L. Ivanov, M. J. Wadhams, R. K. Roby, M. M. Holland, V. W. Weedn, and T. J. Parsons. Mitochondrial DNA sequence heteroplasmy in the grand duke of Russia Georgij Romanov establishes the authenticity of the remains of Tsar Nicholas II. *Nat. Genet.*, 12:417-420, 1996.

[275] T. S. Jaakkola, M. Diekhans, and D. Haussler. Using the Fisher kernel method to detect remore protein homologies. In T. Lengauer, R. Schneider, P. Bork, D. Brutlag, J. Glasgow, H. W. Mewes, and R. Zimmer, editors, *Proceedings of the Seventh International Conference on Intelligent Systems for Molecular Biology (ISMB99)*, pages 149-155. AAAI Press, Menlo Park, CA, 1999.

[276] T. S. Jaakkola and I. Jordan. Recursive algorithms for approximating probabilities in graphical models. In M. C. Mozer, M. I. Jordan, and T. Petsche, editors, *Advances in Neural Information Processing Systems*, volume 9, pages 487–493. MIT Press, Cambridge, MA, 1997.

[277] R. A. Jacobs, M. I. Jordan, S. J. Nowlan, and G. E. Hinton. Adaptive mixtures of local experts. *Neural Comp.*, 3:79–87, 1991.

[278] B. D. James, G. J. Olsen, and N. R. Pace. Phylogenetic comparative analysis of RNA secondary structure. *Meth. Enzymol.*, 180:227–239, 1989.

[279] P. G. Jansen. *Exploring the exon universe using neural networks*. PhD thesis, The Technical University of Denmark, 1993.

[280] E. T. Jaynes. Information theory and statistical mechanics. *Phys. Rev.*, 106:620–630, 1957.

[281] E. T. Jaynes. Information theory and statistical mechanics. II. *Phys. Rev.*, 108:171–190, 1957.

[282] E. T. Jaynes. Prior probabilities. *IEEE Trans. Systems Sci. Cybernet.*, 4:227–241, 1968.

[283] E. T. Jaynes. Bayesian methods: General background. In J. H. Justice, editor, *Maximum entropy and Bayesian methods in statistics*, pages 1–25. Cambridge University Press, Cambridge, 1986.

[284] E. T. Jaynes. Probability theory: The logic of science. Unpublished., 1994.

[285] W. H. Jeffreys and J. O. Berger. Ockham's razor and Bayesian analysis. *Am. Sci.*, 80:64–72, 1992.

[286] F. V. Jensen. *An Introduction to Bayesian Networks*. Springer Verlag, New York, 1996.

[287] F. V. Jensen, S. L. Lauritzen, and K. G. Olesen. Bayesian updating in causal probabilistic networks by local computations. *Comput. Statist. Quart.*, 4:269–282, 1990.

[288] L. J. Jensen, R. Gupta, N. Blom, D. Devos, J. Tamames, C. Kesmir, H. Nielsen, C. Workman, C. A. Andersen, K. Rapacki, H.H. Stærfelt, A. Krogh, S. Knudsen, A. Valencia, and S. Brunak. Using posttranslational modifications to predict orphan protein function for the human genome. *Submitted*, 2001.

[289] H. Jeong, B. Tomber, R. Albert, Z.N. Oltvai, and A.-L. Barabasi. The large-scale organization of metabolic networks. *Nature*, 407:651–654, 2000. in press.

[290] D. T. Jones. Protein secondary structure prediction based on position-specific scoring matrices. *J. Mol. Biol.*, 292:195–202, 1999.

[291] D. T. Jones, C. M. Moody, J. Uppenbrink, J. H. Viles, P. M. Doyle, C. J. Harris, L. H. Pearl, P. J. Sadler, and J. M. Thornton. Towards meeting the Paracelsus challenge: The design, synthesis, and characterization of paracelsin-43, an alpha-helical protein with over 50% sequence identity to an all-beta protein. *Proteins*, 24:502–513, 1996.

[292] M. I. Jordan. *Learning in Graphical Models*. MIT Press, Cambridge, MA, 1999.

[293] M. I. Jordan, Z. Ghahramani, and L. K. Saul. Hidden Markov decision trees. In M. C. Mozer, M. I. Jordan, and T. Petsche, editors, *Advances in Neural Information Processing Systems*, volume 9, pages 501-507. MIT Press, Cambridge, MA, 1997.

[294] T. H. Jukes. Possibilities for the evolution of the genetic code from a preceding form. *Nature*, 246:22-26, 1973.

[295] T. H. Jukes and C. R. Cantor. Evolution of protein molecules. In *Mammalian Protein Metabolism*, pages 21-132. Academic Press, New York, 1969.

[296] B. Jungnickel, T.A. Rapoport, and E. Hartmann. Protein translocation: Common themes from bacteria to man. *FEBS Lett.*, 346:73-77, 1994.

[297] W. Kabsch and C. Sander. Dictionary of protein secondary structure: Pattern recognition of hydrogen-bonded and geometrical features. *Biopolymers*, 22:2577-2637, 1983.

[298] L. P. Kaelbling, M. L. Littman, and A. W. Moore. Reinforcement learning: A survey. *J. Art. Intell. Res.*, 4:237-285, 1996.

[299] P. Kahn. From genome to proteome: Looking at a cell's proteins. *Science*, 270:369-370, 1995.

[300] D. Kaiser and R. Losick. How and why bacteria talk to each other. *Cell*, 73:873-885, 1993.

[301] P. M. Kane, C. T. Yamashiro, D. F. Wolczyk, N. Neff, M. Goebl, and T. H. Stevens. Protein splicing converts the yeast tfp1 gene product to the 69-kd subunit of the vacuolar h(+)-adenosine triphosphatase. *Science*, 250:651-657, 1990.

[302] N. Kaplan and C. H. Langley. A new estimate of sequence divergence of mitochondrial DNA using restriction endonuclease mappings. *J. Mol. Evol.*, 13:295-304, 1979.

[303] J. D. Karkas, R. Rudner, and E. Chargaff. Separation of *B. subtilis* DNA into complementary strands, II. Template functions and composition as determined by transcription with RNA polymerase. *Proc. Natl. Acad. Sci. USA*, 60:915-920, 1968.

[304] S. Karlin, B. E. Blaisdell, and P. Bucher. Quantile distributions of amino acid usage in protein classes. *Prot. Eng.*, 5:729-738, 1992.

[305] S. Karlin and J. Mrazek. What drives codon choices in human genes. *J. Mol. Biol.*, 262:459-472, 1996.

[306] S. Karlin, F. Ost, and B. E. Blaisdell. Patterns in DNA and amino acid sequences and their statistical significance. In M.S. Waterman, editor, *Mathematical methods for DNA sequences*, pages 133-157, Boca Raton, Fla., 1989. CRC Press.

[307] P. Karp, M. Riley, S. Paley, A. Pellegrini-Toole, and M. Krummenacker. EcoCyc: Electronic encyclopedia of e. coli genes and metabolism. *Nucl. Acids Res.*, 27:55-59, 1999.

[308] P. D. Karp. An ontology for biological function based on molecular interactions. *Bioinformatics*, 16:269-285, 2000.

[309] P. D. Karp, M. Krummenacker, S. Paley, and J. Wagg. Integrated pathway-genome databases and their role in drug discovery. *Trends Biotech.*, 17:275–281, 1999.

[310] S. A. Kauffman. Metabolic stability and epigenesis in randomly constructed genetic nets. *J. Theor. Biol.*, 22:437–467, 1969.

[311] S. A. Kauffman. The large scale structure and dynamics of gene control circuits: an ensemble approach. *J. Theor. Biol.*, 44:167–190, 1974.

[312] S. A. Kauffman. Requirements for evolvability in complex systems: orderly dynamics and frozen components. *Physica D*, 42:135–152, 1990.

[313] T. Kawabata and J. Doi. Improvement of protein secondary structure prediction using binary word encoding. *Proteins*, 27:36–46, 1997.

[314] M. J. Kearns and U. V. Vazirani. *An Introduction to Computational Learning Theory.* MIT Press, Cambridge, MA, 1994.

[315] W. J. Kent and A. M. Zahler. The Intronerator: exploring introns and alternative splicing in caenorhabditis elegans. *Nucl. Acids Res.*, 28:91–93, 2000.

[316] D. H. Kenyon and G. Steinman. *Biochemical Predestinations.* McGraw-Hill, New York, 1969.

[317] H. G. Khorana. Bacteriorhodopsin, a membrane protein that uses light to translocate protons. *J. Biol. Chem.*, 263:7439–7442, 1988.

[318] H. G. Khorana, G. E. Gerber, W. C. Herlihy, C. P. Gray, R. J. Anderegg, K. Nihei, and K. Biemann. Amino acid sequence of bacteriorhodopsin. *Proc. Natl. Acad. Sci.*, 76:5046–5050, 1979.

[319] J. L. King and T. H. Jukes. Non-Darwinian evolution. *Science*, 164:788–798, 1969.

[320] R. D. King and M. J. Sternberg. Identification and application of the concepts important for accurate and reliable protein secondary structure prediction. *Prot. Sci.*, 5:2298–2310, 1996.

[321] S. Kirkpatrick, C. D. Gelatt, and M. P. Vecchi. Optimization by simulated annealing. *Science*, 220:671–680, 1983.

[322] T. M. Klingler and D. L. Brutlag. Discovering side-chain correlation in alpha-helices. In R. Altman, D. Brutlag, P. Karp, R. Lathrop, and D. Searls, editors, *Proceedings of the Second International Conference on Intelligent Systems for Molecular Biology*, pages 236–243. AAAI Press, Menlo Park, CA, 1994.

[323] D. G. Kneller, F. E. Cohen, and R. Langridge. Improvements in protein secondary structure prediction by an enhanced neural network. *J. Mol. Biol.*, 214:171–182, 1990.

[324] P. Koehl and M. Levitt. A brighter future for protein structure prediction. *Nat. Struct. Biol.*, 6:108–111, 1999.

[325] L. F. Kolakowski. GCRDb: A G-protein-coupled receptor database. *Receptors Channels*, 2:1–7, 1994.

[326] A. K. Konopka. Sequences and codes: Fundamentals of biomolecular cryptology. In D. W. Smith, editor, *Biocomputing—Informatics and Genome Projects*, pages 119–174, San Diego, 1994. Academic Press.

[327] P. G. Korning, S. M. Hebsgaard, P. Rouze, and S. Brunak. Cleaning the GenBank *Arabidopsis thaliana* data set. *Nucl. Acids Res.*, 24:316-320, 1996.

[328] J. R. Koza. *Genetic Programming: On the Programming of Computers by Means of Natural Selection.* MIT Press, Cambridge MA, 1992.

[329] J. R. Koza. Evolution of a computer program for classifying protein segments as transmembrane domains using genetic programming. In R. Altman, D. Brutlag, P. Karp, R. Lathrop, and D. Searls, editors, *Proceedings of the Second International Conference on Intelligent Systems for Molecular Biology*, pages 244-252. AAAI Press, Menlo Park, CA, 1994.

[330] J. R. Koza. *Genetic Programming II: Automatic Discovery of Reusable Programs.* MIT Press, Cambridge MA, 1994.

[331] A. Kreegipuu, N. Blom, S. Brunak, and J. Jarv. Statistical analysis of protein kinase specificity determinants. *FEBS Lett.*, 430:45-50, 1998.

[332] J. K. Kristensen. Analysis of cis alternatively spliced mammalian genes. Master Thesis, University of Copenhagen, 2000.

[333] A. Krogh. Two methods for improving performance of an HMM and their application for gene finding. In T. Gaasterland et al., editor, *Proceedings of the Fifth International Conference on Intelligent Systems for Molecular Biology*, pages 179-186. AAAI Press, Menlo Park, CA, 1997.

[334] A. Krogh, M. Brown, I. S. Mian, K. Sjölander, and D. Haussler. Hidden Markov models in computational biology: Applications to protein modeling. *J. Mol. Biol.*, 235:1501-1531, 1994.

[335] A. Krogh, B. Larsson, G. von Heijne, and E. L. Sonnhammer. Predicting transmembrane protein topology with a hidden markov model: application to complete genomes. *J. Mol. Biol.*, 305:567-580, 2001.

[336] A. Krogh, I. S. Mian, and D. Haussler. A hidden Markov model that finds genes in *E. coli* DNA. *Nucl. Acids Res.*, 22:4768-4778, 1994.

[337] A. Krogh and G. Mitchinson. Maximum entropy weighting of aligned sequences of proteins of DNA. In C. Rawlings, D. Clark, R. Altman, L. Hunter, T. Lengauer, and S. Wodak, editors, *Proceedings of the Third International Conference on Intelligent Systems for Molecular Biology*, pages 215-221. AAAI Press, Menlo Park, CA, 1995.

[338] A. Krogh and S. K. Riis. Prediction of beta sheets in proteins. In M. C. Mozer S. Touretzky and M. E. Hasselmo, editors, *Advances in Neural Information Processing Systems*, volume 8, pages 917-923. MIT Press, Boston, MA, 1996.

[339] A. Krogh and P. Sollich. Statistical mechanics of ensemble learning. *Phys. Rev. E*, 55:811-825, 1997.

[340] A. Krogh and J. Vedelsby. Neural network ensembles, cross validation and active learning. In G. Tesauro, D. S. Touretzky, and T. K. Leen, editors, *Advances in Neural Information Processing Systems*, volume 7, pages 231-238. MIT Press, Cambridge, MA, 1995.

[341] S. Kullback. *Information Theory and Statistics*. Dover Publications, New York, 1959.

[342] S. Kullback and R. A. Leibler. On information and sufficiency. *Ann. Math. Stat.*, 22:79, 1986.

[343] D. Kulp, D. Haussler, M. G. Reese, and F. H. Eeckman. A generalized hidden Markov model for the recognition of human genes in dna. *ISMB*, 4:134–142, 1996.

[344] A. Lapedes, C. Barnes, C. Burks, R. Farber, and K. Sirotkin. Application of neural networks and other machine learning algorithms to dna sequence analysis. In G. I. Bell and T. G. Marr, editors, *Computers in DNA. The Proceedings of the Interface Between Computation Science and Nucleic Acid Sequencing Workshop.*, volume VII, pages 157–182. Addison Wesley, Redwood City, CA, 1988.

[345] K. Lari and S. J. Young. The estimation of stochastic context-free grammars using the inside-outside algorithm. *Computer Speech and Lang.*, 4:35–36, 1990.

[346] N. Larsen, G. J. Olsen, B. L. Maidak, M. J. McCaughey, R. Overbeek, T. J. Macke, T. L. Marsh, and C. R. Woese. The ribosomal database project. *Nucl. Acids Res.*, 21:3021–3023, 1993.

[347] E. E. Lattman and G. D. Rose. Protein folding–what's the question? *Proc. Natl. Acad. Sci. USA*, 90:439–441, 1993.

[348] S. L. Lauritzen. *Graphical Models*. Oxford University Press, Oxford, 1996.

[349] S. L. Lauritzen, A. P. Dawid, B. N. Larsen, and H. G. Leimer. Independence properties of directed Markov fields. *Networks*, 20:491–505, 1990.

[350] S. L. Lauritzen and D. J. Spiegelhalter. Local computations with probabilities on graphical structures and their application to expert systems. *J. R. Statis. Soc. B*, 50:157–224, 1988.

[351] C. E. Lawrence, S. F. Altschul, M. S. Boguski, J. S. Liu, A. Neuwald, and J. C. Wootton. Detecting subtle sequence signals: A Gibbs sampling strategy for multiple alignment. *Science*, 262:208–214, 1993.

[352] C. E. Lawrence and A. A. Reilly. An expectation maximization (EM) algorithm for the identification and characterization of common sites in unaligned biopolymer sequences. *Proteins*, 7:41–51, 1990.

[353] J. R. Lawton, F. A. Martinez, and C. Burks. Overview of the LiMB database. *Nucl. Acids Res.*, 17:5885–5899, 1989.

[354] C. Lee, R. G. Klopp, R. Weindruch, and T. A. Prolla. Gene expression profile of aging and its retardation by caloric restriction. *Science*, 285:1390–1393, 1999.

[355] M. T. Lee, F. C. Kuo, G. A. Whitmore, and J. Sklar. Importance of replication in microarray gene expression studies: statistical methods and evidence from repetitive cDNA hybridizations. *Proc. Natl. Acad. Sci. USA*, 97:9834–9839, 2000.

[356] N. Lehman and G. F. Joyce. Evolution in vitro of an RNA enzyme with altered metal dependence. *Nature*, 361:182–185, 1993.

[357] E. Levin and R. Pieraccini. Planar hidden Markov modeling: From speech to optical character recognition. In S. J. Hanson, J. D. Cowan, and C. Lee Giles, editors, *Advances in Neural Information Processing Systems*, volume 5, pages 731–738. Morgan Kaufmann, San Mateo, CA, 1993.

[358] J. Levin, S. Pascarella, P. Argos, and J. Garnier. Quantification of secondary structure prediction improvement using multiple alignments. *Prot. Eng.*, 6:849–854, 1993.

[359] S. E. Levinson, L. R. Rabiner, and M. M. Sondhi. An introduction to the application of the theory of probabilistic functions of a Markov process to automatic speech recognition. *Bell Syst. Tech. J.*, 62:1035–1074, 1983.

[360] S. Lewis, M. Ashburner, and M. G. Reese. Annotating eukaryote genomes. *Curr. Opin. Struct. Biol.*, 10:349–354, 2000.

[361] F. Liang, I. Holt, G. Pertea, S. Karamycheva, S.L. Salzberg, and J. Quackenbush. Gene index analysis of the human genome estimates approximately 120, 000 genes. *Nat. Genetics*, 25:239–240, 200.

[362] V. I. Lim. Algorithms for prediction of α-helical and β-structural regions in globular proteins. *J. Mol. Biol.*, 88:873–894, 1974.

[363] S. Lin and A. D. Riggs. The general affinity of lac repressor for *E. coli* DNA: Implications for gene regulation in procaryotes and eucaryotes. *Cell*, 4:107–111, 1975.

[364] T. Lin, B. G. Horne, P. Tiño, and C. L. Giles. Learning long-term dependencies in NARX recurrent neural networks. *IEEE Trans. Neural Networks*, 7:1329–1338, 1996.

[365] H. Lodish, D. Baltimore, A. Berk, S. L. Zipursky, and P. Matsudairas. *Molecular cell biology*. Scientific American Books, New York, 3rd edition, 1995.

[366] A. D. Long, H. J. Mangalam, B. Y. Chan, L. Tolleri, G. W. Hatfield, and P. Baldi. Global gene expression profiling in *escherichia coli* K12: Improved statistical inference from DNA microarray data using analysis of variance and a Bayesian statistical framework. *J. Biol. Chem.*, 276:19937–19944, 2001.

[367] A. V. Lukashin and M. Borodovsky. GeneMark.hmm: new solutions for gene finding. *Nucl. Acids Res.*, 26:1107–1115, 1998.

[368] O. Lund, K. Frimand, J. Gorodkin, H. Bohr, J. Bohr, J. Hansen, and S. Brunak. Protein distance constraints predicted by neural networks and probability density functions. *Prot. Eng.*, 25:1241–1248, 1997.

[369] D. H. Ly, D. J. Lockhart, R. A. Lerner, and P. G. Schultz. Mitotic misregulation and human aging. *Science*, 287:2486–2492, 2000.

[370] M. J. MacGregor, T. P. Flores, and M. J. E. Sternberg. Prediction of beta-turns in proteins using neural networks. *Prot. Eng.*, 2:521–526, 1989.

[371] A. L. Mackay. Optimization of the genetic code. *Nature*, 216:159–160, 1967.

[372] D. J. C. MacKay. Bayesian interpolation. *Neural Comp.*, 4:415–447, 1992.

[373] D. J. C. MacKay. A practical Bayesian framework for back-propagation networks. *Neural Comp.*, 4:448–472, 1992.

[374] D. J. C. MacKay. Density networks and their application to protein modelling. In J. Skilling and S. Sibisi, editors, *Maximum Entropy and Bayesian Methods*, pages 259–268, Dordrecht, 1996. Kluwer.

[375] D. J. C. MacKay. Comparison of approximate methods for handling hyperparameters. *Neural Comp.*, 11:1035–1068, 1999.

[376] D. J. C. MacKay and L. C. Bauman Peto. A hierarchical Dirichlet language model. *Nat. Lang. Eng.*, 1:1–19, 1995.

[377] R. Maclin and J. Shavlik. Using knowledge-based neural networks to improve algorithms: Refining the Chou–Fasman algorithm for protein folding. *Machine Learning*, 11:195–215, 1993.

[378] E. M. Marcotte. Computational genetics: finding protein function by nonhomology methods. *Curr. Opin. Struct. Biol.*, 10:359–365, 2000.

[379] E. M. Marcotte, M. Pellegrini, H. L. Ng, D. L. Rice, T. O. Yeates, and D. Eisenberg. Detecting protein function and protein-protein interactions from genome sequences. *Science*, 285:751–753, 1999.

[380] E. M. Marcotte, M. Pellegrini, M. J. Thompson, T. O. Yeates, and D. Eisenberg. A combined algorithm for genome-wide prediction of protein function. *Nature*, 402:83–86, 1999.

[381] E. Marinari and G. Parisi. Simulated tempering: A new Monte Carlo scheme. *Europhys. Lett.*, 19:451–458, 1992.

[382] B. W. Matthews. Comparison of the predicted and observed secondary structure of T4 phage lysozyme. *Biochim. Biophys. Acta*, 405:442–451, 1975.

[383] H. H. McAdams and A. Arkin. It's a noisy business! Genetic regulation at the nanomolar scale. *Trends Genet.*, 15:65–69, 1999.

[384] P. McCullagh and J. A. Nelder. *Generalized linear models*. Chapman and Hall, London, 1989.

[385] R. J. McEliece, D. J. C. MacKay, and J. F. Cheng. Turbo decoding as an instance of Pearl's belief propagation algorithm. *IEEE J. Sel. Areas Commun.*, 16:140–152, 1998.

[386] L. J. McGuffin, K. Bryson, and J. T. Jones. The PSIPRED protein structure prediction server. *Bioinformatics*, 16:404–405, 2000.

[387] X. L. Meng and D. B. Rubin. Recent extensions to the EM algorithm. In J. M. Bernardo, J. O. Berger, A. P. Dawid, and A. F. M. Smith, editors, *Bayesian statistics*, volume 4, pages 307–320. Oxford University Press, Oxford, 1992.

[388] N. Metropolis, A. W. Rosenbluth, M. N. Rosenbluth, A. H. Teller, and E. Teller. Equations of state calculations by fast computing machines. *J. Chem. Phys.*, 21:1087–1092, 1953.

[389] F. Miescher. Uber die chemische Zusammensetzung der Eiterzellen. In F. Hoppe-Seyler, editor, *Medicinisch-chemische Untersuchungen*, pages 441–460, Berlin, 1871. August Hirschwald.

[390] G. L. G. Miklos and G. M. Rubin. The role of the genome project in determining gene function: Insights from model organisms. *Cell*, 86:521–529, 1996.

[391] E. Mjolsness, D. H. Sharp, and J. Reinitz. A connectionist model of development. *J. Theor. Biol.*, 152:429–453, 1991.

[392] J. M. Modestino and J. Zhang. A Markov random field model-based approach to image interpretation. *IEEE Trans. Pattern Anal. Machine Intell.*, 14:606–615, 1992.

[393] R. N. Moll, M. A. Arbib, and A. J. Koufry. *An Introduction to Formal Language Theory*. Springer-Verlag, New York, 1988.

[394] J. C. Mullikin, S. E. Hunt, C. G. Cole, B. J. Mortimore, C. M. Rice, J. Burton, L. H. Matthews, R. Pavitt, R. W. Plumb, S. K. Sims, R. M. Ainscough, J. Attwood, J. M. Bailey, K. Barlow, R. M. Bruskiewich, P. N. Butcher, N. P. Carter, Y. Chen, C. M. Clee, P. C. Coggill, J. Davies, R. M. Davies, E. Dawson, M.D. Francis, A. A. Joy, R. G. Lamble, C. F. Langford, J. Macarthy, V. Mall, A. Moreland, E. K. Overton-Larty, M. T. Ross, L. C. Smith, C. A. Steward, J. E. Sulston, E. J. Tinsley, K. J. Turney, D. L. Willey, G. D. Wilson, A. A. McMurray, I. Dunham, J. Rogers, and D. R. Bentley. An SNP map of human chromosome 22. *Nature*, 407:516–520, 2000.

[395] R. M. Neal. Connectionist learning of belief networks. *Art. Intell.*, 56:71–113, 1992.

[396] R. M. Neal. Probabilistic inference using Markov chain Monte Carlo methods. Technical report. Department of Computer Science, University of Toronto, 1993.

[397] R. M. Neal. *Bayesian Learning for Neural Networks*. PhD thesis, Department of Computer Science, University of Toronto, 1995.

[398] R. M. Neal. *Bayesian Learning for Neural Networks*. Springer-Verlag, New York, 1996.

[399] R. M. Neal. Monte Carlo implementation of Gaussian process models for Bayesian regression and classification. Technical Report no. 9702. Department of Statistics, University of Toronto, 1997.

[400] R. M. Neal and G. E. Hinton. A new view of the EM algorithm that justifies incremental and other variants. Technical Report, Department of Computer Science, University of Toronto, Canada, 1993.

[401] S. B. Needleman and C. D Wunsch. A general method applicable to the search for similarities in the amino acid sequence of two proteins. *J. Mol. Biol.*, 48:443–453, 1970.

[402] E. J. Neer. G proteins: Critical control points for transmembrane signals. *Prot. Sci.*, 3:3–14, 1994.

[403] M. A. Newton, C. M. Kendziorski, C. S. Richmond, F. R. Blattner, and K. W. Tsui. On differential variability of expression ratios: improving statistical inference about gene expression changes from microarray data. *J. Comp. Biol.*, 8:37-52, 2001.

[404] H. Nielsen, J. Engelbrecht, S. Brunak, and G. von Heijne. Identification of prokaryotic and eukaryotic signal peptides and prediction of their cleavage sites. *Prot. Eng.*, 10:1-6, 1997.

[405] H. Nielsen, J. Engelbrecht, G. von Heijne, and S. Brunak. Defining a similarity threshold for a functional protein sequence pattern: The signal peptide cleavage site. *Proteins*, 24:316-320, 1996.

[406] H. Nielsen and A. Krogh. Prediction of signal peptides and signal anchors by a hidden Markov model. *ISMB*, 6:122-130, 1998.

[407] M. W. Nirenberg, O. W. Jones, P. Leder, B. F. C. Clark, W. S. Sly, and S. Pestka. On the coding of genetic information. *Cold Spring Harbor Symp. Quant. Biol.*, 28:549-557, 1963.

[408] R. Nowak. Entering the postgenome era. *Science*, 270:368-371, 1995.

[409] L. E. Orgel. A possible step in the origin of the genetic code. *Isr. J. Chem.*, 10:287-292, 1972.

[410] R. L. Ornstein, R. Rein, D. L. Breen, and R. D. MacElroy. An optimised potential function for the calculation of nucleic acid interaction energies. I. Base stacking. *Biopolymers*, 17:2341-2360, 1978.

[411] Y. A. Ovchinnikov, N. G. Abdulaev, M. Y. Feigina, A. V. Kiselev, and N. A. Lobanov. The structural basis of the functioning of bacteriorhodopsin: An overview. *FEBS Lett.*, 100:219-234, 1979.

[412] M. Pagel and R. A. Johnstone. Variation across species in the size of the nuclear genome supports the junk-DNA explanation for the c-value paradox. *Proc. R. Soc. Lond. (Biol.)*, 249:119-124, 1992.

[413] A. Pandey and M. Mann. Proteomics to study genes and genomes. *Nature*, 405:837-846, 2000.

[414] L. Pardo, J. A. Ballesteros, R. Osman, and H. Weinstein. On the use of the transmembrane domain of bacteriorhodopsin as a template for modeling the three-dimensional structure of guanine nucleotide-binding regulatory protein-coupled receptors. *Proc. Natl. Acad. Sci. USA*, 89:4009-4012, 1992.

[415] R. Parsons and M. E. Johnson. DNA sequence assembly and genetic programming—new results and puzzling insights. In C. Rawlings, D. Clark, R. Altman, L. Hunter, T. Lengauer, and S. Wodak, editors, *Proceedings of the Third International Conference on Intelligent Systems for Molecular Biology*, pages 277-284. AAAI Press, Menlo Park, CA, 1995.

[416] J. Pearl. *Probabilistic Reasoning in Intelligent Systems*. Morgan Kaufmann, San Mateo, CA, 1988.

[417] W. R. Pearson. Rapid and sensitive sequence comparison with FASTP and FASTA. *Meth. Enzymol.*, 183:63-98, 1990.

[418] W. R. Pearson and D. J. Lipman. Improved tools for biological sequence comparison. *Proc. Nat. Acad. Sci. USA*, 85:2444-2448, 1988.

[419] W.R. Pearson. Effective protein sequence comparison. *Meth. Enzymol.*, 266:227-258, 1996.

[420] E. Pebay-Peyroula, G. Rummel, J. P. Rosenbusch, and E. M. Landau. X-ray structure of bacteriorhodopsin at 2.5 angstroms from microcrystals grown in lipidic cubic phases. *Science*, 277:1676-1681, 1997.

[421] A. G. Pedersen, P. F. Baldi, Y. Chauvin, and S. Brunak. DNA structure in human polymerase II promoters. *J. Mol. Biol.*, 281:663-673, 1998.

[422] A. G. Pedersen and H. Nielsen. Neural network prediction of translation initiation sites in eukaryotes: Perspectives for EST and genome analysis. In *Proceedings of the Fifth International Conference on Intelligent Systems for Molecular Biology*, pages 226-233, Menlo Park, CA., 1997. AAAI Press.

[423] M. Pellegrini, E. M. Marcotte, M. J. Thompson, D. Eisenberg, and T.O Yeates. Assigning protein functions by comparative genome analysis: protein phylogenetic profiles. *Proc. Natl. Acad. Sci. U.S.A.*, 38:667-677, 1999.

[424] M. D. Perlwitz, C. Burks, and M. S. Waterman. Pattern analysis of the genetic code. *Advan. Appl. Math.*, 9:7-21, 1988.

[425] C. M. Perou, S. S. Jeffrey, M. van de Rijn, C. A. Rees, M. B. Eisen, D. T. Ross, A. Pergamenschikov, C. F. Williams, S. X. Zhu, J. C. Lee, D. Lashkari, D. Shalon, P. O. Brown, and D. Botstein. Distinctive gene expression patterns in human mammary epithelial cells and breast cancers. *Proc. Natl. Acad. Sci. USA*, 96:9212-9217, 1999.

[426] M. P. Perrone and L. N. Cooper. When networks disagree: ensemble method for neural networks. In R. J. Mammone, editor, *Neural networks for speech and image processing*, chapter 10. Chapman and Hall, London, 1994.

[427] T. N. Petersen, C. Lundegaard, M. Nielsen, H. Bohr, J. Bohr, S. Brunak, G. P. Gippert, and O. Lund. Prediction of protein secondary structure at 80% accuracy. *Proteins*, 41:17-20, 2000.

[428] P. A. Pevzner. *Computational Molecular Biology—An Algorithmic Approach*. MIT Press, Cambridge, MA, 2000.

[429] G. Pollastri, P. Baldi, P. Fariselli, and R. Casadio. Improved prediction of the number of residue contacts in proteins by recurrent neural networks. *Bioinformatics*, 2001. Proceedings of the ISMB 2001 Conference.

[430] V. V. Prabhu. Symmetry observations in long nucleotide sequences. *Nucl. Acids Res.*, 21:2797-2800, 1993.

[431] J. W. Pratt, H. Raiffa, and R. Schlaifer. *Introduction to Statistical Decision Theory*. MIT Press, Cambridge, MA, 1995.

[432] S. R. Presnell and F. E. Cohen. Artificial neural networks for pattern recognition in biochemical sequences. *Ann. Rev. Biophys. Biomol. Struct.*, 22:283–298, 1993.

[433] S. J. Press. *Bayesian Statistics: Principles, Models, and Applications*. John Wiley, New York, 1989.

[434] W. H. Press, B. P. Flannery, S. A. Teukolsky, and W. T. Vetterling. *Numerical recipes in C*. Cambridge University Press, Cambridge, 1988.

[435] L. G. Presta and G. D. Rose. Helix signals in proteins. *Science*, 240:1632–1641, 1988.

[436] W. C. Probst, L. A. Snyder, D. I. Schuster, J. Brosius, and S. C. Sealfon. Sequence alignment of the G-protein coupled receptor superfamily. *DNA and Cell Biol.*, 11:1–20, 1992.

[437] N. Qian and T. J. Sejnowski. Predicting the secondary structure of globular proteins using neural network models. *J. Mol. Biol.*, 202:865–884, 1988.

[438] M. B. Qumsiyeh. Evolution of number and morphology of mammalian chromosomes. *J. Hered.*, 85:455–465, 1994.

[439] L. R. Rabiner. A tutorial on hidden Markov models and selected applications in speech recognition. *Proc. IEEE*, 77:257–286, 1989.

[440] T. A. Rapoport. Transport of proteins across the endoplasmic reticulum membrane. *Science*, 258:931–936, 1992.

[441] M. G. Reese, D. Kulp, H. Tammana, and D. Haussler. Genie-gene finding in *drosophila melanogaster*. *Genome Res.*, 10:529–538, 2000.

[442] F. M. Richards and C. E. Kundrot. Identification of structural motifs from protein coordinate data: Secondary structure and first-level supersecondary structure. *Proteins*, 3:71–84, 1988.

[443] D. S. Riddle, J. V. Santiago, S. T. Bray-Hall, N. Doshi, V.P. Grantcharova, Q. Yi, and D. Baker. Functional rapidly folding proteins from simplified alphabets. *Nat. Struct. Biol.*, 4:805–809, 1997.

[444] R. Riek, S. Hornemann, G. Wider, M. Billeter, R. Glockshuber, and K. Wuthrich. NMR structure of the mouse prion protein domain PrP(121-321). *Nature*, 382:180–182, 1996.

[445] S. K. Riis and A. Krogh. Improving prediction of protein secondary structure using structured neural networks and multiple sequence alignments. *J. Comput. Biol.*, 3:163–183, 1996.

[446] J. J. Rissanen. Modeling by shortest data description. *Automatica*, 14:465–471, 1978.

[447] É. Rivals, M. Dauchet, J. P. Delahaye, and O. Delgrange. Compression and genetic sequence analysis. *Biochimie*, 78:315–322, 1996.

[448] D. Ron, Y. Singer, and N. Tishby. The power of amnesia. In J. D. Cowan, G. Tesauro, and J. Alspector, editors, *Advances in Neural Information Processing Systems*, volume 6, pages 176–183. Morgan Kaufmann, San Francisco, CA, 1994.

[449] G. D. Rose. Protein folding and the Paracelsus challenge. *Nat. Struct. Biol.*, 4:512–514, 1997.

[450] G. D. Rose and T. P. Creamer. Protein folding: predicting predicting. *Proteins*, 19:1-3, 1994.

[451] B. Rost and C. Sander. Improved prediction of protein secondary structure by use of sequence profiles and neural networks. *Proc. Nat. Acad. Sci. USA*, 90:7558-7562, 1993.

[452] B. Rost and C. Sander. Prediction of protein secondary structure at better than 70% accuracy. *J. Mol. Biol.*, 232:584-599, 1993.

[453] B. Rost and C. Sander. Combining evolutionary information and neural networks to predict protein secondary structure. *Proteins*, 19:55-72, 1994.

[454] B. Rost, C. Sander, and R. Schneider. Redefining the goals of protein secondary structure prediction. *J. Mol. Biol.*, 235:13-26, 1994.

[455] D. E. Rumelhart, R. Durbin, R. Golden, and Y. Chauvin. Backpropagation: The basic theory. In *Backpropagation: Theory, Architectures and Applications*, pages 1-34. Lawrence Erlbaum Associates, Hillsdale, NJ, 1995.

[456] D. E. Rumelhart, G. E. Hinton, and R. J. Williams. Learning internal representations by error propagation. In D. E. Rumelhart, J. L. McClelland, and the PDP Research Group, editors, *Parallel distributed processing: Explorations in the microstructure of cognition.*, volume 1: Foundations, pages 318-362, Cambridge, MA., 1986. MIT Press.

[457] R. Russell and G. Barton. The limits of protein secondary structure prediction accuracy from multiple sequence alignment. *J. Mol. Biol.*, 234:951-957, 1993.

[458] J. R. Saffran, R. N. Aslin, and E. L. Newport. Statistical learning by 8-month-old infants. *Science*, 274:1926-1928, 1996.

[459] Y. Sakakibara. Efficient learning of context-free grammars from positive structural examples. *Info. Comput.*, 97:23-60, 1992.

[460] Y. Sakakibara, M. Brown, R. Hughey, I. S. Mian, K. Sjölander, R. C. Underwood, and D. Haussler. Stochastic context-free grammars for tRNA modeling. *Nucl. Acids Res.*, 22:5112-5120, 1994.

[461] S. L. Salzberg, A. L. Delcher, S. Kasif, and O. White. Microbial gene identification using interpolated Markov models. *Nucl. Acids Res.*, 26:544-548, 1998.

[462] C. Sander and R. Schneider. Database of homology-derived protein structures and the structural meaning of sequence alignment. *Proteins*, 9:56-68, 1991.

[463] F. Sanger, G. M. Air, B. G. Barrell, N. L. Brown, A. R. Coulson, C. A. Fiddes, C. A. Hutchison, P. M. Slocombe, and M. Smith. Nucleotide sequence of bacteriophage phi X174 DNA. *Nature*, 265:687-695, 1977.

[464] D. Sankoff and P. Rousseau. Locating the vertices of a Steiner tree in an arbitrary metric space. *Math. Prog.*, 9:240-246, 1975.

[465] L. K. Saul and M. I. Jordan. Exploiting tractable substructures in intractable networks. In D. S. Touretzky, M. C. Mozer, and M. E. Hasselmo, editors, *Advances in Neural Information Processing Systems*, volume 8, pages 486–492. MIT Press, Cambridge, MA, 1996.

[466] M. A. Savageau. Power-law formalism: a canonical nonlinear approach to modeling and analysis. In V. Lakshmikantham, editor, *World Congress of Nonlinear Analysts 92*, volume 4, pages 3323–3334. Walter de Gruyter Publishers, Berlin, 1996.

[467] R. D. Schachter. Probabilistic inference and influence diagrams. *Operation Res.*, 36:589–604, 1988.

[468] R. D. Schachter, S. K. Anderson, and P. Szolovits. Global conditioning for probabilistic inference in belief networks. In *Proceedings of the Uncertainty in AI Conference*, pages 514–522, San Francisco, CA, 1994. Morgan Kaufmann.

[469] D. Schneider, C. Tuerk, and L. Gold. Selection of high affinity RNA ligands to the bacteriophage r17 coat protein. *J. Mol. Biol.*, 228:862–869, 1992.

[470] F. Schneider. Die funktion des arginins in den enzymen. *Naturwissenschaften*, 65:376–381, 1978.

[471] R. Schneider, A. de Daruvar, and C. Sander. The HSSP database of protein structure-sequence alignments. *Nucleic Acids Res.*, 25:226–230, 1997.

[472] T. D. Schneider. Reading of DNA sequence logos: Prediction of major groove binding by information theory. *Meth. Enzymol.*, 274:445–455, 1996.

[473] T. D. Schneider and R. M. Stephens. Sequence logos: A new way to display consensus sequences. *Nucl. Acids Res.*, 18:6097–6100, 1990.

[474] T. D. Schneider, G. D. Stormo, L. Gold, and A. Ehrenfeucht. Information content of binding sites on nucleotide sequences. *J. Mol. Biol.*, 188:415–431, 1986.

[475] B. Scholkopf, C. Burges, and V. Vapnik. Extracting support data for a given task. In U. M. Fayyad and R. Uthurusamy, editors, *Proceedings First International Conference on Knowledge Discovery and Data Mining*. AAAI Press, Menlo Park, CA, 1995.

[476] H. P. Schwefel and R. Manner, editors. *Parallel Problem Solving from Nature*, Berlin, 1991. Springer-Verlag.

[477] R. R. Schweitzer. Anastasia and Anna Anderson. *Nat. Genet.*, 9:345, 1995.

[478] W. Schwemmler. *Reconstruction of Cell Evolution: A Periodic System of Cells*. CRC Press, Boca Raton, FL, 1994.

[479] D. B. Searls. Linguistics approaches to biological sequences. *CABIOS*, 13:333–344, 1997.

[480] T. J. Sejnowski and C. R. Rosenberg. Parallel networks that learn to pronounce English text. *Complex Syst.*, 1:145–168, 1987.

[481] P. H. Sellers. On the theory and computation of evolutionary distances. *SIAM J. Appl. Math.*, 26:787–793, 1974.

[482] H. S. Seung, H. Sompolinsky, and N. Tishby. Statistical mechanics of learning from examples. *Phys. Rev. A*, 45:6056-6091, 1992.

[483] C. E. Shannon. A mathematical theory of communication. *Bell Syst. Tech. J.*, 27:379-423, 623-656, 1948.

[484] R. Sharan and R. Shamir. CLICK: a clustering algorithm with applications to gene expression analysis. In *Proceedings of the 2000 Conference on Intelligent Systems for Molecular Biology (ISMB00), La Jolla, CA*, pages 307-316. AAAI Press, Menlo Park, CA, 2000.

[485] I. N. Shindyalov, N. A. Kolchanov, and C. Sander. Can three-dimensional contacts in protein structures be predicted by analysis of correlated mutations? *Prot. Eng.*, 7:349-358, 1994.

[486] J. E. Shore and R. W. Johnson. Axiomatic derivation of the principle of maximum entropy and the principle of minimum cross-entropy. *IEEE Trans. Info. Theory*, 26:26-37, 1980.

[487] P. Sibbald and P. Argos. Weighting aligned protein or nucleic acid sequences to correct for unequal representation. *J. Mol. Biol.*, 216:813-818, 1990.

[488] R. R. Sinden. *DNA Structure and Function*. Academic Press, San Diego, 1994.

[489] K. Sjölander, K. Karplus, M. Brown, R. Hughey, A. Krogh, I. S. Mian, and D. Haussler. Dirichlet mixtures: a method for improved detection of weak but significant protein sequence homology. *CABIOS*, 12:327-345, 1996.

[490] A. F. Smith and G. O. Roberts. Bayesian computation via the Gibbs sampler and related Markov chain Monte Carlo methods. *J. R. Statis. Soc.*, 55:3-23, 1993.

[491] A. F. M. Smith. Bayesian computational methods. *Phil. Trans. R. Soc. London A*, 337:369-386, 1991.

[492] T. F. Smith and M. S. Waterman. Identification of common molecular subsequences. *J. Mol. Biol.*, 147:195-197, 1981.

[493] P. Smyth, D. Heckerman, and M. I. Jordan. Probabilistic independence networks for hidden Markov probability models. *Neural Comp.*, 9:227-267, 1997.

[494] E. E. Snyder and G. D. Stormo. Identification of protein coding regions in genomic DNA. *J. Mol. Biol.*, 248:1-18, 1995.

[495] V. V. Solovyev, A. A. Salamov, and C. B. Lawrence. Predicting internal exons by oligonucleotide composition and discriminant analysis of spliceable open reading frames. *Nucl. Acids Res.*, 22:5156-5153, 1994.

[496] V. V. Solovyev, A. A. Salamov, and C. B. Lawrence. Prediction of human gene structure using linear discriminant functions and dynamic programming. In C. Rawling, D. Clark, R. Altman, L. Hunter, T. Lengauer, and S. Wodak, editors, *Proceedings of the Third International Conference on Intelligent Systems for Molecular Biology*, pages 367-375, Cambridge, 1995. AAAI Press.

[497] E. L. L. Sonnhammer, S. R. Eddy, and R. Durbin. Pfam: a comprehensive database of protein domain families based on seed alignments. *Proteins*, 28:405-420, 1997.

[498] P. T. Spellman, G. Sherlock, M. Q. Zhang, V. R. Iyer, K. Anders, M. B. Eisen, P. O. Brown, D. Botstein, and B. Futcher. Comprehensive identification of cell cycle-regulated genes of the yeast *saccharomyces cerevisiae* by microarray hybridization. *Mol. Biol. Cell*, 9:3273-3297, 1998.

[499] D. J. Spiegelhalter, A. P. Dawid, S. L. Lauritzen, and R. G. Cowell. Bayesian analysis in expert systems. *Stat. Sci.*, 8:219-283, 1993.

[500] F. Spitzer. Markov random fields and Gibbs ensembles. *Am. Math. Monthly*, 78:142-154, 1971.

[501] S. Stamm, M. Q. Zhang, T. G. Marr, and D. M. Helfman. A sequence compilation and comparison of exons that are alternatively spliced in neurons. *Nucl. Acids Res.*, 22:1515-1526, 1994.

[502] S. Steinberg, A. Misch, and M. Sprinzl. Compilation of tRNA sequences and sequences of tRNA genes. *Nucl. Acids Res.*, 21:3011-3015, 1993.

[503] G. Stoesser, P. Sterk, M. A. Tull, P. J. Stoehr, and G. N. Cameron. The EMBL nucleotide sequence database. *Nucl. Acids Res.*, 25:7-13, 1997.

[504] A. Stolcke and S. Omohundro. Hidden Markov model induction by Bayesian model merging. In S. J. Hanson, J. D. Cowan, and C. Lee Giles, editors, *Advances in Neural Information Processing Systems*, volume 5, pages 11-18. Morgan Kaufmann, San Mateo, CA, 1993.

[505] P. Stolorz, A. Lapedes, and Y. Xia. Predicting protein secondary structure using neural net and statistical methods. *J. Mol. Biol.*, 225:363-377, 1992.

[506] G. D. Stormo, T. D. Schneider, L. Gold, and A. Ehrenfeucht. Use of the "perceptron" algorithm to distinguish translational initiation sites in *e. coli. Nucl. Acids Res.*, 10:2997-3011, 1982.

[507] G. D. Stormo, T. D. Schneider, and L. M. Gold. Characterization of translational initiation sites in *e. coli. Nucl. Acids Res.*, 10:2971-2996, 1982.

[508] C. D. Strader, T. M. Fong, M. R. Tota, and D. Underwood. Structure and function of G protein-coupled receptors. *Ann. Rev. Biochem.*, 63:101-132, 1994.

[509] R. Swanson. A unifying concept for the amino acid code. *Bull. Math. Biol.*, 46:187-203, 1984.

[510] R. H. Swendsen and J. S. Wang. Nonuniversal critical dynamics in Monte Carlo simulations. *Phys. Rev. Lett.*, 58:86-88, 1987.

[511] P. Tamayo, D. Slonim, J. Mesirov, Q. Zhu, S. Kitareewan, E. Dmitrovsky, E. S. Lander, and T. R. Golub. Interpreting patterns of gene expression with self-organizing maps: methods and application to hematopoietic differentiation. *Proc. Natl. Acad. Sci. USA*, 96:2907-2912, 1999.

[512] R. E. Tarjan and M. Yannakakis. Simple linear-time algorithms to test the chordality of graphs, test acyclicity of hypergraphs, and selectively reduce acyclic hypergraphs. *SIAM J. Computing*, 13:566-579, 1984.

[513] R. L. Tatusov and E. V. Koonin D. J. Lipman. A genomic perspective on protein families. *Science*, 278:631-637, 1997.

[514] F. J. R. Taylor and D. Coates. The code within the codons. *Biosystems*, 22:177–187, 1989.

[515] W. R. Taylor and K. Hatrick. Compensating changes in protein multiple sequence alignments. *Prot. Eng.*, 7:341–348, 1994.

[516] T. A. Thanaraj. A clean data set of EST-confirmed splice sites from Homo sapiens and standards for clean-up procedures. *Nucl. Acids Res.*, 27:2627–2637, 1999.

[517] H. H. Thodberg. A review of Bayesian neural networks with an application to near infrared spectroscopy. *IEEE Trans. Neural Networks*, 7:56–72, 1996.

[518] C. A. Thomas. The genetic organization of chromosomes. *Ann. Rev. Genet.*, 5:237–256, 1971.

[519] J. L. Thorne, H. Kishino, and J. Felsenstein. An evolutionary model for maximum likelihood alignment of DNA sequences. *J. Mol. Evol.*, 33:114–124, 1991.

[520] L. Tierney. Markov chains for exploring posterior distributions. *Ann. Statis.*, 22:1701–1762, 1994.

[521] I. Tinoco, Jr., O. C. Uhlenbeck, and M. D. Levine. Estimation of secondary structure in ribonucleic acids. *Nature*, 230:362–367, 1971.

[522] D. M. Titterington, A. F. M. Smith, and U. E. Makov. *Statistical Analysis of Finite Mixture Distributions*. John Wiley & Sons, New York, 1985.

[523] N. Tolstrup, C. V. Sensen, R. A. Garrett, and I. G. Clausen. Two different and highly organized mechanisms of translation initiation in the archaeon sulfolobus solfataricus. *Extremophiles*, 4:175–179, 2000.

[524] N. Tolstrup, J. Toftgard, J. Engelbrecht, and S. Brunak. Neural network model of the genetic code is strongly correlated to the GES scale of amino-acid transfer free-energies. *J. Mol. Biol.*, 243:816–820, 1994.

[525] E. N. Trifonov. Translation framing code and frame–monitoring mechanism as suggested by the analysis of mRNA and 16S rRNA nucleotide sequences. *J. Mol. Biol.*, 194:643–652, 1987.

[526] M. K. Trower, S. M. Orton, I. J. Purvis, P. Sanseau, J. Riley, C. Christodoulou, D. Burt, C. G. See, G. Elgar, R. Sherrington, E. I. Rogaev, P. St George-Hyslop, S. Brenner, and C. W. Dykes. Conservation of synteny between the genome of the pufferfish (*Fugu rubripes*) and the region on human chromosome 14 (14q24.3) associated with familial Alzheimer disease (AD3 locus). *Proc. Natl. Acad. Sci. USA*, 93:1366–1369, 1996.

[527] D. H. Turner and N. Sugimoto. RNA structure prediction. *Ann. Rev. Biophys. Biophys. Chem.*, 17:167–192, 1988.

[528] E. C. Uberbacher and R. J. Mural. Locating protein-coding regions in human DNA sequences by a multiple sensor-neural network approach. *Proc. Natl. Acad. Sci. USA*, 88:11261–11265, 1991.

[529] E. C. Uberbacher, Ying Xu, and R. J. Mural. Discovering and understanding genes in human DNA sequence using GRAIL. *Meth. Enzymol.*, 266:259–281, 1996.

[530] J. van Helden, B. Andre, and J. Collado-Vides. Extracting regulatory sites from the upstream region of yeast genes by computational analysis of oligonucleotide frequencies. *J. Mol. Biol.*, 281:827-842, 1998.

[531] J. van Helden, M. del Olmo, and J. E. Perez-Ortin. Statistical analysis of yeast genomic downstream sequences reveals putative polyadenylation signals. *Nucl. Acids Res.*, 28:1000-1010, 2000.

[532] E. P. van Someren, L. F. A. Wessels, and M. J. T. Reinders. Linear modeling of genetic networks from experimental data. In *Proceedings of the 2000 Conference on Intelligent Systems for Molecular Biology (ISMB00), La Jolla, CA*, pages 355-366. AAAI Press, Menlo Park, CA, 2000.

[533] V. Vapnik. *The Nature of Statistical Learning Theory.* Springer-Verlag, New York, 1995.

[534] B. Venkatesh, B. H. Tay, G. Elgar, and S. Brenner. Isolation, characterization and evolution of nine pufferfish (*Fugu rubripes*) actin genes. *J. Mol. Biol.*, 259:655-665, 1996.

[535] J. Vilo and A. Brazma. Mining for putative regulatory elements in the yeast genome using gene expression data. In *Proceedings of the 2000 Conference on Intelligent Systems for Molecular Biology (ISMB00), La Jolla, CA*, pages 384-394. AAAI Press, Menlo Park, CA, 2000.

[536] M. Vingron and P. Argos. A fast and sensitive multiple sequence alignment algorithm. *CABIOS*, 5:115-121, 1989.

[537] E. O. Voit. *Canonical Nonlinear Modeling.* Van Nostrand and Reinhold, New York, 1991.

[538] M. V. Volkenstein. The genetic coding of protein structure. *Biochim. Biophys. Acta*, 119:418-420, 1966.

[539] G. von Heijne. A new method for predicting signal sequence cleavage sites. *Nucl. Acids Res.*, 14:4683-4690, 1986.

[540] G. von Heijne. *Sequence Analysis in Molecular Biology: Treasure Trove or Trivial Pursuit?* Academic Press, London, 1987.

[541] G. von Heijne. Transcending the impenetrable: How proteins come to terms with membranes. *Biochim. Biophys. Acta*, 947:307-333, 1988.

[542] G. von Heijne. The signal peptide. *J. Membrane Biol.*, 115:195-201, 1990.

[543] G. von Heijne and C. Blomberg. The beta structure: Inter-strand correlations. *J. Mol. Biol.*, 117:821-824, 1977.

[544] P. H. von Hippel. Molecular databases of the specificity of interaction of transcriptional proteins with genome DNA. In R.F. Goldberger, editor, *Gene expression. Biological regulation and Development, vol. 1*, pages 279-347, New York, 1979. Plenum Press.

[545] S. S. Wachtel and T. R. Tiersch. Variations in genome mass. *Comp. Biochem. Physiol. B*, 104:207-213, 1993.

[546] G. Wahba. *Spline Models of Observational Oata*. Society for Industrial and Applied Mathematics, Philadelphia, PA, 1990.

[547] J. Wang and R. H. Swendsen. Cluster Monte Carlo algorithms. *Physica A*, 167:565–579, 1990.

[548] J. Wang and W. Wang. A computational approach to simplifying the protein folding alphabet. *Nat. Struct. Biol.*, 6:1033–1038, 1999.

[549] Z. X. Wang. Assessing the accuracy of protein secondary structure. *Nat. Struct. Biol.*, 1:145–146, 1994.

[550] M. S. Waterman. *Introduction to Computational Biology*. Chapman and Hall, London, 1995.

[551] T. A. Welch. A technique for high performance data compression. *IEEE Computer*, 17:8–19, 1984.

[552] J. Wess. G-protein-coupled receptors: molecular mechanisms involved in receptor activation and selectivity of g-protein recognition. *FASEB J.*, 11:346–354, 1997.

[553] J. V. White, C. M. Stultz, and T. F. Smith. Protein classification by stochastich modeling and optimal filtering of amino-acid sequences. *Mathem. Biosci.*, 119:35–75, 1994.

[554] K. P. White, S. A. Rifkin, P. Hurban, and D. S. Hogness. Microarray analysis of *drosophila* development during metamorphosis. *Science*, 286:2179–2184, 1999.

[555] S. H. White. Global statistics of protein sequences: Implications for the origin, evolution, and prediction of structure. *Ann. Rev. Biophys. Biomol. Struct.*, 23:407–439, 1994.

[556] S. H. White and R. E. Jacobs. The evolution of proteins from random amino acid sequences. I. Evidence from the lengthwise distribution of amino acids in modern protein sequences. *J. Mol. Evol.*, 36:79–95, 1993.

[557] J. Whittaker. *Graphical Models in Applied Multivariate Statistics*. John Wiley & Sons, New York, 1990.

[558] B. L. Wiens. When log-normal and gamma models give different results: a case study. *The American Statistician*, 53:89–93, 1999.

[559] K. L. Williams, A. A. Gooley, and N. H. Packer. Proteome: Not just a made-up name. *Today's Life Sciences*, June:16–21, 1996.

[560] E. Wingender, X. Chen, R. Hehl, H. Karas, I. liebich, V. Matys, T. Meinhardt, M. Pruss, I. Reuter, and F. Schacherer. TRANSFAC: an integrated system for gene expression regulation. *Nucl. Acids Res.*, 28:316–319, 2000.

[561] H. Winkler. *Verbreitung und Ursache der Parthenogenesis im Pflanzen und Tierreich*. Fischer, Jena, 1920.

[562] C. R. Woese. *The Genetic Code. The Molecular Basis for Genetic Expression*. Harper & Row, New York, 1967.

[563] C. R. Woese, D. H. Dugre, S. A. Dugre, M. Kondo, and W. C. Saxinger. On the fundamental nature and evolution of the genetic code. *Cold Spring Harbor Symp. Quant. Biol.*, 31:723–736, 1966.

[564] C. R. Woese and G. E. Fox. Phylogenetic structure of the prokaryotic domain: The primary kingdoms. *Proc. Natl. Acad. Sci. USA*, 74:5088–5090, 1977.

[565] C. R. Woese, R. R. Gutell, R. Gupta, and H. F. Noller. Detailed analysis of the higher-order structure of 16S-like ribosomal ribonucleic acids. *Microbiol. Rev.*, 47:621–669, 1983.

[566] R. V. Wolfenden, P. M. Cullis, and C. C. F. Southgate. Water, protein folding, and the genetic code. *Science*, 206:575–577, 1979.

[567] T. G. Wolfsberg, A. E. Gabrielian, M. J. Campbell, R. J. Cho, J. L. Spouge, and D. Landsman. Candidate regulatory sequence elements for cell cycle-dependent transcription in *saccharomyces cerevisiae*. *Genome Res.*, 9:775–792, 1999.

[568] D. Wolpert. Stacked generalization. *Neural Networks*, 5:241–259, 1992.

[569] J. T. Wong. A co-evolution theory of the genetic code. *Proc. Natl. Acad. Sci. USA*, 72:1909–1912, 1975.

[570] F. S. Wouters, M. Markman, P. de Graaf, H. Hauser, H. F. Tabak, K. W. Wirtz, and A. F. Moorman. The immunohistochemical localization of the non-specific lipid transfer protein (sterol carrier protein-2) in rat small intestine enterocytes. *Biochim. Biophys. Acta*, 1259:192–196, 1995.

[571] C. H. Wu. Artificial neural networks for molecular sequence analysis. *Comp. Chem.*, 21:237–256, 1997.

[572] C. H. Wu and J.W. McLarty. *Neural Networks and Genome Informatics.* Elsevier, Amsterdam, 2000.

[573] J. R. Wyatt, J. D. Puglisi, and I Tinoco, Jr. Hybrid system for protein secondary structure prediction. *BioEssays*, 11:100–106, 1989.

[574] L. Xu. A unified learning scheme: Bayesian-Kullback Ying-Yang machine. In D. S. Touretzky, M. C. Mozer, and M. E. Hasselmo, editors, *Advances in Neural Information Processing Systems*, volume 8. MIT Press, Cambridge, MA, 1996.

[575] M. Ycas. The protein text. In H. P. Yockey, editor, *Symposium on information theory in biology*, pages 70–102, New York, 1958. Pergamon.

[576] T. Yi, Y. Huang, M. I. Simon, and J. Doyle. Robust perfect adaptation in bacterial chemotaxis through integral feedback control. *Proc. Natl. Acad. Sci. USA*, 97:4649–4653, 2000.

[577] H. P. Yockey. *Information Theory and Molecular Biology.* Cambridge University Press, Cambridge, 1992.

[578] J. York. Use of the Gibbs sampler in expert systems. *Artif. Intell.*, 56:115–130, 1992.

[579] C. H. Yuh, H. Bolouri, and E. H. Davidson. Genomic cis-regulatory logic: experimental and computational analysis of a sea urchin gene. *Science*, 279:1896–1902, 1998.

[580] A. Zemla, C. Venclovas, K. Fidelis, and B. Rost. A modified definition of SOV, a segment-based measure for protein secondary structure prediction assessment. *Proteins*, 34:220–223, 1999.

[581] M. Q. Zhang. Large-scale gene expression data analysis: a new challenge to computational biologists. *Genome Res.*, 9:681–688, 1999.

[582] X. Zhang, J. Mesirov, and D. Waltz. Hybrid system for protein secondary structure prediction. *J. Mol. Biol.*, 225:1049–1063, 1992.

[583] J. Zhu, J. Liu, and C. Lawrence. Bayesian adaptive alignment and inference. In T. Gaasterland, P. Karp, K. Karplus, C. Ouzounis, C. Sander, and A. Valencia, editors, *Proceedings of Fifth International Conference on Intelligent Systems for Molecular Biology*, pages 358–368. AAAI Press, 1997. Menlo Park, CA.

[584] A. Zien, R. Kuffner, R. Zimmer, and T. Lengauer. Analysis of gene expression data with pathway scores. In *Proceedings of the 2000 Conference on Intelligent Systems for Molecular Biology (ISMB00), La Jolla, CA*, pages 407–417. AAAI Press, Menlo Park, CA, 2000.

[585] M. Zuker. Computer prediction of RNA structure. *Meth. Enzymol.*, 180:262–288, 1989.

[586] M. Zuker and P. Stiegler. Optimal computer folding of large RNA sequences using thermodynamic and auxiliary information. *Nucl. Acids Res.*, 9:133–148, 1981.

[587] M. Zvelebil, G. Barton, W. Taylor, and M. Sternberg. Prediction of protein secondary structure and active sites using the alignment of homologous sequences. *J. Mol. Biol.*, 195:957–961, 1987.

Index